CONTEMPORARY ISSUES IN CURRICULUM

SECOND EDITION

Edited by

ALLAN C. ORNSTEIN

Loyola University of Chicago

LINDA S. BEHAR-HORENSTEIN

University of Florida

ALLYN AND BACON

Boston   London   Toronto   Sydney   Tokyo   Singapore

Senior Editor: Virginia Lanigan
Editorial Assistant: Kris Lamarre
Marketing Manager: Kathy Hunter
Editorial-Production Service: Raeia Maes, Maes Associates
Manufacturing Buyer: Suzanne Lareau
Cover Administrator: Linda Knowles

Library of Congress Cataloging-in-Publication Data
Contemporary issues in curriculum / edited by Allan C. Ornstein, Linda
    S. Behar-Horenstein.—2nd ed.
        p.   cm.
    Includes bibliographical references and indexes.
    ISBN 0-205-28323-3
    1. Education—United States—Curricula.   2. Curriculum planning—
-United States.   I. Ornstein, Allan C.   II. Behar-Horenstein, Linda
S.
LB1570.C813   1999
375'.00973—dc21   97-48490
                                                                              CIP

Credits can be found on pages 455–456, which should be considered extensions of the copyright page.

Printed in the United States of America

10 9 8 7 6 5 4 3 2 1   03 02 01 00 99 98

CONTENTS

CONTRIBUTORS

Ellen S. Amatea, University of Florida
Carole A. Ames, University of Illinois at Urbana-Champaign
Lorin W. Anderson, University of South Carolina
Linda S. Behar-Horenstein, University of Florida
David C. Berliner, Arizona State University
Benjamin S. Bloom, Emeritus, University of Chicago
Ronald S. Brandt, Association for Supervision and Curriculum Development
James W. Chapple, Northern Ohio Special Education Regional Resource Center
Katherine S. Cushing, Harrison School District, Colorado
Linda Darling-Hammond, Teachers College, Columbia University
Joyce L. Epstein, Center of School, Family, and Community Partnerships, Johns Hopkins University
Elliot W. Eisner, Stanford University
Michael G. Fullan, University of Toronto
Howard Gardner, Harvard University
Geneva Gay, University of Washington
Henry A. Giroux, Pennsylvania State University
Maxine Greene, Emeritus, Teachers College, Columbia University
Thomas R. Guskey, University of Kentucky
Simon Hooper, University of Minnesota
M. Frances Klein, Emeritus, University of Southern California
Lawrence Kohlberg, Emeritus, Harvard University
Alfie Kohn, Author and Lecturer on Education and Human Behavior
Matthew Lipman, Montclair State College
Susan Loucks-Horsley, Regional Laboratory for Educational Improvement of the Northeast and Islands
Todd I. Lubart, Yale University
Jeannie S. Oakes, University of California at Los Angeles
Allan C. Ornstein, Loyola University of Chicago
Leonard O. Pellicer, University of South Carolina
Lloyd P. Rieber, University of Georgia
Donna S. Sabers, Test Consultant, Arizona State Department of Education
James T. Sears, University of South Carolina
Thomas J. Sergiovanni, Trinity University
Peter A. D. Sherrard, University of Florida
Beverly Showers, Consultant in Staff Development and School Improvement
Lee S. Shulman, Stanford University
Robert E. Slavin, Johns Hopkins University
Dennis Sparks, National Staff Development Council
Robert J. Sternberg, Yale University
Jacqueline S. Thousand, University of Vermont
Ralph W. Tyler, Center for Advanced Study in the Behavioral Sciences
Richard A. Villa, Bayridge Educational Consortium

PREFACE

This second edition of *Contemporary Issues in Curriculum* is a book for students studying curriculum, instruction, administration, teacher education, and educational foundations. It is a text written for those who are exploring the issues that have the potential to influence the implementation, planning, and evaluation of curriculum at all levels of learning. The articles reflect the emergent trends in the field of curriculum.

The book is divided into six parts: philosophy, teaching, learning, instruction, supervision, and policy. Each part consists of six chapters and is preceded by an introduction that focuses the reader's attention on the issues to be discussed. It also provides a brief overview of the articles. Each chapter begins with a set of focusing questions and ends with several discussion questions. A pro-con chart that explores views for and against a current controversial curricular concern and a case study problem appear at the end of each part. These instructional features are designed to help the reader integrate the content and issues of the book.

Most readers focus primarily on issues affecting the theoretical or practical applications of curriculum and present the popularly accepted views in the field. Most readers focus on curriculum and teaching as they relate to the individual, society, and groups, or they emphasize philosophy, teaching, and trends found at various educational levels. We have tried to balance our discussion by focusing on six major areas that influence the field: philosophy, teaching, learning, instruction, supervision, and policy. To ensure that the breadth and depth of viewpoints in the field are represented, we have included articles that portray current trends and illustrate the dynamism within the field of curriculum. The readings consist of views that reflect traditionally held beliefs as well as other perspectives that might be considered more controversial in nature. Students and practitioners should have an opportunity to investigate the breadth of issues that are affecting curriculum and be able to access such information in a single source. Readers are encouraged to examine and debate these issues, formulate their own ideas regarding the issues affecting the field of curriculum, and decide what direction that field should take.

We acknowledge the many authors who granted us permission to reprint their work, as well as the following professors who reviewed the book: Gail J. Gerlach, Indiana University of Pennsylvannia, and James S. Henderson, Kent State University.

Thanks are also extended to Virginia Lanigan, senior editor, Allyn and Bacon, who had faith in our idea and on nothing more than a concept and an outline gave us the green light. Allan Ornstein expresses love for his children, Jason, Stacey, and Joel, and advises them to always take the high road in life. Linda Behar-Horenstein dedicates this book to her husband, Benjamin, whose love, friendship, and encouragement have been the fertilizer for new endeavors, and to her daughter, Rachel, and newborn son, Max, who in their own inimitable styles remind her everyday what an essential curriculum really is.

A.C.O.

L.S.B-H.

PART ONE

Curriculum and Philosophy

INTRODUCTION

How does philosophy influence the curriculum? To what extent does the curriculum reflect personal beliefs and societal views? How do different conceptions of curriculum affect schooling and student achievement? In what way has curriculum been a catalyst in empowering certain segments of society while disenfranchising others?

In Chapter 1, Linda Behar-Horenstein, Ellen Amatea, and Peter Sherrard discuss several different factors that influence educators' conceptions of the theory–practice relationship. They describe the role that curriculum professors can play in helping students to appreciate how an understanding of theory can lead to improved teaching and learning. In the next chapter, Allan Ornstein considers how philosophy guides the organization of the curriculum. He explores how beliefs about the purposes of education are reflected in the subject matter and the process of teaching and learning.

In Chapter 3, Ronald Brandt and Ralph Tyler present a rationale for establishing educational goals. They identify the sources that they believe should be considered before articulating goals, as well as how goals should be used in planning learning activities and evaluation. Next, M. Frances Klein presents an overview of the traditional models of curriculum. She argues that a narrow focus on concepts and procedures has limited curriculum delivery and student outcomes. She suggests that educators might accomplish more by considering different conceptions of curriculum.

In Chapter 5, Henry Giroux describes how language and curriculum discourse influence teaching and outcomes. He discusses how the relationship between politics, bureaucracy, and the teacher's role impacts the curriculum. He offers several strategies for restructuring the curriculum so that teachers and students might become empowered by school experiences. In the last chapter of Part One, Maxine Greene reminds us of the essential role that arts experiences play in helping students to develop an aesthetic awareness. She explains why encounters with the arts are likely to enrich students' learning experiences. She also discusses why experience with the arts is critical to combating the delivery of prescriptive curricula and developing students' metacognitive strategies.

From Theory to Practice:
Contemporary Curriculum Issues[1]

LINDA S. BEHAR-HORENSTEIN
ELLEN S. AMATEA
PETER A. D. SHERRARD

FOCUSING QUESTIONS

1. **What factors affect educators' perceptions of the theory–practice relationship?**
2. **Within professional journals, what issues do curriculum scholars address relevant to conceptualizations of the field?**
3. **How do curriculum professors influence educators' understanding and perceptions of the theory–practice relationship?**
4. **What is the relationship between appropriate and culturally responsive programs of curriculum and the development of student understanding about the theory–practice relationship?**
5. **Why is it important to provide students with instructional experiences beyond the classroom?**
6. **Why should there be a compendium of core competencies in the field of curriculum?**

In the following chapter, the authors discuss the role that curriculum professors play in sustaining the theory–practice dualism and formulating educators' understanding of the practical application of curriculum theory. Scholars' and practitioners' perceptions of the field of curriculum and their interpretation of curriculum professors' written work may be among the primary reasons that collaborative relationships between practitioners and curriculum scholars may be difficult to establish. Several suggestions are offered for bringing about the development of cooperative and supportive relationships among universities, administrators, and teachers. These suggestions include offering instructional experiences that exemplify the reality of school life, establishing professional programs of study that are perceived as credible by both scholars and those outside the field, identifying core competencies for matriculation from professional degree programs, encouraging students to analyze the belief systems that guide their educational practice, and expanding students' world view to encompass a second-order perspective.

THE RELATIONSHIP BETWEEN CURRICULUM THEORY AND PRACTICE

Many factors and issues impinge on the relationship between theory and practice. They range from broad, macro or institutional-based dynamics to micro considerations that are endemic to the vagaries characteristic of human behavior. Rooted at the institutional level as well as within the individual, these issues influence both the nature of the theory–practice relationship and the perceptions that scholars and practitioners form related to this dualism. Individuals at all levels of the academy influence perceptions of the theory–practice relationship. The focus of this chapter is concerned primarily with the role that curriculum professors[2] play in sustaining this dualism. If we accept the supposition that the type of scholarly work published in journals and other media coalesces into the perceptions that others form about professors who teach curriculum, then other questions emerge. For example, what role do curriculum professors play in perpetuating or deconstructing the complex elements of this duality? How do their conversations and writings as scholars influence how others view their position about the theory–practice relationship?

After presenting a brief overview of the conflicts embedded in conceptualizing the field, the authors identify some of the behaviors that may impede a working-together agenda. Next, they discuss how scholarly conversations may be perceived by practitioners. Third, the authors describe how the relationship between students' learning experiences and the status of the field of curriculum as portrayed and perceived influences perceptions of theory–practice. There can be little doubt that the instructional experiences that we offer affect not only students' emergent knowledge base but their perceptions of our commitment to working together. Finally, the authors offer some suggestions for ways that we can work together so that the development of collaborative relationships among universities, administrators, and teachers might become a norm, rather than an occasional pursuit.

CONFLICTING CONCEPTIONS IN THE FIELD

Many curricularists have been engaged in discussions aimed at delineating the parameters of the field of curriculum and identifying which paradigm is appropriate to guiding inquiry into the field (Behar-Horenstein, Amatea, & Sherrard, 1997; Doll, 1993; Johnston, 1994; Hlebowitsh, 1995; Hlebowitsh, 1993; Lincoln, 1992; Schwab, 1970; Short, 1987; Wraga, 1996). Curriculum journals are replete with discussions about the professional and hierarchical structures that perpetuate hegemony and the marginalization of students, as well as debates about which view of curriculum is most efficacious: the modern, progressivist, or postmodern (Giroux, 1994; Pinar, 1988; Slattery, 1995). However, these discussions represent only a microcosm of how curricularists can utilize their scholarship and insight to make schools places where even the disowned and disenfranchised students will feel welcomed into the learning community and can be successful. We must begin to move away from esoteric conversation and address the practical concerns of the teachers and students.

There has been a proliferation of writing about which particular paradigms should guide curriculum development and inquiry. In fact, one may conclude that curriculum scholars have difficulty agreeing on the usefulness and viability of competing paradigms. These discussions exhibit a remarkable similarity to the paradigm debates in research methodologies (Behar-Horenstein & Morgan, 1995). However, paradigmatic conceptions of curriculum are likely to influence student outcomes to a much lesser degree than the epistemological lenses used to train aspiring curricularists. Professors who teach curriculum can influence how curriculum concepts and theory are ultimately applied to classroom teaching. How should curriculum professors teach relevant concepts? We believe that providing effective instruction at any level requires solid grounding in principles of curriculum design, child development, and situational context; a sensitivity to the cultural, economical, emotional, social, political, and familial backgrounds of students (Thurston, Clift, & Schacht, 1993); and an understanding about how our belief systems influence our construction of a particular reality of practice and subsequent actions.

Often conversations about how curriculum concepts facilitate inquiry into classroom phenomena demonstrate little relevance to practice. These discussions may also exhibit little concern about the issues affecting teachers' and students' everyday lives. The disparity between research and actual practice may raise the specter of concern among public and school-based personnel. This incongruity can give rise to questions such as why professors of curriculum spend so much time writing about esoteric topics. Are curriculum professors really interested in working on problems of practical significance?

Historically, conveying practical knowledge has been a central focus in the field of curriculum studies. Alberty & Alberty (1962), Caswell (1932), Dewey (1902), Kilpatrick (1925), and Tyler (1968), among others, were involved in helping practitioners study and resolve school-based problems. Alberty & Alberty (1962) were influential in the emergence of a core curriculum. They suggested a version of the correlated curriculum design for the secondary level. Caswell (1932), Dewey (1902), and Kilpatrick (1925), among others, were influential in promoting the child-centered movement. This approach emphasized teaching based on students' natural development and curiosity. During the mid 1920s and the 1930s, Caswell also tried to improve teacher's instruction and student learning by providing a seven-question framework that teachers could consider while they were involved in curriculum development. Tyler (1968) suggested that curriculum should reach all students and be responsive to the needs of disadvantaged students, especially those who had little or no basis for schoolwork. Tyler also claimed that it was imperative that the curriculum provide "educational opportunities and to assure effective learning for youth from varied backgrounds of training, experience, and outlook" (p. 10). These statements reflect Tyler's recognition of the importance of developing curricula that were practical and useful, yet responsive to the needs of both individual students and society.

However, since Schwab's (1970) identification of the demise of the field and a series of conferences convened by curricularists who were opposed to the mainstream that defined curriculum studies (Pinar, 1988), many curriculum professors seem to be moving away from this practice. Their focus has shifted to elements external to the schools, such as the sociological, cultural, political, and economical context of communities and families that affect students' lives and classroom learning (Apple, 1986; Giroux, 1994; Pinar, 1988; Slattery, 1995).

TEACHING THE KNOWLEDGE BASE OF CURRICULUM

The ways we teach can enhance teachers' and principals' knowledge base in two ways. First, an understanding of the curriculum knowledge base can help them to become informed practitioners. Second, using this information, teachers and principals can help to bring about effective and enduring change. If our goal is to encourage students to become effective team members in educational reform initiatives, then we must help them to grow in professional ways. We must focus our efforts on engaging them as partners in learning.

The way we teach curriculum concepts influences students' interpretation and subsequent use of curriculum ideas. Therefore, it is imperative that professors have a keen understanding of what they want students to learn when they teach. To thwart the perpetuation of the misperceptions that abound about the field of curriculum, we must be succinct and clear about how we use language. We must offer students an opportunity to develop a common platform for discussion about curriculum. Describing the meanings of particular curricular concepts or lecturing them about the important epochs in the field is insufficient. Additionally, we must help students to become active participants. We must encourage them to begin a deliberate and personalized process of translating theory into practice by thinking about the ways in which they observe or practice curriculum.

Helping students visualize the connections between their experience and pedagogy is critical to the formulation of their own ideas. For example, we can design activities that encourage them to construct and interpret their own knowledge about the field of curriculum. Learning how curriculum principles operate in their world can be enormously beneficial to the students' application of new knowledge. These experiences can help students to determine just what essential curriculum knowledge is and how that knowledge can be used in practice. Doing this requires creativity, enthusiasm, responsive teaching, an awareness of students' unique learning needs and styles, and the ability to create learning environments in which students feel encouraged to participate and will become enthusiastic. Most educators would probably agree that if our goal is to engage students actively then the instructional environment will be characterized by the educator's ability to perceive patterns, an awareness of the emergent classroom dynamics, the ability to discern their meaning, and the ingenuity to respond in meaningful ways (Eisner, 1995).

There are many approaches to catalyzing students' construction of knowledge. Portfolios, observations, and interviews can be instrumental in their construction of new ways of seeing. Students can learn much about the practical application of curriculum by interviewing an administrator or curriculum specialist who oversees the effectiveness of the total school curriculum. Designing a portfolio can help them develop a personalized understanding of the ways in which curriculum operates in educational settings. Also, students can discover how theory influences the actual practice of curriculum. Active learning experiences, rather than didactic teaching, are essential to helping teachers and principals to acquire the curriculum skills necessary to modifying the curriculum for the diverse students whom they serve. This goal can be accomplished by providing coursework in curriculum design whereby students construct a curriculum, teach various lessons, and formatively assess its effectiveness. This activity can help stu-

dents to discover the relationship between course assignments and the worlds in which they teach. When students begin to analyze what is taking place in their classrooms and schools, they start to develop more sophisticated ways of seeing and understanding classroom phenomena.

How can articles that reveal the actual practice of curriculum facilitate student learning? When students are given opportunities to talk about readings that offer a synthesis of the current breadth of viewpoints in the field along with their own experiences, they often expand their recognition of the multiplicity of perspectives about issues in practice. Almost reflexively, students begin to appreciate the range of choices that they have in selecting an action. These experiences can illuminate how conceptual kinds of curricular knowledge can be applied to their own classroom practice. For example, these experiences might broaden their awareness of existing educational practice or strategies and lead to different kinds of actions and planning. Professors who teach courses in curriculum pedagogy, design, and evaluation[3] can help teachers to make sense of theoretical or conceptual constructs by translating abstract information into the language of practice. Moreover, we can exercise leadership by moving our conversations beyond the obvious, beyond mere criticism to a more proactive stance and a more hopeful vision of how we can work together.

WORKING TOGETHER WITH PEOPLE IN SCHOOLS

We can make an authentic commitment to help teachers to become better informed and curriculum developers in their own right through the experiences that we provide. An authentic commitment becomes genuine when we take our students into school settings and engage them in the type of problem solving and reflection that are necessary to make schools places where all children can achieve success.

There is little doubt that the creation of appropriately designed programs is in our hands. We must move beyond political agendas, issues of territoriality, and ego toward an appreciation of our responsibility as educators to serve curricularists, teachers, and principals, as well as the children and students whose lives they will affect. Such an agenda presupposes that individuals, endowed with the power and responsibility to develop appropriate and culturally responsive programs, possess a thorough knowledge of the theoretical aspects of curriculum, a keen understanding of how precepts can be applied to practice, supervisory techniques and skills, and sufficient clinical skills to engage in critical reflection.

As professors we must be self-reflective and ask ourselves a number of questions. Why do I promote particular practices? To what end do I believe my behaviors and actions will lead? How can university and school personnel accomplish this work together? How do I hope to influence the lives of my students and the students that they will teach? As a teacher, do I demonstrate a commitment to helping students become problem solvers or capable practitioners? Am I teaching students to make rationale choices so that they develop curricula that meet students' instructional needs? Am I helping students to learn to become the kind of leader who will create school learning communities in which all children can be successful?

How can curriculum professors promote collaborative relationships between universities and schools as well as scholars and practitioners? If we accept that one goal of public education is to help all students to achieve success, then promoting this educational mission should be an integral component of the work that curriculum professors do. While the concept of what constitutes success may be defined in a variety of ways, it can be agreed that creating and sustaining a dialogue between curriculum scholars and practitioners is essential to that goal. This commitment can be achieved in many ways. For example, curriculum professors can help practitioners to conduct systematic inquiry into how classroom phenomena affect student outcomes. Representing one component of this exploratory process, scholars and practitioners might analyze the quality of instruction and teacher–student interaction. Through rigorous

study, they can determine if there are alternative ways to represent the curricular concepts. Together they can discover if there are alternative approaches to facilitating student comprehension.

Curriculum professors can address the current limitations within the field of curriculum studies. Enhancing the status of the field so that it is perceived as a legitimate discipline, with the same privileges and recognition as other professional instructional and noninstructional educational fields, should be a priority. Five suggestions for enhancing the status of the field are offered. First, curriculum professors can create a sense of integrity for both scholars and those outside the field by establishing professional programs of study supported by scholarship. Professors can offer instructional experiences that exemplify the reality of school life. Syllabi can include course assignments that allow students to experience how forces inside and outside schools influence the teaching, learning, and evaluation processes. Scholars can codify a compendium of core competencies that will guide program development and lead to nationally recognized professional certification. Moreover, curriculum professors can identify consensually agreed on language for talking about curriculum phenomena with other educators.

Curriculum professors can encourage students to surface and analyze the belief systems that guide their educational practice. If it is revealed that students favor viewpoints that reflect prejudicial, stereotypical, or preconceived ideas, then curriculum professors must challenge students to expand their world view to encompass a second-order perspective. Building collaborative relationships among universities, school districts, and students is a significant challenge. While acknowledging that there is no single solution to this challenge, three ideas for fostering collaborative relationships are discussed next.

INTEGRATING THE TRIPARTITE FOCUS OF THE PROFESSORS' ROLES

We can offer learning experiences that benefit the student, schools, and the professor through course development projects that integrate the tripartite focus of the professorship: teaching, research, and service. Consider the following example. In an effort to offer students enrolled in an evaluation course the opportunity to apply their emergent knowledge to a practice-based situation, a professor contacted local school district personnel. She offered to help them examine an instructional issue of significant concern throughout their twenty-three schools. The district had been using a computerized integrated learning system package to help Chapter One students to achieve significant gains in reading and mathematics achievement scores. Little information about the efficacy of these instructional materials was available. However, outcomes that emerged from this instruction carried high stakes. Placement decisions and a determination about the breadth of student progress were made on the basis of this instructional intervention (see Behar-Horenstein, 1996)

Essentially, the district program supervisor and teachers were interested in determining the fiscal and instructional effectiveness of this curriculum. They wanted to assess the cost effectiveness of the program, since maintaining the delivery of this program district wide and providing enough individual student work stations represented a considerable expense. Additionally, they wanted to determine the optimal amount of time that students needed computer instruction in order to realize significant academic gains in reading and mathematics.

As a consequence of establishing a relationship with the school, the professor was able to engage university students in an examination of these issues. The data set was used in a number of ways. Initially, it provided students with a means to acquire experience in data management techniques. The data set was also used to help students understand the process of both research design and statistical methods. Data were used to help students learn how to organize and develop a research paper. Finally, the data set was used as a tool to help graduate students analyze Chapter One students' progress in reading and mathematics as a function of computerized instructional time. Students ac-

tively applied conceptual and theoretical concepts of evaluation in a hands-on project.

Findings related to this study concerning minority students were notable. The results revealed that minority children (66%) spent significantly less time engaged in computerized reading instruction than white children. Also, it was reported that minority children received instruction from less experienced teachers than white children (34%) even though they constituted the majority of the Chapter One population. These particular findings stimulated other issues for district supervisors, principals, and teachers to consider related to the instructional component of the program. Moreover, at the conclusion of this study, several more questions had emerged.

Time constraints did not permit a more comprehensive examination. There are other approaches to exploring the primary research questions. A nonexclusive list of suggestions is offered. For example, how did the quality of teachers' and aides' instruction affect student outcomes? How were students' initial placement levels determined? How did teachers' and aides' preparation in and beliefs about the efficacy of computer-based instruction influence student outcomes?

Research initiatives between the university and the school district concerning these issues are continuing. One benefit of this collaborative study is the recognition that the school district is likely to learn more about how computerized instruction is actually delivered. Results from this collaboration are likely to lead to more effective approaches to facilitating successful student learning. The type of collaboration described helps to ensure that we are not responding in ways that cement the archetype of the university professor. That stereotype is perhaps most aptly represented by an illustration of the contemplative scholar who sits among his or her books and research in an enclave isolated from the world at large. We must take a close look at the reality of school life for teachers and students and thoughtfully assess the currency and relevance of the training we provide students. Then we must summon the courage and stamina to create the type of programs that are needed to help all students to become successful.

EXPLORING THE LACK OF CURRICULUM COMPETENCIES AND LICENSURE

A lack of agreed on curriculum competencies and national licensure for curriculum specialists has placed the credibility of the field into question. In a study concerning knowledge requirements in doctoral curriculum programs, it was reported that there is an absence of both core course requirements and program experiences (Behar-Horenstein, 1994). What actions are needed to create comprehensive programs of study? Initially, a compendium of competencies must be identified so that a framework to guide program development and clarify graduation requirements can be established (Behar & Ornstein, 1992). We must also institute professional certification for curricularists throughout each state in the union so that the field may be viewed as an area that is credible and important in its own right.[4]

Curriculum can no longer be considered an orphan that has been adopted neither by principals, the science of administration, or schools of supervision. While acknowledging that it may be difficult to develop a program that would encompass agreed on knowledge, it is essential to determine what practices are important to improve the curriculum process (Behar, 1994). Furthermore, it is important that scholars and practitioners develop a common language for talking about curriculum and related phenomena. We need to define curricular constructs in the same way. Such activities are needed to move the field beyond opaque linguistic and metaphorical discussions about which curriculum knowledge is worth most.

Why is it necessary to identify agreed on knowledge? The most compelling argument for competencies is that most curricular decisions are made in a variety of ways by a variety of people who do not necessarily possess adequate or essential knowledge (Behar & Ornstein, 1992). Furthermore, establishing a compendium for com-petencies can serve as criteria for designing staff development programs and for making curriculum decisions. Clarifying what curricularists need to know and do to function effectively in school settings can benefit the field as well as schoolchildren. Colleges and universities can play an integral role in helping schools to successfully implement initiatives by ensuring that curriculum specialist graduates have the necessary skills to apply curriculum principles in a practical way.

Acquainting teachers and principals with essential curriculum knowledge can help teachers to acquire the skills necessary to develop substantive lessons and promote successful student outcomes. Helping students to appreciate the function of the macrocurriculum, not just the microcurriculum or contextualized classroom experience, can cultivate their understanding regarding how common instruction and learning activities fit into the total school curriculum. Understanding the macrocurriculum can also help teachers recognize how their work facilitates students' subsequent learning and synthesis of knowledge. How can such a compendium of competencies be established? Although this topic will not be discussed in this chapter, ways to establish a compendium that is responsive to the epistemologies of both quantitative and qualitative researchers are not beyond our realization.

EXAMINING OUR EPISTEMOLOGICAL BELIEFS

Most of us are familiar with a mechanistic view of the nature of the world and the way it works. However, we may not be aware of how this world view not only shapes what we know about schools, but also how we know it and how we decide to use the knowledge in formulating a course of action. Clearly, our awareness of how our world view shapes (and limits) our understanding is evoked when we face alternative world views. Alternative world views generate certain kinds of knowledge about schools, while excluding the possibility of other knowledge ever being formed (Amatea, Behar-Horenstein, & Sherrard, 1996).

Each of us, whether school administrator, curriculum specialist, or teacher, formulates our own answer to what knowledge is and how we know it (Held & Pols, 1985). The concept of epistemology has been defined as "the nature of knowledge." This concept refers to "both with *what* knowledge is, as distinct from mere belief or prejudice; and with *how* we know" (Held & Pols, p. 510). The nature of knowledge in this context "is more concerned with what we know (or think we know)," for example, "the inquiry into the nature of the world as it is" (p. 510). Berger and Luckman (1966) claim that when we consciously reflect on "how we know" we become aware of how we "edit" the universe and participate in the "social construction of reality" (Amatea, Behar-Horenstein, & Sherrard, 1996).

This discovery of a set of opposing "truths" reminds us that we participate in choosing from a larger range of options or thought rules. Using thought rules, we construct the particular reality of curriculum practice. Knowledge of these alternative lenses can aid us in identifying the particular epistemological assumptions that support our integration of theoretical and practical applications of curriculum. This knowledge also helps us to recognize that it is our choice of focus, position, and mode of inquiry and explanation that allows us to see different realities (Amatea, Behar-Horenstein, & Sherrard, 1996).

The lens we select to view how curriculum can and/or should operate in school has a significant impact on how we think about the role of the person engaged in the process of curriculum delivery. Many curricularists have been trained to operate from a first-order perspective, assuming that they can more effectively observe and analyze inputs to and outputs from classrooms by standing outside it. In using this first-order way of thinking, it is presumed that difficulties in curriculum delivery, instruction, or learning represent inadequacies in preestablished teacher and student social roles and the hierarchical, contextual, or bureaucratic structures of classroom organization and schools. As an alternative to the first-order lens, the second-order perspective is rooted in social construction

theory and holds that our beliefs about the world are social inventions (Amatea, Behar-Horenstein, & Sherrard, 1996).

Second-order views are really "views about views" that can often make an individual more aware of the way in which his or her relationship to an operation can influence it. So, thinking in these ways about how we teach and what we teach within the larger social context, as well as one's position in it, has radical implications. Using the second-order perspective, we no longer see the locus of teaching or learning dilemmas as residing in the character of a particular teacher, student, or structure of the school. Instead, we begin to view the larger social context in which a teacher, student, and staff are responsible for jointly constructing the stories people in the school live by. Teacher, student, or staff behavior is no longer viewed from a unidimensional perspective or as the result of a linear or sequential causal sequence. Instead, actions and reactions are seen as simultaneously influencing each other (Amatea, Behar-Horenstein, & Sherrard, 1996).

When one chooses a second-order lens, she or he conceptualizes the focus of her or his efforts differently. Thus, the focus of her or his examination is seen as consisting of both the person (for example, the university professor) and the observed group (students, teachers, or parents) as bound together in one large bundle as an "observing system." From this position, the university professor not only views herself or himself as belonging to a group, linked together by a common language and world of meaning, but also as involved in a common search for new meanings when they become constraining (Amatea, Behar-Horenstein, & Sherrard, 1996).

We assume that our selection of the epistemological lenses (or thought rules) by which we construct a particular reality of curriculum practice not only signals our beliefs as to whom we focus on, but also whom we hold accountable for the world in its present state and how we function in relation to them. The first-order view often focuses on changing the outcomes while maintaining the existing school structure. In contrast, the second-order view is often characterized by a change in the very meanings and processes that characterize our interaction in a human system. A second-order perspective emphasizes the multiplicity of perspectives of the various players in school settings and how these perspectives influence the individual thought and action of both the observer and the observed. By more consciously considering the underlying assumptions that guide one's thinking and actions, understanding may take precedence over judgment and analysis may supersede redefined outcomes. As a result, making decisions about appropriate action may be based more on situational demands than individual needs. Obviously, the selection of lenses will be influenced by the individual's comfort level in handling the turbulence generated by considering different ways of defining change initiatives and by one's flexibility in trying out a variety of competing definitions (Amatea, Behar-Horenstein, & Sherrard, 1996).

CONCLUSION

Professors who teach courses in curriculum pedagogy, design, and evaluation are charged with the responsibility to help students to surface their beliefs. We must help individuals who possess narrow, conflicting, or prejudicial views by posing questions that give rise to alternative ways of looking at things. We must also offer experiences that can expand individuals' ways of looking at the world. The guidance we provide is greatly influenced by our own belief system and ability to be authentically reflective. The greater the magnitude of vision that we offer, the larger is the repertoire of options and alternatives that we provide students. We also encourage the development of alternative ways of seeing by modeling. In so doing, we challenge the potential in all of us for ignorance to remain untouched.

ENDNOTES

1. This paper was adapted from an invited panel presentation to the Professors of Curriculum at the 1997 Annual Meeting of the American Educational Research Association, Chicago.

2. For the purposes of this discussion, curriculum professors are those educators who teach courses that deal with a broad range of curriculum concepts covered in generic curriculum courses, such as curriculum theory, curriculum development, curriculum change, and curriculum evaluation (Johnston, 1994).

3. We refer to those courses that cover a broad range of topics related to generic curriculum concepts, such as curriculum theory, curriculum planning and development, curriculum change, and curriculum evaluation (Johnston, 1994).

4. In Behar-Horenstein's (1994) study, it was reported that only eleven states offered programs of study that led to earning a state license as a certified curriculum specialist.

REFERENCES

Alberty, H. B., & Alberty, E. S. (1962). *Reorganizing the high school curriculum,* 3rd ed. New York: Macmillian.

Amatea, E. S., Behar-Horenstein, L. S., & Sherrard, P. E. D. (1996). Creating school change: Discovering a choice of lenses for the school administrator. *Journal of Educational Administration, 34*(3), 49–64.

Apple, M. W. (1986). *Teachers and texts: A political economy of class and gender relations in education.* New York: Routledge & Kegan Paul.

Behar, L. S. (1994). *The knowledge base of curriculum.* Lanham, MD: University Press of America.

Behar, L. S., & Ornstein, A. C. (1992). An overview of curriculum: The theory and practice. *National Association of Secondary School Principals Bulletin, 76*(547), 32–44.

Behar-Horenstein, L. S. (1994). Knowledge requirements in doctoral curriculum programs. *Curriculum and Teaching, 9*(1), 33–44.

Behar-Horenstein, L. S. (1996). Influencing the academic achievement of Chapter 1 students: Does computer technology facilitate student outcomes? Paper presented at the Annual Meeting of the American Educational Research Association, New York, April 1996.

Behar-Horenstein, L. S., Amatea, E. S., & Sherrard, P. E. D. (1997). The dance of dichotomous paradigms of curriculum; let's reconstruct. Paper presented at the Annual Meeting of the American Educational Research Association, Chicago, March 1997.

Behar-Horenstein, L. S., & Morgan, R. R. (1995). Narrative research, teaching and teacher thinking:

Perspectives and possibilities. *Peabody Journal of Education, 70*(2), 139–161.

Berger, P., & Luckman, T. (1966). *The social construction of reality.* Garden City, NY: Doubleday.

Caswell, H. L. (1932). *Program making in small elementary schools.* Nashville, TN: George Peabody College for Teachers.

Dewey, J. (1902). *The child and the curriculum.* Chicago: University of Chicago Press.

Doll, W. E. (1993). Curriculum possibilities in a "post"-future. *Journal of Curriculum and Supervision, 8*(4), 277–292.

Eisner, E. W. (1995). The art and craft of teaching. In Ornstein, A. C., and Behar, L. S. *Contemporary Issues in Curriculum.* Boston: Allyn & Bacon.

Giroux, H. A. (1994). Teachers, public life, and curriculum reform. *Peabody Journal of Education, 69*(3), 35–47.

Held, B., & Pols, B. (1985). The confusion about epistemology and "epistemology" and what to do about it. *Family Process 24,* 509–516.

Hlebowitsh, P. S. (1993). *Radical curriculum theory reconsidered: A historical approach.* New York: Teachers College Press.

Hlebowitsh, P. S. (1995). Interpretations of the Tyler rationale: A reply to Kliebard. *Journal of Curriculum Studies, 27*(1), 89–94.

Johnston, S. (1994). Resolving questions of "why" and "how" about the study of curriculum in teacher education programmes. *Journal of Curriculum Studies, 26*(5), 525–540.

Kilpatrick, W. H. (1925). *Foundations of Method.* New York: Macmillan.

Lincoln, Y. S. (1992). Curriculum studies and the traditions of inquiry: The humanistic tradition. In Philip W. Jackson, ed., *Handbook of research on curriculum.* New York: Macmillan.

Pinar, W. F. (1988). The reconceptualization of curriculum studies, 1987: A personal retrospective. *Journal of Curriculum and Supervision, 3*(2), 157–167.

Schwab, J. J. (1970). *The practical: A language for curriculum.* Washington, DC: National Educational Association.

Short, E. G. (1987). Curriculum research in retrospect. Paper delivered at the Society of the Study of Curriculum History, Washington, DC.

Slattery, P. S. (1995). A postmodern vision of time and learning: A response to the National Education Commission Report Prisoners of Time. *Harvard Educational Review, 65*(4), 612–633.

Thurston, P., Clift, R., & Schacht, M. (1993). Preparing leaders for change-oriented schools. *Phi Delta Kappan, 75,* 259–265.

Tyler, R. W. (1968). Purposes for our schools. *National Association for Secondary School Principals, 52*(332), 1–12.

Wraga, W. (1996). Toward a curriculum theory for the new century: Essay review of Patrick Slattery, *Curriculum development in the postmodern era. Journal of Curriculum Studies, 28*(4), 463–474.

DISCUSSION QUESTIONS

1. How does the nature of the scholarly work written about theory–practice influence educators' perceptions and understanding of that relationship?
2. Why is it important to consider the role that curriculum professors play in sustaining the theory–practice dualism?
3. Why should students develop a common platform for discussions about curriculum?
4. What type of learning environment is essential if students are to become active participants?
5. How has the absence of both curriculum competencies and national licensure influenced perceptions formed by others about the field of curriculum?
6. How do epistemological beliefs affect the way in which (a) curriculum professors teach, (b) educators analyze instructional dilemmas, and (c) curriculum professors teach about the theory–practice relationship?

Philosophy as a Basis for Curriculum Decisions

ALLAN C. ORNSTEIN

FOCUSING QUESTIONS

1. *How does philosophy guide the organization and implementation of curriculum?*
2. *What are the sources of knowledge that shape a person's philosophy of curriculum?*
3. *What are the sources of knowledge that shape your philosophical view of curriculum?*
4. *How do the aims, means, and ends of education differ?*
5. *What is the major philosophical issue that must be determined before we can define a philosophy of curriculum?*
6. *What are the four major educational philosophies that have influenced curriculum in the United States?*
7. *What is your philosophy of curriculum?*

Philosophic issues always have and still do impact on schools and society. Contemporary society and its schools are changing fundamentally and rapidly, much more so than in the past. There is a special urgency that dictates continuous appraisal and reappraisal of the role of schools, and calls for a philosophy of education. Without philosophy, educators are directionless in the whats and hows of organizing and implementing what we are trying to achieve. In short, our philosophy of education influences, and to a large extent determines, our educational decisions, choices, and alternatives.

PHILOSOPHY AND CURRICULUM

Philosophy provides educators, especially curriculum specialists, with a framework for organizing schools and classrooms. It helps them answer what are the school's purpose, what subjects are of value, how students learn, and what methods and materials to use. Philosophy provides them with a framework for broad issues and tasks, such as determining the goals of education, subject content and its organization, the process of teaching and learning, and, in general, what experiences and activities to stress in schools and classrooms. It also provides educators with a basis for making such decisions as what workbooks, textbooks, or other cognitive and noncognitive activities to utilize and how to utilize them, what homework to assign and how much of it, how to test students and how to use the test results, and what courses or subject matter to emphasize.

The importance of philosophy in determining curriculum decisions is expressed well by the classic statement of Thomas Hopkins (1941); "Philosophy has entered into every important decision that has ever been made about curriculum and teaching in the past and will continue to be the basis of every important decision in the future…There is rarely a moment in a school day when a teacher is not confronted with occasions where philosophy is a vital part of action." Hopkins' statement reminds us of how important philosophy is to all aspects of curriculum decisions, whether it operates overtly or covertly. Indeed, almost all elements of curriculum are based on philosophy. As John Goodlad (1979) points out, philosophy is the beginning point in curriculum decision making and is the basis for all subsequent decisions regarding curriculum. Philosophy becomes the criterion for determining the aims, means, and ends of curriculum. The aims are statements of value, based on philosophical beliefs; the means represent processes and methods, which reflect philosophical choices; and the ends connote the facts, concepts, and principles of the knowledge or behavior learned—what is felt to be important to learning.

Smith, Stanley, and Shores (1957) also put great emphasis on the role of philosophy in developing curriculum, asserting it is essential when formulating and justifying educational purposes, selecting and organizing knowledge, formulating basic procedures and activities, and dealing with verbal traps (what we see versus what is read). Curriculum theorists, they point out, often fail to recognize both how important philosophy is to developing curriculum and how it influences aspects of curriculum.

Philosophy and the Curriculum Specialist

The philosophy of curriculum specialists reflects their life experiences, common sense, social and economic background, education, and general beliefs about people. An individual's philosophy evolves and continues to evolve as long as there is personal growth, development, and learning from experience. Philosophy is a description, explanation, and evaluation of the world as seen from personal perspective, or through what some social scientists call "social lenses."

Curriculum specialists can turn to many sources of knowledge, but no matter how many sources upon which they may draw or how many authorities to whom they listen, their decisions are shaped by all the experiences that have affected them and the social groups with which they identify. These decisions are based on values, attitudes, and beliefs that they have developed, involving their knowledge and interpretation of causes, events, and their consequences. Philosophy determines principles for guiding action.

No one can be totally objective in a cultural or social setting, but curriculum specialists can broaden their base of knowledge and experiences by trying to understand other people's sense of values, and to analyze problems from various perspectives. They can also try to modify their own critical analyses and points of view by learning from their experiences and those of others. Curriculum specialists who are unwilling to modify their points of view, or compromise philosophical positions when school officials or their colleagues espouse another philosophy, are at risk of causing conflict and disrupting the school. Ronald Doll (1986) puts it this way: "Conflict among curriculum planners occurs when persons…hold positions along a continuum of [different] beliefs and…persuasions." The conflict may become so intense that "curriculum study grinds to a halt." Most of the time, the differences can be reconciled "temporarily in deference to the demands of a temporary, immediate task." However, Doll further explains that "teachers and administrators who are clearly divided in philosophy can seldom work together in close proximity for long periods of time."

The more mature and understanding, and the less personally threatened and ego-involved individuals are, the more capable they are of reexamining or modifying their philosophy, or at least of being willing to appreciate other points of view. It is important for curriculum specialists to regard their attitudes and beliefs as tentative—as subject to reexamination whenever facts or trends chal-

lenge them. Equally dangerous for curricula specialists is the opposite—indecision or lack of any
philosophy, which can be reflected in attempts to
avoid commitment to sets of values. A measure of
positive conviction is essential to prudent action.
Having a personal philosophy that is tentative or
subject to modification does not lead to lack of
conviction or disorganized behavior. Curriculum
specialists can arrive at their conclusions on the
best evidence available, and they then can change
when better evidence surfaces.

Philosophy as a Curriculum Source

The function of philosophy can be conceived as either the base for the starting point in curriculum
development, or an interdependent function of
other functions in curriculum development. John
Dewey (1916) represents the first school of
thought, by contending that "philosophy may…be
defined as the general theory of education," and
that "the business of philosophy is to provide [the
framework] for the aims and methods" of schools.
For Dewey, philosophy provides a generalized
meaning to our lives and a way of thinking, "an explicit formulation of the…mental and moral attitudes in respect to the difficulties of contemporary
social life." Philosophy is not only a starting point
for schools, it is also crucial for all curriculum activities. For as Dewey adds, "Education is the laboratory in which philosophic distinctions become
concrete and are tested."

Highly influenced by Dewey, Ralph Tyler's
(1949) framework of curriculum includes philosophy as only one of five criteria commonly used for
selecting educational purposes. The relationship
between philosophy and the other criteria—studies
of learners, studies of contemporary life, suggestions from subject specialists, and the psychology
of learning—is the basis for determining the
school's purposes. Although philosophy is not the
starting point in Tyler's curriculum, but rather interacts on an equal basis with the other criteria, it
does seem to place more importance on philosophy for developing educational purposes. Tyler
(1949) writes, "The educational and social philos-

ophy to which the school is committed can serve as
the first screen for developing the social program."
He concludes that "philosophy attempts to define
the nature of the good life and a good society," and
that the "educational philosophies in a democratic
society are likely to emphasize strongly democratic values in schools."

There can be no serious discussion about philosophy until we embrace the question of what is
education. When we agree on what is education,
we can ask what is the school's purpose. We can
then pursue philosophy, aims, and goals of curriculum. According to Goodlad (1979), the school's
first responsibility is to the social order, what he
calls the "nation-state," but in our society the sense
of individual growth and potential is paramount.
This duality—society vs. the individual—has been
a major philosophical issue in western society for
centuries and was a very important issue in
Dewey's works. As Dewey (1916) claimed, we not
only wish "to make [good] citizens and workers"
but also we ultimately want "to make human beings who will live life to the fullest."

The compromise of the duality between
national allegiance and individual fulfillment is a
noble aim that should guide all curriculum specialists—from the means to the ends. When many
individuals grow and prosper, then society flour-
ishes. The original question set forth by Goodlad
can be answered: Education is growth and the focal
point for the individual as well as society; it is a
never ending process of life, and the more refined
the guiding philosophy the better the quality of the
educational process.

Major Educational Philosophies. In considering the influence on philosophic thought on curriculum, several classification schemes are possible;
therefore, no superiority is claimed for the categories used in the tables. The cluster of ideas are organized here as those that often evolve openly or
unwittingly during curriculum planning.

Four major educational philosophies have
influenced curriculum in the United States: Perennialism, Essentialism, Progressivism, and Reconstructionism. Table 2.1 provides an overview of
these education philosophies, and how they affect

TABLE 2.1   Overview of Educational Philosophies

	Philosophical Base	Instructional Objective	Knowledge	Role of Teacher	Curriculum Focus	Related Curriculum Trends
Perennialism	Realism	To educate the rational person; to cultivate the intellect	Focus on past and perm-anent studies; mastery of facts and timeless knowledge	Teacher helps students think rationally; based on Socratic method and oral expo-sition; explicit teaching of traditional values	Classical subjects; literary analysis; constant curriculum	Great books; *Paideia* proposal
Essentialism	Idealism, Realism	To promote the intel-lectual growth of the individ-ual; to educate the competent person	Essential skills and academic subjects; mastery of concepts and principles of subject matter	Teacher is authority in his or her field; explicit teaching of traditional values	Essential skills (three Rs) and essential sub-jects (English, arithmetic, science, history, and foreign language)	Back to basics; excellence in education
Progressivism	Pragmatism	To promote democratic, social living	Knowledge lends to growth and development; a living-learning process; focus on active and interesting learning	Teacher is a guide for problem solving and scientific inquiry	Based on stu-dents' interests; involves the application of human prob-lems and affairs; inter-disciplinary subject matter; activities and projects	Relevant curriculum; humanistic education; alternative and free schooling
Reconstructionism	Pragmatism	To improve and reconstruct society; education for change and social reform	Skills and subjects needed to identify and ameliorate problems of society; learning is active and concerned with contemporary and future society	Teacher serves as an agent of change and reform; acts as a project director and research leader, helps students become aware of problems confronting humankind	Emphasis on social sciences and social research meth-ods; examina-tion of social, economic and political prob-lems; focus on present and fu-ture trends as well as national and interna-tional issues	Equality of education; cultural pluralism; international education; futurism

Source: Allan C. Ornstein and Francis P. Hunkins, *Curriculum: Foundations, Principles, and Theory,* 2nd ed. (Boston: Allyn and Bacon, 1993), p. 62.

curriculum, instruction, and teaching. Teachers and administrators should compare the content of the categories with their own philosophical "lens" in terms of how they view curriculum, and how other views of curriculum and related instructional and teaching issues may disagree.

Another way of interpreting philosophy and its effect on curriculum is to analyze philosophy in terms of polarity. The danger of this method is to simplify it in terms of a dichotomy, not to recognize that there are overlaps and shifts. Table 2.2 illustrates philosophy in terms of traditional and contemporary categories. The traditional philosophy, as shown, tends to overlap with Perennialism and Essentialism. Contemporary philosophy tends to coincide with Progressivism and Reconstructionism.

Table 2.2 shows that traditional philosophy focuses on the past, emphasizes fixed and absolute values, and glorifies our cultural heritage. Contemporary philosophy emphasizes the present and future, and views events as changeable and relative; for the latter, nothing can be preserved forever, for despite any attempt, change is inevitable. The traditionalists wish to train the mind, emphasize subject matter, and fill the learner with knowledge and information. Those who ascribe to contemporary philosophies are more concerned with problem solving and emphasize student interests and needs. Whereas subject matter is considered important for its own sake, according to traditionalists, certain subjects are more important than others. For contemporary educators, subject matter is considered a medium for teaching skills and attitudes, and most subjects have similar value. According to the traditionalists, the teacher is an authority in subject matter, who dominates the lesson with explanations and lectures; as for the contemporary proponent, the teacher is a guide for learning, as well as an agent for change; students and teachers often are engaged in dialogue.

In terms of social issues and society, the traditionalist views education as a means of providing direction, control, and restraint, while their counterparts focus on individual expression and freedom from authority. Citizenship is linked to cognitive development for the traditional educator, and it is linked to moral and social development for the contemporary educator. Knowledge and the disciplines prepare students for freedom, according to the traditional view, but it is direct experience in democratic living and political/social action which prepares students for freedom, according to the contemporary ideal. Traditionalists believe in excellence and contemporary educators favor equality. The traditional view of education maintains that group values come first, where cooperative and conforming behaviors are important for the good of society. Contemporary educators assert that what is good for the individual should come first, and they believe in the individual modifying and perhaps reconstructing society.

The Curriculum Specialist at Work

Philosophy gives meaning to our decisions and actions. In the absence of a philosophy, educators are vulnerable to externally imposed prescriptions, to fads and frills, to authoritarian schemes, and to other "-isms." Dewey (1916) was so convinced of the importance of philosophy that he viewed it as the all-encompassing aspect of the educational process—as necessary for "forming fundamental dispositions, intellectual and emotional, toward nature and fellow man." If this conclusion is accepted, it becomes evident that many aspects of a curriculum, if not most of the educational processes in school, are developed from a philosophy. Even if it is believed that Dewey's point is an overstatement, the pervasiveness of philosophy in determining views of reality, the values and knowledge that are worthwhile, and the decisions to be made about education and curriculum should still be recognized.

Very few schools adopt a single philosophy; in practice, most schools combine various philosophies. Moreover, the author's position is that no single philosophy, old or new, should serve as the exclusive guide for making decisions about schools or about the curriculum. All philosophical groups want the same things of education—that is, they wish to improve the educational process, to enhance the achievement of the learner, to produce better and more productive citizens, and to

TABLE 2.2   Overview of Traditional and Contemporary Philosophies

Philosophical Consideration	Traditional Philosophy	Contemporary Philosophy
Educational philosophy	Perennialism, Essentialism	Progressivism, Reconstructionism
Direction in time	Superiority of past; education for preserving past	Education is growth; reconstruction of present experiences; changing society; concern for future and shaping it
Values	Fixed, absolute, objective and/or universal	Changeable, subjective, and/or relative
Educational process	Education is viewed as instruction; mind is discipline and filled with knowledge	Education is viewed as creative self-learning; active process in which learner reconstructs knowledge
Intellectual emphasis	To train or discipline the mind; emphasis on subject matter	To engage in problem-solving activities and social activities; emphasis on student interest and needs
Worth of subject matter	Subject matter for its own importance; certain subjects are better than others for training the mind	Subject matter is a medium for teaching skills, attitudes and intellectual processes; all subjects have similar value for problem-solving activities
Curriculum content	Curriculum is composed of three Rs, as well as liberal studies or essential academic subjects	Curriculum is composed of three Rs, as well as skills and concepts in arts, sciences, and vocational studies
Learning	Emphasis on cognitive learning; learning is acquiring knowledge and/or competency in disciplines	Emphasis on whole child; learning is giving meaning to experiences and/or active involvement in reform
Grouping	Homogeneous grouping and teaching of students by ability	Heterogeneous grouping and integration of students by ability (as well as race, sex and class)
Teacher	Teacher is an authority on subject matter; teacher plans activities; teacher supplies knowledge to student; teacher talks, dominates lesson; Socratic method	Teacher is a guide for inquiry and change agent; teacher and students plan activities; students learn on their own independent of the teacher; teacher-student dialogue, student initiates much of the discussion and activities
Social roles	Education involves direction, control, and restraint; group (family, community, church, nation, etc.) always comes first	Education involves individual expression and imposition from authority; individual comes first
Citizenship	Cognitive development leads to good citizenship	Moral and social development leads to good citizenship
Freedom and democracy	Acceptance of one's fate, conformity and compliance with authority; knowledge and discipline prepare students for freedom	Emphasis on creativeness, nonconformity and self-actualization; direct experiences in democratic living and political/social action prepare students for freedom
Excellence vs equality	Excellence in education; education as far as human potential permits; academic rewards and jobs based on merit	Equality of education; education which permits more than one chance and more than an equal chance to disadvantaged groups; education and employment sectors consider unequal abilities of individuals and put some restraints on achieving individuals so that different outcomes and group scores, if any, are reduced
Society	Emphasis on group values; acceptance of norms of and roles in society; cooperative and conforming behavior; importance of society; individual restricted by custom and tradition of society	Emphasis on individual growth and development; belief in individual with ability to modify, even reconstruct the social environment; independent and self-realizing, fully functioning behavior; importance of person; full opportunity to develop one's own potential

improve society. Because of their different views of reality, values, and knowledge, however, they find it difficult to agree on how to achieve these ends.

What needs to be done, as curricularists, is to search for the middle ground, a highly elusive and abstract concept, where there is no extreme emphasis on subject matter or student, cognitive development or sociopsychological development, excellence or equality. What we need is a prudent school philosophy, one that is politically and economically feasible, that serves the needs of students and society. Implicit in this view of education is that too much emphasis on any one philosophy may do harm and cause conflict. How much one philosophy is emphasized, under the guise of reform (or for whatever reason), is critical because no one society can give itself over to extreme "-isms" or political views and still remain a democracy. The kind of society which evolves is in part reflected in the education system, which is influenced by the philosophy that is eventually defined and developed.

CONCLUSION

In the final analysis, curriculum specialists must understand that they are continuously faced with curriculum decisions, and that philosophy is important in determining these decisions. Unfortunately, few school people test their notions of curriculum against their school's statement of philosophy. According to Brandt and Tyler (1983), it is not uncommon to find teachers and administrators developing elaborate lists of behavioral objectives with little or no consideration to the overall philosophy of the school. Curriculum workers need to provide assistance in developing and designing school practices that coincide with the philosophy of the school and community. Teaching, learning, and curriculum are all interwoven in school practices and should reflect a school's and a community's philosophy.

REFERENCES

Brandt, R. S., and Tyler, R. W. (1983). "Goals and Objectives," in F. W. English, ed., *Fundamental Curriculum Decisions,* Alexandria, VA: Association for Supervision and Curriculum Development.

Dewey, J. (1916). *Democracy and Education.* New York, N.Y.: Macmillan, p. 383–384.

Doll, R. C. (1986). *Curriculum Improvement: Decision-making and Process,* 6th ed. Boston, MA: Allyn and Bacon, p. 30.

Goodlad, J. I. (1984). *A Place Called School.* New York, N.Y.: McGraw-Hill.

Goodlad, J. I. (1979a). *Curriculum Inquiry.* New York, N.Y.: McGraw-Hill.

Goodlad, J. I. (1979b). *What Schools Are For.* Bloomington, IN: Phi Delta Kappa Educational Foundation.

Hopkins, L. T. (1941). *Interaction: The Democratic Process.* Boston, MA: D. C. Heath, p. 198–200.

Smith, B. O., Stanley, W. O., and Shores, J. H. (1957). *Fundamentals of Curriculum Development,* rev. ed. New York, N.Y.: Worldbook.

Tyler, R. W. (1949). *Basic Principles of Curriculum and Instruction.* Chicago, IL: University of Chicago Press, p. 33–34.

DISCUSSION QUESTIONS

1. Which philosophical approach reflects your beliefs about (a) the school's purpose, (b) what subjects are of value, (c) how students learn, and (d) the process of teaching and learning?
2. What curriculum focus would the perennialists and essentialists recommend for our increasingly diverse school age population?
3. What curriculum would the progressivists and reconstructionists select for a multicultural student population?
4. Should curriculum workers adopt a single philosophy to guide their practices? Why? Why not?
5. Which philosophy is most relevant to contemporary education? Why?

Goals and Objectives

RONALD S. BRANDT
RALPH W. TYLER

FOCUSING QUESTIONS

1. *Why is it important to establish goals for student learning?*
2. *How do goals and objectives differ?*
3. *What are three types of goals?*
4. *What are the factors that should be considered when developing educational goals?*
5. *What is the relationship between goals and learning activities?*
6. *In what ways are curriculum goals integral to the process of evaluation?*
7. *What types of goals should be addressed by schools?*

Whether planning for one classroom or many, curriculum developers must have a clear idea of what they expect students to learn. Establishing goals is an important and necessary step because there are many desirable things students could learn—more than schools have time to teach them—so schools should spend valuable instructional time only on high priority learnings.

Another reason for clarifying goals is that schools must be able to resist pressures from various sources. Some of the things schools are asked to teach are untrue, would hinder students' development, or would help make them narrow, bigoted persons. Some would focus students' learning so narrowly it would reduce, rather than increase, their life options.

FORMS OF GOALS AND OBJECTIVES

Statements of intent appear in different forms, and words such as goals, objectives, aims, ends, out-comes, and purposes are often used interchangeably. Some people find it useful to think of goals as long-term aims to be achieved eventually and objectives as specific learning students are to acquire as a result of current instruction.

Planners in the Portland, Oregon, area schools say these distinctions are not clear enough to meet organizational planning requirements. They use "goal" to mean any desired outcome of a program, regardless of its specificity, and "objective" only in connection with *program change objectives,* which are defined as statements of intent to change program elements in specified ways. Doherty and Peters (1981) say this distinction avoids confusion and is consistent with the philosophy of "management by objectives."

They refer to three types of goals: instructional, support, and management. Educational goals are defined as learnings to be acquired; support goals as services to be rendered; and management goals as functions of management, such as planning, operating, and evaluating. Such a goal structure permits evaluation to focus on measures of learning acquired (educational outcomes), measures of quantity and quality of service delivery (support outcomes), and measures of quality and effectiveness of management functions (management outcomes).

The Tri-County Goal Development Project, which has published 14 volumes containing over 25,000 goal statements,[1] is concerned only with *educational goals*. For these collections, the following distinctions are made within the general category of "goals":

System level goals (set for the school district by the board of education)

Program level goals (set by curriculum personnel in each subject field)

Course level goals (set by groups of teachers for each subject or unit of instruction)

Instructional level goals (set by individual teachers for daily planning)

Examples of this outcome hierarchy are shown in Figure 3.1.

What distinguishes this system of terminology from others is its recognition that a learning outcome has the same essential character at all levels of planning (hence the appropriateness of a single term, goal, to describe it); and that the level of generality used to represent learning varies with the planning requirements at each level of school organization. The degree of generality chosen for

planning at each level is, of course, a matter of judgment; there is no "correct" level but only a sense of appropriateness to purpose.

Teachers, curriculum specialists, and university consultants who write and review course goals use the following guidelines (Doherty and Peters, 1980, pp. 26–27):

1. Is the stated educational outcome potentially significant?
2. Does the goal begin with "The student knows…" if it is a knowledge goal and "The student is able to…" if it is a process goal?
3. Is the goal stated in language that is sufficiently clear, concise, and appropriate? (Can it be stated in simpler language and/or fewer words?)
4. Can learning experiences be thought of that would lead to the goal's achievement?
5. Do curricular options exist for the goal's achievement? (Methodology should not be a part of the learning outcome statement.)
6. Does the goal clearly contribute to the attainment of one or more of the program goals in its subject area?
7. Can the goal be identified with the approximate level of student development?
8. Can criteria for evaluating the goal be identified?

Curriculum developers need to decide the types and definitions of goals most useful to them and to users of their materials. Some authors advise

System Goal:	The student knows and is able to apply basic scientific and technological processes.
Program Goal:	The student is able to use the conventional language, instruments, and operations of science.
Course Goal:	The student is able to classify organisms according to their conventional taxonomic categories.
Instructional Goal:	The student is able to correctly classify cuttings from the following tress as needle-leaf, hemlock, pine, spruce, fir, larch, cypress, redwood, and cedar.

FIGURE 3.1 Examples of Goals at Each Level of Planning

avoiding vagueness by using highly specific language.[2] Mager (1962) and other writers insist that words denoting observable behaviors, such as "construct" and "identify" should be used in place of words like "understand" and "appreciate." Others reject this approach, claiming that behavioral objectives "are in no way adequate for conceptualizing most of our most cherished educational aspirations" (Eisner, 1979, p. 101). Unfortunately this dispute has developed into a debate about behavioral objectives rather than dialogue over the kinds of behavior appropriate for a humane and civilized person.

The debate is partly semantic and partly conceptual. To some persons the word "behavior" carries the meaning of an observable act, like the movement of the fingers in typing. To them, behavioral objectives refer only to overt behavior. Others use the term "behavior" to emphasize the active nature of the learner. They want to emphasize that learners are not passive receptacles but living, reasoning persons. In this sense behavior refers to all kinds of human reactions.

For example, a detailed set of "behavioral goals" was prepared by French and associates (1957). Organized under the major headings of "self-realization," "face-to-face relationships," and "membership in large organizations," *Behavioral Goals of General Education in High School* includes aims such as "Shows growing ability to appreciate and apply good standards of performance and artistic principles." These are expanded by illustrative behaviors such as "Appreciates good workmanship and design in commercial products."

The other aspect of the debate over behavioral objectives arises from focusing on limited kinds of learning, such as training factory workers to perform specific tasks. The term "conditioning" is commonly used for the learning of behaviors initiated by clear stimuli and calling for automatic, fixed responses. Most driving behavior, for example, consists of conditioned responses to traffic lights, to the approach of other cars and pedestrians, and to the sensations a driver receives from the car's movements. Conditioning is a necessary and important type of learning.

In some situations, though, an automatic response is inappropriate. A more complex model of learning compatible with development of responsible persons in a changing society conceives of the learner as actively seeking meaning. This implies understanding and conscious pursuit of one's goals. The rewards of such learning include the satisfaction of coping with problems successfully.

Planning curriculum for self-directed learning requires goals that are not directly observable: ways of thinking, understanding of concepts and principles, broadening and deepening of interests, changing of attitudes, developing satisfying emotional responses to aesthetic experiences, and the like.

Even these goals, however, should use terms with clearly defined meanings. Saying that a student should "understand the concept of freedom" is far too broad and ambiguous, both because the meaning of the term "concept" is not sufficiently agreed on among educators, and because concept words such as "freedom" have too great a range of possible informational loadings to ensure similar interpretation from teacher to teacher. If used at all, such a statement would be at the program level, and would require increasingly specific elaboration at the course and lesson plan levels.

Some educators find it useful to refer to a particular type of goal as a *competency*. Used in the early 1970s in connection with Oregon's effort to relate high school instruction to daily life (Oregon State Board, 1972), the term "minimum competency" has become identified with state and district testing programs designed to ensure that students have a minimum level of basic skills before being promoted or graduated. Spady (1978) and other advocates of performance-based education point out that competency involves more than "capacities" such as the ability to read and calculate; it should refer to *application* of school-learned skills in situations outside of school.

One definition of competency is the ability to perform a set of related tasks with a high degree of skill. The concept is especially useful in vocational education, where a particular competency can be broken down through task analysis into its component skills so that teachers and curriculum planners have both a broad statement of expected performance and an array of skills specific enough to be taught and measured (Chalupsky and others, 1981).

CONSIDERATIONS IN CHOOSING GOALS

Educational goals should reflect three important factors: the nature of organized knowledge, the nature of society, and the nature of learners (Tyler, 1949). An obvious source is the nature of organized fields of study. Schools teach music, chemistry, and algebra because these fields have been developed through centuries of painstaking inquiry. Each academic discipline has its own concepts, principles, and processes. It would be unthinkable to neglect passing on to future generations this priceless heritage and these tools for continued learning.

Another factor affecting school goals is the nature of society. For example, the goals of education in the United States are quite different from those in the Soviet Union. In the United States we stress individuality, competition, creativity, and freedom to choose government officials. Soviet schools teach loyalty to the state and subordination of one's individuality to the welfare of the collective. One result is that most American schools offer a great many electives, while the curriculum in Soviet schools consists mostly of required subjects. For example, all students in the U.S.S.R. must study advanced mathematics and science to serve their technologically advanced nation (Wirszup, 1981).

U.S. schools have assumed, explicitly or implicitly, many goals related to the nature of society. For example, schools offer drug education, sex education, driver education, and other programs because of concerns about the values and behavior of youth and adults. Schools teach visual literacy because of the influence of television, consumer education because our economic system offers so many choices, and energy education because of the shortage of natural resources.

A goal statement by Ehrenberg and Ehrenberg (1978) specifically recognizes the expectations of society. Their model for curriculum development begins with a statement of "ends sought": "It is intended that as a result of participating in the K–12 educational program students will consistently and effectively take *intelligent, ethical action*: (1) to accomplish the tasks society legitimately expects of all its members, and (2) to establish and pursue worthwhile goals of their own choosing."

The curriculum development process outlined by the Ehrenbergs involves preparing a complete rationale for the ends-sought statement and then defining, for example, areas of societal expectations. The work of the curriculum developer consists of defining a framework of "criterion tasks," all derived either from expectations of society or necessary to pursue individual goals. These tasks, at various levels of pupil development, become the focus of day-to-day instruction. In this way, all curriculum is directly related to school system goals.

A third consideration in choosing goals, sometimes overlooked, is the nature of learners. For example, because Lawrence Kohlberg (1980) has found that children pass through a series of stages in their moral development, he believes schools should adopt the goal of raising students' levels of moral reasoning. Sternberg (1981) and other "information processing" psychologists believe that intelligence is, partly at least, a set of strategies and skills that can be learned. Their research suggests, according to Sternberg, that schools can and should set a goal of improving students' intellectual performance.

Recognizing that students often have little interest in knowledge for its own sake or in adult applications of that knowledge, some educators believe goals should not only be based on what we know about students, but should come from students themselves. Many alternative schools emphasize this source of goals more than conventional schools typically do (Raywid, 1981).

While knowledge, society, and learners are all legitimate considerations, the three are sometimes in conflict. For example, many of the products of the curriculum reform movement of the 1960s had goals based almost exclusively on the nature of knowledge. The emphasis of curriculum developers was on the "structure of the disciplines" (Bruner, 1960). Goals of some curriculums failed to fully reflect the nature of society and students, so teachers either refused to use them or gave up after trying them for a year or two (Stake and Easley, 1978).

In the 1970s educators and the general public reacted against this discipline-centered emphasis by stressing practical activities drawn from daily life. Schools were urged to teach students how to balance a checkbook, how to choose economical purchases, how to complete a job application, and how to read a traffic ticket. Career education enthusiasts, not content with the reasonable idea that education should help prepare students for satisfying careers, claimed that *all* education should be career-related in some way.

Conflicts of this sort between the academic and the practical are persistent and unavoidable, but curriculum developers err if they emphasize only one source of goals and ignore the others. If noneducators are preoccupied with only one factor, educational leaders have a responsibility to stress the importance of the others and to insist on balance.

SCOPE OF THE SCHOOL'S RESPONSIBILITY

There have been many attempts to define the general aims of schools and school programs, including the well-known Cardinal Principles listed by a national commission in 1918. The seven goals in that report—health, fundamental processes, worthy home membership, vocation, civic education, worthy use of leisure, and ethical character—encompass nearly every aspect of human existence, and most goal statements written since that time have been equally comprehensive.

Some authors contend that schools are mistaken to assume such broad aims. Martin (1980) argued that intellectual development and citizenship are the only goals for which schools should have primary responsibility and that other institutions should be mainly responsible for such goals

as worthy home membership. He proposed that schools undertake a new role of coordinating educational efforts of all community agencies.

Paul (1982) reported that in three different communities large numbers of teachers, students, and parents agreed on a limited set of goals confined mostly to basic skills. Paul contended that schools often confuse the issue when involving citizens in setting goals because they ask what students should learn rather than what schools should teach. Goal surveys conducted by her organization showed, she said, that adults want young people to develop many qualities for which they do not expect schools to be responsible.

Undeniably, the aims and activities of U.S. schools are multiple and diverse. They not only teach toothbrushing, crafts, religion, care of animals, advertising, cooking, automobile repair, philosophy, hunting, and chess; they also provide health and food services to children, conduct parent education classes, and offer a variety of programs for the elderly. Periodic review of these obligations is clearly in order. However, in trying to delimit their mission schools must not minimize concern for qualities that, though hard to define and develop, distinguish educated persons from the less educated.

A carefully refined statement of goals of schooling in the United States was developed by Goodlad (1979) and his colleagues in connection with their Study of Schooling. Deliberately derived from an analysis of hundreds of goal statements adopted by school districts and state departments of education so as to reflect accurately the currently declared aims of American education, the list comprises 65 goals in 12 categories, including "intellectual development," "self-concept," and "moral and ethical character."

An equally broad set of goals is used in Pennsylvania's Educational Quality Assessment, which includes questions intended to measure such elusive aims as "understanding others" and "self-esteem." School districts must give the tests at least once every five years as part of a plan to make schools accountable for the 12 state-adopted goals

(Seiverling, 1980). An adaptation of the Pennsylvania goals was used by the ASCD Committee on Research and Theory (1980) in connection with their plan for *Measuring and Attaining the Goals of Education.*

In many cases schools contribute modestly or not at all to helping students become loving parents and considerate neighbors. In other cases, school experiences may have lasting effects on values, attitudes, and behavior. We believe school goals should include such aims as "interpersonal relations" and "autonomy," as well as "intellectual development" and "basic skills" (Goodlad, 1979), although the goal statement should specifically recognize that most goals are not the exclusive domain of schools but are a shared responsibility with other institutions.

ESTABLISHING LOCAL GOALS

It is usually helpful to begin identification of goals by listing all the promising possibilities from various sources. Consider contemporary *society.* What things could one's students learn that would help them meet current demands and take advantage of future opportunities? General data about modern society may be found in studies of economic, political, and social conditions. Data directly relevant to the lives of one's students will usually require local studies, which can be made by older students, parents, and other local people.

Consider the *background of the students:* their previous experiences, things they have already learned, their interests and needs; that is, the gaps between desired ways of thinking, feeling, and acting and their present ways. This information should be specific to one's own students, although generalized studies of the development of children and youth in our culture will suggest what to look for.

Consider the potential of the various *subject fields.* What things could one's students learn about their world and themselves from the sciences, history, literature, and so on? What can mathematics provide as a resource for their lives?

Visual arts? Music? Each new generation is likely to find new possibilities in these growing fields of knowledge and human expression.

In the effort to identify possible goals don't be unduly concerned about the form in which you state these "things to be learned." For example, you may find a possibility in "learn new ways of expressing emotions through various experiences provided in literature," and another in "understanding how animal ecologies are disturbed and the consequences of the disturbance." These are in different forms and at different levels of generality, but at this stage the purpose is only to consider carefully all the promising possibilities. Later on, those selected as most important and appropriate for one's students can be refined and restated in common form so as to guide curriculum developers in designing learning experiences. At that point, it will probably be helpful to standardize terms and definitions. At early stages, however, curriculum developers should use terminology familiar and understandable to teachers, principals, parents, and citizens rather than insisting on distinctions that others may have difficulty remembering and using.

The comprehensive list of possible outcomes should be carefully scrutinized to sift out those that appear to be of minor importance or in conflict with the school's educational philosophy. The list should also be examined in the light of the apparent prospects for one's students being able to learn these things in school. For example, we know that things once learned are usually forgotten unless there are continuing opportunities to use them. So one criterion for retaining a goal is that students will have opportunities in and out of school to think, feel, and act as expected. We also know that learning of habits requires continuous practice with few errors, so work and study habits should be selected as goals only if they are to be emphasized consistently in school work.

This procedure for identifying what students are to be helped to learn is designed to prevent a common weakness in curriculum development: selection of goals that are obsolete or irrelevant, inappropriate for students' current level of development, not in keeping with sound scholarship, not in harmony with America's democratic philosophy, or for which the school cannot provide the necessary learning conditions.

A common practice when planning curriculum is to refer to published taxonomies (Bloom and others, 1956; Krathwohl and others, 1964). Taxonomies can be useful for their original purpose—classifying goals already formulated—but they do not resolve the issue of the relevance of any particular goal to contemporary society or to one's own students. The Bloom and Krathwohl taxonomies are organized in terms of what the authors conceive to be higher or lower levels, but higher ones are not always more important or even necessary. In typewriting, for example, so-called "higher mental processes" interfere with the speed and accuracy of typing.

A similar caution applies to uncritically taking goals from curriculum materials of other school systems. The fact that educators in Scarsdale or some other district chose certain goals is not in itself evidence that they are appropriate for your students.

Development of general goals for a school system should be a lengthy process with opportunities for students, parents, and others to participate. This can be done, for example, by sponsoring "town meetings," publishing draft statements of goals in local newspapers with an invitation to respond, and by holding and publicizing hearings on goals sponsored by the board of education.

A factor that complicates the matter is that some sources of goals are simply not subject to a majority vote. Knowledge—whether about physics, poetry, or welding—is the province of specialists. Educators sometimes know more about the nature of children and the learning process than many other adults in the community. Nevertheless, in a democracy there is no higher authority than the people, so the people must be involved in deciding what public schools are to teach.

Most general goals, because they are so broad and because they deal with major categories of human experience, are acceptable to most people.

Few will quarrel with a goal such as "Know about human beings, their environments and their achievements, past and present." The problem in developing a general goal statement is usually not to decide which goals are proper and which are not, but to select among many possibilities those which are most important, are at the proper level of generality, and are at least partially the responsibility of schools.

While general goals are not usually controversial, more specific ones can be. For example, parents might not quarrel with "Understand and follow practices associated with good health," but some would reject "Describe two effective and two ineffective methods of birth control." Thus, parents and other citizens should be involved in formulating course and program goals as well as general system goals.

USING GOALS TO PLAN LEARNING ACTIVITIES

To some extent, well-stated goals imply the kinds of learning activities that would be appropriate for achieving them. For example, if an instructional goal is "Solve word problems requiring estimation involving use of simple fractions such as $1/2$, $1/4$, $2/3$" students would have to practice estimating solutions to practical problems as well as learning to calculate using fractions. In many instances, however, knowing the goal does not automatically help an educator know how to teach it. For example, to enable students to "understand and appreciate significant human achievements," one teacher might have students read about outstanding scientists of the 19th century, supplement the readings with several lectures, and give a multiple choice examination. Another teacher might decide to divide students into groups and have each group prepare a presentation to the class about a great scientist using demonstrations, dramatic skits, and so on. Forging the link between goals and other steps in curriculum development requires professional knowledge, experience, and imagination.

A factor that distorts what might appear to be a straightforward relationship between goals and activities is that every instructional activity has multiple goals. The goal-setting process is sometimes seen as a one-to-one relationship between various levels of goals and levels of school activity. For example, the mission of a local school system might be to "Offer all students equitable opportunities for a basic education plus some opportunities to develop individual talents and interests." "Basic education" would be defined to include "Communicate effectively by reading, writing, speaking, observing, and listening." A middle school in that district might have a goal such as "Read and understand nonfiction at a level of the average article in *Reader's Digest,*" or more specifically, "Students will be able to distinguish between expressions of fact and opinion in writing."

While similar chains of related goals are basic to sound curriculum planning, developers should never assume that such simplicity fully represents the reality of schools. When a teacher is engaged in teaching reading he or she must also be conscious of and teach toward other goals: thinking ability, knowledge of human achievements, relationships with others, positive self-concept, and so on.

Not only must teachers address several officially adopted "outside" goals all at once; they must cope with "inside" goals as well. Although Goodlad (1979) uses declared goals to remind educators and the public what schools are said to be for, he cautions that the ends-means model doesn't do justice to the educational process and offers, as an alternative, an ecological perspective. Insisting that school activities should "be viewed for their intrinsic value, quite apart from their linkage or lack of linkage to stated ends" (p. 76), he points out that in addition to "goals that have been set outside of the system for the system" there are also goals inside the system—"students' goals, teachers' goals, principals' goals, and so on—and...these goals are not necessarily compatible" (p. 77).

The message to curriculum developers is that although "outside" goals and objectives are fundamental to educational planning, the relationship between purposes and practices is more complex than it may seem.

USING GOALS
IN CURRICULUM EVALUATION

Some writers argue that specific objectives are essential in order to design suitable evaluation plans and write valid test items. The work of the National Assessment of Educational Progress shows, however, that even evaluators may not require objectives written in highly technical language.[3] National Assessment objectives do not contain stipulations of conditions or performance standards; in fact they are expected to meet just two criteria: clarity and importance. The educators, citizens, and subject matter experts who review the objectives are asked, "Do you understand what this objective means? How important is it that students learn this in school?" Objectives are often considered clear and important even though they are stated briefly and simply. When the objectives have been identified, National Assessment staff members or consultants develop exercises designed to be operational definitions of the intended outcomes. Conditions, standards of performance, and so on are specified for the exercises, not for the objectives.

Setting goals is difficult because it requires assembling and weighing all the factors to be considered in selecting the relatively few but important goals that can be attained with the limited time and resources available to schools. The demands and opportunities of society, the needs of students, the resources of scholarship, the values of democracy, and the conditions needed for effective learning must all be considered.

A common error is the failure to distinguish purposes appropriate for the school from those attainable largely through experiences in the home and community. The school can reinforce the family in helping children develop punctuality, dependability, self-discipline, and other important habits. The school can be and usually is a community in which children and adults respect each other, treat each other fairly, and cooperate. But the primary task for which public schools were established is to enlarge students' vision and experience by helping them learn to draw upon the resources of scholarship, thus overcoming the limitations of direct experience and the narrow confines of a local environment. Students can learn to use sources of knowledge that are more accurate and reliable than folklore and superstition. They can participate vicariously through literature and the arts with peoples whose lives are both similar to and different from those they have known. The school is the only institution whose primary purpose is enabling students to explore these scholarly fields and to learn to use them as resources in their own lives. Great emphasis should be given to goals of this sort.

Goals are frequently not stated at the appropriate degree of generality-specificity for each level of educational responsibility. Goals promulgated by state education authorities should not be too specific because of the wide variation in conditions among districts in the state. State goals should furnish general guidance for the kinds and areas of learning for which schools are responsible in that state. The school district should furnish more detailed guidance by identifying goals that fall between the general aims listed by the state and those appropriate to the local school. School goals should be adapted to the background of students and the needs and resources of the neighborhood, especially the educational role the parents can assume. The goals of each teacher should be designed to attain the goals of the school. The test of whether a goal is stated at the appropriate degree of generality-specificity is its clarity and helpfulness in guiding the educational activities necessary at that level of responsibility.

CONCLUSION

When states list specific skills as goals and develop statewide testing programs to measure them, they may overlook a significant part of what schools should teach: understanding, analysis, and problem solving. If students are taught only to follow prescribed rules, they will be unable to deal with varied situations. Another common limitation of such lists is their neglect of affective components, such as finding satisfaction in reading and developing the habit of reading to learn.

The form and wording of goals and objectives should be appropriate for the way they are to be used. For clarity, we have generally used the term "goal" for all statements of intended learning outcomes regardless of their degree of specificity, but we recognize that no one formula is best for all situations. The criterion for judging goals and objectives is their usefulness in communicating educational purposes and their helpfulness to teachers in planning educational activities.

ENDNOTES

1. Available from Commercial-Educational Distributing Service, P.O. Box 4791, Portland, OR 97208.
2. Collections of "measurable objectives" may be purchased from Instructional Objectives Exchange, Box 24095-M, Los Angeles, CA 90024-0095.
3. National Assessment has developed objectives for a number of subject areas, including art, citizenship, career and occupational development, literature, mathematics, music, reading, science, social studies, and writing. Because they have been carefully written and thoroughly reviewed, the objectives and accompanying exercises are a helpful resource for local curriculum developers, although they are designed only for assessment, not for curriculum planning.

REFERENCES

ASCD Committee on Research and Theory, Wilbur B. Brookover, Chairman. *Measuring and Attaining the Goals of Education.* Alexandria, Va.: Association for Supervision and Curriculum Development, 1980.

Bloom, Benjamin S., ed. *Taxonomy of Educational Objectives: The Classification of Educational Goals. Handbook 1: Cognitive Domain.* New York: David McKay Co., Inc., 1956.

Bruner, Jerome. *The Process of Education.* Cambridge: Belknap Press, 1960.

Chalupsky, Albert B.; Phillips-Jones, Linda; and Danoff, Malcolm N. "Competency Measurement in Vocational Education: A Review of the State of the Art." Prepared by American Institute for Research. Washington, D.C.: Office of Vocational and Adult Education, U.S. Department of Education, 1981.

Commission on the Reorganization of Secondary Education, U.S. Office of Education. *Cardinal Principles of Secondary Education.* Washington, D.C.: Government Printing Office, 1918.

Doherty, Victor W., and Peters, Linda B. "Introduction to K–12 Course Goals for Educational Planning and Evaluation." 3rd ed. Portland, Oregon: Commercial-Educational Distributing Services, 1980.

Doherty, Victor W., and Peters, Linda B. "Goals and Objectives in Educational Planning and Evaluation." *Educational Leadership* 38 (May 1981): 606.

Ehrenberg, Sydelle D., and Ehrenberg, Lyle, M. *A Strategy for Curriculum Design—The ICI Model.* Miami, Florida: Institute for Curriculum and Instruction, 1978.

Eisner, Eliot W. *The Educational Imagination.* New York: Macmillan Publishing Co., Inc., 1979.

French, Will. *Behavioral Goals of General Education in High School.* New York: Russell Sage Foundation, 1957.

Goodlad, John I. *What Schools Are For?* Bloomington, Indiana: Phi Delta Kappa, 1979.

Kohlberg, Lawrence. "Moral Education: A Response to Thomas Sobol." *Educational Leadership* 38 (October 1980): 19–23.

Krathwohl, David R., and others. *Taxonomy of Educational Objectives: The Classification of Educational Goals, Handbook II: Affective Domain.* New York: David McKay Company, Inc., 1964.

Lindvall, C. M., ed. *Defining Educational Objectives.* Pittsburgh: University of Pittsburgh Press, 1964.

Mager, R. F. *Preparing Instructional Objectives.* Palo Alto: Fearon Publishers, 1962.

Martin, John Henry. "Reconsidering the Goals of High School Education." *Educational Leadership* 37 (January 1980): 278–285.

Mathematics Objectives, Second Assessment. Denver: National Assessment of Educational Programs, 1978.

Oregon State Board of Education. "Minimum State Requirements Standards for Graduation from High School." Salem, Oregon, 1972.

Paul, Regina. "Are You Out On a Limb?" *Educational Leadership* 39 (January 1982): 260–264.

Raywid, Mary Anne. "The First Decade of Public School Alternatives." *Phi Delta Kappan* 62 (April 1981): 551–554.

Saylor, J. Galen; Alexander, William M.; and Lewis, Arthur J. *Curriculum Planning for Better Teaching and Learning.* 4th ed. New York: Holt, Rinehart and Winston, 1981.

Seiverling, Richard F., ed. *Educational Quality Assessment: Getting Out The EQA Results.* Harrisburg, Pa.: Pennsylvania Department of Education, 1980.

Spady, William G. "The Concept and Implications of Competency-Based Education." *Educational Leadership* 36 (October 1978): 16–22.

Stake, R. E., and Easley, J. A., Jr. *Case Studies in Science Education.* 2 vols. Washington, D.C.: U.S. Government Printing Office, 1978.

Sternberg, Robert J. "Intelligence as Thinking and Learning Skills." *Educational Leadership* 39 (October 1981): 18–20.

Tyler, Ralph W. *Basic Principles of Curriculum and Instruction.* 1974 ed. Chicago: University of Chicago Press, 1949.

Ward, Barbara. "The National Assessment Approach to Objectives and Exercise Development." Report No. 12-IP-55. Denver, Colo.: Education Commission of the States, September 1980.

Wirszup, Izaak. "The Soviet Challenge." *Educational Leadership* 38 (February 1981): 358–360.

DISCUSSION QUESTIONS

1. What should the goals of contemporary education be?
2. Should the goals of education be the same for all students?
3. What is the best method for defining goals, by behavioral objectives or by competencies?
4. Who should assume responsibility for determining educational goals: the federal government, the state board of education, local school districts, building principals, or the faculty at each school? Why?
5. What is the best criterion for judging goals and objectives?

Alternative Curriculum Conceptions and Designs

M. FRANCES KLEIN

FOCUSING QUESTIONS

1. *What is the measured curriculum?*
2. *In what ways do alternative curriculum conceptions and designs influence curriculum delivery and evaluation?*
3. *What common ideas do technological, cognitive processes, and academic rationalism embrace?*
4. *How do social reconstructionism and self-actualization differ?*
5. *How do the means-end, naturalistic observation, educational connoisseurship, and case study forms of evaluation differ?*
6. *Which type of curriculum conception and design do you prefer? Why?*

The field of curriculum is not without its critics. Schwab (1978) has called the study of curriculum moribund and Jackson (1981) has even questioned the existence of curriculum as a field of study. Most curriculum scholars, however, are more confident about the existence of the curriculum field since they have spent their careers in an effort to conceptualize it and study those practices which are called curriculum. Although some scholars may debate whether curriculum studies exist and if so, how to conceptualize them, few practitioners would question the existence or importance of curriculum. Curriculum is the substance of schooling—the primary reason why people attend school.

Many educational resources go to direct and support the curriculum. Countless committee meetings are held to develop it; teachers are hired, trained, and supervised in order to implement it; administrators are exhorted to provide curriculum leadership as their primary role; materials are pur-chased or created; learning resource centers are built to support the curriculum; and educational researchers seek bases for improving it.

In the comparatively short time since its generally recognized "birth" with the publication of Bobbitt's book, *The Curriculum* (1918), the growth of the field has been slow and difficult. Curriculum scholars have debated significant ideas and proposed changes, but have not always addressed themselves to what difference their ideas make to the practitioner. Little wonder, then, that the practice of curriculum continues along a single strand of development with few alternative ideas considered.

Tyler's syllabus, *Basic Principles of Curriculum and Instruction* (1950), was selected by the leadership group, Professors of Curriculum, as one of two publications which has had the most influence over the field of curriculum (Shane, 1981).[1] In the Tyler syllabus, concepts and procedures are spelled out as a way to view curriculum and they have been applied in diverse situations all over the world in curriculum development efforts. Some curriculum scholars owe their careers to their refinements and modifications of the Tyler rationale.

Tyler identified three data sources which must be used in curriculum development: society, student, and subject matter. These three data sources have historically stimulated alternative conceptions of curriculum and the development of different curriculum designs. Scholars have long recognized the importance of the three data sources, but too often missed Tyler's message—that the use of one of the data sources alone is inadequate in developing curricula. A comprehensive curriculum must use all three.

Current curriculum practice and research focus almost exclusively on just one of these data sources, subject matter. Curricula have been developed using what Eisner and Vallance (1974) call the technological conception. Referred to here as the measured curriculum, it has emerged into dominance over all other alternative conceptions and designs.

THE MEASURED CURRICULUM

The measured curriculum is familiar to all educators. Behavioral objectives, time on task, sequential learning, positive reinforcement, direct instruction, achievement testing, mastery in skills and content, and teacher accountability are essential concepts used in practice and research. The measured curriculum should neither be condemned nor used exclusively to direct curriculum practice and research. It must be recognized for its strengths and limitations. It is compatible with some of the major educational outcomes valued by society—a store of knowledge about the world, command of the basic processes of communication, and exposure to new content areas. But this conception and design of curriculum cannot accomplish everything students are expected to learn.

Most curriculum scholars have long advocated the use of different designs for a school's curriculum; subject-centered, societal-centered,

and individual-centered designs are the most commonly discussed. Unless alternatives to the technological, subject-matter-based curriculum (i.e., the measured curriculum) are used, some of the time-honored and persistently stated educational outcomes will not be accomplished.

OTHER CONCEPTIONS

Eisner and Vallance (1974) identified four other conceptions of curriculum in addition to the technological process: cognitive processes, self-actualization, social reconstruction, and academic rationalism. These four conceptions propose something the technological process does not—desired outcomes and a focus on the substance of curriculum. Two of the conceptions of curriculum, cognitive processes and academic rationalism, are often planned and implemented through the use of the technological process and a subject matter design. The other two, self-actualization and social reconstruction, require different curriculum designs and different concepts and procedures from the measured curriculum for planning and implementation.

Cognitive Processes
and Academic Rationalism

Most similar to and compatible with the concepts and procedures of the measured curriculum are academic rationalism and cognitive processes. Academic rationalism advocates that the curriculum be based on the storehouse of knowledge which has enabled humankind to advance civilization. This storehouse is defined as organized subject matter in the form of the academic disciplines. The subject-centered curriculum design and the efficient technological process of curriculum building are compatible with this conception. It has been used well in the past and continues to have strong and prestigious advocates—Adler in *The Paideia Proposal* (1982), for example. Classroom practices and research are familiar to all when they are based on this conception. It is a form of the measured curriculum.

Cognitive processes as a conception of curriculum is less tied to specific content than is academic rationalism. Cognitive processes are thought to be "content-free" in the sense that they are generalizable from one subject area to another. The concept emphasizes the ability to think, reason, and engage in problem-solving activities. The specific content used is somewhat less important than the processes to be learned. This conception, too, has its strong proponents—Bruner (1961) and Bloom (1956), for example. Many curricula include this conception of outcomes as a major part of their intent and substance.

Curriculum development in both of these conceptions occurs in a similar way. The technological approach of the Tyler rationale (1950) is commonly used as a basis for planning and implementing curricula. The subject-centered design also is commonly employed, using concepts such as behavioral objectives, sequential organization of content, time on task, appropriate practice, and achievement tests. However, teachers using the cognitive processes conception might operate more from the information processing models of teaching as conceptualized by Joyce and Weil (1980), while academic rationalists might more often employ behavioristic models.

Social Reconstruction and Self-Actualization

The last two conceptions of curriculum, social reconstruction and self-actualization, are quite different and require different approaches to their development. The concepts from the measured curriculum are not automatically transferable to research and practice based on these conceptions.

Social reconstructionists look to society as a basis for the substance of curriculum. In their view, the problems and dilemmas of society are what ought to be studied by students with the intent of creating a more just, equitable, and humane society. Students must be involved in studying how obstacles can be overcome so that a more ideal society can be created. This becomes the content of the curriculum. Students are not to learn about them simply through a subject-centered design, however. The traditional textbook coverage in sociology or political science is not what these cur-

riculum advocates favor. They want the students out in the community, using original sources, interviewing people, formulating solutions, testing hypotheses, and solving real problems—not just reading about them.

This design is societal centered rather than subject centered. The disciplines are used only as they relate to the problems being studied. Science is not studied as science nor history as history, but both subjects may be essential to understanding and developing possible resolutions to a local pollution problem. If so, students are expected to draw upon both disciplines. Through this conception and design of curriculum, students learn how to learn. They attack real problems, become meaningfully involved as citizens of the society, and begin to critically examine and help mold a better society.

Traditional concepts and processes from the measured curriculum are not applicable in practice for social reconstruction. No defined body of content can be spelled out in behavioral objectives. Time on task cannot be tracked easily since schooling is extended beyond the classroom. Time may even be "wasted" in tracking down important resources. Efficiency is not inherent to this design. Achievement also takes on a different definition, relating not to a body of prescribed content or skills but rather to how effectively the problem was studied and potentially resolved.

Testing as a form of evaluation is not applicable since each student or group of students may have studied different problems, used different resources, and posed different solutions. Other forms of evaluation emphasizing process more than content must be used. Students must be more involved in the planning, implementation, and evaluation of such a curriculum. In a social reconstructionist approach, curriculum development is not conducted prior to classroom interaction as in the measured curriculum. The curriculum must be developed jointly with the students.

The planning and implementation of a social reconstructionist's curriculum using a societal-based design would be distinctively different from other conceptions and designs. Rather than using behavioral objectives, practice would be guided by goals or general objectives such as those proposed by Zahorik (1976) or by problem-solving objectives as suggested by Eisner (1979). The use of general objectives such as learning how to study a problem or studying about discrimination, or of problem-solving objectives such as investigating the control of pollutants within the community or how the school could be a more democratic institution, allows for greater diversity in what is learned by students. All students are not expected to have the same experience or learn the same content. General objectives or problem-solving objectives open up the parameters for teaching and learning.

Classroom activities and evaluation procedures in social reconstruction would be developed through the use of criteria as proposed by Raths (1971) instead of according to the concepts of appropriate practice and achievement tests. Rather than activities which primarily provide appropriate practice for the behavior and content of the objectives, activities would be planned which permit students to make informed choices and reflect on their consequences; take risks of success or failure; and share the development, implementation, and evaluation of a plan. Evaluation procedures would focus on the provision of such activities and what is learned through them, not on the mastery of content or skills.

Teacher accountability would shift from a focus on how well students learn content to such considerations as processes used, community involvement achieved, and the diversity of relevant resources available to and used by the students. Learning in this design would not be sequential or like a stairstep as in the measured curriculum, but more like Eisner's (1979) spider-web model of learning. Teachers would draw most often from the social interaction family of teacher models as conceptualized by Joyce and Weil (1980).

Curriculum as self-actualization is even further removed from the traditional curriculum practices and research of the measured curriculum. In this conception, students become the curriculum developers, selecting for study what they are interested in, intrigued by, and curious about. The curriculum is not preplanned by adults, but evolves as a student or a group of students and their teacher explore something of interest. Growth is viewed as the process of becoming a self-actualizing person, not learning a body of content or a set of cognitive processes or studying the problems of society. Content is important to the extent that it is relevant and meaningful to the individual student, not as it is defined by someone else. The design becomes individual centered with the role of the student rather than that of the teacher being dominant.

In this conception and design, traditional concepts guiding practice are incompatible. Objectives are too directing; time on task becomes unmanageable as students pursue different ideas, at different paces, and in different ways; achievement testing is impossible when students learn different things; and appropriate practice becomes idiosyncratically defined based on students' own interests. The classroom becomes an enriched, stimulating environment to challenge and appeal to students, an active, noisy place where students interact with each other as needed, and an extension of a learning resource laboratory with diverse and plentiful materials. Students and teachers become co-learners embarked on a study plan of their own making.

For this conception of curriculum as self-actualization, new concepts and procedures must be developed and legitimatized. Eisner's (1979) concept of expressive outcomes seems uniquely fitted to this conception and design, and educational criticism and connoisseurship are better suited as a mode of evaluation (Eisner, 1979). The personal family of teaching models would be most representative of how teachers and students would interact (Joyce & Weil, 1980).

Macdonald, Wolfson, and Zaret (1973) propose learning organized around a continuous cycle of exploring, integrating, and transcending. They also identify self-evaluation as an important aspect of this conception. Accountability according to them should be social accountability. Is the school exemplifying the values which the society desires to foster within young people? Other compatible concepts will need to be developed through an exploration of this design in practice, an opportunity curriculum workers do not frequently have. From such a curriculum students learn to develop their unique talents and interests, to value learning as a process, to become even more creative, curious, and imaginative, and to become more integrated, humane, caring human beings.

NEEDED CHANGES
IN CURRICULUM RESEARCH

The procedures and concepts used in research help determine what is "seen" in the curriculum. When researchers structure interviews, questionnaires, and observation around behavioral objectives, time on task, appropriate practice, and achievement testing, those are the concepts which are documented. Rather than rely exclusively on those concepts used in the practices of the measured curriculum (upon which much of the current research on curriculum is based), alternative approaches to curriculum research must be applied for different conceptions and designs.

More naturalistic observations in classrooms for the self-actualization conception and individual-based design are needed. New approaches to determining individual perceptions of growth and relating those to classroom practices would be one way to proceed. Eisner's (1979) concepts of educational connoisseurship and criticism seem to have considerable compatibility and already offer an alternative approach to traditional curriculum research. Case studies of classrooms using the social reconstruction conception and societal-centered design may be needed as research documentation.

However the research methodologies and constructs are developed and used in relation to the alternative approaches to curriculum, they must honor and be compatible with the unique expected outcomes of each and the different concepts upon which practice is based. To do otherwise is to destroy the potential any alternative in curriculum conception and design has to enhance the growth of students. This undoubtedly will require the use of ideas other than our traditional research concepts such as validity, reliability, objectivity, and generalizability.

Research methodology and the type of research study conducted must accommodate the alternative shifts in curriculum conceptions and designs which are developed to guide practice. Researchers must learn to operationalize new concepts, to ask different questions, to view curriculum from different conceptions. The new research concepts and procedures must be compatible with the practices and reflective of the differing educational outcomes each design will encourage.

CONCLUSION

For the purposes of this chapter, the placement of basic concepts and procedures has been perhaps too narrow and somewhat rigid in order to make the case for using alternative concepts and processes for different conceptions and designs. It may well be that several concepts have applicability in more than one conception and design. Only as they are given rigorous study in research and practice will this become clear, however.

The extent to which schooling can accommodate these designs—and newer ones being developed—is a matter for debate and experimentation. However, much more can be accomplished with alternative conceptions and designs than is even thought about now. Curriculum does not have to be *either* one conception *or* another. With the use of varying conceptions and designs in each classroom, schools might well become much more attractive, challenging, and relevant places for students. And schooling as a process may become more responsive to the needs and desires of both the individual student and society.

The field of study called curriculum is alive, but not as healthy as it might be. Its health could be enhanced by enriching the diet currently restricted to the measured curriculum with more diverse nutrients from the storehouse of alternative conceptions and designs. This enrichment is a fundamental task to which future curriculum workers must address themselves.

ENDNOTE

1. The other most influential book was Dewey's *Democracy and Education* (1916).

REFERENCES

Adler, M. J. (1982). *The Paideia proposal. An educational manifesto.* New York: Macmillan.

Bloom, B. S. (Ed.). (1956). *Taxonomy of educational objectives: Cognitive domain.* New York: Longmans, Green.

Bobbitt, F. (1918). *The curriculum.* Boston, MA: Houghton Mifflin.

Bruner, J. (1961). *The process of education.* Cambridge, MA: Harvard University Press.

Dewey, J. (1916). *Democracy and education.* New York: Macmillan.

Eisner, E. W. (1979). *The educational imagination.* New York: Macmillan.

Eisner, E. W., & Vallance, E. (1974). *Conflicting conceptions of curriculum.* Berkeley, CA: McCutchan.

Jackson, P. W. (1981). Curriculum and its discontents. In H. A. Giroux, A. N. Penna, & W. F. Pinar (Eds.), *Curriculum and instruction: Alternatives in education* (pp. 367–381). Berkeley, CA: McCutchan.

Joyce, B., & Weil, M. (1980). *Models of teaching.* Englewood Cliffs, NJ: Prentice-Hall

Macdonald, J. B., Wolfson, B. J., & Zaret, E. (1973). *Reschooling society; A conceptual model.* Washington, DC: Association for Supervision and Curriculum Development.

Raths, J. D. (April, 1971). Teaching without specific objectives. *Educational Leadership, 28,* 714–720.

Schwab, J. (1978). The practical: A language for curriculum. In I. Westbury & N. J. Wilkof (Eds.), *Science, curriculum and liberal education* (pp. 287–321). Chicago, IL: University of Chicago Press.

Shane, H. G. (1981, January). Significant writings that have influenced the curriculum: 1906–81. *Phi Delta Kappan, 62* (5), 311–314.

Tyler, R. W. (1950). *Basic principles of curriculum and instruction.* Chicago, IL: University of Chicago Press.

Zahorik, J. A. (1976, April). The virtue of vagueness in instructional objectives. *Elementary School Journal, 76,* 411–419.

DISCUSSION QUESTIONS

1. Which type of curriculum conception is most relevant to contemporary education? Which is the most irrelevant?
2. Which method of evaluation is most relevant to contemporary education?
3. Suppose you are the curriculum director and can determine the curriculum for your school. Which type of curriculum conception and method of evaluation would guide your selection? Would you use a single approach to curriculum design and evaluation?
4. What is the relationship between types of curriculum conceptions and educational philosophies?
5. How might schools become more relevant and challenging places for students?

Teachers, Public Life, and Curriculum Reform

HENRY A. GIROUX

FOCUSING QUESTIONS

1. *How does curriculum discourse influence teaching?*
2. *What role does the language of curriculum play in influencing student outcomes?*
3. *How are curriculum and politics related?*
4. *In what ways does the curriculum reflect dominant social views?*
5. *How does politics influence the role of the teacher?*
6. *Why are the notions of accountability and practicality superordinate to concerns related to equity, equality, community, and social justice?*

REASSERTING THE PRIMACY OF THE POLITICAL IN CURRICULUM THEORY

The connection between curriculum and teaching is structured by a series of issues that are not always present in the language of the current educational reform movement. This is evident, for instance, in the way mainstream educational reformers often ignore the problematic relationship between curriculum as a socially constructed narrative, on the one hand, and the interface of teaching and politics on the other. Mainstream curriculum reformers often view curriculum as an objective text that merely has to be imparted to students.[1]

In opposition to this view, I want to argue that the language used by administrators, teachers, students, and others involved in either constructing, implementing, or receiving the classroom curriculum actively produces particular social identities, "imagined communities," specific competencies, and distinctive ways of life. Moreover, the language of curriculum like other discourses does not merely reflect a pregiven reality; on the contrary, it selectively offers depictions of the larger world through representations that people struggle over to name what counts as knowledge, what counts as communities of learning, what social relationships matter, and what visions of the future can be represented as legitimate (Aronowitz & Giroux, 1993).

Of course, if curriculum is seen as a terrain of struggle, one that is shot through with ethical considerations, it becomes reasonable to assume that talk about teaching and curriculum should not be removed from considerations of history, power, and politics. After all, the language of curriculum is both historical and contingent. Theories of curriculum have emerged from past struggles and are often heavily weighted in favor of those who have power, authority, and institutional legitimation.

Curriculum is also political in that state governments, locally elected school boards, and powerful business and publishing interests exercise enormous influence over teaching practices and curriculum policies (Apple & Christian-Smith,

1991). Moreover, the culture of the school is often representative of those features of the dominant culture that it affirms, sustains, selects, and legitimizes. Thus, the distinction between high and low status academic subjects, the organization of knowledge into disciplines, and the allocation of knowledge and symbolic rewards to different groups indicate how politics works to influence the curriculum.

Within dominant versions of curriculum and teaching, there is little room theoretically to understand the dynamics of power as it works in the schools, particularly around the mechanisms of tracking, racial and gender discrimination, testing, and other mechanisms of exclusion (Oaks, 1985). Mainstream educational reformers such as William Bennett, Chester Finn, and Dianne Ravitch exhibit little understanding of schooling as a site that actively produces different histories, social groups, and student identities who exist under profound conditions of inequality. This is true, in part, because many dominant versions of curriculum and teaching legitimate themselves through unproblematized claims to objectivity and an obsession with empiricist forms of accountability. But, more importantly, many mainstream theorists of curriculum refuse to link schooling to the complex political, economic, and cultural relations that structure it as a borderland of movement and translation rather than as a fixed and unitary site.

When inserted into this matrix of power, difference, and social justice, schools cannot be abstracted from the larger society in which histories mix, languages and identities intermingle, values clash, and different groups struggle over how they are represented and how they might represent themselves. Questions of representation, justice, and power are central to any critical theory of curriculum. This is especially true in a society in which African Americans, women, and other people of color are vastly underrepresented in both schools and other dominant cultural institutions. Of course, the issue of representation as I am using it here suggests that meaning is always political, actively involved in producing diverse social positions and inextricably implicated in relations of power.

Educators generally exhibit a deep suspicion of politics, and this is not unwarranted when politics is reduced to a form of dogmatism. And, yet, it is impossible for teachers to become agents in the classroom without a broader understanding of politics and the emancipatory possibilities that it provides for thinking about and shaping their own practices. Recognizing the politics of one's location as an educator should not imply that one's pedagogical practice is inflexible, fixed, or intolerant. To insist that teachers recognize the political nature of their own work can be understood as part of a broader critical effort to make them self-reflective of the interests and assumptions that shape their classroom practices. Roger Simon (1992) captures this sentiment by arguing that by inserting the political back into the discourse of teaching, educators can "initiate rather than close off the problem of responsibility" (p. 16) for those classroom practices generated by their claim to knowledge and authority.

In what follows, I want to offer an alternative language for defining the purpose and meaning of teacher work. While I have talked about teachers as intellectuals in another context, I want to extend this analysis by analyzing what implications exist for redefining teachers as public intellectuals.[2] In part, I want to explore this position by drawing upon my own training as a teacher and some of the problems I had to face when actually working in the public schools. I will conclude by highlighting some of the defining principles that might structure the content and context of what it means for teachers to assume the role of a public intellectual.

TRADITION AND THE PEDAGOGY OF RISK

> Let me begin by saying that we are living through a very dangerous time.... We are in a revolutionary situation, no matter how unpopular that word has become in this country. The society in which we live is desperately menaced, not by [the cold war] but from within. So any citizen of this country who figures himself as responsible—and particularly those of you who deal with the minds and hearts of young people—must be prepared to "go for

broke." Or to put it another way, you must understand that in the attempt to correct so many generations of bad faith and cruelty, when it is operating not only in the classroom but in society, you will meet the most fantastic, the most brutal, and the most determined resistance. There is no point in pretending that this won't happen.... [And yet] the obligation of anyone who thinks of him or herself as responsible is to examine society and try to change it and to fight it—at no matter what risk. This is the only hope society has. This is the only way societies change (Baldwin, 1988, p. 3).

I read the words of the famed African-American novelist James Baldwin less as a prescription for cynicism and powerlessness than I do as an expression of hope. Baldwin's words are moving because he confers a sense of moral and political responsibility upon teachers by presupposing that they are critical agents who can move between theory and practice in order to take risks, to refine their visions, and to make a difference for both their students and the world in which they live. In order to take up Baldwin's challenge for teachers to "go for broke," to act in the classroom and in the world with courage and dignity, it is important for educators to recognize that the current challenge facing public schools is one of the most serious that any generation of existing and prospective teachers has ever had to face. Politically, the United States has lived through twelve years of reforms in which teachers have been invited to de-skill themselves, to become technicians, or, in more ideological terms, to accept their role as "clerks of the empire." We live at a time when state legislators and federal officials are increasingly calling for the testing of teachers and the implementation of standardized curriculum; at the same time, legislators and government officials are ignoring the most important people in the reform effort, the teachers. Within this grim scenario, the voices of teachers have been largely absent from the debate about education. It gets worse.

Economically, the working conditions of teachers, especially those in the urban districts with a low tax base, have badly deteriorated. The story is a familiar one: overcrowded classrooms, inadequate resources, low salaries, and a rise in teacher-directed violence. In part, this is due to the increased financial cutbacks to the public sector by the federal government, the middle-class tax revolt of the 1970s that has put a ceiling on the ability of cities and states to raise revenue for public services, and the refusal by wide segments of the society to believe that public schooling is essential to the health of a democratic society. Compounding these problems is a dominant vision of schooling defined largely through the logic of corporate values and the imperatives of the marketplace. Schools are being treated as if their only purpose is to train future workers, and teachers are being viewed as corporate foot soldiers whose role is to provide students with the skills necessary for the business world. In short, part of the crisis of teaching is the result of a vision of schooling that subordinates issues of equity, community, and social justice to pragmatic considerations that enshrine the marketplace and accountability schemes that standardize the social relations of schooling. The political and ideological climate does not look favorable for teachers at the moment. But it does offer prospective and existing teachers the challenge to engage in dialogue and debate on important issues such as the nature and purpose of teacher preparation, the meaning of educational leadership, and the dominant forms of classroom teaching.

I think that if existing and future teachers are willing to go for broke, they will need to re-imagine teaching as part of a project of critique and possibility. But there is more at stake here than simply a change in who controls the conditions under which teachers work. Although this is important, what is also needed is a new language, a new way of naming, ordering, and representing how power works in schools. It is precisely through a more critical language that teachers might be able to recognize the power of their own agency to raise and act upon such questions as: What range of purposes should schools serve? What knowledge is of most worth? What does it mean for teachers and students to know something? What direction should teachers and students choose? What notions of authority should structure teaching and learning? These questions are important because they force educators to engage in a process of self-critique while simultaneously they highlight the central role that teachers might play in any viable attempt to reform the public schools.

My own journey into teaching was largely shaped by undergraduate education training and my first year of student teaching. While the content and context of these experiences shaped my initial understanding of myself as a teacher, they did not prepare me for the specific tasks and problems that I had to confront in my first job. In what follows, I want to speak from my own experiences to illuminate the shortcomings of the educational theories that both shaped my perceptions of teaching and the classroom practices I was expected to implement.

LEARNING TO BE A TECHNICIAN

During the time that I studied to be a teacher, for the most part, I learned how to master classroom methods, read Bloom's taxonomy, and became adept at administering tests, but I was never asked to question how testing might be used as a sorting device to track and marginalize certain groups. Like many prospective teachers of my generation, I was taught how to master a body of knowledge defined within separate academic disciplines, but I never learned to question what the hierarchical organization of knowledge meant and how it conferred authority and power. For example, I was never taught to raise questions about what knowledge was worth knowing and why, why schools legitimated some forms of knowledge and ignored others, why English was more important than art, and why it was considered unworthy to take a course in which one worked with one's hands. I never engaged in a classroom discussion about whose interests were served through the teaching and legitimacy of particular forms of school knowledge, or how knowledge served to silence and disempower particular social groups. Moreover, I was not given the opportunity to reflect

upon the authoritarian principles that actually structure classroom life and how these could be understood by analyzing social, political, and economic conditions outside of schools. If a student slept in the morning at his or her desk, I was taught to approach the issue as a problem of discipline and management. I was not taught to recognize the social conditions that may have caused such behavior. That is, to the possibility that the student might have a drug-related problem or might be hungry, sick, or simply exhausted because of the conditions in his or her home life. I learned quickly to separate out the problems of society from the problems of schooling and hence became illiterate in understanding the complexity of the relationship between schools and the larger social order.

My initial teaching assignment was in a school in which the teacher turnover rate exceeded 85% each year. The first day I walked into that school I was met by some students hanging out in the lobby. They greeted me with stares born of territorial rights and suspicion and one of them jokingly asked me: "Hey man, you're new, what's your name?" I remember thinking they had violated some sort of rule regarding teacher-student relationships by addressing me in that way. Questions of identity, culture, and racism had not been factored into my understanding of teaching and schooling. I had no idea that the questions that would be raised for me that year had less to do with the sterile language of methods I had learned as an undergraduate than they did with my becoming culturally and politically literate about the context-specific histories and experiences that revealed the places from which my students came and how they viewed themselves and others. I had no idea of how important it was to create a meaningful and safe classroom so that I could connect my teaching to their own languages, cultures, and life experiences. I soon found out that giving students some sense of power and ownership over their own educational experience has more to do with developing a language that was risk taking and self-critical for me and meaningful, practical, and transformative for them. During that first year, I also learned something about the ways in which many school administrators are educated.

LEADERSHIP WITHOUT VISION

During that first year, I rented movies from the American Friends Service Committee, ignored the officially designated curriculum textbooks, and eventually put my own books and magazine articles on reserve in the school library for my students to read. Hoping to give my students some control over the conditions in which they could produce knowledge, I encouraged them to produce their own texts through the use of school video equipment, cameras, and daily journals. Within a very short time, I came in conflict with the school principal. He was a mix between General Patton and the Encino Man. At six foot three, weighing in at 250 pounds, his presence seemed a bit overwhelming and intimidating. The first time he called me into his office, I learned something about how he was educated. He told me that students should be quiet in classrooms, teachers should stick to giving lectures and writing on the board, and that I was never to ask a student a question that he or she could not answer. He further suggested that rather than developing my own materials in class I should use the curricula packages made available through the good wishes of local businesses and companies. While clearly he was a reflection, if not a parody, of the worst kind of teacher training, he adamantly believed that strict management controls, rigid systems of accountability, and lock-step discipline were at the heart of educational leadership. Hence, I found myself in a secular version of hell. This was a school in which teaching became reduced to the sterile logic of flow charts. Moreover, it was a school in which power was wielded largely by white, male administrators who further reinforced the isolation and despair of most of the teachers. I engaged in forms of guerrilla warfare with this administration. But in order to survive I had to enlist the help of a few other teachers and some members of the community. At the end of the school year, I was encouraged not to come back. Fortunately, I had another teaching job back east and ended up in a much better school.

In retrospect, this dominant view of educational leadership had a resurgence during the Reagan and Bush eras. Its overall effect has been to limit a teacher's control over the development and planning of curriculum, to reinforce the bureaucratic organization of the school, and to remove teachers from the process of judging and implementing classroom instruction. This is evident in the growing call for national testing, national curriculum standards, and the concerted attack on multicultural curricula. The ideology that guides this model and its view of pedagogy is that the behavior of teachers needs to be controlled and made consistent and predictable across different schools and student populations. The effect is not only to remove teachers from the process of deliberation and reflection, but also to routinize the nature of learning and classroom pedagogy. In this approach, it is assumed that all students can learn from the same standardized materials, instructional techniques, and modes of evaluation. That students come from different histories, experiences, and cultures is strategically ignored within this approach. The notion that pedagogy should be attentive to specific contexts is ignored.

TEACHERS AS PUBLIC INTELLECTUALS

I want to challenge these views by arguing that one way to rethink and restructure the nature of a teacher's work is to view teachers as public intellectuals. The unease expressed about the identity and role of teachers as public intellectuals has a long tradition in the United States and has become the focus of a number of recent debates. On one level, there are conservatives who argue that teachers who address public issues from the perspective of a committed position are simply part of what they call the politically correct movement. Thus, there is a deep suspicion of any attempt to open up for educators the possibility of addressing pressing social issues and connecting them to their teaching. Moreover, within the broad parameters of this view, schools are seen as apolitical institutions whose primary purpose is to both prepare students for the work place and to reproduce the alleged common values that define the "American" way of life.[3] At the same time, many liberals have argued that while teachers should address public issues they should do so from the perspective of a particular teaching methodology. This is evident from Gerald Graff's (1992) call for educators to teach the conflicts. In this view, the struggle over representations replaces how a politics of meaning might help students identify, engage, and transform relations of power that generate the material conditions of racism, sexism, poverty, and other oppressive conditions. Moreover, some radical feminists have argued that the call for teachers to be public intellectuals promotes leadership models that are largely patriarchal and overly rational in the forms of authority that they secure. While there may be an element of truth in all of these positions, they all display enormous theoretical shortcomings. Conservatives often refuse to problematize their own version of what is legitimate intellectual knowledge and how it works to secure particular forms of authority by simply labeling as "politically correct" those individuals, groups, or views that challenge the basic tenets of the status quo. Liberals, on the other hand, inhabit a terrain that is conflicted, wavering between rejecting a principled standpoint from which to teach and staunchly arguing for a pedagogy that is academically rigorous and fair. Caught between a discourse of fairness and the appeal to use provocative teaching methods, liberals have no language for clarifying the moral visions that structure their views of the relationship between knowledge and authority and the practices that it promotes. Moreover, increasingly they have come to believe that teaching from a particular standpoint is tantamount to imposing an ideological position upon students. This has led in some cases to a form of McCarthyism in which critical educators are summarily dismissed as being guilty of ideological indoctrination. While the feminist critique is the most interesting, it underplays the possibility for using authority in ways that allow teachers to be more self-critical while simultaneously providing conditions in which students can recognize the possibility for democratic agency in both themselves and others. Operating out of a language of dichotomies, some feminist education critics essentialize the positions of their opponents and in doing so present a dehistoricized and reductionistic view of critical pedagogy. Most importantly, all of these positions share in the failure to address the possibility for teachers to become a force for democratization both within and outside of schools.

As public intellectuals, teachers must bring to bear in their classrooms and other pedagogical sites the courage, analytical tools, moral vision, time, and dedication that are necessary to return schools to their primary task and that are to be places of critical education in the service of creating a public sphere of citizens who are able to exercise power over their own lives and especially over the conditions of knowledge acquisition. Central to any such reform effort is the recognition that democracy is not a set of formal rules of participation, but the lived experience of empowerment for the vast majority. Moreover, the call for schools as democratic public spheres should not be limited to the call for equal access to schools, equal opportunity, or other arguments defined in terms of the principles of equality. Equality is a crucial aspect of school democratization, but teachers should not limit their demands to the call for equality. Instead, the rallying cry of teachers should be organized around the practice of empowerment for the vast majority of students in this country who need to be educated in the spirit of a critical democracy.[4]

This suggests another dimension in defining the role of public intellectuals. Such intellectuals must combine their role as educators and citizens. This implies they must connect the practice of classroom teaching to the operation of power in the larger society. At the same time, they must be attentive to those broader social forces that influence the workings of schooling and pedagogy. What is at issue here is a commitment on the part of teachers as public intellectuals to extend the principles of social justice to all spheres of economic, political, and cultural life. Within this discourse, the experiences that constitute the production of knowledge, identities, and social values in the schools are inextricably linked to the quality of moral and political life of the wider society. Hence, the reform of schooling must be seen as a part of a wider revitalization of public life.

This should not suggest that as public intellectuals, teachers represent a vanguard group dedicated to simply reproducing another master narrative. In fact, as public intellectuals it is important for them to link their role as critical agents to their ability to be critical of their own politics while constantly engaging in dialogue with other educators, community people, various cultural workers, and students. As public intellectuals, teachers need to be aware of the limits of their own positions, make their pedagogies context specific, challenge the current organization of knowledge into fixed disciplines, and work in solidarity with others to gain some control over their working conditions. At the very least, this suggests that teachers will have to struggle on many different fronts in order to transform those conditions of work and learning that exist in the schools. This means not only working with community people, teachers, students, and parents to open up progressive spaces within classrooms but also forming alliances with other cultural workers in order to debate and shape educational policy at the local, state, and federal levels of government.

As public intellectuals, teachers need to provide those conditions for students in which they can learn that knowledge and power can be emancipatory, that their histories and experiences matter, and that what they say and do can play a part in the wider struggle to change the world around them. More specifically, teachers need to argue for forms of pedagogy that close the gap between the school and the real world. The curriculum needs to be organized around knowledge that relates to communities, cultures, and traditions in a way that gives students a sense of history, identity, and place. This suggests pedagogical approaches that do more than make learning context specific; it also points to the need to expand the range of cultural texts that inform what counts as knowledge. As

public intellectuals, teachers need to understand and use those electronically-mediated knowledge forms that constitute the terrain of popular culture. This is the world of media texts-videos, films, music, and other mechanisms of popular culture that exist outside of the technology of print and the book. Put another way, the content of the curriculum needs to affirm and critically enrich the meaning, language, and knowledge that students actually use to negotiate and inform their lives.

While it is central for teachers to expand the relevance of the curriculum to include the richness and diversity of the students they actually teach, they also need to correspondingly decenter the curriculum. That is, students should be actively involved with issues of governance, "including setting learning goals, selecting courses, and having their own, autonomous organizations, including a free press" (Aronowitz, forthcoming). Not only does the distribution of power among teachers, students, and administrators provide the conditions for students to become agents in their learning process, it also provides the basis for collective learning, civic action, and ethical responsibility. Moreover, such agency emerges as a lived experience rather than as the mastery of an academic subject.

In addition, as public intellectuals, teachers need to make the issue of cultural difference a defining principle of curriculum development and research. In an age of shifting demographics, large scale immigration, and multiracial communities, teachers must make a firm commitment to cultural difference as central to the relationship of schooling and citizenship (Giroux, 1992). In the first instance, this means dismantling and deconstructing the legacy of nativism and racial chauvinism that has defined the rhetoric of school reform for the last decade. The Reagan and Bush era witnessed a full fledged attack on the rights of minorities, civil rights legislation, affirmative action, and the legitimation of curriculum reforms pandering to Eurocentric interests. Teachers can affirm their commitment to democratic public life and cultural democracy by struggling in and outside of their classrooms in solidarity with others to reverse these policies in order to make schools more attentive to the cultural resources that students bring to the public schools. At one level, this means working to develop legislation that protects the civil rights of all groups. Equally important is the need for teachers to take the lead in encouraging programs that open school curricula to the narratives of cultural difference, without falling into the trap of merely romanticizing the experience of Otherness. At stake here is the development of an educational policy that asserts public education as part of a broader ethical and political discourse, one that both challenges and transforms those curricula reforms of the last decade that are profoundly racist in context and content. This suggests at least changing the terms of the debate on the relationship between schooling and national identity, moving away from an assimilationist ethic and the profoundly Eurocentric fantasies of a common culture to one that links national identity to diverse traditions and histories.

CONCLUSION

In short, as public intellectuals, teachers need to address the imperatives of citizenship. In part, this means addressing how schools can create the conditions for students to be social agents willing to struggle for expanding the critical public cultures that make a democracy viable. Consequently, any notion of pedagogy must be seen as a form of cultural politics, that is, a politics that highlights the role of education, as it takes place in a variety of public sites, to open up rather than close down the possibilities for keeping justice and hope alive at a time of shrinking possibilities.

ENDNOTES

1. This is particularly true with respect to those mainstream reformers arguing for national standards and testing. In this discourse, students are always on the receiving end of the learning experience. It is as if the histories, experiences, and communities that shape their identities and sense of place are irrelevant to what is taught and how it is taught. See, for example, Hirsch (1987), Finn, Jr., and Ravitch (1987). For an alternative to this position, see Apple (1993), Giroux (1988b), and Giroux (1993). For an examination of schools that view teachers as more than clerks and technicians, see Wood (1993).

2. I have taken up this issue more extensively in Giroux (1988) and Aronowitz and Giroux (1993).

3. For a trenchant analysis of the political correctness movement, see Aronowitz (1993), especially Chapter 1. See also Frank (1993).

4. I take this issue up in Giroux (1988).

REFERENCES

Apple, M. (1993). *Official Knowledge* (New York: Routledge).

Apple, M., and L. K. Christian-Smith, eds. (1992). *The Politics of the Textbook* (New York: Routledge).

Aronowitz, S. (1993). *Roll Over Beethoven: The Return of Cultural Strife* (Hanover: Wesleyan University Press).

Aronowitz, S. (forthcoming). "A Different Perspective on Educational Inequality." *The Review of Education/Pedagogy/Cultural Studies.*

Aronowitz, S., and H. A. Giroux (1993). *Education Still Under Siege* (Westport, Conn.: Bergin and Garvey Press).

Baldwin, J. (1988). "A Talk to Teachers." In Rick Simonson and Scott Waler, eds. *Multicultural Literacy: Opening the American Mind* (Saint Paul, Minn.: Graywolf Press), pp. 3–12.

Finn, Jr. C., and D. Ravitch (1987). *What Our 17-Year-Olds Know* (New York: Harper and Row).

Frank, J. (1993). "In the Waiting Room: Canons, Communities, 'Political Correctness.'" In Mark Edmunson, ed. *Wild Orchids: Messages from American Universities* (New York: Penguin).

Giroux, H. (1988a). *Teachers as Intellectuals* (Westport, Conn.: Bergin and Garvey Press).

Giroux, H. (1988b). *Schooling and the Struggle for Public Life* (Minneapolis: University of Minnesota Press).

Giroux, H. (1992). *Border Crossings* (New York: Routledge).

Giroux, H. (1993). *Living Dangerously: The Politics of Multiculturalism* (New York: Peter Lang).

Graff, G. (1992). "Teaching the Conflicts." In Darryl J. Gless and Barbara Hernstein Smith, eds. *The Politics of Liberal Education* (Durham: Duke University Press), pp. 57–73.

Hirsch, E. D. (1987). *Cultural Literacy* (Boston: Houghton Mifflin).

Oaks, J. (1985). *Keeping Track: How Schools Structure Inequality* (New Haven: Yale University Press).

Simon, R. (1992). *Teaching Against the Grain* (Westport, Conn.: Bergin and Garvey Press).

West, C. (1990). "The New Politics of Difference," *October,* 53: 93–109.

Wood, G. (1993). *Schools That Work.* (New York: Penguin Books).

DISCUSSION QUESTIONS

1. How do bureaucratic organization structures influence the teacher's role?
2. What kinds of organizational changes would be needed to create schools that were authentic democratic institutions?
3. In what ways will the curriculum need to be restructured in order to empower students? Teachers?
4. How can pedagogy influence cultural politics?
5. As public intellectuals, what do teachers need to provide?

6

Art and Imagination: Overcoming a Desperate Stasis

MAXINE GREENE

FOCUSING QUESTIONS

1. *What are the existential contexts of education?*
2. *How do encounters with the arts influence student engagement in learning?*
3. *How might experience with the arts affect student (a) imagination, (b) construction of reality, and (c) depth of perspective?*
4. *What is the relationship between individual freedom and learning?*
5. *What are the contradictory goals of education?*
6. *What is the relationship between encounters with the arts and the goals of education?*

The existential contexts of education reach far beyond what is conceived of in Goals 2000. They have to do with the human condition in these often desolate days, and in some ways they make the notions of world-class achievement, benchmarks, and the rest seem superficial and limited, if not absurd. They extend beyond the appalling actualities of family breakdown, homelessness, violence, and the "savage inequalities" described by Jonathan Kozol, although social injustice has an existential dimension.

Like their elders, children and young persons inhabit a world of fearful moral uncertainty—a world in which it appears that almost nothing can be done to reduce suffering, contain massacres, and protect human rights. The faces of refugee children in search of their mothers, of teenage girls repeatedly raped by soldiers, of rootless people staring at the charred remains of churches and libraries may strike some of us as little more than a "virtual reality." Those who persist in looking feel numbed and, reminded over and over of helplessness, are persuaded to look away.

It has been said that Pablo Picasso's paintings of "weeping women" have become the icons of our time.[1] They have replaced the statues of men on horseback and men in battle; they overshadow the emblems of what once seemed worth fighting for, perhaps dying for. When even the young confront images of loss and death, as most of us are bound to do today, "it is important that everything we love be summed up into something unforgettably beautiful."[2] This suggests one of the roles of the arts. To see sketch after sketch of women holding dead babies, as Picasso has forced us to do, is to become aware of a tragic deficiency in the fabric of life. If we know enough to make those paintings the objects of our experience, to encounter them against the background of our lives, we are likely to strain toward conceptions of a better order of things, in which there will be no more wars that make women weep like that, no more bombs to murder innocent children. We are likely, in rebelling against such horror, to summon up images of smiling mothers and lovely children, metaphors for what *ought* to be.

Clearly, this is not the only role of the arts, although encounters with them frequently do move us to want to restore some kind of order, to repair, and to heal. Participatory involvement with the many forms of art does enable us, at the very least, to *see* more in our experience, to *hear* more on normally unheard frequencies, to *become conscious* of what daily routines, habits, and conventions have obscured.

We might think of what Pecola Breedlove in *The Bluest Eye* has made us realize about the metanarrative implicit in the Dick and Jane basal readers or in the cultural artifact called Shirley Temple, who made so many invisible children yearn desperately to have blue eyes.[3] We might recall the revelations discovered by so many through an involvement with *Schindler's List*. We might try to retrieve the physical consciousness of unutterable grief aroused in us by Martha Graham's dance "Lamentation," with only feet and hands visible outside draped fabric—and agony expressed through stress lines on the cloth. To see more, to hear more. By such experiences we are not only lurched out of the familiar and the taken for granted, but we may also discover new avenues for action. We may experience a sudden sense of new possibilities and thus new beginnings.

The prevailing cynicism with regard to values and the feelings of resignation it breeds cannot help but create an atmosphere in the schools that is at odds with the unpredictability associated with the experience of art. The neglect of the arts by those who identified the goals of Goals 2000 was consistent with the focus on the manageable, the predictable, and the measurable. There have been efforts to include the arts in the official statements of goals, but the arguments mustered in their favor are of a piece with the arguments for education geared toward economic competitiveness, technological mastery, and the rest. They have also helped support the dominant arguments for the development of "higher-level skills," academic achievement, standards, and preparation for the workplace.

The danger afflicting both teachers and students because of such emphases is, in part, the danger of feeling locked into existing circumstances defined by others. Young people find themselves described as "human resources," rather than as persons who are centers of choice and evaluation. It is suggested that young people are to be molded in the service of technology and the market, no matter who they are. Yet, as many are now realizing, great numbers of our young people will find themselves unable to locate satisfying jobs, and the very notion of "all the children" and even of human resources carries with it deceptions of all kinds. Perhaps it is no wonder that the dominant mood in many classrooms is one of passive reception.

Umberto Eco, the Italian critic of popular culture, writes about the desperate need to introduce a critical dimension into such reception. Where media and messages are concerned, it is far more important, he says, to focus on the point of reception than on the point of transmission. Finding a threat in "the universal of technological communication" and in situations where "the medium is the message," he calls seriously for a return to individual resistance. "To the anonymous divinity of Technological Communication, our answer could be: 'Not thy, but *our* will be done.'"[4]

The kind of resistance Eco has in mind can best be evoked when imagination is released. But, as we well know, the bombardment of images identified with "Technological Communication" frequently has the effect of freezing imaginative thinking. Instead of freeing audiences to look at things as if they could be otherwise, present-day media impose predigested frameworks on their audiences. Dreams are caught in the meshes of the salable; the alternative to gloom or feelings of pointlessness is consumerist acquisition. For Mary Warnock, imagination is identified with the belief that "there is more in our experience of the world than can possibly meet the unreflecting eye."[5] It tells us that experience always holds more than we can predict. But Warnock knows that acknowledging the existence of undiscovered vistas and perspectives requires reflectiveness. The passive, apathetic person is all too likely to be unresponsive to ideas of the unreal, the as if, the merely possible. He or she becomes the one who bars the arts as frivolous, mere frills, irrelevant to learning in the postindustrial world.

It is my conviction that informed engagements with the several arts would be the most likely way to release the imaginative capacity and give it play. However, this does not happen automatically or "naturally." We have all witnessed the surface contacts with paintings when groups of tourists hasten through museums. Without time spent, without tutoring, and without dialogue regarding the arts, people merely seek the right labels. They look for the artists' names. There are those who watch a ballet for the story, not for the movement or the music; they wait for Giselle to go mad or for Sleeping Beauty to be awakened or for the white swan to return.

Mere exposure to a work of art is not sufficient to occasion an aesthetic experience. There must be conscious participation in a work, a going out of energy, an ability to notice what is there to be noticed in the play, the poem, the quartet. "Knowing about," even in the most formal, academic manner, is entirely different from creating an unreal world imaginatively and entering it perceptually, affectively, and cognitively. To introduce people to such engagement is to strike a delicate balance between helping learners to pay heed—to attend to shapes, patterns, sounds, rhythms, figures of speech, contours, lines, and so on—and freeing them to perceive particular works as meaningful. Indeed, the inability to control what is discovered as meaningful makes many traditional educators uneasy and strikes them as being at odds with conceptions of a norm, even with notions of appropriate "cultural literacy." This uneasiness may well be at the root of certain administrators' current preoccupation with national standards.

However, if we are to provide occasions for significant encounters with works of art, we have to combat standardization and what Hannah Arendt called "thoughtlessness" on the part of all those involved. What she meant by thoughtlessness was "the heedless recklessness or hopeless confusion or complacent repetition of 'truths' which have become trivial and empty."[6] There is something in that statement that recalls what John Dewey described as a "social pathology"—a condition that still seems to afflict us today. Dewey wrote that it manifests itself "in querulousness, in impotent drifting, in uneasy snatching at distractions, in idealization of the long established, in a facile optimism assumed as a cloak."[7] Concerned about "sloppiness, superficiality, and recourse to sensations as a substitute for ideas," Dewey made the point that "thinking deprived of its normal course takes refuge in academic specialism."[8]

For Arendt, the remedy for this condition is "to think what we are doing." She had in mind developing a self-reflectiveness that originates in situated life, the life of persons open to one another in their distinctive locations and engaging one another in dialogue. Provoked by the spectacle of the Nazi Adolf Eichmann, Arendt warned against "clichés, stock phrases, adherence to conventional, standardized codes of expression and conduct," which have, she said, "the socially recognized function of protecting us against reality, that is, against the claim on our thinking attention that all events and facts make by virtue of their existence."[9] She was not calling for a new intellectualism or for a new concentration on "higher-order skills." She was asking for a way of seeking clarity and authenticity in the face of thoughtlessness, and it seems to me that we might ask much the same thing if we are committed to the release of the imagination and truly wish to open the young to the arts.

Thoughtfulness in this sense is necessary if we are to resist the messages of the media in the fashion Eco suggests, and it is difficult to think of young imaginations being freed without learners finding out how to take a critical and thoughtful approach to the illusory or fabricated "realities" presented to them by the media. To be thoughtful about what we are doing is to be conscious of ourselves struggling to make meanings, to make critical sense of what authoritative others are offering as objectively "real."

I find a metaphor for the reification of experience in the plague as it is confronted in Albert Camus' novel. The pestilence that struck the town of Oran (submerged as it was in habit and "doing business") thrust most of the inhabitants into resignation, isolation, or despair. Gradually revealing itself as inexorable and incurable, the plague froze people in place; it was simply *there*. At first Dr. Rieux fights the plague for the most abstract of reasons: because it is his job. Only later, when the unspeakable tragedies he witnesses make him actually think about what he is doing, does he reconceive his practice and his struggle and talk about not wanting to be complicit with the pestilence. By then he has met Tarrou, who is trying to be a "saint without God" and who has the wit and, yes, the imagination to organize people into sanitary squads to fight the plague and make it the moral concern of all.

Tarrou has the imagination too to find in the plague a metaphor for indifference or distancing or (we might say) thoughtlessness. Everyone carries the microbe, he tells his friend; it is only natural. He means what Hannah Arendt meant—and Dewey and Eco and all the others who resist a lack of concern. He has in mind evasions of complex problems, the embrace of facile formulations of the human predicament, the reliance on conventional solutions—all those factors I would say stand in the way of imaginative thinking and engagement with the arts. "All the rest," says Tarrou, "health, integrity, purity (if you like)—is a product of the human will, of a vigilance that must never falter." He means, of course, that we (and those who are our students) must be given opportunities to choose to be persons of integrity, persons who care.

Tarrou has a deep suspicion of turgid language that obscures the actualities of things, that too often substitutes abstract constructions for concrete particulars. This is one of the modes of the thoughtlessness Arendt was urging us to fight. She,

too, wanted to use "plain, clear-cut language." She wanted to urge people, as does Tarrou, to attend to what is around them, "to stop and think." I am trying to affirm that this kind of awareness, this openness to the world, is what allows for the consciousness of alternative possibilities and thus for a willingness to risk encounters with the "weeping women," with Euripides' *Medea,* with *Moby Dick,* with Balanchine's (and, yes, the Scripture's) *Prodigal Son,* with Mahler's *Songs of the Earth.*

Another novel that enables its readers to envisage what stands in the way of imagination is Christa Wolf's *Accident: A Day's News.* It moves me to clarify my own response to the technical and the abstract. I turn to it not in order to add to my knowledge or to find some buried truth, but because it makes me see, over the course of time, what I might never have seen in my own lived world.

The power the book holds for me may be because it has to do with the accident at Chernobyl, as experienced by a woman writer, who is also a mother and grandmother. She is preoccupied by her brother's brain surgery, taking place on the same day, and by the consequences of the nuclear accident for her grandchildren and for children around the world. She spends no time wondering about her own response to such a crisis; her preoccupation is with others—those she loves and the unknown ones whom she cannot for a moment forget. It is particularly interesting, within the context of an ethic of care, to contain for a moment within our own experience the thoughts of a frightened young mother, the narrator's daughter, picturing what it means to pour away thousands of liters of milk for fear of poisoning children while "children on the other side of the earth are perishing for lack of those foods."

The narrator wants to change the conversation and asks her daughter to "tell me something else, preferably about the children." Whereupon she hears that "the little one had pranced about the kitchen, a wing nut on his thumb, his hand held high. Me Punch. Me Punch. I was thrilled by the image."[10] Only a moment before, another sequence of pictures had come into her mind and caused her to

> admire the way in which everything fits together with a sleepwalker's precision: the desire of most people for a comfortable life, their tendency to believe the speakers on raised platforms and the men in white coats; the addiction to harmony and the fear of contradiction of the many seem to correspond to the arrogance and hunger for power, the dedication to profit, unscrupulous inquisitiveness, and self-infatuation of the few. So what was it that didn't add up in this equation?[11]

This passage seems to me to suggest the kind of questioning, and, yes, the kind of picturing that may well be barred by the preoccupation with "world-class achievement" and by the focus on human resources that permeate Goals 2000.

But it does not have to be so. Cognitive adventuring and inquiry are much more likely to be provoked by the narrator's question about "this equation" than by the best of curriculum frameworks or by the most responsible and "authentic" assessment. To set the imagination moving in response to a text such as Wolf's may well be to confront learners with a demand to choose in a fundamental way between a desire for harmony with its easy answers and a commitment to the risky search for alternative possibilities.

Wolf's narrator, almost as if she were one of Picasso's weeping women, looks at the blue sky and, quoting some nameless source, says, "Aghast, the mothers search the sky for the inventions of learned men."[12] Like others to whom I have referred, she begins pondering the language and the difficulty of breaking through such terms as "half-life," "cesium," and "cloud" when "polluted rain" is so much more direct. Once again, the experience of the literary work may help us to feel the need to break through the mystification of technology and the language to which it has given rise.

The narrator feels the need to battle the disengagement that often goes with knowing and speaking. When she ponders the motives of those who

thought up the procedures for the "peaceful utilization of nuclear energy," she recalls a youthful protest against a power plant and the rebukes and reprimands directed at the protesters for their skepticism with regard to a scientific utopia. And then she lists the activities that the men of science and technology presumably do not pursue and would probably consider a waste of time if they were forced to:

> Changing a baby's diapers. Cooking, shopping with a child on one's arm or in the baby carriage. Doing the laundry, hanging it up to dry, taking it down, folding it, ironing it, darning it. Sweeping the floor, mopping it, polishing it, vacuuming it. Dusting. Sewing. Knitting. Crocheting. Embroidering. Doing the dishes. Doing the dishes. Taking care of a sick child. Thinking up stories to tell. Singing songs. And how many of these activities do I myself consider a waste of time?[13]

Reading this passage and posing a new set of questions, we cannot but consider the role of such concrete images in classroom conversation and in our efforts to awaken persons to talk about what ought to be. The narrator believes that the "expanding monstrous technological creation" may be a substitute for life for many people. She is quite aware of the benevolent aspects of technology: her brother, after all, is having advanced neurosurgery (which he does survive). But she is thinking, as we might well do in the schools, about the consequences of technological expansion for the ones we love. Her thinking may remind us of how important it is to keep alive images of "everything we love." I want to believe that by doing so we may be able to create classroom atmospheres that once again encourage individuals to have hope.

This brings me back to my argument for the arts, so unconscionably neglected in the talk swirling around Goals 2000. It is important to make the point that the events that make up aesthetic experiences are events that occur within and by means of the transactions with our environment that situate us in time and space. Some say that participatory encounters with paintings, dances, stories, and the rest enable us to recapture a lost spontaneity. By breaking through the frames of presuppositions and conventions, we may be enabled to reconnect ourselves with the processes of becoming who we are. By reflecting on our life histories, we may be able to gain some perspective on the men in white coats, even on our own desires to withdraw from complexity and to embrace a predictable harmony. By becoming aware of ourselves as questioners, as makers of meaning, as persons engaged in constructing and reconstructing realities with those around us, we may be able to communicate to students the notion that reality depends on perspective, that its construction is never complete, and that there is always more. I am reminded of Paul Cézanne's several renderings of Mont St. Victoire and of his way of suggesting that it must be viewed from several angles if its reality is to be apprehended.

Cézanne made much of the insertion of the body into his landscapes, and that itself may suggest a dimension of experience with which to ground our thinking and the thinking of those we teach. There are some who suggest that, of all the arts, dance confronts most directly the question of what it means to be human. Arnold Berleant writes that

> in establishing a human realm through movement, the dancer, with the participating audience, engages in the basic act out of which arise both all experience and our human constructions of the world.... [That basic act] stands as the direct denial of that most pernicious of all dualisms, the division of body and consciousness. In dance, thought is primed at the point of action. This is not the reflection of the contemplative mind but rather intellect poised in the body, not the deliberate consideration of alternative courses but thought in process, intimately responding to and guiding the actively engaged body.[14]

The focus is on process and practice; the skill in the making is embodied in the object made. In addition, dance provides occasions for the emergence of the integrated self. Surely, this ought to be taken into account in our peculiarly technical and academic time.

Some of what Berleant says relates as well to painting, if painting is viewed as an orientation in time and space of the physical body—of both perceiver and creator. If we take a participatory stance, we may enter a landscape or a room or an open street. Different modes of perception are asked of us, of course, by different artists, but that ought to mean a widening of sensitivity with regard to perceived form, color, and space. Jean-Paul Sartre, writing about painting, made a point that is significant for anyone concerned about the role of art and the awakening of imagination:

> The work is never limited to the painted, sculpted or narrated object. Just as one perceives things only against the background of the world, so the objects represented by art appear against the backround of the universe.... [T]he creative act aims at a total renewal of the world. Each painting, each book, is a recovery of the totality of being. Each of them presents this totality to the freedom of the spectator. For this is quite the final goal of art: to recover this world by giving it to be seen as it is, but as if it had its source in human freedom.[15]

In this passage Sartre suggests the many ways in which classroom encounters with the arts can move the young to imagine, to extend, and to renew. And surely nothing can be more important than finding the source of learning not in extrinsic demands, but in human freedom.

All this is directly related to developing what is today described as the active learner, here conceived as one awakened to pursue meaning. There are, of course, two contradictory tendencies in education today: one has to do with shaping malleable young people to serve the needs of technology in a postindustrial society; the other has to do with educating young people to grow and to become different, to find their individual voices, and to participate in a community in the making. Encounters with the arts nurture and sometimes provoke the growth of individuals who reach out to one another as they seek clearings in their experience and try to live more ardently in the world. If the significance of the arts for growth, inventiveness, and problem solving is recognized at last, a desperate stasis may be overcome, and people may come to recognize the need for new raids on what T. S. Eliot called the "inarticulate."

I choose to end this extended reflection on art and imagination with some words from "Elegy in Joy," by Muriel Rukeyser:

Out of our life the living eyes
See peace in our own image made,
Able to give only what we can give:
Bearing two days like midnight. "Live,"
The moment offers: the night requires
Promise effort love and praise.

Now there are no maps and no magicians.
No prophets but the young prophet, the sense of the
  world.
The gift of our time, the world to be discovered.
All the continents giving off their several lights,
the one sea, and the air. And all things glow.[16]

These words offer life; they offer hope; they offer the prospect of discovery; they offer light. By resisting the tyranny of the technical, we may yet make them our pedagogic creed.

ENDNOTES

1. Judi Freeman, *Picasso and the Weeping Women* (Los Angeles: Los Angeles Museum of Art, 1994).

2. Michel Leiris. "Faire-part," in E. C. Oppler, ed., *Picasso's Guernica* (New York: Norton, 1988), p. 201.

3. Toni Morrison, *The Bluest Eye* (New York: Washington Square Press, 1970), p. 19.

4. Richard Kearney, *The Wake of Imagination* (Minneapolis: University of Minnesota Press, 1988), p. 382.

5. Mary Warnock, *Imagination* (Berkeley: University of California Press, 1978), p. 202.

6. Hannah Arendt, *The Human Condition* (Chicago: University of Chicago Press, 1958), p. 5.

7. John Dewey, *The Public and Its Problems* (Athens, Ohio: Swallow Press, 1954), p. 170.

8. Ibid., p. 168.

9. Hannah Arendt, *Thinking: Vol. II, The Life of the Mind* (New York: Harcourt Brace Jovanovich, 1978), p. 4.

10. Christa Wolf, *Accident: A Day's News* (New York: Farrar, Straus & Giroux, 1989), p. 17.

11. Ibid.

12. Ibid., p. 27.

13. Ibid., p. 31.

14. Arnold Berleant, *Art and Engagement* (Philadelphia: Temple University Press, 1991), p. 167.

15. Jean-Paul Sartre, *Literature and Existentialism* (New York: Citadel Press, 1949), p. 57.

16. Muriel Rukeyser, "Tenth Elegy: An Elegy in Joy," in idem. *Out in Silence: Selected Poems* (Evanston, Ill.: TriQuarterly Books, 1992), p. 104.

DISCUSSION QUESTIONS

1. What are the implications of understanding the existential contexts of education and educational goals?
2. Why does inclusion of the arts in the school curriculum continue to be a topic of debate among many educators?
3. Why is mere exposure to a work of art insufficient to stimulating an aesthetic experience?
4. How does a neglect of the arts in school experiences affect students?
5. How might repeated significant encounters with the arts be used to combat standardization?
6. What is the relationship between aesthetic experience and the development of metacognitive strategies?

PRO-CON CHART 1

Should the schools introduce a values-centered curriculum for all students?

PRO	CON
1. There are certain basic core values that educators involved in curriculum development should be able to agree upon.	1. Values are not objective or neutral. Therefore, educators involved in curriculum development cannot easily agree upon them.
2. The classroom is a place in which students can define what values are and share a diversity of viewpoints.	2. Engaging students in discussion will lead to peer pressure and indoctrination.
3. Students should be able to explore their values in a classroom setting.	3. Unstated teacher attitudes may impinge upon students' ability to identify their own preferences.
4. Valuing is part of citizenship education and, therefore, schools have a responsibility to teach valuing.	4. Values are not part of civic education. Moreover, values education is the responsibility of the home, not the school.
5. Students need to learn to express themselves forthrightly and to make choices without fear and condemnation.	5. There is no assurance that the teacher can model values or choosing, much less provide appropriate instructional activities that will promote these behaviors.

CASE STUDY 1

A Clash Concerning the Arts Curriculum

Andrea Brown had recently been hired as the assistant principal in charge of curriculum at the Newberry Elementary School. Brown, an advocate for arts education, had a humanistic orientation to curriculum. The principal, Al Sigel, had an essentialist view of the curriculum. Adhering to a back to basics focus, Sigel felt that math, science, and computer education should be emphasized and that arts courses were frivolous.

The state code and the school's educational manuals indicated that all students were required to receive 40 minutes of music, art, and dance per week. Without discussing his intentions with Brown or eliciting faculty reactions, Sigel distributed a memo to the staff at the first faculty meeting of the school year indicating that music, art, and dance courses were to be eliminated from the academic schedule as specific courses and that teachers should integrate these subjects into social studies and English. This extra class time was to be equally distributed to provide additional math, science, and computer education classes.

Upon learning about this decision, several parents approached Brown and asked that she assist them in getting the arts classes placed back into the schedule. Brown felt an ethical and educational obligation to address the parents' concern. While cognizant of the legal implications, she also believed the arts are an essential curriculum component. She pondered how she might approach this situation.

Assume that you are the assistant principal. Consider the circumstances described in the case. How would you propose to handle the parents' concerns?

Consider also the implications of taking one of the following actions in response to the parents' request:

1. Confront the principal and cite the state and school mandated requirements concerning course time allocations?

2. Resign from the position and state that she and Sigel had irresolvable differences regarding their philosophical orientation to curriculum?

3. Take these curriculum-related concerns to the district superintendent in charge of instruction?

4. Present an inservice workshop to the teaching staff about the intrinsic and utilitarian values of an arts education?

5. Lead a coalition of concerned parents and ask for a meeting with the principal?

PART TWO

Curriculum and Teaching

INTRODUCTION

What are the trends in teaching that influence student outcomes and teachers' selection of instructional approaches? What method is most appropriate for teaching a diverse population of learners? How does research on teachers' display of practical knowledge, teacher thinking, and teacher effectiveness affect the ways in which teachers deliver the curriculum?

In Chapter 7, Richard Villa, Jacqueline Thousand, and James Chapple describe how the quality of preservice preparation programs influences teachers' ability to work successfully with students of varying abilities. They suggest ways that teacher preparation programs need to change to ensure that future teachers will be successful instructors with all students. Also, they discuss how inservice training can help teachers create a quality-inclusive learning environment. Next, Allan Ornstein describes the confusion regarding the referents that should be measured in teacher effectiveness research. He explores the limitations of product-oriented research and recommends that we emphasize both process and product teacher research. He suggests that research on teaching should focus on learners, not teachers, and be revised to fit varied teaching contexts.

In Chapter 9, Elliot Eisner criticizes formalized methods and bureaucratized procedures for stifling teacher spontaneity and the potential of unanticipated discoveries. He advocates an instructional approach that would permit teachers to use their intuition. He also suggests that we can learn much from teachers' display of practical knowledge, such as their ability to respond to the nuances that arise in teacher–student interaction on a daily basis.

In Chapter 10, Linda Behar-Horenstein explores the implications of narrative research for understanding teaching and teacher thinking. She suggests that narrative research may expand current thought about how teachers use practical knowledge. She offers several ideas for ensuring that findings from narrative research have application beyond singular case studies. In Chapter 11, Lee Shulman argues that the results of teacher effectiveness research should not constitute the sole basis for defining the knowledge base of teaching. He suggests that teaching involves understanding, reasoning, transformation, and reflection. Shulman presents a six-step model that illustrates his conception of pedagogy and delineates the processes involved in pedagogical reasoning and action.

In the final chapter of this part, Katherine Cushing, Donna Sabers, and David Berliner explore the factors that influence the perceptions of teachers at different stages in their professional development. The authors point out how expert, advanced beginners, and novices differ in the ways that they view classroom processes and the teacher's role.

7

Preparing Teachers to Support Inclusion: Preservice and Inservice Programs

RICHARD A. VILLA
JACQUELINE S. THOUSAND
JAMES W. CHAPPLE

FOCUSING QUESTIONS

1. *Why do teacher preparation programs often fail to prepare future teachers to work successfully with students of varying abilities?*
2. *In what ways will teacher preparation programs need to change to ensure that future teachers will be successful instructors with all students?*
3. *What steps will general and special education faculty need to take to facilitate the merger of professional preparation programs?*
4. *How can collaboration be successfully demonstrated in the merger of general and special education programs?*
5. *What were the outcomes of model demonstration projects initiated by the Ohio State Department of Education?*
6. *In your opinion, what changes are needed in the way that we prepare teachers?*

Parents, students, and educators committed to educating all children in general education settings have a right to expect that teachers coming out of teacher preparation programs are prepared to celebrate and teach to the individual differences of a diverse student population. The reality, unfortunately, is that too many training programs have yet to communicate to their teachers-to-be that they can expect to educate all children (with and without identified disabilities), rather than identify and sort children into general education versus other tracks of education.

Furthermore, teachers report that too few programs explicitly teach future teachers the skills that they actually need to accommodate widely varying student needs (e.g., Lyon, Vaassen, & Toomey, 1989). Nationwide, teachers are being asked to collaborate with one another and others to instruct an increasingly heterogeneous student body. But, in order for them to do this, they need to acquire a common conceptual framework, language, and set of technical skills with which to communicate.

Given that preservice education and the relatively isolated teaching experiences of so many teachers have fallen short of what they report that they need (Lyon et al., 1989), it falls on the shoulders of local school communities to be the primary actors in formulating and delivering a comprehensive inservice training agenda to "gear up" educators to respond to unique student needs. Clearly, any agenda settled on by a school community will need to extend across several years to ensure that instructional personnel have the opportunity to progress from acquisition to mastery of skills in areas of assessment, curriculum and instruction, creativity, collaboration, and student disciplinary systems.

In addition, a quality inservice program must afford faculty and staff experiences for continually upgrading their skills for the purpose of supporting increasingly more inclusive learning communities. This chapter proposes changes in content and format of both preservice teacher preparation and inservice programs and shares examples of programs that exemplify such changes.

RECOMMENDED CHANGES FOR TEACHER PREPARATION PROGRAMS

> School personnel are graduates of our colleges and universities. It is there that they learn there are at least two types of human beings and if you choose to work with one of them you render yourself legally and conceptually incompetent to work with others. (Sarason, 1982, p. 258)

Sarason (1982) asserts that public schools simply mirror image today's colleges and universities. Specifically, the current division of teacher preparation programs into separate, distinct, and categorical programs—general education versus special education and its various subcategories of learning disabilities, emotional and behavioral disorders, severe disabilities, English as a second language, gifted and talented—causes educators-in-preparation to neither expect nor have the know-how to create successful heterogeneous learning experiences for students of differing abilities. Is it any wonder that general and special education evolved as separate systems?

Furthermore, few have graduated from personnel preparation programs having seen modeled for them the act of adults collaborating across areas of expertise. Yet the act of collaboration is the

most important one that they will need to perform to "survive" in a profession in which no one person could possibly meet the needs of all the children in their charge (Johnson & Johnson, 1989; Villa, Thousand, Nevin, & Malgeri, 1996). Sarason and colleagues long ago called teaching the "lonely profession" (Sarason, Levine, Goldenberg, Cherlin, & Bennett, 1966, p. 74); and it no longer can be.

The historically separate general and special education teacher preparation programs have not provided trainees with intensive training and experience to develop the necessary skills and dispositions to be effective collaborators in planning, teaching, and evaluating instruction. To remediate this situation, programs preparing general and special education teachers should place strong emphasis on theory, practice, and experience in collaborative planning, teaching, and problem-solving processes. Special priority should be given to establishing noncategorical programs that merge professional training programs so that general, special, and related service personnel share common coursework and practicum experiences. Continuing education at the university and local level also must focus on in-place local school personnel, community members, and students acquiring and practicing collaborative planning, teaching, and evaluation skills for the purpose of effectively educating all children.

Stainback and Stainback (1989) offer steps for facilitating the merger of personnel preparation programs. First, general and special education faculty need to sit down and analyze their curricula and emerging demands on educators (e.g., proficiency in the use of technology, collaborative teaming) in order to identify the core values, knowledge, and skills that all teachers should acquire. They will likely discover "holes" in the "traditional" curriculum and a need for new courses. A core set of courses, such as those recommended in Figure 7.1, can then be developed or reformulated and required of all education majors. In addition to this core, students would select their own specialty areas (e.g., language arts, alternative communication systems, employment training, history) and take courses to develop extended competence in their selected concentrations. By restructuring professional preparation programs in this manner, graduates would no longer get the message that there are separate systems of education. Instead, they would have the disposition and skill to work collaboratively and creatively with others to merge their unique areas of expertise in order to instruct a diverse student body.

EXEMPLARY TEACHER PREPARATION INITIATIVES

In many institutions of higher education, faculty of the various separate education departments have begun the dialogue with local communities and school personnel to determine how to retool their professional preparation programs to better ready graduates for meeting the challenges of inclusive 21st century education. In a few places, dialogue has resulted in action and the creation of new and innovative training initiatives that model faculty and community collaboration and depart from traditional ways of inducting educators into their profession. Four such places are Trinity College (Burlington, Vermont), Syracuse University (New York), the University of California at San Marco, and Arizona State University-West (Phoenix). The result of these institutions' initiatives has been the merging of the expertise and knowledge of formerly separated or disjointed higher education and school-based education.

COURSES	CREDIT HOURS
Historical and Philosophical Foundations of Education	3
Child and Adolescent Development	3
Human Relations and Sensitivity to Human Differences	3
Classroom Organization, Management, and Motivational Strategies	3
Curriculum Design and Adaptations	3
Educational Measurement and Authentic Assessment	3
Peer-mediated Strategies (cooperative group learning, peer tutoring, students as peacemakers and mediators of conflict)	3
Adapting Instruction to Individual Differences	3
Use of Audiovisual, Media, and Computer Technology	3
Home, School, and Community Relations	3
Issues and Trends in Education	3
Creativity and Collaborative Teaming	3
Total	36

FIGURE 7.1 Professional Coursework for All Educators
Source: Stainback & Stainback (1989; adapted by permission).

Trinity College

The certification program at Trinity College is an example of a teacher preparation program that has restructured in a fashion suggested by Stainback and Stainback (1989). Specifically, all education majors take a common core of courses (i.e., teaching in an integrated environment, foundations of education, educational psychology, child development, senior practicum issues seminar) intended to impart a common core of instructional skills and dispositions to empower them to be teachers of *all* children. Practicum experiences begin the second year, with 3 hours per week spent in the classroom, and culminate with 16 to 32 weeks of classroom experience in the final year.

An option for all education majors is dual certification in general and special education. To receive dual certification, students take an additional core of courses (i.e., education law, assessment methodologies, designing instructional programs and accommodations, collaboration and consultation) typically associated with special education teacher preparation programs. Additionally, to gain the perspective of both a general and special educator, candidates devote half of their final practicum year serving in the role of general educator and the other half in the role of a special educator, generally within the same classroom.

The Trinity program is continually evolving as faculty examine exemplary educational practices and question the match between the college's offerings and the demands that the inclusive schools in Vermont and the nation place on new teachers. For example, beginning in the fall of 1995, traditionally separate methods seminars (e.g., mathematics instruction, science instruction, elementary education, special education) will be merged so that students in all content areas attend common methods courses designed to model an interdisciplinary–thematic instructional approach. Additionally, the faculty of the general education concentrations has led the college to question the wisdom of multiple, separate concentrations and actively explores the development of a singular, unified teacher preparation program (D. Gurney, personal communication, May 1995). The faculty is studying several colleges that have done just this and has taken particular interest in the Syracuse University model described next.

Syracuse University

The School of Education of Syracuse University has merged its previously separate elementary and special education programs and created a single Inclusive Elementary and Special Education Teacher Preparation Program (Meyer & Biklen, 1992) expressly designed to ready all its candidates to educate an increasingly diverse student population and certify graduates in both elementary and special education. A major program objective is to graduate education professionals who are able to lead communities to a vision of schooling in which equity and excellence are both celebrated. A critical feature of the program is its focus on multicultural education and student acquisition of the knowledge and skills needed for the cultural pluralism of today's schools. A series of practicum experiences in inclusive inner city, urban, and suburban schools affords education students opportunities to develop and apply skills to educate students with diverse needs, including students identified as eligible for special education.

Students in the inclusive program benefit from the program's modeling of collaboration and cultural pluralism. Specifically, the program's faculty is drawn from a wide variety of departments within and outside the School of Education (Teaching and Leadership; Cultural Foundations of Education; Instructional Design, Development, and Evaluation; Communication Sciences and Disorders; Reading and Language Arts; College for Human Development, Child and Family Studies).

University of California at San Marco

Collaborative planning and teaming have repeatedly been identified as critical to successfully educating children with and without disabilities in general education (Cross & Villa, 1992; Thousand et al., 1986; Thousand, Villa, Meyers, & Nevin, 1994). Taking this information to heart and recognizing that teachers-in-preparation need to see their professors model the practices that they "preach," the teacher preparation program of the University of California at San Marco has chosen to structure courses so that general and special education faculty team teach and model an interdisciplinary, collaborative approach to curriculum and instruction. The faculty works closely with local school personnel and are encouraged to collaboratively conduct research and author scholarly work.

Arizona State University-West

Arizona State University-West launched the Quality Undergraduate Education Through Site-based Teaching (QUEST) Program (Zambo et al., 1994), a new collaborative relationship between university education faculty, student teachers, and local education agencies (Harris & Cleland, 1994). In the spring of 1994, 25 education majors (11 special education majors and 14 elementary education majors) and 5 Arizona State University-West faculty joined with the K–6 Orangewood Elementary School faculty in a mutual teaching–learning partnership. Desert Sage Elementary School welcomed 23 education majors (11 special education majors and 12 elementary education majors) and 3

Arizona State University-West faculty. The dual goals of the collaborative effort are to enhance all participants' skill in accommodating students' individual differences in style and rate of learning, while simultaneously developing the student teachers' competence in methods for teaching children mathematics, science, social studies, and language arts.

A unique collaborative feature of the program is that faculty who teach general and special education methods classes team teach and deliver the instruction at the local elementary schools where students are placed for their internships. Additionally, in their internship placements, general and special education majors are assigned to schools in pairs and triads so that they can collaboratively co-develop and co-teach their lessons in their classroom placements.

INSERVICE PROGRAMS

Sadly, innovations in teacher preparation such as those just described are not what many educators recall as their preservice preparation experience. Instead, they report being ill prepared to expect and effectively respond to the needs of a widely diverse student body (Lyon et al., 1989). Fortunately, local communities, school districts, and state departments of education need not wait for higher education to "get its act together" in order to ready teachers to educate all children in general education settings (Villa, 1989, p. 175). We now have models of local school and joint state department, community, and university collaborative ventures in comprehensive inservice training to support inclusive education. In this section, three professional development approaches that have succeeded in creating and/or maintaining systems change for inclusive schooling are described.

A Local Community and School Program

Through a long-range inservice training agenda, a community and its teachers can "gear up" to create quality-inclusive learning environments. Such an agenda was formulated and carried out over a 5-

year period in a school district that committed itself to and successfully transformed from an exclusionary to a fully inclusive educational system (Cross & Villa, 1992). The inservice agenda included four tiers of training. The first tier was designed for *any member of the community* and included content regarding general education research on the characteristics of effective schools (e.g., Block, Efthim, & Burns, 1989), exemplary practices for educating all children in heterogeneous learning environments (e.g., Fox & Williams, 1991), and models for adult collaboration and the development of small-group interpersonal skills (Johnson & Johnson, 1987a, 1987b; Thousand et al., 1986; Thousand, Villa, Paolucci-Whitcomb, & Nevin, 1992; Thousand & Villa, 1992). The second tier of training was intended to respond to the *self-identified needs of parents and community members* and addressed such issues as legal rights and procedural safeguards for children with and without disabilities, discipline policies, community-referenced instruction, and transition to adult services and continuing education opportunities.

The third tier of training experiences was designed expressly for *people who work with and for children on a day-to-day basis*—teachers, paraeducators, volunteers, and administrators. Training introduced concepts and practices in the following areas:

- Outcome-based instructional models (e.g., Block & Anderson, 1975; Guskey, 1985; Spady & Marshall, 1991)
- Alternatives to standardized assessment models (e.g., Deno, 1985; Giangreco, Cloninger, & Iverson, 1993; Idol, Nevin, & Paolucci-Whitcomb, 1994; Perrone, 1991; Ysseldyke & Christenson, 1987)
- Curriculum adaptation approaches (e.g., Campbell, Campbell, Collicott, Perner, & Stone, 1988; Giangreco & Meyer, 1988; Udvari-Solner, 1994; Wood, 1992)
- Strategies for peer-mediated instruction (cooperative group learning, peer tutoring) and conflict management (e.g., Davidson, 1994; Harper, Maheady, & Mallette, 1994; Johnson

& Johnson, 1987a; LaPlant & Zane, 1994; Schrumpf, 1994)

- Use of technology (Dutton & Dutton, 1990; Heerman, 1988; "Realizing the Promise," 1994; Thornburg, 1992)
- Responsibility-based classroom and school-wide behavior management and discipline approaches (e.g., Becker, 1986; Brendtro, Brokenleg, & Van Bockern, 1990; Curwin & Mendler, 1988; Glasser, 1986)
- Methods for teaching and reinforcing students' use of positive social skills (e.g., Elias & Clabby, 1992; Goldstein, 1988; Hazel, Schumaker, Sherman, & Sheldon-Wildgen, 1981; Vernon, 1989)

The fourth tier of training focused on providing *supervisors and professional teaching personnel* with peer coaching and clinical supervision approaches to assist teachers to be reflective practitioners (Cummings, 1985; Glickman, 1995; Joyce & Showers, 1980, 1988). Interestingly, this local school agenda was consistent with results of qualitative research (see Figure 7.2) in which teachers from a wide variety of schools were interviewed in focus groups (Bradley, 1993).

Both teachers (Bradley, 1993) and findings on exemplary practices (Joyce & Showers, 1988) emphasize the importance of avoiding "one-shot" training experiences and making available a variety of training formats (e.g., summer institutes, graduate courses, workshops, required inservice presentations, staff meetings, one-on-one consultation and conversation, mentoring, team teaching, videotaping, and coaching). Every effort must be made to employ principles of effective teaching by having instructors provide expert models and structure opportunities to develop generalized skill use in actual school and community situations through clinical supervision and peer coaching (Cummings, 1985).

Personnel charged with arranging inservice opportunities also need to consider a menu of incentives for encouraging participation of school and community members in training efforts. Every effort should be made to highlight for staff the in-

trinsic incentives of (1) opportunity for professional and personal growth, (2) opportunity to advance knowledge and practice in the educational

---

1.0 *Program modifications*
   Includes an expressed need for information for adapting curriculum and teaching more than one curriculum at a time.

2.0 *Working with others*
   Includes collaborative methods for teaching and team building; communication, negotiation, and listening skills; and creative problem-solving skills such as brainstorming.

3.0 *Impact on students*
   Includes gaining information about the effects of inclusion on students with and without disabilities and strategies for preparing students without disabilities to welcome and be meaningful helping partners to a new student with disabilities.

4.0 *Parent involvement*
   Involves communication with parents about the general education program and inclusive-practices.

5.0 *Knowledge of specific disabilities*
   Includes an overview of the various disabilities teachers might encounter as well as specific training, as needed, for working with a student with a particular disability.

6.0 *Attitudes of educator*
   Involves formats to discuss and be listened to about feelings regarding the topic of inclusion; also includes some direction in establishing a philosophy of inclusion.

7.0 *Expectations for included students*
   Concerns role clarification for adults and peers regarding responsibilities, including methods for becoming knowledgeable about and accomplishing individual student goals through the existing curriculum.

8.0 *Background of inclusion*
   Involves context setting—familiarizing educators with the rationale for and history of the inclusion movement; also, exploring definitions of inclusion and policies and procedures of the school district to promote inclusion.

FIGURE 7.2 Teacher-Identified Training Components

fields, (3) increased potential for success in teaching a heterogeneous student body, (4) opportunity to experience collegiality through participation in common training, and (5) meeting expectations of members of the school and greater community, including district leadership.

Extrinsic motivators include (1) graduate or recertification credit, (2) salary column movement due to training, (3) remuneration for the cost of training, (4) release time for training, (5) "escape" to a pleasant, nurturing, nonschool setting, and (6) availability of child care during training. The key, of course, is to always ask teachers what it is that they individually and collectively consider rewarding (Villa & Thousand, 1990).

Statewide Summer Leadership Institutes

Since the mid-1980s the Vermont state department of education, the university, and local school leadership have collaborated to provide summer inservice training to increase schools' capacities to be inclusive communities. The effort grew out of a recognized need for training of school personnel to respond to the transition of children with intensive needs back to their home schools, which already had occurred as a state initiative. The Vermont Department of Education, the University of Vermont, and local Vermont school districts collaborate to jointly plan and deliver an annual, intensive, week-long summer leadership institute. The institute's goal is to give family, school, and community members critical knowledge and skills to accommodate the needs of students presenting intensive challenges.

For a school team to attend the institute, it must be heterogeneous—with representation from constituency groups within the school and among community agencies (e.g., administrators, general educators, special educators, other specialists, parents, students, human service providers). Participants learn about and practice communication and small-group skills; collaborative teaming processes (Thousand & Villa, 1992); processes for transitioning students into inclusive local school and community settings (Thousand et al., 1986);

and creative problem-solving strategies for adapting curriculum and instruction to enable successful inclusion of learners with intensive challenges (e.g., Giangreco, 1993; Parnes, 1988).

The instructional format alternates between team work sessions and more formal instruction by parents, students, administrators, teachers, related service personnel, and instructional assistants from schools with experience in creating inclusion-oriented educational opportunities. Each team has an assigned *facilitator* who answers technical questions, guides team work, and observes and processes the team's effectiveness in collaborating and managing conflict. By the week's end, each team has developed a comprehensive *action plan* for delivering support to a targeted student and/or meeting a challenge to inclusive education in their school.

An overarching objective of the institute is to create a sense of group cohesion and build a common conceptual framework and language among team members, so that they will be better able to support one another in transferring their newly acquired knowledge and skills to colleagues in their home school when school resumes. This collaborative "trainer of trainers" inservice model has been highly successful in promoting and sustaining systems change in support of inclusive educational practices and has been replicated in many states and communities across North America.

Regional Summer and School-Year Training

For the 1991 and 1992 school years, the Ohio State Department of Education for the first time afforded local school districts the opportunity to design and implement alternative service delivery models for meeting the needs of children eligible for special education. Each district selected for participation had a choice of trying one of four experimental service delivery models that were exceptions to the Ohio standards for educating children with special needs. The outcomes of these model demonstration projects were examined as part of the process of developing new state standards for serving students eligible for special education.

In Model I, special and general educators jointly served students with and without disabilities in the general education classroom full time through a team teaching model. The primary curriculum used for all children was the general education curriculum. In Model II, special educators worked with children eligible for special education and at-risk students in special classes or learning centers. In Model III, special educators served special-education-eligible students cross-categorically in special classes or learning centers. In Model IV, a team determined the most appropriate way to meet individual students' needs, and special educators supported students in a variety of fashions (e.g., team teaching, consultation, providing modified materials to the teacher, small-group instruction). In Model IV, teachers could instruct all students in the same curriculum or use multilevel, overlapping, or alternative curriculum (Giangreco & Meyer, 1988). Models I and IV were the most inclusive models and the ones that were selected by most districts.

Inservice education was provided to initial and subsequent Model I and IV personnel and took a variety of forms. First, university and special education regional resource center (SERRC) staff were available to provide technical assistance and training upon request at any time during the school year. Additionally, SERRCs provided "leadership teams" from Model I and IV sites in their region with specific training in collaboration and creative problem solving. Each leadership team was comprised of five people—a building administrator, a special educator, a general educator, a parent of a child with disabilities, and a fifth member who could be an additional general or special educator, speech-language pathologist, school psychologist, instructional assistant, or guidance counselor. Teams participated in an initial intensive, 2-day inservice program and three 1-day workshops throughout the school year.

For the second and subsequent years, new sites could opt for this school-year training format or have their leadership teams receive the same content through a 3-day summer institute and 2-day school-year format. Teams from "old" sites could either apply for training as many times as desired or reapply with new team members, in order to expand the cadre of school and community members with the knowledge and skills to promote inclusive schooling. Both summer and school-year training formats required each team to develop an action plan for creating a more inclusive school. Incentives for people to participate were continuing education units and a team stipend to be used to purchase materials, pay for substitutes or future workshop participation, throw a team celebration, or whatever the team deemed important.

To determine the viability and success of each model, data were collected at the end of the first and second years of the project's initiation and compared with the same outcomes measured at the end of the preintervention year (Chapple, 1994; Ohio Department of Education Division of Special Education, 1993). Quantitative student data included the percentage of academic and social IEP (individualized education plan) objectives accomplished and reading and mathematics scores. Results showed that students (in every disability category) served through Models I and IV achieved higher percentages of academic and social IEP objectives at the end of the two experimental years as compared with preintervention year-end results. The greatest gains were made by students with multiple disabilities.

Qualitative data were collected largely on site through interviews of parents, teachers, and administrators. Analysis of the data revealed increases in positive comments about the benefits of inclusive education on the part of teachers, parents, and administrators. Parents emphasized that their children had learned more, felt better about themselves, and were able to make and keep new friends.

In addition to collecting data on student outcomes, a major purpose of the study was to solicit from the innovators their perception of the training needed to successfully apply alternative service delivery approaches. Overwhelmingly, teachers recognized staff development as critical to their success in this venture and noted that much of what they needed had not been a part of their preservice training program. The content areas that emerged as highest priority were collaboration, co-operative learning, team teaching, problem solving, and decision making. Participants believed that they should have received training in these areas *before* implementation of the program and that they should have been involved in every step of planning from the start of the initiative.

As the examples above illustrate, systems change cannot occur and be successful without an accompanying, thoughtful program of staff development. Furthermore, staff development can and should be organized and delivered in a variety of ways. Additional examples of staff development approaches taken by U.S. and Canadian school systems attempting to include all children in general education are offered by Villa, Thousand, Stainback, and Stainback (1992).

SUMMARY

The creation of inclusive schools and classrooms depends on the development of a new collaborative relationship between local education agencies, school districts, and training institutions. Model preservice and inservice programs can be developed. This requires, however, the coordinated actions of local school, higher education, and state department of education personnel. Working together in all aspects of systems change, people concerned with school reform can successfully (1) identify the most meaningful and helpful training content, formats, and incentives; (2) develop successful demonstration sites; (3) provide ongoing training and supervision in real, live school situations; and (4) conduct research that answers our current questions and, probably more importantly, helps us to discover the really important questions to ask next (Villa, 1989).

REFERENCES

Becker, W. (1986). *Applied psychology for teachers: A behavioral cognitive approach.* Chicago: Science Research Associates.

Block, J., & Anderson, L. (1975). *Mastery learning in classroom instruction.* New York: Macmillan.

Block, J., Efthim, H., & Burns, B. (1989). *Building effective mastery learning schools.* New York: Longman.

Bradley, D. (1993). *Staff training for the inclusion of students with disabilities: Visions from educators.* Unpublished doctoral dissertation, Walden University, Baltimore.

Brendtro, L., Brokenleg, M., & Van Bockern, S. (1990). *Reclaiming youth at risk: Our hope for the future.* Bloomington, IN: National Education Service.

Campbell, S., Campbell, S., Collicott, J., Perner, D., & Stone, J. (1988). Individualized instruction. *Education New Brunswick-Journal of Education, 3,* 17–20.

Chapple, J. (1994, October). *Data demonstrates inclusion works in Ohio.* Paper presented at the Common Goals: Effective Practice and Preparation for the 21st Century Conference, Fourth International Conference on Mental Retardation and Developmental Disabilities, Arlington Heights, IL.

Cross, G., & Villa, R. (1992). The Winooski school system: An evolutionary perspective of a school restructuring for diversity. In R. Villa, J. Thousand, W. Stainback, & S. Stainback (Eds.), *Restructuring for caring and effective education: An administrative guide to creating heterogeneous schools* (pp. 219–237). Baltimore: Paul H. Brookes.

Cummings, C. (1985). *Peering in on peers.* Edmonds, WA: Snohomish Publishing.

Curwin, R., & Mendler, A. (1988). *Discipline with dignity.* Alexandria, VA: Association for Supervision & Curriculum Development.

Davidson, N. (1994). Cooperative and collaborative learning: An integrative perspective. In J. Thousand, R. Villa, & A. Nevin (Eds.), *Creativity and collaborative learning: A practical guide to empowering students and teachers* (pp. 13–30). Baltimore: Paul H. Brookes.

Deno, S. L. (1985). Curriculum-based measurement: The emerging alternative. *Exceptional Children, 52,* 219–232.

Dutton, D. H., & Dutton, D. L. (1990). Technology to support diverse needs in regular classes. In W. Stainback & S. Stainback (Eds.), *Support networks for inclusive schooling: Interdependent integrated education* (pp. 167–183). Baltimore: Paul H. Brookes.

Elias, M., & Clabby, J. (1992). *Building social problem-solving skills.* San Francisco: Jossey–Bass.

Fox, T. J., & Williams, W. (1991). *Implementing best practices for all students in their local school—Inclusion for all students through family and* community involvement, collaboration, and the use of school planning teams and individual student planning teams. Burlington: Center for Developmental Disabilities, University of Vermont.

Giangreco, M. F. (1993). Using creative problem-solving methods to include students with severe disabilities in general education classroom activities. *Journal of Educational and Psychological Consultation, 4*(2), 113–135.

Giangreco, M. F., Cloninger, C. J., & Iverson, V. S. (1993). *Choosing options and accommodations for children (COACH): A guide to planning inclusive education.* Baltimore: Paul H. Brookes.

Giangreco, M. F., & Meyer, L. H. (1988). Expanding service delivery options in regular schools and classes for students with disabilities. In J. L. Graden, J. E. Zins, & M. J. Curtis (Eds.), *Alternative educational delivery systems: Enhancing instructional options for all students* (pp. 241–267). Washington, DC: National Association of School Psychologists.

Glasser, W. (1986). *Control theory in the classroom.* New York: Harper & Row.

Glickman, C. (1995). *Supervision of instruction: A developmental approach* (3rd ed.). Boston: Allyn & Bacon.

Goldstein, A. (1988). *The prepare curriculum.* Champaign, IL: Research Press.

Guskey, T. (1985). *Implementing mastery learning.* Belmont, CA: Wadsworth Publishing.

Harper, G., Maheady, L., & Mallette, B. (1994). The power of peer-mediated instruction. In J. Thousand, R. Villa, & A. Nevin (Eds.), *Creativity and collaborative learning: A practical guide to empowering students and teachers* (pp. 229–241). Baltimore: Paul H. Brookes.

Harris, K., & Cleland, J. (1994, April). *A collaborative undergraduate teacher education program: QUEST.* Paper presented at the Council for Exceptional Children annual conference, San Diego, CA.

Hazel, J., Schumaker, J., Sherman, J., & Sheldon-Wildgen, J. (1981). *Asset: A social skills program for adolescents.* Champaign, IL: Research Press.

Heerman, B. (1988). *Teaching and learning with computers.* San Francisco: Jossey–Bass.

Idol, L., Nevin, A., & Paolucci-Whitcomb, P. (1994). *Collaborative consultation.* Austin, TX: Pro-Ed.

Johnson, D. W., & Johnson, R. T. (1987a). *Learning together and alone: Cooperation, competition, and individualization* (2nd ed.). Upper Saddle River, NJ: Prentice Hall.

Johnson, D. W., & Johnson, R. T. (1987b). *A meta-analysis of cooperative, competitive, and individualistic goal structures.* Hillsdale, NJ: Lawrence Erlbaum.

Johnson, D. W., & Johnson, R. T. (1989). *Cooperation and competition: Theory and research.* Edina, MN: Interaction Book.

Joyce, B., & Showers, B. (1980). Improving inservice training: The messages of research. *Educational Leadership, 37,* 379–385.

Joyce, B., & Showers, B. (1988). *Student achievement through staff development.* New York: Longman.

LaPlant, L., & Zane, N. (1994). Partner learning systems. In J. Thousand, R. Villa, & A. Nevin (Eds.), *Creativity and collaborative learning: A practical guide to empowering students and teachers* (pp. 261–273). Baltimore: Paul H. Brookes.

Lyon, G. R., Vaassen, M., & Toomey, F. (1989). Teachers' perceptions of their undergraduate and graduate preparation. *Teacher Education and Special Education, 12,* 164–169.

Meyer, L., & Biklen, D. (1992). *Inclusive elementary and special education teacher preparation program.* Syracuse, NY: Syracuse University, Division for the Study of Teaching and Division of Special Education and Rehabilitation.

Ohio Department of Education Division of Special Education. (1993). *Highlights in Special Education, 14,* 2–3.

Parnes, S. J. (1988). *Visionizing: State-of-the-art processes for encouraging innovative excellence.* East Aurora, NY: D. O. K. Publishers.

Perrone, V. (1991). *Expanding student assessment.* Alexandria, VA: Association for Supervision & Curriculum Development.

Realizing the promise of technology [Special section] (1994). *Educational Leadership, 51*(7), 4–82.

Sarason, S. (1982). *The culture of the school and the problem of change.* Boston: Allyn & Bacon.

Sarason, S., Levine, M., Goldenberg, I., Cherlin, D., & Bennett, E. (1966). *Psychology in community settings: Clinical, educational, vocational, social aspects.* New York: Wiley.

Schrumpf, F. (1994). The role of students in resolving conflicts. In J. Thousand, R. Villa, & A. Nevin (Eds.), *Creativity and collaborative learning: A practical guide to empowering students and teachers* (pp. 275–291). Baltimore: Paul H. Brookes.

Spady, W., & Marshall, K. (1991). Beyond traditional outcome-based education. *Educational Leadership, 49*(2), 67–72.

Stainback, S., & Stainback, W. (1989). Facilitating merger through personnel preparation. In S. Stainback, W. Stainback, & M. Forest (Eds.), *Educating all students in the mainstream of regular education* (pp. 139–150). Baltimore: Paul H. Brookes.

Thornburg, D. (1992). *Edutrends 2010.* San Carlos, CA: Starsong Publications.

Thousand, J., & Villa, R. (1992). Collaborative teams: A powerful tool in school restructuring. In R. Villa, J. Thousand, W. Stainback, & S. Stainback (Eds.), *Restructuring for caring and effective education: An administrative guide for creating heterogeneous schools* (pp. 73–108). Baltimore: Paul H. Brookes.

Thousand, J., Fox, T., Reid, R., Godek, J., Williams, W., & Fox, W. (1986). *The homecoming model: Educating students who present intensive educational challenges within regular education environments* (Monograph No. 7–1). Burlington: University of Vermont, Center for Developmental Disabilities.

Thousand, J., Villa, R., Meyers, H., & Nevin, A. (1994, April). *The heterogeneous education teacher survey: A retrospective analysis of heterogeneous (full inclusion) education.* Paper presented at the annual meeting of the American Education Research Association, New Orleans.

Thousand, J., Villa, R., Paolucci-Whitcomb, P., & Nevin, A. (1992). A rationale for collaborative consultation. In S. Stainback & W. Stainback (Eds.), *Divergent perspectives in special education* (pp. 223–232). Boston: Allyn & Bacon.

Udvari-Solner, A. (1994). A decision-making model for curricular adaptations in cooperative groups. In J.

Thousand, R. Villa, & A. Nevin (Eds.), *Creativity and collaborative learning: A practical guide to empowering students and teachers* (pp. 59–77). Baltimore: Paul H. Brookes.

Vernon, A. (1989). *Thinking, feeling, behaving.* Champaign, IL: Research Press.

Villa, R. (1989). Model public school inservice programs: Do they exist? *Teacher Education and Special Education, 12,* 173–176.

Villa, R., & Thousand, J. (1990). Administrative supports to promote inclusive schooling. In W. Stainback & S. Stainback (Eds.), *Support networks for inclusive schooling: Integrated interdependent education* (pp. 201–218). Baltimore: Paul H. Brookes.

Villa, R., Thousand, J., Nevin, A., & Malgeri, C. (1996). Instilling collaboration for inclusive schooling as a way of doing business in public schools. *Remedial and Special Education, 17,* 169–181.

Villa, R., Thousand, J., Stainback, W., & Stainback, S. (1992). *Restructuring for caring and effective education: An administrative guide to creating heterogeneous schools.* Baltimore: Paul H. Brookes.

Wood, J. (1992). *Adapting instruction for mainstreamed and at-risk students* (2nd ed.). New York: Merrill/Macmillan.

Ysseldyke, J., & Christenson, S. L. (1987). *The instructional environment scale.* Austin, TX: Pro-Ed.

Zambo, R., Moore, S., Nevin, A., Harris, K., Fedock, P., Cobern, W., & Cleland, J. (1994). *The Quality Undergraduate Education through Site-based Teaching (QUEST) Program.* Phoenix: Arizona State University-West [P.O. Box 37100].

DISCUSSION QUESTIONS

1. Why don't teachers learn the skills that they need to accommodate students' varying instructional needs in their preservice programs?
2. How can inservice training help teachers to create a quality-inclusive learning environment?
3. What were the goals of the statewide summer leadership institute?
4. In what ways did the statewide summer leadership institute serve as a model of collaboration?
5. How can local education agencies, school districts, and colleges and universities work together to create inclusive schools and classrooms?

8

Research for Improving Teaching[1]

ALLAN C. ORNSTEIN

FOCUSING QUESTIONS

1. *What factors have restricted teacher effectiveness research?*
2. *In what ways is theory advantageous and disadvantageous to the practice of teaching?*
3. *How do the art and science of teaching differ?*
4. *Do you prefer a scientific or artistic approach to education? Why?*
5. *What aspects of teaching are not evaluated in the product-oriented teaching model?*
6. *Why should research on teacher styles be incorporated into the study of teacher effectiveness?*

It is not an exaggeration to say that the literature on teaching is a morass of ill-defined and changing concepts. Investigators have examined teacher personality, traits, behaviors, attitudes, values, abilities, competencies, and many other characteristics. A host of measuring instruments have been employed: personality tests, attitudinal scales, observation instruments, rating scales, checklists, bipolar descriptors, and close-ended and open-ended written statements. The results of teaching have been studied in terms of student achievement, adjustment, attitudes, socioeconomic status, and creativity. Despite all this activity and thousands of studies conducted in the last fifty years, common denominators and agreed-on generalizations are hard to come by; hence, few facts concerning teacher effectiveness have been established (Borich, 1986; Ornstein, 1986a, 1990).

Confusion over terms, measurement problems, and the complexity of the teaching act are major reasons for the negligible results in judging teacher effectiveness. The studies themselves are often confirmations of common sense (a "democratic" teacher is an effective teacher) or contradictory ("direct" behaviors are effective; "indirect" behaviors are effective), or the contexts within which the studies take place have little bearing on classroom settings, subject, or grade level of the individual teacher.

Because we are unable to agree on or precisely define what a good teacher is, we can use almost any definition, so long as it makes sense or seems logical. Despite the elusive and complex nature of teaching, research on teaching should continue with the hope we can better understand it. This chapter, then, is concerned with the understanding of teacher effectiveness—and with some of the theoretical issues related to defining effective teaching.

THEORY VERSUS THE PRACTICE OF TEACHING

The test of a good theory is whether it can guide practice. In reverse, good practice is based on theory. By practice, we mean the methods, strategies, and skills that apply to the working world, when a person is on the job and actively involved in his or her profession. These theoretical procedures are teachable and can be applied in different situations. When applied, they should result in the practitioner (the teacher) being considered "successful" or "effective" (Ornstein, 1987). By theory, we mean knowledge gained by research and experience that is generalizable and whereby potential users (teachers) can make informed estimates of the probable effects and effectiveness of practices (Bolin, 1988; Wise et al., 1985). Without theory, we cannot assess whether a particular method or strategy will suit the purpose or effect we are trying to achieve. Also, without theory, we operate haphazardly, intuitively, and instinctively. This is not always bad, but it is often difficult to put confidence in our judgments while teaching because of its swift and complex nature. The nature of teaching, therefore, makes it difficult to repeat and interpret what we are doing when we teach.

Regardless of our theories, those who work with or prepare teachers in one way or another have to deal with practice—that is, with what works. Good theories are workable for practitioners, make sense, can be applied to the real world of classrooms and schools, and are generalizable to the greatest number of real situations. Theories that are not workable and generalizable are not good theories and cannot be translated into practice. Theories about teaching may not provide specific answers or quick solutions to vexing problems. Theories must be adjusted to the situation, given the fact that people (teachers and students) differ—they are not nuts and bolts on an assembly line or tiny transistors in a computer, which can be shaped precisely to specifications. Thus, we commonly hear teachers saying, "That's all good theory, but it doesn't work in practice."

In defense of teachers, most teaching experts have difficulty fusing theory and practice. Perhaps we have trouble connecting theory and practice because the methods of inquiry lend themselves more to theoretical discussions and less to practical matters. Also, while discovering good theory is recognized as a worthwhile endeavor, a repertoire of good practice is often misconstrued by theoreticians as a "cookbook" or as "do's and don'ts" that are second-rate or unimportant. Despite the claims of some theoreticians, we seem unable to make the leap from theory to practice, from the textbook and college course to the classroom and school. Good theory in teaching often gets lost as practitioners try to apply what they have learned in college to the classroom setting in a search for practical solutions to common, everyday problems.

The problem of translating theory into practice is further aggravated by researchers and professors, many of whom are more concerned with the teacher "knowing that" than with the teacher "knowing how." This distinction "refers to the difference between being able to state factual propositions [theory] and being able to perform skills or operations [practice]" (Gage, 1978, p. 44). The one kind of knowledge does not necessarily follow from the other; this is the reason why teaching texts and courses can stress either theory or practice. According to Gage, "much of the teacher education program is given over to providing teachers with a great deal of knowledge that certain things are true, in the subject [and grade levels] to be taught" (p. 44). This kind of knowledge is acquired by most prospective teachers at the expense of theory that could help them understand the basic principles and phenomena underlying their work.

The problem is further compounded by practitioners, including teachers, supervisors, and administrators, who feel that practical considerations are more worthwhile than theory; most teachers and supervisors view theory as impractical and "how-to" approaches as helpful. Thus, while many theoreticians ignore the practitioners, at the same time many practitioners ignore the theoreticians. Moreover, many theoretical discussions of teaching are divorced from practical application in the classroom, and many practical discussions of teaching rarely consider theoretical relationships.

Practice involves selecting strategies and methods that apply to specific situations. Theory involves principles and propositions that can be generalized to many situations. The problem is that every situation is unique. This becomes especially evident when practitioners try to apply the theory they learn from the professional literature. Adopting the right method for the appropriate situation is not an easy task and involves a good deal of common sense and experience, which no one can learn from a theoretical discussion. No matter how good our theories may be, they are not always predictable or generalizable from one situation to another.

THE SCIENCE VERSUS THE ART OF TEACHING

Another problem with preparing teachers is that we cannot agree on whether teaching is a science or an art. Some readers may say that this is a hopeless dichotomy, similar to that of theory versus practice, because the real world rarely consists of neat packages or either/or situations. Gage (1978) uses this distinction between teaching as a science and as an art to describe the elements of predictability in teaching and what constitutes "good" teaching. A science of teaching is attainable, he contends, because it "implies that good teaching will some day be attainable by closely following vigorous laws that yield high predictability and control." Teaching is more than a science, he observes, because it also involves "artistic judgment about the best ways to teach" (p. 17). When teaching leaves the laboratory or textbook and goes face to face with students, "the opportunity for artistry expands enormously." No science can prescribe successfully all the twists and turns as teaching unfolds, or as teachers respond with "judgment, sudden insight, sensitivity, and agility to promote learning" (p. 15). These are expressions of art that depart from the rules and principles of science.

Is such a limited scientific basis of teaching even worthwhile to consider? Yes, but the practitioner must learn as a teacher to draw not only from his or her professional knowledge (which is grounded in scientific principles), but also from a set of personal experiences and resources that are uniquely defined and exhibited by the teacher's own personality and "gut" reaction to classroom events that unfold (which form the basis for the art of teaching). For Jackson (1990), the hunches, judgments, and insights of the teacher, as he or she responds spontaneously to events in the classroom, are as important as, and perhaps even more important than, the science of teaching.

To some extent, the act of teaching must be considered intuitive and interactive, not prescriptive or predictable. According to Eisner (1983), teaching is based primarily on feelings and artistry, not scientific rules. In an age of science and technology, there is a special need to consider teaching as an "art and craft." Eisner condemns the scientific movement in psychology, especially behaviorism, and the scientific movement in education, especially in school management, as reducing the teaching act to trivial specifications. He regards teaching as a "poetic metaphor," more suited to satisfying the soul than informing the head, more concerned with the whole than with a set of discrete skills or stimuli. Our role as teachers, he claims, should not be that of a "puppeteer," an "engineer," or a manager; rather, it is "to orchestrate the dialogue [as the conductor of a symphony] moving from one side of the room to the other" (p. 8). The idea is to perceive patterns in motion, to improvise within the classroom, and to avoid mechanical or prescribed rules.

Rubin (1985) has a similar view of teaching—that effectiveness and artistry go hand in hand. The interplay of students and teacher is crucial and cannot be predetermined with carefully devised strategies. Confronted with everyday problems that cannot be easily predicted, the teacher must rely on intuition and on "insight acquired through long experience" (p. 61). Rubin refers to such terms as "with-it-ness," "instructional judgments," "quick cognitive leaps," and "informal guesses" to explain the difference between the effective teacher and the ineffective teacher. Recognizing limits to rationality, he claims that for the artistic teacher a "feel for what is right often is more productive than prolonged analysis" (p. 69). In the final analysis, Rubin compares the teacher's pedagogy with the "artist's colors, poet's words, sculptor's clay, and musician's notes" (p. 60)—in all of which a certain amount of artistic judgment is needed to get the right mix, medium, or blend.

Dawe (1984a, 1984b) is most extreme in his analysis of teaching solely as an art, providing romantic accounts and tales of successful teaching and teaching strategies, described in language that could hardly be taken for social science research. He considers the act of teaching akin to drama, and feels that those who wish to teach should audition in a teaching studio before teachers trained as performing artists. Good teaching is likened to good theater, and a good teacher is likened to a good actor.

Blending Science and Art

The more we consider teaching as an art, packed with emotions, feelings, and excitement, the more difficult it is to derive rules or generalizations. If teaching is more of an art than a science, then principles and practices cannot be easily codified or developed in the classroom or easily learned by others. Hence, there is little reason to offer to teachers methods courses in education. If, however, teaching is more of a science, or at least partly a science, then pedagogy is predictable to that extent; it can be observed and measured with some accuracy, and the research can be applied to the practice of teaching (as a physician applies scientific knowledge to the practice of medicine) and also learned in a university or on the job (Bolster, 1983; Ornstein, 1985, 1990).

But a word of caution is needed. The more we rely on artistic interpretations or on old stories and accounts about teachers, the more we fall victim to fantasy, wit, and romantic rhetoric, and the more we depend on hearsay and conjecture rather than on social science or objective data in evaluating teacher competency. On the other hand, the more we rely on the scientific interpretations of teaching, the more we overlook those commonsense and spontaneous processes of teaching, and the sounds, smells, and visual flavor of the classroom. The more scientific we are in our approach to teaching, the more we ignore what we cannot accommodate

to our empirical assumptions or principles. What sometimes occurs, according to Eisner (1993), is that the educationally significant but difficult to measure or observe is replaced by what is insignificant but comparatively easy to measure or observe.

It is necessary to blend artistic impressions and relevant stories about teaching, because good teaching involves emotions and feelings, with the objectivity of observations and measurements and the precision of language. There is nothing wrong with considering good teaching to be art, but we must also consider it to lend itself to a prescriptive science or practice. If it does not, then there is little assurance that prospective teachers can be trained to be teachers—told what to do, how to instruct students, how to manage students, and so forth—and educators will be extremely vulnerable to public criticism and to people outside the profession telling them how and what to teach.

TEACHER–STUDENT VARIABLES

The kind of teacher effectiveness studies that make up the mainstream of educational research considers relationships between variables. We can have *predictive* relationships and *causal* relationships. For example, Flanders (1965) in his classic study shows that students who are taught by an "indirect" teacher learn more and exhibit more constructive behaviors than do those who are taught by a "direct" teacher. The results of that study have been cited in thousands of studies on teaching, including some fifteen times in the most recent edition of the *Handbook of Research on Teaching,* edited by Wittrock (1986).

However, such a predictive relationship may not really reflect a causal relationship or a cause-effect relationship. It is possible that students who are nonachievers or unruly cause teachers to exhibit direct behaviors and that students who are achievers and well mannered permit teachers to exhibit indirect behaviors. We can raise this point with about 90 percent of the research on teacher effectiveness, since the results are overwhelmingly correlational. Furthermore, many teacher behaviors and methods that seem to have a positive effect in one situation may be ineffective and inappropriate in another. Different teacher behaviors and methods have different effects on different students, in different grades, subjects, classrooms, and schools. For example, does the "warm" teacher have the same effect on first graders and twelfth graders? In mathematics, history, and physical education? With low-income and middle-income students, with low achievers and high achievers, with boys and girls, and so on? Moreover, it is difficult to isolate the teacher effects from the effects of other agents such as parents, peer group, television, and other teachers (Ornstein, 1986b, 1989). Failure to control for these variables and their interaction effects leads to inappropriate research findings and to nonrelevant and misleading data for the teacher. But once we start to analyze the various relationships among the variables, we come to numerous interactions and still other new and untested interactions, which in turn can be analyzed. This process is endless; we enter a hall of mirrors that extends to infinity.

Not only do process variables (different behaviors and/or methods) mean different things to different researchers, but also similar behaviors or methods are sometimes considered effective in one study and ineffective in another study. These are constructs that interact with numerous presage and context variables, and they entail such a diversity of specifics that they defy precise definitions and exact quantification. Moreover, if we break them down into precise, agreed-on, quantifiable constructs and variables, the number would vastly increase to the point of trivia and the importance of each would be reduced to the specific study. How far we extend our analysis depends on our purpose and knowledge; nonetheless, the existing relationships are not linear or clear, but rather multiple and sketchy.

Process Versus Product

Most of the research from the turn of the century to the early 1970s focused on process variables in terms of their relationships to presage or context variables. The idea was to focus on teacher behaviors or methods and to use such measures as ratings, classroom observations, and personality tests to obtain information on what the teacher was doing in the classroom. A basic assumption of many investigators during this period was that assessment of teacher behavior sufficed for describing teaching and learning. The focus was on what the teacher was doing, with little consideration given to the resulting behavior or performance of the students. Although one can make a good case for focusing on teachers, more emphasis should have been given to student outcomes.

Only recently has the research moved from the processes to the products of teaching. Emphasis on the products of teaching makes the behavior of the teacher, or what the teacher is doing, of secondary importance to student outcomes or results, and these are usually measured through standardized tests of achievement. Process variables are still considered part of the research; but, they are often used as part of a process-product paradigm whereby certain teacher behaviors or methods are determined to be "effective" in contributing to student achievement (which is usually based on reading or mathematics tests).

TEACHER EFFECTIVENESS RESEARCH

The current research on teacher effectiveness delineates a host of easily measured businesslike, structured, and tasklike behaviors (i.e., Doyle, 1985, 1986; Evertson, 1993; Good and Brophy, 1990; Rosenshine, 1987, Rosenshine and Meister, 1992). But these models fail to consider that teachers differ, and that many successful teachers do not exhibit such direct behaviors.

The new and popular teacher effectiveness models lock us into a narrow mold that misses many nuances of teaching. Many of these prescriptions (sometimes called principles) themselves are old ideas bottled under new labels such as "with-it-ness," "smoothness," "clarity," "alertness," "pacing," "momentum," "overlapping," and "student accountability." These terms are rooted in Kounin's (1970) research on classroom management, and in some cases it is not clear that the current crop of researchers on teacher effectiveness gives Kounin his full credit. This explains in part the current emphasis on routines, rules, and control—in short, on teaching behaviors and methods that enhance classroom management. Furthermore, much of the new research deals with low achievers and at-risk students—another reason why many of its recommended teacher behaviors and methods coincide with managerial and structured techniques. Indeed, the new research tends to confirm that effective teachers are good classroom managers, which is something most teachers already know and knew even before Kounin established his "principles" of classroom management.

In our efforts to identify good teaching, the teacher effectiveness research is often published as if its findings are new or groundbreaking. But the findings are nothing more than behaviors and methods that good teachers have been using for many years. What these product-oriented researchers have done is to summarize what we have known for a long time but have often passed on as "tips for teachers" or "practical suggestions." (And we were once criticized by researchers as being recipe oriented.) These researchers confirm the basic behaviors and methods of experienced teachers; however, they give beginning teachers a better yardstick or starting point to understand effective teaching than did previous researchers, and they give credibility to the teachers' practices by correlating their behaviors (processes) with student achievement (products).

The Purposes of Teacher Effectiveness Research

The fundamental question in the conduct and appreciation of research into teacher effectiveness is whether or not teachers influence student outcomes and, if so, to what extent. The need to establish the relative contribution of the teacher to student learning is particularly important for four reasons:

1. *It provides teacher educators a rationale for their job.* Teacher educators must screen and prepare future teachers, as well as provide in-service education for experienced teachers. If teachers have little or no impact on student outcomes, then there is no reason to guard the gates with credentials or to make such a fuss about teacher education. If teachers have minimal or no impact on students, then there is little or no reason to provide pedagogical knowledge in order to enhance professional competence.

2. *It provides a rationale for the recent reforms regarding teacher evaluation, teacher accountability, teacher performance, and teacher competence.* If teachers have little effect on student outcomes, or if replicable findings of teacher effectiveness cannot be found, then all these new reform policies are at best theoretical exercises and at worst politicize the evaluation of teachers. If such data are lacking, then various methods for effective teaching have been sold unproven, and sound teacher evaluation policies cannot be formulated. Moreover, assessing teachers or making judgments about their competence cannot be supported; making inferences from observations or rating scales to support personnel decisions is invalid; and labels such as "incompetent," "competent," or "master" teacher are premature. The absence of teacher influence on student performance suggests that remediation, probation, or performance-related programs cannot be statistically or legally supported, and it is difficult for supervisors and administrators to give constructive evaluation and feedback to teachers.

3. *It provides support for the ideas that teacher differences exist and that teachers make a difference.* Since the 1980s, the prominent view is that teachers affect student outcomes. This new research assumes that the process (teacher behaviors and/or methods) can be controlled, modified, or taught, and that teacher-student interactions can be analyzed and predicted; it also assumes that what teachers do in the classroom does affect students and that narrowly defined teacher behaviors or methods affect student performance (Ornstein, 1990).

4. *It provides a professional knowledge base for teacher educators and teacher training institutions.* If this knowledge base continues to develop and is appropriately used, it can help provide information to use when making decisions about appropriate teaching techniques—even who should teach. This information base allows us to act confidently on a theoretical basis, whereby we establish certain principles or methods of teaching. Whether these theoretical generalizations apply to the real world of teaching, that is, the practice of teaching, is not clear. It is assumed that much of the teacher effectiveness research can be integrated into what teachers already know or think they know about teaching, and it is also assumed that the behaviors that are codified and measured lead to desired learning outcomes.

In general, the new research on teacher effectiveness opposes a wealth of large-scale research considered conventional wisdom in the 1960s and 1970s, which held that teacher effects were secondary or irrelevant and that each student's IQ, family, home life, peer group, and social class were crucial in determining his or her achievement (Coleman, 1966; Husén, 1967; Jencks, 1972; Moynihan, 1965; Thorndike, 1973). This research attributed only a small fraction of the independent variation in student achievement to school variables (about 15 to 20 percent, depending on the research study), and only a small part to teachers. Their analysis points the finger of responsibility for achievement to students, not teachers; thus we should remember their findings and discuss publicly the influence of family structure and parental responsibility on student outcomes.

Caution and Criticism

There is some danger in the new research. The conclusions overwhelmingly portray the effective teacher as task-oriented, organized, and structured—nothing more than Ryans's (1960) Pattern Y or businesslike teacher and Flanders's (1965) direct teacher (who was considered ineffective). These teacher effectiveness models tend to overlook the friendly, warm, and democratic teacher; the creative teacher who is stimulating and imaginative; the dramatic teacher who bubbles with energy and enthusiasm; the philosophical teacher who encourages students to play with ideas and concepts; and the problem-solving teacher who requires that students think out the answers. In their desire to identify and prescribe measurable and quantifiable behaviors, the new researchers overlook the emotional, qualitative, and interpretive descriptions of classrooms, and the joys of teaching. Most of the new research has been conducted at the elementary grade levels, where one would expect more social, psychological, and humanistic factors to be observed, recorded, and recommended as effective.

The new teacher effectiveness models fail to consider that a good deal of effective teaching may not directly correlate with student performance measured by achievement tests. For Greene (1986, 1993), good teaching and learning involve such intangibles as values, experiences, insights, and appreciation—the "stuff" that cannot be easily observed or measured. Teaching and learning are an "existential" encounter, a philosophical process involving creative ideas and inquiries that cannot be easily quantified. We might add that much of teaching involves caring, nurturing, and valuing behaviors—attributes not easily assessed by evaluation instruments.

Much of teaching also deals with hunches and intuitive judgments that teachers make as classroom events and interactions evolve; the teachers' behaviors or responses are not preplanned, and they cannot easily be categorized or made to fit into measurable units that correspond with the classroom context. Indeed, teaching is a holistic enterprise and trying to slice, isolate, or categorize it into some set of recommendations or hierarchy of principles and methods may not be realistic. It may be the best we can offer as researchers continue the struggle to define good teaching, but it is merely an abstraction from a host of classroom events that rarely considers prior teacher-student experiences and the thinking and feelings that interact with behaviors to influence learning.

What is not measurable goes unnoticed in a process-product teaching model. By breaking down the teaching act into behaviors, competencies, or criteria that can be defined operationally and quantified, educators overlook the hard-to-measure aspects of teaching, the personal and humanistic aspects of teaching. To say that excellence in teaching requires measurable behaviors and outcomes is to miss a substantial part of teaching—what some educators refer to as artistry, drama, tone, and flavor. It can be argued, too, that teacher behaviors that correlate with measurable outcomes often lead to rote learning, drill, and automatic responses.

In their attempts to observe and measure what teachers do and to detail whether students improve their performance (usually on reading or mathematics tests), these models ignore the learners' imaginations, fantasies, and aesthetic thoughts, including their dreams, hopes, and aspirations, and how teachers influence these hard-to-define but very important aspects of students' lives. The chief variable in this current research is knowledge of facts, as evidenced by scores on achievement tests (Ornstein, 1989, 1990).

The fact is that the research on teaching tends to neglect the "subject knowledge" of the teacher—how it relates to student understanding, how it is taught and how it is integrated with "pedagogical knowledge"—the genetic principles and methods of teaching. Teacher effectiveness research also neglects learning experiences that deal with metacognition, critical thinking, and learning how to learn, as well as more global learning outcomes such as cultural sensitivity, spiritual outlook, and philosophy. It correlates with specific knowledge—the content of Walt Whitman's poems and the outcomes of Hiroshima—but not how students feel about these subjects, or how it has affected their own learning or outlook on life. In the same view, teacher behavior research seems to miss moral and ethical outcomes, as well as social, personal, and self-actualizing processes related to life—the affective domain of learning and the psychology of being human.

Quantifiable Research Methods

The traditional world of measuring teacher behavior assumes that educational research is a matter of identifying and adding more variables and providing sophisticated analysis to a one-way, or input-output, explanation of human behavior. The intent is to discover a number of "right" input variables that will define human behavior as output in educational settings (Cziko, 1992). But this basic model and its assumptions, which drive group-based statistics, miss the mark for fully explaining purposeful behavior.

Regardless of the statistical procedures used—correlation tests, t-tests, analysis of variances, and multiple regression, among others—proponents are convinced that human behavior can be explained by causality, where an independent variable (usually some condition or treatment effect) causes or affects the dependent variable (an outcome). This is a quick and snappy method of exhibiting "expertise," especially when mixed with professional or research jargon. Well, life is not that simple, especially when it comes to teaching and learning. Outcomes in life, as well as life in classrooms, depend on a host of complex interactions that cannot be fully explained by isolating or breaking down abstractions of human behavior into discrete categories or statistical units, at least not without interpreting the data within the context of what is happening. All these quantifiable (independent-dependent variables) procedures merely provide the researcher with frequency of outcomes; they assume a one-way cause-effect explanation—similar to classical behaviorist psychology—but are inadequate for fully explaining the complex aspect of teaching and learning.

Many of us who are satisfied in analyzing the world of psychology or education in term of quantifiable outcomes believe that if research or evaluation problems exist it is because the methods need to be improved. When critics mention that causality is sometimes unknown, or blurred by other factors not accounted for, the most common reaction is to ignore or criticize the information.

Even worse, once we try to analyze the various relationships among variables, we come to numerous interactions and still other new and untested interactions. The process is endless, especially in the teaching-learning equation, and we enter into a hall of mirrors that extends into infinity.

How far we carry our analysis depends on our knowledge and purposes; nonetheless, the relationships are not linear or clear, but rather multiple and sketchy.

The traditional, quantifiable model of research on teaching is hard to criticize, because it represents mainstream thinking and is derived from predictable behavior. To discuss human behavior with fuzzy phenenoma or hard-to-define processes or products is to leave oneself open to professional ridicule, especially in a world governed by "technocratic" researchers and Skinnerian logic.

THE HUMAN FACTOR IN TEACHING

Good teachers know, although they may not be able to prove it, that good teaching is really about caring and sharing; the capacity to accept, understand, and appreciate students on their terms and through their world; making students feel good about themselves; having positive attitudes and setting realistic achievement goals; and getting all fired up with enthusiasm and a cheerful presence.

These are basically fuzzy qualities that the scientific theories and paradigms of effective teaching tend to overlook. Indeed teachers who place high priority on humanistic and effective practices, and on the personal and social development of their students, are not really interested in devoting much time to the empirical or behavioral literature, or in teaching small pieces of information that can be measured and correlated with their own teaching behaviors.

Teachers who are confident about themselves are not overly concerned about their evaluation ratings, or even what the research has to say about their teacher behaviors. How does the profession reconcile the fact that so many competent teachers consider teacher research as "irrelevant and counterintuitive" to their own practice of teaching? Why do we often hear the complaint—"That's all good theory, but it does not work in practice."

Teaching is a people industry, and people (especially young people) perform best in places in which they feel wanted and respected. To be sure, it is possible for a teacher to "disengage" or "disin-

vite" students by belittling them, ignoring them, undercutting them, comparing them to other siblings or students, or even "yessing" them (failing to hold them accountable for the right answer), and still perform high on other discrete competencies or behaviors associated with the teacher as a technician: "The teacher came to class on time." "The teacher's objectives were clearly stated." "The teacher checked homework on a regular basis." "The teacher's expectations were clearly stated." "The teacher graded quizzes on a timely basis." Such a checklist or behaviorist approach is common today, as we search for a research-based model of what is a "good" or "effective" teacher. This mentality can make us technically right but never really describe good teaching; it coincides with the bureaucratic process, where rules, regulations, and memos prevail. But it misses the essence of classroom teaching, where feelings, attitudes, and imagination are crucial and should take precedence over tiny, measurable pieces of information that border on silliness and trivia. Of course, some of the research that characterizes good teaching is reasonable and warranted, but most of this "wisdom" is old hat, and what experienced teachers already know.

The focus of teacher research should be on the learner, not on the teacher; on the feelings and attitudes of the students, not on knowledge and information (since feelings and attitudes will eventually determine what knowledge and information are sought after and acquired); and on long-term objectives or specific tasks. But if teachers spend more time on the learner, on his or her feelings and attitudes, and on the social or personal growth and development of their students, they may be penalized when cognitive outcomes (little pieces of information) are correlated with their teaching behaviors.

Students need to be encouraged and nurtured by their teachers, especially when they are young. They are too dependent on approval from significant adults—first their parents, then their teachers. Because of this, parents and teachers need to help young children and adolescents establish a source of self-esteem within themselves by focusing on their strengths, supporting them, and by discouraging negative self-talk while helping them to take control of their lives and living by their own values.

People (including young people) with high self-esteem achieve at high levels, and the more one achieves, the better one feels about oneself. The opposite is also true. Students who fail to master the subject matter get down on themselves and eventually give up. Students with low self-esteem give up quickly. In short, student self-esteem and achievement are related, as are student self-esteem and self-reliance (Ames, 1990; Corno, 1993). Put in different words, if we can nurture the students' self-esteem, almost everything else should fall into place, including achievement scores and academic outcomes. If we can get the students' feelings and emotions on track, cognition will follow. Cognition cannot be successful if teachers fail to guide students who have serious social or personal problems.

This builds a strong argument for creating success experiences for students to help them feel good about themselves. The long-term benefits are obvious. The more students learn to like themselves, the more they will achieve, and the more they achieve, the more they will like themselves. But that takes time, that is nurturing learners for future benefits. However, these benefits do not show up on a classroom or standardized test within a semester or school year; it doesn't help the teacher who is being evaluated by a content-driven or test-driven school administrator. It certainly does not benefit the teacher who is being evaluated for how many times he or she attended departmental meetings, whether the shades in the classroom were even, or whether the instructional objectives were clearly stated.

The current research on teaching is primarily concerned with the present—with processes and products that are measured in one term (or year) and by a standardized test of cognitive outcomes (not affective outcomes). Thus, one might conclude that the new teacher effectiveness research misses the humanistic mark. Students need to engage in growth-enhancing experiences and we need to recognize that the most effective teachers endow their students with a "you can do it" attitude, with good feelings about themselves, which

are indirectly and eventually related to cognitive achievement. While every teacher needs to demand high academic standards and teach the content, there needs to be understanding that the content interacts with the process. If the process can be cultivated in a humanistic way, then the outcomes of the content should be improved.

Beyond Effective Teaching

The current research on teacher effectiveness needs to be revised to fit varied teaching contexts. Teachers must be permitted to incorporate specific teacher behaviors and methods according to their personality, philosophy, and goals—to pick and choose from a wide range of research and theory and to discard other teacher behaviors and methods that conflict with their style, without being considered ineffective. It also needs to include, according to Prawat (1992), what students do outside of school because the time spent outside of school surpasses the time spent in classrooms. Out-of-school variables are certainly more important than school variables, but that brings us back to Coleman, Jencks, and Moynihan and the family and peer group—which many educators would rather not discuss; moreover, it is the research that the current model on teacher effectiveness wishes to refute.

It is obvious that certain behaviors contribute to good teaching. The trouble is, there is little agreement on exactly what behaviors or methods are most important. There will be some teachers who gain theoretical knowledge of "what works," but will be unable to put the ideas into practice. Some teachers will act effortlessly in the classroom and others will consider teaching a chore. All this suggests that teaching cannot be described in terms of a checklist or a precise model. It also suggests that teaching is a holistic activity that deals with people (not tiny behaviors or competencies) and how they (teachers and students) develop and behave in a variety of classroom and school settings.

While the research on teacher effectiveness provides a vocabulary and system for improving our insight into good teaching, there is a danger that it may lead to some of us becoming too rigid in our view of teaching. Following only research on teaching effectiveness can lead to too much emphasis on specific behaviors that can be easily measured or prescribed in advance, at the expense of ignoring humanistic behaviors and hard-to-measure behaviors.

Most teacher evaluation instruments tend to deemphasize the human side of teaching, because it is difficult to measure. In an attempt to be scientific, to predict and control behavior, and to assess group patterns, we sometimes lose sight of effective behaviors and individual preferences. Although some educators have moved to a search for humanistic factors that influence teaching, we continue to mainly define most teacher behaviors in terms of behaviorist and cognitive factors.

Similarly, most teacher evaluation instruments still do not address the question of how to change teacher behavior. The developers of evaluation instruments assume that once they have discovered what ought to be done, teachers will naturally do what is expected. If our purpose is to change or improve the practices of teachers, then it is necessary to come to grips with teachers' beliefs and attitudes and with their concepts of "good" and "effective."

In providing feedback and evaluation for teachers many factors need to be considered so that advice or information does not fall on deaf ears. Teachers appreciate feedback processes whereby they can improve their teaching, so long as the processes are honest and fair and are professionally planned and administered; so long as teachers are permitted to make mistakes; and so long as more than one model of effectiveness is considered so that they can adopt recommended behaviors and methods that fit their personality and philosophy of teaching.

The current research on teacher effectiveness needs to be revised to include varied teaching styles. Teachers must be permitted to incorporate specific teacher behaviors and methods according to their own unique personality, philosophy, and goals; to pick and choose from a wide range of research and theory; and to discard those teacher behaviors that conflict with their own style, without

fear of being considered ineffective. A good many school districts, even state departments of education, have developed evaluation instruments and salary plans based exclusively on these prescriptive and product-oriented behaviors. Even worse, teachers who do not exhibit these behaviors are often penalized or labeled as "marginal" or "incompetent" (Holdzkom, 1987; Milner, 1991; Ornstein, 1988a, 1988b). There is an increased danger that many more school districts and states will continue to jump on this bandwagon and make decisions based on these models without recognizing or giving credibility to other teacher effectiveness research.

CONCLUSION

Few, if any, activities are as crucial in schooling as teaching; and, as elusive and complex as teaching may be, research toward understanding it must continue. The problem, however, is that most of the research on teaching is not read by the most important group—teachers, who can and should benefit by knowing, understanding, and integrating the concepts and principles of the research on teaching.

It is obvious that certain behaviors contribute to good teaching. The trouble is that there is little agreement on exactly what behaviors or methods are most important. Some teachers will learn most of the rules about good teaching, yet be unsuccessful. Other teachers will break the rules of "good" teaching, yet be profoundly successful. Some teachers will gain theoretical knowledge of "what works," but be unable to put the ideas into practice. And yet other teachers will act effortlessly in the classroom, while others will consider teaching a chore. All this suggests that teaching is more art than science and practice is more important than theory.

While the research on teacher effectiveness provides a vocabulary and system for improving our insight into good teaching, there is a danger that it may lead to some of us becoming too rigid in our view of teaching. Following only the research on teaching can lead to too much emphasis on specific behaviors that cannot be easily measured or prescribed in advance.

Most teacher evaluation processes do not address the question of how to change teacher behavior. The developers of evaluation instruments assume that once they have discovered what ought to be done, teachers will naturally do what is expected. If our purpose is to change or improve the practices of teachers, then it is necessary to come to grips with teachers' beliefs and attitudes and with their concepts of "good" or "effective."

In providing feedback and evaluation to teachers, many factors need to be considered so that the advice or information does not fall on deaf ears. Teachers appreciate feedback processes whereby they can improve their teaching, if the processes are honest and fair and are professionally planned and administered; if teachers are permitted to make mistakes; and if more than one model of effectiveness is considered so that teachers can adopt recommended behaviors and methods that fit their own personality and philosophy of teaching.

ENDNOTE

1. This article is based on three of the author's works: "Teacher Effectiveness Research: Theoretical Considerations," in H. C. Waxman and H. J. Walberg, eds., *Effective Teaching: Current Research.* Berkeley: McCutchan Press, 1991, pp. 63–80; "How to Recognize Good Teaching," *American School Board Journal,* 180 (1993), pp. 24–29; and "The Human Dimension of Teaching," *Educational Forum,* in print (1995).

REFERENCES

Ames, Carol. "Motivation: What Teachers Need to Know." *Teachers College Record* 91 (1990): 409–421.

Bolin, Frances G. "Helping Student Teachers Think about Teaching." *Journal of Teacher Education* 39 (1988): 48–55.

Bolster, Arthur S. "Toward a More Effective Model of Research on Teaching." *Harvard Educational Review* 53 (1983): 294–398.

Borich, G. D. "Paradigms of Teacher Effectiveness Research." *Education and Urban Society* 18 (1986): 143–167.

Brophy, Jere E. "Classroom Management Techniques." *Education and Urban Society* 18 (1986): 182–194.

Brophy, Jere E. "Educating Teachers about Managing Classrooms and Students." *Teaching and Teacher Education* 4 (1988): 1–18.

Coleman, James S. *Equality of Educational Opportunity.* Washington, D.C.: U.S. Government Printing Office, 1966.

Corno, Lyn. "Modern Conceptions of Volition and Educational Research." *Educational Researcher* 22 (1993): 14–22.

Cziko, Gary A. "Purposeful Behavior as the Control of Perception." *Educational Researcher* 21 (1992): 10–18.

Dawe, Harry A. "Teaching: A Performing Art." *Phi Delta Kappan* 65 (1984a): 548–552.

Dawe, Harry A. "Teaching: Social Science or Performing Art?" *Harvard Educational Review* 54 (1984b): 111–114.

Doyle, Walter E. "Effective Teaching and the Concept of Master Teacher." *Elementary School Journal* 86 (1985): 27–34.

Doyle, Walter E. "Classroom Organization and Management." In *Handbook of Research on Teaching,* 3rd ed. Edited by Merlin C. Wittrock. New York: Macmillan, 1986.

Eisner, Elliot W. "The Art and Craft of Teaching." *Educational Leadership* 40 (1983): 4–13.

Eisner, Elliot W. *The Educational Imagination,* 3rd ed. New York: Macmillan, 1993.

Evertson, Carolyn M. "Do Teachers Make a Difference?" *Education and Urban Society* 18 (1986): 195–210.

Evertson, Carolyn M., et al. *Classroom Management for Secondary Teachers,* 3rd ed. Englewood Cliffs, N.J.: Prentice-Hall, 1993.

Flanders, Ned. *Teacher Influence, Pupil Attitudes and Achievement.* Washington, D.C.: U.S. Government Printing Office, 1965.

Gage, N. L. *The Scientific Basis of the Art of Teaching.* New York: Teachers College Press, 1978.

Good, Thomas L., and Jere E. Brophy. *Looking in Classrooms,* 5th ed. New York: HarperCollins, 1990.

Greene, Maxine. "Philosophy and Teaching." In *Handbook of Research on Teaching,* 3rd ed. Edited by Merlin C. Wittrock. New York: Macmillan. 1986.

Greene, Maxine. "The Passions of Pluralism." *Educational Researcher,* 22 (1993): 13–18.

Holdzkom, David. "Appraising Teacher Performance in North Carolina." *Educational Leadership* 44 (1987): 40–44.

Husen, Torsten. *International Study of Achievement in Mathematics: A Comparison of Twelve Countries.* New York: Wiley, 1967.

Jencks, Christopher, et al. *Inequality: A Reassessment of the Effect of Family and Schooling in America.* New York: Basic Books, 1972.

Kounin, Jacob. *Discipline and Group Management in Classrooms.* New York: Holt, Rinehart, 1970.

Milner, Joseph O. "Working Together For Better Evaluation," *Phi Delta Kappan* 72 (1991): 788–789.

Moynihan, D. P. *The Negro Family: The Case for National Action.* Washington, D.C.: U.S. Government Printing Office, 1965.

Ornstein, Allan C. "Research on Teaching: Issues and Trends." *Journal of Teacher Education* 36 (1985): 27–31.

Ornstein, Allan C. "Research on Teacher Behavior: Trends and Policies." *High School Journal* 69 (1986a): 399–402.

Ornstein, Allan C. "Teacher Effectiveness: Current Research and Issues." *Educational and Urban Society* 18 (1986b): 168–175.

Ornstein, Allan C. "Theory and Practice of Curriculum." *Kappa Delta Pi Record* 24 (1987): 15–17.

Ornstein, Allan C. "The Changing Status of the Teaching Profession." *Urban Education* 23 (1988a): 261–279.

Ornstein, Allan C. "The Evolving Accountability Movement." *Peabody Journal of Education* 65 (1988b): 12–20.

Ornstein, Allan C. "Theoretical Issues Related To Teaching." *Education and Urban Society* 22 (1989): 95–104.

Ornstein, Allan C. "A Look at Teacher Effectiveness Research." *NASSP Bulletin* 74 (1990): 78–88.

Prawat, Richard S. "From Individual Differences to Learning Communities." *Educational Leadership* 49 (1992): 9–13.

Rosenshine, Barak V. "Explicit Teaching and Teacher Training." *Journal of Teacher Education* 38 (1987): 34–36.

Rosenshine, Barak V., and Carla Meister. "The Use of Scaffolds for Higher-Level Cognitive Strategies." *Educational Leadership* 49 (1992): 26–33.

Rubin, Louis J. *Artistry in Teaching.* New York: Random House, 1985.

Ryans, David G. *Characteristics of Teachers.* Washington, D.C.: America Council on Education, 1960.

Thorndike, Robert L. *Reading Comprehension Education in Fifteen Countries.* New York: Wiley, 1973.

Wise, Arthur, Darling-Hammond, Linda, McLaughlin, Milbrey, and Berstein, Harriet. "Teacher Evaluation: A Study of Effective Practices." *Elementary School Journal* 86 (1985): 61–121.

Wittrock, Merlin C., ed. *Handbook of Research on Teaching,* 3rd ed. New York: Macmillan, 1986.

DISCUSSION QUESTIONS

1. How do presage, context, process, and product variables differ?
2. What are some of the limitations of current teacher effectiveness research?
3. Why should researchers study teacher effectiveness?
4. What is the fallacy associated with attempting to correlate teacher effectiveness behaviors and student achievement?
5. Should graduate students in education be required to demonstrate an understanding of the literature on teacher effectiveness research? Why? Why not?

9

The Art and Craft of Teaching

ELLIOT W. EISNER

FOCUSING QUESTIONS

1. *What are the pros and cons of a science of education and a science of curriculum?*
2. *How has the history of psychology and business influenced teaching and curriculum?*
3. *Why is it important for curriculum workers to be reflective practitioners?*
4. *In what ways is teaching both an art and a science?*
5. *How do the art and craft of teaching differ?*
6. *Why is aesthetics an integral aspect of teaching?*

My aim in this essay is to recover on a theoretical level what I believe practitioners—teachers and school administrators—have never relinquished in the private, quiet moments of their professional lives. I wish to help re-establish, to legitimatize, to publicly acknowledge the art and craft of teaching. To write about the art and craft of teaching in a period in which we are sending a space shuttle through the heavens, when we are able to place man on the moon and, as Frank Buck used to say, "to bring 'em back alive" is seemingly to hearken back to a bygone era. We pride ourselves, and we should, on the achievements of science and the technology science has made possible.

Indeed, to write about the craft of teaching today is likely to evoke images of the elderly working painstakingly on a handcrafted item in a tiny cottage located in a small village sitting next to the delicate but limited glow of a flickering fire. Our images of science and technology are much sleeker, and these images have penetrated contemporary education. In education we talk about diagnosis and prescription, of entry and exit skills, of the use of token economies, and of feedback loops for inputs that fail to meet specifications when they become output. Such talk reminds me of the story of a conversation between the senior officer of a large corporation and a new business school graduate:

> "Sir, I think that by bringing up a small model to simulate aggregate income-expenditure alternatives over various time frames, by integrating those results with appropriate ZBB reviews to assess minimum core expenditure levels, and then by relating to managers in an MBO framework, we can get this administration moving again," said the young colleague with eagerness and authority.
>
> The senior man gazed out the window, pondered the words so redolent with modern techniques, then spoke:
>
> "Shut up," he explained.[1]

Why is it the art and craft of teaching—and of school administration—should seem so quaint? Why is it that the art of teaching should be regarded as a poetic metaphor, but like poetry, more suited to satisfy the soul than to inform the head? Why is it that one so seldom hears of workshops or conferences devoted to the art and craft of teaching? And what would re-emergence of such concepts mean for the improvement of teaching and for educational administrators? To find out we must first look back in time.

When one examines the intellectual history of American education, particularly as it emerged during the 19th century, one finds that a distinctive form of professional preparation developed with the creation of the first state normal school in 1839.[2] By the end of the 1870s, 80 such schools had been established and by 1900 there were over 150.[3] When schools are established for training practitioners, it's nice to have something to teach them. During the same period in Europe and later in America the field of psychology was itself being formalized, and the work of Wilhelm Wundt in Germany, Francis Galton in England, and G. Stanley Hall and William James in the United States provided much of the substance on which to build a profession of education.[4] Hall, the first person to receive a Ph.D. in psychology from Harvard University in 1878,[5] was the father of the child study movement[6] and editor of the influential *Pedagogical Seminary*.[7] James, whose *Talks to Teachers*[8] remains a classic, was himself influenced by Wundt and later was to train the giant of American psychology, the man to whom B. F. Skinner once wrote: "I seem to identify your point of view with the modern psychological view taken as a whole. It has always been obvious that I was merely carrying on your puzzle box experiments...."[9] That man was Edward L. Thorndike.

Thorndike was a great psychologist. He did about everything. He studied children's drawings, he studied handwriting, he studied aptitude and motivation, he wrote yards of books and articles, but what he did most was study learning. It was Thorndike who developed the idea of the S-R bond and who coined the term "Connectionism"[10]: Learning, he argued, was the result of connections in the cortex, connections strengthened by reinforcements provided to responses to particular stimuli. To the extent to which each stimulus was

unique, the responses to be learned were also unique. Rationality was a concept fit for philosophy of mind, but not for a scientific psychology of learning.

As for the transfer of learning, Thorndike believed it was quite limited: One was able to transfer what one had learned only insofar as the elements in one situation were identical with those in the next. It was, as he called it, a theory of identical elements.[11] Memory drums, rat mazes, positive and negative reinforcement, frequency, recency, and intensity were the metaphors with which he worked. Thorndike's task was to develop a science of learning so that brick by brick a science of education could be built. For those seeking a respectable basis for teacher training and school administration, such a view was understandably attractive.

When the first issue of the *Journal of Educational Psychology* was published in 1910, it was Edward L. Thorndike who had the lead article. He wrote:

> A complete science of psychology would tell every fact about everyone's intellect and character and behavior, would tell the cause of every change in human nature, would tell the result which every educational force—every act of every person that changed any other or the agent himself—would have. It would aid us to use human beings for the world's welfare with the same surety of the result that we now have when we use falling bodies or chemical elements. In proportion we get such a science we shall become masters of heat and light. Progress toward such a science is being made.[12]

What we see here is a noble ambition, an expression of faith in the power of scientific inquiry to shape, indeed to determine the future, and thus to enable humankind to create a better, more predictable world. Science is, after all, associated with progress. To have a science of education is to have know-how, to understand not only what works, but why. A scientific technology of teaching would reduce noise in the system, make the system more systematic, more efficient, and hence give taxpayers the products they wanted schools to produce.

Science became the faith: scientific technology, the good works that the faith made possible.

It is hard to underestimate Thorndike's legacy. His ideas, his research, but even more his faith in science, helped set the tone for educational research for the next 70 years. To understand that tone is to understand why it is that the art and craft of teaching were and are regarded as relics having only marginal relevance to the study and practice of education.

But even as influential as Thorndike was, he was not alone in shaping assumptions on which current conceptions of teaching and education rest. During the same period the concept of scientific management, developed by Francis Taylor and applied to the problems of making industrial plants more efficient, also entered the educational scene.[13]

School administrators embraced scientific management as a way to reduce their vulnerability to public criticism and to make schools more efficient. In this approach management of education was hyper-rationalized. Teachers were regarded as workers to be supervised by specialists who made sure that goals were being attained, that teachers were performing as prescribed, and that the public who paid for the schools were getting their money's worth.

The guiding metaphor was industrial and the scope for personal ingenuity on the teacher's part was accordingly diminished.[14] The task was to get teachers to follow the one best method, a method that scientific management of education would prescribe. Thorndike's ideas, working in conceptual tandem with Taylor's, set a tone for American education that is still with us.

There are several characteristics of scientifically oriented ideology in education that deserve more than a casual mention. I say ideology because any perspective one embraces comes replete with values and assumptions about what is valid and trustworthy, what methods are legitimate, what counts as evidence, and hence helps determine the ends that are worth pursuing. If an aim cannot be accommodated within the dominant ideology, it is dropped from view; it is not considered meaningful.[15]

One assumption used in the effort to build a science of educational practice is that education cannot in principle become a discipline in its own right. It is rather "an area of study" and the most promising way to study that area is through the social science disciplines. The ramifications of this view were then and are today substantial. Consider only one—its impact on theory.

Since the concepts and categories that constitute theory in the social sciences were originally designed for noneducationally specific phenomena—rat maze learning, socialization in prisons, churches, and the home, for example—what such categories and theories illuminate is largely what education has in common with other phenomena rather than what is unique or special about schools, classrooms, teaching, or curriculum. The theoretical windows through which we peer circumscribe that portion of the landscape we shall see.

A second widely accepted assumption is that what we can learn through research about learning will be less ambiguous if the units treated are segmented and small. The operating belief is that once these small units are brought under control, variables can be isolated, effective educational treatments identified and then, finally, aggregated in order to build a technology of educational practice. First you learn how to introduce a lesson, then how to pose questions to students, then how to demonstrate a principle, then how to bring a lesson to closure, and when these and several other dozen—dare I say hundreds?—of teaching skills are learned, the ability to teach skillfully will have been achieved.[16]

Because long periods of experimental treatment time tend to lead to confounding—that is, long experimental periods increase the probability that uncontrolled variability will contaminate the treatment making the results difficult to explain—experiments in classrooms tend to be "cleaner" if they are brief.[17] The result is that much educational experimentation takes the form of commando raids designed to get in and out of classrooms in as little time as possible or consists of very short microexperiments that compare the effects of bits and pieces. The modal amount of experimental treatment time in experimental studies reported in the *American Education Research Journal* in 1977–78 was about 45 minutes. Studies are undertaken that are designed to determine if giving an example first and then an explanation, or an explanation first and then an example make any difference. The tacit assumption is that such knowledge, although discrete, is cumulative and independent of context. The variations that are possible in such approaches are, of course, endless. Like tadpoles they come forth filling the pages of learned journals.

Third, because the believability of conclusions can be no greater than the reliability of the instruments used, instruments used to measure classroom practice and student learning need to be very reliable indeed. What this has meant all too often is that what is educationally significant but difficult to measure or observe is replaced with what is insignificant but comparatively easy to measure or observe.

Hence, we have a spate of studies that use the majestic to treat the trivial and others whose results are so qualified in character, for example, "The results hold for classrooms when the children are of low socioeconomic status if grouped homogeneously by reading score and taught by a male teacher who participated in at least five sessions of inservice education," that their practical utility is next to nil.

Fourth, and finally—although this critique could be extended further—is the assumption, and the primary one as far as I am concerned, that (1) a prescriptive educational science will make prediction and control of human behavior possible, and (2) such achievements are educationally desirable: the more prediction and control, the better. Prediction and control are of course virtues in the space program. The last place we want surprises is on the launching pad or on the moon. The best thing that can be said for such operations is that they were uneventful. But are such aspirations quintessential in education? Do we want—even if we could achieve it—to be able to predict and control all or even most of what a student will think, feel, or be? Is E. L. Thorndike's aspiration an appropriate one for education? Is Francis Taylor's model of scientific management what students need today? By this time you might have guessed that I have my doubts.

The critique I have provided concerning the aspiration to develop a science of education and the assumptions and consequences of that approach should not lead you to believe that I see no place for scientific study in education or that I believe that scientific metaphors should be replaced with artistic ones. This is not the case. What I do not believe holds promise in education is a prescriptive view of science. I do not believe that with greater specificity or by reducing the whole to its most essential parts we can produce the kind of prescriptions that have made the space shuttle, radar, or laser beam possible. The aspiration to create a prescriptive science of educational practice is, I believe, hopeless.

What I think scientific inquiry can provide in education are rules of thumb, not rules.[18] Rules of thumb are schematics that make interpretation and judgment more acute. Scientific inquiry can provide frames of reference that can sophisticate our perceptions, not mechanisms that will control the behavior of students, teachers, or administrators. In short, if a distinction can be made between the *prescriptive* and the *interpretive,* between rules and schematics, between algorithms and heuristics, in the human situation I opt for interpretation, schematics, and heuristics, rather than prescriptions, rules, and algorithms.

To assert these views is not to provide for holding them. Let me provide a few. First, those of us who work with human beings work with people who do not, despite Thorndike's view, simply respond to stimuli. Human beings *construe* situations, they make sense of classrooms, they anticipate the world in which they live. What constitutes a stimulus depends not simply on what is injected in the classroom but what students take from it. And what various students take from the classroom, and what they make of what they take, differs. It differs because of their prior experience, their capabilities, their friends, their predispositions, and their relationship with the teacher. Because the perspectives they bring are multiple, no teacher can depend on a script or a prestructured sequence for guarantees about effective teaching. Indeed, the more opportunities a teacher provides to students to idiosyncratically construe and express what they have gotten out of a lesson, the less the teacher controls what they are likely to learn: the students teach each other.

Second, what students learn from educational encounters increases the differences among them.[19] Students with high levels of interest and aptitudes for particular subjects are likely to go further and faster. Their satisfactions are likely to be greater than their opposite. Students who are ingenious arrive at answers that are often unpredictable. Where in all of this is the power of a prescribed method of instruction? Unlike automobiles rolling down an assembly line where an additive model works fairly well (interaction effects are small), the children a classroom teacher deals with are unique configurations that change over time. Unlike electrons or billiard balls, students have ambitions and purposes and refuse to be treated as lumps of clay or sheets of steel passively awaiting the impact of a scientifically based teaching technology that provides little or no scope in its assumptions for what the students make of all of this. Our roles as teachers are closer to those of negotiators than to puppeteers or engineers. And even when we succeed in shaping our students' surfaces, unless we touch their souls we will be locked out of their inner lives. Much of contemporary education in both the public school and the university seldom gets more than skin deep.

Third, the idea that the skills of teaching can be treated as discrete elements and then aggregated to form a whole reflects a fundamental misconception of what it means to be skilled in teaching. What skilled teaching requires is the ability to recognize dynamic patterns, to grasp their meaning, and the ingenuity to invent ways to respond to them. It requires the ability to both lose oneself in the act and at the same time maintain a subsidiary awareness of what one is doing. Simply possessing a set of discrete skills ensures nothing.

The importance of perceiving patterns in motion while at the same time being able to monitor oneself should not come as a surprise to anyone who has reflected on what being in a social situation requires. Humans have a built-in need to seek structures of signification. They find it necessary to make sense of the world. They learn to improvise within a changing field, whether in the classroom, the board room, or the principal's office. The mechanical application of prescribed routines is the surest way I know of to get into trouble.

But what of the art and craft of teaching? Thus far I have discussed our intellectual heritage in education, but have said little that is explicit about the art and craft of teaching. The time has come to address these concepts.

Given what I have already said about the kind of science appropriate for education, it should be clear that the space is very large between the ideas that science can provide and the kinds of decisions and actions a teacher must take. Classrooms and students are particular in character. Theory is general. What the teacher must be able to do is see the connection—if there is one—between the principle and the case. But even where such a connection exists, the fit is never perfect.

An imaginative leap is always required. But if we have no rules to follow, then how shall we take this leap? How shall we decide how to act? How do we fill the space between the theoretical frameworks and scientific findings we get from educational research and the concrete realities that we face on the job?

I suggest that it is in this space—the interstices between framework and action—that the art and craft of teaching are most crucial. We face a class, we raise a question, we get little or no response. Theoretical frameworks and the findings of research studies provide only limited help. What we do is to look for clues. We try to read the muted and enigmatic messages in our students' faces, in their posture, in their comportment. We look for a light at one end of the room and then at the other. Our sensibilities come into play as we try to construe the meaning of the particular situation we face.

And what do we face? Do we call on a particular student to get the ball rolling? Do we recast the question? Do we keep on talking and hope for the best? Our educational imagination begins to operate and we consider options. Theory helps, but as a guide not a prescription. It helps us consider options and once selected, we listen for messages given in the tone and pace of our students' conversations and questions. But even these options are options considered in the preactive, rather than in the interactive, phase of teaching.

Teaching is typically too dynamic for the teacher to stop in order to formulate hypotheses or to run through a series of theories to form a productive eclectic relationship among them as the basis for deciding on a course of action. Students are not inclined to wait—and teachers know this. Teaching action is more immediate than reflective—unless we have a problem that we cannot solve—and even then reflection is likely to occur outside of the class. The teacher reads the qualitative cues of the situation as it unfolds and thinks on her feet, in many cases like a stand-up comedian. Reflection is not absent, theory is not irrelevant, even research conclusions might be considered, but they provide guidance, not direction. They are more in the background than the forefront of the action.

What we do as teachers is to orchestrate the dialogue moving from one side of the room to the other. We need to give the piccolos a chance—indeed to encourage them to sing more confidently—but we also need to provide space for the brass. And as for the violins, they always seem to have a major part to play. How is it going? What does the melody sound like? Is the music full enough? Do we need to stretch the orchestra further? When shall we pause and recapitulate the introductory theme? The clock is reaching ten and we have not yet crescendoed? How can we bring it to closure when we can't predict when a stunning question or an astute observation will bring forth a new melodic line and off we go again? Such are the pleasures and trials of teaching and when it goes well, there is nothing more that we would rather do.

Is such a story apocryphal? Clearly teachers are not orchestra conductors. Yet teachers orchestrate. The analogue rings true. Is artistry involved? Clearly it is. But where does it occur and of what does it consist? Let me suggest that it occurs first of all in those places—and they are legion—in the conduct of teaching when rules fail.

When rules cannot be used to decode meaning and when prescriptions cannot be used to control practice, the teacher must rely on art and craft. To function as an artist or a craftsperson one must be able to read the ineffable yet expressive messages of classroom life. It requires a level of what I have called in previous writings "educational connoisseurship"—the ability to appreciate what one has encountered.[20]

But appreciation, even by an educational connoisseur, is not enough. A teacher—like a school administrator—must act. And it is here that another characteristic of the art and craft of teaching comes into play: The ability to draw on the educational imagination. Like an artist, a teacher must be able to invent moves that will advance the situation from one place in a student's intellectual biography to another. What to do? What kind of question to raise? Do I keep on talking? Do I raise another question? Or do I do something that I never did before? Do I create a new move in another way? Do I let myself fly and thus take the risk of failing? It is here in this pedagogical space that the distinction found in the tide of this essay can be explained—"The Art and Craft of Teaching."

What is it that distinguishes the art of teaching from the craft of teaching? It is precisely the willingness and ability to create new forms of teaching—new teaching moves—moves that were not a part of one's existing repertoire.[21] The craftsperson in the classroom has the repertoire, is skilled in its use, and manages the performance quite well indeed. But the craftsperson creates essentially nothing new as a performer. This person's mark is known by the skill with which he or she uses known routines.

The artist in the classroom invents new ones in the process. Such modes of performance are not plentiful, and they require ingenuity and all of the skill that the person possesses. The artist is rarer than the craftsperson. Is the notion of the artist in the classroom really obsolete?

What can we say thus far about what the art and craft of teaching means? First, it means that we recognize that no science of teaching exists, or can exist, that will be so prescriptive as to make teaching routine. The best we can hope for—and it is substantial—is to have better tools from science with which teachers can use their heads.

Second, because the classroom, when not hog-tied or mechanically regimented, is a dynamic enterprise, teachers must be able to read the dynamic structures of signification that occur in such settings. Such reading requires attention to pattern and expressive nuance created by the students and the teacher's own activities.

Third, appreciation is not enough. The teacher must be able to call on or invent a set of moves that create an educationally productive tempo within a class. When we say of some lesson, "It went flat," we mean it both visually and aurally: It had no life, it didn't take hold. What is needed is either, or both, a better reading of the class by the teacher or a more imaginative set of teaching acts.

Fourth, it means that we acknowledge that artistry in teaching represents the apotheosis of educational performance and rather than try to diminish or replace it with rule-governed prescriptions, we ought to offer it a seat of honor. Artistry in teaching is always likely to be rare but it is even rarer when one works in an educational climate that is so concerned about academic achievement that it often stifles intellectual risk-taking on the part of both students and teachers.

This leads me to the final points I wish to address in my examination of the art and craft of teaching. One of those points deals with what it is that we have come to expect from art and craft: the provision of a very special kind of experience we sometimes call aesthetic. Just what does the aesthetic have to do with teaching and education? What is its import? Is it the frosting that makes the cake palatable or is it the marrow of education?

By art in education I am not talking about the visual arts, or music, or dance, but rather about the fact that activities motivated by the aesthetic satisfactions they provide—those that are intrinsic— are among the few that have any durability.[22] Extrinsic rewards for teachers are always likely to be small compared to those secured by people working in other fields. Despite longer vacation periods and sabbaticals, professional opportunities and satisfactions for teachers are limited largely to the lives they lead in their classrooms. Few people regard teachers as receiving handsome salaries—and

they are right. The perks related to sabbaticals and vacation periods are distant and short-lived.

When one finds in schools a climate that makes it possible to take pride in one's craft, when one has the permission to pursue what one's educational imagination adumbrates, when one receives from students the kind of glow that says you have touched my life, satisfactions flow that exceed whatever it is that sabbaticals and vacations can provide. The aesthetic in teaching is the experience secured from being able to put your own signature on your own work—to look at it and say it was good. It comes from the contagion of excited students discovering the power of a new idea, the satisfaction of a new skill, or the dilemma of an intellectual paradox that once discovered creates. It means being swept up in the task of making something beautiful—and teachers do make their own spaces and places. They provide, perhaps more than they realize, much of the score their students will experience.

Such moments of aesthetic experience will not of course be constant. We could not, I am convinced, endure it if they were. Only a few scattered throughout the week are enough to keep us going. But without them teaching will be draining rather than nourishing and the likelihood of keeping in teaching those who need and value intellectual stimulation and challenge is very small. The aesthetic moments of teaching are among the deepest and most gratifying aspects of educational life.

But such moments in teaching are not the children of mechanical routine, the offspring of prescriptive rules for teaching, the progeny of rigid lesson plans that stifle spontaneity and discourage exploring the adventitious. Formalized method, bureaucratized procedures, and pressure to get students to perform at any price are their eviscerating conditions. Teachers need the psychological space and the permission to maintain a sense of excitement and discovery for themselves as teachers so that such excitement can be shared with their students.

Does the unabashedly romantic image of teaching I have portrayed have any implications for what we ought to be doing in the schools or is it simply an unrealistic conception of what it means to teach? A conception that will be amply corrected by a Betty Crocker view of teaching or by a teacher-proof curriculum?

I believe the image of the teacher as craftsperson and artist is an ideal toward which we should strive. I believe that our intellectual roots have mistakenly regarded such images as suspect. I believe that many of the solutions being proposed to cure what people believe to be educational ills, solutions such as minimum competency testing, state mandated evaluation procedures, and other legislative panaceas, to be fundamentally misguided. They were born of suspicion and tend to motivate by the stick. Human growth and development, whether for teachers or for students, need richer soil in which to flourish. How might such conditions be provided and what might they be? First teachers need to be de-isolated in schools. Hardly anyone knows how or even what their colleagues are doing.

What is the logic in assuming that teachers can be trained once and for all in preservice university programs and then assigned to classrooms for the bulk of their careers with nothing more than brief excursions for inservice education that are usually provided by university professors who themselves have not taught in an elementary or secondary school classroom for a decade or two? The school needs to become a professional community with space enough for teachers to grow as professionals. They have much to offer each other, but these contributions are not easily made when teachers are isolated.

It is well past the time that schools create the organizational structure in which teachers and administrators can reflect on their activities as a regular part of their jobs, not simply within the scope of an inservice education program. Staff development needs to be a continuing part of what it means to be a teacher. The overstaffing of one teacher for every ten would be a step in the right direction. Joint planning could help contribute to it. And a school community that would not judge the quality of its educational program by SAT scores or enrollment in AP courses would also help. Is our educational imagination so impoverished that the only thing we can think of doing for the most able col-

lege-bound students is to give them what they will get in college a semester or two later?

We also need administrators who are at least as interested in teaching and curriculum as in organizational maintenance and public relations. We need principals who think of themselves *both* as teachers of teachers and as their teachers' staff. We need school superintendents who can help close the breach between administration and faculty and who remember from whence they came. But how can a principal be an instructional leader when he believes that he knows little about teaching or curriculum?

While it's true that legal mandates, problems between teachers and administrators, increasingly vocal community concern with the quality of schooling need attention and appropriate professional skills, it is the instructional program and the skill with which it is mediated for which all of the former issues are to be instrumental. Without attention to the instructional program and to the quality of teaching provided, successful arbitration and positive relationships with the community will amount to little from an educational point of view.

At a time when programs in educational administration are focusing on "policy studies" and the "politics of education," it would be ironic if administrators learned how to survive but forgot what survival was for. Our beneficiaries are the students—and without teachers skilled in the craft of teaching, and a curriculum worth teaching, schooling is likely to be educationally vapid.

We need, too, an attitude in schools that expects that experimentation in educational practices is a normal part of doing educational business. Where are the equivalents of Varian's, Xerox's, and IBM's think tanks in our schools? Where are our educational studios? Must we always be in a responsive posture or can we too dream dreams and pursue them?

CONCLUSION

I said at the beginning of this essay that I was intent on re-establishing the legitimacy of the art and craft of teaching. The image I portrayed at the outset was that of a single individual working painstakingly on something about which he or she cared a great deal. Craftspersons and artists tend to care a great deal about what they do, they get a great deal of satisfaction from the journey as well as from the destination, they take pride in their work, and they are among the first to appreciate quality. Is such an image really inappropriate today? I hope not. I hope such an image always has a place in our schools. And somehow, just somehow, I think that in the private, quiet moments of our professional lives, we do too.

ENDNOTES

1. I am indebted to Ray Bachetti for this tale. Its source is a case study paper that he wrote for Education 279X, Managing in Higher Education, School of Education, Stanford University.

2. Elwood P. Cubberley, *Public Education in the United States* (Boston: Houghton Mifflin Company, 1934), p. 380.

3. Ibid., p. 384.

4. Lawrence Cremin, *The Transformation of the School* (New York: Alfred Knopf, 1961).

5. Ibid., p. 101

6. Ibid., pp. 100–103.

7. Hall was not only the first editor of *Pedagogical Seminary,* he was its founder. He served as editor from its inception in 1881 to 1924.

8. William James, *Talks to Teachers on Psychology* (New York: H. Holt & Co., 1901).

9. Geraldine Joncich, *The Sane Positivist: The Biography of Edward L. Thorndike* (Middletown, Conn.: Wesleyan University Press, 1968).

10. Ibid., p. 336.

11. Edward L. Thorndike and Robert S. Woodworth, "The Influences of Special Training on General Ability," *Psychological Abstracts* 7 (March 1900).

12. Edward L. Thorndike, "The Contribution of Psychology to Education," *Journal of Educational Psychology* 1 (1910): 618.

13. For a brilliant discussion of this period, see Raymond Callahan, *Education and the Cult of Efficiency* (Chicago: The University of Chicago Press, 1962).

14. Ibid.

15. Alfred Jules Ayer, *Language, Truth and Logic* (New York: Dover, no date).

16. The concept of micro-teaching as the practice of discrete teaching skills is related to this view of the skills of teaching.

17. The average amount of experimental treatment time for experimental studies reported in the *American Educational Research Journal* in 1977–78 is approximately 45 minutes per subject.

18. The distinction I wish to underscore is between sciences like anthropology, archeology, and psychoanalysis that aim at explication and those like physics that not only explain but lead to prediction and control.

19. Because aptitudes for learning different skills and concepts differ among human beings, the effective school will tend to increase individual differences among students rather than diminish them.

20. Elliot W. Eisner, *The Educational Imagination: On the Design and Evaluation of School Programs* (New York: The Macmillan Company, 1979).

21. This view of art is based on the work of R. G. Collingwood. See his *Principles of Art* (New York: Oxford University Press, 1958).

22. Mark Lepper, ed., *The Hidden Cost of Reward* (Hillsdale, N.J.: Erlbaum Associates, 1978).

DISCUSSION QUESTIONS

1. What curricular changes will be needed to encourage teachers to function as craft persons and artists?

2. How can preservice university training programs help shape the development of artist-teachers?

3. How might the organizational structure of a school be altered to help teachers pursue continuing professional development?

4. What role should principals and superintendents assume in developing artist-teachers?

5. What does the metaphor of teacher as orchestra conductor suggest about teaching?

10

Narrative Research: Understanding Teaching and Teacher Thinking[1]

LINDA S. BEHAR-HORENSTEIN

FOCUSING QUESTIONS

1. *What are the benefits of narrative research?*
2. *What is narrative research?*
3. *What are the limitations associated with doing narrative research?*
4. *In what ways might interpretations resulting from narrative research be methodologically flawed?*
5. *Does narrative research yield information that is useful for the practitioner? Why? Why not?*
6. *What are some of the epistemological issues that narrative researchers and empiricists must resolve?*
7. *In what ways might methodological approaches from other fields be instructive to educators conducting research on teacher thinking?*

The use of narrative inquiry as an educational research method for analyzing teaching and teacher thinking has generated controversy and excitement among educators. Advocates of narrative inquiry believe that story research offers rich descriptions of the experiences that teachers live in context-specific situations. Such descriptions are thought to play a powerful meditational role for teachers who engage in active reflection. These descriptions have been credited with guiding practice through the illumination of tacit wisdom and assisting teachers in the generation of practice-based theory. Narrative researchers proclaim that story represents an enormous database from which to develop new understandings about the relationships among phenomena in educational contexts. However, empiricists have raised several questions about the authenticity and veracity of storytelling research.

They also question the validity of this approach. Essentially, empiricists are asking what can be learned from one teacher's contextually embedded story. These concerns beg the question of whether the research community will ultimately sanctify storytelling work as a viable methodological approach. Debates between narrative and empirical researchers have reached new levels of argumentation, while educators continue to ponder the question of which research paradigm is the best approach for analyzing teachers' behavior.

This chapter examines the legitimacy of narrative as a research tool. A framework for this discussion is provided by the (1) definitions and conceptions of narrative–story inquiry, (2) conceptual and theoretical framework that supports narrative research, (3) advantages, criticisms, and limitations of story, and (4) epistemological issues that influence the interpretation and conceptualization of story research. The chapter concludes with the presentation of a conceptual framework designed to move us beyond philosophical musings about the viability of story research as methodological approach and offer story a vital role in research initiatives about teachers.

CONCEPTIONS OF STORY–NARRATIVE FORMS OF INQUIRY

Characteristically, story is a narrative with very specific syntactical shape (Scholes, 1981, 1982) and subject matter that allows for or encourages the projection of human values on this material. Story places an emphasis on the connections between what humans think, know, and do, as well as on the reciprocal relationships between the way that human thinking shapes behavior and knowing shapes thinking. As an entity with its own parameters (beginning, middle, and end), story has a dynamic that is created and interpreted through the lived experiences of a person or a participant observer who offers a vicarious interpretation of an individual's personal story. A synthesis of the lived experiences results in a narration that occurs through a process of active construction and reconstruction. Temporality and causality are involved in this reconstruction process. These factors, related to the time, place, specific situation, and cultural context, provide a framework for interpreting the events and outcomes within a story.

Many similarities may be found between story and musical compositions. When comparing story and musical works, it becomes evident that the structure of a story parallels that of a musical exposition. Consider the elements embedded in a composer's production. Musical works have an introduction, development, recapitulation, variation on a theme, or denouement. As the theme is developed, the listener may become acutely engaged in attending to the melody (perceived as the thematic content) or may focus on the harmony, dynamics, tonality, metric movement, intervalic patterns, or tempo.

Comparable to the ways in which an individual processes hearing or reading a story, the listener constructs his or her own personal experience and meaning while listening. There is no assurance that the listener's experience is synonymous with that of the composer's intentions. The representation of the listener's experience is contextualized and embedded in his or her previous experiences, tacit knowledge, and connectedness to the exposition. The components that help listeners to construct meaning when they hear a musical composition can also be found in narrative research methods. Narrative researchers employ codes and conventions to construct stories, relay their interpretations (as exemplified by melody, dynamics, or harmony), convey the sequence of incidents (demonstrated by meter, intervalic patterns, or tempo), and describe a synthesis of events that occurs by way of a story (also illustrated by development, recapitulation, variation on a theme, or denouement). By its very nature, a story involves an agent who acts to achieve goals that can be interpreted in understandable ways. Story establishes the "ordinary" and the demonstration of the truth as it is experienced.

Story or narrative inquiry belongs to the classroom ecology paradigm that includes sociolinguistic meditational research on teaching, as well as qualitative, interpretive, and psychoanalytic forms of inquiry (Martin & Sugarman, 1993). Story–narrative inquiry is an ethnographic form of qualitative research that involves telling or recounting. The use of narrative forms of inquiry has been exemplified in a variety of research studies by Clandinin and Connelly's (1988) and Connelly & Clandinin's (1990, 1988, 1986) microanalyses of teacher–student classroom interactions within specific curriculum areas, documentations of teachers' reflections (Cochran-Smith & Lytle, 1993, 1990; Elbaz, 1991; Kagan, 1988; Leinhardt, 1990; Schon 1987; Shulman, 1987; and Yinger, 1987), and microanalyses of social and community factors that influence schooling, teaching, and learning (Peshkin, 1978).

Story research emphasizes learning how to teach and is often used as a way to demonstrate teachers' ways of knowing. The use of narrative inquiry is grounded in the belief that teachers' thought processes, not solely their behavior, are essential to the knowledge base on research on teacher thinking. To appreciate the value of story research, it is important to bear in mind that the knowledge that results from narratives is qualitatively different from formal theoretical knowledge. Formal theoretical knowledge represents the synthesis of interactions taking place within a particular context and the classroom situations in which knowledge is transformed into action. In contrast, story knowledge attempts to relate predefined observables to a theoretical context. In story, the teacher is the unit of analysis.

By highlighting the teacher, credence is given to an assumption that teachers bring a specialized set of social relationships and experiences to the classroom. These particular social relationships and experiences are considered to be important components in the development of knowledge. Although the practical knowledge that coalesces as practitioners interact in the classroom results in knowledge in action, this quality of knowledge is integrally interwoven with the teachers' level of expertise. One must exercise caution when interpreting the meaning of practical knowledge. The validity of classroom experience may be misleading since teachers are generally very isolated while experiencing and perceiving events. The perceptions that teachers form may be limited by the depth and breadth of their own experience or bias. Furthermore, variability among individuals underscores the difficulty in codifying teachers' analyses. In contrast, others have argued that the interaction of classroom experience and active reflection acts as a powerful instructor that facilitates teachers' development of beliefs and perceptions of themselves as learners and helps them to acquire practical knowledge (Connelly & Clandinin, 1986). Narrative research acknowledges the importance of the teacher's role by underscoring the value of teacher autonomy and reflection.

The overall purpose of story research is to fill a gap in the knowledge base of teaching by crafting a mode for teacher voice and providing a means to understand the interpretive frames that teachers use to improve their classroom practices (Cochran-Smith & Lytle, 1990). Narratives emphasize teachers' own interpretations of context-specific classrooms by elucidating the context in which decisions are made. Narrative research provides an avenue to bring about a conscious awareness of teachers' professional reasoning. The common thread in narrative studies is the overarching emphasis on the validity of teachers' judgments drawn from their own experiences.

Sparks-Langer and Bernstein-Colton (1991) claim that several benefits are derived from research that utilizes teacher narrative. First, by creating a detailed description of a teacher's everyday life, these studies are believed to heighten an awareness regarding what motivates teacher action. Second, teacher narratives provide material for instructional case study. Third, as teachers engage in self-reflection, narratives can encourage the development of their insight. Sparks-Langer and Bernstein-Colton (1991) contend that narrative research represents a bridge to a new way of thinking about teacher thinking. In contradistinction, it is thought that many contemporary researchers who are philosophically opposed to the use of empirical forms of methodological inquiry have chosen to project the sociolinguistic techniques (literary analysis and psychoanalysis) of the humanities onto the context of educational research.

Meaning that evolves from using the narrative inquiry paradigm emerges from the use of interpretive and analytical frameworks. Narrative inquiry attempts to explicate an understanding of the events in the specific educational contexts under investigation by generating rich and thick descriptions without reliance on causal, associative data treatments and analyses. One of the fundamental assumptions underlying the application of narrative methodology lies in the belief that the interaction of teachers' personal biographies with particular situations helps them to understand their use and application of practical knowledge. Narrative inquiry also seeks to explicate teachers' ways and origins of knowing by analyzing their reflective thought processes and related behaviors.

Few would disagree that other environmental factors, such as the contextual, organizational, or bureaucratic structures indigenous to specific school environments, also influence teachers' thinking, behaviors, and reflection in action. However, it is somewhat remarkable that little attention has been given to understanding the ways in which these environmental structures actually influence teachers' behavior or mediate their display of practical knowledge. Generally, it is understood that individual responses can perhaps be predicted in laboratory settings or role-play situations. Although in real-world or actual contexts, planned responses may be sacrificed for behaviors that are perceived as normative within the context of the culture in which they are expressed. Teachers may experience pressure to conform to the contextual influences of the power structures within which they have to coexist. Having provided a framework for what constitutes story and narrative forms of research, we now turn our attention to the conceptual frameworks that amplify the utility of story in context-specific situations.

CONCEPTUAL FRAMEWORKS

Advantages of Story

Advocates for story as a form of inquiry assert that it has unique benefits. They claim that these benefits cannot be realized solely by the use of empirical methodologies. Proponents for story research claim the following:

1. Stories give meaning and convey a sense of experience.
2. Stories act as a frame to counter the technical–empirical modes of inquiry that have dominated research on teacher thinking.
3. Stories portray women's specialized way of knowing (Belensky, Clinchy, Goldberger, & Tarule, 1986; Helle, 1991) and provide them with a representative voice in the research literature.
4. Storied knowledge can be organized into explanatory frameworks in which the cultural and contextual variables that serve as interpre-

tive lenses for comprehending one's experiences can be analyzed.

Advocates for storytelling research also suggest that experienced teachers use narrative structures (story) as a framework for organizing, interpreting, and integrating their use and application of curriculum knowledge (Gudmundsdottir, 1991). Moreover, since teaching is experienced as a complexity of social events that is driven (in part) by knowledge derived from teachers' stories, it is believed that the knowledge thus derived results in the acquisition of event-structured knowledge (Carter, 1993; Carter & Doyle, 1987; Carter & Gonzalez, 1990) that promotes expertise in teaching.

Criticisms of Story

Critics of story claim that storytelling suffers from an absence of an "authenticity judge" (Kleine and Greene, 1993) and an inability to "distinguish a scholarly interpretation of a classroom event from that of a delirious observer" (Salomon, 1991, p. 10). Some researchers suggest that the use of story research results from a researcher's inability to utilize experimental design methods and statistical techniques for data analysis. Essentially, story is portrayed as an indefensible form of inquiry and a victim of the fluidity that characterizes the context in which data are collected. Even Connelly and Clandinin (1990), who rely heavily on narrative inquiry in their own research, seem to suggest that perhaps narrative inquiry provides a research agenda that gives "curriculum professors something to do" (Schwab, 1983). Others have criticized story for placing extreme emphasis on teachers' personal meaning and exaggerating the significance of the writer. Such an unbalanced presentation tends to confer unwarranted authenticity on teacher experience and rewards narcissism. Basic problems of knowledge claims associated with elevating teachers' stories to a "privileged status" have yet to be systematically addressed.

In an overall sense, storytelling is a variation on reflection. Reflection may be an experience in which individuals analyze, question, or privately reevaluate their behavior and perceptions. While engaged in reflection, individuals may consider or incorporate the wisdom and perceptions of others. While reflection is essential to the processes involved in analysis, clearly this technique is not emergent; reflection has been around for more than 50 years. Reflection seems to be a quality of good practitioners who are generally thought to be intuitive individuals. As such, some researchers assert that the use of the term reflection is equivalent to faddism.

Limitations of Story–Narrative

Several limitations regarding the disadvantages of story have been cited:

1. The relationship between story and reality as defined by the experiences of an outside observer does not necessarily portray a one-to-one correspondence.
2. Selecting a story for teaching purposes conveys a particular conception of teaching to students. Since these descriptions are open to multiple meanings, the complexities portrayed sometimes lead to confusion in teaching. The possibilities for different interpretations are also a function of the perspectives and experiences that students engaged in the study of story bring to the task.
3. Story does not represent a consensually agreed on and/or scholarly curriculum. Therefore, the use of story as curriculum for training teachers raises questions regarding what knowledge is worth most. One must wonder, if told stories solely represent those of the dominant culture, how does this curriculum promote pedagogical practice for people of color, women, underrepresented populations, and/or the underprivileged classes? How do the contextualized ethnography research findings embedded in case studies help us to better understand what teachers should consider doing in classrooms?
4. The interpretations that emerge from narrative inquiry are not open to verification since they emanate from beliefs that are the collaborative construction of the teacher (interviewee) and/or researcher (interviewer).
5. The generalizability and utility of interpretations are also open to argumentation. Interpretations of narratives are influenced by belief systems that are a product of one's own cultural framework. Are neutrality or unbiased perceptions possible? Can we claim that the evidence derived from interpretations truly corresponds to an objective reality or renders any universally valid principles or laws (Greene, 1994)?
6. Paradigmatic assumptions about the value of various research methodologies also play a role in interpretations that emerge from narrative research. Story has been criticized for amplifying moralistic, narcissistic, and omnipotent representations. Calling our attention to these concerns, Hargreaves (1994) suggests that the voice given to teachers through narrative research has come to represent teachers as an entity. He claims that this notion is a highly morally laden and prescriptive voice, not an empirical or actual representation of all teachers. Hargreaves points out that later-career teachers do not necessarily exemplify "care" for their students. Research on teachers' thought and voice is replete with teachers who are humanistic and caring, but not those who are cynical, lack knowledge or pedagogy. Although the research literature amplifies the positive, moral characteristics of teachers, these qualities are not grounded in representation of all teachers.

According to Hargreaves (1994), this moral singularity of teachers' voice needs to be deconstructed. Research on teaching shows that teachers' didactic moralistic instruction seems to dominate classrooms even today. Many teachers tend to see classrooms from the position of power, authority, privileged status, and role, instead of from the viewpoint of their students. One can build a strong case for the notion that understanding teachers' voice should be a priority, but we must be careful not to romanticize these "voices" or accord them unwarranted authenticity. One of the most poignant criticisms leveled against stories is that they amplify a sense of narcissism by exemplifying delusions of omnipotence and highlighting the sense of a boundless self (Hargreaves, 1994). If narrative inquiry is likely to be accepted by the research community at large, these concerns obligate disputation or serious consideration about whether to modify the techniques involved in the process of gathering and analyzing storytelling data.

EPISTEMOLOGICAL ISSUES

Assumptions Underlying Interpretation

Connelly and Clandinin (1990) claim that the primary value of narrative inquiry resides in its quality as subject matter and its capacity to render life experiences. However, certain difficulties exist, since falsehood may be substituted for meaning and narrative truth by using criteria that give rise to significance, value, and intention. Meanings told do not necessarily represent the interpretation of teacher (interviewee). Furthermore, secondary or tertiary levels or interpretations may be falsely created. Methodological errors in interpretation of narrative can occur from attempts to generalize the events of story. One may misrepresent the truth and alter actualities by fabricating a recounting of the events. Narrative smoothing (Spence, 1986) may result from an obscurity of facts, leaving open questions of what is not being told. Gadamer (1960) concurs and reminds us that "The interpreter experiences two claims: one from the object of the interpretation…and one from the interpreters' own lived circumstances" (pp. 124–125). "Prejudgments and prejudices cannot be set aside, since they have so much to do with shaping those *interpretations*" (italics added) (Greene, 1994, p. 438).

Sanctifying and formulating an epistemology to support storytelling work is insufficient for creating a new paradigm for research on teacher thinking without addressing the assumptions that underlie this method or without considering those posited by empirical researchers. Researchers are still grappling with the issue that story has been criticized on epistemological grounds because the criteria of acceptance are rooted in contextualism. Moreover, the interpretations gathered from story data do not necessarily yield practical information because the meanings embedded in story are not always accessible to the reader. Nespor and Barlyske (1991) contend that, when researchers use narratives as a tool for constructing knowledge, they are describing, discovering, or identifying objects that really exist. However, they use teachers' constructions of the object that has been fashioned according to the needs of the researcher. In this sense, narratives are used to express relations of power and political agendas of researchers, not as a tool to discover truth and expand the pluralistic knowledge base of research on teacher thinking.

Nespor and Barlyske (1991) point out the fallacy associated with the premise that narratives index fundamental structures of thought or experience, as Bruner (1986), Connelly & Clandinin (1990), Gergen & Gergen (1986), Polkinghorne (1988), and others suggest. The representational fallacy is that entities that emerge within story actually preexist and contribute to the creation of that discourse. Researchers reify narrative discourse, make inferences from nonobservable mental processes, and then use discourse as evidence for the existence of the inferred processes. Thus sophisticated and esoteric but circular and indefensible systems of reasoning have been created to forge the acceptance of a nontraditional method of research. In spite of these epistemological issues, the number of publications and presentations grounded in narrative research has recently burgeoned. One must also ask if narrative research is actually more prevalent than the empirical–technical (traditional) forms of inquiry than previously acknowledged. How much of our current research, case studies, and the like, are grounded in empirical interpretations that represent forms of story?

Connelly and Clandinin (1990, pp. 7–9) have defined criteria for narrative as grounded in white, educated, and Anglo-American society. This perspective contradicts their assumption that narrative reflects basic human cognitive structures that mirror normative methodological inquiry. The historical specificity that defines criteria for narrative is class biased, gender biased, and culturally biased if the criteria of acceptance are based solely on the value system of the dominant culture and middle-class standards. Using these criteria as the standard ignores the diversity, richness, and thickness of experience, which narrative portends to exemplify.

Narrative is a culturally specific communication that imposes certain societal structural characteristics. For example, there may be difficulty in determining whose narrative is being told, that of the teacher (interviewee) or the researcher (interviewer). According to Willinsky (1989), representation is always a matter of power that should be treated with skepticism. Recounting one's history and related social events does not always portray the lived experience of the teacher's discourse. An account may be told through the lived experiences or interpretation of the researcher; however, the latter may reflect the researcher's desire for recognition (Crapanzano, 1980, pp. 9–10).

Conceptual Roots of Story

On an epistemological level, story is conceptually rooted in mentalistic psychology as opposed to behavioral psychology. Kendler (1993) stated that the differences between the two are methodological, not theoretical. He asserted that selecting behavior as the dependent variable does not negate the use of hypotheses about mentalistic processes as long as theoretical mentalistic assumptions have testable behavioral implications. In contrast, the behaviorists argue that by promoting techniques of self-observation "the unbiased scrutiny of experience" (MacLeod, 1968) is unachievable, because conscious experience is private and only available to the self-observer, although most people are incapable of self-awareness. Behaviorists also claim that it is only when an event can be observed by more than one person that socially agreed on criteria can be adopted that might lead to observational agreement.

The overarching dilemma is that researchers engaged in narrative inquiry cannot provide veracity or socially agreed on criteria by which to judge the content and/or value of story. Pondering the notion of either–or perspectives, Keller (1985) contends that this dichotomy is akin to the male–female opposition. She links the abstract and objectivist to masculine modes of thinking and self-interpretation, but challenges male claims to universalism and neutrality. Greene (1994) concurs with Keller (1985) and states that "For mainstream and technical thinkers (often including some of the doctrinal Marxists), so-called *subjective* views are suspect in part because they are associated with embeddedness or situatedness and, by extension, with the female" (p. 433).

Psychology cannot resolve the conflict that ensues during a debate related to which is better, qualitative or quantitative methodology. However, psychology can shed light on the consequences of adopting competing principles. The dilemma facing the empiricists is that they cannot provide value-free information devoid of expressions that reveal the researcher's political or value commitments. Some will insist that behavioral methodology seeks to attain political power control, not truth (explanation). On the other hand, the subjective conceptions associated with qualitative research can be criticized for failure to distinguish between those value judgments (emphasis on controlled observations, use of comparisons groups, statistical significance) intrinsically associated with empiricism and those that can be detached from empirical evidence.

One major issue that empiricists have yet to grapple with lies in the limitations associated with the knowledge claims that empirical researchers offer. Greene (1994) asserts the following:

> Too many researchers still find it difficult to confront the effects of technicism on their thinking or to face the problem of objectivity. The desire for precision and disinterestedness continues on, sometimes as a corrective against what is viewed as uncontained relativism and reliance on mere *opinion* (p. 432).

Another limitation associated with empiricism lies in its inability to discern if the quality of research illuminates the social consequences associated with competing methodologies. Technocratic research varies in its ability to empirically predict consequences associated with assumptions underlying qualitative and quantitative methods of research. Second, knowledge claims that emanate from the notional quality of behavioral concepts may or may not be socially defensible.

The difficulty associated with narrative inquiry as a phenomenological and mentalistic conception of psychology resides in the observation that it suffers from an inability to offer persuasive knowledge claims that society can trust. Kendler's (1993) claim that empirical researchers need to abandon their assumptions that quantifiable research can identify definitive principles that describe predictable human behavior should be instructive to those who believe that a strict use of empirical methodology can guide teaching and teacher education programs. Kendler (1993) also suggests that empiricists must give up the notion that a gap between what is and what ought to be can be bridged only by empirical evidence.

Kendler (1993) receives support from Martin and Sugarman (1993), who contend that research on teaching that relies primarily on an empirical enterprise is ill-fated because of an overemphasis on methodology. Furthermore, they assert that empirical researchers have failed to adequately address the epistemological problems that confront assumptions underlying their work. Much of the empirical research on teaching (1) lacks an underlying theory that identifies specific variables, (2) provides an insufficient description of the characteristics of focal variables that are particularly worthy of empirical scrutiny, or (3) fails to explain why empirically based evidence is pragmatically unmanageable (Martin & Sugarman, 1993). One might ask how research based on narrative inquiry can be advocated when it seems to be based purely on rationally biased assumptions.

Current debates about research on teachers have focused primarily on methodological and epistemological paradigms instead of providing a theoretically defensible argument for the empirical preoccupation. However, as Martin and Sugarman (1993) have pointed out, during the proliferation of empirical studies, no new scientific understandings or heuristics have been made available for practitioners.

FUTURE DIRECTIONS

Although the use of story has become an emergent power in educational research, teachers' stories do not provide us with a political or paradigmatic base from which to create new understandings. Contextual parameters need to be established in order to illuminate the potential contributions of research that relies on story (Goodson, personal communication, April 8, 1994). One avenue to capitalize on the unrealized benefits of story research may involve *macrolizing* the location of story. *Macrolizing* refers to the process of creating a quantifiable database and analyzing all the stories that emerge in a particular location by assessing common themes, patterns, or traits that emerge across locations. Macrolizing means to take a macro or global perspective and move beyond the analysis of individual stories as they exist in micro or singular educational contexts. Since the ultimate aim of story–narrative research is to mediate pedagogically, politically, and educationally what we want to share, the categorization and organization of information gleaned from story research seem to be a logical progression from accumulating individual stories.

A review of the research literature on narrative inquiry reveals that the predominant purpose of story resides in its ongoing efforts to create an awareness about what teachers do and how they teach. Each teacher's story seeks to impart something of a practical nature regarding how that particular teacher copes with instructional and curricular matters in the context of his or her environment. However, the emergent insights derived from one's own story or a study of stories have implications only in the context in which the story was located. What does continued research on classroom ecology using narrative as the methodological vehicle portend for training teachers? Perhaps the time is ripe to create teacher education programs that use individualistic, sociolinguistic, and psychoanalytically anchored approaches to teacher preparation (Combs, 1965). Perhaps storytelling research offers unrealized instructional potential to teacher educators.

Clearly, we need to reassess the potential utility of story and bring narrative methodology to a more sophisticated level of productiveness. Suppose, for example, that we obtained narratives from teachers in several schools and created a database of multiple stories. With a large database, researchers would be able to organize the descriptive findings emergent in narrative studies and compile analytical or classificatory systems that might be used in understanding relationships among variables. During the process of data analysis, patterns or classificatory systems of action that reveal how teachers use story or how professional reasoning guides their practice might become apparent. An analysis of these classificatory systems of action might also highlight the reciprocal relationships between teachers' thinking process and behaviors. Subsequently, tangible connections between practice and theory might be synthesized. By organizing the data into logical categories and quantifying multiple stories, as well as the contextual and demographic variables related to the occurrences of and characterizations of self-awareness, the applicability of story research might be substantiated.

Methodological approaches in other fields might be instructive to educators conducting research on teachers. Consider the potential utility of methods used in health care. Within medicine, particularly psychiatry, patients' case histories have been documented and chronicled. They became codified sources for illustrating classificatory systems of mental disorders. Subsequently, this information became a database for the diagnostic statistical manuals in which characterizations of symptomatology have been organized. Volumes of case studies have been written into books to guide the effective treatment of patients.

These textbooks continue to be used as primary sources for training psychiatrists, psychoanalysts, and psychologists. Using the sociolinguistic approaches employed by narrative inquiry, the findings from story research might serve to highlight effective teaching practices for students in "characteristic" or "chronicled" situations or within context-specific environments.

CONCLUSION

Stories are important because they constitute a legitimate arena of formal knowledge about teaching. Storied research makes knowledge about teachers' expertise accessible and provides perspectives on teaching and learning that cannot be known by other forms of inquiry. However, while all forms of research rely on assumptions, it is crucial to question assumptions that underlie different conceptions of research inquiry. Most of us would probably support the notion that absolute truths will never be known about the truths of assumptions.

Concerns about the limitations of narrative research techniques have focused on the descriptive nature of narrative and have highlighted the lack of objective standards to guide improvement or gauge effectiveness. To be truly effective, narrative research should be evaluated in consideration of standards that would be used to ensure appropriate classroom practice. Changes in teacher practice will also be necessary. Teachers will need to progress beyond the development of their own idiosyncratic theory and/or practice to use these standards in classroom practice (Buchmann, 1986). Furthermore, incomplete considerations about story should involve examining the possibilities for the use of story that have not been suggested previously. Using narrative as the sole form of methodological inquiry will require agreed on and rigorous methodological procedures, clear conceptualizations, the formulation of key assumptions, and common referents that have precise meanings and consistent usage.

Given the importance of stories, the next step should focus on rendering story knowledge accessible. Looking at recurring patterns across different contexts and variables will be essential. To aid in this process, a conceptual framework consisting of four process-oriented principles is offered: (1) situating teachers' stories in relationship to other stories, (2) contextualizing stories in relationship to other considerations, (3) raising questions about story in relationship to social and political considerations, and (4) regrounding stories (Hargreaves, 1994).

The implementation of the first principle is predicated on increasing the use of story and building large databases of multiple stories. For example, suppose that teachers' stories were compiled for all teachers within several public and private (elementary, middle, junior high, special education, and secondary) schools. Teachers would maintain daily journals. Using content analysis procedures, the entries in each journal would be examined. As a result, recurrent themes could be identified, categorized, and quantified within and across all journals.

Related to the second principle, themes would be categorized in relationship to demographic teacher variables (gender, age, level of education, area of subject matter expertise, socioeconomic status, race and ethnic orientation) and school variables (the geographical location and type of school). If similarities across variables and contexts within thematic categories became apparent, techniques might be employed to test for significance. Correlation techniques might be used to test for significant relationships among various subgroups and across variables and themes. Path analysis, a technique that permits testing the validity of causal inferences for pairs of variables while controlling for the effects of others, might also be used.

Path models can be specified using sophisticated statistical programs. Using the framework of the model, the influence of exogenous variables (which correspond to independent constructs) on endogenous variables (which correspond to dependent variables) as influenced by other variables (which correspond to moderator, control, or intervening variables) present in an educational context (location) can be estimated. Limitations on the meaningfulness of parameters are predicated on the researcher's ability to demonstrate the extent to which models can be shown to fit the data. If the pattern of variances and covariances derived from the model does not differ significantly from the pattern of variances and covariances related to the observed variables, a given model is said to fit the data (Leithwood, Jantzi, & Fernandez, 1993). This evidence might serve to identify the strengths and weaknesses of storytelling as a research tool. Corresponding to the third principle, these activities would cause researchers to raise questions about story themes that emerged in relationship to social and political considerations. A total analysis of the findings would then lead to regrounding stories, as suggested by the fourth principle.

Another way to expand the use of story might involve examining the outcomes of certain emergent themes among teachers, such as teacher isolation, working with a student with disabilities, or professional disequilibrium (Cochran-Smith & Lytle, 1993, p. 231) during a teacher's transition from a novice to advanced beginner. If teachers' actions were dissimilar for each situation reported, we might ponder if their behavior was coincidental or influenced by one or more variables. Having actual data to look at, rather than relying on preferences or hunches, is the most appropriate means for exploring the meaning of teachers' behavior.

Finally, it is important to respond to critics' concerns about the validity of story research findings and consider ways in which the believability of these findings might be addressed. There can be little doubt that the interviewer interjects his or her interpretive reality while recounting a teacher's story. An approach that would strengthen the validity of findings associated with story research would require that several researchers use codified means of analysis to examine and interpret teachers' stories simultaneously. Consider if one teacher's story was distributed among a group of researchers, rather than just to one or two. What is the likelihood that the analysis or identification of thematic content would be the same? How do we separate the framework of one's own culture, experiences, or tacit knowledge from one's interpretation of teachers' stories? If we gathered seven to ten teacher stories and asked five to seven researchers to analyze the content, what degree of agreement or interrater reliability might be achieved? This approach to analyzing the data might minimize the obvious bias that is likely to result from a single researcher's subjective interpretation of his or her findings.

There have been voracious debates about the limitations of story and empiricism. While many of these arguments are difficult to evaluate, proaction rather than reaction is needed. Surely, there are other productive approaches to take in addressing this matter, instead of remaining paralyzed in unresolvable debates. A marriage of empiricism and mentalistic psychology is not unreasonable, given that the underlying assumptions from both camps have not been verified. Research in the field may be strengthened by a combination of these methods. The power of story to make new things possible and important in educational research becomes a reality when the researchers' aims are focused on expanding our understanding, rather than providing the one right methodology. If we begin to quantify the contexts in which teachers' themes occur, the potential value of story as an educational research tool may be known. The substantial and quantified framework offered by these approaches may affirm the belief that, by engaging educators, regardless of gender, class, and culture, and giving them a voice, story–narrative research can be used as a vehicle to direct and change lives (Noddings, 1991).

We are coming full circle in our exploration of what constitutes truth, knowledge, and viable educational research approaches. However, ultimately, we must disengage from the notion of renegotiating which research method is worth most for understanding teachers' behavior. Instead, we must examine the essential means by which research methodology can inform practice. If we do not challenge and develop the value or utility of story as a viable methodology, we will remain mired in the undisciplined and circular discourse that characterizes the debates between narrative and empirical researchers. To challenge these assumptions might give rise to an emergent linkage that I believe exists in *macrolizing* the location of multiple stories. Operationalizing this concept will require the creation of a classificatory system supported by empirical analyses. The development of this classificatory system will help illustrate the inherent relationships between teachers' reflection, thought, beliefs, and actions. Finally, attempts to codify thematic material will exemplify the notional value of story and illustrate the importance of this methodology in the training of future educators.

ENDNOTE

1. This chapter was adapted from L. S. Behar-Horenstein and R. R. Morgan, (1995), Narrative, teaching, and teacher thinking: Perspectives and possibilities. *Peabody Journal of Education 70*(2), 139–161 and a presentation made by the author at the Annual Meeting of the American Educational Research (San Francisco, CA, April 1995) entitled "Toward an understanding of teaching and teacher thinking: Contributions from story research."

This manuscript has been accepted by H. C. Waxman and H. Walberg (eds.) for their forthcoming textbook *New Directions for Research on Teaching*. The textbook will be published by McCutchan Publishers, Berkeley, CA, in 1998.

REFERENCES

Belensky, M., Clinchy, B., Goldberger, N., & Tarule, J. (1986). *Women's ways of knowing.* New York: Basic Books.

Bruner, J. (1986). *Actual minds, possible worlds.* Cambridge, MA: Harvard University Press.

Buchmann, M. (1986). Role over person: Morality and authenticity in teaching. *Teachers' College Record, 87,* 529–544.

Carter, K. (1993). The place of story in the study of teaching and teacher education. *Educational Researcher, 22*(1), 5–12, 18.

Carter, K., & Doyle, W. (1987). Teachers' knowledge structures and comprehension processes. In J. Calderhead (Ed.), *Exploring teachers' thinking,* pp. 79–98. Hillsdale, NJ: Lawrence Erlbaum.

Carter, K., & Gonzalez, L. (1990, April). Beginning teachers' knowledge of classroom events. Paper presented at the Annual Meeting of the American Educational Research Association, Boston.

Clandinin, D. J., & Connelly, F. M. (1988). Studying teachers' knowledge of classrooms: Collaborative research, ethics, and the negotiation of narrative. *Journal of Educational Thought, 22*(2A), 269–282.

Cochran-Smith, M., and Lytle, S. (1990). Research on teaching and teacher research: The issues that divide. *Educational Researcher, 19*(2), 2–11.

Cochran-Smith, M., and Lytle, S. (1993). *Inside/outside: Teacher research and knowledge.* New York: Teachers College Press.

Combs, A. W. (1965). *The professional education of teachers: A perceptual view of teacher preparation.* Boston: Allyn & Bacon.

Connelly, F. M., & Clandinin, D. J. (1986). On narrative method, biography, and narrative unities in the study of teaching. *Journal of Research in Science on Teaching, 24*(4), 293–320.

Connelly, F. M., & Clandinin, D. J. (1988). *Teachers as curriculum planners: Narratives of experience.* New York: Teachers College Press.

Connelly, F. M., and Clandinin, D. J. (1990). Stories of experience and narrative inquiry. *Educational Researcher, 19*(5), 2–14.

Crapanzano, V. (1980). *Tuhami.* Chicago: University of Chicago Press.

Elbaz, F. (1991). Research on teachers' knowledge: The evolution of a discourse. *Journal of Curriculum Studies, 23,* 1–19.

Gadamer, H.-G. (1960). *Truth and method.* New York: Seabury Press.

Gergen, M., & Gergen, K. (1986). The social construction of narrative accounts. In K. Gergen and M. Gergen (Eds.), *Historical social psychology,* pp. 173–189. Hillsdale, NJ: Lawrence Erlbaum.

Greene, M. (1994). Epistemology and educational research: The influence of recent approaches to knowledge. *Review of Research in Education, 20,* 223–264.

Gudmundsdottir, S. (1991). Story-maker, story-teller: Narrative structures in curriculum. *Journal of Curriculum Studies, 23,* 207–218.

Hargreaves, A. (1994). Dissonant voices: Teachers and the multiple realities of restructuring. Paper presented at the Annual Meeting of the American Educational Research Association, New Orleans, April 1994.

Helle, A. P. (1991). Reading women's autobiographies: A map of reconstructed knowing. In C. Witherell &

N. Noddings (Eds.), *Stories lives tell: Narrative and dialogue in education,* pp. 233–249. Chicago: University of Chicago Press.

Kagan, D. M. (1988). Teaching as critical problem solving: A critical examination of the analogy and its implications. *Review of Educational Research, 58*(4), 482–505.

Keller, E. F. (1985). *Reflections on gender and science.* New Haven, CT: Yale University Press.

Kendler, H. H. (1993). Psychology and the ethics of social psychology. *American Psychologist, 48*(10), 1046–1053.

Kleine, P. F., & Greene, B. A. (1993). Story telling: A rich history and a sordid past—a response to Berliner (1992). *Educational Psychologist, 28*(2), 185–190.

Leinhardt, G. (1990). Capturing craft knowledge in teaching. *Educational Researcher, 19*(2), 18–25.

Leithwood, K., Jantzi, D., & Fernandez, A. (1993). Secondary school teachers' commitment to change: The contributions of transformational leadership. Paper presented at the Annual Meeting of the American Educational Research Association, Atlanta, GA, April 1993.

MacLeod, R. B. (1986). Phenomenology. In D. L. Stills (Ed.), *International encyclopedia of the social sciences, 12,* pp. 68–72. New York: Macmillan & Free Press.

Martin, J., & Sugarman, J. (1993). Beyond methodolatry: Two conceptions of relations between theory and research in research on teaching. *Educational Researcher, 22*(8), 17–24.

Nespor, J., and Barylske, J. (1991). Narrative discourse and teacher knowledge. *American Educational Research Journal, 28*(4), 805–823.

Noddings, N. (1991). Stories in dialogue: Caring and interpersonal reasoning. In C. Witherell & N. Noddings (Eds.), *Stories lives tell: Narrative and dialogue in education,* pp. 155–170. New York: Teachers College Press.

Peshkin, A. (1978). *Growing up in America: Schooling and the survival of community.* Chicago: University of Chicago Press.

Polkinghorne, D. (1988). *Narrative knowing and the human sciences.* Albany, NY: State University of New York.

Salomon, G. (1991). Transcending the qualitative–quantitative debate: The analytic and systematic approaches to educational research. *Educational Researcher, 20,* 10–18.

Scholes, R. (1981). Language, narrative, and anti-narrative. In W. J. T. Mitchell (Ed.), *On narrative,* pp. 200–208. Chicago: University of Chicago Press.

Scholes, R. (1982). *Semiotics and interpretation.* New Haven, CT: Yale University Press.

Schon, D. A. (1987). *Educating the reflective practitioner.* San Francisco: Jossey-Bass.

Schwab, J. J. (1983). The practical 4: Something for curriculum professors to do. *Curriculum Inquiry, 13*(3), 239–265.

Shulman, L. S. (1987). Knowledge and teaching: Foundations of the new reform. *Harvard Educational Review, 57*(1), 1–22.

Sparks-Langer, G. M., and Bernstein-Colton, A. (1991). Synthesis of research on teachers' reflective thinking. *Educational Leadership, 48*(6), 37–44.

Spence, D. P. (1986). *Narrative truth and historical method.* New York: Norton & Company.

Willinsky, J. (1989). Getting personal and practical with personal practical knowledge. *Curriculum Inquiry, 19*(3), 247–264.

Yinger, R. (1987). Learning the language of practice. *Curriculum Inquiry, 17*(3), 293–318.

DISCUSSION QUESTIONS

1. Why must one carefully scrutinize interpretations related to the meanings emerging from practical knowledge?
2. In your opinion, why is the empirical paradigm sufficient (insufficient) to revealing insights into teachers' ways of thinking?
3. What are the difficulties associated with romanticizing or according teachers' voice with unwarranted authenticity?
4. What steps will be needed if findings from narrative research are to have application beyond singular case studies?
5. How might an increased use of narrative research influence (a) preservice teacher training programs, (b) doctoral programs in teacher education, (c) early childhood, and (d) educational leadership?

11

Knowledge and Teaching: Foundations of the New Reform

LEE S. SHULMAN

FOCUSING QUESTIONS

1. *Why is a codified compendium of knowledge and skills insufficient for articulating a knowledge base of teaching?*
2. *What sources should comprise teaching the knowledge base according to the author?*
3. *What is pedagogical content knowledge?*
4. *Which role should the liberal arts college, school, and departments of education assume in training teachers for the twenty-first century?*
5. *What is the purpose of transformation and reflection in the process of pedagogical reasoning and action?*
6. *What should be the goal of teacher education?*

Lee S. Shulman builds his foundation for teaching reform on an idea of teaching that emphasizes comprehension and reasoning, transformation and reflection. "This emphasis is justified," he writes, "by the resoluteness with which research and policy have so blatantly ignored those aspects of teaching in the past." To articulate and justify this conception, Shulman responds to four questions: What are the sources of the knowledge base for teaching? In what terms can these sources be conceptualized? What are the processes of pedagogical reasoning and action? and What are the implications for teaching policy and educational reform? The answers—informed by philosophy, psychology, and a growing body of casework based on young and experienced practitioners—go far beyond current reform assumptions and initiatives. The outcome for educational practitioners, scholars, and policymakers is a major redirection in

how teaching is to be understood and teachers are to be trained and evaluated.

This chapter was selected for the November 1986 special issue on "Teachers, Teaching, and Teacher Education," but appears here because of the exigencies of publishing.

PROLOGUE: A PORTRAIT OF EXPERTISE

Richly developed portrayals of expertise in teaching are rare. While many characterizations of effective teachers exist, most of these dwell on the teacher's management of the classroom. We find few descriptions or analyses of teachers that give careful attention not only to the management of students in classrooms, but also to the management of *ideas* within classroom discourse. Both kinds of emphasis will be needed if our portrayals of good practice are to serve as sufficient guides to the design of better education. Let us examine one brief account.

A twenty-five-year veteran English teacher, Nancy, was the subject of a continuing study of experienced teachers that we had been conducting. The class was nearing the end of the second week of a unit on *Moby Dick.* The observer had been well impressed with the depth of Nancy's understanding of that novel and her skill as a pedagogue, as she documented how Nancy helped a group of California high school juniors grasp the many faces of that masterpiece. Nancy was a highly active teacher, whose classroom style employed substantial interaction with her students, both through recitations and more open-ended discussion. She was like a symphony conductor, posing questions, probing for alternative views, drawing out the shy while tempering the boisterous. Not much happened in the classroom that did not pass through Nancy, whose pacing and ordering, structuring and expanding, controlled the rhythm of classroom life.

Nancy characterized her treatment of literature in terms of a general theoretical model that she employed.

Basically, I break reading skills into four levels:

Level 1 is simply translation…. It is understanding the literal meaning, denotative, and frequently for students that means getting a dictionary.

Level 2 is connotative meaning and again you are still looking at the words…. What does that mean, what does that tell us about the character?…We looked at *The Scarlet Letter.* Hawthorne described a rose bush in the first chapter. Literal level is: What is a rose bush? More important, what does a rose bush suggest, what is it that comes to mind, what did you picture?

Level 3 is the level of interpretation…. It is the implication of Levels 1 and 2. If the author is using a symbol, what does that say about his view of life? In *Moby Dick,* the example I used in class was the boots. The boots would be the literal level. What does it mean when he gets under the bed? And the students would say, he is trying to hide something. Level 3 would be what does Melville say about human nature? What is the implication of this? What does this tell us about this character?

Level 4 is what I call application and evaluation and I try, as I teach literature, to get the students to Level 4, and that is where they take the literature and see how it has meaning for their own lives. Where would we see that event occur in our own society? How would people that we know be behaving if they are doing what these characters are doing? How is this piece of literature similar to our common experiences as human beings?…So my view of reading is basically to take them from the literal on the page to making it mean something in their lives. In teaching literature I am always working in and out of those levels (Gudmundsdottir, in preparation).

Nancy employed this conceptual framework in her teaching, using it to guide her own sequencing of material and formulation of questions. She taught the framework explicitly to her students over the semester, helping them employ it like a scaffolding to organize their own study of the texts, to monitor their own thinking. Although as a teacher she maintained tight control of the classroom discourse, her teaching goals were to liberate her students' minds through literacy, eventually to use great works of literature to illuminate their own lives. Whichever work she was teaching, she understood how to organize it, frame it for teaching, divide it appropriately for assignments and activities. She seemed to possess a mental index for these books she had taught so often—*The Red Badge of Courage, Moby Dick, The Scarlet Letter, The Adventures of Huckleberry Finn*—with key episodes organized in her mind for different pedagogical purposes, different levels of difficulty, different kinds of pupils, different themes or emphases. Her combination of subject-matter understanding and pedagogical skill was quite dazzling.

When the observer arrived at the classroom one morning, she found Nancy sitting at her desk as usual. But her morning greeting elicited no response from Nancy other than a grimace and motion toward the pad of paper on her desktop. "I have laryngitis this morning and will not be able to speak aloud," said the note. What's more, she appeared to be fighting the flu, for she had little energy. For a teacher who managed her classroom through the power of her voice and her manner, this was certainly a disabling condition. Or was it?

Using a combination of handwritten notes and whispers, she divided the class into small groups by rows, a tactic she had used twice before during this unit. Each group was given a different character who has a prominent role in the first chapters of the novel, and each group was expected to answer a series of questions about that character. Ample time was used at the end of the period for representatives of each group to report to the whole class. Once again the class had run smoothly, and the subject matter had been treated with care. But the style had changed radically, an utterly different teaching technology was employed, and still the students were engaged, and learning appeared to occur.

Subsequently, we were to see many more examples of Nancy's flexible style, adapted to the characteristics of learners, the complexities of subject matter, and her own physical condition. When learners experienced serious problems with a particular text, she self-consciously stayed at the lower levels of the reading ladder, helping the students with denotative and connotative meanings, while emphasizing literary interpretations somewhat less. When teaching *Huck Finn,* a novel she saw as less difficult than *Moby Dick,* her style changed once again. She gave much more autonomy to the students and did not directly run the classroom as much.

> For *Huck Finn,* she abandoned the stage early on and let the students teach each other. She had the students working independently in eight multi-ability groups, each group tracing one of eight themes: hypocrisy; luck and superstition; greed and materialism; romantic ideas and fantasy; religion and the Bible; social class and customs; family, racism, and prejudice; freedom and conscience. There were only two reading checks at the beginning and only two rounds of reporting. Once the groups were underway, Nancy took a seat at the back of the class and only interacted with students when she was called upon, and during group presentations (Gudmundsdottir, in preparation).

Thus Nancy's pattern of instruction, her style of teaching, is not uniform or predictable in some simple sense. She flexibly responds to the difficulty and character of the subject matter, the capacities of the students (which can change even over the span of a single course), and her educa-

tional purposes. She can not only conduct her orchestra from the podium, she can sit back and watch it play with virtuosity by itself.

What does Nancy believe, understand, and know how to do that permits her to teach as she does? Can other teachers be prepared to teach with such skill? The hope that teaching like Nancy's can become typical instead of unusual motivates much of the effort in the newly proposed reforms of teaching.

THE NEW REFORMS

During the past year the U.S. public and its professional educators have been presented with several reports on how to improve teaching as both an activity and a profession. One of the recurring themes of these reports has been the professionalization of teaching—the elevation of teaching to a more respected, more responsible, more rewarding and better rewarded occupation. The claim that teaching deserves professional status, however, is based on a more fundamental premise: that the standards by which the education and performance of teachers must be judged can be raised and more clearly articulated. The advocates of professional reform base their arguments on the belief that there exists a "knowledge base for teaching"—a codified or codifiable aggregation of knowledge, skill, understanding, and technology, of ethics and disposition, of collective responsibility—as well as a means for representing and communicating it. The reports of the Holmes Group (1986) and the Carnegie Task Force (1986) rest on this belief and, furthermore, claim that the knowledge base is growing. They argue that it should frame teacher education and directly inform teaching practice.

The rhetoric regarding the knowledge base, however, rarely specifies the character of such knowledge. It does not say what teachers should know, do, understand, or profess that will render teaching more than a form of individual labor, let alone be considered among the learned professions.

In this paper, I present an argument regarding the content, character, and sources for a knowledge base of teaching that suggests an answer to the question of the intellectual, practical, and normative basis for the professionalization of teaching. The questions that focus the argument are: What are the sources of the knowledge base for teaching? In what terms can these sources be conceptualized? What are the implications for teaching policy and educational reform?[1]

In addressing these questions I am following in the footsteps of many eminent scholars, including Dewey (1904), Scheffler (1965), Green (1971), Fenstermacher (1978), Smith (1980), and Schwab (1983), among others. Their discussions of what qualities and understandings, skills and abilities, and what traits and sensibilities render someone a competent teacher have continued to echo in the conference rooms of educators for generations. My approach has been conditioned, as well, by two current projects: a study of how new teachers learn to teach and an attempt to develop a national board for teaching.

First, for the past three years, my colleagues and I have been watching knowledge of pedagogy and content grow in the minds of young men and women. They have generously permitted us to observe and follow their eventful journeys from being teacher education students to becoming neophyte teachers. In this research, we are taking advantage of the kinds of insights Piaget provided from his investigations of knowledge growth. He discovered that he could learn a great deal about knowledge and its development from careful observation of the very young—those who were just beginning to develop and organize their intelligence. We are following this lead by studying those just learning to teach. Their development from students to teachers, from a state of expertise as learners through a novitiate as teachers exposes and highlights the complex bodies of knowledge and skill needed to function effectively as a teacher. The result is that error, success, and refinement—in a word, teacher-knowledge growth—are seen in high profile and in slow motion. The neophyte's stumble becomes the scholar's window.

Concurrently, we have found and explored cases of veteran teachers such as Nancy (Baxter, in preparation; Gudmundsdottir, in preparation; Hashweh, 1985) to compare with those of the nov-

ices. What these studies show is that the knowledge, understanding, and skill we see displayed haltingly, and occasionally masterfully, among beginners are often demonstrated with ease by the expert. But, as we have wrestled with our cases, we have repeatedly asked what teachers knew (or failed to know) that permitted them to teach in a particular manner.

Second, for much of the past year, I have engaged in quite a different project on the role of knowledge in teaching. In conjunction with the recent Carnegie initiative for the reform of the teaching profession, my colleagues and I have been studying ways to design a national board assessment for teaching, parallel in several ways to the National Board of Medical Examiners (Shulman & Sykes, 1986; Sykes, 1986). This challenge renders the questions about the definition and operationalization of knowledge in teaching as far more than academic exercises. If teachers are to be certified on the basis of well-grounded judgments and standards, then those standards on which a national board relies must be legitimized by three factors: they must be closely tied to the findings of scholarship in the academic disciplines that form the curriculum (such as English, physics, and history) as well as those that serve as foundations for the process of education (such as psychology, sociology, or philosophy); they must possess intuitive credibility (or "face validity") in the opinions of the professional community in whose interests they have been designed; and they must relate to the appropriate normative conceptions of teaching and teacher education.

The new reform proposals carry assumptions about the knowledge base for teaching: when advocates of reform suggest that requirements for the education of teachers should be augmented and periods of training lengthened, they assume there must be something substantial to be learned. When they recommend that standards be raised and a system of examinations introduced, they assume there must exist a body of knowledge and skill to examine. Our research and that of others (for example, Berliner, 1986; Leinhardt & Greeno, 1986) have identified the sources and suggested outlines of that knowledge base. Watching veterans such as

Nancy teach the same material that poses difficulties for novice teachers helped focus our attention on what kinds of knowledge and skill were needed to teach demanding materials well. By focusing on the teaching of particular topics—*Huck Finn,* quadratic equations, the Indian subcontinent, photosynthesis—we learned how particular kinds of content knowledge and pedagogical strategies necessarily interacted in the minds of teachers.

What follows is a discussion of the sources and outlines of the required knowledge base for teaching. I divide this discussion into two distinct analyses. First, after providing an overview of one framework for a knowledge base for teaching, I examine the *sources* of that knowledge base, that is, the domains of scholarship and experience from which teachers may draw their understanding. Second, I explore the processes of pedagogical reasoning and action within which such teacher knowledge is used.

THE KNOWLEDGE BASE

Begin a discussion on the knowledge base of teaching, and several related questions immediately arise: What knowledge base? Is enough known about teaching to support a knowledge base? Isn't teaching little more than personal style, artful communication, knowing some subject matter, and applying the results of recent research on teaching effectiveness? Only the last of these, the findings of research on effective teaching, is typically deemed a legitimate part of a knowledge base.

The actions of both policymakers and teacher educators in the past have been consistent with the formulation that teaching requires basic skills, content knowledge, and general pedagogical skills. Assessments of teachers in most states consist of some combination of basic-skills tests, an examination of competence in subject matter, and observations in the classroom to ensure that certain kinds of general teaching behavior are present. In this manner, I would argue, teaching is trivialized, its complexities ignored, and its demands diminished. Teachers themselves have difficulty in articulating what they know and how they know it.

Nevertheless, the policy community at present continues to hold that the skills needed for teaching are those identified in the empirical research on teaching effectiveness. This research, summarized by Brophy and Good (1986), Gage (1986), and Rosenshine and Stevens (1986), was conducted within the psychological research tradition. It assumes that complex forms of situation-specific human performance can be understood in terms of the workings of underlying generic processes. In a study of teaching context, the research, therefore, seeks to identify those general forms of teaching behavior that correlate with student performance on standardized tests, whether in descriptive or experimental studies. The investigators who conduct the research realize that important simplifications must be made, but they believe that these are necessary steps for conducting scientific studies. Critical features of teaching, such as the subject matter being taught, the classroom context, the physical and psychological characteristics of the students, or the accomplishment of purposes not readily assessed on standardized tests, are typically ignored in the quest for general principles of effective teaching.

When policymakers have sought "research-based" definitions of good teaching to serve as the basis for teacher tests or systems of classroom observation, the lists of teacher behaviors that had been identified as effective in the empirical research were translated into the desirable competencies for classroom teachers. They became items on tests or on classroom-observation scales. They were accorded legitimacy because they had been "confirmed by research." While the researchers understood the findings to be simplified and incomplete, the policy community accepted them as sufficient for the definitions of standards.

For example, some research had indicated that students achieved more when teachers explicitly informed them of the lesson's objective. This seems like a perfectly reasonable finding. When translated into policy, however, classroom-observation competency-rating scales asked whether the teacher had written the objective on the blackboard and/or directly told the students the objectives at the beginning of class. If the teacher had not, he or she was marked off for failing to demonstrate a desired competency. No effort was made to discover whether the withholding of an objective might have been consistent with the form of the lesson being organized or delivered.

Moreover, those who hold with bifurcating content and teaching processes have once again introduced into policy what had been merely an act of scholarly convenience and simplification in the research. Teaching processes were observed and evaluated without reference to the adequacy or accuracy of the ideas transmitted. In many cases, observers were not expected to have content expertise in the areas being observed, because it did not matter for the rating of teacher performance. Thus, what may have been an acceptable strategy for research became an unacceptable policy for teacher evaluation.

In this paper I argue that the results of research on effective teaching, while valuable, are not the sole source of evidence on which to base a definition of the knowledge base of teaching. Those sources should be understood to be far richer and more extensive. Indeed, properly understood, the actual and potential sources for a knowledge base are so plentiful that our question should not be, Is there really much one needs to know in order to teach? Rather, it should express our wonder at how the extensive knowledge of teaching can be learned at all during the brief period allotted to teacher preparation. Much of the rest of this paper provides the details of the argument that there exists an elaborate knowledge base for teaching.

A View of Teaching

I begin with the formulation that the capacity to teach centers around the following commonplaces of teaching, paraphrased from Fenstermacher (1986). A teacher knows something not understood by others, presumably the students. The teacher can transform understanding, performance skills, or desired attitudes or values into pedagogical representations and actions. These are ways of talking, showing, enacting, or otherwise representing ideas so that the unknowing can come to know,

those without understanding can comprehend and discern, and the unskilled can become adept. Thus, teaching necessarily begins with a teacher's understanding of what is to be learned and how it is to be taught. It proceeds through a series of activities during which the students are provided specific instruction and opportunities for learning,[2] though the learning itself ultimately remains the responsibility of the students. Teaching ends with new comprehension by both the teacher and the student.[3] Although this is certainly a core conception of teaching, it is also an incomplete conception. Teaching must properly be understood to be more than the enhancement of understanding; but if it is not even that, then questions regarding performance of its other functions remain moot. The next step is to outline the categories of knowledge that underlie the teacher understanding needed to promote comprehension among students.

Categories of the Knowledge Base

If teacher knowledge were to be organized into a handbook, an encyclopedia, or some other format for arraying knowledge, what would the category headings look like?[4] At minimum, they would include:

—content knowledge;
—general pedagogical knowledge, with special reference to those broad principles and strategies of classroom management and organization that appear to transcend subject matter;
—curriculum knowledge, with particular grasp of the materials and programs that serve as "tools of the trade" for teachers;
—pedagogical content knowledge, that special amalgam of content and pedagogy that is uniquely the province of teachers, their own special form of professional understanding;
—knowledge of learners and their characteristics;
—knowledge of educational contexts, ranging from the workings of the group or class-

room, the governance and financing of school districts, to the character of communities and cultures; and

—knowledge of educational ends, purposes, and values, and their philosophical and historical grounds.

Among those categories, pedagogical content knowledge is of special interest because it identifies the distinctive bodies of knowledge for teaching. It represents the blending of content and pedagogy into an understanding of how particular topics, problems, or issues are organized, represented, and adapted to the diverse interests and abilities of learners, and presented for instruction. Pedagogical content knowledge is the category most likely to distinguish the understanding of the content specialist from that of the pedagogue. While far more can be said regarding the categories of a knowledge base for teaching, elucidation of them is not a central purpose of this chapter.

Enumerating the Sources

There are at least four major sources for the teaching knowledge base: (1) scholarship in content disciplines, (2) the materials and settings of the institutionalized educational process (for example, curricula, textbooks, school organizations and finance, and the structure of the teaching profession), (3) research on schooling, social organizations, human learning, teaching and development, and the other social and cultural phenomena that affect what teachers can do, and (4) the wisdom of practice itself. Let me elaborate on each of these.

Scholarship in content disciplines. The first source of the knowledge base is content knowledge—the knowledge, understanding, skill, and disposition that are to be learned by school children. This knowledge rests on two foundations: the accumulated literature and studies in the content areas, and the historical and philosophical scholarship on the nature of knowledge in those fields of study. For example, the teacher of English should know English and American prose and poetry,

written and spoken language use and comprehension, and grammar. In addition, he or she should be familiar with the critical literature that applies to particular novels or epics that are under discussion in class. Moreover, the teacher should understand alternative theories of interpretation and criticism, and how these might relate to issues of curriculum and of teaching.

Teaching is, essentially, a learned profession. A teacher is a member of a scholarly community. He or she must understand the structures of subject matter, the principles of conceptual organization, and the principles of inquiry that help answer two kinds of questions in each field: What are the important ideas and skills in this domain? and How are new ideas added and deficient ones dropped by those who produce knowledge in this area? That is, what are the rules and procedures of good scholarship or inquiry? These questions parallel what Schwab (1964) has characterized as knowledge of substantive and syntactic structures, respectively. This view of the sources of content knowledge necessarily implies that the teacher must have not only depth of understanding with respect to the particular subjects taught, but also a broad liberal education that serves as a framework for old learning and as a facilitator for new understanding. The teacher has special responsibilities in relation to content knowledge, serving as the primary source of student understanding of subject matter. The manner in which that understanding is communicated conveys to students what is essential about a subject and what is peripheral. In the face of student diversity, the teacher must have a flexible and multifaceted comprehension, adequate to impart alternative explanations of the same concepts or principles. The teacher also communicates, whether consciously or not, ideas about the ways in which "truth" is determined in a field and a set of attitudes and values that markedly influence student understanding. This responsibility places special demands on the teacher's own depth of understanding of the structures of the subject matter, as well as on the teacher's attitudes toward and enthusiasms for what is being taught and learned. These many aspects of content knowledge, therefore, are properly understood as a central feature of the knowledge base of teaching.

Educational materials and structures. To advance the aims of organized schooling, materials and structures for teaching and learning are created. These include: curricula with their scopes and sequences; tests and testing materials; institutions with their hierarchies, their explicit and implicit systems of rules and roles; professional teachers' organizations with their functions of negotiation, social change, and mutual protection; government agencies from the district through the state and federal levels; and general mechanisms of governance and finance. Because teachers necessarily function within a matrix created by these elements, using and being used by them, it stands to reason that the principles, policies, and facts of their functioning comprise a major source for the knowledge base. There is no need to claim that a specific literature undergirds this source, although there is certainly abundant research literature in most of these domains. But if a teacher has to "know the territory" of teaching, then it is the landscape of such materials, institutions, organizations, and mechanisms with which he or she must be familiar. These comprise both the tools of the trade and the contextual conditions that will either facilitate or inhibit teaching efforts.

Formal educational scholarship. A third source is the important and growing body of scholarly literature devoted to understanding the processes of schooling, teaching, and learning. This literature includes the findings and methods of empirical research in the areas of teaching, learning, and human development, as well as the normative, philosophical, and ethical foundations of education.

The normative and theoretical aspects of teaching's scholarly knowledge are perhaps most important. Unfortunately, educational policymakers and staff developers tend to treat only the findings of empirical research on teaching and learning as relevant portions of the scholarly knowledge base. But these research findings, while important and worthy of careful study, represent only one

facet of the contribution of scholarship. Perhaps the most enduring and powerful scholarly influences on teachers are those that enrich their images of the possible: their visions of what constitutes good education, or what a well-educated youngster might look like if provided with appropriate opportunities and stimulation.

The writings of Plato, Dewey, Neill, and Skinner all communicate their conceptions of what a good educational system should be. In addition, many works written primarily to disseminate empirical research findings also serve as important sources of these concepts. I count among these such works as Bloom's (1976) on mastery learning and Rosenthal and Jacobson's (1968) on teacher expectations. Quite independent of whether the empirical claims of those books can be supported, their impact on teachers' conceptions of the possible and desirable ends of education is undeniable. Thus, the philosophical, critical, and empirical literature which can inform the goals, visions, and dreams of teachers is a major portion of the scholarly knowledge base of teaching.

A more frequently cited kind of scholarly knowledge grows out of the empirical study of teaching effectiveness. This research has been summarized recently by Gage (1978, 1986), Shulman (1986a), Brophy and Good (1986), and Rosenshine and Stevens (1986). The essential goal of this program of research has been to identify those teacher behaviors and strategies most likely to lead to achievement gains among students. Because the search has focused on generic relationships— teacher behaviors associated with student academic gains irrespective of subject matter or grade level— the findings have been much more closely connected with the management of classrooms than with the subtleties of content pedagogy. That is, the effective-teaching principles deal with making classrooms places where pupils can attend to instructional tasks, orient themselves toward learning with a minimum of disruption and distraction, and receive a fair and adequate opportunity to learn. Moreover, the educational purposes for which these research results are most relevant are the teaching of skills. Rosenshine (1986) has observed that effective teaching research has much less to offer to the teaching of understanding, especially of complex written material; thus, the research applies more to teaching a skill like multiplication than to teaching critical interpretations of, say, the *Federalist Papers*.

There are a growing number of such generic principles of effective teaching, and they have already found their way into examinations such as the National Teachers Examination and into state-level assessments of teaching performance during the first teaching year. Their weakness, that they essentially ignore the content-specific character of most teaching, is also their strength. Discovering, explicating, and codifying general teaching principles simplify the otherwise outrageously complex activity of teaching. The great danger occurs, however, when a general teaching principle is distorted into prescription, when maxim becomes mandate. Those states that have taken working principles of teaching, based solely on empirical studies of generic teaching effectiveness, and have rendered them as hard, independent criteria for judging a teacher's worth, are engaged in a political process likely to injure the teaching profession rather than improve it.

The results of research on learning and development also fall within the area of empirical research findings. This research differs from research on teaching by the unit of investigation. Studies of teaching typically take place in conventional classrooms. Learning and development are ordinarily studied in individuals. Hence, teaching studies give accounts of how teachers cope with the inescapable character of schools as places where groups of students work and learn in concert. By comparison, learning and development studies produce principles of individual thought or behavior that must often be generalized to groups with caution if they are to be useful for schoolteaching.

The research in these domains can be both generic and content-specific. For example, cognitive psychological research contributes to the development of understanding of how the mind works to store, process, and retrieve information. Such general understanding can certainly be a source of knowledge for teachers, just as the work of Piaget, Maslow, Erikson, or Bloom has been and continues to be. We also find work on specific subject matter and student developmental levels that is enormously useful; for example, we learn about student misconceptions in the learning of arithmetic by elementary school youngsters (Erlwanger, 1975) or difficulties in grasping principles of physics by university and secondary school students (for example, Clement, 1982). Both these sorts of research contribute to a knowledge base for teaching.

Wisdom of practice.   The final source of the knowledge base is the least codified of all. It is the wisdom of practice itself, the maxims that guide (or provide reflective rationalization for) the practices of able teachers. One of the more important tasks for the research community is to work with practitioners to develop codified representations of the practical pedagogical wisdom of able teachers. As indicated above, much of the conception of teaching embodied in this chapter is derived from collecting, examining, and beginning to codify the emerging wisdom of practice among both inexperienced and experienced teachers.

The portrait of Nancy with which this paper began is only one of the many descriptions and analyses of excellent teaching we have been collecting over the past few years. As we organize and interpret such data, we attempt to infer principles of good practice that can serve as useful guidelines for efforts of educational reform. We attempt to keep the accounts highly contextualized, especially with respect to the content-specificity of the pedagogical strategies employed. In this manner we contribute to the documentation of good practice as a significant source for teaching standards. We also attempt to lay a foundation for a scholarly literature that records the details and rationales for specific pedagogical practice.

One of the frustrations of teaching as an occupation and profession is its extensive individual and collective amnesia, the consistency with which the best creations of its practitioners are lost to both contemporary and future peers. Unlike fields such as architecture (which preserves its creations in both plans and edifices), law (which builds a case literature of opinions and interpretations), medicine (with its records and case studies), and even unlike chess, bridge, or ballet (with their traditions of preserving both memorable games and choreographed performances through inventive forms of notation and recording), teaching is conducted without an audience of peers. It is devoid of a history of practice.

Without such a system of notation and memory, the next steps of analysis, interpretation, and codification of principles of practice are hard to pursue. We have concluded from our research with teachers at all levels of experience that the potentially codifiable knowledge that can be gleaned from the wisdom of practice is extensive. Practitioners simply know a great deal that they have never even tried to articulate. A major portion of the research agenda for the next decade will be to collect, collate, and interpret the practical knowledge of teachers for the purpose of establishing a case literature and codifying its principles, precedents, and parables (Shulman, 1986b). A significant portion of the research agenda associated with the Carnegie program to develop new assessments for teachers involves the conducting of "wisdom-of-practice" studies. These studies record and organize the reasoning and actions of gifted teachers into cases to establish standards of practice for particular areas of teaching.[5]

A knowledge base for teaching is not fixed and final. Although teaching is among the world's oldest professions, educational research, especially the systematic study of teaching, is a relatively new enterprise. We may be able to offer a compelling argument for the broad outlines and categories of the knowledge base for teaching. It will, however, become abundantly clear that much, if not most, of the proposed knowledge base remains to be discovered, invented, and refined. As more is learned about teaching, we will come to recognize new categories of performance and understanding that are characteristic of good teachers, and will have to reconsider and redefine other domains. Our current "blueprint" for the knowledge base of teaching has many cells or categories with only the most rudimentary placeholders, much like the chemist's periodic table of a century ago. As we proceed, we will know that something can be known in principle about a particular aspect of teaching, but we will not yet know what that principle or practice entails. At base, however, we believe that scholars and expert teachers are able to define, describe, and reproduce good teaching.

THE PROCESSES OF PEDAGOGICAL REASONING AND ACTION

The conception of teaching I shall discuss has emerged from a number of sources, both philosophical and empirical. A key source has been the several dozen teachers whom we have been studying in our research during the past three years. Through interviews, observations, structured tasks, and examination of materials, we have attempted to understand how they commute from the status of learner to that of teacher,[6] from being able to comprehend subject matter for themselves, to becoming able to elucidate subject matter in new ways, reorganize and partition it, clothe it in activities and emotions, in metaphors and exercises, and in examples and demonstrations, so that it can be grasped by students.

As we have come to view teaching, it begins with an act of reason, continues with a process of reasoning, culminates in performances of imparting, eliciting, involving, or enticing, and is then thought about some more until the process can begin again. In the discussion of teaching that follows, we will emphasize teaching as comprehension and reasoning, as transformation and reflection. This emphasis is justified by the resoluteness with which research and policy have so blatantly ignored those aspects of teaching in the past.

Fenstermacher (1978, 1986) provides a useful framework for analysis. The goal of teacher education, he argues, is not to indoctrinate or train teachers to behave in prescribed ways, but to educate teachers to reason soundly about their teaching as well as to perform skillfully. Sound reasoning requires both a process of thinking about what they are doing and an adequate base of facts, principles, and experiences from which to reason. Teachers must learn to use their knowledge base to provide the grounds for choices and actions. Therefore, teacher education must work with the beliefs that guide teacher actions, with the principles and evidence that underlie the choices teachers make. Such reasons (called "premises of the practical argument" in the analysis of Green, 1971, on which Fenstermacher bases his argument) can be predominantly arbitrary or idiosyncratic ("It sure seemed like the right idea at the time!" "I don't know much about teaching, but I know what I like."), or they can rest on ethical, empirical, theoretical, or practical principles that have substantial support among members of the professional community of teachers. Fenstermacher argues that good teaching not only is effective behaviorally, but must rest on a foundation of adequately grounded premises.

When we examine the quality of teaching, the idea of influencing the grounds or reasons for teachers' decisions places the emphasis precisely where it belongs: on the features of pedagogical reasoning that lead to or can be invoked to explain pedagogical actions. We must be cautious, however, lest we place undue emphasis upon the ways teachers reason to achieve particular ends, at the expense of attention to the grounds they present for selecting the ends themselves. Teaching is both effective and normative; it is concerned with both means and ends. Processes of reasoning underlie both. The knowledge base must therefore deal with the purposes of education as well as the methods and strategies of educating.

This image of teaching involves the exchange of ideas. The idea is grasped, probed, and comprehended by a teacher, who then must turn it about in his or her mind, seeing many sides of it. Then the idea is shaped or tailored until it can in turn be grasped by students. This grasping, however, is not a passive act. Just as the teacher's comprehension requires a vigorous interaction with the ideas, so students will be expected to encounter ideas actively as well. Indeed, our exemplary teachers present ideas in order to provoke the constructive

processes of their students and not to incur student dependence on teachers or to stimulate the flatteries of imitation.[7]

Comprehension alone is not sufficient. The usefulness of such knowledge lies in its value for judgment and action. Thus, in response to my aphorism, "those who can, do; those who understand, teach" (Shulman, 1986b, p. 14), Petrie (1986) correctly observed that I had not gone far enough. Understanding, he argued, must be linked to judgment and action, to the proper uses of understanding in the forging of wise pedagogical decisions.

Aspects of Pedagogical Reasoning

I begin with the assumption that most teaching is initiated by some form of "text": a textbook, a syllabus, or an actual piece of material the teacher or student wishes to have understood. The text may be a vehicle for the accomplishment of other educational purposes, but some sort of teaching material is almost always involved. The following conception of pedagogical reasoning and action is taken from the point of view of the teacher, who is presented with the challenge of taking what he or she already understands and making it ready for effective instruction. The model of pedagogical reasoning and action is summarized in Table 11.1.

Given a text, educational purposes, and/or a set of ideas, pedagogical reasoning and action involve a cycle through the activities of comprehension, transformation, instruction, evaluation, and reflection.[8] The starting point and terminus for the process is an act of comprehension.

Comprehension.   To teach is first to understand. We ask that the teacher comprehend critically a set of ideas to be taught.[9] We expect teachers to understand what they teach and, when possible, to understand it in several ways. They should understand how a given idea relates to other ideas within the same subject area and to ideas in other subjects as well.

Comprehension of purposes is also central here. We engage in teaching to achieve educational purposes, to accomplish ends having to do with student literacy, student freedom to use and enjoy, student responsibility to care and care for, to believe and respect, to inquire and discover, to develop understandings, skills, and values needed to function in a free and just society. As teachers, we also strive to balance our goals of fostering individual excellence with more general ends involving equality of opportunity and equity among students of different backgrounds and cultures. Although most teaching begins with some sort of text, and the learning of that text can be a worthy end in itself, we should not lose sight of the fact that the text is often a vehicle for achieving other educational purposes. The goals of education transcend the comprehension of particular texts, but may be unachievable without it.

Saying that a teacher must first comprehend both content and purposes, however, does not particularly distinguish a teacher from non-teaching peers. We expect a math major to understand mathematics or a history specialist to comprehend history. But the key to distinguishing the knowledge base of teaching lies at the intersection of content and pedagogy, in the capacity of a teacher to transform the content knowledge he or she possesses into forms that are pedagogically powerful and yet adaptive to the variations in ability and background presented by the students. We now turn to a discussion of transformation and its components.

Transformation. Comprehended ideas must be transformed in some manner if they are to be

TABLE 11.1 A Model of Pedagogical Reasoning and Action

Comprehension
Of purposes, subject matter structures, ideas within and outside the discipline

Transformation
Preparation: critical interpretation and analysis of texts, structuring and segmenting, development of a curricular repertoire, and clarification of purposes
Representation: use of a representational repertoire which includes analogies, metaphors, examples, demonstrations, explanations, and so forth
Selection: choice from among an instructional repertoire which includes modes of teaching, organizing, managing, and arranging
Adaptation and Tailoring to Student Characteristics: consideration of conceptions, preconceptions, misconceptions, and difficulties, language, culture, and motivations, social class, gender, age, ability, aptitude, interests, self concepts, and attention

Instruction
Management, presentations, interactions, group work, discipline, humor, questioning, and other aspects of active teaching, discovery or inquiry instruction, and the observable forms of classroom teaching

Evaluation
Checking for student understanding during interactive teaching
Testing student understanding at the end of lessons or units
Evaluating one's own performance, and adjusting for experiences

Reflection
Reviewing, reconstructing, reenacting, and critically analyzing one's own and the class's performance, and grounding explanations in evidence

New Comprehensions
Of purposes, subject matter, students, teaching, and self
Consolidation of new understandings, and learnings from experience

taught. To reason one's way through an act of teaching is to think one's way from the subject matter as understood by the teacher into the minds and motivations of learners. Transformations, therefore, require some combination or ordering of the following processes, each of which employs a kind of repertoire: (1) preparation (of the given text materials) including the process of critical interpretation, (2) representation of the ideas in the form of new analogies, metaphors, and so forth, (3) instructional selections from among an array of teaching methods and models, and (4) adaptation of these representations to the general characteristics of the children to be taught, as well as (5) tailoring the adaptations to the specific youngsters in the classroom. These forms of transformation, these aspects of the process wherein one moves from personal comprehension to preparing for the comprehension of others, are the essence of the act of pedagogical reasoning, of teaching as thinking, and of planning—whether explicitly or implicitly—the performance of teaching.

Preparation involves examining and critically interpreting the materials of instruction in terms of the teacher's own understanding of the subject matter (Ben-Peretz, 1975). That is, one scrutinizes the teaching material in light of one's own comprehension and asks whether it is "fit to be taught." This process of preparation will usually include (1) detecting and correcting errors of omission and commission in the text, and (2) the crucial processes of structuring and segmenting the material into forms better adapted to the teacher's understanding and, in prospect, more suitable for teaching. One also scrutinizes educational purposes or goals. We find examples of this preparation process in a number of our studies. Preparation certainly draws upon the availability of a curricular repertoire, a grasp of the full array of extant instructional materials, programs, and conceptions.

Representation involves thinking through the key ideas in the text or lesson and identifying the alternative ways of representing them to students. What analogies, metaphors, examples, demonstrations, simulations, and the like can help to build a bridge between the teacher's comprehen-

sion and that desired for the students? Multiple forms of representation are desirable. We speak of the importance of a representational repertoire in this activity.[10]

Instructional selections occur when the teacher must move from the reformulation of content through representations to the embodiment of representations in instructional forms or methods. Here the teacher draws upon an instructional repertoire of approaches or strategies of teaching. This repertoire can be quite rich, including not only the more conventional alternatives such as lecture, demonstration, recitation, or seatwork, but also a variety of forms of cooperative learning, reciprocal teaching, Socratic dialogue, discovery learning, project methods, and learning outside the classroom setting.

Adaptation is the process of fitting the represented material to the characteristics of the students. What are the relevant aspects of student ability, gender, language, culture, motivations, or prior knowledge and skills that will affect their responses to different forms of representation and presentation? What student conceptions, misconceptions, expectations, motives, difficulties, or strategies might influence the ways in which they approach, interpret, understand, or misunderstand the material? Related to adaptation is tailoring, which refers to the fitting of the material to the specific students in one's classrooms rather than to students in general. When a teacher thinks through the teaching of something, the activity is a bit like the manufacture of a suit of clothing. Adaptation is like preparing a suit of a particular style, color, and size that can be hung on a rack. Once it is prepared for purchase by a particular customer, however, it must be tailored to fit perfectly.

Moreover, the activity of teaching is rarely engaged with a single student at a time. This is a process for which the special term "tutoring" is needed. When we speak of teaching under typical school circumstances, we describe an activity which brings instruction to groups of at least fifteen—or more typically, twenty-five to thirty-five—students. Thus, the tailoring of instruction entails fitting representations not only to particular students, but also to a group of a particular size, disposition, receptivity, and interpersonal "chemistry."

All these processes of transformation result in a plan, or set of strategies, to present a lesson, unit, or course. Up to this point, of course, it is all a rehearsal for the performances of teaching which have not yet occurred. Pedagogical reasoning is as much a part of teaching as is the actual performance itself. Reasoning does not end when instruction begins. The activities of comprehension, transformation, evaluation, and reflection continue to occur during active teaching. Teaching itself becomes a stimulus for thoughtfulness as well as for action. We therefore turn next to the performance that consummates all this reasoning in the act of instruction.

Instruction.   This activity involves the observable performance of the variety of teaching acts. It includes many of the most crucial aspects of pedagogy: organizing and managing the classroom; presenting clear explanations and vivid descriptions; assigning and checking work; and interacting effectively with students through questions and probes, answers and reactions, and praise and criticism. It thus includes management, explanation, discussion, and all the observable features of effective direct and heuristic instruction already well-documented in the research literature on effective teaching.

We have compelling reasons to believe that there are powerful relationships between the comprehension of a new teacher and the styles of teaching employed. An example, based on the research of Grossman (1985), will illustrate this point.

> Colleen had completed a master's degree in English before entering a teacher education program. She expressed confidence in her command of the subject matter and began her internship with energy and enthusiasm. Her view of literature and its teaching was highly interpretive and interactive. She saw fine literature as layered communication, capable of many diverse readings and interpretations. Moreover, she felt that these various readings should be provided by her students through their own careful reading of the texts.

> Colleen was so committed to helping students learn to read texts carefully, a habit of mind not often found among the young or old, that she constructed one assignment in which each student was asked to bring to school the lyrics of a favorite rock song. (She may have realized that some of these song lyrics were of questionable taste, but preferred to maximize motivation rather than discretion in this particular unit.) She then asked them to rewrite each line of the song, using synonyms or paraphrases to replace every original word. For many, it was the first time they had looked at any piece of text with such care.

> When teaching a piece of literature, Colleen performed in a highly interactive manner, drawing out student ideas about a phrase or line, accepting multiple competing interpretations as long as the student could offer a defense of the construction by reference to the text itself. Student participation was active and hearty in these sessions. Based on these observations, one would have characterized Colleen's teaching style with descriptors such as student-centered, discussion-based, occasionally Socratic, or otherwise highly interactive.

> Several weeks later, however, we observed Colleen teaching a unit on grammar. Although she had completed two university degrees in English, Colleen had received almost no preparation in prescriptive grammar. However, since a typical high school English class includes some grammar in addition to the literature and writing, it was impossible to avoid teaching the subject. She expressed some anxiety about it during a pre-observational interview.

> Colleen looked like a different teacher during that lesson. Her interactive style evaporated. In its place was a highly didactic, teacher-directed, swiftly paced combination of lecture and tightly-controlled recitation: Socrates replaced by DISTAR. I sometimes refer to such teaching as the Admiral Farragut style, "Damn the questions, full speed ahead." Students were not given opportunities to raise questions or offer alternative views. After the session, she confessed to the observer that she had actively avoided making eye contact with one particular student in the front row because that youngster always had good questions or ideas and in this particular lesson Colleen really didn't want to encourage either, because she wasn't sure of the answers. She was uncertain about the content and adapted her instructional style to allay her anxiety.[11]

Colleen's case illustrates the ways in which teaching behavior is bound up with comprehension and transformation of understanding. The flexible and interactive teaching techniques that she uses are simply not available to her when she does not understand the topic to be taught. Having examined the processes of pedagogical reasoning and performance that are prospective and enactive in nature, we now move to those that are retrospective.

Evaluation.   This process includes the on-line checking for understanding and misunderstanding that a teacher must employ while teaching interactively, as well as the more formal testing and evaluation that teachers do to provide feedback and grades. Clearly, checking for such understanding requires all the forms of teacher comprehension and transformation described above. To understand what a pupil understands will require a deep grasp of both the material to be taught and the processes of learning. This understanding must be specific to particular school subjects and to individual topics within the subject. This represents another way in which what we call pedagogical content knowledge is used. Evaluation is also directed at one's own teaching and at the lessons and materials employed in those activities. In that sense it leads directly to reflection.

Reflection.   This is what a teacher does when he or she looks back at the teaching and learning that has occurred, and reconstructs, reenacts, and/or recaptures the events, the emotions, and the accomplishments. It is that set of processes through which a professional learns from experience. It can be done alone or in concert, with the help of recording devices or solely through memory. Here again, it is likely that reflection is not merely a disposition (as in, "she's such a reflective person!") or a set of strategies, but also the use of particular kinds of analytic knowledge brought to bear on one's work (Richert, in preparation). Central to this process will be a review of the teaching in comparison to the ends that were sought.

New comprehension.   Thus we arrive at the new beginning, the expectation that through acts of

teaching that are "reasoned" and "reasonable" the teacher achieves new comprehension, both of the purposes and of the subjects to be taught, and also of the students and of the processes of pedagogy themselves. There is a good deal of transient experiential learning among teachers, characterized by the "aha" of a moment that is never consolidated and made part of a new understanding or a reconstituted repertoire (Brodkey, 1986). New comprehension does not automatically occur, even after evaluation and reflection. Specific strategies for documentation, analysis, and discussion are needed.

Although the processes in this model are presented in sequence, they are not meant to represent a set of fixed stages, phases, or steps. Many of the processes can occur in different order. Some may not occur at all during some acts of teaching. Some may be truncated, others elaborated. In elementary teaching, for example, some processes may occur that are ignored or given short shrift in this model. But a teacher should demonstrate the capacity to engage in these processes when called upon, and teacher education should provide students with the understandings and performance abilities they will need to reason their ways through and to enact a complete act of pedagogy, as represented here.

KNOWLEDGE, TEACHING POLICY, AND EDUCATIONAL REFORM

The investigations, deliberations, and debates regarding what teachers should know and know how to do have never been more active. Reform efforts are underway: they range from raising standards for admission into teacher education programs, to establishing state and national examinations for teachers; from insisting that teacher preparation require at least five years of higher education (because there is so much to learn), to organizing elaborate programs of new-teacher induction and mentoring (because the most important learning and socialization can occur only in the workplace).

Most of the current reforms rest on the call for greater professionalization in teaching, with higher standards for entry, greater emphasis on the scholarly bases for practice, more rigorous programs of theoretical and practical preparation, better strategies for certification and licensure, and changes in the workplace that permit greater autonomy and teacher leadership. In large measure, they call for teaching to follow the model of other professions that define their knowledge bases in systematic terms, require extended periods of preparation, socialize neophytes into practice with extended periods of internship or residency, and employ demanding national and state certification procedures.

Implicit in all these reforms are conceptions of teacher competence. Standards for teacher education and assessment are necessarily predicated on images of teaching and its demands. The conception of the knowledge base of teaching presented in this chapter differs in significant ways from many of those currently existing in the policy community. The emphasis on the integral relationships between teaching and the scholarly domains of the liberal arts makes clear that teacher education is the responsibility of the entire university, not the schools or departments of education alone. Moreover, teachers cannot be adequately assessed by observing their teaching performance without reference to the content being taught.

The conception of pedagogical reasoning places emphasis upon the intellectual basis for teaching performance rather than on behavior alone. If this conception is to be taken seriously, both the organization and content of teacher education programs and the definition of the scholarly foundations of education will require revision. Teacher education programs would no longer be able to confine their activity to the content-free domains of pedagogy and supervision. An emphasis on pedagogical content knowledge would permeate the teacher preparation curriculum. A national board examination for teachers would focus upon the teacher's ability to reason about teaching and to teach specific topics, and to base his or her actions on premises that can bear the scrutiny of the professional community.

We have an obligation to raise standards in the interests of improvement and reform, but we must avoid the creation of rigid orthodoxies. We must achieve standards without standardization. We must be careful that the knowledge-base approach does not produce an overly technical image of teaching, a scientific enterprise that has lost its soul. The serious problems in medicine and other health professions arise when doctors treat the disease rather than the person, or when the professional or personal needs of the practitioner are permitted to take precedence over the responsibilities to those being served.

CONCLUSION

Needed change cannot occur without risk. The currently incomplete and trivial definitions of teaching held by the policy community comprise a far greater danger to good education than does a more serious attempt to formulate the knowledge base. Nancy represents a model of pedagogical excellence that should become the basis for the new reforms. A proper understanding of the knowledge base of teaching, the sources for that knowledge, and the complexities of the pedagogical process will make the emergence of such teachers more likely.

ENDNOTES

Preparation of this paper was made possible, in part, by grants to Stanford University from the Spencer Foundation for the project, Knowledge Growth in a Profession, and from the Carnegie Corporation of New York for research on the development of new modes of assessment for teachers, Lee S. Shulman, principal investigator. Suzanne Wilson, Pamela Grossman, and Judy Shulman provided criticism and counsel when it was most needed. A longer version of this paper will be available from the Carnegie Forum on Education and the Economy. The views expressed are the author's and are not necessarily shared by these organizations or individuals.

1. Most of the empirical work on which this essay rests has been conducted with secondary-school teachers, both new and experienced. While I firmly believe that much of the emphasis to be found here on the centrality of content knowledge in pedagogy holds reasonably well for the elementary level as well, I am reluctant to make that claim too boldly. Work currently underway at the elementary level, both by Leinhardt (1983) and her colleagues (for example,

Leinhardt & Greeno, 1985; Leinhardt & Smith, 1986) and by our own research group, may help clarify this matter.

2. There are several aspects of this formulation that are unfortunate, if only for the impression they may leave. The rhetoric of the analysis, for example, is not meant to suggest that education is reduced to knowledge transmission, the conveying of information from an active teacher to a passive learner, and that this information is viewed as product rather than process. My conception of teaching is not limited to direct instruction. Indeed, my affinity for discovery learning and inquiry teaching is both enthusiastic and ancient (for example, Shulman & Keislar, 1966). Yet even in those most student-centered forms of education, where much of the initiative is in the hands of the students, there is little room for teacher ignorance. Indeed, we have reason to believe that teacher comprehension is even more critical for the inquiry-oriented classroom than for its more didactic alternative.

Central to my concept of teaching are the objectives of students learning how to understand and solve problems, learning to think critically and creatively as well as learning facts, principles, and rules of procedure. Finally, I understand that the learning of subject matter is often not an end in itself, but rather a vehicle employed in the service of other goals. Nevertheless, at least at the secondary level, subject matter is a nearly universal vehicle for instruction, whatever the ultimate goal.

3. This formulation is drawn from the teacher's perspective and, hence, may be viewed by some readers as overly teacher-centered. I do not mean to diminish the centrality of student learning for the process of education, nor the priority that must be given to student learning over teacher comprehension. But our analyses of effective teaching must recognize that outcomes *for teachers* as well as pupils must be considered in any adequate treatment of educational outcomes.

4. I have attempted this list in other publications, though, admittedly, not with great cross-article consistency (for example, Shulman, 1986b; Shulman & Sykes, 1986; Wilson, Shulman & Richert, in press).

5. It might be argued that the sources of skilled performances are typically tacit, and unavailable to the practitioner. But teaching requires a special kind of expertise or artistry, for which explaining and showing are the central features. Tacit knowledge among teachers is of limited value if the teachers are held responsible for explaining what they do and why they do it, to their students, their communities, and their peers.

6. The metaphor of commuting is not used idly. The journey between learner and teacher is not one-way. In the best teachers, as well as in the more marginal, new learning is constantly required for teaching.

7. The direction and sequence of instruction can be quite different as well. Students can literally initiate the process, proceeding by discovering, inventing, or inquiring, to prepare their own representations and transformations. Then it is the role of the teacher to respond actively and creatively to those student initiatives. In each case the teacher needs to possess both the comprehension and the capacities for transformation. In the student-initiated case, the flexibility to respond, judge, nurture, and provoke student creativity will depend on the teacher's own capacities for sympathetic transformation and interpretation.

8. Under some conditions, teaching may begin with "given a group of students." It is likely that at the early elementary grades, or in special education classes or other settings where children have been brought together for particular reasons, the starting point for reasoning about instruction may well be at the characteristics of the group itself. There are probably some days when a teacher necessarily uses the youngsters as a starting point.

9. Other views of teaching will also begin with comprehension, but of something other than the ideas or text to be taught and learned. They may focus on comprehension of a particular set of values, of the characteristics, needs, interests, or propensities of a particular individual or group of learners. But some sort of comprehension (or self-conscious confusion, wonder, or ignorance) will always initiate teaching.

10. The centrality of representation to our conception of pedagogical reasoning is important for relating our model of teaching to more general approaches to the study of human thinking and problem solving. Cognitive psychologists (for example, Gardner, 1986; Marton, 1986; Norman, 1980) argue that processes of internal representation are key elements in any cognitive psychology. "To my mind, the major accomplishment of cognitive science has been the clear demonstration of the validity of positing a level of mental representation: a set of constructs that can be invoked for the explanation of cognitive phenomena, ranging from visual perception to story comprehension" (Gardner, 1986, p. 383). Such a linkage between models of pedagogy and models of more general cognitive functioning can serve as an important impetus for the needed study of teacher thinking.

11. In no way do I wish to imply that effective lectures are out of place in a high school classroom. On the contrary, good lecturing is an indispensable teaching technique. In this case I am more interested in the relationship between knowledge and teaching. It might be suggested

that this teaching style is more suited to grammar than to literature because there is little to discuss or interpret in a grammar lesson. I do not agree, but will not pursue the matter here. In Colleen's case, the rationale for a linear lecture was not grounded in such an argument, but quite clearly in her concern for limiting the range of possible deviations from the path she had designed.

REFERENCES

Baxter, J. (in preparation). *Teacher explanations in computer programming: A study of knowledge transformation.* Unpublished doctoral dissertation in progress, Stanford University.

Ben-Peretz, M. (1975). The concept of curriculum potential. *Curriculum Theory Network, 5,* 151–159.

Berliner, D. (1986). In pursuit of the expert pedagogue. *Educational Researcher, 15*(7), 5–13.

Bloom, B. S. (1976). *Human characteristics and school learning.* New York: McGraw-Hill.

Brodkey, J. J. (1986). *Learning while teaching: Self-assessment in the classroom.* Unpublished doctoral dissertation, Stanford University.

Brophy, J. J., & Good, T. (1986). Teacher behavior and student achievement. In M. C. Wittrock (Ed.), *Handbook of research on teaching* (3rd ed., pp. 328–375). New York: Macmillan.

Carnegie Task Force on Teaching as a Profession. (1986). *A nation prepared: Teachers for the 21st century.* Washington, DC: Carnegie Forum on Education and the Economy.

Clement, J. (1982). Students' preconceptions in introductory mechanics. *American Journal of Physics, 50,* 67–71.

Dewey, J. (1904). The relation of theory to practice in education. In C. A. McMurry (Ed.), *The relation of theory to practice in the education of teachers* (Third Yearbook of the National Society for the Scientific Study of Education, Part I). Bloomington, IL: Public School Publishing.

Erlwanger, S. H. (1975). Case studies of children's conceptions of mathematics, Part I. *Journal of Children's Mathematical Behavior, 1,* 157–283.

Fenstermacher, G. (1978). A philosophical consideration of recent research on teacher effectiveness. In L. S. Shulman (Ed.), *Review of research in education* (Vol. 6, pp. 157–185). Itasca, IL: Peacock.

Fenstermacher, G. (1986). Philosophy of research on teaching: Three aspects. In M. C. Wittrock (Ed.), *Handbook of research on teaching* (3rd ed., pp. 37–49). New York: Macmillan.

Gage, N. L. (1978). *The scientific basis of the art of teaching.* New York: Teachers College Press.

Gage, N. L. (1986). *Hard gains in the soft sciences: The case of pedagogy.* Bloomington, IN: Phi Delta Kappa.

Gardner, H. (1986). *The mind's new science: A history of cognitive revolution.* New York: Basic Books.

Green, T. F. (1971). *The activities of teaching.* New York: McGraw-Hill.

Grossman, P. (1985). *A passion for language: From text to teaching* (Knowledge Growth in Teaching Publications Series). Stanford: Stanford University, School of Education.

Gudmundsdottir, S. (in preparation). *Knowledge use among experienced teachers: Four case studies of high school teaching.* Unpublished doctoral dissertation in progress, Stanford University.

Hashweh, M. Z. (1985). *An exploratory study of teacher knowledge and teaching: The effects of science teachers' knowledge of subject-matter and their conceptions of learning on their teaching.* Unpublished doctoral dissertation, Stanford University.

The Holmes Group (1986). *Tomorrow's teachers: A report of the Holmes Group.* East Lansing, MI: Author.

Leinhardt, G. (1983). Novice and expert knowledge of individual students' achievement. *Educational Psychologist, 18,* 165–179.

Leinhardt, G., & Greeno, J. G. (1986). The cognitive skill of teaching. *Journal of Educational Psychology, 78,* 75–95.

Leinhardt, G., & Smith, D. A. (1985). Expertise in mathematics instruction: Subject matter knowledge. *Journal of Educational Psychology, 77,* 247–271.

Marton, F. (1986). *Towards a pedagogy of content.* Unpublished manuscript, University of Gothenburg, Sweden.

Norman, D. A. (1980). What goes on in the mind of the learner? In W. J. McKeachie (Ed.), *New directions for teaching and learning: Learning, cognition, and college teaching* (Vol. 2). San Francisco: Jossey-Bass.

Petrie, H. (1986, May). *The liberal arts and sciences in the teacher education curriculum.* Paper presented at the Conference on Excellence in Teacher Preparation through the Liberal Arts, Muhlenberg College, Allentown, PA.

Richert, A. (in preparation). *Reflex to reflection: Facilitating reflection in novice teachers.* Unpublished doctoral dissertation in progress, Stanford University.

Rosenshine, B. (1986, April). *Unsolved issues in teaching content: A critique of a lesson on Federalist Paper No. 10.* Paper presented at the meeting of the American Educational Research Association, San Francisco, CA.

Rosenshine, B., & Stevens, R. S. (1986). Teaching functions. In M. C. Wittrock (Ed.), *Handbook of research on teaching* (3rd ed., pp. 376–391). New York: Macmillan.

Rosenthal, R., & Jacobson, L. (1968). *Pygmalion in the classroom.* New York: Holt, Rinehart & Winston.

Scheffler, I. (1965). *Conditions of knowledge: An introduction to epistemology and education.* Chicago: University of Chicago Press.

Schwab, J. J. (1964). The structure of the disciplines: Meanings and significances. In G. W. Ford & L. Pugno (Eds.), *The structure of knowledge and the curriculum.* Chicago: Rand McNally.

Schwab, J. J. (1983). The practical four: Something for curriculum professors to do. *Curriculum Inquiry, 13,* 239–265.

Shulman, L. S. (1986a). Paradigms and research programs for the study of teaching. In M. C. Wittrock (Ed.), *Handbook of research on teaching* (3rd ed., pp. 3–36). New York: Macmillan.

Shulman, L. S. (1986b). Those who understand: Knowledge growth in teaching. *Educational Researcher, 15*(2), 4–14.

Shulman, L. S., & Keislar, E. R. (Eds.). (1966). *Learning by discovery: A critical appraisal.* Chicago: Rand McNally.

Shulman, L. S., & Sykes, G. (1986, March). *A national board for teaching?: In search of a bold standard* (Paper commissioned for the Task Force on Teaching as a Profession, Carnegie Forum on Education and the Economy).

Smith, B. O. (1980). *A design for a school of pedagogy.* Washington, DC: U.S. Department of Education.

Sykes, G. (1986). *The social consequences of standardsetting in the professions* (Paper commissioned for the Task Force on Teaching as a Profession, Carnegie Forum on Education and the Economy).

Wilson, S. M., Shulman, L. S., & Richert, A. (in press). "150 different ways" of knowing: Representations of knowledge in teaching. In J. Calderhead (Ed.), *Exploring teacher thinking.* Sussex, Eng.: Holt, Rinehart & Winston.

DISCUSSION QUESTIONS

1. Why is research on teacher effectiveness on its own an insufficient source for defining the knowledge base of teaching?
2. In what ways are (a) content area scholarship, (b) educational materials and structures, (c) formal educational scholarship, and (d) wisdom of practice integral components of the teacher knowledge base?
3. Which domains should comprise the conception of teacher competence?
4. What do you think teachers should know and be able to do as a result of their training?
5. Should teacher education require national board examinations for certification? Why? Why not?

12

Investigations of Expertise in Teaching

KATHERINE S. CUSHING
DONNA S. SABERS
DAVID C. BERLINER

FOCUSING QUESTIONS

1. *What factors distinguish expert and novice teachers?*
2. *What elements influence the ways in which experts, advanced beginners, and novices view classrooms?*
3. *How do experts, advanced beginners, and novices define instruction?*
4. *How do experts, advanced beginners, and novices differ in their perception of the teacher's role?*
5. *In what ways do experts, advanced beginners, and novices interpret "typicality" within classrooms?*

What makes an expert teacher an expert? The authors conducted studies aimed at unraveling the nature of expertise in teaching. Following the general model of expertise in many fields, they studied expert teachers, advanced beginners, and novices. This chapter contains their findings, conclusions, and recommendations for developing and nurturing expertise in all teachers.

In this year of the 25th Summer Olympiad we are intrigued by the performances of experts. We hold our collective breath as one-by-one each competitor takes to the track, court, or arena. Who will win the Gold, the Silver, the Bronze? Will the Unified Team from the former Soviet Union and the German Unified Team perform as well as they did in the XV Olympic Winter Games? It is not so much the medal count that intrigues us, but the instinctiveness with which the athletes perform. We know this level of skill comes from years of practice, but these Olympic athletes make it look so easy and graceful.

Like Olympians, the performances of expert teachers also intrigue us. Expert teachers make classroom management and instruction look easy. Yet we know that teaching is a complex task, and that good teaching requires a teacher to do many things at the same time. Griffin has described the ideal teacher as: "well-organized, alert to classroom events, concerned about classroom groups as well as about individuals, and skillful in the management of a complex social system.... The teacher [is able to] diagnose cognitive and social behaviors of students...monitor the understanding of the students...monitor learning as well as...behavior.... The ideal teacher is in command of subject matter and [of] delivering that subject matter so that effective, efficient, and long-term learning takes place."[1] This description of the ideal teacher only serves to draw our attention to the many performance demands on classroom teachers. Some researchers have suggested that elementary teachers have many hundreds of distinct interactions with individual students each day[2]; a teacher's ability to manage these interactions, maintain order, and maintain the instruction flow is testimony to their level of expertise.

In a series of studies conducted at the University of Arizona and Arizona State University we have attempted to unravel the nature of expertise in teaching. In our efforts to add to the knowledge base about pedagogical expertise we asked: What is it that makes an expert teacher an expert? We were particularly interested in whether expert teachers resemble experts in other fields. Further, we believed that if we found differences in the perceptions, understanding, and problem-solving skills of expert and beginning teachers, such findings would have implications for teacher training and certification as well as for discussions about master teacher and career ladder plans.

Three studies, each part of a larger research project, assessed expert-novice differences in processing and using information about students, in perceiving and processing static visual classroom information, and in perceiving and processing dynamic and simultaneous events within a classroom.

The data presented here follow the general model of the development of expertise across many fields proposed by Dreyfus and Dreyfus.[3] They describe five stages: in the novice stage (stage one) behavior is relatively inflexible as context-free rules are followed; the advanced beginner (stage two) begins to meld on-the-job experience with book learning; however, they are still not very flexible in behavior. At the third stage, that of competent performer, behavior becomes more flexible, whereas the proficient performer (stage four) recognizes patterns and inter-relationships and has a holistic understanding of the processes involved. Experts (stage five) have the same integrated, holistic view and also respond effortlessly, fluidly, and appropriately to the demands of the situations with which they are confronted. This heuristic way of thinking about pedagogical expertise and the policy implications of such a model have been described in detail by Berliner.[4]

For these studies we compared the perceptions and performances of three groups of partici-

pants. Experts were junior or senior high school teachers of science or mathematics, identified as outstanding teachers by their supervisors and by members of the research team. Advanced Beginners were those who had completed student teaching or who were in their first year of classroom teaching and who were viewed by supervisory personnel as having the potential to develop into an "excellent" teacher. A third group of participants was designated as Novices. These were individuals employed by business and industry who expressed an interest in classroom teaching but who had no formal teacher training or experience in public school teaching. These individuals had expertise in fields such as computer technology, chemistry, and physics. They indicated an interest in teaching, and we believe they represent those individuals who might enter the teaching profession through an alternative certification route. Details regarding the identification and selection of these individuals are described elsewhere[5]; however, it is important to note that by our criteria they represented the best in each category.

FINDINGS FROM THREE INVESTIGATIONS OF EXPERTISE

Because we were particularly interested in differences in how experts, advanced beginners, and novices see and understand classroom events, we designed three research studies to assess these differences. In the Student Information Task[6] participants were presented with a simulation in which they were asked to "take over" a science or mathematics class six weeks into the school year. After reviewing classroom materials and information about individual students and student performance, participants were asked to plan the first two days of instruction, and then to explain their lesson plans and answer questions about students, instruction, and classroom management.

In the Slide Task[7] participants were asked to view and interpret static information: slides of classroom instruction. This included both a one-second viewing of particular slides, and the viewing of a sequence of 50 slides depicting a classroom lesson. While viewing the sequence of slides, participants had control of the pace of the slide presentation, and were asked to stop and comment on slides that caught their attention.

In the Simultaneity Task[8] participants were asked to simultaneously view three video monitors of classroom instruction and then to answer both general and specific questions about what they saw. During a second viewing participants were asked to "talk aloud" about what they were viewing and to indicate which monitor they were referring to by touching a designated computer key.

For each task, propositions suggested interesting contrasts among groups. Patterns of differences across tasks were also discernable. This article presents findings in the form of propositions that appear consistent in these three tasks. Each proposition is followed by an explanation and excerpts from individual protocols, which instantiate these findings.

PROPOSITION ONE: EXPERTS, ADVANCED BEGINNERS, AND NOVICES DIFFER IN THEIR PERCEPTIONS AND UNDERSTANDING OF CLASSROOM EVENTS

Perhaps because of their classroom experience, experts viewed the visual materials presented to them differently than did either advanced beginners or novices. In all three tasks, experts acted in one of two very different ways: either they made hypotheses to explain or interpret the information presented, or they were very cautious and refrained from interpreting the information presented to them. On the other hand, advanced beginners and novices provided literal and often valid descriptions of the information presented, seeming to appreciate and accept as valid the information provided to them. Lacking in the protocols of the advanced beginners and novices was interpretation of the meaning of this information for instructional purposes.

For example, on the Student Information Task experts were much less interested than either advanced beginners or novices in remembering specific "facts" about students, but instead indicated that they would like to develop their own, very personal feeling for the students. In describing this preference experts stated:

> Expert 6: I didn't read the [student information] cards. I never do, unless there's a comment about a physical impairment such as hearing or sight or something I get from the nurse. I never want to place a judgment on the students before they start. I find I have a higher success rate if I don't.... My expectations going in are the same for everybody. So if I bias that by any knowledge other than the fact that I presume they can succeed, then I feel that I might not give them a fair chance going into the class.
>
> Expert 8: I think it's good reference material [information left by the previous teacher], but I sure wouldn't put a whole lot of stock in it.

Novices, however, paid serious attention to the comments left by the previous teacher on the student information cards and used that information for categorizing students. For example, novices reported:

> Novice 1: I sorted the bad kids from the good kids from some of the ones that were just good-natured, if they liked to work, that type of thing.
>
> Novice 4: I went through her student cards and also went through test scores and tried to divide the students into three groups, one group which I thought might be disruptive, one which I thought would not be disruptive and that wouldn't need intense watching, and the third group I really didn't know because the back of the card was blank.

Thus, novices appeared to consider the teacher's comments on the student information cards as accurately reflecting the students in the classroom. As such, they believed that information was relevant when planning instruction. Perhaps due to inexperience or a lack of confidence in their own instructional skills, novices heeded all the material presented them and appeared unable to filter and judge the relevancy of different information.

This interpretative-descriptive distinction in the responses among group members was also apparent in the Slide Task where participants viewed static information of classroom scenes. The following typical comments were provided by experts after a one second viewing of a classroom slide:

> Expert 1: It's a hands-on activity of some type. Group work with a male and female of maybe late junior high school age.
>
> Expert 8: A group of students maybe doing small group discussion or a project as seats were not in rows.

Expert responses indicate that what is important to "see" during this brief viewing is what is happening instructionally for students in the classroom. Advanced beginners and novices, on the other hand, provided literal, and quite accurate, descriptions of the slides:

> Advanced Beginner 3: A room full of students sitting at tables.
>
> Advanced Beginner 4: Two students at the chalkboard working.
>
> Novice 3: A fellow and girl in the foreground standing. She had her hand near her face—other activity in the background.
>
> Novice 4: Whole classroom—teacher standing up front, windows behind him. Chalkboard to left of room.

Such limited information, while accurate, emphasizes the different meanings group members bring to classroom observations. Only the experts provided an instructional interpretation of what was observed.

Findings from the Slide Task were confirmed in the Simultaneity Task where participants were asked to view and respond to dynamic rather than static information. In this task, experts were better able to monitor all three screens and to respond to the audio cues, whereas advanced beginners experienced difficulty, and novices reported it was "almost impossible" to watch all three video monitors at once. Further, the responses of the experts indicated they were, once again, interpreting and making sense of the classroom events they were viewing. Examples from protocols follow:

> Expert 2: In the center monitor, I hear a buzzer and nobody is getting up, so I assume that's some sort of a warning bell that…indicates a certain length of time till the end of the period.
>
> Expert 3: On the left-hand monitor, when the bell rings it appears that students know exactly what they're supposed to do without any prior instruction. They get right to work.
>
> Expert 4: Again viewing the middle monitor, I think there is an indication here of the type of structure of the classroom. It's pretty loose, the kids come in and go out without checking with the teacher.

On the other hand, advanced beginners and novices generally focused on the middle monitor and, for the most part, described what they observed happening in a step-by-step, almost radio announcer-type fashion:

> Advanced Beginner 2: Middle monitor, the boy in red, was talking to someone else, while the teacher was talking.
>
> Advanced Beginner 3: In the middle monitor, the teacher's reminding the students that it's very important to label all their work, or they will receive no credit.

In all three tasks, experts were better able than either advanced beginners or novices to make sense of and interpret classroom phenomena, whether presented as archival and anecdotal information, static visual information, or dynamic, simultaneous information. The experts focused on events that had instructional implications. In contrast, advanced beginners and novices, not knowing what was important instructionally, provided descriptions of what they saw, but did not provide interpretations. This interpretative-descriptive difference has important implications for classroom management and instruction. If we extrapolate from these studies, we would expect the expert teachers to better understand and make sense of what was happening in the classroom than beginning teachers. Expert teachers would attend to different information, whether presented through the visual or auditory mode, and would be better able to monitor instructional activities and management issues.

PROPOSITION TWO: EXPERTS, ADVANCED BEGINNERS, AND NOVICES DIFFER IN THE ROLE THEY ASSUME IN CLASSROOM INSTRUCTION

In all three tasks, participants were asked to attend to, focus on, or comment about anything they believed important for classroom management or instruction. We have already noted differences among group members in how they perceive and understand classroom events—now we find differences among group members in how they define instruction and the role of the teacher. Experts' comments focused on the role of the teacher as instructor and monitor of student learning; they made evaluative comments or suggestions on ways in which instruction might be modified or improved to ensure student learning. While advanced beginners and novices were generally as aware of "off-task" student behaviors as experts, the comments of advanced beginners and novices generally focused on issues of management or control, rather than on issues of instructional methodology or content.

In the Student Information Task, experts thought differently about preparing to take over a class than did either advanced beginners or novices. Experts talked about how to get the classroom going, and about how to determine where the students were in terms of understanding the course content. Experts emphasized the importance of breaking the old ties and "starting over"; they stressed that this was a new beginning. Experts' protocols documented routines for beginning a new class and finding out just what it is that students already know. For example, when asked about instructional activities for the first day experts responded:

> Expert 5: Well, Day One, I just wanted to meet the kids and find out who they were. I would lay down what my rules are, what my grading would be, and my policies. Then I would question them to find out what chapters they had covered in this book. And then what I wanted to do was verbally review with them and ask questions to find out the techniques they've been taught….

> Expert 7: The first day I had in mind that I'm going into a brand new class, they possibly don't know me at all. I would quickly go over what I would expect for rules and expectations, raising their hand before talking, courtesy to teacher and students…. I'd give them some rules to follow to get us started.

Both advanced beginners and novices were willing to begin wherever the previous teacher had left off, and although they might spend some time introducing themselves, it was with the idea of continuing, not starting over

> Advanced Beginner 1: I would first introduce myself…. I might have them introduce themselves. Then I would ask them what their prior teacher expected from them and how she ran the class and what they liked or disliked.
> Novice 2: I guess my biggest problem with the lesson plan was to figure out where they are now and where they were going.

Thus we see that experts choose to make the classroom their own, often changing the instructional techniques and focus of the previous teacher. Advanced beginners and novices, on the other hand, were planning to follow in the previous teacher's footsteps.

This notion of the teacher's role in monitoring instruction emerged clearly in the Slide Task when participants were asked to talk about and make sense of the sequence of classroom slides. Although experts, advanced beginners, and novices all commented about "on-task" and "off-task" behaviors, experts talked, to a much greater degree, about their role (as teacher) of "monitoring" the laboratory experiments, calculations, and laboratory write-ups. For example, about the science slides experts commented: Expert 1: [Slide 61] I would remind people that if they have long hair…it can be a real hazard and it needs to be tied back or somehow held back.

> Expert 1: [Slide 9] [I would] monitor situations where you've got water up on high (boiling water above a Bunsen burner)…[these are] not real stable situations that you could get burns on.

Expert 1: [Slide 21] [I would] probably go around and just monitor making sure that they're reading the right kinds of observations. Just make some visual checks on their data that they're recording…[maybe] give them a little guidance.

Throughout the rest of the slides this expert continually offered suggestions about what he would do to ensure student learning was "on track" and to alleviate management concerns before they became issues needing attention. This expert's comments were not atypical—examples from protocols of other experts who participated in this study document consistent monitoring of the class activity and student behavior to ensure optimal learning.

Only one advanced beginner discussed the instructional role of monitoring, and none of the novices commented on this instructional activity. Instead, members of both groups made more comments related to behavioral management and control. For example, from the science lesson protocol:

Novice 2: [Slide 20] The one girl isn't paying attention while the other is adding something to her test tube.

Novice 2: [Slide 24] We've got a lot of movement, conversing back and forth between groups. That's potentially a problem.

Novice 3: [Slide 11] Something is going on in the background. I don't know what they are doing.

Novice 3: [Slide 34] Now they're horsing around in the back.

And from the mathematics protocols:

Advanced Beginner 4: [Slide 13] This is where the young fellow…was out of his seat. A potential problem.

Advanced Beginner 5: [Slide 9] This is the type of picture you like to see…all the students are doing work…

Thus, advanced beginners and novices again described what they saw and expressed concerns about behavior, but appeared less likely to focus on the role of the teacher in either classroom management or instruction. Experts, on the other hand, appeared comfortable with the role of assessing classroom events in terms of the teacher's role in instructional activities, and they seemed less worried about management issues.

In the Simultaneity Task, experts, advanced beginners, and novices differed in their interpretations of what instructional strategies were used by the teacher. While all agreed that lecture was the primary instructional methodology, experts provided details, explanations, and interpretations of the instruction, whereas advanced beginners and novices tended to focus on the materials the teacher used rather than the actual instruction, as if the materials, themselves, were the instruction. Examples from representative protocols follow:

Expert 4: The teacher wanted to have, I think, a lot of classroom interaction…. I think the technique that she used was very low-key, perhaps a process type approach to teaching science, rather than a very structured approach.

Expert 5: It was generally a "stand-up-in-front" type lecture over the material. It wasn't a guided practice or anything. It wasn't keyed toward questions and answers of what they were looking at.

Expert 6: This was a teacher-centered class! The teacher had the information to present. The students were there to listen and to assimilate. There wasn't any evidence of any inquiry or any hands-on activities.

Excerpts from the advanced beginner and novice protocols revealed different concerns:

Advanced Beginner 1: It looks…well, mostly lecture…. Some use of media. She used the overhead a little bit.

Advanced Beginner 4: She did lecture near the beginning with the overhead projector. She was using some audio-visual things.

Novice 1: She gave them a diagram and then she explained it with an overhead projector.

Novice 2: There was an attempt by the teacher to, you know, lecture with some questioning of the students.

From this data, it seems that advanced beginners and novices view instruction as the presentation or use of materials with which one teaches a lesson: methodology (lecture) and materials used (overhead projector) became "instruction" for these participants. On the other hand, experts attempted to understand and interpret the instructional activity they observed and were not particularly interested in the materials the classroom teacher used. To experts, instruction was an interactive process, and they appeared concerned about student participation and the effect of that interactive process (or lack of it) on student learning.

Again, if we extrapolate from this data we would expect the expert teachers to define their role differently than beginning teachers. Experts would perceive themselves as "teachers,"—as instructors of content. Their focus would be on the interactive nature of learning, and on monitoring to ensure that learning occurs. We would expect beginning teachers to be less comfortable with this interactive role and instead focus on classroom management and on the instructional materials or activities needed to present a lesson. Furthermore, we might expect the expert and beginning teachers to begin the school year differently, to interact differently with students, and to focus on different issues.

PROPOSITION THREE: EXPERTS, ADVANCED BEGINNERS, AND NOVICES DIFFER IN THEIR NOTION OF "TYPICALITY" WITHIN THE CLASSROOM ENVIRONMENT

Throughout these studies experts responded to the information presented them, whether visual or auditory, whether as a single event or as multiple events, based on a notion of typicality. Experts talked about typical students, typical classrooms, typical student behavior. In this sense, they were already familiar with management and instructional issues in ways that advanced beginners and novices could never be because they lack the rich experiential base of the experts.

This notion of typicality was apparent in the Student Information Task where experts paid little attention to the student information cards presented to them. After deciding that this new class of students was somehow "typical" of classes in general, the experts seemed to have a clear sense of what kinds of students they would be teaching— most likely this was a result of their numerous years of teaching experience. This finding was not unexpected, for it replicates work done by Calderhead. In his study comparing experienced, student, and novice teachers, Calderhead noted that experienced teachers had acquired a large amount of information about students and, in a sense, "they seemed to 'know' their students before they met them."[9] Advanced beginners and novices did not show that same kind of well developed schemata for students.

In the Slide Task, expert protocols revealed sensitivity to unusual situations that attracted their attention. Experts focused on these atypical situations until they could explain them. When a situation was assessed as "typical," the need for additional processing was reduced. These concerns about "typicality" were rare in the protocols of either advanced beginners or novices.

In the Simultaneity Task, the notion of "typicality" emerged as experts discussed the demands of the task. Experts commented that the task of viewing three monitors, touching a computer key, and talking aloud simultaneously was a fair representation of what they were required to do all day long as classroom teachers. Advanced beginners and novices, on the other hand, found the task difficult and often overwhelming. One novice acknowledged an awareness that he "probably ought" to be able to perform the task better, but found it simply too difficult to do all that was requested of him at once!

Again, based on these studies we might expect beginning and expert teachers to have a different understanding of events within a classroom. Beginning teachers would not always know what to expect, or what was "normal" student behavior, and might respond in ways that increase the confusion or lead to management problems within a classroom. Expert teachers, on the other hand, appear able to identify a wide range of events as typical. Thus, they almost automatically know how to respond or handle those events.

CONCLUSION

We began this paper by comparing the performance of Olympic competitors and expert teachers. We suggested that, as a result of practice, Olympic athletes make their performances look easy and graceful. But it is not just practice. As with teaching expertise, it is much, much more. Expert teachers don't just practice the same techniques over and over again. They stop, reflect on what they are doing, and try different methods. They attend workshops and collaborate with colleagues—always searching for a better way to perfect their craft.

What is it that makes an expert teacher an expert? We believe we have some plausible answers to that question.

Like experts in other fields, expert teachers perceive and understand information in their area of expertise differently from novices. Thus, expert teachers see and make sense of classroom events differently than do beginning teachers. This appears to be the case regardless of how information about those events is presented to the experts. Perhaps because they see and understand classroom events differently they also plan for and deliver instruction differently. Planning differences were evident in the Student Information Task, and more recent studies have documented behavioral and affective differences among expert, advanced beginner, and novice teachers.[10]

Because of these differences it makes little sense to expect the same performances from beginning teachers as we do from experienced and expert teachers. It seems that the first year or two will most likely be spent trying to figure out what is important about students and instruction and management in a classroom. If there are many variables to attend to (students come and go, several different content preparations, the most difficult students to teach) those first few years are likely to be even more difficult. Providing support and help for beginning teachers makes sense. Help could come in many forms: observations of expert performances, mentor experiences, or seminar-discussion-type groups to name but a few. The help offered, however, should not be overwhelming.

Learning to teach is difficult enough so that additional requirements for learning during the first year on the job should be minimal.

Our data suggest that qualitative differences of considerable importance exist among expert teachers, beginning teachers with some training, and those who want to be teachers through the alternative certification route. One example of the importance of these findings concerns alternative certification. However well-meaning these individuals are, and however good they may ultimately become, we believe that when they enter teaching they are fundamentally unenlightened about classrooms. What shall we do about that? As another example, our data suggests that evaluative instruments are unfair if they do not recognize differences between expert and novice teachers. What may be appropriate evaluative criteria for the novice may not be appropriate for the expert.

These data also lead us to conclude that teacher education programs must re-think the nature of their graduates. Teacher education programs do not graduate competent teachers, merely beginners. Thus, the colleges may need to have an educational program that follows up their graduates over the first few years. Perhaps colleges should provide only provisional degrees, certifying only that their graduates are ready for an apprenticeship. Permanent degrees might be issued after three or so years. Our data lead us to believe, also, that the pool of experts, as in chess and other fields, is likely to be small. While such individuals need to be honored and ways must be found to have them stay in classroom teaching, the primary goal of preservice and inservice education in America may be the development and the maintenance of competence. This is a level of performance that virtually all who enter teaching should reach in a few years. The building up of competence, however, and the subsequent growth to a level regarded as expert, does require time. There seem to be few shortcuts since experience is the necessary, though not sufficient, condition for this kind of growth. Episodic and strategic knowledge must be built up and reflected upon, and this cannot occur in a few months or years. This has implications for the tenure laws in states. We would think that five years, rather than three, would be a better point at which to make these important judgments.

Learning the ways one grows from novice to expert in pedagogy is not easy, either for the practitioner or the researcher. But for both of them, the rewards for studying the process are likely to be quite high.

ENDNOTES

1. Gary A. Griffin, "Clinical Teacher Education," *Reality and Reform in Clinical Teacher Education,* eds. J. V. Hoffman and S. A. Edwards (New York: Random House, 1986), 1–24.
2. P. V. Gump, *The Classroom Behavior Setting: Its Nature and Relation to Student Behavior,* final report prepared by the U.S. Office of Education, Bureau of Research (Washington, D.C., 1967) (ED 015 515); P. W. Jackson, *Life in Classrooms* (New York: Holt, Rinehart & Winston, 1968).
3. Hubert L. Dreyfus and Stuart E. Dreyfus, *Mind Over Machine* (New York: Free Press, 1986); see also Patricia Benner, *From Novice to Expert* (Reading, MA: Addison-Wesley, 1984).
4. David C. Berliner, "Implications of Studies of Expertise in Pedagogy for Teacher Education and Evaluation," *New Directions for Teacher Assessment: Proceedings of the 1988 ETS Invitational Conference* (Princeton, NJ: Educational Testing Service, 1989).
5. Donna S. Sabers, Katherine S. Cushing, and David C. Berliner, "Differences Among Teachers in a Task Characterized by Simultaneity, Multidimensionality, and Immediacy," *American Educational Research Journal,* 28 (Spring 1991): 63–88.
6. Kathy Carter, Donna Sabers, Katherine Cushing, Stefinee Pinnegar, and David C. Berliner, "Processing and Using Information About Students: A Study of Expert, Novice, and Postulant Teachers," *Teaching and Teacher Education* 3 (1987): 147–157.
7. Kathy Carter, Katherine Cushing, Donna Sabers, Pamela Stein, and David Berliner, "Expert-Novice Differences in Perceiving and Processing Visual Classroom Information," *Journal of Teacher Education* 39 (May–June, 1988): 25–31.
8. Sabers, Cushing, and Berliner, pp. 63–88.
9. James Calderhead, "Research into Teachers' and Student Teachers' Cognitions: Exploring the Nature of Classroom Practice" (Paper presented at the annual meeting of the American Educational Research Association, Montreal, 1983).
10. Donna Sabers, Katherine Cushing, and David C. Berliner, "Students' Evaluations of Teachers Who Differ in Experience and Expertise" (Paper presented at the annual meeting of the American Educational Research Association, New Orleans, 1988); and Pamela Stein and David C. Berliner, "Expert, Novice and Postulant Teachers' Thoughts During Teaching" (Paper presented at the annual meeting of the American Educational Research Association, New Orleans, 1988).

DISCUSSION QUESTIONS

1. How might the Dreyfus and Dreyfus model of expertise development be used to guide teacher training?
2. What should the role of reflection in teacher training be?
3. Should colleges provide only provisional degrees for teachers? Why? Why not?
4. What changes might be implemented in teacher training programs to facilitate teachers' professional growth during their first few years in the field?
5. How do experts, advanced beginners, and novices perceive the teacher's role?

PRO-CON CHART 2

Should teachers be held accountable for their teaching?

PRO	CON
1. Teaching should be guided by clear objectives and outcomes.	1. Many factors influence teaching and learning that have little to do with measurable objectives and outcomes.
2. Students have a right to receive a quality education, whereby professionals are held accountable for their behavior.	2. Educational accountability is a cooperative responsibility of students, teachers, parents, and taxpayers.
3. Accountability will encourage teachers to uphold high standards for instruction.	3. Teachers can provide instruction but they cannot force students to learn.
4. Feedback from accountability evaluation measures will provide teachers with information about their instructional strengths and weaknesses.	4. Mandating accountability will demoralize teachers and reduce their professional status.
5. Accountability will provide standards that are derived through consensual agreement and will offer objective assessment.	5. There will always be disagreement on who is accountable, for what, and by whom.

CASE STUDY 2

School District Proposes Evaluations by Students

Kamhi County School District in West Suburb had proposed to vote on implementing a change to their current teacher evaluation procedures. The proposed change would permit junior high students to participate in the evaluation process of their teachers, beginning in the spring. As a way of gathering feedback, all thirty principals were asked to complete an anonymous three-part survey. In Parts One and Two, the principals were asked to cite the advantages and disadvantages of this proposed change. In Part Three, they were asked to provide a plan that outlined how they would implement this approach in their building site if it were enacted.

While reading the survey responses, Marilyn Lauter, assistant superintendent for instruction, noticed two items, unsigned letters from both a student and a teacher, that caught her attention. The student argued that because students are consumers of teachers' services, they should have a right to have their voices heard. The teacher's letter expressed complete opposition to the proposed change, citing that students lacked the maturity to provide feedback. The teacher's letter also stated that such a change would advocate the philosophy and teaching styles of certain administrators, thereby limiting the teacher's voice. Furthermore, the letter stated that if the district voted to enact this change as policy, the teachers would probably strike. Lauter was feeling very uncomfortable with both letters, but also knew that more discussion was needed before any policy change should be taken to a vote.

Discuss the issues raised by the student and the teacher and consider the following questions:

1. Should junior high students be involved in the evaluation of their teachers? Why? Why not?

2. If you were the assistant superintendent for instruction, how would you handle this situation?

3. What other approaches might have been used to elicit feedback from the teachers, parents, and students concerning the proposed policy change to the teacher evaluation process?

4. In what ways might students' evaluations of teachers affect their instruction or your own instruction?

5. What evidence does research provide about the ability of junior high students to evaluate teachers?

6. How might teachers and parents in your school district react to this proposed policy change in teacher evaluation procedures?

PART THREE

Curriculum and Learning

INTRODUCTION

What is the relationship between learning and curriculum? What role does motivation play in student achievement? To what extent is higher-order thinking, creativity, and moral education emphasized in curriculum delivery? How have cooperative learning and the use of standards influenced student outcomes? What is the role of character education in students' learning experiences?

In Chapter 13, Carole Ames explains the relationship between motivational concepts and student learning. She points out how teachers, classrooms, and family context influence student motivation. She describes how teachers can plan instruction that enhances student motivation. In Chapter 14, Matthew Lipman distinguishes between critical and ordinary thinking. He suggests that an emphasis on critical thinking will promote intellectual responsibility. He also describes the processes that encourage critical thinking.

Next, Robert Sternberg and Todd Lubart discuss the factors that characterize creative thinking. The authors describe the type of instruction that fosters creative thinking. They suggest that students should be given more responsibility for selecting the type of problems that they investigate, rather than relying on teacher-constructed problems. In Chapter 16, Lawrence Kohlberg describes how moral education promotes the aims of education. He compares the cognitive–developmental approach with other approaches to moral education and discusses the school's role in moral and civic education. Next, Alfie Kohn presents a critical analysis of the limitations of current character education program strategies. He describes why divergent approaches would exemplify a program different from traditional approaches to moral development. He suggests ways that reflection can be used to enhance students' moral growth.

In the final chapter of Part III, Robert Slavin describes how cooperative learning results in improved academic achievement. He describes how cooperative learning techniques enhance the quality of interpersonal relationships.

13

Motivation: What Teachers Need to Know

CAROLE A. AMES

FOCUSING QUESTIONS

1. *Why should teachers be concerned with the concept of motivation?*
2. *How does working for extrinsic versus intrinsic rewards influence student learning?*
3. *Why is the quantitative view of motivation that focuses on intensity, duration, and direction of behavior insufficient in helping teachers understand how motivation influences student learning? Do you agree or disagree?*
4. *How are self-efficacy and attribution related to the concept of motivation?*
5. *What factors influence whether students adopt mastery or performance goals?*

Motivation, one of the foremost problems in education, is often inadequately addressed in typical foundational (educational psychology) courses. In this chapter, Ames clarifies the complex construct of motivation as it relates to learning and offers a revamped curriculum that applies motivation theory and research to practice. She recommends instruction in how motivation constructs relate to each other, to developmental changes, to individual and culturally related differences, and to the classroom context.

There are three things to remember about education. The first one is motivation. The second one is motivation. The third one is motivation.

—Terrell H. Bell

What is it about the academic motivation of students that teachers should know? Certainly, knowledge of motivation concepts, principles, and theories should be basic elements in a foundations course in educational psychology, but this is not really what educational psychology should be about. Teachers need to know how this conceptual knowledge relates to the classroom and to their instructional role in the classroom. Teachers also need to know how to rely on this knowledge when dealing with issues that involve motivational concerns and when making instructional decisions.

For example, consider a not very unusual problem facing a teacher about homework. How can a teacher set homework policy so that students complete the homework and still maintain their interest in the material? Teacher A's policy states that all homework must be turned in daily, that all homework will be graded daily with letter or percentage grades, and that homework counts for 30 percent of the quarter grade. Teacher B's policy states that students are to spend no more than thirty minutes per night on homework, that homework will be graded satisfactory or unsatisfactory, that students can redo and correct their work, and that homework counts for 10 percent of the quarter grade. We may think the stringency of Teacher A's policy might be more effective, but research on motivation would suggest that Teacher B's policy is more likely to fulfill both objectives. At the classroom level, teachers are often faced with a child who continually avoids challenge. At the beginning level, teachers must come together and decide how to structure a reading program so that students will read more but also enjoy reading more. These are simple examples of everyday problems and decisions that involve motivation questions.

Student motivation has, for some time, been described as one of the foremost problems in education.[1] It is certainly one of the problems most commonly cited by teachers. Motivation is important because it contributes to achievement, but it is also important itself as an outcome.

Motivation is not synonymous with achievement, and student motivation cannot necessarily be inferred by looking at achievement test scores. Immediate achievement and test performance are determined by a variety of factors and may even be assured through a variety of ways, and some practices that serve to increase immediate achievement may actually have the effect of diminishing students' interest in learning as well as their long-term involvement in learning. When we talk about motivation as an outcome, we are concerned with students' "motivation to learn."[2] If we place a value on developing a motivation to learn in students, we are concerned with whether students initiate learning activities and maintain an involvement in learning as well as a commitment to the process of learning. Effective schools and effective teachers are those who develop goals, beliefs, and attitudes in students that will sustain a long-term involvement and that will contribute to quality involvement in learning.

If we evaluate our schools and classrooms strictly by how much students achieve, we can easily lose sight of these other educational goals and values. We not only want students to achieve, we want them to value the process of learning and the improvement of their skills, we want them to willingly put forth the necessary effort to develop and apply their skills and knowledge, and we want them to develop a long-term commitment to learning.[3] It is in this sense that motivation is an outcome of education. Students who elect to take advanced science classes because they want to learn more and not just because they think they can do well is an example of this outcome.

It is therefore a first priority to help teachers develop an understanding of why motivation is important. This, indeed, may be a challenge when educational psychology textbooks typically allot only one chapter to motivation, and this chapter usually provides little more than an overview of theories and concepts. Moreover, topics that are intricately related to motivation, such as classroom management, individual differences, testing and evaluation, grouping, and family, are often treated in separate chapters with little or no linkage to motivational concepts and without discussion of motivational processes. Educational psychology is about application; it is not enough to highlight theories or review basic constructs and dot these presentations with a few examples.

Motivation has often been characterized within what has been called a quantitative view of motivation,[4] in which motivation has been described as the *intensity* of behavior, the *direction* of behavior, and the *duration* of behavior.[5] The question for classroom teachers is how to get students to do what you want them to do and to do it consistently over time. This focus, however, does not help us in thinking about how to develop and nurture a motivation to learn in students.

Rather than the duration of behavior (or what has been called engaged time), we need to think about the quality of task engagement. Students need to develop motivational thought patterns that contribute to self-regulated learning. Observing students' time on task does not tell us about what they are attending to, how they are processing information, how they are reacting to their performance, and how they are interpreting feedback. What is critical is the quality of engaged time, not the duration of engaged time.

Rather than the direction of behavior, we need to think about students' goals or reasons for learning. Two students may choose to work on a science project or complete a math worksheet, but they may pursue quite different goals in doing so. A student who works for extrinsic rewards such as grades is likely to engage in very different thought processes and behaviors compared with the student who wants to learn something new about the subject matter or improve a skill. Students' reasons for learning have important consequences for how they approach and engage in learning.

Motivation is also not a matter of increasing the intensity of behavior. The task facing teachers is not one of maximizing or even optimizing the level of motivation; to suggest so perpetuates a view that motivation is a state of arousal or energy. What is assumed is that by increasing or optimizing this state, performance will be enhanced. What we often find, however, is that students can be equally motivated but for very different reasons. Often, it is not that the child is not motivated, but that the child is not motivated to do what *we* want him to do. Rather than focus on differentiating high, low, and optimally motivated students, we instead need to define adaptive and maladaptive or positive and negative motivation patterns and to understand how and why these patterns develop over time.

MOTIVATION CONSTRUCTS

To teach quantitative concepts such as duration, intensity, and direction is not going to help teachers understand how or why students develop adaptive, positive, or effective thought patterns. At a very general level, these thought patterns include goals, beliefs, and attitudes that are involved in how students approach learning situations, engage in the process of learning, and respond to learning experiences. Some examples are self-worth or self-concept of ability, attributions, self-regulated learning, and achievement goals. We need to pay more attention to how teachers can become more successful in socializing these adaptive motivation patterns in students. To set the stage for some later points, let me briefly describe just a few of these constructs.

Self-Worth

Students' self-worth is intricately tied to their self-concept of ability in school settings.[6] This self-concept of ability or self-efficacy has significant consequences for student achievement behavior. Self-efficacy is an expectation or belief that one is capable of performing a specific task, organizing and carrying out required behaviors in a situation.[7] Efficacy is not self-concept of ability in a general sense; it is task- or situation-specific. One's self-worth is implicated when the task is important and when one's ability is threatened. Clearly, in the classroom, all tasks can be made important through the use of external rewards and certain evaluation procedures. Indeed, it is very difficult to look in a classroom and determine what is or is not important to different children. As a consequence, self-efficacy is often a critical factor predicting children's task choices, willingness to try and persist on difficult tasks, and even actual performance in many classrooms.

At first glance, it may appear that increasing student's self-efficacy is merely a matter of increasing children's confidence that they can do well. This is not necessarily the case. Consider an example where a teacher tells all her students that everyone's story is going to become part of the class newspaper. Although all the children can expect success in getting their stories "published," a child may still harbor intense doubts about whether he or she can write a story. The child's self-confidence of ability to write the story has not been changed. Children's self-efficacy does respond positively when they learn to set short-term, realistic goals and are shown how to make progress toward these goals. It is not a matter of convincing them they can do well or even guaranteeing it; it is giving them the strategies to do so.

Children's understanding about their ability is responsive to developmental changes as well as situational influences, and this also has important implications for practice. Young children tend to have an optimistic view of their ability, high expectations for success, and a sort of resilience after failure.[8] Moreover, young children tend to equate effort with ability. To them, hard workers are smart and smart children work hard. As children progress through school, their perceptions of their ability decrease and tend to reflect the teacher's evaluation of their ability. Older children's self-evaluations are more responsive to failure or negative feedback, meaning that they are more likely to adjust their expectations downward after failing. Older children also develop a more differentiated view of effort and ability. While effort can increase the chance for success, ability sets the boundaries of what one's effort can achieve. Effort now becomes the "double-edged sword."[9] Trying hard and failing threatens one's self-concept of ability.

What does this mean to teachers? First, for young children, praising their effort may actually convey to them a sense of confidence in their ability. Because ability and effort are not well differentiated, praise for children's efforts can enhance their self-confidence. However, this does not work with older children. To them, effort and ability are not the same, and they are more concerned with being perceived as able. It is at this point that teachers' and students' preferences diverge. While teachers may value effort and hard work, students prefer to maximize their chances for success and at the same time minimize their effort expenditure. Ability is important in most classrooms; when students' self-concept of ability is threatened, they display failure-avoidance motivation.[10] They engage in failure-avoiding tactics such as not trying, procrastinating, false effort, and even the denial of effort. Why would they do this when these behaviors most assuredly will increase the likelihood of failure? What these behaviors accomplish is reducing the negative implications of failure. From the students' point of view, failure without effort does not negatively reflect on their ability. What they have achieved is "failure with honor."[11]

Attributions and Related Metacognitive Beliefs

The consequences of students' attributions for success and failure for their subsequent achievement behavior have been well described in the research literature. Attributions are related to expectations about the likelihood of success, to judgments about one's own ability, to emotional reactions of pride or hopelessness, and to a willingness to engage in effort-driven cognitions as in self-regulated learning. Over time, children who believe that failure is caused by a lack of ability are likely to exhibit a sense of helplessness. Low expectations, negative affect, and ineffective strategies characterize these children. Children with this dysfunctional attribution pattern are less likely to develop or enact those metacognitive skills that will enable them to tackle a wide range of classroom tasks. By contrast, children who perceive a relationship between their own effort and success are likely to respond to failure or problem situations with a sense of hopefulness and engage in strategic task behavior.[12]

Related to attributional beliefs is students' use of learning strategies and other self-regulated thought processes. These are effort-driven processes, and in that sense, they are motivational. They include, for example, organizing and planning, goal-setting, self-monitoring, and self-instruction. These strategies have been called generic or general learning strategies in that they can be applied across situations and across domains. Of course, students have to have knowledge of the strategies and an awareness of their appropriateness to the situation, but beyond knowledge and awareness is the volitional (motivational) question of whether students will apply the strategies. Whether students choose to engage in such strategic thinking is largely dependent on whether they are willing to apply the necessary effort and whether they believe effort will lead to success. Thus, there are two issues concerning students' strategy use. The first issue concerns whether students have and can apply the necessary skills or strategies. The second issue is motivational: whether students believe that effort is linked to success and that the outcome is worth the effort, and whether they are willing to expend the effort.[13]

Achievement Goals

Related to attributions are students' reasons for learning and their achievement-related goals.[14]

The issue here is *why* students engage in learning and choose to engage in academic tasks rather than whether they choose to do so. For example, students may choose to participate in specific activities to gain external rewards, to develop their skills and ability, or to demonstrate that they are smart by outperforming others or by trying to achieve success with minimal effort.

Students who are interested in learning new things and developing their skills and ability have been described as mastery-oriented. These students are willing to expend the necessary effort to learn something new and confront challenging tasks. It is this mastery-goal orientation that is more likely to produce independent learning and sustained involvement in achievement activities. These students are motivated to learn.

Students who instead perceive that normative performance is important and want to demonstrate that they have ability or to protect their ability when threatened are labeled performance-oriented. Such students tend to think more about their ability than about "how to do the task." Their strategies, such as memorizing facts or reading or studying only what they think will be on a test, tend to serve their performance only over the short term.

Whether students adopt mastery or performance goals is, in part, dependent on their classroom experiences, essentially their perceptions of how the teacher structures the classroom.[15] Many children enter school with mastery or learning goals but many become socialized into a performance-goal orientation.[16] When we consider the preponderance of public evaluation practices, normative comparisons, extrinsic rewards, ability grouping, and emphasis on production, speed, and perfection, it is no wonder that children find it difficult to maintain a learning or mastery orientation.

ENHANCING MOTIVATION

In most of our foundational courses, we stop once we have covered the basic theories or motivational constructs. We cannot assume, however, that teachers are prepared to translate these ideas into classroom practice. This is a major problem for foundations courses. We give too little attention to how motivation concepts interface with the instructional program, too little attention to how the social context of the classroom can undermine or facilitate the development of students' motivation to learn, and too little attention to how motivation principles relate to each other. What we do is cover the basics, highlight a few principles, maybe even review a case study or two, and then hope that the teacher's intuition has somehow been enlightened and that the teacher will be able to apply this knowledge. Many textbooks, when it comes to dealing with applications, rely on conventional wisdom. There are several major texts that present a problem (e.g., how to deal with a child who exhibits poor motivation) and then present teachers' solutions. These solutions are not linked to any conceptual framework. There is even an implicit endorsement of these ideas and solutions as credible, viable, and conceptually sound because the source is practicing teachers. Unfortunately, it is often the case that this is not so. The problem is that many strategies for enhancing student-motivation involve the use of principles that are counterintuitive. Let me illustrate this point with examples that are related to the motivation constructs described in the preceding section.

1. If children lack confidence in their ability to succeed, we might infer that these low-confident children should receive a heavy dose of success experience. The considerable literature on learned helplessness and attribution retraining, however, has shown that success alone does not alleviate a helplessness syndrome.[17] In contrast to what we might surmise, providing or ensuring successful outcomes or feedback does not necessarily bolster children's confidence in their abilities. Such a prescription ignores the role of cognitive motivational factors in determining how children interpret their classroom experiences. For many children success is not sufficient to create or maintain a belief that they have the ability to reverse failure. Children who are convinced that they lack the necessary ability to do school tasks do not take responsibility for success and even underestimate their performance when they do well. Thus, it is not a matter of persuading them they can do well or even guaranteeing it; instead, practice should involve giving them short-term goals and strategies for making progress toward the goals.[18] Once students understand how to reach a goal and focus on strategies, rather than outcomes, they are more likely to "own" the outcome.

2. Related to an emphasis on success is the prescription "try to find *something* positive to say about a child's work." Reinforcing children's work even if it involves some small aspect of the total effort should be a step in the direction of giving the child more confidence. Unfortunately, for the very children who most need positive feedback, the "something positive" is often something unimportant and irrelevant to the task requirements. For example, if the task is to write a book report in a certain format, commenting positively on the child's neat handwriting is not likely to have the intended effect.

On the one hand, the generous use of praise would seem to be an obvious and salient way of encouraging children who generally perform poorly, but as Brophy has shown, the way praise is often used in elementary school classrooms can undermine the achievement behavior of these children.[19] The praise children receive is often on irrelevant aspects of a task; in these instances, children discount the praise. Praise on easy tasks or praise that is noncontingent on children's effort or performance quality can be interpreted by children as evidence that they lack ability; it can, therefore, have unintended negative effects on children's self-confidence.

The effects of praise must also be considered from a developmental perspective. Praise can be interpreted quite differently by younger and older children. Praising young children's effort conveys to them a positive expectation that they can do the work and can enhance their perceptions of their competence. Because older children have differentiated concepts of ability and effort, praising their effort may actually be interpreted by them as low expectations for their ability. It is therefore important to understand how developmental changes in

cognition mediate the effects of well-intended behaviors. The application of basic psychological principles requires more than just a casual understanding of how cognition gives meaning to actions and classroom events.

3. One of the seeming paradoxes of research on student learning concerns the effects of rewards and incentives on student motivation. We have been taught that, if we want to increase the probability of a behavior, the most efficient method is to apply reinforcement principles. In fact, it seems that we have been indoctrinated into this way of thinking so well that these extrinsic reinforcements are often overused. Recent research by Boggiano and her colleagues certainly supports this assertion.[20] They presented a number of scenarios that described children involved in both high- and low-interest activities to adults, college students, and parents and asked them to judge how well certain strategies would maintain or increase the child's interest over time. For example, they described one ten-year-old child as one "who really enjoys reading and particularly likes to read books to learn about new things." Another ten-year-old was described as a child who "does not enjoy reading and chooses the easiest books to read when asked to write a book report." What is particularly striking is that regardless of the child's interest level, extrinsic rewards (such as adding 50 percent extra to the child's allowance) were preferred over other strategies as a way of maintaining or increasing the child's interest. Reward was preferred to reasoning, punishment, and even noninterference. Moreover, Boggiano et al. found that adults consistently preferred large rewards over small rewards, which they interpreted as reflecting a belief that interest level would vary with the size of the reward.

Certainly programs involving extrinsic rewards tend to be pervasive in our schools as a mechanism for increasing achievement behavior. In many schools and classrooms, extrinsic incentives are seen as necessary to get children to spend time on various tasks and lessons. Over twenty years ago, Jackson suggested that many of children's schooling experiences involve a hidden curriculum of controls and social constraints.[21] As students progress through school, they become more and more extrinsically controlled.

What are the consequences of using extrinsic incentives to try to shape children's achievement behaviors, to get them to complete their work, to increase the quality of work, and to get them to spend more time on particular tasks? The evidence from considerable research converges in identifying the "hidden cost" of using extrinsic rewards to motivate children.[22] This is not to say that incentives cannot be effective in some situations and for some children. The fundamental problem is that when we look into classrooms, we see the same incentive system being used for all the children in the classroom.

I am not suggesting that we need to inculcate the idea that incentives are ineffective or motivationally detrimental. The use of extrinsic incentives can have multiple effects on children's motivation; predicting the specific effects requires an analysis of a number of component processes. For instance, it is important to consider the relationship of extrinsic incentives to other motivation variables. In certain instances, rewards may have the effect of increasing self-efficacy, which can positively influence students' motivation or willingness to learn. The relation of extrinsic rewards to individual differences is of critical importance. In the classroom, extrinsic incentives are often intended to motivate the least attentive students or those who typically perform poorly; however, the rewards are typically applied to the entire classroom or even the entire school population, as in many reading incentive programs. The hidden costs become most apparent when they are applied to these larger groups where individual differences in interest, performance, and ability are ignored.

4. From the work on intrinsic motivation comes the recommendation to give children choices and thus a sense of personal control in the classroom.[23] Choice of tasks or activities is viewed as fostering belief in personal control and increasing interest and involvement in learning. This is easy enough to endorse and gives us a nice, simple application of intrinsic motivation theory to the classroom. A problem arises when we consider the context or structure of many classrooms. When normative evaluation and public comparisons are expected, students' choices reflect an avoidance of challenge and a preference for tasks that ensure success. In other words, a choice is not an equal choice in some contexts. When evaluation is pending on one's final product, choices are not based on interest; they more likely reflect a protection of one's ability and concern for one's level of performance. In this case, motivation theory cannot be applied without considering the context of the classroom.

5. On the basis of attribution theory, we might infer that it is a good idea to try to persuade students that they are not working hard enough or that they need to work harder on occasions of failure or poor performance. The implication is that students must perceive that outcome varies with effort expenditure and that increased effort will result in more positive outcomes.

The first consideration here is that the admonishment to try harder is to no avail to the student who believes he or she is already trying hard. This is a very likely scenario for young children, who believe they always try hard because it is not smart not to try. Telling these children that they did not work hard enough may actually decrease their sense of efficacy.

Second, problems arise when we put too much emphasis on effort. We do not want to impress on students that sustained maximal effort is what leads to success. Students may feel very satisfied when they have worked very hard and achieved success, but this is usually accompanied by the feeling that "I don't want to work that hard again." Conveying the expectation that a maximized effort is necessary may spark a child's investment once in a while, but over time students are more likely to become discouraged. In classrooms where the goal is to demonstrate one's ability over the long term, continuously maximizing one's effort is not desirable.

Finally, in most classrooms, students do not perceive the classroom hierarchy as effort-determined. As Nicholls suggests, students at the bottom of the hierarchy are not there because they are not effortful;[24] convincing students that this is, in fact, the case has little credence. If we want teachers to apply attribution theory to classroom practice, they need to know that whether they convey to students that effort is important depends on how they structure tasks, evaluate students, and give recognition and rewards.

These examples illustrate the complex nature of classroom learning and motivation. One of the major problems in our training of teachers is that we do not adequately address how motivation theory, constructs, and principles relate to practice: How can teachers develop in students a motivation to learn? As the preceding five examples illustrate, we currently rely on the wisdom of experience or derive applications without regard to the complexities involved. We need to consider how motivation constructs relate to each other, to developmental changes, to individual and culturally related differences, and to the context or structure of the classroom itself when we apply motivation theory and research to practice.

CONTEXT OF MOTIVATION

Finally, if we want teachers to apply these constructs in order to develop these motivational patterns in students, it is important to recognize that motivation occurs within a context—the school, the classroom, and the family. We spend a great deal of time discussing individual differences in motivation, treating motivation as a trait, but not enough time attending to how the organization and structure of the classroom shapes and socializes adaptive and maladaptive motivation patterns. Moreover, developing a positive motivational orientation in students is necessarily a matter of dealing with diversity among students in the classroom.[25] Teachers need to know ways of dealing with this diversity, and these methods ought to involve a comprehensive look at the classroom.

Thus, the teacher must first be guided by goals that assign primary importance to developing in students a motivation to learn. Second, we need a framework for identifying those aspects or structures of the classroom that are manipulable. These structures must represent the classroom organiza-

tion and must relate to instructional planning. Then we need to identify strategies that will serve to enhance the motivation of all students. These strategies or applications must be grounded in theory and research and evaluated in relation to developmental factors and in relation to other motivation constructs, as well as individual differences. Many educational psychology textbooks describe one or two ideas for application but do not provide a comprehensive view of classroom organization.

When we look at the classroom, there are six areas of organization that are manipulable and that involve motivational concerns: task, authority, recognition, grouping, evaluation, and time. These structures have been described in considerable detail by Epstein.[26] There is considerable research that relates to each area, and there are many motivational strategies that can be extracted from the research; the point is to apply appropriate strategies in all of these areas frequently and consistently. Preservice teachers often learn a great deal about only one area, and practicing teachers often focus on one or two areas but do little in the others. As a consequence, motivation becomes restricted to one area of the classroom. Often that area is reward or recognition (providing rewards and incentives), and even in that area inappropriate strategies are used.

CONCLUSION

This framework offers a starting point for extracting motivational strategies and applications from research and theory, and for relating them to all areas of classroom organization and instructional planning. This is important because motivation enhancement cannot be reserved for Friday afternoons, or be viewed as something to be used during free time or extra time or as superfluous to academic activities. Nor can motivational concerns surface only when a student does not do well. Motivation as an outcome is important to all students in the classroom all the time. This view gives student motivation a central place as an educational outcome, important in its own right. The emphasis is on identifying strategies that will foster a mastery-goal orientation in students and that relate to all aspects of classroom learning and organization. It requires a comprehensive approach to looking at how motivation theory and research interface with classroom learning.

ENDNOTES

1. See Lawrence A. Cremin, *The Transformation of the School* (New York: Random House, 1961).

2. See Carole Ames and Jennifer Archer, "Achievement Goals and Learning Strategies," *Journal of Educational Psychology* 80 (1989): 260–67; Jere Brophy, "Conceptualizing Student Motivation," *Educational Psychologist* 18 (1983): 200–15; Elaine S. Elliott and Carol S. Dweck, "Goals; An Approach to Motivation and Achievement," *Journal of Personality and Social Psychology* 54 (1988): 5–12; Martin L. Maehr, "Meaning and Motivation: Toward a Theory of Personal Investment," in *Research on Motivation in Education, Vol. 1: Student Motivation,* ed. Russell Ames and Carole Ames (Orlando: Academic Press, 1984), pp. 115–44; and John Nicholls, "Quality and Equality in Intellectual Development," *American Psychologist* 34 (1979): 1071–84.

3. Brophy, "Conceptualizing Student Motivation," pp. 200–15.

4. Carole Ames and Russell Ames, "Systems of Student and Teacher Motivation: Toward a Qualitative Definition," *Journal of Educational Psychology* 76 (1984): 535–56.

5. For example, Nathan Gage and David C. Berliner, *Educational Psychology* (Boston: Houghton-Mifflin, 1984).

6. See Martin Covington and Richard Beery, *Self-Worth and School Learning* (New York: Holt, Rinehart & Winston, 1976); and Martin Covington, "The Motive for Self-Worth," in *Research on Motivation in Education, Vol. 1,* pp. 77–113.

7. Dale Schunk, "Self-efficacy and Cognitive Skill Learning," in *Research on Motivation in Education, Vol. 3: Goals and Cognitions,* ed. Carole Ames and Russell Ames (San Diego: Academic Press, 1989), pp. 13–44.

8. Deborah Stipek, "The Development of Achievement Motivation," in *Research on Motivation in Education, Vol. 1,* pp. 145–74.

9. Martin Covington and Carol Omelich, "Effort: The Double-Edged Sword in School Achievement," *Journal of Educational Psychology* 71 (1979): 169–82.

10. Covington and Beery, *Self-Worth and School Learning.*

11. Ibid.

12. Ames and Archer, "Achievement Goals," pp. 260–67; and Carole Diener and Carol Dweck, "An Analysis of Learned Helplessness: Continuous Changes in Performance, Strategy, and Achievement Cognitions following Failure," *Journal of Personality and Social Psychology* 36 (1978): 451–62.

13. Ames and Archer, "Achievement Goals," p. 260.

14. Ibid.; Elliott and Dweck, "Goals," pp. 5–12; Nicholls, "Quality and Equality," pp. 1071–84; and Maehr, "Meaning and Motivation," pp. 115–44.

15. Covington and Beery, *Self-Worth and School Learning;* Ames and Archer, "Achievement Goals," pp. 260–67; and Ames and Ames, "Systems of Student and Teacher Motivation," pp. 535–56.

16. John Nicholls, *The Competitive Ethos and Democratic Education* (Cambridge: Harvard University Press, 1989).

17. Carole Dweck, "Motivation," in *Handbook of Psychology and Education,* ed. R. Glaser and A. Lesgold (Hillsdale, N.J.: Erlbaum, 1985).

18. Schunk, "Self-efficacy and Cognitive Skill Learning."

19. Jere Brophy, "Teacher-Praise: A Functional Analysis," *Review of Educational Research* 51 (1981): 5–32.

20. Ann Boggiano et al., "Use of Maximal-Operant Principle to Motivate Children's Intrinsic Interest," *Journal of Personality and Social Psychology* 53 (1987): 866–79.

21. Philip W. Jackson, *Life in Classrooms* (New York: Holt, Rinehart & Winston, 1968); see also Mark Lepper and Melinda Hodell, "Intrinsic Motivation in the Classroom," in *Research on Motivation in Education, Vol. 3,* pp. 73–105.

22. Mark Lepper, "Extrinsic Reward and Intrinsic Motivation: Implications for the Classroom," in *Teacher and Student Perceptions: Implications for Learning,* ed. J. Levine and M. Wang (Hillsdale, N.J.: Erlbaum, 1983a), pp. 281–317; and idem, "Social Control Processes and the Internalization of Social Values: An Attributional Perspective," in *Developmental Social Cognition: A Sociocultural Perspective,* ed. E. Tory Higgins et al. (New York: Cambridge University Press, 1983), pp. 294–330.

23. See Richard deCharms, *Enhancing Motivation: Change in the Classroom* (New York: Irvington, 1976); Edward Deci and Richard Ryan, *Intrinsic Motivation and Self-determination in Human Behavior* (New York: Plenum, 1985); and Richard Ryan, James Connell, and Edward Deci, "A Motivational Analysis of Self-determination and Self-regulation in Education," in *Research on Motivation in Education, Vol. 2: The Classroom Milieu,* ed. Carole

Ames and Russell Ames (Orlando: Academic Press, 1985), pp. 13–51.

24. Nicholls, *The Competitive Ethos and Democratic Education.*

25. Joyce Epstein, "Effective Schools or Effective Students: Dealing with Diversity," in *Policies for America's Public Schools: Teachers, Equity, Indicators,* ed. Ron Haskins and Duncan MacRae (Norwood, N.J.: Ablex, 1988).

26. Ibid.; and idem, "Family Structures and Student Motivation: A Developmental Perspective," in *Research on Motivation in Education, Vol. 3,* pp. 259–95.

DISCUSSION QUESTIONS

1. How does a teacher's understanding of motivation influence his or her instruction?

2. In what ways does classroom and family context influence student motivation?

3. How does motivation influence student outcomes?

4. How can teachers plan instruction that enhances the students' motivation in relationship to motivational concerns such as task, authority, grouping, and evaluation?

5. What are the effects of rewards and incentives on student learning?

14

Critical Thinking—What Can It Be?

MATTHEW LIPMAN

FOCUSING QUESTIONS

1. *What are the characteristics of critical thinking?*
2. *In what ways does critical thinking differ from ordinary thinking?*
3. *How does critical thinking assist students in becoming self-regulated learners?*
4. *What kind of curriculum needs to be implemented to encourage the development of critical thinking students?*
5. *How does the critical thinking model differ from (a) explicit instruction, (b) generative model of teaching, (c) cooperative learning methods, and (d) mastery model of learning?*

If we are to foster and strengthen critical thinking in schools and colleges, we need a clear conception of what it is and what it can be. We need to know its defining features, its characteristic outcomes, and the underlying conditions that make it possible.

THE OUTCOMES OF CRITICAL THINKING ARE JUDGMENTS

Let's begin with outcomes. If we consult current definitions of critical thinking, we cannot help being struck by the fact that the authors stress the *outcomes* of such thinking but generally fail to note its essential characteristics. What is more, they specify outcomes that are limited to *solutions* and *decisions*. Thus, one writer defines critical thinking as "the mental processes, strategies, and representations people use to solve problems, make decisions, and learn new concepts."[1] Another conceives of critical thinking as "reasonable

reflective thinking that is focused on deciding what to believe and do."[2]

These definitions provide insufficient enlightenment because the outcomes (solutions, decisions, concept-acquisition) are too narrow, and the defining characteristics (reasonable, reflective) are too vague. For example, if critical thinking is *thinking that results in decisions,* then selecting a doctor by picking a name at random out of a phone book would count as critical thinking. *We must broaden the outcomes, identify the defining characteristics, and then show the connection between them.*

Our contemporary conception of education as inquiry combines two aims—the transmission of knowledge and the cultivation of wisdom. But what is wisdom? Consulting a few dictionaries will yield such phrases as "intelligent judgment," "excellent judgment," or "judgment tempered by experience." But what is judgment?[3] Here again, recourse to dictionaries suggests that judgment is "the forming of opinions, estimates, or conclusions." It therefore includes such things as solving problems, making decisions, and learning new concepts; but it is more inclusive and more general.

The line of inquiry we are taking shows wisdom to be the characteristic outcome of good judgment and good judgment to be the characteristic of critical thinking. Perhaps the point where we are now, where we want to know how ordinary judgment and good judgment differ, is a good place to consider some illustrations.

Wherever knowledge and experience are not merely possessed but *applied to practice,* we see clear instances of judgment. Architects, lawyers, and doctors are professionals whose work constantly involves the making of judgments. It is true of any of us when we are in moral situations: we have to make moral judgments. It is true of teachers and farmers and theoretical physicists as well: all must make judgments in the practice of their occupations and in the conduct of their lives. There are practical, productive, and theoretical judgments, as Aristotle would have put it. Insofar as we make such judgments well, we can be said to behave wisely.

It should be kept in mind that good professionals make good judgments about their own practice as well as about the subject-matter of their practice. A good doctor not only makes good diagnoses of patients and prescribes well for them, but also makes good judgments about the field of medicine and his or her ability to practice it. Good judgment takes everything into account, including itself.

A judgment, then, is a determination—of thinking, of speech, of action, or of creation. A gesture, such as the wave of a hand, can be a judgment; a metaphor, like "John is a worm," is a judgment; an equation, like $E = mc^2$, is a judgment. They are judgments because, in part, they have been reached in certain ways, relying on certain instruments or procedures in the process. They are likely to be *good* judgments if they are the products of *skillfully* performed acts guided by or facilitated by appropriate instruments and procedures. If we now look at the process of critical thinking and identify its essential characteristics, we can better understand its relationship to judgment. I will ar-gue that critical thinking is *skillful, responsible thinking that facilitates good judgment because it (1) relies upon criteria,*[4] *(2) is self-correcting, and (3) is sensitive to context.*

CRITICAL THINKING RELIES ON CRITERIA

We suspect an association between the terms *critical* and *criteria* because they have a common ancestry. We are also aware of a relationship between criteria and judgments, for the very meaning of *criterion* is "a rule or principle utilized in the making of judgments." A criterion is an instrument for judging as an ax is an instrument for chopping. It seems reasonable to conclude, therefore, that there is some sort of logical connection between "critical thinking" and "criteria" and "judgment." The connection, of course, is to be found in the fact that judgment is a skill, critical thinking is skillful thinking, and skills cannot be defined without criteria by means of which allegedly skillful performances can be evaluated. So critical thinking is thinking that both employs criteria and that can be assessed by appeal to criteria.

The fact that critical thinking relies upon criteria suggests that it is well-founded, structured, and reinforced thinking, as opposed to "uncritical" thinking, which is amorphous, haphazard, and unstructured. Critical thinking seems to be defensible and convincing. How does this happen?

Whenever we make a claim or utter an opinion, we are vulnerable unless we can back it up with *reasons.* What is the connection between reasons and criteria? Criteria *are* reasons: they are one kind of reason, but it is a particularly *reliable* kind. When we have to sort things out descriptively or evaluationally—and these are two very important tasks—we have to use the most reliable reasons we can find, and these are classificatory and evaluational criteria. Criteria may or may not have a high level of acceptance and respect in the community of inquiry. The competent use of such respected criteria is a way of establishing the objectivity of our prescriptive, descriptive, and evaluative judgments. Thus, architects will judge a building by employing such criteria as *utility, safety,* and *beauty;* and presumably, critical thinkers rely upon such time-tested criteria as *validity, evidential warrant,* and *consistency.* Any area of practice—architectural, cognitive, and the like—should be able to cite the criteria by which that practice is guided.

The intellectual domiciles we inhabit are often of flimsy construction; we can strengthen them by learning to reason more logically. But this will help little if their foundations are soft and spongy. We need to rest our claims and opinions—all of our thinking—upon footings as firm as bedrock. One way of putting our thinking upon a solid foundation is to rely upon sound criteria.

Here then is a brief list of the sorts of things we invoke or appeal to and that therefore represent specific kinds of criteria:

- standards;
- laws, by-laws, rules, regulations;
- precepts, requirements, specifications;
- conventions, norms, regularities;
- principles, assumptions, presuppositions, definitions;
- ideals, goals, objectives;
- tests, credentials, experimental findings;
- methods, procedures, policies.

All of these instruments are part of the apparatus of rationality. Isolated in categories in a taxonomy, as they are here, they appear inert and sterile. But when they are at work in the process of inquiry, they function dynamically—and critically.

As noted, by means of logic we can validly extend our thinking; by means of reasons such as criteria we can justify and defend it. The improvement of student thinking—from ordinary thinking to good thinking—depends heavily upon students' ability to identify and cite good reasons for their opinions (see Figure 14.1). Students can be brought to realize that, for a reason to be called good, it must be *relevant* to the opinion in question and *stronger* (in the sense of being more readily accepted, or assumed to be the case) than the opinion in question.

Critical thinking is a sort of *cognitive accountability.*[5] When we openly state the criteria we employ—for example, in assigning grades to students—we encourage students to do likewise. By demonstrating models of *intellectual responsibility,* we invite students to assume responsibility for their own thinking and, in a larger sense, for their own education.

When we have to select among criteria, we must of course rely on other criteria to do so. Some criteria serve this purpose better than others and can therefore be said to operate as *meta-criteria.* For example, when I pointed out earlier that criteria are especially reliable reasons and that good reasons are those that reveal strength and relevance, I was saying that *reliability, strength,* and

Ordinary Thinking.	Critical Thinking/Reasoning
Guessing.	Estimating
Preferring	Evaluating
Grouping	Classifying
Believing.	Assuming
Inferring	Inferring logically
Associating concepts.	Grasping principles
Noting relationships	Noting relationships among other relationships
Supposing.	Hypothesizing
Offering opinions without reasons.	Offering opinions with reasons
Making judgments without criteria	Making judgments with criteria

FIGURE 14.1   Comparing Ordinary Thinking to Good Thinking

relevance are important meta-criteria. *Coherence* and *consistency* are others.

Some criteria have a high level of generality and are often presupposed, explicitly or implicitly, whenever critical thinking takes place. Thus the notion of knowledge presupposes the criterion of *truth,* and so wherever scientific knowledge is claimed, the concomitant claim being made is that it is true. In this sense, philosophical domains such as epistemology, ethics, and aesthetics do not dictate the criteria relevant to them; rather, the criteria define the domains. Epistemology consists of judgments to which truth and falsity are the relevant criteria; ethics compromises judgments to which right and wrong are relevant; and aesthetics contains judgments to which beautiful and not-beautiful are relevant. *Truth, right, wrong, just, good, beautiful*—all of these are such vast scope that we should probably consider them *mega-criteria.* And they in turn are instances of the great galactic criterion of *meaning.*

One of the primary functions of criteria is to provide a basis for comparisons. When a comparison is made and no basis or criterion is given (for example, "Tokyo is better than New York"), confusion results. On the other hand, if several competing criteria might be applicable (as when someone says, "Tokyo is larger than New York" but does not specify whether in size or in population), the situation can be equally confusing. Just as opinions should generally be backed up with reasons, comparisons should generally be accompanied by criteria.

Sometimes criteria are introduced "informally" and extemporaneously, as when someone remarks that Tuesday's weather was good compared with Monday's, while Wednesday's weather was bad compared with Monday's. In this case, Monday's weather is being used as an informal criterion. Even figurative language can be understood as involving the use of informal criteria. Thus, an open simile such as "The school was like an army camp" suggests the regimentation of an army camp as an informal criterion against which to measure the orderliness of the school.

On the other hand, when criteria are considered by an authority or by general consent to be a basis of comparison, we might speak of them as "formal" criteria. When we compare the quantities of liquid in two tanks in terms of gallons, we are employing the unit of the gallon on the say-so of the Bureau of Weights and Measures. The gallon measure at the Bureau is the institutionalized paradigm case to which our gallon measure is comparable.

So things are compared by means of more or less formal criteria. But there is also the distinction between comparing things with one another and comparing them with an ideal standard, a distinction Plato addresses in *The Statesman.*[6] For example, in grading test papers, we may compare a student's performance with the performances of other students in the class (using "the curve" as a criterion); or we may compare it with the standard of an error-free performance.[7]

Standards and *criteria* are terms often used interchangeably in ordinary discourse. Standards, however, represent a vast subclass of criteria. It is vast because the concept of *standard* can be understood in many different ways. There is the interpretation cited in the preceding paragraph, where we are talking about a standard of perfection. There are, in contrast, standards as *minimal* levels of performance, as in the oft-heard cry, "We must not lower our standards!" There is a sense in which standards are conventions of conduct: "When in Rome, do as the Romans do." There is also the sense in which standards are the units of measurement defined authoritatively by a bureau of standards.

There is, of course, a certain arbitrariness about even the most reliable standards, such as units of measurement, in that we are free to define them as we like. We could, if we liked, define a yard as containing fewer inches than it presently does. But the fact is that, once defined, we prefer such units to be unchanging: they are so much more reliable that way.

Perhaps we can sum up the relationship between criteria and standards by saying that criteria specify general requirements, while standards represent the degree to which these requirements need be satisfied in particular instances. Criteria—and particularly standards among them—are among the most valuable instruments of rational procedure. Teaching students to use them is essential to the teaching of critical thinking (see Figure 14.2).

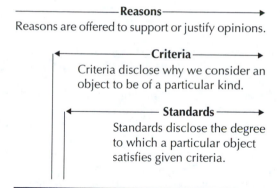

FIGURE 14.2 Relationship of Standards to Criteria to Reasons

CRITICAL THINKING IS SELF-CORRECTING

The most characteristic feature of inquiry is that it aims to discover its own weaknesses and rectify what is at fault in its own procedures. Inquiry, then, is *self-correcting.*[8]

Much of our thinking unrolls impressionistically, from association to association, with little concern for either truth or validity, and with even less concern for the possibility that it might be erroneous. Among the many things we may reflect upon is our own thinking, yet we can do so in a way that is still quite uncritical. And so, "metacognition," or thinking about thinking, need not be equivalent to critical thinking.

One of the most important advantages of converting the classroom into a community of inquiry (in addition to the improvement of moral climate) is that the members of the community not only become conscious of their own thinking but begin looking for and correcting each other's methods and procedures. Consequently, insofar as each participant can internalize the methodology of the community as a whole, each participant is able to become self-correcting in his or her own thinking.

CRITICAL THINKING IS SENSITIVE TO CONTEXT

Just as critical thinking is sensitive to uniformities and regularities that are genetic and intercontextual, it is sensitive to situational characteristics that are holistic or context-specific. Thinking that is sensitive to context takes into account:

(a) *exceptional or irregular circumstances and conditions*—for example, a line of investigation ordinarily considered *ad hominem* and therefore fallacious might be found permissible in a trial

(b) *special limitations, contingencies, or constraints*—for example, the rejection of certain Euclidean theorems, such as that parallel lines never meet, in non-Euclidean geometries

(c) *overall configurations*—for instance, a remark taken out of context may seem to be flagrantly in error but in the light of the discourse taken as a whole appears valid and proper, or vice versa;

(d) *the possibility that evidence is atypical*—for example, a case of overgeneralizing about national voter preferences based on a tiny regional sample of ethnically and occupationally homogeneous individuals.

(e) *the possibility that some meanings do not translate from one context or domain to another*—there are terms and expressions for which there are no precise equivalents in other languages and whose meanings are therefore wholly context-specific.

With regard to *thinking with criteria* and *sensitivity to context,* a suitable illustration might be an exercise involving the application of a particular criterion to a set of fictional situations. Suppose the criterion in question is *fairness* (which is itself a way of construing the still broader criterion of justice). One form that fairness assumes is *taking turns.* Figure 14.3 is an exercise taken from *Wondering at the World,*[9] the instructional manual accompanying *Kio and Gus,*[10] a Philosophy for Children program for children 9 to 10 years of age.

In performing this exercise, students apply the criterion of *turn-taking* (i.e., *fair play* or *justice*) to six situations requiring sensitivity to context. Classroom discussion should distinguish between those situations in which the procedure of turn-taking is appropriate and those in which it is dubious. Using exercises like these in a community of inquiry sets the stage for critical thinking in the classroom. It is not the only way to accomplish this, but it is one way.

Taking Turns

To the teacher: There are times when people engage in sharing. For example, they go to a movie and share the pleasure of looking at the movie together. Or they can share a piece of cake by each taking half.

In other cases, however, simultaneous sharing is not so easily accomplished. If two people ride a horse, someone has to ride in front. They can take turns riding in front, but they can't both ride in front at the same time. Children understand this very well. They recognize that certain procedures must be followed in certain ways.

For example, ask your students to discuss the number of ways they "take turns" in the classroom during the ordinary day. They take turns washing the blackboard, going to the bathroom, going to the cloakroom, and passing out the papers. On the playground, they take turns at bat, they take turns lining up for basketball, and they take turns at the high bar.

Ask your students what they think the connection is between "taking turns" and "being fair." The resulting discussion should throw light on the fact that sometimes being fair involves the way children are to be treated simultaneously, while at other times it involves the way they are to be treated sequentially. For example, if it is one child's birthday and there is going to be a party with cupcakes, there should be at least one cupcake for every child. This is being fair simultaneously. Later, if you want to play "Pin the Tail on the Donkey," children should sequentially take turns in order to be fair. (The prospect of everyone *simultaneously* being blindfolded and searching about with a pin boggles the mind.)

Exercise: When is it appropriate to take turns?

	Appropriate	Not Appropriate	?
1. Pam: "Louise, let's take turns riding your bike. I'll ride it Mondays, Wednesdays, and Fridays, and you ride it Tuesdays, Thursdays, and Saturdays."	☐	☐	☐
2. Gary: "Burt, let's take turns taking Louise to the movies. I'll take her the first and third Saturday of every month, and you take her the second and fourth Saturday."	☐	☐	☐
3. Jack: "Louise, let's take turns doing the dishes. You wash and I'll dry."	☐	☐	☐
4. Chris: "Okay, Louise, let's take turns with the TV. You choose a half-hour program, then I'll choose one."	☐	☐	☐
5. Melissa: "Louise, what do you say we take turns doing our homework? Tonight I'll do yours and mine, and tomorrow you can do mine and yours."	☐	☐	☐
6. Hank: "Louise, I hate to see you struggle to school each day, carrying those heavy books! Let me carry yours and mine today, and you can carry yours and mine tomorrow."	☐	☐	☐

FIGURE 14.3   "Taking Turns" Exercise
Reprinted from Matthew Lipman and Ann Margaret Sharp. *Wondering at the World.* Lanham, Md: University Press of America and IAPC, co-publishers, 1986.

THE PROMISE OF
INTELLECTUAL EMPOWERMENT

What, then, is the relevance of critical thinking to the enhancement of elementary school, secondary school, and college education? Part of the answer lies in the gradual shift that is occurring in the focus of education—the shift from *learning* to *thinking*. We want students to think for themselves and not merely to learn what other people have thought.

But another part of the answer lies in the fact that we want students who can do more than merely think: it is equally important that they exercise good judgment. It is good judgment that characterizes the sound interpretation of written text; the well-balanced, coherent composition; the lucid comprehension of what one hears; and the persuasive argument. It is good judgment that enables one to weigh and grasp what a statement or passage states, assumes, implies, or suggests. And this good judgment cannot be operative unless it rests upon proficient reasoning skills that can ensure competency in inference, as well as upon proficient inquiry, concept-formation, and translation skills. Students who are *not* taught to use criteria in a way that is both sensitive to context and self-corrective are *not* being taught to think critically. If teaching critical thinking can improve education, it will be because it increases the quantity and quality of meaning that students derive from what they read and perceive and that they express in what they write and say.

CONCLUSION

Last, a word about the employment of criteria in critical thinking that facilitates good judgment. Critical thinking, as we know, is skillful thinking, and skills are proficient performances that satisfy relevant criteria. When we think critically, we are required to orchestrate a vast variety of cognitive skills, grouped in families such as reasoning skills, concept-formation skills, inquiry skills, and translation skills. Without these skills, we would be unable to draw meaning from written text or from conversation, nor could we impart meaning to a conversation or to what we write.

We all know that an otherwise splendid musical performance can be ruined if so much as a single instrumentalist performs below acceptable standards. Likewise, the mobilization and perfection of the cognitive skills that make up critical thinking cannot omit any of these skills without jeopardizing the process as a whole. We cannot be content, then, to give students practice in a handful of cognitive skills while neglecting all the others necessary for the competency in inquiry, in language, and in thought that is the hallmark of proficient critical thinkers. Instead of selecting and polishing a few skills that we think will do the trick, we must begin with the raw subject matter of communication and inquiry—with reading, listening, speaking, writing, and reasoning—and we must cultivate all the skills that the mastery in such processes entails. It is only when we do this that we realize that the philosophical disciplines alone provide both the skills and the criteria that are presently lacking in the curriculum.

ENDNOTES

1. Robert Sternberg, "Critical Thinking: Its Nature, Measurement, and Improvement" in *Essays on the Intellect,* ed. Frances R. Link (Alexandria, Va.: Association for Supervision and Curriculum Development, 1985), p. 46.
2. Robert H. Ennis, "A Taxonomy of Critical Thinking Dispositions and Abilities" in *Teaching Thinking Skills: Theory and Practice,* ed. Joan Boykoff Baron and Robert J. Sternberg (New York: W. H. Freeman and Co., 1987), p. 10.
3. For a penetrating discussion of judgment, see Justus Buchler, *Toward a General Theory of Human Judgment* (New York: Columbia University Press, 1951).
4. Useful discussions of the nature of criteria are to be found in Michael Anthony Slote, "The Theory of Important Criteria," *The Journal of Philosophy* LXIII, 8 (April 1966): 221–224; Michael Scriven, "The Logic of Criteria," *The Journal of Philosophy* 56 (October 1959): 857–868; and Stanley Cavell, *The Claim of Reason* (Oxford: The Clarendon Press, 1979), pp. 3–36.
5. I see no inconsistency between urging "cognitive accountability" and urging the development of intellectual autonomy among students. There are times when we

cannot let other people do our thinking for us; we must think for ourselves. And we must learn to think for ourselves by thinking for ourselves; no one can instruct us in how to do it, although a community of inquiry makes it relatively easy. The point is that students must be encouraged to become reasonable for their own good (i.e., as a step toward their own autonomy) and not just for our good (i.e., because the growing rationalization of the society requires it).

6. The Stranger remarks to young Socrates, "We must posit two types and two standards of greatness and smallness...The standard of relative comparison will remain, but we must acknowledge a second standard, which is a standard of comparison with the due measure." *Statesman* (283e) in *Plato: The Collected Dialogues,* ed. Edith Hamilton and Huntington Cairns (Princeton: Princeton University Press, 1969), p. 1051.

7. For a contemporary interchange regarding comparison of things with one another vs. comparison of things with an ideal, see Gilbert Ryle, "Perceiving" in *Dilemmas* (London: Cambridge University Press, 1966), pp. 93–102; and D. W. Hamlyn, *The Theory of Knowledge* (London: Doubleday and Company and Macmillan, 1970), pp. 16–21.

8. Charles Peirce, "Ideals of Conduct" in *Collected Papers of Charles Sanders Peirce,* ed. by Charles Hartshorne and Paul Weiss (Cambridge, Mass.: Harvard University Press, 1931–35) discusses the connection between self-correcting inquiry, self-criticism, and self-control.

9. Matthew Lipman and Ann Margaret Sharp, *Wondering at the World* (Lanham, Md.: University Press of America and IAPC, co-publishers, 1986), pp. 226–299.

10. Matthew Lipman, *Kio and Gus* (Upper Montclair, N.J.: IAPC, 1982).

DISCUSSION QUESTIONS

1. How does critical thinking promote intellectual responsibility?
2. How do standards, criteria, and reasons differ?
3. How is good judgment related to critical thinking?
4. How can critical thinking be promoted in classroom instruction?
5. What modifications would you make to specific subject area content such as the art, science, reading, math, social studies, or science curriculum to help students become critical thinkers?

15

Creating Creative Minds

ROBERT J. STERNBERG
TODD I. LUBART

FOCUSING QUESTIONS

1. *How are intelligence and creativity related?*
2. *What is the relationship between knowledge and creativity?*
3. *How are intellectual styles related to creativity?*
4. *What are the advantages and disadvantages for giving students the responsibility for selecting problems they would like to solve?*
5. *What distinguishes creative thinking and ordinary thinking?*
6. *How can the use of ill-structured problems help students to think insightfully?*
7. *How do the norms of a school's environment influence the development of creativity?*

Creativity is not simply inborn. On the contrary, schooling can create creative minds—though it often doesn't. To create creativity, we need to understand the resources on which it draws and to determine how we can help children develop these resources. In particular, we need to know how we can invest in our children's futures by helping them invest in their own creative endeavors.

We propose an "investment theory of creativity."[1] The basic notion underlying our theory is that, when making any kind of investment, including creative investment, people should "buy low and sell high." In other words, the greatest creative contributions can generally be made in areas or with ideas that at a given time are undervalued. Perhaps people in general have not yet realized the importance of certain ideas, and hence there is a potential for making significant advances. The more in favor an idea is, the less potential there is for it to appreciate in value, because the idea is already valued.

A theory of creativity needs to account for how people can generate or recognize undervalued ideas. It also needs to specify who will actually pursue these undervalued ideas rather than join the crowd and make contributions that, while of some value, are unlikely to turn around our existing ways of thinking. Such a theory will enable us and our children to invest in a creative future.[2] As is sometimes said, nothing is as practical as a good theory.

We hold that developing creativity in children—and in adults—involves teaching them to use six resources: intelligence, knowledge, intellectual style, personality, motivation, and environmental context. Consider each of these resources in turn.

INTELLIGENCE

Two main aspects of intelligence are relevant to creativity. These aspects, based on the triarchic theory of human intelligence, are the ability to define and redefine problems and the ability to think insightfully.[3]

Problem Definition and Redefinition

Major creative innovations often involve seeing an old problem in a new way. For example, Albert Einstein redefined the field of physics by proposing the theory of relativity; Jean Piaget redefined the field of cognitive development by conceiving of the child as a scientist; Pablo Picasso redefined the field of art through his cubist perspective on the world.

In order to *re*define a problem, a student has to have the option of defining a problem in the first place. Only rarely do schools give students this luxury. Tests typically pose the problems that students are to solve. And if a student's way of seeing a problem is different from that of the test constructor, the student is simply marked wrong. Similarly, teachers typically structure their classes so that they, not the students, set the problems to be solved. Of course, textbooks work the same way. Even when papers or projects are assigned, teachers often specify the topics. Some teachers, who view themselves as more flexible, allow students to define problems for themselves. These same teachers may then proceed to mark students down when students' definitions of problems do not correspond to their own.

In the "thinking-skills movement," we frequently hear of the need for schools to emphasize more heavily the teaching of problem-solving skills. Educators are then pleased when students do not merely memorize facts but rather use the facts to solve problems. Certainly, there is much to be said for a problem-solving approach to education. But we need to recognize that creative individuals are often most renowned not for solving problems, but for posing them. It is not so much that they have found the "right" answers (often there are none); rather, they have asked the right questions—they recognized significant and substantial problems and chose to address them. One only has to open almost any professional journal to find articles that are the fruit of good problem solving on bad—or at least fairly inconsequential—problems.

If we are to turn schooling around and emphasize creative definition and redefinition of problems, we need to give our students some of the control we teachers typically maintain. Students need to take more responsibility for the problems they choose to solve, and we need to take less. The students will make mistakes and attempt to solve inconsequential or even wrongly posed problems. But they learn from their mistakes, and, if we do not give them the opportunity to make mistakes, they will have no mistakes to learn from. Instead of almost always giving children the problems, we more often need to let them find the problems that they are to solve. We need to help them develop their skills in defining and redefining problems, not just in solving them.

Insight Skills

Insight skills are involved when people perceive a high-quality solution to an ill-structured problem to which the solution is not obvious. Being truly creative involves "buying low"—that is, picking up on an idea that is out of favor. But just picking up on any idea that is out of favor is not sufficient. Insight is involved in spotting the *good* ideas. We have proposed a theory of insight whereby insights are of three kinds.[4]

The first kind of insight involves seeing things in a stream of inputs that most people would not see. In other words, in the midst of a stream of mostly irrelevant information, an individual is able to zero in on particularly relevant information for his or her purposes. For example, the insightful reader observes clues to an author's meaning that others may miss. An insightful writer is often one whose observations about human behavior, as revealed through writing, go beyond those of the rest of us.

The second kind of insight involves seeing how to combine disparate pieces of information whose connection is nonobvious and usually elusive. For example, proving mathematical theorems requires seeing how to fit together various axioms and theorems into a coherent proof. Interpreting data from a scientific experiment often involves making sense of seemingly disparate pieces of information.

The third kind of insight involves seeing the nonobvious relevance of old information to a new problem. Creative analogies and metaphors are representative of this kind of insight. For example, the student of history comes to see how understanding events of long ago can help us understand certain events in the present. A scientist might recall a problem from the past that was solved by using a certain methodology and apply this methodology to a current scientific problem.

Problems requiring insightful solution are almost always ill-structured; that is, there are no readily available paths to solution. Rather, much of the difficulty in solving the problem is figuring out what the steps toward solution might be. For example, when James Watson and Francis Crick sought to find the structure of DNA, the nature of the problem was clear. The way in which to solve it was not clear at all.

Problems presented in schools, however, are usually well-structured; that is, there is a clear path—or several paths—to a prompt and expedient solution. In standardized tests, for example, there is always a path that guarantees a "correct" solution. The examinee's problem is, in large part, to find that guaranteed path. Similarly, textbook problems are often posed so that there can be an answer key for the teacher that gives the "correct" answers. Problems such as these are unlikely to require insightful thinking. One ends up trying to "psych out" the thought processes of the person who formulated the problem, rather than to generate one's own insightful thought processes.

While not exclusively limited to ill-structured problems, creative innovations tend to address such problems—not the well-structured ones that we typically use in school settings. If we want students to think insightfully, we need to give them opportunities to do so by increasing our use of ill-

structured problems that allow insightful thinking. Project work is excellent in this regard, for it requires students not only to solve problems but also to structure the problems for themselves.

KNOWLEDGE

In order to make a creative contribution to a field of knowledge, one must, of course, have knowledge of that field. Without such knowledge, one risks rediscovering what is already known. Without knowledge of the field, it is also difficult for an individual to assess the problems in the field and to judge which are important. Indeed, during the past decade or so, an important emphasis in psychology has been on the importance of knowledge to expertise.

Schools can scarcely be faulted for making insufficient efforts to impart knowledge. Indeed, that seems to be their main function. Yet we have two reservations about the extent to which the knowledge they impart is likely to lead to creativity.

First, there is a difference between knowledge and usable knowledge. Knowledge can be learned in a way that renders it inert. Knowledge may be stored in the brain, but an individual may nonetheless be unable to use it. For example, almost every college undergraduate who majors in psychology takes a course in statistics as a part of that major. Yet very few undergraduates who have taken statistics are able to use what they have learned in the design and analysis of scientific experiments. (At the secondary level, many physics and chemistry students are unable to use basic algebra when they need to apply it.) Undergraduates in psychology do fine as long as they are given highly structured problems in which it is obvious which statistical technique applies. But they have trouble when they have to figure out which technique to apply and when to apply it. The context in which they acquired their knowledge is so different from the context in which they must use it that their knowledge is simply unavailable.

Our experience with knowledge learned in statistics courses is, we believe, the rule rather than the exception. Students do not generally learn knowledge in a way that renders it useful to them. To the contrary, they are likely to forget much of what they learn soon after they are tested on it. We have all had the experience of studying for an exam and then quickly forgetting what we studied. The information was learned in such a way as to make it useful in the context of a structured exam; once the exam is finished, so is that use of the knowledge.

Our second reservation about the knowledge that schools typically impart is that students are not taught in a way that makes clear to them why the information they are learning is important. Students do much better in learning if they believe that they can use what they learn. Foreign language provides a good example. People who need to use a foreign language learn it. Those who don't need it rarely retain much of it. Unless we show students why what they are learning should matter to them, we cannot expect them to retain what they are taught. Unfortunately, we often don't really know ourselves how students might use what we are teaching them. And if we don't know, how can we expect them to?

We also need to be concerned about the tradeoff that can develop between knowledge and flexibility. We have suggested that increased expertise in terms of knowledge in a given domain often comes at the expense of flexibility in that domain.[5] We can become so automatic about the way we do certain things that we lose sight of the possibility of other ways. We can become entrenched and have trouble going beyond our very comfortable perspective on things. Because creativity requires one to view things flexibly, there is a danger that, with increasing knowledge, one will lose creativity by losing the ability to think flexibly about the domain in which one works. We need to recognize that sometimes students see things that we do not see—that they may have insights we have not had (and that initially we may not even recognize as insights). Teachers who have been doing the same thing year after year can become so self-satisfied and happy with the way they do things that they are closed to new ways of doing these things. They are unwilling to "buy low"—to try an idea that is different from those they have favored in the past.

On the one hand, we do not wish to underemphasize the importance of knowledge to creativity. On the other hand, we cannot overemphasize the importance of usable knowledge that does not undermine flexibility. Often we need to adopt the maintenance of flexibility as a goal to be achieved self-consciously. We might go to inservice training sessions, read new kinds of books, learn about a new domain of knowledge, seek to learn from our students, or whatever. If we want students to be creative, we have to model creativity for them, and we won't be able to do that if we seek to turn students' minds into safe-deposit boxes in which to store our assorted and often undigested bits of knowledge.

INTELLECTUAL STYLES

Intellectual styles are the ways in which people choose to use or exploit their intelligence as well as their knowledge. Thus intellectual styles concern not abilities, but how these abilities and the knowledge acquired through them are used in day-to-day interactions with the environment.

Elsewhere one of the authors has presented details of a theory of intellectual styles based on a notion of "mental self-government."[6] Hence we need not cover the theory in detail here. The basic idea is that people need to govern themselves mentally and that styles provide them with ways to do so. The ways in which people govern themselves are internal mirrors of the kinds of government we see in the external world.

Creative people are likely to be those with a legislative proclivity. A legislative individual is someone who enjoys formulating problems and creating new systems of rules and new ways of seeing things. Such a person is in contrast to an individual with an executive style: someone who likes implementing the systems, rules, and tasks of others. Both differ from an individual with a judicial style: someone who enjoys evaluating people, things, and rules. Thus the creative person not only has the ability to see things in new ways but likes to do so. The creative person is also likely to have a global—not just a local—perspective on problems. Seeing the forest despite all the trees is the mark of creative endeavor.

PERSONALITY

Creative people seem to share certain personality attributes. Although one can probably be creative in the short term without these attributes, long-term creativity requires most of them. The attributes are tolerance of ambiguity, willingness to surmount obstacles and persevere, willingness to grow, willingness to take risks, and courage of one's convictions.

Tolerance for ambiguity. In most creative endeavors, there is a period of time during which an individual is groping—trying to figure out what the pieces of the puzzle are, how to put them together, how to relate them to what is already known. During this period, an individual is likely to feel some anxiety—possibly even alarm—because the pieces are not forming themselves into a creative solution to the problem being confronted. Creative individuals need to be able to tolerate such ambiguity and to wait for the pieces to fall into place.

In many schools, most of the assignments students are given are due the next day or within a very short period of time. In such circumstances students cannot develop a tolerance for ambiguity because they cannot spare the time to allow a situation to be ambiguous. If an assignment is due in a day or two, ambiguities need to be resolved quickly. A good way to help students develop a tolerance for ambiguity is to give them more long-term assignments and encourage them to start thinking about the assignments early on so that they can mull over whatever problems they face. Moreover, students need to realize that a period of ambiguity is the rule, not the exception, in creative work and that they should welcome this period as a chance to hatch their ideas, rather than dread it as a time when their ideas are not fully formed.

Willingness to Surmount Obstacles and Persevere

Almost every major creative thinker has surmounted obstacles at one time or another, and the willingness not to be derailed is a crucial element of success. Confronting obstacles is almost a certainty in creative endeavor because most such endeavors threaten some kind of established and entrenched interest. Unless one can learn to face adversity and conquer it, one is unlikely to make a creative contribution to one's field.

We need to learn to think of obstacles and the need to surmount them as part of the game, rather than as outside it. We should not think of obstacles as something only we have, but as something that everyone has. What makes creative people special is not that they have obstacles but how they face them.

Schools can be fairly good proving grounds for learning to surmount obstacles because we face so many of them while we are in school (whether as students or as teachers). But students sometimes leave school with the feeling that society is more likely to get in the way of creativity than to support it. Sometimes they are right, of course. And ultimately, they may have to fight for their ideas, as creative people have done before them. However, training to overcome resistance to new ideas shouldn't be the main contribution of the schools to students' creativity.

Willingness to Grow

When a person has a creative idea and is able to have others accept it, that person may be highly rewarded for the idea. It then becomes difficult to move on to still other ideas. The rewards for staying with the first idea are often great, and it feels comfortable to stick with that idea. At the same time, the person who has had a creative idea often acquires a deep-seated fear that his or her next idea won't be as good as the first one. Indeed, the phenomenon of "statistical" regression toward the mean would suggest that subsequent ideas actually will not be as good—that they will regress toward the mean. This is the same phenomenon that operates when the "rookie of the year" in baseball doesn't play as well in his second year as in his first or when a restaurant that seems outstanding when we first eat there isn't quite as good the second time. In short, there is a fair amount of pressure to stay with what one has and knows. But creativity exhibited over prolonged periods of time requires one to move beyond that first creative idea and even to see problems with what at one time may have seemed a superb idea. While schools often encourage the growth of a student's knowledge, such growth will by no means lead automatically to creativity, in part because schools do not encourage students to take risks with their newly acquired knowledge and abilities.

Willingness to Take Risks

A general principle of investment is that, on the average, greater return entails greater risk. For the most part, schools are environments that are not conducive to risk taking. On the contrary, students are as often as not punished for taking risks. Taking a course in a new area or in an area of weakness is likely to lead to a low grade, which in turn may dim a student's future prospects. Risking an unusual response on an exam or an idiosyncratic approach in a paper is a step likely to be taken only with great trepidation because of the fear that a low or failing grade on a specific assignment may ruin one's chances for a good grade in the course. Moreover, there is usually some safe response that is at least good enough to earn the grade for which one is aiming.

In addition, many teachers are not themselves risk-takers. Teaching is not a profession that is likely to attract the biggest risk-takers, and hence many teachers may feel threatened by students who take large risks, especially if the teacher perceives those risks to be at his or her expense. Unfortunately, students' unwillingness to take risks derives from their socialization in the schools, which are environments that encourage conformity to societal norms. The result is often stereotyped thinking.

Courage of One's Convictions and Belief in Oneself

There are times in the lives of almost all creative people when they begin to doubt their ideas—and themselves. Their work may not be achieving the recognition it once achieved, or they may not have succeeded in getting recognition in the first place. At these times, it is difficult to maintain a belief in one's ideas or in oneself. It is natural for people to go through peaks and valleys in their creative output, and there are times when creative people worry that their most recent good idea will end up being their final good idea. At such times, one needs to draw upon deep-seated personal resources and to believe in oneself, even when others do not.

Schools do teach some students to believe in themselves: namely, those who consistently receive high grades. But the skills one needs to earn high grades are often quite different from those one needs to be creative. Thus those who go out and set their own course may receive little encouragement, whereas those who play the game and get good grades may develop a confidence in themselves that, though justified, is not necessarily related to their past or potential creative contributions. Those who most need to believe in themselves may be given every reason not to.

MOTIVATION

There is now good evidence to suggest that motivation plays an important part in creative endeavors. Two kinds of motivation are particularly important: intrinsic motivation and the motivation to excel. Both kinds of motivation lead to a focus on tasks rather than on the external rewards that performance of these tasks might generate.

Intrinsic Motivation

Teresa Amabile has conducted and reviewed a number of studies suggesting the importance of intrinsic motivation to creativity.[7] People are much more likely to respond creatively to a task that they enjoy doing for its own sake, rather than a task that they carry out exclusively or even primarily for such extrinsic motivators as grades. Indeed, research suggests that extrinsic rewards undermine intrinsic motivation.[8]

There is little doubt as to the way in which most schools motivate students today: namely, through grades. Grades are the ultimate criterion of one's success in school, and, if one's grades are not good, love of one's work is unlikely to be viewed as much compensation. Therefore, many students chart a path in school that is just sufficient to get them an A. (If they put too much effort into a single course, they risk jeopardizing their performance in the other courses they are taking.) Students who once may have performed well for love of an intellectual challenge may come to perform well only to get their next A. Whatever intrinsic motivation children may have had at the start is likely to be drummed out of them by a system that rewards extrinsically, not intrinsically.

Motivation to Excel

Robert White identified as an important source of motivation a desire to achieve competence in one or more of a person's endeavors.[9] In order to be creative in a field, one generally will need to be motivated not only to be competent, but also to excel. The best "investors" are almost always those who put in the work necessary to realize their goals. Success does not just come to them—they work for it.

Schools vary in the extent to which they encourage students to excel. Some schools seem to want nothing more than for all their students to be at some average or "golden mean." Many schools, however, encourage excellence. Unfortunately, it is rare in our experience for the kind of excellence that is encouraged to be *creative* excellence. It may be excellence in grades, which generally does not require great creativity to attain; it may be excellence in sports or in extracurricular activities. There is nothing wrong with excellence of these kinds. Indeed, they are undoubtedly important in today's world. But seeking such excellences does not foster creativity—and may even interfere with

it. When a student is simultaneously taking five or six courses, there is not much opportunity to spend the time or to expend the effort needed to be creative in any of them.

ENVIRONMENTAL CONTEXT

Creativity cannot be viewed outside an environmental context. What would be viewed as creative in one context might be viewed as trivial in another. The role of context is relevant to the creative enterprise in at least three different ways: in sparking creative ideas, in encouraging follow-up of these ideas, and in rewarding the ideas and their fruits.

Sparking Creative Ideas

Some environments provide the bases for lots of creative sparks, whereas other environments may provide the basis for none at all. Do schools provide environments for sparking creative ideas? Obviously, the answer to this question is necessarily subjective. Given the discussion above, we would have difficulty saying that they do. Schools provide environments that encourage learning about and dealing with existing concepts rather than inventing new ones. There is a lot of emphasis on memorization and some emphasis on analysis, but there is little emphasis on creative synthesis. Indeed, it is difficult for us to remember more than a handful of tests we ever took in school that encouraged creative thinking. On the contrary, the tests students typically take reward them for spitting back what they have learned—or, at best, analyzing it in a fairly noncreative way.

Encouraging Follow-up of Creative Ideas

Suppose a student has a genuinely creative idea and would like to pursue it within the school setting. Is there any vehicle for such follow-up? Occasionally, students will be allowed to pursue projects that encourage them to develop their creative thinking. But again, spending a great deal of time on such projects puts them at risk in their other courses and in their academic work. It is quite rare that any allowance is made whereby students can be excused from normal requirements in order to pursue a special interest of their own.

Evaluating and Rewarding Creative Ideas

Most teachers would adamantly maintain that, when grading papers, they reward creativity. But, if the experience of other teachers is similar to that of the teachers with whom we have worked, they don't find a great deal of creativity to reward. And we sometimes worry whether they would recognize creativity in student work were they to meet it. Please note that we do not except ourselves from this charge. We have failed more than once to see the value of a student's idea when we first encountered it, only to see that value later on—after the student had decided to pursue some other idea, partly at our urging. Teachers genuinely believe that they reward creativity. But the rewards are few and far between.

Look at any school report card, and assess the skills that the report card values. You will probably not find creativity anywhere on the list. One of us actually analyzed the report cards given to children in several elementary schools. A number of skills were assessed. However, not a single one of the report cards assessed creativity in any field whatsoever. The creative child might indeed be valued by the teacher, but it would not show up in the pattern of check marks on the report card.

TEACHING FOR CREATIVITY

How can we help develop students' creativity in the classroom? Consider an example. A few weeks ago, one of us had the opportunity to teach a class of 9- and 10-year-olds in a New York City school. The children ranged fairly widely in abilities and came from various socioeconomic backgrounds. The guest teacher was asked to demonstrate how to "teach for thinking" and decided to do so in the context of teaching about psychology. However, he wanted to impart not merely a set of decontextualized "facts" about the field, but rather the way psy-

chologists think when they develop ideas for creative scientific theory and research.

He didn't tell the students what problem they were going to solve or even offer them suggestions. Rather, he asked each of them to share with the class some aspect of human behavior—their own, their parents', their friends'—that intrigued them and that they would like to understand better. In other words, the students were asked to *define problems* rather than have the teacher do it for them. At first, no one said anything. The children may never have been asked to formulate problems for themselves. But the teacher waited. And then he waited some more (so as not to teach them that, if only they said nothing, he would panic and start to answer his own questions).

Eventually, one student spoke up, and then another, and then another. The ice broken, the children couldn't wait to contribute. Rather than adopting the executive and largely passive style to which they were accustomed, they were adopting a *legislative style* whereby they enjoyed and actively participated in the opportunity to create new ideas. And create ideas they did. Why do parents make children dress up on special occasions? Why do parents sometimes have unreasonable expectations for their children? Why do some siblings fight a lot while others don't? How do we choose our friends?

Because these problems were the children's own problems and not the teacher's, the children were *intrinsically motivated* to seek answers. And they came up with some very perceptive answers indeed. We discussed their ideas and considered criteria for deciding which potential experiment to pursue as a group. The criteria, like the ideas, were the students' own, not the teacher's. And the students considered such factors as *taking risks* in doing experiments, *surmounting obstacles to doing an experiment,* and so on.

The children entered the class with almost no formal knowledge about psychology. But they left it with at least a rudimentary *procedural knowledge* of how psychologists formulate research. The teacher didn't give them the knowledge; they created it for themselves, in an environment that *sparked* and then *rewarded* creative ideas. To be sure, not all of the ideas were creative or even particularly good. But the students were encouraged to give it their best shot, and that's what they did.

The class didn't have time in one 75-minute period to complete the full design of an experiment. However, it did have time to demonstrate that even children can do the kind of creative work that we often reserve until graduate school. We can teach for creativity at any level, in any field. And if we want to improve our children and our nation, this is exactly what we need to do.

Does teaching for creativity actually work? We believe that it does. Moreover, the effectiveness of such teaching has been demonstrated.[10] After five weeks of insight training involving insight problems in language arts, mathematics, science, and social studies, students in grades 4 through 6 displayed significant and substantial improvements (from a pretest to a posttest) over an untrained control group on insight skills and general intelligence. In addition, the training transferred to insight problems of kinds not covered in the course, and, a year later, the gains were maintained. These children had improved their creative skills with only a relatively small investment of instructional time.

Those who invest are taught that most obvious of strategies: buy low and sell high. Yet few people manage to do so. They don't know when a given security is really low or when it is really high. We believe that those who work in the schools do not have much better success in fostering creativity. We often don't recognize creativity when we see it. And although most of us believe that we encourage it, our analysis suggests that schools are probably as likely to work against the development of creativity as in its favor. The conventional wisdom is likely correct: schools probably do at least as much to undermine creativity as to support it.

It is important to realize that our theory of creativity is a "confluence" theory: the elements of creativity work together interactively, not alone. The implication for schooling is that addressing just one—or even a few—of the resources we have discussed is not sufficient to induce creative thinking. For example, a school might teach "divergent thinking," encouraging students to see multiple solutions to problems. But children will not suddenly become creative in the absence of an environment that tolerates ambiguity, encourages risk taking, fosters task-focused motivation, and supports the other aspects of creativity that we have discussed.

It is also important to realize that obtaining transfer of training from one domain to another is at least as hard with creative thinking as with critical thinking. If you use trivial problems in your classroom (e.g., "What are unusual uses of a paper clip?"), you are likely to get transfer only to trivial problems outside the classroom. We are not enthusiastic about many so-called tests of creativity, nor about many training programs, because the problems they use are trivial. We would encourage the use of serious problems in a variety of disciplines in order to maximize the transfer of training. Better to ask students to think of unusual ways to solve world problems—or school problems, for that matter—than to ask them to think of unusual ways to use a paper clip!

CONCLUSION

Perhaps the greatest block to the enhancement of creativity is a view of the "ideal student" that does not particularly feature creativity. Paul Torrance used an "Ideal Child Checklist," composed of characteristics that had been found empirically to differentiate highly creative people from less creative people.[11] A total of 264 teachers in the state of New York ranked the items in terms of desirability. The teachers' rankings showed only a moderate relation with the rankings of 10 experts on creativity. The teachers supported more strongly than the experts such attributes as popularity, social skills, and acceptance of authority. The teachers disapproved of asking questions, being a good guesser, thinking independently, and risk taking. A replication of this study in Tennessee showed only a weak relation between the views of teachers and those of experts on creativity.[12] Clearly, to engender creativity, first we must value it!

Schools could change. They could let students define problems, rather than almost always doing it for them. They could put more emphasis on ill-structured rather than well-structured problems. They could encourage a legislative rather than (or in addition to) an executive style, by providing assignments that encourage students to see things in new ways. They could teach knowledge for use, rather than for exams; they could emphasize flexibility in using knowledge, rather than mere recall. They could encourage risk taking and other personality attributes associated with creativity, and they could put more emphasis on motivating children intrinsically rather than through grades. Finally, they could reward creativity in all its forms, rather than ignore or even punish it.

But for schools to do these things, it would take a rather fundamental re*valuation* of what schooling is about. We, at least, would like to see that process start now. Rather than put obstacles in their paths, let's do all that we can to *value* and encourage the creativity of students in our schools.

ENDNOTES

1. Robert J. Sternberg, "A Three-Facet Model of Creativity," in idem, ed., *The Nature of Creativity* (New York: Cambridge University Press, 1988), pp. 125–47; and Robert J. Sternberg and Todd I. Lubart, "An Investment Theory of Creativity and Its Development," *Human Development,* vol. 34, 1991, pp. 1–31.
2. Herbert J. Walberg, "Creativity and Talent as Learning," in Sternberg, *The Nature of Creativity,* pp. 340–61.
3. Robert J. Sternberg, *Beyond IQ: A Triarchic Theory of Human Intelligence* (New York: Cambridge University Press, 1985); and idem, *The Triarchic Mind: A New Theory of Human Intelligence* (New York: Viking, 1988).
4. Janet E. Davidson and Robert J. Sternberg, "The Role of Insight in Intellectual Giftedness," *Gifted Child Quarterly,* vol. 28, 1984, pp. 58–64; and Robert J. Sternberg and Janet E. Davidson, "The Mind of the Puzzler," *Psychology Today,* June 1982, pp. 37–44.
5. Robert J. Sternberg and Peter A. Frensch, "A Balance-Level Theory of Intelligent Thinking," *Zeitschrift für Pädagogische Psychologie,* vol. 3, 1989, pp. 79–96.
6. Robert J. Sternberg, "Mental Self-Government: A Theory of Intellectual Styles and Their Development," *Human Development,* vol. 31, 1988, pp. 197–224; and idem, "Thinking Styles: Keys to Understanding Student Performance," *Phi Delta Kappan,* January 1990, pp. 366–71.
7. Teresa M. Amabile, *The Social Psychology of Creativity* (New York: Springer-Verlag, 1983).
8. Mark Lepper, David Greene, and Richard Nisbett, "Undermining Children's Intrinsic Interest with Extrinsic Rewards: A Test of the 'Overjustification' Hypothesis," *Journal of Personality and Social Psychology,* vol. 28, 1973, pp. 129–37.
9. Robert White, "Motivation Reconsidered: The Concept of Competence," *Psychological Review,* vol. 66, 1959, pp. 297–323.
10. Davidson and Sternberg, op. cit.
11. E. Paul Torrance, *Role of Evaluation in Creative Thinking* (Minneapolis: Bureau of Educational Research, University of Minnesota, 1964).
12. Bill Kaltsounis, "Middle Tennessee Teachers' Perceptions of Ideal Pupil," *Perceptual and Motor Skills,* vol. 44, 1977, pp. 803–6.

DISCUSSION QUESTIONS

1. How can curriculum workers plan instruction that encourages students to use legislative intellectual styles?
2. In what ways will the curriculum need to be structured to promote creative thinking?
3. What kinds of changes at the school level might be necessary to foster creative thinking?
4. What instructional approaches are most likely to promote creative thinking?
5. What personality attributes do creative people seem to share?

16

The Cognitive-Developmental Approach to Moral Education

LAWRENCE KOHLBERG

FOCUSING QUESTIONS

1. *How does moral education promote the aims of education?*
2. *What are the levels of moral development?*
3. *How do moral judgment, content of moral judgment, and moral action differ?*
4. *How do conventional rules and principles influence moral choice?*
5. *How do indoctrination and values clarification differ as approaches to moral education?*
6. *What is the cognitive developmental approach to moral education?*

In this chapter, I present an overview of the cognitive-developmental approach to moral education and its research foundations, compare it with other approaches, and report the experimental work my colleagues and I are doing to apply the approach.

MORAL STAGES

The cognitive-developmental approach was fully stated for the first time by John Dewey. The approach is called *cognitive* because it recognizes that moral education, like intellectual education, has its basis in stimulating the *active thinking* of the child about moral issues and decisions. It is called developmental because it sees the aims of moral education as movement through moral stages. According to Dewey:

The aim of education is growth or *development,* both intellectual and moral. Ethical and psychological principles can aid the school in the *greatest of all the constructions—the building of a free and powerful character.* Only knowledge of the *order and connection of the stages in psychological development can insure this.* Education is the work of *supplying the conditions* which will enable the psychological functions to mature in the freest and fullest manner.[1]

Dewey postulated three levels of moral development: (1) the *pre-moral* or *preconventional* level "of behavior motivated by biological and social impulses with results for morals," (2) the *conventional* level of behavior "in which the individual accepts with little critical reflection the standards of his group," and (3) the *autonomous* level of behavior in which "conduct is guided by the individual thinking and judging for himself whether a purpose is good, and does not accept the standard of his group without reflection."[2]

Dewey's thinking about moral stages was theoretical. Building upon his prior studies of cognitive stages, Jean Piaget made the first effort to define stages of moral reasoning in children through actual interviews and through observations of children (in games with rules).[3] Using this interview material, Piaget defined the premoral, the conventional, and the autonomous levels as follows: (1) the *premoral stage,* where there was no sense of obligation to rules; (2) the *heteronomous stage,* where the right was literal obedience to rules and an equation of obligation with submission to power and punishment (roughly ages four to eight); and (3) the *autonomous stage,* where the purpose and consequences of following rules are considered and obligation is based on reciprocity and exchange (roughly ages eight to twelve).[4]

In 1955 I started to redefine and validate (through longitudinal and cross-cultural study) the Dewey-Piaget levels and stages. The resulting stages are presented in Table 16.1.

We claim to have validated the stages defined in Table 1. The notion that stages can be *validated* by longitudinal study implies that stages have definite empirical characteristics.[5] The concept of stages (as used by Piaget and myself) implies the following characteristics:

1. Stages are "structured wholes," or organized systems of thought. Individuals are *consistent* in level of moral judgment.
2. Stages form an *invariant sequence.* Under all conditions except extreme trauma, movement is always forward, never backward. Individuals never skip stages; movement is always to the next stage up.
3. Stages are "hierarchical integrations." Thinking at a higher stage includes or comprehends within it lower-stage thinking. There is a tendency to function at or prefer the highest stage available.

Each of these characteristics has been demonstrated for moral stages. Stages are defined by responses to a set of verbal moral dilemmas classified according to an elaborate scoring scheme. Validating studies include:

1. A twenty-year study of fifty Chicago-area boys, middle- and working-class. Initially in-

terviewed at ages ten to sixteen, they have been reinterviewed at three-year intervals thereafter.
2. A small, six-year longitudinal study of Turkish village and city boys of the same age.
3. A variety of other cross-sectional studies in Canada, Britain, Israel, Taiwan, Yucatan, Honduras, and India.

With regard to the structured whole or consistency criterion, we have found that more than 50 percent of an individual's thinking is always at one stage, with the remainder at the next adjacent stage (which he is leaving or which he is moving into).

With regard to invariant sequence, our longitudinal results have been presented in the *American Journal of Orthopsychiatry* (see endnote 12), and indicate that on every retest individuals were either at the same stage as three years earlier or had moved up. This was true in Turkey as well as in the United States.

With regard to the hierarchical integration criterion, it has been demonstrated that adolescents exposed to written statements at each of the six stages comprehend or correctly put in their own words all statements at or below their own stage but fail to comprehend any statements more than one stage above their own.[6] Some individuals comprehend the next stage above their own; some do not. Adolescents prefer (or rank as best) the highest stage they can comprehend.

To understand moral stages it is important to clarify their relations to stage of logic or intelligence, on the one hand, and to moral behavior on the other. Maturity of moral judgment is not highly correlated with IQ or verbal intelligence (correlations are only in the 30s, accounting for 10 percent of the variance). Cognitive development, in the stage sense, however, is more important for moral development than such correlations suggest. Piaget has found that after the child learns to speak there are three major stages of reasoning: the intuitive, the concrete operational, and the formal operational. At around age seven, the child enters the stage of concrete logical thought: He can make logical inferences, classify, and handle quantitative

TABLE 16.1   Definition of Moral Stages

I. Preconventional level

At this level, the child is responsive to cultural rules and labels of good and bad, right or wrong, but interprets these labels either in terms of the physical or the hedonistic consequences of action (punishment, reward, exchange of favors) or in terms of the physical power of those who enunciate the rules and labels. The level is divided into the following two stages:

Stage 1: *The punishment-and-obedience orientation.* The physical consequences of action determine its goodness or badness, regardless of the human meaning or value of these consequences. Avoidance of punishment and unquestioning deference to power are valued in their own right, not in terms of respect for an underlying moral order supported by punishment and authority (the latter being Stage 4).

Stage 2: *The instrumental-relativist orientation.* Right action consists of that which instrumentally satisfies one's own needs and occasionally the needs of others. Human relations are viewed in terms like those of the marketplace. Elements of fairness, of reciprocity, and of equal sharing are present, but they are always interpreted in a physical, pragmatic way. Reciprocity is a matter of "You scratch my back and I'll scratch yours," not of loyalty, gratitude, or justice.

II. Conventional level

At this level, maintaining the expectations of the individual's family, group, or nation is perceived as valuable in its own right, regardless of immediate and obvious consequences. The attitude is not only one of *conformity* to personal expectations and social order, but of loyalty to it, of actively *maintaining,* supporting, and justifying the order, and of identifying with the persons or group involved in it. At this level, there are the following two stages:

Stage 3: *The interpersonal concordance or "good boy-nice girl" orientation.* Good behavior is that which pleases or helps others and is approved by them. There is much conformity to stereotypical images of what is majority or "natural" behavior. Behavior is frequently judged by intention—"he means well" becomes important for the first time. One earns approval by being "nice."

Stage 4: *The "law and order" orientation.* There is orientation toward authority, fixed rules, and the maintenance of the social order. Right behavior consists of doing one's duty, showing respect for authority, and maintaining the given social order for its own sake.

III. Postconventional level

At this level, there is a clear effort to define moral values and principles that have validity and application apart from the authority of the groups or persons holding these principles and apart from the individual's own identification with these groups. This level also has two stages:

Stage 5: *The social-contract, legalistic orientation,* generally with utilitarian overtones. Right action tends to be defined in terms of general individual rights and standards, which have been critically examined and agreed upon by the whole society. There is a clear awareness of the relativism of personal values and opinions and a corresponding emphasis upon procedural rules for reaching consensus. Aside from what is constitutionally and democratically agreed upon, the right is a matter of personal "values" and "opinion." The result is an emphasis upon the "legal point of view," but with an emphasis upon the possibility of changing law in terms of rational considerations of social utility (rather than freezing it in terms of Stage 4 "law and order"). Outside the legal realm, free agreement and contract is the binding element of obligation. This is the "official" morality of the American government and Constitution.

Stage 6: *The universal-ethical-principle orientation.* Right is defined by the decision of conscience in accord with self-chosen *ethical principles* appealing to logical comprehensiveness, universality, and consistency. These principles are abstract and ethical (the Golden Rule, the categorical imperative); they are not concrete moral rules like the Ten Commandments. At heart, these are universal principles of *justice,* of the *reciprocity* and *equality* of human *rights,* and of respect for the dignity of human beings as *individual persons* ("From Is to Ought," pp. 164, 165).

relations about concrete things. In adolescence individuals usually enter the stage of formal operations. At this stage they can reason abstractly, i.e., consider all possibilities, form hypotheses, deduce implications from hypotheses, and test them against reality.[7]

Since moral reasoning clearly is reasoning, advanced moral reasoning depends upon advanced logical reasoning; a person's logical stage puts a certain ceiling on the moral stage he can attain. A person whose logical stage is only concrete operational is limited to the preconventional moral stages (Stages 1 and 2). A person whose logical stage is only partially formal operational is limited to the conventional moral stages (Stages 3 and 4). While logical development is necessary for moral development and sets limits to it, most individuals are higher in logical stage than they are in moral stage. As an example, over 50 percent of late adolescents and adults are capable of full formal reasoning, but only 10 percent of these adults (all formal operational) display principled (Stages 5 and 6) moral reasoning.

The moral stages are *structures of moral judgment* or *moral reasoning. Structures* of moral judgment must be distinguished from the *content* of moral judgment. As an example, we cite responses to a dilemma used in our various studies to identify moral stage. The dilemma raises the issue of stealing a drug to save a dying woman. The inventor of the drug is selling it for ten times what it costs him to make it. The woman's husband cannot raise the money, and the seller refuses to lower the price or wait for payment. What should the husband do?

The choice endorsed by a subject (steal, don't steal) is called the *content* of his moral judgment in the situation. His reasoning about the choice defines the structure of his moral judgment. This reasoning centers on the following ten universal moral values or issues of concern to persons in these moral dilemmas:

1. Punishment
2. Property
3. Roles and concerns of affection
4. Roles and concerns of authority
5. Law
6. Life
7. Liberty
8. Distributive justice
9. Truth
10. Sex

A moral choice involves choosing between two (or more) of these values as they *conflict* in concrete situations of choice.

The stage or structure of a person's moral judgment defines: (1) *what* he finds valuable in each of these moral issues (life, law), i.e., how he defines the value, and (2) *why* he finds it valuable, i.e., the reasons he gives for valuing it. As an example, at Stage 1 life is valued in terms of the power or possessions of the person involved; at Stage 2, for its usefulness in satisfying the needs of the individual in question or others; at Stage 3, in terms of the individual's relations with others and their valuation of him; at Stage 4, in terms of social or religious law. Only at Stages 5 and 6 is each life seen as inherently worthwhile, aside from other considerations.

MORAL JUDGMENT VS. MORAL ACTION

Having clarified the nature of stages of moral *judgment,* we must consider the relation of moral judgment to moral *action.* If logical reasoning is a necessary but not sufficient condition for mature moral judgment, mature moral judgment is a necessary but not sufficient condition for mature moral action. One cannot follow moral principles if one does not understand (or believe in) moral principles. However, one can reason in terms of principles and not live up to these principles. As an example, Richard Krebs and I found that only 15 percent of students showing some principled thinking cheated as compared to 55 percent of conventional subjects and 70 percent of preconventional subjects.[8] Nevertheless, 15 percent of the principled subjects did cheat, suggesting that factors additional to moral judgment are necessary for principled moral reasoning to be translated into "moral action." Partly, these factors include the situation and its pressures.

Partly, what happens depends upon the individual's motives and emotions. Partly, what the individual does depends upon a general sense of will, purpose, or "ego strength." As an example of the role of will or ego strength in moral behavior, we may cite the study by Krebs: Slightly more than half of his conventional subjects cheated. These subjects were also divided by a measure of attention/will. Only 26 percent of the "strong-willed" conventional subjects cheated; however, 74 percent of the "weak-willed" subjects cheated.

If maturity of moral reasoning is only one factor in moral behavior, why does the cognitive-developmental approach to moral education focus so heavily upon moral reasoning? For the following reasons:

1. Moral judgment, while only one factor in moral behavior, is the single most important or influential factor yet discovered in moral behavior.
2. While other factors influence moral behavior, moral judgment is the only distinctively *moral* factor in moral behavior. To illustrate, we noted that the Krebs study indicated that "strong-willed" conventional stage subjects resisted cheating more than "weak-willed" subjects. For those at a preconventional level of moral reasoning, however, "will" had an opposite effect. "Strong-willed" Stages 1 and 2 subjects cheated more, not less, than "weak-willed" subjects, i.e., they had the "courage of their (amoral) convictions" that it was worthwhile to cheat. "Will," then, is an important factor in moral behavior, but it is not distinctively moral; it becomes moral only when informed by mature moral judgment.
3. Moral judgment change is long-range or irreversible; a higher stage is never lost. Moral behavior as such is largely situational and reversible or "losable" in new situations.

AIMS OF MORAL AND CIVIC EDUCATION

Moral psychology describes what moral development is, as studied empirically. Moral education must also consider moral philosophy, which strives to tell us what moral development ideally *ought to be*. Psychology finds an invariant sequence of moral stages; moral philosophy must be invoked to answer whether a later stage is a better stage. The "stage" of senescence and death follows the "stage" of adulthood, but that does not mean that senescence and death are better. Our claim that the latest or principled stages of moral reasoning are morally better stages, then, must rest on considerations of moral philosophy.

The tradition of moral philosophy to which we appeal is the liberal or rational tradition, in particular the "formalistic" or "deontological" tradition running from Immanuel Kant to John Rawls.[9] Central to this tradition is the claim that an adequate morality is *principled,* i.e., that it makes judgments in terms of *universal* principles applicable to all mankind. *Principles* are to be distinguished from *rules.* Conventional morality is grounded on rules, primarily "thou shalt nots" such as are represented by the Ten Commandments, prescriptions of kinds of actions. Principles are, rather, universal guides to making a moral decision. An example is Kant's "categorical imperative," formulated in two ways. The first is the maxim of respect for human personality, "Act always toward the other as an end, not as a means." The second is the maxim of universalization, "Choose only as you would be willing to have everyone choose in your situation." Principles like that of Kant's state the formal conditions of a moral choice or action. In the dilemma in which a woman is dying because a druggist refuses to release his drug for less than the stated price, the druggist is not acting morally, though he is not violating the ordinary moral rules (he is not actually stealing or murdering). But he is violating principles: He is treating the woman simply as a means to his ends of profit, and he is not choosing as he would wish anyone to choose (if the druggist were in the dying woman's place, he would not want a druggist to choose as he is choosing). Under most circumstances, choice in terms of conventional moral rules and choice in terms of principles coincide. Ordinarily, principles dictate not stealing (avoiding stealing is implied by acting in terms of a regard for others as ends and in terms of what one would want everyone to do). In a situation where stealing is the only means to save a life, however, principles contradict the ordinary rules and would dictate stealing. Unlike rules which are supported by social authority, principles are freely chosen by the individual because of their intrinsic moral validity.[10]

The conception that a moral choice is a choice made in terms of moral principles is related to the claim of liberal moral philosophy that moral principles are ultimately principles of justice. In essence, moral conflicts are conflicts between the claims of persons, and principles for resolving these claims are principles of justice, "for giving each his due." Central to justice are the demands of *liberty, equality,* and *reciprocity.* At every moral stage, there is a concern for justice. The most damning statement a school child can make about a teacher is that "he's not fair." At each higher stage, however, the conception of justice is reorganized. At Stage 1, justice is punishing the bad in terms of "an eye for an eye and a tooth for a tooth." At Stage 2, it is exchanging favors and goods in an equal manner. At Stages 3 and 4, it is treating people as they desire in terms of the conventional rules. At Stage 5, it is recognized that all rules and laws flow from justice, from a social contract between the governors and the governed designed to protect the equal rights of all. At Stage 6, personally chosen moral principles are also principles of justice, the principles any member of a society would choose for that society if he did not know what his position was to be in the society and in which he might be the least advantaged.[11] Principles chosen from this point of view are, first, the maximum liberty compatible with the like liberty of others and, second, no inequalities of goods and respect which are not to the benefit of all, including the least advantaged.

As an example of stage progression in the orientation to justice, we may take judgments about capital punishment.[12] Capital punishment is only firmly rejected at the two principled stages, when the notion of justice as vengeance or retribution is abandoned. At the sixth stage, capital punishment is not condoned even if it may have some useful deterrent effect in promoting law and order. This is because it is not a punishment we would choose for a society if we assumed we had as much chance of being born into the position of a criminal or murderer as being born into the position of a law abider.

Why are decisions based on universal principles of justice better decisions? Because they are decisions on which all moral men could agree. When decisions are based on conventional moral rules, men will disagree, since they adhere to conflicting systems of rules dependent on culture and social position. Throughout history men have killed one another in the name of conflicting moral rules and values, most recently in Vietnam and the Middle East. Truly moral or just resolutions of conflicts require principles which are, or can be, universalizable.

Alternative Approaches

We have given a philosophic rationale for stage advance as the aim of moral education. Given this rationale, the developmental approach to moral education can avoid the problems inherent in the other two major approaches to moral education. The first alternative approach is that of indoctrinative moral education, the preaching and imposition of the rules and values of the teacher and his culture on the child. In America, when this indoctrinative approach has been developed in a systematic manner, it has usually been termed "character education."

Moral values, in the character education approach, are preached or taught in terms of what may be called the "bag of virtues." In the classic studies of character by Hugh Hartshorne and Mark May, the virtues chosen were honesty, service, and self-control.[13] It is easy to get superficial consensus on such a bag of virtues—until one examines in detail the list of virtues involved and the details of their definition. Is the Hartshorne and May bag more adequate than the Boy Scout bag (a Scout should be honest, loyal, reverent, clean, brave, etc.)? When one turns to the details of defining each virtue, one finds equal uncertainty or difficulty in reaching consensus. Does honesty mean one should not steal to save a life? Does it mean that a student should not help another student with his homework?

Character education and other forms of indoctrinative moral education have aimed at teaching universal values (it is assumed that honesty or service is a desirable trait for all men in all societies), but the detailed definitions used are relative; they are defined by the opinions of the teacher and the conventional culture and rest on the authority of the teacher for their justification. In this sense character education is close to the unreflective valuings by teachers which constitute the hidden curriculum of the school.[14] Because of the current unpopularity of indoctrinative approaches to moral education, a family of approaches called "values clarification" has become appealing to teachers. Values clarification takes the first step implied by a rational approach to moral education: the eliciting of the child's own judgment or opinion about issues or situations in which values conflict, rather than imposing the teacher's opinion on him. Values clarification, however, does not attempt to go further than eliciting awareness of values; it is assumed that becoming more self-aware about one's values is an end in itself. Fundamentally, the definition of the end of values education as self-awareness derives from a belief in ethical relativity held by many value-clarifiers. As stated by Peter Engel, "One must contrast value clarification and value inculcation. Value clarification implies the principle that in the consideration of values there is no single correct answer." Within these premises of "no correct answer," children are to discuss moral dilemmas in such a way as to reveal different values and discuss their value differences with each other. The teacher is to stress that "our values are different," not that one value is more adequate than others. If this program is systematically followed, students will themselves become relativists, believing there is no "right" moral answer. For instance, a student caught cheating might argue that he did nothing wrong, since his own hierarchy of values, which may be different from that of the teacher, made it right for him to cheat.

Like values clarification, the cognitive-developmental approach to moral education stresses open or Socratic peer discussion of value dilemmas. Such discussion, however, has an aim: stimulation of movement to the next stage of moral reasoning. Like values clarification, the developmental approach opposes indoctrination. Stimulation of movement to the next stage of reasoning is not indoctrinative, for the following reasons:

1. Change is in the way of reasoning rather than in the particular beliefs involved.
2. Students in a class are at different stages; the aim is to aid movement of each to the next stage, not convergence on a common pattern.
3. The teacher's own opinion is neither stressed nor invoked as authoritative. It enters in only as one of many opinions, hopefully one of those at a next higher stage.
4. The notion that some judgments are more adequate than others is communicated. Fundamentally, however, this means that the student is encouraged to articulate a position which seems most adequate to him and to judge the adequacy of the reasoning of others.

In addition to having more definite aims than values clarification, the moral development approach restricts value education to that which is moral or, more specifically, to justice. This is for two reasons. First, it is not clear that the whole realm of personal, political, and religious values is a realm which is nonrelative, i.e., in which there are universals and a direction of development. Second, it is not clear that the public school has a right or mandate to develop values in general.[15] In our view, value education in the public schools should be restricted to that which the school has the right and mandate to develop: an awareness of justice, or of the rights of others in our Constitutional system. While the Bill of Rights prohibits the teaching of religious beliefs, or of specific value systems, it does not prohibit the teaching of the awareness of rights and principles of justice fundamental to the Constitution itself.

When moral education is recognized as centered in justice and differentiated from value education or affective education, it becomes apparent that moral and civic education are much the same thing. This equation, taken for granted by the classic philosophers of education from Plato and Aristotle to Dewey, is basic to our claim that a concern for moral education is central to the educational objectives of social studies.

The term *civic education* is used to refer to social studies as more than the study of the facts and concepts of social science, history, and civics. It is education for the analytic understanding, value principles, and motivation necessary for a citizen in a democracy if democracy is to be an effective process. It is political education. Civic or political education means the stimulation of development of more advanced patterns of reasoning about political and social decisions and their implementation directly derivative of broader patterns of moral reasoning. Our studies show that reasoning and decision making about political decisions are directly derivative of broader patterns of moral reasoning and decision making. We have interviewed high school and college students about concrete political situations involving laws to govern open housing, civil disobedience for peace in Vietnam, free press rights to publish what might disturb national order, and distribution of income through taxation. We find that reasoning on these political decisions can be classified according to moral stage and that an individual's stage on political dilemmas is at the same level as on nonpolitical moral dilemmas (euthanasia, violating authority to maintain trust in a family, stealing a drug to save one's dying wife). Turning from reasoning to action, similar findings are obtained. In 1963 a study was made of those who sat in at the University of California, Berkeley, administration building and those who did not in the Free Speech Movement crisis. Of those at Stage 6, 80 percent sat in, believing that principles of free speech were being compromised, and that all efforts to compromise and negotiate with the administration had failed. In contrast, only 15 percent of the conventional (Stage 3 or Stage 4) subjects sat in. (Stage 5 subjects were in between.)[16]

From a psychological side, then, political development is part of moral development. The same is true from the philosophic side. In the *Republic,* Plato sees political education as part of a broader education for moral justice and finds a rationale for such education in terms of universal philosophic principles rather than the demands of a particular society. More recently, Dewey claims the same.

In historical perspective, America was the first nation whose government was publicly founded on postconventional principles of justice, rather than upon the authority central to conventional moral reasoning. At the time of our founding, postconventional or principled moral and political reasoning was the possession of the minority, as it still is. Today, as in the time of our founding, the majority of our adults are at the conventional level, particularly the "law and order" (fourth) moral stage. (Every few years the Gallup Poll circulates the Bill of Rights unidentified, and every year it is turned down.) The Founding Fathers intuitively understood this without benefit of our elaborate social science research; they constructed a document designing a government which would maintain principles of justice and the rights of man even though principled men were not the men in power. The machinery included checks and balances, the independent judiciary, and freedom of the press. Most recently, this machinery found its use at Watergate. The tragedy of Richard Nixon, as Harry Truman said long ago, was that he never understood the Constitution (a Stage 5 document), but the Constitution understood Richard Nixon.[17]

Watergate, then, is not some sign of moral decay of the nation, but rather of the fact that understanding and action in support of justice principles are still the possession of a minority of our society. Insofar as there is moral decay, it represents the weakening of conventional morality in the face of social and value conflict today. This can lead the less fortunate adolescent to fixation at the preconventional level, the more fortunate to movement to principles. We find a larger proportion of youths at the principled level today than was the case in their fathers' day, but also a larger proportion at the preconventional level.

Given this state, moral and civic education in the schools becomes a more urgent task. In the high school today, one often hears both preconventional adolescents and those beginning to move beyond convention sounding the same note of disaffection for the school. While our political institutions are in principle Stage 5 (i.e., vehicles for maintaining universal rights through the democratic process), our schools have traditionally been Stage 4 institutions of convention and authority. Today more than ever, democratic schools systematically engaged in civic education are required.

Our approach to moral and civic education relates the study of law and government to the actual creation of a democratic school in which moral dilemmas are discussed and resolved in a manner which will stimulate moral development.

Planned Moral Education

For many years, moral development was held by psychologists to be primarily a result of family upbringing and family conditions. In particular, conditions of affection and authority in the home were believed to be critical, some balance of warmth and firmness being optimal for moral development. This view arises if morality is conceived as an internalization of the arbitrary rules of parents and culture, since such acceptance must be based on affection and respect for parents as authorities rather than on the rational nature of the rules involved.

Studies of family correlates of moral stage development do not support this internalization view of the conditions for moral development. Instead, they suggest that the conditions for moral development in homes and schools are similar and that the conditions are consistent with cognitive-developmental theory. In the cognitive-developmental view, morality is a natural product of a universal human tendency toward empathy or role taking, toward putting oneself in the shoes of other conscious beings. It is also a product of a universal human concern for justice, for reciprocity or equality in the relation of one person to another. As an example, when my son was four, he became a morally principled vegetarian and refused to eat meat, resisting all parental persuasion to increase his protein intake. His reason was, "It's bad to kill an-

imals." His moral commitment to vegetarianism was not taught or acquired from parental authority; it was the result of the universal tendency of the young self to project its consciousness and values into other living things, other selves. My son's vegetarianism also involved a sense of justice, revealed when I read him a book about Eskimos in which a real hunting expedition was described. His response was to say, "Daddy, there is one kind of meat I would eat—Eskimo meat. It's all right to eat Eskimos because they eat animals." This natural sense of justice or reciprocity was Stage 1—an eye for an eye, a tooth for a tooth. My son's sense of the value of life was also Stage 1 and involved no differentiation between human personality and physical life. His morality, though Stage 1, was, however, natural and internal. Moral development past Stage 1, then, is not an internalization but the reconstruction of role taking and conceptions of justice toward greater adequacy. These reconstructions occur in order to achieve a better match between the child's own moral structures and the structures of the social and moral situations he confronts. We divide these conditions of match into two kinds: those dealing with moral discussions and communication and those dealing with the total moral environment or atmosphere in which the child lives.

In terms of moral discussion, the important conditions appear to be:

1. Exposure to the next higher stage of reasoning
2. Exposure to situations posing problems and contradictions for the child's current moral structure, leading to dissatisfaction with his current level
3. An atmosphere of interchange and dialogue combining the first two conditions, in which conflicting moral views are compared in an open manner

Studies of families in India and America suggest that morally advanced children have parents at higher stages. Parents expose children to the next higher stage, raising moral issues and engaging in open dialogue or interchange about such issues.[18]

Drawing on this notion of the discussion conditions stimulating advance, Moshe Blatt conducted classroom discussions of conflict-laden hypothetical moral dilemmas with four classes of junior high and high school students for a semester.[19] In each of these classes, students were to be found at three stages. Since the children were not all responding at the same stage, the arguments they used with each other were at different levels. In the course of these discussions among the students, the teacher first supported and clarified those arguments that were one stage above the lowest stage among the children; for example, the teacher supported Stage 3 rather than Stage 2. When it seemed that these arguments were understood by the students, the teacher then challenged that stage, using new situations, and clarified the arguments one stage above the previous one: Stage 4 rather than Stage 3. At the end of the semester, all the students were retested; they showed significant upward change when compared to the controls, and they maintained the change one year later. In the experimental classrooms, from one-fourth to one-half of the students moved up a stage, while there was essentially no change during the course of the experiment in the control group.

Given the Blatt studies showing that moral discussion could raise moral stage, we undertook the next step: to see if teachers could conduct moral discussions in the course of teaching high school social studies with the same results. This step we took in cooperation with Edwin Fenton, who introduced moral dilemmas in his ninth- and eleventh-grade social studies texts. Twenty-four teachers in the Boston and Pittsburgh areas were given some instruction in conducting moral discussions around the dilemmas in the text. About half of the teachers stimulated significant developmental change in their classrooms—upward stage movement of one-quarter to one-half a stage. In control classes using the text but no moral dilemma discussions, the same teachers failed to stimulate any moral change in the students. Moral discussion, then, can be a usable and effective part of the curriculum at any grade level. Working with

filmstrip dilemmas produced in cooperation with Guidance Association, second-grade teachers conducted moral discussions yielding a similar amount of moral stage movement.

Moral discussion and curriculum, however, constitute only one portion of the conditions stimulating moral growth. When we turn to analyzing the broader life environment, we turn to a consideration of the *moral atmosphere* of the home, the school, and the broader society. The first basic dimension of social atmosphere is the role-taking opportunities it provides, the extent to which it encourages the child to take the point of view of others. Role taking is related to the amount of social interaction and social communication in which the child engages, as well as to his sense of efficacy in influencing attitudes of others. The second dimension of social atmosphere, more strictly moral, is the level of justice of the environment or institution. The justice structure of an institution refers to the perceived rules or principles for distributing rewards, punishments, responsibilities, and privileges among institutional members. This structure may exist or be perceived at any of our moral stages. As an example, a study of a traditional prison revealed that inmates perceived it as Stage 1, regardless of their own level.[20] Obedience to arbitrary command by power figures and punishment for disobedience were seen as the governing justice norms of the prison. A behavior-modification prison using point rewards for conformity was perceived as a Stage 2 system of instrumental exchange. Inmates at Stage 3 or 4 perceived this institution as more fair than the traditional prison, but not as fair in their own terms.

These and other studies suggest that a higher level of institutional justice is a condition for individual development of a higher sense of justice. Working on these premises, Joseph Hickey, Peter Scharf, and I worked with guards and inmates in a women's prison to create a more just community.[21] A social contract was set up in which guards and inmates each had a vote of one and in which rules were made and conflicts resolved through discussions of fairness and a democratic vote in a community meeting. The program has been operating four years and has stimulated moral stage advance in inmates, though it is still too early to draw conclusions as to its overall long-range effectiveness for rehabilitation.

One year ago, Fenton, Ralph Mosher, and I received a grant from the Danforth Foundation (with additional support from the Kennedy Foundation) to make moral education a living matter in two high schools in the Boston area (Cambridge and Brookline) and two in Pittsburgh. The plan had two components. The first was training counselors and social studies and English teachers in conducting moral discussions and making moral discussion an integral part of the curriculum. The second was establishing a just community school within a public high school.

We have stated the theory of the just community high school, postulating that discussing real-life moral situations and actions as issues of fairness and as matters for democratic decision would stimulate advance in both moral reasoning and moral action. A participatory democracy provides more extensive opportunities for role taking and a higher level of perceived institutional justice than does any other social arrangement. Most alternative schools strive to establish a democratic governance, but none we have observed has achieved a vital or viable participatory democracy. Our theory suggested reasons why we might succeed where others failed. First, we felt that democracy had to be a central commitment of a school, rather than a humanitarian frill. Democracy as moral education provides that commitment. Second, democracy in alternative schools often fails because it bores the students. Students prefer to let teachers make decisions about staff, courses, and schedules, rather than to attend lengthy, complicated meetings. Our theory said that the issues a democracy should focus on are issues of morality and fairness. Real issues concerning drugs, stealing, disruptions, and grading are never boring if handled as issues of fairness. Third, our theory told us that if large democratic community meetings were preceded by small-group moral discussion, higher-stage thinking by students would win out in later decisions, avoiding the disasters of mob rule.[22]

Currently, we can report that the school based on our theory makes democracy work or function where other schools have failed. It is too early to make any claims for its effectiveness in causing moral development, however.

Our Cambridge just community school within the public high school was started after a small summer planning session of volunteer teachers, students, and parents. At the time the school opened in the fall, only a commitment to democracy and a skeleton program of English and social studies had been decided on. The school started with six teachers from the regular school and sixty students, twenty from academic professional homes and twenty from working-class homes. The other twenty were dropouts and troublemakers or petty delinquents in terms of previous record. The usual mistakes and usual chaos of a beginning alternative school ensued. Within a few weeks, however, a successful democratic community process had been established. Rules were made around pressing issues: disturbances, drugs, hooking. A student discipline committee or jury was formed. The resulting rules and enforcement have been relatively effective and reasonable. We do not see reasonable rules as ends in themselves, however, but as vehicles for moral discussion and an emerging sense of community. This sense of community and a resulting morale are perhaps the most immediate signs of success. This sense of community seems to lead to behavior change of a positive sort. An example is a fifteen-year-old student who started as one of the greatest combinations of humor, aggression, light-fingeredness, and hyperactivity I have ever known. From being the principal disturber of all community meetings, he has become an excellent community meeting participant and occasional chairman. He is still more ready to enforce rules for others than to observe them himself, yet his commitment to the school has led to a steady decrease in exotic behavior. In addition, he has become more involved in classes and projects and has begun to listen and ask questions in order to pursue a line of interest.

CONCLUSION

We attribute such behavior change not only to peer pressure and moral discussion but to the sense of community which has emerged from the democratic process in which angry conflicts are resolved through fairness and community decision. This sense of community is reflected in statements of the students to us that there are no cliques—that the blacks and the whites, the professors' sons and the project students, are friends. These statements are supported by observation. Such a sense of community is needed where students in a given classroom range in reading level from fifth-grade to college.

Fenton, Mosher, the Cambridge and Brookline teachers, and I are now planning a four-year curriculum in English and social studies centering on moral discussion, on role taking and communication, and on relating the government, laws, and justice system of the school to that of the American society and other world societies. This will integrate an intellectual curriculum for a higher level of understanding of society with the experiential components of school democracy and moral decision.

There is very little new in this—or in anything else we are doing. Dewey wanted democratic experimental schools for moral and intellectual development seventy years ago. Perhaps Dewey's time has come.

ENDNOTES

1. John Dewey, "What Psychology Can Do for the Teacher," in Reginald Archambault, ed., *John Dewey on Education: Selected Writings* (New York: Random House, 1964).

2. These levels correspond roughly to our three major levels: the preconventional, the conventional, and the principled. Similar levels were propounded by William McDougall, Leonard Hobhouse, and James Mark Baldwin.

3. Jean Piaget, *The Moral Judgment of the Child,* 2nd ed. (Glencoe, Ill.: Free Press, 1948).

4. Piaget's stages correspond to our first three stages: Stage 0 (premoral), Stage 1 (heteronomous), and Stage 2 (instrumental reciprocity).

5. Lawrence Kohlberg, "Moral Stages and Moralization: The Cognitive-Developmental Approach," in Thomas

Lickona, ed., *Man, Morality, and Society* (New York: Holt, Rinehart and Winston, in press).

6. James Rest, Elliott Turiel, and Lawrence Kohlberg, "Relations Between Level of Moral Judgment and Preference and Comprehension of the Moral Judgment of Others," *Journal of Personality,* vol. 37, 1969, pp. 225–52, and James Rest, "Comprehension, Preference, and Spontaneous Usage in Moral Judgment," in Lawrence Kohlberg, ed., *Recent Research in Moral Development* (New York: Holt, Rinehart and Winston, in preparation).

7. Many adolescents and adults only partially attain the stage of formal operations. They do consider all the actual relations of one thing to another at the same time, but they do not consider all possibilities and form abstract hypotheses. A few do not advance this far, remaining "concrete operational."

8. Richard Krebs and Lawrence Kohlberg, "Moral Judgment and Ego Controls as Determinants of Resistance to Cheating," in Lawrence Kohlberg, ed., *Recent Research.*

9. John Rawls, *A Theory of Justice* (Cambridge, Mass.: Harvard University Press, 1971).

10. Not all freely chosen values or rules are principles, however. Hitler chose the "rule," "exterminate the enemies of the Aryan race," but such a rule is not a universalizable principle.

11. Rawls, *A Theory of Justice.*

12. Lawrence Kohlberg and Donald Elfenbein, "Development of Moral Reasoning and Attitudes Toward Capital Punishment," *American Journal of Orthopsychiatry,* Summer, 1975.

13. Hugh Hartshorne and Mark May, *Studies in the Nature of Character: Studies in Deceit,* vol. 1; *Studies in Service and Self-Control,* vol. 2; *Studies in Organization of Character,* vol. 3 (New York: Macmillan, 1928–30).

14. As an example of the "hidden curriculum," we may cite a second-grade classroom. My son came home from this classroom one day saying he did not want to be "one of the bad boys." Asked "Who are the bad boys?" he replied, "The ones who don't put their books back and get yelled at."

15. Restriction of deliberate value education to the moral may be clarified by our example of the second-grade teacher who made tidying up of books a matter of moral indoctrination. Tidiness is a value, but it is not a moral value. Cheating is a moral issue, intrinsically one of fairness. It involves issues of violation of trust and taking advantage. Failing to tidy the room may under certain conditions be an issue of fairness, when it puts an undue burden on others. If it is handled by the teacher as a matter of cooperation among the group in this sense, it is a le-

gitimate focus of deliberate moral education. If it is not, it simply represents the arbitrary imposition of the teacher's values on the child.

16. The differential action of the principled subjects was determined by two things. First, they were more likely to judge it right to violate authority by sitting in. But second, they were also in general more consistent in engaging in political action according to their judgment. Ninety percent of all Stage 6 subjects thought it right to sit in, and all 90 percent lived up to this belief. Among the Stage 4 subjects, 45% thought it right to sit in, but only 33% lived up to this belief by acting.

17. No public or private word or deed of Nixon ever rose above Stage 4, the "law and order" stage. His last comments in the White House were of wonderment that the Republican Congress could turn on him after so many Stage 2 exchanges of favors in getting them elected.

18. Bindu Parilch, "A Cross-Cultural Study of Parent-child Moral Judgment," unpublished doctoral dissertation, Harvard University, 1975.

19. Moshe Blatt and Lawrence Kohlberg, "Effects of Classroom Discussions upon Children's Level of Moral Judgment," in Lawrence Kohlberg, ed., *Recent Research.*

20. Lawrence Kohlberg, Peter Scharf, and Joseph Hickey, "The Justice Structure of the Prison: A Theory and an Intervention," *The Prison Journal,* Autumn-Winter, 1972.

21. Lawrence Kohlberg, Kelsey Kauffman, Peter Scharf, and Joseph Hickey, *The Just Community Approach to Corrections: A Manual, Part I* (Cambridge, Mass.: Education Research Foundation, 1973).

22. An example of the need for small-group discussion comes from an alternative school community meeting called because a pair of the students had stolen the school's video-recorder. The resulting majority decision was that the school should buy back the recorder from the culprits through a fence. The teachers could not accept this decision and returned to a more authoritative approach. I believe if the moral reasoning of students urging this solution had been confronted by students at a higher stage, a different decision would have emerged.

DISCUSSION QUESTIONS

1. Should moral and civic education be the responsibility of the schools? Why? Why not?

2. What type of curriculum design lends itself to promoting the aims of moral education?

3. How do the family and norms of school cultures influence children's moral development?

4. What is the role of the social atmosphere in moral education?

5. Should values be infused into the curriculum or explicitly taught? Why? Why not?

17

A Critical Examination of Character Education

ALFIE KOHN

FOCUSING QUESTIONS

1. *What meanings are generally used to describe character education?*
2. *Why is understanding how individuals behave in context-specific situations relevant to analyzing the assumptions underlying character education programs?*
3. *In your opinion, is a negative view of human beings an appropriate orientation for creating character education programs? Why? Why not?*
4. *What essential components would traditional moralist and constructivists suggest for a character education program?*
5. *What should be the teachers' role in promoting students' moral development?*

Teachers and schools tend to mistake good behavior for good character. What they prize is docility, suggestibility; the child who will do what he is told; or even better, the child who will do what is wanted without even having to be told. They value most in children what children least value in themselves. Small wonder that their effort to build character is such a failure; they don't know it when they see it.

—John Holt
How Children Fail

Were you to stand somewhere in the continental United States and announce, "I'm going to Hawaii," it would be understood that you were heading for those islands in the Pacific that collectively constitute the 50th state. Were you to stand in Honolulu and make the same statement, however, you would probably be talking about one specific island in the chain—the big one to your southeast.

The word *Hawaii* would seem to have two meanings, a broad one and a narrow one; we depend on context to tell them apart.

The phrase *character education* also has two meanings. In the broad sense, it refers to almost anything that schools might try to provide outside of academics, especially when the purpose is to help children grow into good people. In the narrow sense, it denotes a particular style of moral training, one that reflects particular values as well as particular assumptions about the nature of children and how they learn.

Unfortunately, the two meanings of the term have become blurred, with the narrow version of character education dominating the field to the point that it is frequently mistaken for the broader concept. Thus educators who are keen to support children's social and moral development may turn, by default, to a program with a certain set of methods and a specific agenda that, on reflection, they might very well find objectionable.

My purpose in this chapter is to subject these programs to careful scrutiny and, in so doing, to highlight the possibility that there are other ways to achieve our broader objectives. I address myself not so much to those readers who are avid proponents of character education (in the narrow sense), but to those who simply want to help children become decent human beings and may not have thought carefully about what they are being offered.

Let me get straight to the point. What goes by the name of character education nowadays is, for the most part, a collection of exhortations and extrinsic inducements designed to make children work harder and do what they're told. Even when other values are also promoted—caring or fairness, say—the preferred method of instruction is tantamount to indoctrination. The point is to drill students in specific behaviors, rather than to engage them in deep, critical reflection about certain ways of being. This is the impression one gets from reading articles and books by contemporary proponents of character education, as well as the curriculum materials sold by the leading national programs. The impression is only strengthened by visiting schools that have been singled out for their commitment to character education. To wit:

> A huge, multiethnic elementary school in Southern California uses a framework created by the Jefferson Center for Character Education. Classes that the principal declares "well behaved" are awarded Bonus Bucks, which can eventually be redeemed for an ice cream party. On an enormous wall near the cafeteria, professionally painted Peanuts characters instruct children: "Never talk in line." A visitor is led to a fifth-grade classroom to observe an exemplary lesson on the current character education topic. The teacher is telling students to write down the name of the person they regard as the "toughest worker" in school. The teacher then asks them, "How many of you are going to be tough workers?" (Hands go up.) "Can you be a tough worker at home, too?" (Yes.)

> A small, almost entirely African American school in Chicago uses a framework created by the Character Education Institute. Periodic motivational assemblies are used to "give children a good pep

talk," as the principal puts it, and to reinforce the values that determine who will be picked as Student of the Month. Rule number one posted on the wall of a kindergarten room is "We will obey the teachers." Today students in this class are listening to the story of "Lazy Lion," who orders each of the other animals to build him a house, only to find each effort unacceptable. At the end, the teacher drives home the lesson: "Did you ever hear Lion say thank you?" (No.) "Did you ever hear Lion say please?" (No.) "It's good to always say...what?" (Please.) The reason for using these words, she points out, is that by doing so we are more likely to get what we want.

> A charter school near Boston has been established specifically to offer an intensive, homegrown character education curriculum to its overwhelmingly white, middle-class student body. At weekly public ceremonies, certain children receive a leaf that will then be hung in the Forest of Virtue. The virtues themselves are "not open to debate," the headmaster insists, since moral precepts in his view enjoy the same status as mathematical truths. In a first-grade classroom, a teacher is observing that "it's very hard to be obedient when you want something. I want you to ask yourself, 'Can I have it—and why not?'" She proceeds to ask the students, "What kinds of things show obedience?" and, after collecting a few suggestions, announces that she's "not going to call on anyone else now. We could go on forever, but we have to have a moment of silence and then a spelling test."

Some of the most popular schoolwide strategies for improving students' character seem dubious on their face. When President Clinton mentioned the importance of character education in his 1996 State of the Union address, the only specific practice he recommended was requiring students to wear uniforms. The premises here are, first, that children's character can be improved by forcing them to dress alike and, second, that if adults object to students' clothing the best solution is not to invite them to reflect together about how this problem might be solved, but instead to compel them all to wear the same thing.

A second strategy, also consistent with the dominant philosophy of character education, is an exercise that might be called "If It's Tuesday, This Must Be Honesty." Here, one value after another is targeted, with each assigned its own day, week, or month. This seriatim approach is unlikely to result in a lasting commitment to any of these values, much less a feeling for how they may be related. Nevertheless, such programs are taken very seriously by some of the same people who are quick to dismiss other educational programs, such as those intended to promote self-esteem, as silly and ineffective.

Then there is the strategy of offering students rewards when they are "caught" being good, an approach favored by right-wing religious groups[1] and orthodox behaviorists but also by leaders of—and curriculum suppliers for—the character education movement.[2] Because of its popularity and because a sizable body of psychological evidence germane to the topic is available, it is worth lingering on this particular practice for a moment.

In general terms, what the evidence suggests is this: the more we reward people for doing something, the more likely they are to lose interest in whatever they had to do to get the reward. Extrinsic motivation, in other words, is not only quite different from intrinsic motivation but actually tends to erode it.[3] This effect has been demonstrated under many different circumstances and with respect to many different attitudes and behaviors. Most relevant to character education is a series of studies showing that individuals who have been rewarded for doing something nice become less likely to think of themselves as caring or helpful people and more likely to attribute their behavior to the reward.

"Extrinsic incentives can, by undermining self-perceived altruism, decrease intrinsic motivation to help others," one group of researchers concluded on the basis of several studies. "A person's kindness, it seems, cannot be bought."[4] The same applies to a person's sense of responsibility, fairness, perseverance, and so on. The lesson a child learns from Skinnerian tactics is that the point of being good is to get rewards. No wonder researchers have found that children who are frequently rewarded—or, in another study, children who receive positive reinforcement for caring, sharing,

and helping—are less likely than other children to keep doing those things.[5]

In short, it makes no sense to dangle goodies in front of children for being virtuous. But even worse than rewards are *a*wards—certificates, plaques, trophies, and other tokens of recognition whose numbers have been artificially limited so only a few can get them. When some children are singled out as "winners," the central message that every child learns is this: "Other people are potential obstacles to my success."[6] Thus the likely result of making students beat out their peers for the distinction of being the most virtuous is not only less intrinsic commitment to virtue but also a disruption of relationships and, ironically, of the experience of community that is so vital to the development of children's character.

Unhappily, the problems with character education (in the narrow sense, which is how I'll be using the term unless otherwise indicated) are not restricted to such strategies as enforcing sartorial uniformity, scheduling a value of the week, or offering students a "doggie biscuit" for being good. More deeply troubling are the fundamental assumptions, both explicit and implicit, that inform character education programs. Let us consider five basic questions that might be asked of any such program: At what level are problems addressed? What is the view of human nature? What is the ultimate goal? Which values are promoted? And, finally, what is the theory of learning?

1.   At what level are problems addressed? One of the major purveyors of materials in this field, the Jefferson Center for Character Education in Pasadena, California, has produced a video that begins with some arresting images—quite literally. Young people are shown being led away in handcuffs, the point being that crime can be explained on the basis of an "erosion of American core values," as the narrator intones ominously. The idea that social problems can be explained by the fact that traditional virtues are no longer taken seriously is offered by many proponents of character education as though it were just plain common sense.

But if people steal or rape or kill solely because they possess bad values—that is, because of their personal characteristics—the implication is that political and economic realities are irrelevant and need not be addressed. Never mind staggering levels of unemployment in the inner cities or a system in which more and more of the nation's wealth is concentrated in fewer and fewer hands; just place the blame on individuals whose characters are deficient. A key tenet of the "Character Counts!" Coalition, which bills itself as a nonpartisan umbrella group devoid of any political agenda, is the highly debatable proposition that "negative social influences can [be] and usually are overcome by the exercise of free will and character."[7] What is presented as common sense is, in fact, conservative ideology.

Let's put politics aside, though. If a program proceeds by trying to "fix the kids"—as do almost all brands of character education—it ignores the accumulated evidence from the field of social psychology demonstrating that much of how we act and who we are reflects the situations in which we find ourselves. Virtually all the landmark studies in this discipline have been variations on this theme. Set up children in an extended team competition at summer camp and you will elicit unprecedented levels of aggression. Assign adults to the roles of prisoners or guards in a mock jail, and they will start to become their roles. Move people to a small town, and they will be more likely to rescue a stranger in need. In fact, so common is the tendency to attribute to an individual's personality or character what is actually a function of the social environment that social psychologists have dubbed this the "fundamental attribution error."

A similar lesson comes to us from the movement concerned with Total Quality Management associated with the ideas of the late W. Edwards Deming. At the heart of Deming's teaching is the notion that the "system" of an organization largely determines the results. The problems experienced in a corporation, therefore, are almost always due to systemic flaws, rather than to a lack of effort or ability on the part of individuals in that organization. Thus, if we are troubled by the way students are acting, Deming, along with most social psychologists, would presumably have us transform the structure of the classroom, rather than try to re-

make the students themselves—precisely the opposite of the character education approach.

2. What is the view of human nature? Character education's "fix-the-kids" orientation follows logically from the belief that kids need fixing. Indeed, the movement seems to be driven by a stunningly dark view of children—and, for that matter, of people in general. A "comprehensive approach [to character education] is based on a somewhat dim view of human nature," acknowledges William Kilpatrick, whose book *Why Johnny Can't Tell Right from Wrong* contains such assertions as "Most behavior problems are the result of sheer 'willfulness' on the part of children."[8]

Despite—or more likely because of—statements like that, Kilpatrick has frequently been invited to speak at character education conferences.[9] But that shouldn't be surprising in light of how many prominent proponents of character education share his views. Edward Wynne says his own work is grounded in a tradition of thought that takes a "somewhat pessimistic view of human nature."[10] The idea of character development "sees children as self-centered," in the opinion of Kevin Ryan, who directs the Center for the Advancement of Ethics and Character at Boston University, as well as heading up the character education network of the Association for Supervision and Curriculum Development.[11] Yet another writer approvingly traces the whole field back to the bleak world view of Thomas Hobbes: it is "an obvious assumption of character education," writes Louis Goldman, that people lack the instinct to work together. Without laws to compel us to get along, "our natural egoism would lead us into 'a condition of warfare one against another.'"[12] This sentiment is echoed by F. Washington Jarvis, headmaster of the Roxbury Latin School in Boston, one of Ryan's favorite examples of what character education should look like in practice. Jarvis sees human nature as "mean, nasty, brutish, selfish, and capable of great cruelty and meanness. We have to hold a mirror up to the students and say, 'This is who you are. Stop it.'"[13]

Even when proponents of character education don't express such sentiments explicitly, they give themselves away by framing their mission as a campaign for self-control. Amitai Etzioni, for example, does not merely include this attribute on a list of good character traits; he *defines* character principally in terms of the capacity "to control impulses and defer gratification."[14] This is noteworthy because the virtue of self-restraint—or at least the decision to give special emphasis to it—has historically been preached by those, from St. Augustine to the present, who see people as basically sinful.

In fact, at least three assumptions seem to be at work when the need for self-control is stressed: (1) we are all at war not only with others but with ourselves, torn between our desires and our reason (or social norms); (2) these desires are fundamentally selfish, aggressive, or otherwise unpleasant; and (3) these desires are very strong, constantly threatening to overpower us if we don't rein them in. Collectively, these statements describe religious dogma, not scientific fact. Indeed, the evidence from several disciplines converges to cast doubt on this sour view of human beings and, instead, supports the idea that it is as "natural" for children to help as to hurt. I will not rehearse that evidence here, partly because I have done so elsewhere at some length.[15] Suffice it to say that even the most hard-headed empiricist might well conclude that the promotion of prosocial values consists to some extent of supporting (rather than restraining or controlling) many facets of the self. Any educator who adopts this more balanced position might think twice before joining an educational movement that is finally inseparable from the doctrine of original sin.

3. What is the ultimate goal? It may seem odd even to inquire about someone's reasons for trying to improve children's character. But it is worth mentioning that the whole enterprise—not merely the particular values that are favored—is often animated by a profoundly conservative, if not reactionary, agenda. Character education based on "acculturating students to conventional norms of 'good' behavior…resonates with neoconservative concerns for social stability," observed David Purpel.[16] The movement has been described by another critic as a "yearning for some halcyon days of moral niceties and social tranquillity."[17] But it is

not merely a *social* order that some are anxious to preserve (or recover): character education is vital, according to one vocal proponent, because "the development of character is the backbone of the economic system" now in place.[18]

Character education, or any kind of education, would look very different if we began with other objectives—if, for example, we were principally concerned with helping children to become active participants in a democratic society (or agents for transforming a society *into* one that is authentically democratic). It would look different if our top priority were to help students to develop into principled and caring members of a community or advocates for social justice. To be sure, these objectives are not inconsistent with the desire to preserve certain traditions, but the point would then be to help children to decide which traditions are worth preserving and why, based on these other considerations. That is not at all the same as endorsing anything that is traditional or making the preservation of tradition our primary concern. In short, we want to ask character education proponents what goals they emphasize—and ponder whether their broad vision is compatible with our own.

4. Which values? Should we allow values to be taught in school? The question is about as sensible as asking whether our bodies should be allowed to contain bacteria. Just as humans are teeming with microorganisms, so schools are teeming with values. We can't see the former because they're too small; we don't notice the latter because they're too similar to the values of the culture at large. Whether or not we deliberately adopt a character or moral education program, we are always teaching values. Even people who insist that they are opposed to values in school usually mean that they are opposed to values other than their own.[19]

And that raises the inevitable question: Which values, or whose, should we teach? It has already become a cliché to reply that this question should not trouble us because, while there may be disagreement on certain issues, such as abortion, all of us can agree on a list of basic values that children ought to have. Therefore, schools can vigorously and unapologetically set about teaching all those values.

But not so fast. Look at the way character education programs have been designed and you will discover, alongside such unobjectionable items as "fairness" or "honesty," an emphasis on values that are, again, distinctly conservative—and, to that extent, potentially controversial. To begin with, the famous Protestant work ethic is prominent: children should learn to "work hard and complete their tasks well and promptly, even when they do not want to," says Ryan.[20] Here the Latin question *Cui bono?* comes to mind. Who benefits when people are trained not to question the value of what they have been told to do but simply to toil away at it—and to regard this as virtuous?[21] Similarly, when Wynne defines the moral individual as someone who is not only honest but also "diligent, obedient, and patriotic,"[22] readers may find themselves wondering whether these traits really qualify as *moral*—as well as reflecting on the virtues that are missing from this list.

Character education curricula also stress the importance of things like "respect," "responsibility," and "citizenship." But these are slippery terms, frequently used as euphemisms for uncritical deference to authority. Under the headline "The Return of the 'Fourth R'"—referring to "respect, responsibility, or rules"—a news magazine recently described the growing popularity of such practices as requiring uniforms, paddling disobedient students, rewarding those who are compliant, and "throwing disruptive kids out of the classroom."[23] Indeed, William Glasser observed some time ago that many educators "teach thoughtless conformity to school rules and call the conforming child 'responsible.'"[24] I once taught at a high school where the principal frequently exhorted students to "take responsibility." By this he meant specifically that they should turn in their friends who used drugs.

Exhorting students to be "respectful" or rewarding them if they are caught being "good" may likewise mean nothing more than getting them to do whatever the adults demand. Following a lengthy article about character education in the *New York Times Magazine,* a reader mused, "Do you suppose that if Germany had had character education at the time, it would have encouraged children to fight Nazism or to support it?"[25] The more time I spend in schools that are enthusiastically implementing character education programs, the more I am haunted by that question.

In place of the traditional attributes associated with character education, Deborah Meier and Paul Schwarz of the Central Park East Secondary School in New York nominated two core values that a school might try to promote: "empathy and skepticism: the ability to see a situation from the eyes of another and the tendency to wonder about the validity of what we encountered."[26] Anyone who brushes away the question "Which values should be taught?" might speculate on the concrete differences between a school dedicated to turning out students who are empathic and skeptical and a school dedicated to turning out students who are loyal, patriotic, obedient, and so on.

Meanwhile, in place of such personal qualities as punctuality or perseverance, we might emphasize the cultivation of autonomy so that children come to experience themselves as "origins" rather than "pawns," as one researcher put it.[27] We might, in other words, stress self-determination at least as much as self-control. With such an agenda, it would be crucial to give students the chance to participate in making decisions about their learning and about how they want their classroom to be.[28] This stands in sharp contrast to a philosophy of character education like Wynne's, which decrees that "it is specious to talk about student choices" and offers students no real power except for when we give "some students authority over other students (for example, hall guard, class monitor)."[29]

Even with values that are widely shared, a superficial consensus may dissolve when we take a closer look. Educators across the spectrum are concerned about excessive attention to self-interest and are committed to helping students to transcend a preoccupation with their own needs. But how does this concern play out in practice? For some of us, it takes the form of an emphasis on *compassion;* for the dominant character education approach, the alternative value to be stressed is *loyalty,* which is, of course, altogether different.[30] Moreover, as John Dewey remarked at the turn of the century, anyone seriously troubled about rampant individualism among children would promptly target for extinction the "drill-and-skill" approach to instruction: "The mere absorbing of facts and truths is so exclusively individual an affair that it tends very naturally to pass into selfishness."[31] Yet conservative champions of character education are often among the most outspoken supporters of a model of teaching that emphasizes rote memorization and the sequential acquisition of decontextualized skills.

Or take another example: all of us may say we endorse the idea of "cooperation," but what do we make of the practice of setting groups against one another in a quest for triumph, such that cooperation becomes the means and victory is the end? On the one hand, we might find this even more objectionable than individual competition. (Indeed, we might regard a "We're Number One!" ethic as a reason for schools to undertake something like character education in the first place.) On the other hand, "school-to-school, class-to-class, or row-to-row academic competitions" actually have been endorsed as part of a character education program,[32] along with contests that lead to awards for things like good citizenship.

The point, once again, is that it is entirely appropriate to ask which values a character education program is attempting to foster, notwithstanding the ostensible lack of controversy about a list of core values. It is equally appropriate to put such a discussion in context—specifically, in the context of which values are *currently* promoted in schools. The fact is that schools are already powerful socializers of traditional values—although, as noted above, we may fail to appreciate the extent to which this is true because we have come to take these values for granted. In most schools, for example, students are taught—indeed, compelled—to follow the rules regardless of whether the rules are reasonable and to respect authority regardless of whether that respect has been earned. (This process isn't always successful, of course, but that is a different matter.) Students are led to accept competition as natural and desirable and to see themselves

more as discrete individuals than as members of a community. Children in American schools are even expected to begin each day by reciting a loyalty oath to the Fatherland, although we call it by a different name. In short, the question is not whether to adopt the conservative values offered by most character education programs, but whether we want to consolidate the conservative values that are already in place.

5. What is the theory of learning? We come now to what may be the most significant, and yet the least remarked on, feature of character education: the way values are taught and the way learning is thought to take place.

> The character education coordinator for the small Chicago elementary school also teaches second grade. In her classroom, where one boy has been forced to sit by himself for the last two weeks ("He's kind of pesty"), she is asking the children to define tolerance. When the teacher gets the specific answers she is fishing for, she exclaims, "Say that again," and writes down only those responses. Later comes the moral: "If somebody doesn't think the way you think, should you turn them off?" (No.)
>
> Down the hall, the first-grade teacher is fishing for answers on a different subject. "When we play games, we try to understand the—what?" (Rules.) A moment later, the children scramble to get into place so she will pick them to tell a visitor their carefully rehearsed stories about conflict resolution. Almost every child's account, narrated with considerable prompting by the teacher, concerns name-calling or some other unpleasant incident that was "correctly" resolved by finding an adult. The teacher never asks the children how they felt about what happened or invites them to reflect on what else might have been done. She wraps up the activity by telling the children, "What we need to do all the time is clarify—make it clear—to the adult what you did."

The schools with character education programs that I have visited are engaged largely in exhortation and directed recitation. At first one might assume that this is due to poor implementation of the programs on the part of individual educators. But the programs themselves—and the theorists who promote them—really do seem to regard teaching as a matter of telling and compelling. For example, the broad-based "Character Counts!" Coalition offers a framework of six core character traits and then asserts that "young people should be specifically and repeatedly told what is expected of them." The leading providers of curriculum materials walk teachers through highly structured lessons in which character-related concepts are described and then students are drilled until they can produce the right answers.

Teachers are encouraged to praise children who respond correctly, and some programs actually include multiple-choice tests to ensure that students have learned their values. For example, here are two sample test questions prepared for teachers by the Character Education Institute, based in San Antonio, Texas: "Having to obey rules and regulations (a) gives everyone the same right to be an individual, (b) forces everyone to do the same thing at all times, (c) prevents persons from expressing their individually [sic]"; and "One reason why parents might not allow their children freedom of choice is (a) children are always happier when they are told what to do and when to do it, (b) parents aren't given a freedom of choice; therefore, children should not be given a choice either, (c) children do not always demonstrate that they are responsible enough to be given a choice." The correct answers, according to the answer key, are (a) and (c), respectively.

The Character Education Institute recommends "engaging the students in discussions," but only discussions of a particular sort: "Since the lessons have been designed to logically guide the students to the right answers, the teacher should allow the students to draw their own conclusions. However, if the students draw the wrong conclusion, the teacher is instructed to tell them why their conclusion is *wrong*."[33]

Students are told what to think and do, not only by their teachers but by highly didactic stories, such as those in the Character Education Institute's "Happy Life" series, which end with characters saying things like "I am glad that I did not cheat," or "Next time I will be helpful," or "I will never be selfish again." Most character education programs also deliver homilies by way of posters and banners and murals displayed throughout the school. Chil-

dren who do as they are told are presented with all manner of rewards, typically in front of their peers.

Does all of this amount to indoctrination? Absolutely, says Wynne, who declares that "school is and should and must be inherently indoctrinative."[34] Even when character education proponents tiptoe around that word, their model of instruction is clear: good character and values are *instilled in* or *transmitted to* students. We are "planting the ideas of virtue, of good traits in the young," says William Bennett.[35] The virtues or values in question are fully formed and, in the minds of many character education proponents, divinely ordained. The children are—pick your favorite metaphor— so many passive receptacles to be filled, lumps of clay to be molded, pets to be trained, or computers to be programmed.

Thus, when we see Citizen-of-the-Month certificates and "Be a good sport!" posters, when we find teachers assigning preachy stories and principals telling students what to wear, it is important that we understand what is going on. These techniques may appear merely innocuous or gimmicky; they may strike us as evidence of a scattershot, let's-try-anything approach. But the truth is that these are elements of a systematic pedagogical philosophy. They are manifestations of a model that sees children as objects to be manipulated, rather than as learners to be engaged.

Ironically, some people who accept character education without a second thought are quite articulate about the bankruptcy of this model when it comes to teaching academic subjects. Plenty of teachers have abandoned the use of worksheets, textbooks, and lectures that fill children full of disconnected facts and skills. Plenty of administrators are working to create schools where students can actively construct meaning around scientific and historical and literary concepts. Plenty of educators, in short, realize that memorizing right answers and algorithms doesn't help anyone to arrive at a deep understanding of ideas.

And so we are left scratching our heads. Why would all these people, who know that the "transmission" model fails to facilitate intellectual development, uncritically accept the very same model to promote ethical development? How could they understand that mathematical truths cannot be shoved down students' throats, but then participate in a program that essentially tries to shove moral truths down the same throats? In the case of individual educators, the simple answer may be that they missed the connection. Perhaps they just failed to recognize that "a classroom cannot foster the development of autonomy in the intellectual realm while suppressing it in the social and moral realms," as Constance Kamii and her colleagues put it not long ago.[36]

In the case of the proponents of character education, I believe the answer to this riddle is quite different. The reason they are promoting techniques that seem strikingly ineffective at fostering autonomy or ethical development is that, as a rule, they are not *trying* to foster autonomy or ethical development. The goal is not to support or facilitate children's social and moral growth, but simply to "demand good behavior from students," in Ryan's words.[37] The idea is to get compliance, to *make* children act the way we want them to.

Indeed, if these are the goals, then the methods make perfect sense—the lectures and pseudo-discussions, the slogans and the stories that conk students on the head with their morals. David Brooks, who heads the Jefferson Center for Character Education, frankly states, "We're in the advertising business." The way you get people to do something, whether it's buying Rice Krispies or becoming trustworthy, is to "encourage conformity through repeated messages"[38] The idea of selling virtues like cereal nearly reaches the point of self-parody in the Jefferson Center's curriculum, which includes the following activity: "There's a new product on the market! It's Considerate Cereal. Eating it can make a person more considerate. Design a label for the box. Tell why someone should buy and eat this cereal. Then list the ingredients."[39]

If "repeated messages" don't work, then you simply force students to conform: "Sometimes compulsion is what is needed to get a habit started," says William Kilpatrick.[40] We may recoil from the word "compulsion," but it is the premise of that sentence that really ought to give us pause.

When education is construed as the process of inculcating *habits*—which is to say, unreflective actions—then it scarcely deserves to be called education at all. It is really, as Alan Lockwood saw, an attempt to get "mindless conformity to externally imposed standards of conduct."[41]

Notice how naturally this goal follows from a dark view of human nature. If you begin with the premise that "good conduct is not our natural first choice," then the best you can hope for is "the development of good habits"[42]—that is, a system that gets people to act unthinkingly in the manner that someone else has deemed appropriate. This connection recently became clear to Ann Medlock, whose Giraffe Project was designed to evoke "students' own courage and compassion" in thinking about altruism, but which, in some schools, was being turned into a traditional, authoritarian program in which students were simply told how to act and what to believe. Medlock recalls suddenly realizing what was going on with these educators: "Oh, *I* see where you're coming from. You believe kids are no damn good!"[43]

The character education movement's emphasis on habit, then, is consistent with its view of children. Likewise, its process matches its product. The transmission model, along with the use of rewards and punishments to secure compliance, seems entirely appropriate if the values you are trying to transmit are things like obedience and loyalty and respect for authority. But this approach overlooks an important distinction between product and process. When we argue about which traits to emphasize—compassion or loyalty, cooperation or competition, skepticism or obedience—we are trafficking in value judgments. When we talk about how best to teach these things, however, we are being descriptive rather than just prescriptive. Even if you like the sort of virtues that appear in character education programs, and even if you regard the need to implement those virtues as urgent, the attempt to transmit or instill them dooms the project because that is just not consistent with the best theory and research on how people learn. (Of course, if you have reservations about many of the values that the character educators wish to instill, you may be *relieved* that their favored method is unlikely to be successful.)

I don't wish to be misunderstood. The techniques of character education may succeed in temporarily buying a particular behavior. But they are unlikely to leave children with a *commitment* to that behavior, a reason to continue acting that way in the future. You can turn out automatons who utter the desired words or maybe even "emit" (to use the curious verb favored by behaviorists) the desired actions. But the words and actions are unlikely to continue—much less transfer to new situations—because the child has not been invited to integrate them into his or her value structure. As Dewey observed, "The required beliefs cannot be hammered in; the needed attitudes cannot be plastered on."[44] Yet watch a character education lesson in any part of the country and you will almost surely be observing a strenuous exercise in hammering and plastering.

For traditional moralists, the constructivist approach is a waste of time. If values and traditions and the stories that embody them already exist, then surely "we don't have to reinvent the wheel," remarks Bennett.[45] Likewise an exasperated Wynne: "Must each generation try to completely reinvent society?"[46] The answer is no—and yes. It is not as though everything that now exists must be discarded and entirely new values fashioned from scratch. But the process of learning does indeed require that meaning, ethical or otherwise, be actively invented and reinvented, from the inside out. It requires that children be given the opportunity to make sense of such concepts as fairness or courage, regardless of how long the concepts themselves have been around. Children must be invited to reflect on complex issues, to recast them in light of their own experiences and questions, to figure out for themselves—and with one another—what kind of person one ought to be, which traditions are worth keeping, and how to proceed when two basic values seem to be in conflict.[47]

In this sense, reinvention is necessary if we want to help children to become moral people, as opposed to people who merely do what they are told—or reflexively rebel against what they are

told. In fact, as DeVries and Zan add (in a recent book that offers a useful antidote to traditional character education), "If we want children to resist [peer pressure] and not be victims of others' ideas, we have to educate children to think for themselves about all ideas, including those of adults."[48]

Traditionalists are even more likely to offer another objection to the constructivist approach, one that boils down to a single epithet: *relativism!* If we do anything other than insert moral absolutes in students, if we let them construct their own meanings, then we are saying that anything goes, that morality collapses into personal preferences. Without character education, our schools will just offer programs such as Values Clarification, in which adults are allegedly prohibited from taking a stand.

In response, I would offer several observations. First, the Values Clarification model of moral education, popular in some circles a generation ago, survives today mostly in the polemics of conservatives anxious to justify an indoctrinative approach. Naturally, no statistics are ever cited as to the number of school districts still telling students that any value is as good as any other—assuming the program actually said that in the first place.[49] Second, conservative critics tendentiously try to connect constructivism to relativism, lumping together the work of the late Lawrence Kohlberg with programs like Values Clarification.[50] The truth is that Kohlberg, while opposed to what he called the "bag of virtues" approach to moral education, was not much enamored of Values Clarification either, and he spent a fair amount of time arguing against relativism in general.[51]

If Kohlberg can fairly be criticized, it is for emphasizing moral reasoning, a cognitive process, to the extent that he may have slighted the affective components of morality, such as caring. But the traditionalists are not much for the latter either: caring is seen as an easy or soft virtue (Ryan) that isn't sufficiently "binding or absolute" (Kilpatrick). The objection to constructivism is not that empathy is eclipsed by justice, but that children—or even adults—should not have an active role to play in making decisions and reflecting on how to live. They should be led instead to an uncritical acceptance of ready-made truths. The character educator's job, remember, is to elicit the right answer from students and tell those who see things differently "why their conclusion is *wrong*." Any deviation from this approach is regarded as indistinguishable from full-blown relativism; we must "plant" traditional values in each child or else morality is nothing more than a matter of individual taste. Such either/or thinking, long since discarded by serious moral philosophers,[52] continues to fuel character education and to perpetuate the confusion of education with indoctrination.

To say that students must construct meaning around moral concepts is not to deny that adults have a crucial role to play. The romantic view that children can basically educate themselves so long as grown-ups don't interfere is not taken seriously by any constructivists I know of—certainly not by Dewey, Piaget, Kohlberg, or their followers. Rather, like Values Clarification, this view seems to exist principally as a straw man in the arguments of conservatives. Let there be no question, then: educators, parents, and other adults are desperately needed to offer guidance, to act as models (we hope), to pose challenges that promote moral growth, and to help children to understand the effects of their actions on other people, thereby tapping and nurturing a concern for others that is present in children from a very young age.[53]

Character education rests on three ideological legs: behaviorism, conservatism, and religion. Of these, the third raises the most delicate issues for a critic; it is here that the charge of *ad hominem* argument is most likely to be raised. So let us be clear: it is of no relevance that almost all the leading proponents of character education are devout Catholics. But it is entirely relevant that, in the shadows of their writings, there lurks the assumption that only religion can serve as the foundation for good character. (William Bennett, for example, has flatly asserted that the difference between right and wrong cannot be taught "without reference to religion."[54]) It is appropriate to consider the personal

beliefs of these individuals if those beliefs are ensconced in the movement they have defined and directed. What they do on Sundays is their own business, but if they are trying to turn our public schools into Sunday schools, that becomes everybody's business.

Even putting aside the theological underpinnings of the character education movement, the five questions presented in this chapter can help us to describe the natural constituency of that movement. Logically, its supporters should be those who firmly believe that we should focus our efforts on repairing the characters of children, rather than on transforming the environments in which they learn, those who assume the worst about human nature, those who are more committed to preserving than to changing our society, those who favor such values as obedience to authority, and those who define learning as the process of swallowing whole a set of preexisting truths. It stands to reason that readers who recognize themselves in this description would enthusiastically endorse character education in its present form.

The rest of us have a decision to make. Either we define our efforts to promote children's social and moral development as an *alternative* to "character education," thereby ceding that label to the people who have already appropriated it, or we try to *reclaim* the wider meaning of the term by billing what we are doing as a different kind of character education.

The first choice—opting out—seems logical: it strains the language to use a single phrase to describe practices as different as engaging students in reflecting about fairness, on the one hand, and making students dress alike, on the other. It seems foolish to pretend that these are just different versions of the same thing, and thus it may be unreasonable to expect someone with a constructivist or progressive vision to endorse what is now called character education. The problem with abandoning this label, however, is that it holds considerable appeal for politicians and members of the public at large. It will be challenging to explain that "character education" is not synonymous with helping children to grow into good people and, indeed, that the movement associated with the term is a good deal more controversial than it first appears.

The second choice, meanwhile, presents its own set of practical difficulties. Given that the individuals and organizations mentioned in this chapter have succeeded in putting their own stamp on character education, it will not be easy to redefine the phrase so that it can also signify a very different approach. It will not be easy, that is, to organize conferences, publish books and articles, and develop curricular materials that rescue the broad meaning of "character education."

Whether we relinquish or retain the nomenclature, though, it is vital that we work to decouple most of what takes place under the banner of "character education" from the enterprise of helping students become ethically sophisticated decision makers and caring human beings. Wanting young people to turn out that way doesn't require us to adopt traditional character education programs, any more than wanting them to be physically fit requires us to turn schools into Marine boot camps.

What does the alternative look like? Return once more to those five questions: in each case, an answer different from that given by traditional character education will help us to sketch the broad contours of a divergent approach. More specifically, we should probably target certain practices for elimination, add some new ones, and reconfigure still others that already exist. I have already offered a catalogue of examples of what to eliminate, from Skinnerian reinforcers to lesson plans that resemble sermons. As examples of what to add, we might suggest holding regular class meetings in which students can share, plan, decide, and reflect together.[55] We might also provide children with explicit opportunities to practice "perspective taking"—that is, imagining how the world looks from someone else's point of view. Activities that promote an understanding of how others think and feel, that support the impulse to imaginatively reach beyond the self, can provide the same benefits realized by holding democratic class meet-

ings—that is, helping students become more ethical and compassionate while simultaneously fostering intellectual growth.[56]

A good example of an existing practice that might be reconfigured is the use of literature to teach values. In principle, the idea is splendid: it makes perfect sense to select stories that not only help students develop reading skills (and an appreciation for good writing) but also raise moral issues. The trouble is that many programs use simplistic little morality tales in place of rich, complex literature. Naturally, the texts should be developmentally appropriate, but some character educators fail to give children credit for being able to grapple with ambiguity. (Imagine the sort of stories likely to be assigned by someone who maintains that "it is ridiculous to believe children are capable of objectively assessing most of the beliefs and values they must absorb to be effective adults."[57])

Perhaps the concern is not that students will be unable to make sense of challenging literature, but that they will not derive the "correct" moral. This would account for the fact that, even when character education curricula include impressive pieces of writing, the works tend to be used for the purpose of drumming in simple lessons. As Kilpatrick sees it, a story "points to these [characters] and says in effect, 'Act like this; don't act like that.'"[58] This kind of lesson often takes the form of hero worship, with larger-than-life characters—or real historical figures presented with their foibles airbrushed away—held up to students to encourage imitation of their actions.

Rather than employ literature to indoctrinate or induce mere conformity, we can use it to spur reflection. Whether the students are 6-year-olds or 16-year-olds, the discussion of stories should be open ended rather than relentlessly didactic. Teachers who refrain from tightly controlling such conversations are impressed again and again by the levels of meaning students prove capable of exploring and the moral growth that they exhibit in such an environment. Instead of announcing, "This man is a hero; do what he did," such teachers may involve the students in *deciding* who (if anyone) is heroic in a given story—or in contemporary culture[59]—and why. They may even invite students to reflect on the larger issue of whether it is desirable to have heroes. (Consider the quality of discussion that might be generated by asking older students to respond to the declaration of playwright Bertolt Brecht: "Unhappy is the land that needs a hero.")

More than specific practices that might be added, subtracted, or changed, a program to help children grow into good people begins with a commitment to change the way classrooms and schools are structured—and this brings us back to the idea of transcending a fix-the-kid approach. Consider the format of classroom discussions. A proponent of character education, invoking such traditional virtues as patience or self-control, might remind students that they must wait to be recognized by the teacher. But what if we invited students to think about the best way to conduct a discussion? Must we raise our hands? Is there another way to avoid having everyone talk at once? How can we be fair to those who aren't as assertive or as fast on their feet? Should the power to decide who can speak always rest with the teacher? Perhaps the problem is not with students who need to be more self-disciplined, but with the whole instructional design that has students waiting to be recognized to answer someone else's questions. And perhaps the real learning comes only when students have the chance to grapple with such issues.

One more example. A proponent of character education says we must make students understand that it is wrong to lie; we need to teach them about the importance of being honest. But why do people lie? Usually because they don't feel safe enough to tell the truth. The real challenge for us as educators is to examine that precept in terms of what is going on in our classrooms, to ask how we and the students together can make sure that even unpleasant truths can be told and heard. Does pursuing this line of inquiry mean that it's acceptable to fib? No. It means that the problem has to be dissected and solved from the inside out. It means behaviors oc-

cur in a context that teachers have helped to establish; therefore, teachers have to examine (and consider modifying) that context even at the risk of some discomfort to themselves. In short, if we want to help children grow into compassionate and responsible people, we have to change the way the classroom works and feels, not just the way each separate member of that class acts. Our emphasis should not be on forming individual characters so much as on transforming educational structures.

Happily, programs do exist whose promotion of children's social and moral development is grounded in a commitment to change the culture of schools. The best example of which I am aware is the Child Development Project, an elementary school program designed, implemented, and researched by the Developmental Studies Center in Oakland, California. The CDP's premise is that, by meeting children's needs, we increase the likelihood that they will care about others. Meeting their needs entails, among other things, turning schools into caring communities. The CDP offers the additional advantages of a constructivist vision of learning, a positive view of human nature, a balance of cognitive and affective concerns, and a program that is integrated into all aspects of school life (including the curriculum).[60]

Is the CDP an example of what character education ought to be—or of what ought to replace character education? The answer to that question will depend on tactical, and even semantic, considerations. Far more compelling is the need to reevaluate the practices and premises of contemporary character education. To realize a humane and progressive vision for children's development, we may need to look elsewhere.

ENDNOTES

1. See, for example, Linda Page, "A Conservative Christian View on Values," *School Administrator,* September 1995, p. 22.

2. See, for example, Kevin Ryan, "The Ten Commandments of Character Education," *School Administrator,* September 1995, p. 19; and program materials from the Character Education Institute and the Jefferson Center for Character Education.

3. See Alfie Kohn, *Punished by Rewards: The Trouble with Gold Stars, Incentive Plans, A's, Praise, and Other Bribes* (Boston: Houghton Mifflin, 1993); and Edward L. Deci and Richard M. Ryan, *Intrinsic Motivation and Self-determination in Human Behavior* (New York: Plenum, 1985).

4. See C. Daniel Batson et al., "Buying Kindness: Effect of an Extrinsic Incentive for Helping on Perceived Altruism," *Personality and Social Psychology Bulletin,* vol. 4, 1978, p. 90; Cathleen L. Smith et al., "Children's Causal Attributions Regarding Help Giving," *Child Development,* vol. 50, 1979, pp. 203–10; and William Edward Upton III, "Altruism, Attribution, and Intrinsic Motivation in the Recruitment of Blood Donors," *Dissertation Abstracts International* 34B, vol. 12, 1974, p. 6260.

5. Richard A. Fabes et al., "Effects of Rewards on Children's Prosocial Motivation: A Socialization Study," *Developmental Psychology,* vol. 25, 1989, pp. 509–15; and Joan Grusec, "Socializing Concern for Others in the Home," *Developmental Psychology,* vol. 27, 1991, pp. 338–42.

6. See Alfie Kohn, *No Contest: The Case Against Competition,* rev. ed. (Boston: Houghton Mifflin, 1992).

7. This statement is taken from an eight-page brochure produced by the "Character Counts!" Coalition, a project of the Josephson Institute of Ethics. Members of the coalition include the American Federation of Teachers, the National Association of Secondary School Principals, the American Red Cross, the YMCA, and many other organizations.

8. William Kilpatrick, *Why Johnny Can't Tell Right from Wrong* (New York: Simon & Schuster, 1992), pp. 96, 249.

9. For example, Kilpatrick was selected in 1995 to keynote the first in a series of summer institutes on character education sponsored by Thomas Lickona.

10. Edward Wynne, "Transmitting Traditional Values in Contemporary Schools," in Larry P. Nucci, ed., *Moral Development and Character Education: A Dialogue* (Berkeley, Calif.: McCutchan, 1989), p. 25.

11. Kevin Ryan, "In Defense of Character Education," in Nucci, p. 16.

12. Louis Goldman, "Mind, Character, and the Deferral of Gratification," *Educational Forum,* vol. 60, 1996, p. 136. As part of "educational reconstruction," he goes on to say, we must "connect the lower social classes to the middle classes who may provide role models for self-discipline" (p. 139).

13. Jarvis is quoted in Wray Herbert, "The Moral Child," *U.S. News & World Report,* 3 June 1996, p. 58.

14. Amitai Etzioni, *The Spirit of Community: The Reinvention of American Society* (New York: Simon & Schuster, 1993), p. 91.

15. See Alfie Kohn, *The Brighter Side of Human Nature: Altruism and Empathy in Everyday Life* (New York: Basic Books, 1990); and "Caring Kids: The Role of the Schools," *Phi Delta Kappan,* March 1991, pp. 496–506.

16. David E. Purpel, "Moral Education: An Idea Whose Time Has Gone," *The Clearing House,* vol. 64, 1991, p. 311.

17. This description of the character education movement is offered by Alan L. Lockwood in "Character Education: The Ten Percent Solution," *Social Education,* April/May 1991, p. 246. It is a particularly apt characterization of a book like *Why Johnny Can't Tell Right from Wrong,* which invokes an age of "chivalry" and sexual abstinence, a time when moral truths were uncomplicated and unchallenged. The author's tone, however, is not so much wistful about the past as angry about the present: he denounces everything from rock music (which occupies an entire chapter in a book about morality) and feminism to the "multiculturalists" who dare to remove "homosexuality from the universe of moral judgment" (p. 126).

18. Kevin Walsh of the University of Alabama is quoted in Eric N. Berg, "Argument Grows That Teaching of Values Should Rank with Lessons," *New York Times,* 1 January 1992, p. 32.

19. I am reminded of a woman in a Houston audience who heatedly informed me that she doesn't send her child to school "to learn to be nice." That, she declared, would be "social engineering." But a moment later this woman added that her child ought to be "taught to respect authority." Since this would seem to be at least as apposite an example of social engineering, one is led to conclude that the woman's real objection was to the teaching of *particular* topics or values.

20. Kevin Ryan, "Mining the Values in the Curriculum," *Educational Leadership,* November 1993, p. 16.

21. Telling students to "try hard" and "do their best" begs the important questions. *How,* exactly, do they do their best? Surely it is not just a matter of blind effort. And *why* should they do so, particularly if the task is not engaging or meaningful to them, or if it has simply been imposed on them? Research has found that the attitudes students take toward learning are heavily influenced by whether they have been led to attribute their success (or failure) to innate ability, to effort, or to other factors—and that traditional classroom practices such as grading and competition lead them to explain the results in terms of

ability (or its absence) and to minimize effort whenever possible. What looks like "laziness" or insufficient perseverance, in other words, often turns out to be a rational decision to avoid challenge; it is rational because this route proves most expedient for performing well or maintaining an image of oneself as smart. These systemic factors, of course, are complex and often threatening for educators to address; it is much easier just to impress on children the importance of doing their best and then blame them for lacking perseverance if they seem not to do so.

22. Edward A. Wynne, "The Great Tradition in Education: Transmitting Moral Values," *Educational Leadership,* December 1985/January 1986, p. 6.

23. Mary Lord, "The Return of the 'Fourth R,'" *U.S. News & World Report,* 11 September 1995, p. 58.

24. William Glasser, *Schools Without Failure* (New York: Harper & Row, 1969), p. 22.

25. Marc Desmond's letter appeared in the *New York Times Magazine,* 21 May 1995, p. 14. The same point was made by Robert Primack, "No Substitute for Critical Thinking: A Response to Wynne," *Educational Leadership,* December 1985/January 1986, p. 12.

26. Deborah Meier and Paul Schwarz, "Central Park East Secondary School," in Michael W. Apple and James A. Beane, eds., *Democratic Schools* (Alexandria, Va.: Association for Supervision and Curriculum Development, 1995), pp. 29–30.

27. See Richard de Charms, *Personal Causation: The Internal Affective Determinants of Behavior* (Hillsdale, N.J.: Erlbaum, 1983). See also the many publications of Edward Deci and Richard Ryan.

28. See, for example, Alfie Kohn, "Choices for Children: Why and How to Let Students Decide," *Phi Delta Kappan,* September 1993, pp. 8–20; and Child Development Project, *Ways We Want Our Class to Be: Class Meetings That Build Commitment to Kindness and Learning* (Oakland, Calif.: Developmental Studies Center, 1996).

29. The quotations are from Wynne, "The Great Tradition," p. 9; and Edward A. Wynne and Herbert J. Walberg, "The Complementary Goals of Character Development and Academic Excellence," *Educational Leadership,* December 1985/January 1986, p. 17. William Kilpatrick is equally averse to including students in decision making; he speaks longingly of the days when "schools were unapologetically authoritarian," declaring that "schools can learn a lot from the Army," which is a "hierarchial [sic], authoritarian, and undemocratic institution" (see *Why Johnny Can't,* p. 228).

30. The sort of compassion I have in mind is akin to what the psychologist Ervin Staub described as a "prosocial orientation" (see his *Positive Social Behavior and Morality,* vols. 1 and 2 [New York: Academic Press, 1978 and 1979])—a generalized inclination to care, share, and help across different situations and with different people, including those we don't know, don't like, and don't look like. Loyally lending a hand to a close friend is one thing; going out of one's way for a stranger is something else.

31. John Dewey, *The School and Society* (Chicago: University of Chicago Press, 1900; reprint, 1990), p. 15.

32. Wynne and Walberg, p. 17. For another endorsement of competition among students, see Kevin Ryan, "In Defense," p. 15.

33. This passage is taken from page 21 of an undated 28-page "Character Education Curriculum" produced by the Character Education Institute. Emphasis in original.

34. Wynne, "Great Tradition," p. 9. Wynne and other figures in the character education movement acknowledge their debt to the French social scientist Emile Durkheim, who believed that "all education is a continuous effort to impose on the child ways of seeing, feeling, and acting which he could not have arrived at spontaneously.... We exert pressure upon him in order that he may learn proper consideration for others, respect for customs and conventions, the need for work, etc." (See Durkheim, *The Rules of Sociological Method* [New York: Free Press, 1938], p. 6.)

35. This is from Bennett's introduction to *The Book of Virtues* (New York: Simon & Schuster, 1993), pp. 12–13.

36. Constance Kamii, Faye B. Clark, and Ann Dominick, "The Six National Goals: A Road to Disappointment," *Phi Delta Kappan,* May 1994, p. 677.

37. Kevin Ryan, "Character and Coffee Mugs," *Education Week,* 17 May 1995, p. 48.

38. The second quotation is a reporter's paraphrase of Brooks. Both it and the direct quotation preceding it appear in Philip Cohen, "The Content of Their Character: Educators Find New Ways to Tackle Values and Morality," *ASCD Curriculum Update,* Spring 1995, p. 4.

39. See B. David Brooks, *Young People's Lessons in Character: Student Activity Workbook* (San Diego: Young People's Press, 1996), p. 12.

40. Kilpatrick, p. 231.

41. To advocate this sort of enterprise, he adds, is to "caricature the moral life." See Alan L. Lockwood, "Keeping Them in the Courtyard: A Response to Wynne," *Educational Leadership,* December 1985/January 1986, p. 10.

42. Kilpatrick, p. 97.

43. Personal communication with Ann Medlock, May 1996.

44. John Dewey, *Democracy and Education* (New York: Free Press, 1916; reprint, 1966), p. 11.

45. Bennett, p. 11.

46. Wynne, "Character and Academics," p. 142.

47. For a discussion of how traditional character education fails to offer guidance when values come into conflict, see Lockwood, "Character Education."

48. Rheta DeVries and Betty Zan, *Moral Classrooms, Moral Children: Creating a Constructivist Atmosphere in Early Education* (New York: Teachers College Press, 1994), p. 253.

49. For an argument that critics tend to misrepresent what Values Clarification was about, see James A. Beane, *Affect in the Curriculum* (New York: Teachers College Press, 1990), pp. 104–6.

50. Wynne, for example, refers to the developers of Values Clarification as "popularizers" of Kohlberg's research (see "Character and Academics," p. 141), while Amitai Etzioni, in the course of criticizing Piaget's and Kohlberg's work, asserts that "a typical course on moral reasoning starts with something called 'values clarification'" (see *The Spirit of Community,* p. 98).

51. Kohlberg's model, which holds that people across cultures progress predictably through six stages of successively more sophisticated styles of moral reasoning, is based on the decidedly nonrelativistic premise that the last stages are superior to the first ones. See his *Essays on Moral Development, Vol. 1: The Philosophy of Moral Development* (San Francisco: Harper & Row, 1981), especially the essays titled "Indoctrination versus Relativity in Value Education" and "From *Is* to *Ought.*"

52. See, for example, James S. Fishkin, *Beyond Subjective Morality* (New Haven, Conn.: Yale University Press, 1984); and David B. Wong, *Moral Relativity* (Berkeley: University of California Press, 1984).

53. Researchers at the National Institute of Mental Health have summarized the available research as follows: "Even children as young as 2 years old have (a) the cognitive capacity to interpret the physical and psychological states of others, (b) the emotional capacity to effectively experience the other's state, and (c) the behavioral repertoire that permits the possibility of trying to alleviate discomfort in others. These are the capabilities that, we believe, underlie children's caring behavior in the presence of another person's distress…. Young children seem to show patterns of moral internalization that are not simply fear based or solely responsive to pa-rental commands. Rather, there are signs that children feel responsible for (as well as connected to and dependent on) others at a very young age." (See Carolyn Zahn-Waxler et al., "Development of Concern for Others," *Developmental Psychology,* vol. 28, 1992, pp. 127, 135. For more on the adult's role in light of these facts, see Kohn, *The Brighter Side.*)

54. "Education Secretary Backs Teaching of Religious Values," *New York Times,* 12 November 1985, p. B-4.

55. For more on class meetings, see Glasser, chaps. 10–12; Thomas Gordon, *T.E.T: Teacher Effectiveness Training* (New York: David McKay Co., 1974), chaps. 8–9; Jane Nelsen, Lynn Lott, and H. Stephen Glenn, *Positive Discipline in the Classroom* (Rocklin, Calif.: Prima, 1993); and Child Development Project, op. cit.

56. For more on the theory and research of perspective taking, see Kohn, *The Brighter Side,* chaps. 4–5; for practical classroom activities for promoting perspective-taking skills, see Norma Deitch Feshbach et al., *Learning to Care: Classroom Activities for Social and Affective Development* (Glenview, Ill.: Scott, Foresman, 1983). While specialists in the field distinguish between perspective taking (imagining what others see, think, or feel) and empathy (*feeling* what others feel), most educators who talk about the importance of helping children to become empathic really seem to be talking about perspective taking.

57. Wynne, "Great Tradition," p. 9.

58. Kilpatrick, p. 141.

59. It is informative to discover whom the proponents of a hero-based approach to character education themselves regard as heroic. For example, William Bennett's nominee for "possibly our greatest living American" is Rush Limbaugh. (See Terry Eastland, "Rush Limbaugh: Talking Back," *American Spectator,* September 1992, p. 23.)

60. See Victor Battistich et al., "The Child Development Project: A Comprehensive Program for the Development of Prosocial Character," in William M. Kurtines and Jacob L. Gewirtz, eds., *Moral Behavior and Development: Advances in Theory, Research, and Applications* (Hillsdale, N.J.: Erlbaum, 1989); and Daniel Solomon et al., "Creating a Caring Community: Educational Practices That Promote Children's Prosocial Development," in Fritz K. Oser, Andreas Dick, and Jean-Luc Patry, eds., *Effective and Responsible Teaching* (San Francisco: Jossey-Bass, 1992). For more information about the CDP program or about the research substantiating its effects, write the Developmental Studies Center at 2000 Embarcadero, Suite 305, Oakland, CA 94606.

DISCUSSION QUESTIONS

1. According to the author, how is character education most accurately described?
2. What are the fundamental limitations of current character education program strategies?
3. Why do many educators contest the goals and values that typify character education programs?
4. What divergent approaches would exemplify a program that is different from traditional approaches to moral development?
5. How can reflection be used to enhance students' moral growth?
6. How can classroom norms thwart or facilitate students' moral development?

18

Synthesis of Research on Cooperative Learning

ROBERT E. SLAVIN

FOCUSING QUESTIONS

1. *What are the concepts that underlie the cooperative learning methods?*
2. *What ideas are common to all student learning teams?*
3. *How do STAD and TGT differ from TAI and CIRC cooperative learning methods?*
4. *How might cooperative learning methods be used to facilitate mainstreaming?*
5. *What type of curriculum design is most appropriate for cooperative learning methods?*
6. *How do cooperative learning methods promote the aims of education?*

There was once a time when it was taken for granted that a quiet class was a learning class, when principals walked down the hall expecting to be able to hear a pin drop. Today, however, many schools are using programs that foster the hum of voices in classrooms. These programs, called *cooperative learning,* encourage students to discuss, debate, disagree, and ultimately to teach one another.

Cooperative learning has been suggested as the solution for an astonishing array of educational problems: it is often cited as a means of emphasizing thinking skills and increasing higher-order learning; as an alternative to ability grouping, remediation, or special education; as a means of improving race relations and acceptance of mainstreamed students; and as a way to prepare students for an increasingly collaborative work force. How many of these claims are justified? What effects do the various cooperative learning methods have on student achievement and other outcomes? Which forms of cooperative learning are most ef-

fective, and what components must be in place for cooperative learning to work?

To answer these questions, I've synthesized in this chapter the findings of studies of cooperative learning in elementary and secondary schools that have compared cooperative learning to traditionally taught control groups studying the same objectives over a period of at least four weeks (and up to a full school year or more). Here I present a brief summary of the effects of cooperative learning on achievement and noncognitive outcomes; for a more extensive review, see *Cooperative Learning: Theory, Research, and Practice* (Slavin 1990).

COOPERATIVE LEARNING METHODS

There are many quite different forms of cooperative learning, but all of them involve having students work in small groups or teams to help one another learn academic material. Cooperative learning usually supplements the teacher's instruction by giving

---

Highlights of Research on Cooperative Learning

In cooperative learning, students work in small groups to help one another master academic material. There are many quite different forms of cooperative learning, and the effectiveness of cooperative learning (particularly for achievement outcomes) depends on the particular approach used.

- For enhancing student achievement, the most successful approaches have incorporated two key elements: group goals and individual accountability. That is, groups are rewarded based on the individual learning of all group members.
- When group goals and individual accountability are used, achievement effects of cooperative learning are consistently positive; 37 of 44 experimental/control comparisons of at least four weeks' duration have found significantly positive effects, and none have favored traditional methods.
- Achievement effects of cooperative learning have been found to about the same degree at all grade levels (2–12), in all major subjects, and in urban, rural, and suburban schools. Effects are equally positive for high, average, and low achievers.
- Positive effects of cooperative learning have been consistently found on such diverse outcomes as self-esteem, intergroup relations, acceptance of academically handicapped students, attitudes toward school, and ability to work cooperatively.

—Robert E. Slavin

---

students an opportunity to discuss information or practice skills originally presented by the teacher; sometimes cooperative methods require students to find or discover information on their own. Cooperative learning has been used—and investigated—in every imaginable subject in grades 2–12, and is increasingly used in college.

Small-scale laboratory research on cooperation dates back to the 1920s (see Deutsch 1949; Slavin 1977a); research on specific applications of cooperative learning to the classroom began in the early 1970s. At that time, four research groups, one in Israel and three in the U.S., began independently to develop and study cooperative learning methods in classroom settings.

Now researchers all over the world are studying practical applications of cooperative learning principles, and many cooperative learning methods have been evaluated in one or more experimental/control comparisons. The best evaluated of the cooperative models are described below (adapted from Slavin 1990). These include four Student Team Learning variations, Jigsaw, Learning Together, and Group Investigation.

Student Team Learning

Student Team Learning (STL) techniques were developed and researched at Johns Hopkins University. More than half of all experimental studies of practical cooperative learning methods involve STL methods.

All cooperative learning methods share the idea that students work together to learn and are responsible for one another's learning as well as their own. STL methods, in addition to this idea, emphasize the use of team goals and team success, which can only be achieved if all members of the team learn the objectives being taught. That is, in Student Team Learning the students' tasks are not to *do* something as a team but to *learn* something as a team.

Three concepts are central to all Student Team Learning methods: *team rewards, individual accountability,* and *equal opportunities for success.* Using STL techniques, teams earn certificates or other team rewards if they achieve above a designated criterion. The teams are not in competition to earn scarce rewards; all (or none) of the teams may achieve the criterion in a given week. *Individual accountability* means that the team's success depends on the individual learning of all team members. This focuses the activity of the team members on explaining concepts to one another and making sure that everyone on the team is ready for a quiz or other assessment that they will take without teammate help. *Equal opportunities for success* means that students contribute to their teams by improving over their own past performances. This ensures that high, average, and low achievers are equally challenged to do their best and that the contributions of all team members will be valued.

The findings of these experimental studies (summarized in this section) indicate that team rewards and individual accountability are essential elements for producing basic skills achievement (Slavin 1983a, 1983b, 1990). It is not enough to simply tell students to work together. They must have a reason to take one another's achievement seriously. Further, if students are rewarded for doing better than they have in the past, they will be more motivated to achieve than if they are rewarded based on their performance in comparison to others, because rewards for improvement make success neither too difficult nor too easy for students to achieve (Slavin 1980).

Four principal Student Team Learning methods have been extensively developed and researched. Two are general cooperative learning methods adaptable to most subjects and grade levels: Student Teams-Achievement Divisions (STAD) and Teams-Games-Tournament (TGT). The remaining two are comprehensive curriculums designed for use in particular subjects at particular grade levels: Team Assisted Individualization (TAI) for mathematics in grades 3–6 and Cooperative Integrated Reading and Composition (CIRC) for reading and writing instruction in grades 3–5.

Student Teams-Achievement Divisions (STAD). In STAD (Slavin 1978, 1986), students are assigned to four-member learning teams mixed in performance level, sex, and ethnicity. The teacher presents a lesson, and then students work within their teams to make sure that all team members have mastered the lesson. Finally, all students take individual quizzes on the material, at which time they may *not* help one another.

Students' quiz scores are compared to their own past averages, and points are awarded based on the degree to which students can meet or exceed their own earlier performances. These points are then summed to form team scores, and teams that meet certain criteria earn certificates or other rewards. The whole cycle of activities, from teacher presentation to team practice to quiz, usually takes three to five class periods.

STAD has been used in a wide variety of subjects, from mathematics to language arts and social studies. It has been used from grade 2 through college. STAD is most appropriate for teaching well-defined objectives with single right answers, such as mathematical computations and applications, language usage and mechanics, geography and map skills, and science facts and concepts.

Teams-Games-Tournament (TGT). Teams-Games-Tournament (DeVries and Slavin 1978; Slavin 1986) was the first of the Johns Hopkins cooperative learning methods. It uses the same teacher presentations and teamwork as in STAD, but replaces the quizzes with weekly tournaments. In these, students compete with members of other teams to contribute points to their team scores. Students compete at three-person "tournament tables" against others with similar past records in mathematics. A "bumping" procedure changes table assignments to keep the competition fair. The winner at each tournament table brings the same number of points to his or her team, regardless of which table it is; this means that low achievers (competing with other low achievers) and high achievers (competing with other high achievers) have equal opportunities for success. As in STAD, high-performing teams earn certificates or other forms of team rewards. TGT is appropriate for the same types of objectives as STAD.

Team Assisted Individualization (TAI). Team Assisted Individualization (TAI; Slavin et al. 1986) shares with STAD and TGT the use of four-member mixed ability learning teams and certificates for high-performing teams. But where STAD and TGT use a single pace of instruction for the class, TAI combines cooperative learning with individualized instruction. Also, where STAD and TGT apply to most subjects and grade levels, TAI is specifically designed to teach mathematics to students in grades 3–6 (or older students not ready for a full algebra course).

In TAI, students enter an individualized sequence according to a placement test and then proceed at their own rates. In general, team members work on different units. Teammates check each others' work against answer sheets and help one another with any problems. Final unit tests are taken without teammate help and are scored by student monitors. Each week, teachers total the number of units completed by all team members and give certificates or other team rewards to teams that exceed a criterion score based on the number of final tests passed, with extra points for perfect papers and completed homework.

Because students take responsibility for checking each others' work and managing the flow of materials, the teacher can spend most of the class time presenting lessons to small groups of students drawn from the various teams who are working at the same point in the mathematics sequence. For example, the teacher might call up a decimals group, present a lesson, and then send the students back to their teams to work on problems. Then the teacher might call the fractions group, and so on.

Cooperative Integrated Reading and Composition (CIRC). The newest of the Student Team Learning methods is a comprehensive program for teaching reading and writing in the upper elementary grades called Cooperative Integrated Reading and Composition (CIRC) (Stevens et al. 1987). In CIRC, teachers use basal or literature-based readers and reading groups, much as in traditional reading programs. However, all students are assigned to teams composed of two pairs from two different reading groups. For example, a team might have two "Bluebirds" and two "Redbirds." While the teacher is working with one reading group, the paired students in the other groups are working on a series of cognitively engaging activities, including reading to one another, making predictions about how narrative stories will come out, summarizing stories to one another, writing responses to stories, and practicing spelling, decoding, and vocabulary. If the reading class is not divided into homogeneous reading groups, all students in the teams work with one another. Students work as a total team to master "main idea" and other comprehension skills. During language arts periods, students engage in writing drafts, revising and editing one another's work, and preparing for "publication" of team books.

In most CIRC activities, students follow a sequence of teacher instruction, team practice, team pre-assessments, and quizzes. That is, students do not take the quiz until their teammates have determined that they are ready. Certificates are given to teams based on the average performance of all team members on all reading and writing activities.

Other Cooperative Learning Methods

Jigsaw. Jigsaw was originally designed by Elliot Aronson and his colleagues (1978). In Aronson's Jigsaw method, students are assigned to six-member teams to work on academic material that has been broken down into sections. For example, a biography might be divided into early life, first accomplishments, major setbacks, later life, and impact on history. Each team member reads his or her section. Next, members of different teams who have studied the same sections meet in "expert groups" to discuss their sections. Then the students return to their teams and take turns teaching their teammates about their sections. Since the only way students can learn sections other than their own is to listen carefully to their teammates, they are motivated to support and show interest in one another's work.

Slavin (1986) developed a modification of Jigsaw at Johns Hopkins University and then incorporated it in the Student Team Learning program. In this method, called Jigsaw II, students work in four- or five-member teams as in TGT and STAD. Instead of each student's being assigned a particular section of text, all students read a common narrative, such as a book chapter, a short story, or a biography. However, each student receives a topic (such as "climate" in a unit on France) on which to become an expert. Students with the same topics meet in expert groups to discuss them, after which they return to their teams to teach what they have learned to their teammates. Then students take individual quizzes, which result in team scores based on the improvement score system of STAD. Teams that meet preset standards earn certificates. Jigsaw is primarily used in social studies and other subjects where learning from text is important.

Learning Together.   David Johnson and Roger Johnson at the University of Minnesota developed the Learning Together models of cooperative learning (Johnson and Johnson 1987). The methods they have researched involve students working on assignment sheets in four- or five-member heterogeneous groups. The groups hand in a single sheet and receive praise and rewards based on the group product. Their methods emphasize team-building activities before students begin working together and regular discussions within groups about how well they are working together.

Group Investigation.   Group Investigation, developed by Shlomo Sharan and Yael Sharan at the University of Tel Aviv, is a general classroom organization plan in which students work in small groups using cooperative inquiry, group discussion, and cooperative planning and projects (Sharan and Sharan 1976). In this method, students form their own two- to six-member groups. After choosing subtopics from a unit being studied by the entire class, the groups further break their sub-topics into individual tasks and carry out the activities necessary to prepare group reports. Each group then makes a presentation or display to communicate its findings to the entire class.

RESEARCH ON COOPERATIVE LEARNING

Cooperative learning methods are among the most extensively evaluated alternatives to traditional instruction in use today. Outcome evaluations include:

- academic achievement,
- intergroup relations,
- mainstreaming,
- self-esteem,
- others.

Academic Achievement.   More than 70 high-quality studies have evaluated various cooperative learning methods over periods of at least four weeks in regular elementary and secondary schools; 67 of these have measured effects on student achievement (see Slavin 1990). All these studies compared the effects of cooperative learning to those of traditionally taught control groups on measures of the same objectives pursued in all classes. Teachers and classes were either randomly assigned to cooperative or control conditions or matched on pretest achievement level and other factors.

Overall, of 67 studies of the achievement effects of cooperative learning, 41 (61 percent) found significantly greater achievement in cooperative than in control classes. Twenty-five (37 percent) found no differences, and in only one study did the control group outperform the experimental group. However, the effects of cooperative learning vary considerably according to the particular methods used. As noted earlier, two elements must be present if cooperative learning is to be effective: *group goals* and *individual accountability* (Slavin 1983a, 1983b, 1990). That is, groups must be working to achieve some goal or to earn rewards or recognition, and the success of the group must depend on the individual learning of every group member.

In studies of methods such as STAD, TGT, TAI, and CIRC, effects on achievement have been consistently positive; 37 out of 44 such studies (84 percent) found significant positive achievement effects. In contrast, only 4 of 23 studies (17 percent) lacking group goals and individual accountability found positive effects on student achievement. Two of these positive effects were found in studies of Group Investigation in Israel (Sharan et al. 1984; Sharan and Shachar 1988). In Group Investigation, students in each group are responsible for one unique part of the group's overall task, ensuring individual accountability. Then the group's overall performance is evaluated. Even though there are no specific group rewards, the group evaluation probably serves the same purpose.

Why are group goals and individual accountability so important? To understand this, consider the alternatives. In some forms of cooperative learning, students work together to complete a single worksheet or to solve one problem together. In such methods, there is little reason for more able students to take time to explain what is going on to their less able groupmates or to ask their opinions. When the group task is to *do* something, rather than to *learn* something, the participation of less able students may be seen as interference rather than help. It may be easier in this circumstance for students to give each other answers than to explain concepts or skills to one another.

In contrast, when the group's task is to ensure that every group member *learns* something, it is in the interests of every group member to spend time explaining concepts to his or her groupmates. Studies of students' behaviors within cooperative groups have consistently found that the students who gain most from cooperative work are those who give and receive elaborated explanations (Webb 1985). In contrast, Webb found that giving and receiving answers without explanations were *negatively* related to achievement gain. What group goals and individual accountability do is to motivate students to give explanations and to take one another's learning seriously, instead of simply giving answers.

Cooperative learning methods generally work equally well for all types of students. While occasional studies find particular advantages of high or low achievers, boys or girls, and so on, the great majority find equal benefits for all types of students. Sometimes teachers or parents worry that cooperative learning will hold back high achievers. The research provides absolutely no support for this claim; high achievers gain from cooperative learning (relative to high achievers in traditional classes) just as much as do low and average achievers (see Slavin, this issue, p. 63).

Research on the achievement effects of cooperative learning has more often taken place in grades 3–9 than 10–12. Studies at the senior high school level are about as positive as those at earlier grade levels, but there is a need for more research at that level. Cooperative learning methods have been equally successful in urban, rural, and suburban schools and with students of different ethnic groups (although a few studies have found particularly positive effects for black students; see Slavin and Oickle 1981).

Among the cooperative learning methods, the Student Team Learning programs have been most extensively researched and most often found instructionally effective. Of 14 studies of STAD and closely related methods, 11 found significantly higher achievement for this method than for traditional instruction, and two found no differences. For example, Slavin and Karweit (1984) evaluated STAD over an entire school year in inner-city Philadelphia 9th grade mathematics classes. Student performance on a standardized mathematics test increased significantly more than in either a mastery learning group or a control group using the same materials. Substantial differences favoring STAD have been found in such diverse subjects as social studies (e.g., Allen and Van Sickle 1984), language arts (Slavin and Karweit 1981), reading comprehension (Stevens, Slavin, Farnish, and Madden 1988), mathematics (Sherman and Thomas 1986), and science (Okebukola 1985). Nine of 11 studies of TGT found similar results (DeVries and Slavin 1978).

The largest effects of Student Team Learning methods have been found in studies of TAI. Five of six studies found substantially greater learning of mathematics computations in TAI than in control classes, while one study found no differences (see Slavin 1985b). Experimental control differences were still substantial (though smaller) a year after the students were in TAI (Slavin and Karweit 1985). In mathematics concepts and applications, one of three studies (Slavin et al. 1984) found significantly greater gains in TAI than control methods, while two found no significant differences (Slavin and Karweit 1985).

In comparison with traditional control groups, three experimental studies of CIRC have found substantial positive effects on scores from standardized tests of reading comprehension, reading vocabulary, language expression, language mechanics, and spelling (Madden et al. 1986, Stevens et al. 1987, Stevens et al. 1990). Significantly greater achievement on writing samples was also found favoring the CIRC students in the two studies which assessed writing.

Other than STL methods, the most consistently successful model for increasing student achievement is Group Investigation (Sharan and Sharan 1976). One study of this method (Sharan et al. 1984) found that it increased the learning of English as a foreign language, while Sharan and Shachar (1988) found positive effects of Group Investigation on the learning of history and geography. A third study of only three weeks' duration (Sharan et al. 1980) also found positive effects on social studies achievement, particularly on higher-level concepts. The Learning Together methods (Johnson and Johnson 1987) have been found instructionally effective when they include the assignment of group grades based on the average of group members' individual quiz scores (e.g., Humphreys et al. 1982, Yager et al. 1985). Studies of the original Jigsaw method have not generally supported this approach (e.g., Moskowitz et al. 1983); but studies of Jigsaw II, which uses group goals and individual accountability, have shown positive effects (Mattingly and Van Sickle 1990, Ziegler 1981).

Intergroup Relations.   In the laboratory research on cooperation, one of the earliest and strongest findings was that people who cooperate learn to like one another (Slavin 1977b). Not surprisingly, the cooperative learning classroom studies have found quite consistently that students express greater liking for their classmates in general as a result of participating in a cooperative learning method (see Slavin 1983a, 1990). This is important in itself and even more important when the students have different ethnic backgrounds. After all, there is substantial evidence that, left alone, ethnic separateness in schools does not naturally diminish over time (Gerard and Miller 1975).

Social scientists have long advocated interethnic cooperation as a means of ensuring positive intergroup relations in desegregated settings. Contact Theory (Allport 1954), which is in the U.S. the dominant theory of intergroup relations, predicted that positive intergroup relations would arise from school desegregation if and only if students participated in cooperative, equal-status interaction sanctioned by the school. Research on cooperative learning methods has borne out the predictions of Contact Theory. These techniques emphasize cooperative, equal-status interaction between students of different ethnic backgrounds sanctioned by the school (Slavin 1985a).

In most of the research on intergroup relations, students were asked to list their best friends at the beginning of the study and again at the end. The number of friendship choices students made outside their own ethnic groups was the measure of intergroup relations.

Positive effects on intergroup relations have been found for STAD, TGT, TAI, Jigsaw, Learning Together, and Group Investigation models (Slavin 1985b). Two of these studies, one on STAD (Slavin 1979) and one on Jigsaw II (Ziegler 1981), included follow-ups of intergroup friendships several months after the end of the studies. Both found that students who had been in cooperative learning classes still named significantly more friends outside their own ethnic groups than did students who had been in control classes. Two studies of Group Investigation (Sharan et al. 1984, Sharan and Shachar 1988) found that students' improved attitudes and behaviors toward classmates of different ethnic backgrounds extended to classmates who had never been in the same groups, and a study of TAI (Oishi 1983) found positive effects of this method on cross-ethnic interactions outside as well as in class. The U.S. studies of cooperative learning and intergroup relations involved black, white, and (in a few cases) Mexican-American students. A study of Jigsaw II by Ziegler (1981) took place in Toronto, where the major ethnic groups were Anglo-Canadians and children of recent European immigrants. The Sharan (Sharan et al. 1984, Sharan and Shachar 1988) studies of Group Investigation took place in Israel and involved friendships between Jews of both European and Middle Eastern backgrounds.

Mainstreaming.   Although ethnicity is a major barrier to friendship, it is not so large as the one between physically or mentally handicapped children and their normal-progress peers. Mainstreaming, an unprecedented opportunity for handicapped children to take their place in the school and society, has created enormous practical problems for classroom teachers, and it often leads to social rejection of the handicapped children. Because cooperative learning methods have been successful in improving relationships across the ethnicity barrier—which somewhat resembles the barrier between mainstreamed and normal-progress students—these methods have also been applied to increase the acceptance of the mainstreamed student.

The research on cooperative learning and mainstreaming has focused on the academically handicapped child. In one study, STAD was used to attempt to integrate students performing two years or more below the level of their peers into the social structure of the classroom. The use of STAD significantly reduced the degree to which the normal-progress students rejected their mainstreamed classmates and increased the academic achievement and self-esteem of all students, mainstreamed as well as normal-progress (Madden and Slavin 1983). Similar effects have been found for TAI

(Slavin et al. 1984), and other research using cooperative teams has also shown significant improvements in relationships between mainstreamed academically handicapped students and their normal-progress peers (Ballard et al. 1977, Cooper et al. 1980).

In addition, one study in a self-contained school for emotionally disturbed adolescents found that the use of TGT increased positive interactions and friendships among students (Slavin 1977a). Five months after the study ended, these positive interactions were still found more often in the former TGT classes than in the control classes. In a study in a similar setting, Janke (1978) found that the emotionally disturbed students were more on-task, were better behaved, and had better attendance in TGT classes than in control classes.

Self-Esteem.   One of the most important aspects of a child's personality is his or her self-esteem. Several researchers working on cooperative learning techniques have found that these methods do increase students' self-esteem. These improvements in self-esteem have been found for TGT and STAD (Slavin 1990), for Jigsaw (Blaney et al. 1977), and for the three methods combined (Slavin and Karweit 1981). Improvements in student self-concepts have also been found for TAI (Slavin et al. 1984).

Other Outcomes.   In addition to effects on achievement, positive intergroup relations, greater acceptance of mainstreamed students, and self-esteem, effects of cooperative learning have been found on a variety of other important educational outcomes. These include liking school, development of peer norms in favor of doing well academically, feelings of individual control over the student's own fate in school, and cooperativeness and altruism (see Slavin 1983a, 1990). TGT (DeVries and Slavin 1978) and STAD (Slavin 1978, Janke 1978) have been found to have positive effects on students' time-on-task. One study found that lower socioeconomic status students at risk of becoming delinquent who worked in cooperative groups in 6th grade had better attendance, fewer contacts with the police, and higher behavioral ratings by teachers in grades 7–11 than did control students (Hartley 1976). Another study implemented forms of cooperative learning beginning in kindergarten and continuing through the 4th grade (Solomon et al. 1990). This study found that the students who had been taught cooperatively were significantly higher than control students on measures of supportive, friendly, and prosocial behavior; were better at resolving conflicts; and expressed more support for democratic values.

CONCLUSION

Returning to the questions at the beginning of this chapter, we now see the usefulness of cooperative learning strategies for improving such diverse outcomes as student achievement at a variety of grade levels and in many subjects, intergroup relations, relationships between mainstreamed and normal-progress students, and student self-esteem. Further, their widespread and growing use demonstrates that cooperative learning methods are practical and attractive to teachers. The history of the development, evaluation, and dissemination of cooperative learning is an outstanding example of the use of educational research to create programs that have improved the educational experience of thousands of students and will continue to affect thousands more.

ENDNOTE

Author's note. This chapter was written under funding from the Office of Educational Research and Improvement, U.S. Department of Education (Grant No. OERI-R-117-R90002). However, any opinions expressed are mine and do not represent OERI positions or policy.

REFERENCES

Allen, W. H., and R. L. Van Sickle. (1984). "Learning Teams and Low Achievers." *Social Education:* 60–64.

Allport, G. (1954). *The Nature of Prejudice.* Cambridge, Mass.: Addison-Wesley.

Aronson, E., N. Blaney, C. Stephan, J. Sikes, and M. Snapp. (1978). *The Jigsaw Classroom.* Beverly Hills, Calif.: Sage.

Ballard, M., L. Corman, J. Gottlieb, and M. Kauffman. (1977). "Improving the Social Status of Mainstreamed Retarded Children." *Journal of Educational Psychology* 69: 605–611.

Blaney, N. T., S. Stephan, D. Rosenfeld, E. Aronson, and J. Sikes. (1977). "Interdependence in the Classroom: A Field Study." *Journal of Educational Psychology* 69: 121–128.

Cooper, L., D. W. Johnson, R. Johnson, and F. Wilderson. (1980). "Effects of Cooperative, Competitive, and Individualistic Experiences on Interpersonal Attraction Among Heterogeneous Peers." *Journal of Social Psychology* 111: 243–252.

Deutsch, M. (1949). "A Theory of Cooperation and Competition." *Human Relations* 2: 129–152.

DeVries, D. L., and R. E. Slavin. (1978). "Teams-Games-Tournament (TGT): Review of Ten Classroom Experiments." *Journal of Research and Development in Education* 12: 28–38.

Gerard, H. B., and N. Miller. (1975). *School Desegregation: A Long-Range Study.* New York: Plenum.

Hartley, W. (1976). *Prevention Outcomes of Small Group Education with School Children: An Epidemiologic Follow-Up of the Kansas City School Behavior Project.* Kansas City: University of Kansas Medical Center.

Humphreys, B., R. Johnson, and D. W. Johnson. (1982). "Effects of Cooperative, Competitive, and Individualistic Learning on Students' Achievement in Science Class." *Journal of Research in Science Teaching* 19: 351–356.

Janke, R. (April 1978). "The Teams-Games-Tournament (TGT) Method and the Behavioral Adjustment and Academic Achievement of Emotionally Impaired Adolescents." Paper presented at the annual convention of the American Educational Research Association, Toronto.

Johnson, D. W., and R. T. Johnson. (1987). *Learning Together and Alone.* 2nd ed. Englewood Cliffs, N.J.: Prentice-Hall.

Madden, N. A., and R. E. Slavin. (1983). "Cooperative Learning and Social Acceptance of Mainstreamed Academically Handicapped Students." *Journal of Special Education* 17: 171–182.

Madden, N. A., R. J. Stevens, and R. E. Slavin. (1986). *A Comprehensive Cooperative Learning Approach to Elementary Reading and Writing: Effects on Student*

Achievement. Report No. 2. Baltimore, Md.: Center for Research on Elementary and Middle Schools, Johns Hopkins University.

Mattingly, R. M., and R. L. Van Sickle. (1990). *Jigsaw II in Secondary Social Studies: An Experiment.* Athens, Ga.: University of Georgia.

Moskowitz, J. M., J. H. Malvin, G. A. Schaeffer, and E. Schaps. (1983). "Evaluation of a Cooperative Learning Strategy." *American Educational Research Journal* 20: 687–696.

Oishi, S. (1983). "Effects of Team-Assisted Individualization in Mathematics on Cross-Race Interactions of Elementary School Children." Doctoral diss., University of Maryland.

Okebukola, P. A. (1985). "The Relative Effectiveness of Cooperative and Competitive Interaction Techniques in Strengthening Students' Performance in Science Classes." *Science Education* 69: 501–509.

Sharan, S., and C. Shachar. (1988). *Language and Learning in the Cooperative Classroom.* New York: Springer.

Sharan, S., and Y. Sharan. (1976). *Small-group Teaching.* Englewood Cliffs, N.J.: Educational Technology Publications.

Sharan, S., R. Hertz-Lazarowitz, and Z. Ackerman. (1980). "Academic Achievement of Elementary School Children in Small-group vs. Whole Class Instruction." *Journal of Experimental Education* 48: 125–129.

Sharan, S., P. Kussell, R. Hertz-Lazarowitz, Y. Bejarano, S. Raviv, and Y. Sharan. (1984). *Cooperative Learning in the Classroom: Research in Desegregated Schools.* Hillsdale, N.J.: Erlbaum.

Sherman, L. W., and M. Thomas. (1986). "Mathematics Achievement in Cooperative Versus Individualistic Goal-structured High School Classrooms." *Journal of Educational Research* 79: 169–172.

Slavin, R. E. (1977a). "A Student Team Approach to Teaching Adolescents with Special Emotional and Behavioral Needs." *Psychology in the Schools* 14: 77–84.

Slavin, R. E. (1977b). "Classroom Reward Structure: An Analytical and Practical Review." *Review of Educational Research* 47: 633–650.

Slavin, R. E. (1978). "Student Teams and Achievement Divisions." *Journal of Research and Development in Education* 12: 39–49.

Slavin, R. E. (1979). "Effects of Biracial Learning Teams on Cross-Racial Friendships." *Journal of Educational Psychology* 71: 381–387.

Slavin, R. E. (1983a). *Cooperative Learning.* New York: Longman.

Slavin, R. E. (1983b). "When Does Cooperative Learning Increase Student Achievement?" *Psychological Bulletin* 94: 429–445.

Slavin, R. E. (March 1985a). "Cooperative Learning: Applying Contact Theory in Desegregated Schools." *Journal of Social Issues* 41: 45–62.

Slavin, R. E. (1985b). "Team Assisted Individualization: A Cooperative Learning Solution for Adaptive Instruction in Mathematics." In *Adapting Instruction to Individual Differences,* edited by M. Wang and H. Walberg. Berkeley, Calif.: McCutchan.

Slavin, R. E. (1986). *Using Student Team Learning.* 3rd ed. Baltimore, Md.: Center for Research on Elementary and Middle Schools, Johns Hopkins University.

Slavin, R. E. (1990). *Cooperative Learning: Theory, Research, and Practice.* Englewood Cliffs, N.J.: Prentice-Hall.

Slavin, R. E. (February 1991). "Are Cooperative Learning and 'Untracking' Harmful to the Gifted?" *Educational Leadership* 48: 63–74.

Slavin, R. E., and N. Karweit. (1981). "Cognitive and Affective Outcomes of an Intensive Student Team Learning Experience." *Journal of Experimental Education* 50: 29–35.

Slavin, R. E., and N. Karweit. (1984). "Mastery Learning and Student Teams: A Factorial Experiment in Urban General Mathematics Classes." *American Educational Research Journal* 21: 725–736.

Slavin, R. E., and N. L. Karweit. (1985). "Effects of Whole-Class, Ability Grouped, and Individualized Instruction on Mathematics Achievement." *American Educational Research Journal* 22: 351–367.

Slavin, R. E., M. Leavey, and N. A. Madden. (1984). "Combining Cooperative Learning and Individualized Instruction: Effects on Student Mathematics Achievement Attitudes and Behaviors." *Elementary School Journal* 84: 409–422.

Slavin, R. E., M. B. Leavey, and N. A. Madden. (1986). *Team Accelerated Instruction-Mathematics.* Watertown, Mass.: Mastery Education Corporation.

Slavin, R. E., N. A. Madden, and M. B. Leavey. (1984). "Effects of Team Assisted Individualization on the Mathematics Achievement of Academically Handicapped and Nonhandicapped Students." *Journal of Educational Psychology* 76: 813–819.

Slavin, R. E., and E. Oickle. (1981). "Effects of Cooperative Learning Teams on Student Achievement and

Race Relations: Treatment × Race Interactions." *Sociology of Education* 54: 174–180.

Solomon, D., M. Watson, E. Schaps, V. Battistich, and J. Solomon. (1990). "Cooperative Learning as Part of a Comprehensive Classroom Program Designed to Promote Prosocial Development." In *Current Research on Cooperative Learning,* edited by S. Sharan, New York: Praeger.

Stevens, R. J., N. A. Madden, R. E. Slavin, and A. M. Farnish. (1987). "Cooperative Integrated Reading and Composition: Two Field Experiments." *Reading Research Quarterly* 22: 433–454.

Stevens, R. J., R. E. Slavin, and A. M. Farnish. (April 1990). "A Cooperative Learning Approach to Elementary Reading and Writing Instruction: Long-Term Effects." Paper presented at the annual convention of the American Educational Research Association, Boston.

Stevens, R. J., R. E. Slavin, A. M. Farnish, and N. A. Madden. (April 1988). "The Effects of Cooperative

Learning and Direct Instruction in Reading Comprehension Strategies on Main Idea Identification." Paper presented at the annual convention of the American Educational Research Association, New Orleans.

Webb, N. (1985). "Student Interaction and Learning in Small Groups: A Research Summary." In *Learning to Cooperate, Cooperating to Learn,* edited by R. Slavin, S. Sharan, S. Kagan, R. Hertz-Lazarowitz, C. Webb, and R. Schmuck. New York: Plenum.

Yager, S., D. W. Johnson, and R. T. Johnson. (1985). "Oral Discussion, Group-to-Individual Transfer, and Achievement in Cooperative Learning Groups." *Journal of Educational Psychology* 77: 60–66.

Ziegler, S. (1981). "The Effectiveness of Cooperative Learning Teams for Increasing Cross-Ethnic Friendship: Additional Evidence." *Human Organization* 40: 264–268.

DISCUSSION QUESTIONS

1. What are the pros and cons of the cooperative learning strategies?
2. Which approaches have been most successful in enhancing student achievement?
3. How does the cooperative learning model differ from conventional teaching methods, generative teaching, and explicit instruction?
4. Should cooperative learning models be used with special needs students?
5. What are the advantages and disadvantages of implementing the cooperative learning models during the process of mainstreaming?

PRO-CON CHART 3

Should special education students be grouped (mainstreamed) into regular education classes?

PRO	CON
1. Schools should be organized so that all students achieve their maximum potential.	1. Serving the special education population diminishes resources from students who are most likely to benefit from public schooling.
2. Schools should implement curriculum that is student-centered and responsive to the students' learning needs.	2. Schools should not have to provide alternative curriculum designed for a small group of special needs students within a regular classroom setting.
3. Students need to work side by side with peers who have different learning needs.	3. Legislating teachers to fulfill the role of parent, home, and counselor for special education students is unrealistic and unproductive.
4. Teachers must develop a broad-based repertoire of instructional strategies so that they can teach students with different needs and abilities in the same classroom.	4. Students who cannot conform to classroom structure and attend to learning tasks will not benefit from regular education instruction.
5. Mainstreaming can improve the social acceptance of special education students.	5. Most educators have not been adequately prepared to work with special education students.

CASE STUDY 3

Parents Seek to Dismantle the Tracking System

Benjamin High School had a long history of placing students in fixed and homogeneous curriculum tracks. Observation by both the administration and teachers led them to conclude that several undesirable consequences were occurring. The faculty noted that within the school there seemed to be a competitive atmosphere, racial and social isolation, and a community of under and unachieving students who exhibited lower self-esteem. More importantly, achievement test scores demonstrated that tracking by ability groups did not result in significant gains in student test scores.

A group of parents threatened to sue the district, stating that it was their contention that some students were not receiving a quality education. The parent group claimed that the school was in direct violation of federal law by not providing equal access to educational opportunity to all students.

To avert the possibility of litigation, the Benjamin staff voted to implement a revised plan and promised the parent group that they would rectify the inequities that resulted from curriculum segregation. The staff explained that they planned to teach honors and regular students in the same classrooms. The parent group accepted the staff's proposed action as a promise of good faith and withdrew the suit. Now Benjamin's administration and faculty were faced with the more difficult issue of how to structure the curriculum to teach students of different ability levels in the same class.

Consider the implications of such a plan and discuss the following:

1. What are the advantages and disadvantages of teaching honors and regular students in the same classrooms?

2. Which curriculum model would be most effective for teaching a heterogeneous group of students?

3. How might teachers use grouping for instruction without substantially increasing the amount of planning and preparation they already do?

4. Is ability group teaching an appropriate instructional approach? Why? Why not?

5. What kind of teaching strategies are most appropriate for the teaching model proposed in this case study?

6. What type of learning styles should be used to foster the development of critical thinking skills for students of different ability levels?

7. Should a discipline-based, separate-subject, multidisciplinary, integrative, or problem-centered curriculum model be used? Why? Why not?

PART FOUR

Curriculum and Instruction

INTRODUCTION

In what ways are curriculum and instruction related? Which instructional strategies are most effective for learners? Why are students' learning experiences still based on highly structured curricula? How has an understanding of multiple intelligences influenced instruction? In what ways are technological and electronic achievements affecting instruction?

In Chapter 19, Benjamin Bloom describes the advantages and disadvantages of conventional instruction, mastery learning, and tutoring. He explains how context variables including home environment, school learning, and teachers' differential interaction with students are related to outcomes.

In the next chapter, Jeannie Oakes explains how the policy of tracking has affected student outcomes. Despite evidence to the contrary, she explores reasons that the practice of tracking tends to persist. She explains how educators tend to justify the practice of tracking. Through actual case studies, she examines the relationship between the practice of tracking, in-school segregation, and educational equality.

In Chapter 21, Howard Gardner explains why education is enhanced by a multiple intelligence perspective. Yet he cautions the reader that it is fallacious to believe that multiple intelligence is a prescription for educational practice. He also discusses the benefits associated with using pluralistic approaches to instruction.

In Chapter 22, Lorin Anderson and Leonard Pellicer describe the intended goals and actual outcomes associated with compensatory and remedial education. They point out how teacher staffing, organizational structure, and administrative leadership support or impede the efforts of Chapter One programs.

Next, Simon Hooper and Lloyd Rieber follow with a discussion of how educational technology is influencing classroom instruction. The authors present a model that characterizes the adoption of technology in education. Hooper and Rieber describe the role of contemporary educational technology and suggest several teaching strategies to guide effective teaching.

In Chapter 24, Allan Ornstein outlines the contemporary technical advancements and social developments that have the potential to influence curriculum content and delivery. He recommends that, while curriculum should reflect the needs of the changing society, achieving a balance between integrating new knowledge and preserving the time-tested enduring aspects of former curricula is important.

19

The Search for Methods of Instruction

BENJAMIN S. BLOOM

FOCUSING QUESTIONS

1. *What is the difference between conventional instruction, mastery learning, and tutoring?*
2. *How does mastery learning influence student achievement?*
3. *What are the advantages and disadvantages of the mastery learning model and tutoring?*
4. *In what ways are home environment processes and a student's school learning related?*
5. *How does tutoring influence student achievement?*

Two University of Chicago doctoral students in education, Anania (1982, 1983) and Burke (1984), completed dissertations in which they compared student learning under the following three conditions of instruction:

1. *Conventional.* Students learn the subject matter in a class with about 30 students per teacher. Tests are given periodically for marking the students.

2. *Mastery Learning.* Students learn the subject matter in a class with about 30 students per teacher. The instruction is the same as in the conventional class (usually with the same teacher). Formative tests (the same tests used with the conventional group) are given for feedback followed by corrective procedures and parallel formative tests to determine the extent to which the students have mastered the subject matter.

3. *Tutoring.* Students learn the subject matter with a good tutor for each student (or for two or three students simultaneously). This tutoring instruction is followed periodically by formative tests, feedback-corrective procedures, and parallel formative tests as in the mastery learning classes. It should be pointed out that the need for corrective work under tutoring is very small.

The students were randomly assigned the three learning conditions, and their initial aptitude tests scores, previous achievement in the subject, and initial attitudes and interests in the subject were similar. The amount of time for instruction was the same in all three groups except for the corrective work in the mastery learning and tutoring groups. Burke (1984) and Anania (1982, 1983) replicated the study with four different samples of students at grades four, five, and eight and with two different subject matters, Probability and Cartography. In each sub-study, the instructional treatment was limited to 11 periods of instruction over a 3-week block of time.

Most striking were the differences in final achievement measures under the three conditions. Using the standard deviation (sigma) of the control (conventional) class, it was typically found

209

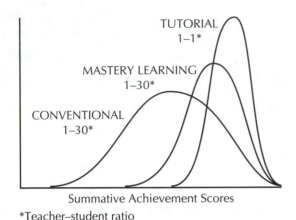

Summative Achievement Scores

*Teacher–student ratio

FIGURE 19.1 Achievement Distribution for Students Under Conventional, Mastery Learning, and Tutorial Instruction.

that the average student under tutoring was about two standard deviations above the average of the control class (the average tutored student was above 98% of the students in the control class).[1] The average student under mastery learning was about one standard deviation above the average of the control class (the average mastery learning student was above 84% of the students in the control class).

The variation of the students' achievement also changed under these learning conditions such that about 90% of the tutored students and 70% of the mastery learning students attained the level of summative achievement reached by only the highest 20% of the students under conventional instructional conditions. (See Figure 19.1.)

There were corresponding changes in students' time on task in the classroom (65% under conventional instruction, 75% under Mastery Learning, and 90+% under tutoring) and students' attitudes and interests (least positive under conventional instruction and most positive under tutoring). There were great reductions in the relations between prior measures (aptitude or achievement) and the summative achievement measures. Typically, the aptitude-achievement correlations changed from +.60 under conventional to +.35 under mastery learning and

+.25 under tutoring. It is recognized that the correlations for the mastery learning and tutoring groups were so low because of the restricted range of scores under these learning conditions. However, the most striking of the findings is that under the best learning conditions we can devise (tutoring), the average student is 2 sigma above the average control student taught under conventional group methods of instruction.

The tutoring process demonstrates that *most* of the students do have the potential to reach this high level of learning. I believe an important task of research and instruction is to seek ways of accomplishing this under more practical and realistic conditions than the one-to-one tutoring, which is too costly for most societies to bear on a large scale. This is the "2 sigma" problem. Can researchers and teachers devise teaching-learning conditions that will enable the majority of students under *group instruction* to attain levels of achievement that can at present be reached only under good tutoring conditions?

It has taken almost a decade and a half to develop the Mastery Learning (ML) strategy to a point where large numbers of teachers at every level of instruction and in many countries can use the feedback-corrective procedures to get the 1 sigma effect (the average ML student is above 84% of the students under conventional instruction—even with the same teacher teaching both the ML and the conventional classes). If the research on the 2 sigma problem yields *practical methods* (methods that the average teacher or school faculty can learn in a brief period of time and use with little more cost or time than conventional instruction), it would be an educational contribution of the greatest magnitude. It would change popular notions about human potential and would have significant effects on what the schools can and should do with the educational years each society requires of its young people.

This paper is a brief presentation of the work on solutions to the 2 sigma problem. It is hoped that it will interest both educational researchers and teachers in further research and application of these ideas.

THE SEARCH

In a number of articles, my graduate students and I have attempted to contrast alterable educational variables with more stable or static variables (Bloom, 1980). In our treatment of this topic, we summarized the literature on such alterable variables as the *quality of teaching,* the *use of time* by teachers and students, *cognitive* and *affective* entry characteristics of students, *formative testing, rate of learning,* and the *home environment.* In each case, we contrasted these alterable variables with the more *stable* variables (e.g., personal characteristics of teachers, intelligence measures, achievement tests for grading purposes, socioeconomic status of the family, etc.) and indicated some of the ways in which the alterable variables influence learning and the processes by which these variables have been altered.

But not all alterable variables are likely to have equal effects on learning. Our research summaries were intended to emphasize the alterable variables that have had the strongest effects on school learning. Within the last 3 years, this search has been aided by the rapid growth of the meta-analysis literature. In this literature, each writer has summarized the research literature on a particular set of alterable variables to indicate the effect size between control and experimental groups of students. They have standardized the results in terms of the *difference* between the experimental and control groups divided by the standard deviation of the control group.[2]

In each study, the reviewer also analyzed the effect size under different conditions, level of school, sex of student, school subject, size of sample, and so on. Such reviews are very useful in selecting alterable variables that are most likely to contribute significantly to the 2 sigma solution.

Table 19.1 is adapted from a summary of effect sizes of key variables by Walberg (1984) who, with other co-authors, has contributed greatly to this literature. In Table 19.1 he has listed the selected variables in order of magnitude of effect size. (We have added other variables and indicated the equivalent percentile for each effect size.)

Thus, in the first entry, *tutorial instruction,* we have indicated the effect size (2 sigma) and indicated that under tutorial instruction, the average student is above 98% of the students under the control teaching conditions. A list of effect size studies appears in the Appendix at the end of this chapter.

In our own attempts to solve the 2 sigma problem we assume that two or three alterable variables must be used that *together* contribute more to the learning than any one of them alone. Because of more than 15 years of experience with ML at different levels of education and in different countries, we have come to rely on ML as one of the possible variables to be combined with selected other variables. ML (the feedback corrective process) under good conditions yields approximately a 1 sigma effect size. We have systematically tried other variables which, in combination with ML, might approach the 2 sigma effect size. So far, we have *not* found any two variable combination that has exceeded the 2 sigma effect. Thus, some of our present research reaches the 2 sigma effect but does not go beyond it.

We have classified the variables in Table 19.1 in terms of the direct object of the change process: (a) the learner; (b) the instructional material; (c) the home environment or peer group; and (d) the teacher and the teaching process.

We have speculated that two variables involving different objects of the change process may, in some instances, be additive, whereas two variables involving the same object of the change process are less likely to be additive (unless they occur at different times in the teaching-learning process). Our research is intended to determine when these rules are true and when they are not. Several of the studies done so far suggest that they may be true. Thus the ML process (which affects the learner most directly), when combined with changes in the teaching process (which affects the teacher most directly), yield additive results. (See Tenenbaum, p. 13 of this article and Mevarech, p. 14 of this article). Although we do not believe these two rules are more than *suggestive* at present, future research on this problem will undoubtedly yield a stronger

TABLE 19.1   Effect of Selected Alterable Variables on Student Achievement (See Appendix)

		EFFECT SIZE	PERCENTILE EQUIVALENT
D[a]	Tutorial instruction	2.00	98
D	Reinforcement	1.20	
A	Feedback-corrective (ML)	1.00	84
D	Cues and explanations	1.00	
(A)D	Student classroom participation	1.00	
A	Student time on task	1.00[b]	
A	Improved reading/study skills	1.00	
C	Cooperative learning	.80	79
D	Homework (graded)	.80	
D	Classroom morale	.60	73
A	Initial cognitive prerequisites	.60	
C	Home environment intervention	.50[b]	69
D	Peer and cross-age remedial tutoring	.40	66
D	Homework (assigned)	.30	62
D	Higher order questions	.30	
(D)B	New science & math curricula	.30[b]	
D	Teacher expectancy	.30	
C	Peer group influence	.20	58
B	Advance organizers	.20	
	Socio-economic status (for contrast)	.25	60

Note. This table was adapted from Walberg (1984) by Bloom.
[a]*Object of change process*—A-Learner; B-Instructional Material; C-Home environment or peer group; D-Teacher.
[b]Averaged or estimated from correlational data or from several effect sizes.

set of generalizations about how the effects of separable variables may be best combined.

In our work so far we have restricted the search to two or three variables, each of which is likely to have a .5 sigma effect or greater. We suspect that the research, as well as the applications to school situations, would get too complex if more than three alterable variables are used. In any case, our work has begun with variables in the top half of Table 19.1. Perhaps as the research moves on, it will be necessary to include some of the variables in the lower part of Table 19.1.

In our research with two variables, we have made use of a 2 × 2 randomized design with ML and one other variable. So far we have not done research with three variables. Where possible, we try to replicate the study with at least two subject fields, two levels of schooling, or some combination of subject fields and levels of schooling. We hope that others will take up this 2 sigma search and that some guidelines for the research can be set up to make the combined results more useful and to reduce the time and costs for experimental and demonstration studies.

IMPROVING STUDENT PROCESSING OF CONVENTIONAL INSTRUCTION

In this section of the paper we are concerned with ways in which students can learn more effectively without basically changing the teaching. If students develop good study habits, devote more time to the learning, improve their reading skills, and so on, they will be better able to learn from a particular teacher and course—even though neither the course nor the teacher has undergone a change process.

For example, the ML feedback-corrective approach is addressed primarily to providing students with the cognitive and affective prerequisites for each new learning task. As we have noted before, when the ML procedures are done systematically and well, the school achievement of the average student under ML is approximately 1 sigma (84 percentile) above the average student in the control class, even when both classes are taught by the *same teacher* with much the same instruction and instructional material. As we view the ML process, we regard it as a method of improving the students' learning from the same teaching over a series of learning tasks.

The major changes under the ML process are that more of the students have the cognitive prerequisites for each new learning task, they become more positive about their ability to learn the subject, and they put in more active learning time than do the control students. As we observe the students' learning and the test results in the ML and the conventional class, we note the improvements in the student learning under ML and the lack of such improvement in conventional classes.

One of our University of Chicago doctoral students, Leyton (1983), suggested that one approach to the 2 sigma problem would be to use ML during the advanced course in a sequence, but in addition attempt to *enhance the students' initial cognitive entry prerequisites* at the beginning of the course. Working with high school teachers in Algebra 2 and French 2, they developed an initial test of the prerequisites for each of these courses. The procedure in developing the initial test was to take the final examination in the prior course (Algebra 1 or French 1) and have a committee of four to six teachers in the subject independently check each test item that they believed measured an idea or skill that was a necessary prerequisite for the next course in the subject. There was very high agreement on most of the selected items, and dis-

cussion among the teachers led to consensus about some of the remaining items.

Two of the classes were helped to review and relearn the specific prerequisites they lacked. This was not done for the students in the other two classes—they spent the time on a more general and informal review of the content taught in the previous course (Algebra 1 or French 1). The method of enhancing the prerequisites was much like the ML feedback-corrective process where the teacher retaught the items that the majority of students had missed, small groups of students helped each other over items that had been missed, and the students reviewed items they were not sure about by referring to the designated pages in the instructional material. The corrective process took about 3 to 4 hours during the first week of the course. After the students completed the corrective process, they were given a parallel test. As a result of the corrective process, most of the students reached the mastery standard (80%) on the parallel test given at the end of the first week of the course. In a few cases, students who didn't reach this standard were given further help.

More important was the improved performance of the enhanced classes over the other two classes on the first *formative* test in the advanced course (French 2 or Algebra 2). The two enhanced classes, which had been helped on the initial prerequisites, were approximately .7 sigma higher than the other two classes on the first formative test given at the end of a 2-week period of learning in the advanced course.

When one of the enhanced classes was also provided with ML feedback-corrective procedures over a series of learning tasks, the final result after a 10- to 12-week period of instruction was that this experimental group was approximately 1.6 sigma above the control group on the summative examination. (The average student in the ML plus enhanced initial prerequisites was above 95% of the control students on this examination.) There were also attitudinal and other affective differences in students related to these achievement differences. These included positive academic self-concept,

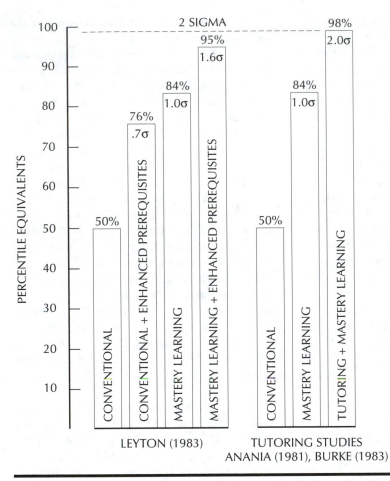

FIGURE 19.2   Average Summative Achievement Scores Under Different Learning Conditions. Comparison of Tutoring Studies, Mastery Learning, and Enhanced Prerequisites.

greater interest in the subject, and greater desire to learn more in the subject field.

In Leyton's (1983) study, he found that the average effect of initial enhancement of prerequisites alone is about .6 sigma (see differences between conventional and conventional plus enhanced prerequisites and between ML and ML plus enhanced prerequisites in Figure 19.2). That is, we have two processes—*ML* and *initial enhancement of cognitive prerequisites*—that have sizable but separate effects. When they are combined, their separate effects tend to be additive. We believe these two variables are additive because they occur at different times. The enhancement of the initial prerequisites is completed during the first week of the new course, while the ML feedback-corrective process takes place every 2 or 3 weeks during the course, after the initial enhancement.

This solution to the 2 sigma problem is likely to be applicable to sequential courses in most school subjects. (In the United States, over two-thirds of the academic courses in elementary-secondary schools are sequential courses.) This solution, of course, applies most clearly to the second courses in a sequence. It probably will not work as well with the third, fourth, or later courses in a sequence if there has been no earlier use of initial enhancement of prerequisites or ML procedures. We hope these ideas will be further explored in the United States as well as in other countries. We believe this solution is relevant at all levels of education, including elementary-secondary, college, and even the graduate and professional school level.

We also regard this approach as widely applicable within a country because the prerequisites for a particular sequential subject or course are likely to be very similar even though different textbooks and teachers may be involved. Thus, a well-made test of the initial prerequisites for a particular sequential course—Arithmetic 2, French 2, Reading 2, and so on—may with only minor changes apply to other versions of the same course within a particular country. Also, the procedures that work well in enhancing these prerequisites in one school should work equally well in other schools. Further research is needed to establish the sequential courses in which this approach is most effective.

Finally, the time cost of the initial enhancement procedures is limited to the class hours of the course during the first week of the sequential course, while the time or other costs of the ML procedures have usually been very small. We hope that this approach to the 2 sigma problem will be found to be a widely applicable as well as economical solution available to most teachers who wish to improve student learning, student academic self-concept, and student attitudes and interest in the learning.

Our graduate students have written papers on several other approaches for improving student processing of conventional instruction:

1. Help students develop a student support system in which groups of two or three students study together, help each other when they encounter difficulties in the course, help each other review in advance of taking tests, and review their learning periodically. A student support system that provides support, encouragement and even help when needed can do much to raise the level of learning of the participants. There is evidence that these and other cooperative learning efforts are almost as effective as ML procedures. (Cooperative Learning—Effect size .80 (79 percentile) Slavin, 1980.)

2. There is evidence that students who take special programs to improve their reading and/or their study and learning methods tend to learn more effectively. Ideally, such special programs should be available at the beginning of each new school level, that is, junior high school, high school, and so on. One would hope that the special programs would be closely related to the academic courses the student is currently taking. (Improved reading/study skills—Effect size 1.00 (84 percentile) (Pflaum, Walberg, Karegianes, & Rasher, 1980).

IMPROVE INSTRUCTIONAL MATERIALS AND EDUCATIONAL TECHNOLOGY

The textbook in the United States, as well as in most advanced countries in the world, is an almost universal part of school instruction. There has been much work on the improvement of the textbooks for reading and, to some extent, arithmetic, mathematics, and science subjects. Most of these are in relation to special curricular improvements, which include improvements in the sequential nature of the topics, the attempt to find important ideas or schema that help to interrelate the different parts of the subject, and improvements in the illustrations and exercises in the books. However, as far as we can find, these improvements have not had very significant effects on student achievement unless the teachers were provided with much inservice education for the new curriculum or the new textbook.

My graduate students and I have been intrigued by the possibility that the organization of a particular section (or chapter) of the textbook might be better integrated or the parts of the section more closely related to each other. Preorganizers or advanced organizers (Ausubel, 1960) have been moderately effective when provided in the textbook or provided by the teacher at the beginning of the new unit of the course. These may be provided in the form of objectives, some ideas about what will be learned in the unit, or a brief discussion of the relation between what has already been learned and what will be learned in the unit. Such advanced organizers (Luiten, Ames, & Ackerson, 1980) appear to have an average effect size on achievement of about .2 sigma. (Incidentally, such advance organizers have about a .4 sigma effect on retention of the learning.) Although this effect is rather consistent, by itself it is not enough to contribute significantly to the 2 sigma effect. It is likely that a *combination* of advance organizers at the beginning of a new topic, further organizational aids during the chapter or unit, as well as appropriate questions, summaries, or other organizational aids at the end of the unit, may have a substantial effect on the student's learning of that chapter.

In Process

One of our students, Carlos Avalos, is working on a study of the effect of *organizational aids* in the instructional material combined with the *initial enhancement of cognitive prerequisites* and the ML *feedback-corrective* procedures. Avalos is planning a research design that will enable him to determine the separate effects of each of the three processes, the effect of any two of the processes, and the combined effect of all three processes. At the least, it is anticipated that the combination of any two of the processes will be greater than the effects of any one of the same processes. It is hoped that the effect of any two will be above 1.3 sigma (90 percentile). If this is found, it will provide several new solutions to the 2 sigma problem—some of which can be done with very little cost or effort by the teachers or the school system.

Avalos expects the results noted above because the organizational aids can be built into new textbooks and can be used by the students with a minimum of emphasis by the teachers. The initial enhancement of the prerequisites is completed before the students begin the study of the new course subject matter, whereas the ML feedback-corrective procedures take place every 2 or 3 weeks dur-

ing the course. We believe that each of these processes is somewhat independent of the other processes.

Other suggestions for the improvement of instructional materials and educational technology include the following:

1. Some of our students have used computer learning courses, such as the Plato system, which appear to work very well for highly motivated students. We believe that it should be possible to determine whether particular computer courses enable sizeable proportions of students to attain the 2 sigma achievement effect. The effectiveness of the computer courses can be determined in terms of the time required, completion rates, student performance on achievement tests, and student retention of the learned material. It is hoped that the more effective computer courses will also have positive effects on such affective characteristics as academic self-concept, interest in the subject, and desire to learn further with computer learning methods.

2. Although the average effect size for new science and math curricula in the United States is only .3 sigma, some of the new curricula (or textbooks) in these and other subjects may be much more effective than others. We propose a careful search of the new curricula and textbooks to determine which ones are more effective and to determine what characteristics make them more effective than the others.

HOME ENVIRONMENT AND THE PEER GROUP

In this section, we are primarily concerned with the out-of-school support that the student receives from the home or the peer group. We are interested in the ways in which the student's achievement, academic aspirations and goals, and progress in learning are influenced by these types of support. We know that the home environment does have great influence on the pupil's school learning and that this influence is especially effective at the elementary school level or earlier. The peer group's influence is likely to be strongest (both positively or negatively) at the secondary school level.

Home Environment Processes

There have been a large number of studies of the home environment processes that affect the students' school learning. These studies involve interviews and observations directed at determining the relevant interactions between parents and their children. The studies find correlations of +.70 to +.80[3] between an index of the home environment processes and the children's school achievement. Some of the home environment processes that appear to have high relationships with school achievement include the following:

1. Work habits of the family—the degree of routine in the home management, the emphasis on regularity in the use of space and time, and the priority given to schoolwork over other more pleasurable activities.

2. Academic guidance and support—the availability and quality of the help and encouragement parents give the child for his or her schoolwork and the conditions they provide to support the child's schoolwork.

3. Stimulation in the home—the opportunity provided by the home to explore ideas, events, and the larger environment.

4. Language development—opportunities in the home for the development of correct and effective language usage.

5. Academic aspirations and expectations—the parents' aspirations for the child, the standards they set for the child's school achievement, and their interests in and knowledge of the child's school experiences.

These studies of the home environment processes began with the work of Dave (1963) and Wolf (1964, 1966), and since then have been replicated in other studies done in the United States and other countries (Marjoribanks, 1974; Kalinowski & Sloane, 1981).

These previous studies of the relationship between the home and the children's school achievement suggest a strong effect of the home environment on the school learning of the children, but they do not provide evidence on the extent to which the home environment can be *altered* and the effect of such alteration on changes in the children's school achievement.

A recent study done in Thailand by Janhom (1983) involved a control group and three experimental groups of parents (and their children). In this study, the most effective treatment of the parents was for the group of parents to meet with a parent educator for about 2 hours twice a month for 6 months. In these meetings, the parents discussed ways in which they could support their children's learning in the school. There was usually an initial presentation made by the parent educator on one of the home environment processes and then the parents discussed what they did as well as what they hoped to do to support their children's school learning.

Another experimental approach included visits to each home separately by a parent educator twice a month for 6 months. A third experimental approach was that newsletters about the same topics were sent to the home twice a month for 6 months.

The parents of all four groups were observed and interviewed at the beginning and end of the 6-month period using the Dave (1963) interview and observational methods. Although the three experimental approaches show significantly greater changes in the parents' home environment index than the control group, the most effective method was the series of meetings between groups of parents and the parent educator. The changes in the home environment of this group were highly significant when compared with the changes in the other three groups of parents.

The fourth grade children of all these parents were given a national standardized test on reading and mother tongue as well as arithmetic at the beginning and end of the 6-month period. It was found that the children of the meeting group of parents had changed by 1 sigma in achievement, as contrasted with the change in the control group of children. In comparison, the parent educators' visit to each of the homes every other week had only a .5 sigma effect on the children's school achievement.

Other methods of changing the home environment have been reported by Dolan (1980), Bronfenbrenner (1974), and Kalinowski and Sloane (1981). Again, the most effective approaches to changing the home environment processes result in changes in the children's school achievement. (Home Environment—Effect size .50 (69 percentile), Iverson & Walberg, 1982.)

The methods of changing the home environments are relatively costly in terms of parent educators meeting with groups of parents over a series of semi-monthly meetings, but the payoff of this approach is likely to be very great. If parents continue to encourage and support each of their children to learn well in school throughout the elementary school years, this should greatly help the children during the years they will attend schools and colleges.

Although such research has not been done as yet, we hope that others will explore an approach to the 2 sigma problem of providing effective parent education combined with the mastery learning method. Because parent support takes place in the home and ML takes place in the school, we expect that these two effects will be additive. The result should be close to a 2 sigma improvement in student learning.

Ideally, if both methods began with first or second grade children, one might hope that the combination would result in consistently good learning, at least through the elementary school years, with less and less need for effort expended by the parents or by the use of ML procedures in the school.

Peer Group

During the adolescent years, it is likely that the peer group will have considerable influence on the student's activities, behavior, attitudes, and academic expectations. The peer group(s) to which the individual "belongs" also has some effect on the student's high school achievement level as well as further academic aspirations. These effects appear to be greatest in urban settings. Although it is difficult to influence the student's choice of friends and peer groups, the availability in the school of a variety of extracurricular activities and clubs (e.g., athletics, music, science, mathematics, social, etc.) should enable students to be more selective in their peer choices within the school setting. (Peer Group Influence—Effect size .20 (58 percentile) (Ide, Haertel, Parkerson, & Walberg, 1981.)

IMPROVEMENT OF TEACHING

When we compare student learning under conventional instruction and tutoring we note that approximately 20% of the students under conventional instruction do about as well as the tutored students. (See Figure 19.1.) That is, tutoring probably would not enable these top students to do any better than they already do under conventional instruction. In contrast, about 80% of the students do relatively poorly under conventional instruction as compared with what they might do under tutoring. We have pondered these facts and believe that this in part results from the unequal treatment of students within most classrooms.

Observations of teacher interaction with students in the classroom reveal that teachers frequently direct their teaching and explanations to some students and ignore others. They give much positive reinforcement and encouragement to some students but not to others, and they encourage active participation in the classroom from some students and discourage it from others. The studies find that typically teachers give students in the top third of the class the greatest attention and students in the bottom third of the class receive the least attention and support. These differences in the interaction between teachers and students provide some students with much greater opportunity and encouragement for learning than is provided for other students in the same classroom (Brophy & Good, 1970).

It is very different in a one-to-one tutoring situation where there is a constant feedback and corrective process between the tutor and the tutee. If the explanation is not understood by the tutee, the tutor soon becomes aware of it and explains it further. There is much reinforcement and encouragement in the tutoring situation, and the tutee must be actively participating in the learning if the tutoring process is to continue. In contrast, there is less feedback from each student in the group situation to the teacher—and frequently the teacher gets most of the feedback on the clarity of his or her explanations, the effect of the reinforcements, and the degree of active involvement in the learning from a *small* number of high achieving students in the typical class of 30 students.

Teachers are frequently unaware of the fact that they are providing more favorable conditions of learning for some students than they are for other students. Generally, they are under the impression that all students in their classes are given equality of opportunity for learning. One basic assumption of our work on teaching is the belief that when teachers are helped to secure a more accurate picture of their own teaching methods and styles of interaction with their students, they will increasingly be able to provide more favorable learning conditions for more of their students, rather than just for the top fraction of the class.

In some of our research on the 2 sigma problem, we have viewed the task of teaching as providing for more equal treatment of students. We have been trying to give teachers feedback on their differential treatment of students. We attempt to provide teachers with a mirror of what they are now doing and have them develop techniques for equalizing their interactions with the students. These include such techniques as: (a) attempt to find something positive and encouraging in each student's response, (b) find ways of involving more of the students in active engagement in the learning process, (c) secure feedback from a small random sample of students to determine when they comprehend the explanations and illustrations, and (d) find ways of supplying additional clarification and illustrations as needed. The major emphasis in this work was *not* to change the teachers' *methods* of instruction, but to have the teacher become more aware of the ways in which he or she could more directly teach to a cross section of the students at each class section.

The first of our studies on improving instruction was done by Nordin (1979, 1980), who found ways of improving the cues and explanations for students as well as increasing the active participation of students.

He found it helpful to meet frequently with the teachers to explain these ideas as well as to observe the teachers and help them determine when they still needed to improve these qualities of the instruction. He also had independent observers noting the frequency with which the experimental teachers were using these ideas well or poorly. Similarly, he had students note the frequency with which they were actively participating in the learning and any problems they had with understanding the ideas or explanations.

In this research he compared student learning under conventional instruction and under enhanced cues (explanations) and participation conditions. During the experiment, observers noted that the student participation and the explanations and directions were positive in about 57% of the observations in the control class as compared with about 67% in the enhanced cue + participation classes. Students in the control classes noted that the cues and participation were positive for them about 50% of the time as compared with about 80% of the time for the students in the enhanced cue + participation classes.

In terms of final achievement, the average student in the enhanced cue and participation group was 1.5 sigma higher than the average student in the control classes. (The average student in the enhanced group was above 93% of the students in the control classes.) (See Figure 19.3.) Nordin (1979, 1980) also made use of the ML procedures in other classes and found that they worked even better than the enhanced cue + participation procedures. Unfortunately, he did not use the ML in combination with the enhanced cue + participation methods.

In any case, Nordin (1979, 1980) did demonstrate that teachers could be taught ways to be more responsive to most of the students in the class, secure increased participation of the students, and ensure that most of the students understood the explanations and illustrations that the

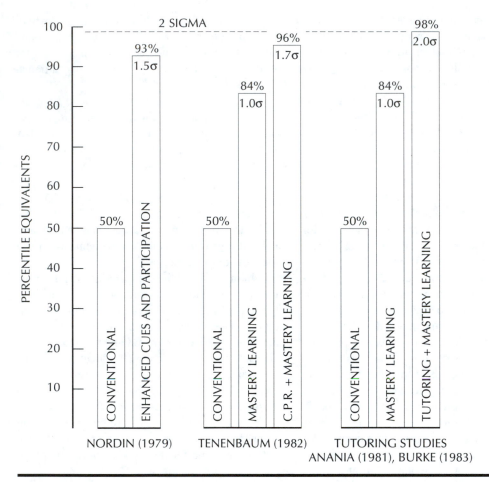

FIGURE 19.3   Average Summative Achievement Scores Under Different Learning Conditions. Comparison of Tutoring Studies, Mastery Learning, and Enhanced Instructional Methods.

teacher provided. The observers noted that the students in the enhanced participation and cue classes were actively engaged in learning (time on task) about 75% of the classroom time, whereas the control students were actively learning only about 57% of the time.

In a later study, Tenenbaum (1982) compared control groups, ML groups, and Enhanced Cues, Participation, and Reinforcement in combination with ML (CPR + ML). Tenenbaum studied these three methods of teaching with randomly assigned students in two different courses—sixth grade science and ninth grade algebra.

Tenenbaum also used student observation of their own classroom processes on cues, participation, and reinforcement. He found that under the CPR + ML, students responded positively about their own participation about 87% of the time as contrasted with 68% in the control classes.

The results of this study demonstrated large differences between the three methods of instruction with the final achievement scores of the CPR + ML group about 1.7 sigmas above the control students (the average student in this group was above 96% of the students in the control group). The average student in the ML groups was the usual 1 sigma above the control students. (See Figure 19.3.)

We believe that this research makes it clear that teachers in both the Nordin and Tenenbaum studies could (at least temporarily) change their teaching methods to provide more equal treatment of the students in their classes. When this more equal treatment is provided and supplemented with the ML feedback and corrective procedures, the average student approaches the level of learning found under tutoring methods of instruction.

We believe there are a variety of methods of giving feedback to teachers on the extent to which they are providing equality of interaction with their students. The tactic of providing a "mirror" to the teacher of the ways in which he or she is providing cues and explanations, appropriate reinforcement, and securing overt as well as covert participation of the students in the learning seems to us to be an excellent approach. This may be in the form of an observer's notes on what the teacher and students did, student observations of their own interactions with the teaching (preferably anonymous, but coded as to whether the students are in the top third, middle third, or the bottom third of the class in achievement), such as their understanding of the cues and explanations, the extent of their overt and covert participation, and the amount of reinforcement they are getting. Perhaps a videotape or audiotape recording of the class could serve the same purpose if the teacher is given brief training on ways of summarizing the classroom interaction between the teacher and the students in the class.

It is our hope that when teachers are helped to secure a more accurate picture of their own teaching methods and styles of interaction with their students, they will be better able to provide favorable learning conditions for most of their students.

IMPROVEMENT OF TEACHING OF THE HIGHER MENTAL PROCESSES

Although there is much of rote learning in schools through the world, in some of the national curriculum centers in different countries (e.g., Israel, Malaysia, South Korea) I find great emphasis on problem-solving, application of principles, analytical skills, and creativity. Such higher mental processes are emphasized because these centers believe that they enable the student to relate his or her learning to the many problems he or she encounters in day-to-day living. These abilities are also stressed because they are retained and used long after the individual has forgotten the detailed specifics of the subject matter taught in the schools. These abilities are regarded as one set of essential characteristics needed to continue learning and to cope with a rapidly changing world. Some curriculum centers believe that these higher mental processes are important because they make learning exciting and constantly new and playful.

In these countries, subjects are taught as methods of inquiry into the nature of science, mathematics, the arts, and the social studies. The subjects are taught as much for the ways of thinking they represent as for their traditional content. Much of this learning makes use of observations, reflections on these observations, experimentation with phenomena, and the use of first hand data and daily experiences, as well as the use of primary printed sources. All of this is reflected in the materials of instruction, the learning and teaching processes used, and the questions and problems used in the quizzes and formative testing, as well as on the final summative examinations.

In sharp contrast with some of these other countries, teachers in the United States typically make use of textbooks that rarely pose real problems. These textbooks emphasize specific content to be remembered and give students little opportunity to discover underlying concepts and principles and even less opportunity to attack real problems in the environments in which they live. The teacher-made tests (and standardized tests) are largely tests of remembered information. After the sale of over one million copies of the *Taxonomy of Educational Objectives—Cognitive Domain* (Bloom, Engelhart, Furst, Hill, & Krathwohl, 1956) and over a quarter of a century of use of this domain in preservice and in-service teacher training, it is estimated that over 90% of test questions that U.S. public school students are *now* expected to answer deal with little

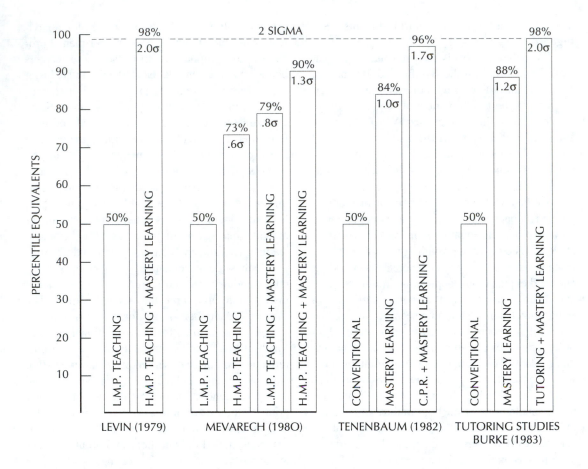

FIGURE 19.3   Average Higher Mental Process Achievement Scores Under Different Learning Conditions. Comparison of Tutoring Studies, Mastery Learning, and Higher Mental Process Instructional Methods.

more than information. Our instructional material, our classroom teaching methods, and our testing methods rarely rise above the lowest category of the Taxonomy-knowledge.

In the tutoring studies reported at the beginning of this paper, it was found that the tutored students' Higher Mental Process (HMP) achievement was 2.0 sigma above the control students. (See Figure 19.4.) (The average tutored student was above 98% of the control students on the HMP part of the summative examination.) It should be noted that in these studies higher mental processes as well as lower mental process questions were in-

cluded in the formative tests used in the feedback-corrective processes for both the ML and tutored groups. Again, the point is that students can learn the higher mental processes if they become more central in the teaching-learning process.

Several studies have been made in which the researcher was seeking to improve the higher mental processes.

We have already referred to the Tenenbaum (1982) study, which emphasized changing teacher-student interaction. In this study, the Cue-Participation-Reinforcement + Mastery Learning student group was 1.7 sigma higher than the control students on the higher mental process part of the summative examination. (The average CPR + ML student was above 96% of the control students on the higher mental processes.) (See Figure 19.4.)

Another study done by Levin (1979) was directed to improving the higher mental processes by emphasizing the mastery of the lower mental processes and providing learning experiences in which the students applied principles in a variety of different problem situations. On the summative examinations, the students were very high on the knowledge of principles and facts and in their ability to apply the principles in new problem situations. These experimental students were compared with a control group that was only taught the principles (but not their application). On the higher mental processes, the experimental group was 2 sigma above the control students (the average experimental student was above 98% of the control students) in the ability to apply the principles to new problem situations.

A third study by Mevarech (1980) was directed at improving the higher mental processes by emphasizing heuristic problem solving and including higher and lower mental process questions in the formative testing and in the feedback-corrective processes. On the higher mental process part of the summative tests, the group using the heuristic methods + ML (HMP Teaching + ML) was 1.3 sigma above the control group (L.M.P. Teaching) taught primarily by learning algorithms—a set of rules and procedures for solving particular math problems (the average student in this experimental group was above 90% of the control students).

In all of these studies, attempts to improve higher mental processes included group instruction emphasizing higher mental processes and feedback-corrective processes, which also emphasized higher mental processes. In addition, the tutoring studies included an instructional emphasis on both higher and lower mental processes, as well as the feedback-corrective processes, which included both higher and lower mental processes. It was evident in all of these studies that in the formative feedback and corrective processes the students needed and received more corrective help on the higher mental

processes questions and problems than they did on the lower mental process questions.

CONCLUSION

The Anania (1982, 1983) and Burke (1984) studies comparing student learning under one-to-one tutoring, ML, and conventional group instruction began in 1980. As the results of these separate studies at different grade levels and in different school subjects began to emerge, we were astonished at the consistency of the findings as well as the great differences in student cognitive achievement, attitudes, and academic self-concept under tutoring as compared with the group methods of instruction.

During the past 4 years, the graduate students in my seminars at the University of Chicago and Northwestern University considered various approaches to the search for group methods of instruction that might be as effective as one-to-one tutoring. This chapter reports on the research studies these students have completed, the studies that are still in process, and some of the other ideas we explored in these seminars.

Although all of us at first thought it was an impossible task, we did agree that if we succeeded in finding *one* solution, there would soon be a great many solutions. In this chapter, I report on six solutions to the 2 sigma problem. In spite of the difficulties, our graduate students found the problem to be very intriguing because the goal was so clear and specific—*find methods of group instruction as effective as one-to-one tutoring.*

Early in the work, it became evident that more than group instruction in the school had to be considered. We also needed to find ways of improving the students' learning processes, the curriculum and instructional materials, as well as the home environmental support of the students' school learning. This chapter is only a preliminary report on what has been accomplished to date, but it should be evident that much can now be done to improve student learning in the schools. However, the search is far from complete. We look for additional solutions to the 2 sigma problem to be reported in the next few years. I hope some of the readers of this chapter will also find this problem challenging.

APPENDIX: EFFECT SIZE REFERENCES

Tutorial Instruction*

Anania, J. (1982). The effects of quality of instruction on the cognitive and affective learning of students (Doctoral dissertation, University of Chicago, 1981). *Dissertation Abstracts International, 42,* 4269A.

Burke, A. J. (1984). Students' potential for learning contrasted under tutorial and group approaches to instruction (Doctoral dissertation, University of Chicago, 1983). *Dissertation Abstracts International, 44,* 2025A.

Reinforcement

Lysakowski, R. S., & Walberg, H. J. (1981). Classroom reinforcement: A quantitative synthesis. *Journal of Educational Research, 75,* 69–77.

Feedback-Corrective, Cues & Explanations, and Student Classroom Participation

Lysakowski, R. S., & Walberg, H. J. (1982). Instructional effects of cues, participation, and corrective feedback: A quantitative synthesis. *American Educational Research Journal, 19,* 559–578.

Student Time on Task (in the classroom)

Frederick, W. C., & Walberg, H. J. (1980). Learning as a function of time. *Journal of Educational Research, 73,* 183–194.

Improved Reading/Study Skills

Pflaum, S. W., Walberg, H. J., Karegianes, M. L., & Rasher, S. (1980). Reading instruction: A quantitative synthesis. *Educational Researcher, 9,* 12–18.

Cooperative Learning

Slavin, R. E. (1980). Cooperative learning. *Review of Educational Research, 50,* 315–342.

Home Work (graded) and Home Work (assigned)

Paschal, R., Weinstein, T., & Walberg, H. J. (in press). Effects of homework: A quantitative synthesis. *Journal of Educational Research.*

*Not effect size studies

Classroom Morale

Haertel, G. D., Walberg, H. J., & Haertel, E. H. (1981). Social-psychological environments and learning: A quantitative synthesis. *British Educational Research Journal, 7,* 27–36.

Initial Cognitive Prerequisites*

Leyton, F. S. (1983). The extent to which group instruction supplemented by mastery of the initial cognitive prerequisites approximates the learning effectiveness of one-to-one tutorial instruction (Doctoral dissertation, University of Chicago, 1983). *Dissertation Abstracts International, 44,* 974A.

Home Environment Intervention (parental educational program)

Iverson, B. K., & Walberg, H. J. (1982). Home environment and learning: A quantitative synthesis. *Journal of Experimental Education, 50,* 144–151.

Peer & Cross-Age Remedial Tutoring

Cohen, P. A., Kulik, J. A., & Kulik, C. C. (1982). Educational outcomes of tutoring: A meta-analysis of findings. *American Educational Research Journal 19,* 237–248.

Higher Order Questions

Redfield, D. L., & Rousseau, E. W. (1981). Meta-analysis of experimental research on teacher questioning behavior. *Review of Educational Research, 51,* 235–245.

New Science & Math Curricula and Teacher Expectancy

Walberg, H. J. (1984). Improving the productivity of America's schools. *Educational Leadership, 41,* 8, 19–27.

Peer Group Influence

Ide, J., Haertel, G. D., Parkerson, J. A., & Walberg, H. J. (1981). Peer-group influences on learning: A quantitative synthesis. *Journal of Educational Psychology, 73,* 472–484.

Advance Organizers

Luiten, J., Ames, W., & Ackerson, G. (1980). A meta-analysis of the effects of advance organizers on learning and retention. *American Educational Research Journal, 17,* 211–218.

ENDNOTES

1. In giving the percentile equivalent we make use of the normal curve distribution. The control class distributions were approximately normal, although the mastery learning and tutoring groups were highly skewed.

2. $\dfrac{\text{Mean experimental–Mean control}}{\text{Standard deviation of the control}} =$

$$\dfrac{\text{Mex–Mc}}{\text{Sigma of control}} = \textit{effect size.}$$

3. When questionnaires rather than interviews and observations have been used, the correlations are somewhat lower, with the average being between +.45 and +.55.

REFERENCES

Anania, J. (1982). The effects of quality of instruction on the cognitive and affective learning of students. (Doctoral dissertation, University of Chicago, 1981). *Dissertation Abstracts International, 42,* 4269A.

Anania, J. (1983). The influence of instructional conditions on student learning and achievement. *Evaluation in Education: An International Review Series, 7,* 1, 1–92.

Ausubel, D. (1960). The use of advanced organizers in the learning and retention of meaningful verbal material. *Journal of Educational Psychology, 51,* 267–272.

Bloom, B. S. (1980). The new direction in educational research: Alterable variables. *Phi Delta Kappan, 61,* 6, 382–385.

Bloom, B. S., Engelhart, M. D., Furst, E. J., Hill, W. H., & Krathwohl, D. R. (1956). *Taxonomy of Educational Objectives: Handbook I, Cognitive Domain.* New York: Longman.

Bronfenbrenner, U. (1974). Is early intervention effective? In H. J. Leichter, (Ed.), *The Family as Educator.* New York: Teachers College Press.

Brophy, J. E., & Good, T. L. (1970). Teachers' communication of differential expectations for children's classroom performance: Some behavioral data. *Journal of Educational Psychology, 61,* 365–374.

Burke, A. J. (1984). Students' potential for learning contrasted under tutorial and group approaches to instruction. (Doctoral dissertation, University of Chicago, 1983). *Dissertation Abstracts International, 44,* 2025A.

Dave, R. H. (1963). The identification and measurement of environment process variables that are related to educational achievement. (Unpublished doctoral dissertation, University of Chicago).

Dolan, L. J. (1980). The affective correlates of home concern and support, instructional quality, and achievement. (Unpublished doctoral dissertation, University of Chicago).

Ide, J., Haertel, G. D., Parkerson, J. A., & Walberg, H. J. (1981). Peer group influences on learning: A quantitive synthesis. *Journal of Educational Psychology, 73,* 472–484.

Iverson, B. K., & Walberg, H. J. (1982). Home environment and learning: A quantitative synthesis. *Journal of Experimental Education, 50,* 144–151.

Janhom S. (1983) Educating parents to educate their children. (Unpublished doctoral dissertation, University of Chicago).

Kalinowski, A., & Sloane, K. (1981). The home environment and school achievement. *Studies in Educational Evaluation, 7,* 85–96.

Levin, T. (1979). Instruction which enables students to develop higher mental processes. *Evaluation in Education: An International Review Series, 3,* 3, 173–220.

Leyton, F. S. (1983). The extent to which group instruction supplemented by mastery of the initial cognitive prerequisites approximates the learning effectiveness of one-to-one tutorial methods. (Doctoral dissertation, University of Chicago, 1983). *Dissertation Abstracts International, 44,* 974A.

Luiten, J., Ames, W., & Ackerson, G. (1980). A meta-analysis of the effects of advance organizers on learning and retention. *American Educational Research Journal, 17,* 211–218.

Marjoribanks, K. (1974). *Environments for Learning.* London: National Foundation for Educational Research.

Mevarech, Z. R. (1980). The role of teaching-learning strategies and feedback-corrective procedures in developing higher cognitive achievement. (Unpublished doctoral dissertation, University of Chicago).

Nordin, A. B. (1979). The effects of different qualities of instruction on selected cognitive, affective, and time variables. (Unpublished doctoral dissertation, University of Chicago).

Nordin, A. B. (1980). Improving learning: An experiment in rural primary schools in Malaysia. *Evaluation in Education: An International Review Series, 4,* 2, 143–263.

Pflaum, S. W., Walberg, H. J., Karegianes, M. L., & Rasher, S. (1980). Reading instruction: A quantitative synthesis. *Educational Researcher, 9,* 12–18.

Slavin, R. E. (1980). Cooperative learning. *Review of Educational Research, 50,* 315–342.

Tenenbaum, G. (1982). A method of group instruction which is as effective as one-to-one tutorial instruction. (Doctoral dissertation, University of Chicago, 1982). *Dissertation Abstracts International, 43,* 1822A.

Walberg, H. J. (1984). Improving the productivity of America's schools. *Educational Leadership, 41,* 8, 19–27.

Wolf, R. M. (1964). The identification and measurement of home environmental process variables that are related to intelligence. (Upublished doctoral dissertation, University of Chicago).

Wolf, R. M. (1966). The measurement of environments. In A. Anastasi (Ed.), *Testing Problems in Perspective.* Washington, D.C.: American Council on Education.

DISCUSSION QUESTIONS

1. Is the mastery learning approach appropriate for all students?
2. How does a teacher's differential interaction with students influence student achievement?
3. How are conditions of learning integrally related to student outcomes?
4. What type of staff development initiatives might be undertaken to provide teachers with an accurate perception of the quality of learning conditions that they provide for their students?
5. How effective are conventional instruction, mastery learning, and tutoring?

20

Limiting Students' School Success and Life Chances: The Impact of Tracking

JEANNIE S. OAKES

FOCUSING QUESTIONS

1. *Why has tracking been considered to be a fair educational practice among educators and psychologists?*
2. *How has tracking affected student outcomes?*
3. *How do educators tend to justify the practice of tracking?*
4. *In what ways were criteria used to assign students to tracks?*
5. *What procedures were used to ensure that parents were informed about tracking and their rights to influence placements?*
6. *What role did teacher assessment and perception play in assigning students to tracks?*

Evidence from two school systems whose ability-grouping and tracking systems were subject to scrutiny in 1993 in conjunction with school desegregation cases demonstrates how grouping practices can create within-school segregation and discrimination against African-American and Latino students. In both school systems, tracking created racially unbalanced classes at all three levels—elementary, middle, and senior high, with African-American or Latino students consistently overrepresented and white and Asian students consistently underrepresented in low-ability tracks in all subjects. Neither district's placement practices created classrooms with a range of measured student ability and achievement in classrooms sufficiently narrow to be considered homogeneous "ability groups," and African-American and Latino students were much less likely than whites or Asians with comparable scores to be placed in high-track courses. These disproportionate lower-track placements worked to disadvantage minority students' achievement outcomes. Whether students began with relatively high or relatively low achievement, those who were placed in lower-level courses showed lesser gains over time than similarly situated students placed in higher-level courses. In both systems, grouping practices created a cycle of restricted opportunities and diminished outcomes and exacerbated differences between African-American and Latino and white students.

Since the 1920s, most elementary and secondary schools have tracked their students into separate "ability" groups designed for bright, average, and slow learners and into separate programs for students who are expected to follow different career routes after high school graduation. Tracking has seemed appropriate and fair, given the way psychologists have defined differences in students' intellectual abilities, motivation, and aspirations. Tracking has seemed logical because it supports a nearly century old belief that a crucial job of schools is to ready students for an economy that requires workers with quite different knowledge and skills. According to this logic, demanding academic classes would prepare bright, motivated students heading for jobs that require college degrees, while more rudimentary academic classes and vocational programs would ready less able and less motivated students for less-skilled jobs or for post-high school technical training. With the development early in the century of standardized tests for placement, most people viewed a tracked curriculum with its ability-grouped academic classes as functional, scientific, and democratic—an educationally sound way to accomplish two important tasks: (1) providing students with the education that best suits their abilities and (2) providing the nation with the array of workers it needs.

Despite its widespread legitimacy, there is no question that tracking, the assessment practices that support it, and the differences in educational opportunity that result from it limit many students' schooling opportunities and life chances. These limits affect schoolchildren from all racial, ethnic, and socioeconomic groups. However, schools far more often judge African-American and Latino students to have learning deficits and limited potential. Not surprisingly, then, schools place these students disproportionately in low-track, remedial programs.

Educators justify these placements by pointing out that African-American and Latino children typically perform less well on commonly accepted assessments of ability and achievement. Moreover, conventional school wisdom holds that low-track, remedial, and special education classes help these students, since they permit teachers to target instruction to the particular learning deficiencies of low-ability students. However, considerable research demonstrates that students do not profit from enrollment in low-track classes; they do not learn as much as comparably skilled students in heterogeneous classes; they have less access than other students to knowledge, engaging learning experiences, and resources.[1] Thus, school tracking practices create racially separate programs that provide minority children with restricted educational opportunities and outcomes.

In what follows, I will illustrate these points with evidence from two school systems whose ability grouping and tracking systems have been subject to scrutiny in the past year in conjunction with school desegregation cases. The first system, Rockford Public Schools, in Rockford, Illinois (previously under an interim court order), was the target of a liability suit brought by a community group, The People Who Care. Among other complaints, the group charged the school system with within-school segregation through ability grouping and discrimination against the district's nearly 30 percent African-American and Latino students. The second system, San Jose Unified School District, in San Jose, California, approached the court hoping to be released from its desegregation order of 1985. The plaintiffs in the San Jose case argued, among other things, that the district had used its ability-grouping system to create within-school segregation and, thereby, circumvented the intent of the court order with regard to its approximately 30 percent Latino student population. I analyzed data about the grouping practices in both these cities, prepared reports for the court, and testified. The San Jose system reached a settlement prior to the formal hearing date. The Rockford system was found liable by the court.

To shed light on the grouping practices in these two systems, I conducted analyses and reported my conclusions about tracking and ability-grouping practices around several questions:

1. Does the school system employ tracking and/or ability grouping? If so, what is the specific nature of these practices?
2. Does the system's use of tracking and/or ability grouping create racially imbalanced classrooms?
3. Does the system's use of these grouping practices reflect sound, consistent, and educationally valid considerations?
4. Are the racial disproportionalities created by the system's ability-grouping practices explained by valid educational considerations?
5. What are the consequences of the system's grouping and tracking practices for the class-

room instructional opportunities of Latino children?

6. What are the consequences of the system's grouping and tracking practices for the educational outcomes of Latino children?

7. Does the system have the necessary support and capacity to dismantle racially identifiable tracking and create heterogeneously grouped classrooms?

I addressed these questions with analyses using data specific to the two school systems. These data were gathered from a variety of sources: district and individual school curriculum documents (e.g., curriculum guides, course catalogs, course descriptions, etc.); school plans; computerized student enrollment and achievement data; prior reports prepared by court monitors; and depositions taken from school district employees in the course of the discovery process.[2]

Several analytic methods were applied to these data, all of which had been used in prior published research on tracking and ability grouping. In both systems, I used statistical methods to calculate the achievement range within each track, the distribution of students from various ethnic groups into various tracks, and the probability of placement of students from each ethnic group whose prior achievement "qualified" them for various tracks. In San Jose, but not in Rockford, I was also able to calculate rather precisely the impact of track placement on achievement gains of students with comparable prior achievement. I applied content analysis techniques to district and school curriculum documents in order to classify courses into various track levels, determine placement criteria and processes, and identify curricular goals, course content, and learning opportunities. These documents constitute official district policy statements about the levels and content of the districts' programs and courses, as well as the criteria and procedures by which students enroll in various programs and courses.

The scope of possible analyses was limited, more in Rockford than in San Jose, by a lack of some essential data. Even so, the available data permitted comprehensive analyses of many aspects of the district's grouping practices. They provided a clear picture of tracking and ability grouping in the two systems and enabled me to place the district's practices in light of national research.

PROLIFERATION OF TRACKING

Grouping practices and their effects on minority children were remarkably similar in both systems. Both systems used tracking extensively. At most grade levels and in most academic subject areas at nearly all schools, educators assigned students to classes based on judgments about students' academic abilities. The schools then tailored the curriculum and instruction within classes to the students' perceived ability levels. The districts' tracking systems were not only very comprehensive (in terms of the subject areas and grade levels that are tracked), but they were also very rigid and stable. That is, the districts tended to place students at the same ability level for classes in a variety of subject areas and to lock students into the same or a lower ability-level placement from year to year.

RACIALLY DISPROPORTIONATE TRACK ENROLLMENTS

In both school systems, tracking had created racially imbalanced classes at all three levels—elementary, middle, and senior high. This imbalance took two forms: (1) white (and Asian, in San Jose) students are consistently overrepresented and African-American and Latino students are consistently underrepresented in high-ability classes in all subjects; (2) in contrast, African-American or Latino students were consistently overrepresented, while white and Asian students were consistently underrepresented, in low-ability tracks in all subjects.

INCONSISTENT APPLICATION OF PLACEMENT CRITERIA

The criteria used to assign students to particular tracks were neither clearly specified nor consistently applied. Accordingly, neither district's tracking policies and practices could be construed as the enactment of valid educational purposes; neither did either district present an educational justification for the racial imbalance that results from tracking. Moreover, my analyses demonstrate clearly that neither district's placement practices—practices that result in racially imbalanced tracked classrooms—could be justified by a racially neutral policy of creating classrooms that are distinctly different from one another in terms of students' academic ability or achievement. To the contrary, neither district had enacted ability grouping and tracking in ways that narrow the range of measured student ability and achievement in classrooms sufficiently so that these classrooms can be considered bona fide ability groups.

Both school systems honored parent requests for students' initial track placements and for subsequent changes. This policy undermined the basis of student assignments in either objective measures of students' abilities or more subjective professional judgments. Making matters worse, not all parents were informed about tracking practices or about parents' right to influence their children's placements. Specifically, African-American and Latino parents had less access than others to this knowledge.

Additionally, teacher and counselor recommendations at the critical transitions between elementary and middle school and between middle and high school included a formal mechanism to take into account highly subjective judgments about students' personalities, behavior, and motivation. For example, the screening process for gifted programs usually began with a subjective teacher identification of potentially gifted children, who were then referred for formal testing. Such referrals were often based on subjective judgments about behavior, personality, and attitudes.

TRACKS ACTUALLY HETEROGENEOUS GROUPS

The theory of tracking argues that, to facilitate learning, children should be separated into groups so that they may be taught together with peers of similar ability and apart from those with higher or lower abilities. But in both school systems, classes that were supposed to be designated for students at a *particular* ability level actually enrolled students who spanned *a very wide range* of measured ability. These ranges demonstrate dramatically that in both Rockford and San Jose racially imbalanced tracked classes have borne little resemblance to homogeneous ability groups—even though they have been labeled and treated as such by schools. While the mean scores in each of the tracks followed expected patterns—with average achievement score for students in the low track less than average score for students in the standard or accelerated tracks—the extraordinarily broad range of achievement in each of the three tracks makes clear how far these classes are from being homogeneous ability groups. In sum, the district's practices do not represent what tracking advocates would claim is a trustworthy enactment of a "theory" of tracking and ability grouping.

For example, at one Rockford middle school, the range of eighth-grade reading scores in Honors English (31–99 National Percentile [NP]) overlapped considerably with the range in Regular English (1–95 NP), which overlapped considerably with the range in Basic English (1–50 NP). At one of the senior highs, the math scores of tenth graders in the normal progress college prep math track (26–99 NP) overlapped considerably with those in the slow progress college prep courses (1–99), and both overlapped considerably with the scores of those in non-college preparatory classes (1–99). I found similar patterns of large, overlapping ranges of qualifying scores throughout the system.

The same was true in San Jose. For example, sixth graders placed in a low-track mathematics course demonstrated abilities that ranged all the way from rock-bottom Normal Curve Equivalent (NCE) achievement scores of 1 to extraordinarily high scores of 86. Even more striking, sixth graders in standard-track math classes had achievement scores that spanned the entire range, from NCE scores of 1 to 99. And, while sixth graders in accelerated courses had a somewhat more restricted ability range, they too scored all the way from 52 to 99 NCE scores. I found similar patterns in a number of other subjects in most middle and senior high school grades.

PLACEMENTS RACIALLY SKEWED BEYOND THE EFFECTS OF ACHIEVEMENT

As a group, African-American and Latino students scored lower on achievement tests than whites and Asians in Rockford and San Jose. However, African-American and Latino students were much less likely than white or Asian students *with the same test scores* to be placed in accelerated courses. For example, in San Jose, Latino eighth graders with average scores in mathematics were three times less likely than whites with the same scores to be placed in an accelerated math course. Among ninth graders, the results were similar. Latinos scoring between 40 and 49, 50 and 59, and 60 and 69 NCEs were less than half as likely as their white and Asian counterparts to be placed in accelerated tracks. The discrimination is even more striking among the highest scoring students. While only 56 percent of Latinos scoring between 90 and 99 NCEs were placed in accelerated classes, 93 percent of whites and 97 percent of Asians gained admission to these classes.

In Rockford's tracks and class ability levels, the groups of *higher*-track students whose scores fell within a range that would qualify them for participation in either a higher or lower track (i.e., their scores were the same as students in the lower track) were consistently "whiter" than groups of students whose scores fell within that same range but were placed in the *lower* track. In a number of cases, Rockford's high-track classes included students with exceptionally low scores, but rarely were these students African Americans. Conversely, high-scoring African Americans were enrolled in low-track classes; again, this was seldom the case for high-scoring whites. For example, in 1987, none of the African-American students who scored in the top quartile (75–99 NP) on the California Assessment Program (CAP) reading comprehension test at two of Rockford's large high schools were placed in high-track English, compared with about 40 percent of top-quartile whites who were enrolled in the high track at those schools. In contrast, at three of the system's senior high schools a small fraction of white students who scored in the bottom quartile (1–25 NP) were in high-track classes, while no similarly low scoring African Americans were so placed. At two other senior highs, while some top-quartile African Americans were placed in Honors English, many more top-scoring African Americans were in the basic classes. No low-scoring whites were so placed. I found similar patterns in other subjects at the district's high schools.

I found other striking examples of racially skewed placements in Rockford's junior highs. For example, at one, the range of reading comprehension scores among eighth graders enrolled in Basic English classes was from the first to the seventy-second national percentile. Of these, ten students scored above the national average of 50 NP. Six of the highest scoring, above-average students were African American, including the highest achieving student in the class. One other of the above-average students was Latino.

In both San Jose and Rockford, placement practices skewed enrollments in favor of whites over and above that which can be explained by measured achievement.

LOW TRACKS PROVIDING LESS OPPORTUNITY

In both school systems, African-American and Latino students in lower-track classes had fewer learning opportunities. Teachers expected less of them and gave them less exposure to curriculum and instruction in essential knowledge and skills. Lower-track classes also provided African-American and Latino students with less access to a whole range of resources and opportunities: to highly qualified teachers, to classroom environments conducive to learning, to opportunities to earn extra grade points that can bolster their grade-point averages, and to courses that would qualify them for college entrance and a wide variety of careers as adults.

LOW TRACKS AND LOWER ACHIEVEMENT

Not only did African-American and Latino students receive a lower-quality education as a result of tracking in San Jose and Rockford; their academic achievement suffered as well. In Rockford the initial average achievement gap (i.e., the difference in group mean achievement scores) between white and African-American and/or white and Latino students (i.e., that found on district-administered achievement tests in first grade) did not diminish in higher grades. To the contrary, eleventh graders exhibited gaps somewhat larger than first graders. For example, on the 1992 Stanford Achievement Test in reading comprehension, the gap between African-American and white first graders was 25 percent; that between African-American and white eleventh graders was 30 percent. Undoubtedly more telling, at the time of the seventh-grade test—probably the last point before considerable numbers of lower-achieving minority students drop out of school—the achievement gap between African Americans and whites had grown considerably wider, to 36 percent. A similar pattern was found in students' raw scores in reading comprehension and mathematics for grades 1–6 on the 1992 Stanford Achievement Test. Here, the reading achievement gap between African-American and white students at first grade was .88 of a standard deviation and grew to .99 by grade 6. The Latino–white gap grew from .67 to .70 over the same grades. In math, the African-American–white gap grew from .87 to 1.01; in contrast, the Latino–white gap dropped from .98 to .79. Clearly, the district's tracked programs failed to close the minority–white gap between average group scores. Neither did these practices correct the overrepresentation of black and Latino students in the group of lowest-scoring students in the district. For example, in 1992, 37 percent of the first-grade children scoring between the first and the twenty-fifth national percentiles in reading comprehension on the Stanford Achievement Test were African American; at seventh grade, the percentage of African Americans in this low-scoring group had

risen to 46 percent, and by grade 11 (following a disproportionately high incidence of dropping out by low-achieving African-American students), African-American students still made up 35 percent of this group. Neither did student placements in various instructional programs enable minority students to rise into the group of the district's highest achievers. In fact, *the proportion of minority students in the highest-achieving group of students dropped precipitously.* For example, in 1992, 10 percent of the first-grade children scoring between the seventy-fifth and the ninety-ninth national percentiles in reading comprehension on the Stanford Achievement Test were African American; at seventh grade, the percentage of African Americans in this high-scoring group had dropped by half, to only 5 percent (28 in number); this low proportion was also found at grade 11 (even though the actual number of students, twenty, was smaller).

Rockford's grouping practices that created racially identifiable classrooms and provided unequal opportunities to learn (with fewer such opportunities provided to minority students) *did not serve a remedial function for minority students.* To the contrary, these practices did not even enable minority students to sustain their position, relative to white students, in the district's achievement hierarchy.

In San Jose, better data permitted me to analyze the impact of track placement on individual students over time. Students who were placed in lower-level courses—disproportionately Latino students—consistently demonstrate lesser gains in achievement over time than their peers placed in high-level courses. For example, among the students with preplacement math achievement between 50 and 59 NCEs, those who were placed in a low-track course began with a mean of 54.4 NCEs, but lost an average of 2.2 NCEs after one year and had lost a total of 1.9 NCEs after three years. Students who scored between 50 and 59 NCEs and were placed in a standard-track course, by contrast, began with a mean of 54.6 NCEs, gained 0.1 NCEs after one year, and had gained 3.5 NCEs after three years. The largest gains were experienced by students who were placed in an accelerated course, who began with a mean of 55.4 NCEs, gained 6.5 NCEs after one year, and had gained a total of 9.6 NCEs after three years.

These results are consistent across achievement levels: Whether students began with relatively high or relatively low achievement, those who were placed in lower-level courses showed lesser gains over time than similarly situated students who were placed in higher-level courses.

IN SUM, CONSIDERABLE HARM

The findings from my analyses of San Jose and Rockford support disturbing conclusions about tracking and within-school segregation and discrimination. The districts' tracking systems pervade their schools. The harm that accrues to African Americans and Latinos takes at least three demonstrable forms: (1) unjustifiable, disproportionate, and segregative assignment to low-track classes and exclusion from accelerated classes; (2) inferior opportunities to learn; and (3) lower achievement. In both systems, grouping practices have created a cycle of restricted opportunities and diminished outcomes and have exacerbated differences between African-American and Latino and white students. That these districts have not chosen to eliminate grouping practices that so clearly discriminate against their African-American and Latino children warrants serious concern and strong remedial action.

IMPLICATIONS FOR REMEDIAL ACTIVITIES AND SCHOOL REFORM

Is it technically possible or politically feasible to abandon these discriminatory practices in San Jose, Rockford, or other school systems that are like them? The two systems are currently charged with making significant progress toward that end.

Both Rockford and San Jose school systems have considerable technical capacity to reform their placement practices so that they teach all children in heterogeneous settings, including the gifted, for part or all of the school day in most or all core aca-

demic courses. Conspicuous examples of successful heterogeneous grouping exist currently in San Jose schools. Much of the professional expertise and some of the support structures needed to implement such practices districtwide are already in place. Moreover, in both systems, administrative and teaching staff demonstrate considerable knowledge of the harms of tracking and ample ability to implement educationally sound alternatives.

Furthermore, both districts are situated in a national and state policy environment that encourages the development and use of such alternatives. For example, such national policy groups such as the National Governors' Association and federally supported efforts to create national standards in each of the curriculum areas all recommend against tracking. In California, the State Department of Education's major policy documents on the reform of K–12 schooling (*It's Elementary, Caught in the Middle,* and *Second to None*) and the state's subject matter frameworks caution schools about problems with tracking and strongly recommend that they not use it.[3] Similar state-led initiatives promote heterogeneity in Illinois—for example, the state's involvement in middle-school reform and its adoption of the Accelerated Schools model.

However, racially mixed school systems that have tackled this issue around the country have experienced considerable difficulty creating alternatives. Amy Stuart Wells and I are currently studying ten such schools.[4] While each has made considerable progress toward integrated classrooms and a more even distribution of educational opportunities, most have been the target of considerable fear and anger. As with the nation's experiences with between-school segregation, the pursuit of court sanctions against tracking and ability grouping may be critical to ensuring educational equality. However, like that earlier effort, remedies are neither easily specified nor readily accepted.

ENDNOTES

1. For a comprehensive review of the literature, see Jeannie Oakes, Adam Gamoran, and Reba Page, "Curriculum

Differentiation: Opportunities, Outcomes, and Meanings," in *Handbook of Research on Education,* ed. Philip Jackson (New York: Macmillan, 1992).

2. These previously unpublished analyses are available in the form of a 1993 report to the court in *The People Who Care* v. *Rockford Board of Education School District no. 205* and in my July 1993 deposition in conjunction with *Jose B. Vasquez* v. *San Jose Unified School District et al.*

3. California State Department of Education, *It's Elementary* (Sacramento: Author, 1993); idem, *Caught in the Middle* (Sacramento: Author, 1988); and idem, *Second to None* (Sacramento: Author, 1991).

4. The study in progress, "Beyond Sorting and Stratification: Creating Alternatives to Tracking in Racially Mixed Schools," is sponsored by the Lilly Endowment.

DISCUSSION QUESTIONS

1. What important tasks was tracking designed to fulfill?
2. In your opinion, is tracking (a) a fair practice, (b) a beneficial practice, or (c) a disadvantageous practice? Why? Why not?
3. Does research support the practice of tracking? Why? Why not?
4. What educational opportunities are typically provided to students in lower-class tracks?
5. How did lower track placement affect students' quality of education and student outcomes?
6. What is the relationship between the practice of tracking, in-school segregation, and educational equality?

21

Reflections on Multiple Intelligences: Myths and Messages

HOWARD GARDNER

FOCUSING QUESTIONS

1. *What is an intelligence-fair set of measures?*
2. *How do domains and intelligence differ?*
3. *In what ways does intelligence differ from a learning style, a cognitive style, or a working style?*
4. *What are the similarities and differences between (a) g, (b) the study of heritability of intelligence, and (c) multiple intelligences?*
5. *What additional intelligences might the author write about in the future?*
6. *Why is it fallacious to believe that multiple intelligence is a prescription for educational practice?*
7. *What are the benefits of using pluralistic approaches to instruction?*

A silence of a decade's length is sometimes a good idea. I published *Frames of Mind,* an introduction to the theory of multiple intelligences (MI theory) in 1983.[1] Because I was critical of current views of intelligences within the discipline of psychology, I expected to stir controversy among my fellow psychologists. This expectation was not disappointed.

I was unprepared for the large and mostly positive reaction to the theory among educators. Naturally, I was gratified by this response and was stimulated to undertake some projects exploring the implications of MI theory. I also took pleasure from—and was occasionally moved by—the many attempts to institute an MI approach to education in schools and classrooms. By and large, however, except for a few direct responses to criticisms,[2] I did not speak up about new thoughts concerning the theory itself.

In 1993 my self-imposed silence was broken in two ways. My publisher issued a 10th-anniversary edition of *Frames of Mind,* to which I contributed a short, reflective introductory essay. In tandem with that release, the publisher issued *Multiple Intelligences: The Theory in Practice,* a set of articles chronicling some of the experiments undertaken in the wake of MI theory—mostly projects pursued by colleagues at Harvard Project Zero, but also other MI initiatives.[3] This collection gave me the opportunity to answer some other criticisms leveled against MI theory and to respond publicly to some of the most frequently asked questions.

In the twelve years since *Frames of Mind* was published, I have heard, read, and seen several hundred different interpretations of what MI theory is and how it can be applied in the schools.[4] Until now, I have been content to let MI theory take on a life of its own. As I saw it, I had issued an "ensemble of ideas" (or "memes") to the outer world, and I was inclined to let those "memes" fend for themselves.[5] Yet, in light of my own reading and observations, I believe that the time has come for me to issue a set of new "memes" of my own.

In the next part of this chapter, I will discuss seven myths that have grown up about multiple intelligences and, by putting forth seven complementary "realities," I will attempt to set the record straight. Then, in the third part of the chapter, reflecting on my observations of MI experiments in the schools, I will describe three primary ways in which education can be enhanced by a multiple-intelligences perspective.

In what follows, I make no attempt to isolate MI theory from MI practice. "Multiple intelligences" began as a theory but was almost immediately put to practical use. The commerce between theory and practice has been ready, continuous, and, for the most part, productive.

MYTHS OF MULTIPLE INTELLIGENCES

Myth 1.   Now that seven intelligences have been identified, one can—and perhaps should—create seven tests and secure seven scores.

Reality 1.   MI theory represents a critique of "psychometrics-as-usual." A battery of MI tests is inconsistent with the major tenets of the theory.

Comment.   My concept of intelligences is an outgrowth of accumulating knowledge about the human brain and about human cultures, not the result of a priori definitions or of factor analyses of test scores. As such, it becomes crucial that intelligences be assessed in ways that are *intelligent fair,* that is, in ways that examine the intelligence directly rather than through the lens of linguistic or logical intelligence (as ordinary paper-and-pencil tests do).

Thus, if one wants to look at spatial intelligence, one should allow an individual to explore a terrain for a while and see whether she can find her way around it reliably. Or if one wants to examine

musical intelligence, one should expose an individual to a new melody in a reasonably familiar idiom and see how readily the person can learn to sing it, recognize it, transform it, and the like.

Assessing multiple intelligences is not a high priority in every setting. But when it is necessary or advisable to assess an individual's intelligences, it is best to do so in a comfortable setting with materials (and cultural roles) that are familiar to that individual. These conditions are at variance with our general conception of testing as a decontextualized exercise using materials that are unfamiliar by design, but there is no reason in principle why an intelligence-fair set of measures cannot be devised. The production of such useful tools has been our goal in such projects as Spectrum, Arts PROPEL, and Practical Intelligence for School.[6]

Myth 2.   An intelligence is the same as a domain or a discipline.

Reality 2.   An intelligence is a new kind of construct, and it should not be confused with a domain or a discipline.

Comment.   I must shoulder a fair part of the blame for the propagation of the second myth. In writing *Frames of Mind,* I was not as careful as I should have been in distinguishing intelligences from other related concepts. As I have now come to understand, largely through my interactions with Mihaly Csikszentmihalyi and David Feldman,[7] an *intelligence* is a biological and psychological potential; that potential is capable of being realized to a greater or lesser extent as a consequence of the experiential, cultural, and motivational factors that affect a person.

In contrast, a *domain* is an organized set of activities within a culture, one typically characterized by a specific symbol system and its attendant operations. Any cultural activity in which individuals participate on more than a casual basis and in which degrees of expertise can be identified and nurtured should be considered a domain. Thus, physics, chess, gardening, and rap music are all domains in Western culture. Any domain can be realized through the use of several intelligences; thus the domain of musical performance involves bodily kinesthetic and personal as well as musical intelligences. By the same token, a particular intelligence, like spatial intelligence, can be put to work in a myriad of domains, ranging from sculpture to sailing to neuroanatomical investigations.

Finally, a *field* is the set of individuals and institutions that judge the acceptability and creativity of products fashioned by individuals (with their characteristic intelligences) within established or new domains. Judgments of quality cannot be made apart from the operation of members of a field, though it is worth noting that both the members of a field and the criteria that they employ can and do change over time.

Myth 3.   An intelligence is the same as a "learning style," a "cognitive style," or a "working style."

Reality 3.   The concept of *style* designates a general approach that an individual can apply equally to every conceivable content. In contrast, an *intelligence* is a capacity, with its component processes, that is geared to a specific content in the world (such as musical sounds or spatial patterns).

Comment.   To see the difference between an intelligence and a style, consider this contrast. If a person is said to have a "reflective" or an "intuitive" style, this designation assumes that the individual will be reflective or intuitive with all manner of content, ranging from language to music to social analysis. However, such an assertion reflects an empirical assumption that actually needs to be investigated. It might well be the case that an individual is reflective with music but fails to be reflective in a domain that requires mathematical thinking or that a person is highly intuitive in the social domain but not in the least intuitive when it comes to mathematics or mechanics.

In my view, the relation between my concept of intelligence and the various conceptions of style needs to be worked out empirically on a style-by-style basis. We cannot assume that "style" means the same thing to Carl Jung, Jerome Kagan, Tony

Gregoric, Bernice McCarthy, and other inventors of stylistic terminology.[8] There is little authority for assuming that an individual who evinces a style in one milieu or with one content will necessarily do so with other, diverse contents—and even less authority for equating styles with intelligences.

Myth 4.   MI theory is not empirical. (A variant of Myth 4 alleges that MI theory is empirical but has been disproved.)

Reality 4.   MI theory is based wholly on empirical evidence and can be revised on the basis of new empirical findings.

Comment.   Anyone who puts forth Myth 4 cannot have read *Frames of Mind*. Literally hundreds of empirical studies were reviewed in that book, and the actual intelligences were identified and delineated on the basis of empirical findings. The seven intelligences described in *Frames of Mind* represented my best-faith effort to identify mental abilities of a scale that could be readily discussed and critiqued.

No empirically based theory is ever established permanently. All claims are at risk in the light of new findings. In the last decade, I have collected and reflected on empirical evidence that is relevant to the claims of MI theory, 1983 version. Thus work on the development in children of a "theory of mind," as well as the study of pathologies in which an individual loses a sense of social judgment, has provided fresh evidence for the importance and independence of interpersonal intelligence.[9] In contrast, the finding of a possible link between musical and spatial thinking has caused me to reflect on the possible relations between faculties that had previously been thought to be independent.[10]

Many other lines of evidence could be mentioned here. The important point is that MI theory is constantly being reconceptualized in terms of new findings from the laboratory and from the field (see also Myth 7).

Myth 5.   MI theory is incompatible with *g* (general intelligence),[11] with hereditarian accounts, or with environmental accounts of the nature and causes of intelligence.

Reality 5.   MI theory questions not the existence but the province and explanatory power of *g*. By the same token, MI theory is neutral on the question of heritability of specific intelligences, instead underscoring the centrality of genetic–environmental interactions.

Comment.   Interest in *g* comes chiefly from those who are probing scholastic intelligence and those who traffic in the correlations between test scores. (Recently, people have become interested in the possible neurophysiological underpinnings of *g*[12] and, sparked by the publication of *The Bell Curve*,[13] in the possible social consequences of "low *g*.") While I have been critical of much of the research in the *g* tradition, I do not consider the study of *g* to be scientifically improper, and I am willing to accept the utility of *g* for certain theoretical purposes. My interest, obviously, centers on those intelligences and intellectual processes that are not covered by *g*.[14]

While a major animating force in psychology has been the study of the heritability of intelligence(s), my inquiries have not been oriented in this direction. I do not doubt that human abilities—and human differences—have a genetic base. Can any serious scientist question this at the end of the 20th century? And I believe that behavioral genetic studies, particularly of twins reared apart, can illuminate certain issues.[15] However, along with most biologically informed scientists, I reject the "inherited versus learned" dichotomy and instead stress the interaction, from the moment of conception, between genetic and environmental factors.

Myth 6.   MI theory so broadens the notion of intelligence that it includes all psychological constructs and thus vitiates the usefulness, as well as the usual connotation, of the term.

Reality 6.   This statement is simply wrong. I believe that it is the standard definition of intelligence that narrowly constricts our view, treating a certain form of scholastic performance as if it encompassed the range of human capacities and leading to disdain for those who happen not to be psychometrically bright. Moreover, I reject the distinction between talent and intelligence: in my view, what we call "intelligence" in the vernacular is simply a certain set of "talents" in the linguistic and/or logical–mathematical spheres.

Comment.   MI theory is about the intellect, the human mind in its cognitive aspects. I believe that a treatment in terms of a number of semi-independent intelligences presents a more sustainable conception of human thought than one that posits a single "bell curve" of intellect.

Note, however, that MI theory makes no claims whatsoever to deal with issues beyond the intellect. MI theory is not and does not pretend to be about personality, will, morality, attention, motivation, and other psychological constructs. Note as well that MI theory is not connected to any set of morals or values. An intelligence can be put to an ethical or an antisocial use. Poet and playwright Johann Wolfgang von Goethe and Nazi propagandist Joseph Goebbels were both masters of the German language, but how different were the uses to which they put their talents!

Myth 7.   There is an eighth (or ninth or tenth) intelligence.

Reality 7.   Not in my writings so far. But I am working on it.

Comment.   For the reasons suggested above, I thought it wise not to attempt to revise the principal claims of MI theory before the 1983 version of the theory had been debated. But recently I have turned my attention to possible additions to the list. If I were to rewrite *Frames of Mind* today, I would probably add an eighth intelligence—the intelligence of the naturalist. It seems to me that the individual who is able readily to recognize flora and fauna, to make other consequential distinctions in the natural world, and to use this ability productively (in hunting, in farming, in biological science) is exercising an important intelligence and one that is not adequately encompassed in the current list. Individuals like Charles Darwin or E. O. Wilson embody the naturalist's intelligence, and, in our consuming culture, youngsters exploit their naturalist's intelligence as they make acute discriminations among cars, sneakers, or hairstyles.

I have read in several secondary sources that there is a spiritual intelligence and, indeed, that I have endorsed a spiritual intelligence. That statement is not true. It is true that I have become interested in understanding better what is meant by "spirituality" and by "spiritual individuals"; as my understanding improves, I expect to write about this topic. Whether it proves appropriate to add "spirituality" to the list of intelligences, this human capacity certainly deserves discussion and study in nonfringe psychological circles.

MESSAGES ABOUT MI IN THE CLASSROOM

If one were to continue adding myths to the list, a promising candidate would read: There is a single educational approach based on MI theory.

I trust that I have made it clear over the years that I do not subscribe to this myth.[16] On the contrary, MI theory is in no way an educational prescription. There is always a gulf between psychological claims about how the mind works and educational practices, and such a gulf is especially apparent in a theory that was developed without specific educational goals in mind. Thus, in educational discussions, I have always taken the position that educators are in the best position to determine the uses to which MI theory can and should be put.

Indeed, contrary to much that has been written, MI theory does not incorporate a "position" on tracking, gifted education, interdisciplinary curricula, the layout of the school day, the length of the school year, or many other "hot button" educational issues. I have tried to encourage certain "applied MI efforts," but in general my advice has echoed the traditional Chinese adage "Let a hundred flowers bloom." And I have often been surprised and delighted by the fragrance of some of these fledgling

plants—for example, the use of a "multiple-intelligences curriculum" in order to facilitate communication between youngsters drawn from different cultures or the conveying of pivotal principles in biology or social studies through a dramatic performance designed and staged by students.

I have become convinced, however, that, while there is no "right way" to conduct a multiple-intelligences education, some current efforts go against the spirit of my formulation and embody one or more of the myths sketched above. Let me mention a few applications that have jarred me.

- *The attempt to teach all concepts or subjects using all the intelligences.* As I indicate below, most topics can be powerfully approached in a number of ways. But there is no point in assuming that every topic can be effectively approached in at least seven ways, and it is a waste of effort and time to attempt to do this.
- *The belief that it suffices, in and of itself, just to go through the motions of exercising a certain intelligence.* I have seen classes in which children are encouraged simply to move their arms or to run around, on the assumption that exercising one's body represents in itself some kind of MI statement. Don't read me as saying that exercise is a bad thing; it is not. But random muscular movements have nothing to do with the cultivation of the mind…or even of the body!
- *The use of materials associated with an intelligence as background.* In some classes, children are encouraged to read or to carry out math exercises while music is playing in the background. Now I myself like to work with music in the background. But unless I focus on the performance (in which case the composition is no longer serving as background), the music's function is unlikely to be different from that of a dripping faucet or a humming fan.
- *The use of intelligences primarily as mnemonic devices.* It may well be the case that it is easier to remember a list if one sings it or even

if one dances while reciting it. I have nothing against such aids to memory. However, these uses of the materials of an intelligence are essentially trivial. What is not trivial—as I argue below—is to think musically or to draw on some of the structural aspects of music in order to illuminate concepts like biological evolution or historical cycles.

- *The conflating of intelligences with other desiderata.* This practice is particularly notorious when it comes to the personal intelligences. Interpersonal intelligence has to do with understanding other people, but it is often distorted as a license for cooperative learning or applied to individuals who are extroverted. Intrapersonal intelligence has to do with understanding oneself, but it is often distorted as a rationale for self-esteem programs or applied to individuals who are loners or introverted. One receives the strong impression that individuals who use the terms in this promiscuous way have never read my writings on intelligence.

- *The direct evaluation (or even grading) of intelligences, without regard to context or content.* Intelligences ought to be seen at work when individuals are carrying out productive activities that are valued in a culture. And that is how reporting of learning and mastery in general should take place. I see little point in grading individuals in terms of how "linguistic" or how "bodily kinesthetic" they are; such a practice is likely to introduce a new and unnecessary form of tracking and labeling. As a parent (or as a supporter of education living in the community), I am interested in the *uses* to which children's intelligences are put; reporting should have this focus.

Note that it is reasonable, for certain purposes, to indicate that a child seems to have a relative strength in one intelligence and a relative weakness in another. However, these descriptions should be mobilized in order to help students perform better in meaningful activities and perhaps even to show that a label was premature or erroneous.

Having illustrated some problematic applications of MI theory, let me now indicate three more positive ways in which MI can be—and has been—used in the schools.

1. *The cultivation of desired capabilities.* Schools should cultivate those skills and capacities that are valued in the community and in the broader society. Some of these desired roles are likely to highlight specific intelligences, including ones that have usually been given short shrift in the schools. If, say, the community believes that children should be able to perform on a musical instrument, then the cultivation of musical intelligence toward that end becomes a value of the school. Similarly, emphasis on such capacities as taking into account the feelings of others, being able to plan one's own life in a reflective manner, or being able to find one's way around an unfamiliar terrain are likely to result in an emphasis on the cultivation of interpersonal, intrapersonal, and spatial intelligences, respectively.

2. *Approaching a concept, subject matter, or discipline in a variety of ways.* Along with many other school reformers, I am convinced that schools attempt to cover far too much material and that superficial understandings (or nonunderstandings) are the inevitable result. It makes far more sense to spend a significant amount of time on key concepts, generative ideas, and essential questions and to allow students to become thoroughly familiar with these notions and their implications.

Once the decision has been made to dedicate time to particular items, it then becomes possible to approach those topics or notions in a variety of ways. Not necessarily seven ways, but in a number of ways that prove pedagogically appropriate for the topic at hand. Here is where MI theory comes in. As I argue in *The Unschooled Mind,* nearly every topic can be approached in a variety of ways, ranging from the telling of a story, to a formal argument, to an artistic exploration, to some kind of hands-on experiment or simulation. Such pluralistic approaches should be encouraged.[17]

When a topic has been approached from a number of perspectives, three desirable outcomes ensue. First, because children do not all learn in the same way, more children will be reached. I term this desirable state of affairs "multiple windows leading into the same room." Second, students secure a sense of what it is like to be an expert when they behold that a teacher can represent knowledge in a number of different ways and discover that they themselves are also capable of more than a single representation of a specified content. Finally, since understanding can also be demonstrated in more than one way, a pluralistic approach opens up the possibility that students can display their new understandings—as well as their continuing difficulties—in ways that are comfortable for them and accessible to others. Performance-based examinations and exhibitions are tailor-made for the foregrounding of a student's multiple intelligences.

3. *The personalization of education.* Without a doubt, one of the reasons that MI theory has attracted attention in the educational community is because of its ringing endorsement of an ensemble of propositions:we are not all the same; we do not all have the same kinds of minds; education works most effectively for most individuals if these differences in mentation and strengths are taken into account rather than denied or ignored. I have always believed that the heart of the MI perspective—in theory and in practice—inheres in taking human differences seriously. At the theoretical level, one acknowledges that all individuals cannot be profitably arranged on a single intellectual dimension. At the practical level, one acknowledges that any uniform educational approach is likely to serve only a minority of children.

When I visit an "MI school," I look for signs of personalization: evidence that all involved in the educational encounter take such differences among human beings seriously; evidence that they construct curricula, pedagogy, and assessment insofar as possible in the light of these differences. All the MI posters, indeed all the references to me personally, prove to be of little avail if the youngsters continue to be treated in homogenized fashion. By the same token, whether or not members of the staff have even heard of MI theory, I would be happy to send my children to a school with the following characteristics: differences among youngsters are taken seriously, knowledge about differences is shared with children and parents, children gradually assume responsibility for their own learning, and materials that are worth knowing are presented in ways that afford each child the maximum opportunity to master those materials and to show others (and themselves) what they have learned and understood.

CLOSING COMMENTS

I am often asked for my views about schools that are engaged in MI efforts. The implicit question may well be, "Aren't you upset by some of the applications that are carried out in your name?"

In truth, I do not expect that initial efforts to apply any new ideas are going to be stunning. Human experimentation is slow, difficult, and filled with zigs and zags. Attempts to apply any set of innovative ideas will sometimes be half-hearted, superficial, even wrongheaded.

For me the crucial question concerns what has happened in a school (or class) two, three, or four years after it has made a commitment to an MI approach. Often, the initiative will be long since forgotten—the fate, for better or worse, of most educational experiments. Sometimes, the school has gotten stuck in a rut, repeating the same procedures of the first days without having drawn any positive or negative lessons from this exercise. Needless to say, I am not happy with either of these outcomes.

I cherish an educational setting in which discussions and applications of MI have catalyzed a more fundamental consideration of schooling—its overarching purposes, its conceptions of what a productive life will be like in the future, its pedagogical methods, and its educational outcomes, particularly in the context of the values of that specific community. Such examination generally leads to more thoughtful schooling. Visits with other schools and more extended forms of networking among MI enthusiasts (and critics) constitute important parts of this building process. If, as a result of these discussions and experiments, a more personalized education is the outcome, I feel that the heart of MI theory has been embodied. And if this personalization is fused with a commitment to the achievement of worthwhile (and attainable) educational understandings for all children, then the basis for a powerful education has indeed been laid.

The MI endeavor is a continuing and changing one. There have emerged over the years new thoughts about the theory, new understandings and misunderstandings, and new applications, some very inspired, some less so. Especially gratifying to me has been the demonstration that this process is dynamic and interactive: no one, not even its creator, has a monopoly on MI wisdom or foolishness. Practice is enriched by theory, even as theory is transformed in the light of the fruits and frustrations of practice. The burgeoning of a community that takes MI issues seriously is not only a source of pride to me but also the best guarantor that the theory will continue to live in the years ahead.

ENDNOTES

1. Howard Gardner, *Frames of Mind: The Theory of Multiple Intelligences* (New York: Basic Books. 1983). A 10th-anniversary edition, with a new introduction, was published in 1993.

2. Howard Gardner, "On Discerning New Ideas in Psychology," *New Ideas in Psychology,* vol. 3, 1985, pp. 101–104; and idem, "Symposium on the Theory of Multiple Intelligences," in David N. Perkins, Jack Lochhead, and John C. Bishop, eds., *Thinking: The Second International Conference* (Hillsdale, N.J.: Erlbaum, 1983), pp. 77–101.

3. Howard Gardner, *Multiple Intelligences: The Theory in Practice* (New York: Basic Books, 1993).

4. For a bibliography through 1992, see the appendices to Gardner, *Multiple Intelligences.*

5. The term "memes" is taken from Richard Dawkins, *The Selfish Gene* (New York: Oxford University Press, 1976).

6. See Gardner, *Multiple Intelligences.*

7. Mihaly Csikszentmihalyi, "Society, Culture, and Person: A Systems View of Creativity," in Robert J. Sternberg, ed., *The Nature of Creativity* (New York: Cambridge University Press, 1988), pp. 325–339; idem, *Creativity: Flow and the Psychology of Discovery and Convention* (New York: HarperCollins, 1996); David H.

Feldman, "Creativity: Dreams, Insights, and Transformations," in Sternberg, op. cit., pp. 271–97; and David H. Feldman, Mihaly Csikszentmihalyi, and Howard Gardner, *Changing the World: A Framework for the Study of Creativity* (Westport, Conn.: Greenwood, 1994).

8. For a comprehensive discussion of the notion of cognitive style, see Nathan Kogan, "Stylistic Variation in Childhood and Adolescence," in Paul Mussen, ed., *Handbook of Child Psychology,* vol. 3 (New York: Wiley, 1983), pp. 630–706.

9. For writings pertinent to the personal intelligences, see Janet Astington, *The Child's Discovery of the Mind* (Cambridge, Mass.: Harvard University Press, 1993); and Antonio Damasio, *Descartes' Error* (New York: Grosset/Putnam, 1994).

10. On the possible relation between musical and spatial intelligence, see Frances Rauscher, G. L. Shaw, and X. N. Ky, "Music and Spatial Task Performance," *Nature,* 14 October 1993, p. 611.

11. The most thorough exposition of g can be found in the writings of Arthur Jensen. See, for example, *Bias in Mental Testing* (New York: Free Press, 1980). For a critique, see Stephen J. Gould, *The Mismeasure of Man* (New York: Norton, 1981).

12. Interest in the neurophysiological bases of g is found in Arthur Jensen, "Why Is Reaction Time Correlated with Psychometric 'G'?," *Current Directions of Psychological Science,* vol. 2, 1993, pp. 53–56.

13. Richard Herrnstein and Charles Murray, *The Bell Curve* (New York: Free Press, 1994).

14. For my view on intelligences not covered by $g,$ see Howard Gardner, "Review of Richard Hernstein and Charles Murray, *The Bell Curve,*" *American Prospect,* Winter 1995, pp. 71–80.

15. On behavioral genetics and psychological research, see Thomas Bouchard and P. Propping, eds., *Twins as a Tool of Behavioral Genetics* (Chichester, England: Wiley, 1993).

16. On the many approaches that can be taken in implementing MI theory, see Mara Krechevsky, Thomas Hoerr, and Howard Gardner, "Complementary Energies: Implementing MI Theory from the Lab and from the Field," in Jeannie Oakes and Karen H. Quartz, eds., *Creating New Educational Communities: Schools and Classrooms Where All Children Can Be Smart: 94th NSSE Yearbook* (Chicago: National Society for the Study of Education, University of Chicago Press, 1995), pp. 166–86.

17. Howard Gardner, *The Unschooled Mind: How Children Learn and How Schools Should Teach* (New York: Basic Books, 1991).

DISCUSSION QUESTIONS

1. How does an intelligence-fair set of measures differ from current conceptions of testing as a decontextualized exercise?
2. What types of empirical evidence support the seven intelligences?
3. According to the author, what is the relationship between talent and intelligence?
4. Why is Gardner critical of some of the efforts to conduct a multiple-intelligence education?
5. In what ways is education enhanced by a multiple-intelligence perspective?

22

Synthesis of Research on Compensatory and Remedial Education

LORIN W. ANDERSON
LEONARD O. PELLICER

FOCUSING QUESTIONS

1. *What are the goals of compensatory and remedial education programs?*
2. *How do differences in staffing impact the effectiveness of such programs?*
3. *How does coordination with the regular education program influence student outcomes?*
4. *What are some of the disadvantages of compensatory and remedial education?*
5. *What role should educators play in reforming compensatory and remedial programs?*

Over the past quarter century, programs designed to provide quality education for children who are economically disadvantaged and educationally deficient have received substantial funding. The major federally-funded program of this type, Chapter 1, accounts for 20 percent of the U.S. Department of Education's total budget, or almost four billion dollars a year. Approximately one of every nine school-age children is enrolled in the Chapter 1 program (OERI 1987).

In recent years, individual states have begun to fund their own programs targeted toward students who fail to meet state achievement standards. In South Carolina, for example, at least one-fourth of the children enrolled in public schools are in state-funded compensatory and remedial programs.[1] Since 1985, the cost of the program in South Carolina has averaged over $55 million per year, a figure which represents approximately 20

percent of the total monies raised in support of the school reform legislation (Anderson et al. 1989).

Whether the money is supplied by federal, state, or local funds, large amounts of money are spent on the education of these children. But what do we know about the operation and effectiveness of these programs? Do the academic gains made by the children served in these programs justify the large expenditure of funds? Are changes needed in the programs to increase their effectiveness? These are the issues we will examine in this chapter, basing our generalizations on the results of numerous studies conducted during the past 15 years.

COSTS AND FUNDING

Compensatory and remedial programs are more costly than regular programs. Carter (1984) estimated that Chapter 1 services cost about $436 more per student than the services provided to non-Chapter 1 students. In South Carolina, services provided to students in compensatory and remedial programs cost approximately $362 and $159 more per student, respectively, than those provided to students not in special programs (Anderson et al. 1989). While these figures must be continually adjusted for increases in the cost of living, it is apparent that compensatory and remedial programs require substantial amounts of additional funds.

Compensatory and remedial programs are funding programs, not educational programs. The criteria and guidelines for these programs specify quite clearly *which* students are to be served, but tend to avoid specifying *how* students are to be served. For the federally-funded program, schools are selected on the basis of economic indicators (e.g., free or reduced price lunch status), while the eligibility of the students in those schools for the program depends on their levels of achievement. State-funded programs often rely exclusively on student achievement to determine which students are eligible for inclusion. In South Carolina, for example, all students who fail to achieve a passing score on one or more of the state's basic skills tests are eligible for placement in the program. Funding for both federal and state programs is based solely on the total number of students served.

The criteria and guidelines for monitoring the programs also have a funding orientation. School districts are expected to avoid co-mingling federal, state, and local funds. For example, Chapter 1 programs are intended to "supplement, not supplant" programs funded locally or at the state level. School districts are also expected to serve only those students who are eligible (OERI 1987).

The only educational advice provided to local educators concerns the available program models and the nature of the services provided to the students. The recommended models (e.g., in-class floating aide, special class or pull out, alternate class or replacement) are quite generic. District personnel are told that services should be of "sufficient size, scope, and quality to give reasonable promise of substantial progress toward meeting students' needs" (OERI 1987, p. 54). As a conse-

quence, any one model is staffed and implemented differently in different districts and schools (Rowan et al. 1986, Anderson et al. 1989). Thus, it should not be surprising that the educational treatments provided to students in these programs are "as varied as can be imagined" (Carter 1984, p. 12).

ORGANIZATION AND ADMINISTRATION

Integration of compensatory and remedial programs into the total school program is often lacking. In addition, administrative leadership for these programs within the school often does not exist or exists at some minimal level. Schools' compensatory and remedial programs typically exist in isolation (Johnston et al. 1985, OERI 1987). Regular classroom teachers hold less than positive attitudes toward compensatory and remedial programs partly because of a perceived lack of coordination with the regular school program and partly because of a perceived lack of difficulty of the content and material included in the compensatory and remedial programs. (Anderson et al. 1989). Regular classroom teachers complain that the scheduling of compensatory and remedial programs takes precedence over the scheduling of regular classes (Rowan et al. 1986).

In addition, "weak or absent" coordination of the Chapter 1 program with the regular program tends to impede student learning (OERI 1987). District administrators usually make decisions concerning the models to use to deliver educational services to compensatory and remedial students without the involvement or even the knowledge of school principals. As a consequence, principals may not have a "clear understanding of the rationale for selecting particular remedial and compensatory models for their schools, much less an understanding of how to integrate these special programs within the regular school curriculum" (Anderson et al. 1989, p. 42).

The district administrators' decisions concerning the models to use often reflect their own preferences or the availability of resources (e.g., space, personnel) (OERI 1987, Anderson et al. 1989), rather than concerns for meeting the needs

---

Highlights of Research on Compensatory and Remedial Education

The research on compensatory and remedial educational programs shows that:

- Chapter 1 programs are often so poorly coordinated with regular programs that student learning is actually impeded. Along with some federal programs for the handicapped and state programs for the gifted, Chapter 1 programs contribute to a fragmentation of the curriculum.
- Although they generally lack qualifications, teacher's aides often serve as instructional staff in Chapter 1 programs because they are less expensive than certified teachers—they are chosen for pragmatic, rather than educational, reasons.
- Students in remedial and compensatory classes often spend inordinate amounts of time working alone at their desks.
- Chapter 1 teachers often have low expectations for their students and a tendency to teach to their present levels of functioning rather than to the levels they will need to be successful in the future. As a result, Chapter 1 students may do well on classroom tests and worksheets, but they often perform poorly on state or national tests.
- Chapter 1 programs are substantially less effective for students with severe learning problems than for "marginal" students, whose problems are associated with an inability or unwillingness to learn in regular classroom settings.
- Rather than exiting from the programs once they achieve better skills, Chapter 1 students often become "lifers." A primary cause of this phenomenon is the poor quality of instruction they receive.

---

of students or evidence concerning the effectiveness of particular models. The models they choose usually remain quite stable from year to year (OERI 1987). Furthermore, in schools which operate both state-funded and federally-funded programs, the two programs generally use the same delivery model (Rowan et al. 1986).

Finally, in addition to the lack of coordination with the "regular" program, there may be a problem with the coordination of these programs with other special programs. For example, Anderson et al. (1989) found less effective state-funded programs in those schools which housed both federally-funded and state-funded compensatory and remedial programs. Along with federal programs for the handicapped and state programs for gifted and talented students, compensatory and remedial programs may be contributing to both a fragmentation of the school curriculum and an administrative nightmare for principals.

Staffing decisions may be more important to program effectiveness than decisions concerning the delivery model. There is increasing evidence that the delivery model chosen does not *by itself* affect the quality of the instruction provided (Rowan et al. 1986) or the effectiveness of the program (Anderson et al. 1989). Excellent instruction, as well as poor quality instruction, has been observed in all delivery models (Rowan et al. 1986, Anderson et al. 1989).

The selection of instructional staff, on the other hand, may be quite important in influencing the effectiveness of the model. Specifically, using aides in compensatory and remedial programs is particularly problematic because of their general lack of qualifications (OERI 1987) and training (Anderson and Reynolds 1990). Furthermore, aides vary greatly in the quality of instruction they provide to the students (Rowan et al. 1986). Finally, less effective programs rely more on aides than do more effective programs (Anderson et al. 1989).

The two reasons for using aides are: (1) they are less expensive than certified teachers, and (2) they are less likely to cause role conflict between instructional personnel within the classroom (OERI 1987). Like the choice of models, the choice of personnel to staff the models seems more pragmatic than educational.

INSTRUCTION AND TEACHING

Students in compensatory and remedial programs receive instruction in smaller groups or classes, typically eight or fewer students. One thing we know about elementary compensatory and remedial programs, in general, is that the staff/student ratio is substantially lower than that of the regular program (Carter 1984, Rowan et al. 1986, OERI 1987). But, interestingly, some remedial high school classes in South Carolina have *larger* numbers of students than do the regular classes.

While classes with smaller numbers of students are likely to allow teachers to provide the type of instruction and teacher-student interaction associated with higher levels of student achievement (OERI 1987), a simple reduction in class or group size does not necessarily guarantee quality teaching or higher levels of achievement. Some teachers use the same general approach to teaching regardless of class size or the achievement levels of their students (Robinson 1990).

Students in compensatory and remedial programs spend large amounts of time engaged in seatwork activities, particularly those students at the upper levels. Despite their smaller class or group sizes, students in compensatory and remedial programs (particularly those at the middle or junior high and high school levels) are seldom taught as a group. (Rowan et al. 1986). Their teachers spend little class time actively or interactively teaching, where the teacher explains material to a group of students and students interact with the teacher and one another by asking questions and making comments. Instead, the students spend large amounts of time working by themselves at their seats on written assignments. During this time, teachers circu-

late among the students, monitor their work, and provide tutoring as necessary (OERI 1987, Anderson et al. 1989). And in elementary reading classes, students may work for extended periods of time *without* supervision as the teacher interacts with another reading group (Lee et al. 1986).

Students in compensatory and remedial programs have very high success rates (in terms of the percentage of correct responses to classroom questions and the percentage of correct answers or solutions to exercises included on worksheets or other written assignments). Unfortunately, however, the demands placed on these students by the academic content that is the basis for these questions and worksheets are often far lower than those typically included on the state or national tests they may have to pass to exit from the programs. Teachers of students enrolled in compensatory and remedial programs appear to be caught between the proverbial rock and a hard place. They want to target their instruction to the current levels at which their students are functioning. At the same time, however, they want to ensure that their students achieve those levels of learning they must achieve to do well on the end-of-year tests. Unfortunately, the data suggest that teachers teach to the students' present levels of academic functioning, rather than to the levels they will need to achieve to be successful in the future (Rowan et al. 1986, Anderson et al. 1989). As a consequence, many compensatory and remedial students appear to be very successful in the short term but remain largely unsuccessful over the long haul.

In general, expectations for students in compensatory and remedial programs are very low. In this regard, there is some evidence that these students would benefit greatly from increased expectations and demands. This generalization follows quite naturally from the previous one. Teachers of students in compensatory and remedial programs tend to perceive that their students live in "intellectually deficient" home environments, lack self-esteem, are unable to work without supervision, and are "slow learners" (Rowan et al. 1986). Furthermore, as we have mentioned, the assignments they give to students at the middle or junior high and high school levels are frequently below the level at which they are functioning, let alone the level at which they need to function in order to pass the test which is the basis for exiting the programs (Anderson et al. 1989). Finally, compensatory and remedial programs rarely teach the development of higher-order skills (Rowan et al. 1986). Rather, their emphasis is on the acquisition of basic facts and skills (Pogrow 1990).

Peterson (1989) suggests that when teachers hold higher expectations for remedial students' mathematics achievement (i.e., they teach algebra rather than review previously taught mechanical skills), the students actually do reach higher levels of achievement. Similarly, Anderson et al. (1989) concluded that giving middle or junior high school students more challenging assignments that result in a greater number of errors is more beneficial over the long term than giving them easier assignments on which they make fewer errors. Finally, Pogrow (1990) contends that emphasizing higher-order thinking skills (HOTS) "can develop the natural intellectual potential of at-risk students in a way that dramatically improves their basic skills" (p. 397).

THE EFFECTIVENESS OF COMPENSATORY AND REMEDIAL PROGRAMS

Compensatory and remedial programs are more effective for "marginal" students (those closest to the standard set for program inclusion) and substantially less effective for the remainder of the students enrolled in these programs. Clearly two distinct groups of students are served by compensatory and remedial programs: the compensatory students (who have severe learning problems as a result of cumulative environmental and/or intellectual deficits) and the remedial students (who have less serious learning problems, problems associated with their inability or unwillingness to learn in regular classroom settings). Carter (1984) concluded that Chapter 1 has been effective for "students who were only moderately disadvantaged, but it did not improve the relative achievement of the most disadvantaged part of the school population" (p. 7). As a consequence, Rowan et al. (1986) contend that the delivery models and assignments

provided to "marginal" remedial students vs. the compensatory students should be very different. Presently, they are not (Anderson et al. 1989).

The majority of students enrolled in compensatory and remedial programs remain in or periodically return to those programs for the better part of their school lives. The percentage of students who remain in compensatory and remedial programs from one year to the next ranges from 40 percent to 75 percent (Carter 1984, Davidoff et al. 1989, Potter and Wall 1990). In addition, approximately one-half of those who exit the program at the end of any given year qualify for re-entry to the program at the next testing date (Davidoff et al. 1989). As a consequence, almost one-half of the students initially enrolled in a compensatory and remedial program spend more of their school years in the program than out of the program (Potter and Wall 1990).

Many of these students experience particular difficulty negotiating the transition from one school level to the next. In a longitudinal study, Jenkins (1990) found that the number of students enrolled in the program increased by almost 40 percent from 5th grade (often the end of elementary school) to 6th grade (often the beginning of middle school). Similarly, in a cross-sectional study, Anderson et al. (1989) found that the number of students enrolled in Chapter 1 and state compensatory and remedial programs increased from 25 percent in 2nd grade to 38 percent by 7th grade. Possible reasons for this increase are higher passing standards on basic skills tests associated with higher school levels (Anderson et al. 1990) and generally less effective programs at the higher grade levels (Carter 1984).

RECOMMENDATIONS FOR CHANGE

There are three recommendations for change that we believe to be of primary importance in ameliorating some of the shortcomings of remedial and compensatory education programs.

Compensatory and remedial programs should be reconceptualized as educational programs rather than funding programs. The availability and allocation of sufficient funding for these programs is a necessary but not sufficient condition for their effectiveness. A number of researchers have documented a wide variety of approaches and strategies used in providing services to these students. As a consequence, there is no single identifiable educational program that we can reliably term "compensatory and remedial." Program input is the focus in the administration of these programs, not program implementation or outcomes. Thus, a student's *access* to a compensatory or remedial program is, in effect, of greater importance than his or her *exit* from it. In fact, many funding formulas actually reward school districts for having greater numbers of students *in* compensatory and remedial programs.

The use of the normal curve equivalent (NCE) metric in evaluating these programs should be reconsidered. An NCE gain of one unit (currently used as a standard in judging the success of federal and state programs in several states) requires that students, on the average, attain marginally higher test scores than they might have been expected to attain given their previous test scores. But for students to re-enter and achieve success in the regular school program they must attain substantially, *not* marginally, higher test scores. Program success should be equated with individual student success, not with the marginal success of students "on the average." Stated somewhat differently, compensatory and remedial programs should be judged successful only when large numbers of their students return to and remain in the academic mainstream.

Compensatory and remedial programs must be more completely integrated into the total school program. If the goals of these special programs are to be reached, they must achieve greater integration into the total school program. Several aspects of this needed integration must be addressed simultaneously.

Principals are the key players in integrating special programs into the total school program in individual schools. Presently, many building administrators are unfamiliar with compensatory and remedial programs and the students served by these programs. Principals must acquaint themselves with compensatory and remedial programs

and actively involve themselves in important decisions about the programs.

Teachers also have a role to play in cross-program coordination. Rowan and his colleagues (1986) concluded that informal coordination was an important factor in program integration. However, regular classroom teachers and special program teachers must develop mutual respect and must function as colleagues if informal coordination is to occur. In the words of Rowan and his colleagues: "Schools that showed the tightest coupling between Chapter 1 and regular instruction were those in which staff endorsed a norm of collegiality and had developed shared beliefs about instruction" (p. 94).

Finally, several curriculum issues must be resolved if integration across programs is to be complete. Sufficient comparability of the curriculum across programs is necessary if students are to be able to move from program to program. The likelihood that students will remain in programs for the duration of their academic careers increases with curriculum diversity across programs because, quite literally, there is nowhere else to go. Teachers must increase the pace at which compensatory and remedial students move through the curriculum if these students are not to fall further behind their same-age peers.

The ultimate goal of compensatory and remedial programs—to bring academically deficient students back into the academic mainstream—will be better served if all administrators and teachers see these programs as an integral part of the total school program and as an important component in the school's educational mission. For programs to be seen in this light, principals and teachers must be better informed about the philosophical basis of and rationale for these programs as well as their organization, structure, integration, and evaluation. Once informed, they must use this knowledge to make important program and student decisions.

The quality of the education provided to compensatory and remedial students must be increased substantially. Once children are placed in compensatory and remedial programs, they usually remain in or return to those programs throughout their school careers. The evidence for this is so compelling that Anderson and his colleagues (1989) referred to these students as "lifers," while Pogrow (1990) termed them "professional Chapter 1 students." The specific reasons for this phenomenon are not completely clear, but there is ample reason to believe that the level and quality of instruction provided to these students are among the primary causes. (Anderson et al. 1990).

In order to improve the level and quality of instruction provided to compensatory and remedial students, we must first admit that smaller classes and greater individual student attention do not guarantee excellence in teaching or learning. The qualifications and training of those providing the services, the quality of the services provided (as opposed to whether the services have been provided), and the accomplishments of those receiving the services must be considered in determining program effectiveness.

Two aspects of quality instruction, expectations and teaching, need further elaboration. Many teachers hold low expectations for compensatory and remedial students. These teachers assign them less difficult work than necessary for students to develop the knowledge and skills needed to "pass the test" and move out of the program. Too often, these teachers accept effort ("they tried") rather than accomplishment ("they learned") in judging student success. They emphasize the learning of facts and discrete skills over the ability to think and reason. Students in these programs spend large amounts of time working on worksheets by themselves. Little interaction with peers has been observed; little whole-class or whole-group dialogue with teachers has been noted. Given the relatively smaller number of students in the classes, this level of student isolation is quite surprising.

Based on the above analysis, we suggest several changes in the level or quality of instruction provided to these students. First, students should be assigned more challenging content and associated tasks at a more rapid pace. Second, teachers should direct more active teaching to the entire class or to small groups of students. Third, at the very least, teachers and administrators should see that their programs incorporate higher-order thinking skills.

Finally, schools should create substantially different instructional programs for compensatory and for remedial students.

CONCLUSION

In 25 years, we have apparently learned very little as a result of our efforts to provide appropriate educational experiences for culturally and educationally deprived children. Our neediest students are enrolled in the neediest programs. Rather than truly compensating or remediating these students, we have contented ourselves with merely slowing the rate at which they fall further and further behind. We continue to justify continuing huge financial commitments to programs that simply don't work very well, year after year after year. Those who make key decisions about compensatory programs are obviously reluctant to deviate very much from the established norms in program delivery, content, and measures of success. Unfortunately, the grim reality is that if you do what you did—you will get what you got!

This reluctance is inexplicable and tragic because we have both the technical expertise and sufficient resources to provide appropriate and effective services to compensatory and remedial students. But can we muster the necessary commitment, and are we willing to dedicate the resources and apply the know-how to ensure the educational success of a very large, but politically less than powerful, segment of our school population?

Throwing money at the problem in no way absolves policymakers and society in general of the responsibility for providing these students with a set of educational experiences that are both appropriate and effective. In the final analysis, successful programs can be realistically defined only in terms of individual student success. And the ultimate measure of success can only be the ability of large numbers of remedial and compensatory students to exit these special programs and return to and remain in the academic mainstream.

ENDNOTE

1. The total number of students served in state compensatory and remedial programs is difficult to calculate pre-

cisely because the South Carolina Department of Education "double counts" students. That is, if a student is concurrently enrolled in both remedial reading and remedial mathematics, that student would appear twice in the overall total.

REFERENCES

Anderson, L. W., N. R. Cook, L. O. Pellicer, and R. L. Spradling. (1989). *A Study of EIA-Funded Remedial and Compensatory Programs in South Carolina.* Columbia, S.C.: The South Carolina Educational Policy Center.

Anderson, L. W., L. O. Pellicer, R. L. Spradling, N.R., Cook, and J. T. Sears. (1990). "No Way Out: Some Reasons for the Stability of Student Membership in State Compensatory and Remedial Programs," paper presented at the Annual Meeting of the American Educational Research Association, Boston.

Anderson, L. W., and E. Reynolds. (1990). "The Training, Qualifications, Duties, and Responsibilities of Teacher Aides in Compensatory and Remedial Programs in South Carolina," Unpublished manuscript, University of South Carolina.

Carter, L. F. (1984). "The Sustaining Effects Study of Compensatory and Elementary Education," *Educational Researcher,* 13, 7: 4–13.

Davidoff, S. H., R. J. Fishman, and E. M. Pierson. (1989). "Indicator Based Evaluation for Chapter 1," paper presented at the Annual Meeting of the American Educational Research Association, San Francisco.

Jenkins, B. S. (1990). "EIA Compensatory/Remedial Programs in Chesterfield County," paper presented at the Annual Meeting of the South Carolina Educators for the Practical Use of Research, Columbia, S. C.

Johnston, P., R. Allington, and P. Afflerbach. (1985). "The Congruence of Classroom and Remedial Instruction." *Elementary School Journal,* 85, 4: 465–477.

Lee, G. V., B. Rowan, R. Allington, L. W. Anderson, S. T. Bossert, A. Harnischseger, and J. A. Stallings. (1986). *The Management and Delivery of Instructional Services to Chapter 1 Students: Case Studies of 12 Schools.* San Francisco: Far West Laboratory for Educational Research and Development.

Office of Educational Research and Improvement. (1987). *The Current Operation of the Chapter 1 Program.* Washington D. C.: OERI.

Peterson, J. M. (1989). "Remediation Is No Remedy," *Educational Leadership,* 46,6: 24–25.

Pogrow, S. (1990). "Challenging At-Risk Students: Findings From the HOTS Program." *Phi Delta Kappan,* 71: 389–397.

Potter, D., and M. Wall. (1990). "An Analysis of Five Years of State Remedial/Compensatory Program Evaluation Data," paper presented at the Annual Meeting of the South Carolina Educators for the Practical Use of Research, Columbia, S.C.

Robinson, G. E. (1990). "Synthesis of Research on the Effects of Class Size." *Educational Leadership,* 47, 7:80–90.

Rowan, B., L. F. Guthrie, G. V. Lee, and G. P. Guthrie. (1986). *The Design and Implementation of Chapter 1 Instructional Services: A Study of 24 Schools.* San Francisco, Cal.: Far West Laboratory of Educational Research and Development.

DISCUSSION QUESTIONS

1. Are compensatory and remedial education programs effective? Why? Why not?
2. What organizational and administrative changes are needed to ensure the integrity of compensatory and remedial efforts?
3. How does the district administrator influence the success of such programs?
4. What types of programmatic changes might enhance the effectiveness of curriculum delivery and student outcomes?
5. What is the role of the teacher in cross-program coordination?

23

Teaching, Instruction, and Technology

SIMON HOOPER
LLOYD P. RIEBER

FOCUSING QUESTIONS

1. *How does educational technology differ from teaching with technology?*
2. *In what ways is teaching with technology affecting classroom instruction?*
3. *What roles do the familiarization, utilization, integration, reorientation, and evolution phases play in applications of technology in education?*
4. *What are the advantages and disadvantages of product technologies?*
5. *What pedagogical principles are likely to guide effective technology-based teaching?*

Classroom teaching is a demanding job. Most people outside education probably think teachers spend most of their time teaching, but teachers are responsible for many tasks that have little to do with classroom instruction. Beyond planning and implementing instruction, teachers are also expected to be managers, psychologists, counselors, custodians, and community "ambassadors," not to mention entertainers. If teaching sounds like an unreasonable almost impossible job, perhaps it is.

It is easy to understand how a teacher might become frustrated and disillusioned. Most teachers enter the profession expecting to spark the joy of learning in their students. Unfortunately, the other demands of the classroom are very distracting and consuming. We envision technology as a teacher's liberator to help reestablish the role and value of the individual classroom teacher. To do so, two things must happen. First the perspective of the classroom must change to become learner-centered. Second, students and teachers must enter into a collaboration or partnership with technology

to create a "community" that nurtures, encourages, and supports the learning process (Cognition and Technology Group at Vanderbilt, 1992).

It is important to note that the focus in this chapter is on *educational technology* as compared to technology in education. There is a difference. Technology in education is often perceived in terms of how many computers or videocassette recorders are in a classroom and how they might be used to support traditional classroom activities, but this is a misleading and potentially dangerous interpretation. It not only places an inappropriate focus on hardware, but fails to consider other potentially useful "idea" technologies that result from the application of one or more knowledge bases such as learning theory. Educational technology involves applying ideas from various sources to create the best learning environments possible for students. Educational technologists also ask questions such as how a classroom might change or adapt when a computer is integrated into the curriculum. This integration means that the curriculum and setting may also need to change to meet the opportunities that the technology may offer.

There are four purposes to this chapter. First, we will examine several different stages of technology adoption. Second, we will review national roles that technology has served in the classroom. Third, we will examine what a classroom might be like when attention is given to educational technology. Fourth, we will provide some specific examples that incorporate contemporary educational principles. This chapter will try to present ways in which educational technology may be useful to teachers given current classroom conditions as well as how it might influence the course that many schools may chart in the future.

A MODEL OF TECHNOLOGY ADOPTION IN THE CLASSROOM

Educational technology is often considered, erroneously, as synonymous with instructional innovation. Technology, by definition, applies current knowledge to some useful purpose. Therefore, technology uses evolving knowledge (whether about a kitchen or a classroom) to adapt and improve the system to which the knowledge applies (such as a kitchen's microwave oven or educational computing). In contrast, innovations represent only change for change sake. Given this distinction, it is easy to argue that educators are correct to resist mere innovation, but they should welcome educational technology. Unfortunately, the history of educational technology does not support this hypothesis (Saettler, 1990).

Although education has witnessed a multitude of both technology and innovation over the past fifty years (Reiser, 1987), the educational system has scarcely changed during that time. Few would argue that doctors and dentists of fifty years ago would be competent and capable enough to practice with the technology of today. Yet, a teacher from fifty years ago would probably feel right at home in most of today's classrooms as most technologies and innovations introduced during this time have been discarded. It is difficult to account for the rapid abandonment of technologies and in-

novations in education over the past fifty years. Has the educational system reached the point of development at which no further improvement can be expected from current educational technology? Have all educational technologies really just been fads of innovation that educators have correctly denounced as irrelevant and unnecessary? We think not in both cases. It seems appropriate to consider these questions as a way to understand both traditional and contemporary roles of educational technology. We will use a simple model as a tool to help explain the patterns of adoption by teachers after they are first introduced to educational technology. Understanding these adoption patterns of the past may give us insights to which technologies may be adopted or discarded in the future.

There have been many attempts to understand patterns of adoption in education (Dalton, 1989; Dwyer, Ringstaff, & Sandholtz, 1991). In this section, we present one such model in simplified form in order to better understand both traditional and contemporary applications of technology in education. The model, as illustrated in Figure 23.1, has five steps or phases: familiarization, utilization, integration, reorientation, and evolution. The full potential of any educational technology can only be realized when educators progress through all five phases; otherwise, the technology will likely be misused or discarded (Rieber & Welliver, 1989; Marcinkiewicz, in press). The *traditional* role of technology in education is necessarily limited to the first three phases, whereas contemporary views hold the promise to reach the evolution phase.

Familiarization

The familiarization phase is concerned with one's initial exposure to and experience with a technology. A typical example of familiarization is a teacher participating in an in-service workshop covering the "how to's" of a technology, such as word processing, spreadsheets, assertive discipline, cooperative learning, motivational strategies, etc. In this phase, the teacher simply becomes acquainted with a technology. Once the workshop ends, so too do the teacher's experience and

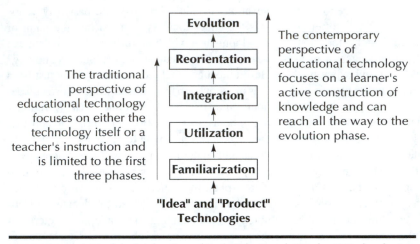

FIGURE 23.1   A Model of Adoption of Both "Idea" and "Product" Technologies in Education.

growth with the technology. All that remains is a memory of the experience. The teacher may discuss the experience and the ideas represented in the experience, even with some degree of authority, but no further action takes place. A great deal of instructional innovation begins and ends with this phase.

Utilization

The utilization phase, in contrast, occurs when the teacher tries out the technology or innovation in the classroom. An example is a social studies teacher who uses role-playing simulations learned in a workshop or graduate course. Obviously, teachers who reach this phase have progressed further than familiarization, but there is the inherent danger that a teacher will become prematurely satisfied with his or her limited use of the technology. The attitude of "At least I gave it a try" will likely interfere with any enduring and long-term adoption of the technology. Teachers who progress only to this phase will probably discard the technology at the first sign of trouble because they have made no commitment to it. This is probably the highest phase of adoption reached by most teachers who use contemporary educational media, including the computer. If the

technology were taken away on Monday, hardly anyone would notice on Tuesday.

Integration

Integration represents the "break through" phase. This occurs when a teacher consciously decides to designate certain tasks and responsibilities to the technology, so, if the technology is suddenly removed or is unavailable, the teacher cannot proceed with the instruction as planned. The most obvious technology that has reached this phase of adoption in education is the book and its derivatives, such as worksheets and other handouts. Most teachers could not function without the support of such print-based technologies. Another example, though perhaps amusing to some, is the chalkboard. Most teachers would find it extremely difficult to teach without it. Hence, the "expendability" of the technology is the most critical attribute or characteristic of this phase (Marcinkiewicz, in press). Although integration is the end of the adoption model for many, it really only represents the beginning of understanding educational technology. For some teachers, the integration phase marks the beginning of a professional "metamorphosis," but only if they progress even further in their adoption pattern.

Reorientation

The reorientation phase requires that educators reconsider and reconceptualize the purpose and function of the classroom. It is marked by many characteristics, probably the most important of which is that the focus of the classroom is now centered on a student's learning, as opposed to the teacher's instruction. A teacher who has reached the reorientation phase does not view good teaching as the delivery of content (i.e., the teaching "acts" of explaining, managing, or motivating). Instead, the teacher's role is to establish a learning environment that supports and facilitates students as they construct and shape their own knowledge. In this phase, the learner becomes the *subject* rather than the *object* of education.

Teachers in the reorientation phase are open to technologies that enable this knowledge construction process and they are not threatened by being "replaced" by technology. In fact, these teachers will probably include technology in their classrooms without necessarily feeling the need to be an "expert" themselves. Their interest is on how technology allows their students to engage the subject matter. It would not be unusual for the students to be more competent than their teachers with the technology. For example, consider a history teacher who discovers that students prefer to create HyperCard stacks, replacing the traditional term paper assignment (Hoffmeister, 1990). If the teacher has a reoriented view of education that is student-centered, the teacher will focus on how intensely the student has engaged the content, not on how well the stack is "programmed." The teacher will emphasize (and evaluate) how well the student has become both a researcher and explorer because of the availability of the computing tool. Whether the teacher possesses more or less technical skill with HyperCard than the student is inconsequential. In addition, the teacher learns about history and HyperCard along with the student. Of course, the teacher's greater experience is an indispensable resource and guide to the student. Rather than view a technology as something that must be mastered beforehand and presented to students in a con-

trolled and systematic way, a teacher at the reorientation phase would encourage and expect students to appropriate the technology in ways that could not be anticipated.

Evolution

The final phase, evolution, serves as a reminder that the educational system must continue to evolve and adapt to remain effective. There will never be a final solution or conclusion and to be searching for one means that one is missing the point. The classroom learning environment should constantly change to meet the challenge and potential provided by new understandings of how people learn. As previously discussed, this appropriate application of basic knowledge for some useful purpose is what defines educational technology, and living up to this definition is the hallmark of the evolution phase.

TRADITIONAL ROLE OF TECHNOLOGY IN EDUCATION

There have been two main types of technology in education that we choose to label as "product technologies" and "idea technologies." Product technologies include (1) hardware, or machine-oriented, technologies that people most often associate with educational technology, such as the range of audio-visual equipment, both traditional (i.e., film strips, movies, audiocassette player/recorders) and contemporary (i.e., videocassette players/recorders, laserdiscs, computers, CD-ROM) and (2) software technologies such as print-based material (i.e., books, worksheets, overhead transparencies) and computer software (i.e., computer-assisted instruction). In contrast, idea technologies do not have such tangible forms.

Of course, idea technologies are usually represented in or through some product technology. For example, simulations are, by and large, idea technologies. Simulations try to give people experiences with events and concepts not generally possible (e.g., travel back in time), probable (e.g., ride aboard the space shuttle), or desirable (e.g., the greenhouse effect) under normal conditions. The idea of a simulation must be realized through some product, such as computer software. In this way, the idea is supported or made possible by the product. A classic example of the distinction between product and idea technologies is Henry Ford's assembly line. The concept of the assembly line is an idea technology that transformed industry in the United States. However, the conveyor belts, workstations, and factories that one sees in old photographs show the product technologies that were used to support the original idea.

The distinction between product technologies and idea technologies is important because most of the historical attempts to use technology in education have focused on product technologies such as teaching machines, educational television and films, and, most currently, computers (Reiser, 1987). Consequently, the role and value of these product technologies were defined by how they supported the established beliefs and practices of classroom teachers. These established practices were largely based on behavioral models that emphasized the transmission and delivery of predetermined content. These approaches exemplify the "student as bucket" metaphor in which the emphasis is on "pouring knowledge" into students' minds by designing and delivering well-planned and controlled instruction. Learning is viewed as a consequence of receiving the information. We believe that contemporary notions of educational technology must go well beyond this philosophy of learning and education. Teachers who adopt technologies without considering the belief structure into which these products and ideas are introduced are necessarily limited to the third phase of integration, though, as previously mentioned, few progress that far.

Consider an example of a product technology reaching the integration phase of adoption—the hand-held graphing calculator. Many high school math teachers use graphing calculators in their teaching. In fact, there are several brands on the market that use a transparent liquid crystal display (LCD) so that the calculator can be placed on an overhead projector. The use of these calculators easily passes the expendability test for many teach-ers—their teaching would be seriously disrupted if the calculators were removed. They would be unable to convey the same information given a quick and sudden return to the static medium of the overhead or chalkboard.

However, the degree to which the teacher's instruction has been altered because of the graphing calculator is critical to determining if the teacher is on the verge of entering the reorientation phase. If the calculator allows the teacher to focus on a student's conceptual understanding of the mathematical function, perhaps because of the calculator's ability to draw a graph using real-time animation, then the teacher has begun to rethink and reflect on the partnership between how product and idea technologies can help a student's learning. The teacher will derive satisfaction from how the technology was harnessed to enable and empower students to understand and apply the mathematical ideas. This teacher is on the brink of entering the reorientation phase. Such a teacher will probably seek to turn the technology (i.e., the calculator) over to the students so that they can begin constructing mathematics.

On the other hand, if the instructional strategies employed by the teacher are virtually the same as those used before the graphing calculator was introduced, then it is very likely that the teacher's adoption of the technology will end with integration because nothing has changed or improved other than the mode of delivery. In this case, although the product technology of the calculator has been integrated, the underlying idea technology of "present, practice, and test" remains unchanged and unchallenged.

The distinction between educators who enter and stall at the integration phase versus those who are "transformed" and enter the reorientation phase is best characterized as a magical line on an "instruction/construction" continuum, as illustrated in Figure 23.2. The utilization and integration of any one technology can be defined by this continuum. The technology of a computer spreadsheet, for example, when used only by a teacher for grade management or as part of an instructional presentation of, say, the principle of averages in a math class, is integrating only the product technology without changing the

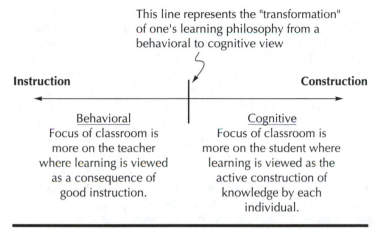

FIGURE 23.2   Philosophies of Learning and Teaching Can Be Viewed as a Continuum with Extreme Educational Interpretations of Behaviorism (e.g., Instruction) and Cognitivism (e.g., Construction) at Either End. Any One Educator's Philosophy Resides Somewhere on This Line. The Threshold Between the Two Views Marks a Critical Point of "Transformation" for an Educator.

underlying philosophical base in which it is applied. The philosophical base, in this example, would be an instruction-centered classroom in which a teacher manages the presentation and practice of predetermined and preselected content.

Consider instead a teacher who uses the same spreadsheet to have students build and construct the knowledge themselves, whether it be the principle of mathematical average or a range of "what if" relationships in economics or history. In this case, the product technology of the spreadsheet directly supports the idea technology of a "microworld" in which students live and experience the content rather than just study it (Dede, 1987; Papert, 1981; Rieber, 1992).

What fundamental principles of learning underlie the most contemporary views of idea technologies that help all educators enter into the reorientation phase of adoption? This is the goal of the next section.

CONTEMPORARY ROLE OF TECHNOLOGY IN EDUCATION

Among the many educational goals are three cognitive outcomes, and they are that students should be able to remember, understand, and use information (Perkins, 1992). One of these outcomes is apparently very difficult to achieve. After more than a decade of schooling, many students leave school unable to use much of the content that they have learned.

Students' inability to apply their learning is attributable to the shallow processing that often occurs in school. Schoolwork often focuses on remembering and organizing lesson content, but rarely on making information meaningful. Meaningful learning is the product of building external connections between existing and new information. Mayer (1984) identified three learning strategies that affect meaningfulness: selection, organization, and integration. Information must initially be selected. Selected information must be organized in working memory if it is to be transferred to long-term memory. Information that is not organized is meaningless. The nature of the organization determines the degree of meaningfulness. Information that is integrated within familiar knowledge or experiences is more durable than information that is not associated to prior knowledge. In school, students select information that they memorize and organize sufficiently to enable satisfactory performance on tests, but they often fail to integrate the information by relating it to previous experiences or knowledge stored in long-term memory. Consequently, one outcome of education, it seems, is a large reserve of inert information that is eventually forgotten (Cognition and Technology Group at Vanderbilt, 1992). For example, how many of us can remember how to compute the sine of a triangle?

How can teaching with technology facilitate deeper, more meaningful cognitive processing? Moreover, what framework should be used to inform such decisions? In a sense, teaching with technology is unlikely to differ greatly from teaching in general. Effective technology-based teaching is more likely the result of teachers' abilities to design lessons based upon robust instructional principles than of the technology per se (Savenye, Davidson, & Smith, 1991). Consequently, guidance for designing effective technology-based classrooms should be grounded in the literature on effective pedagogy in general.

Recently, researchers have identified several principles to guide effective teaching (Koschman, Myers, Feltovich, & Barrows, in press). Although designed primarily for instruction in complex and ill-structured domains, the principles are relevant for many instructional tasks. Most real-world tasks are ill-structured. Problems that are "well-structured" generally occur only in classroom settings. In the following section we will examine three principles and consider the implications of each for using technology in the classroom.

Principle 1: Effective Learners Actively Process Lesson Content

During the past thirty years the shift from behaviorism to cognitivism has modified our conceptions of effective learning and instruction. One of the most consistent themes to emerge from the transition is that learning is an active process. By this it is meant that effective learning requires students to do more than simply respond to stimuli. Instead, learners must actively seek and generate relationships between lesson content and prior knowledge.

One common myth is that product technologies increase interactivity and thereby improve learning. The source of this perception is not difficult to trace. The results of research on students attitudes toward working with product technologies, especially computers, are generally positive (Martin, Heller, & Mahmoud, 1991). Furthermore, research appears to support the belief that product technologies improve learning (Kulik, Bangert, & Williams, 1983). Yet product technologies alone do not ensure learning (Clark, 1983). Indeed, in some cases they may detract from learning by diminishing the amount of effort a student invests.

In general, learning requires students to invest considerable mental effort in the task. However, students appear to vary the effort they invest during learning according to their self-perceptions and their beliefs gained from different media about the difficulty of learning. Salomon (1984) found that children who believed themselves to be effective learners invested greater effort when a learning task was perceived to be challenging than when it was perceived to be easy. However, children with low self-efficacy invested greater effort when learning was perceived to be more attainable than challenging. In other words, high-ability learners may invest more mental effort in a challenging task, such as reading a book, than in a task perceived to be easy, such as learning from television. Low-ability students may invest more effort in a task that they believe to be attainable than one that they perceive to be challenging.

We are by no means opponents of product technologies in education. However, we recognize the importance of blending product and idea technologies into "technological partnerships." An example of an effective technological marriage is that of a musical symphony. A good symphony combines an ideal blend of musical instruments (product technologies) and musical compositions (idea technologies). Misusing the capabilities of the instruments or underemphasizing the composition of the musical score will detract from the final production of the symphony. Similarly, effective uses of technology in education require a blend of product and idea technologies. Together, they form environments that unite technological capability with pedagogical necessity—combining what can be done with what should be done.

Too often in education we have failed to find the right blend of technologies. In particular, the capabilities of product technologies are overemphasized. For example, product technologies are often used to increase cost efficiency by replacing the classroom teacher or by transmitting lessons to larger audiences via satellites and telephone lines. Such approaches are often misdirected. Although the importance of increasing access to education should not be devalued, reproducing existing materials is unlikely to improve educational quality. Rather, using technology as delivery media may perpetuate or even exacerbate existing problems. The benefit of technology is not simply its potential to replicate existing educational practice, but its ability to combine idea and product technologies to encourage students to engage in deeper cognitive activity.

Principle 2: Presenting Information from Multiple Perspectives Increases the Durability of Instruction

Although instruction has traditionally focused on learning specific content, much of contemporary curriculum development focuses on solving problems that require learners to develop ever evolving networks of facts, principles, and procedures. The National Council of Teachers of Mathematics (1989), for example, suggested that greater emphasis be placed on solving open-ended "real world" problems in small groups, connecting mathematics with other content areas, and using computer-based tools to allow students to speculate and explore interrelationships among concepts rather than to spend time on time-consuming calculations. To achieve such goals, learning should take place in environments that emphasize the interconnectedness of ideas across content domains and that help learners develop flexible networks of propositions and productions (Gagné, 1985). Presenting content from a single perspective is unlikely to reflect the complexity inherent in many concepts. In contrast,

repeated exposure to information from varying perspectives helps learners to establish the interrelationships necessary to mediate deep processing and effective retrieval of lesson concepts.

Cooperative learning and hypermedia represent technologies with significant potential for developing multiple perspectives. Cooperative learning is an idea technology that stimulates the development of alternative perspectives through exposure to multiple viewpoints. Two important differences exist between cooperative learning and traditional instruction. First, information to be learned by the students is not transmitted by the teacher. Instead, students teach each other in small groups of between two and five students. Second, students are made responsible for each other's learning. Students must ensure that every member of their group achieves the lesson's objectives. These experiences appear to benefit students of all abilities. More able students gain from the cognitive restructuring associated with teaching, and less able students benefit from the personalized attention available from group members. Moreover, groups appear to create environments in which all members benefit from exposure to diverse attitudes and opinions that are often unavailable in the traditional classroom.

Hypermedia is a product technology that represents a shift in beliefs about how information should be presented to and accessed by students. Hypermedia refers to computer programs that organize information nonsequentially. Information is structured around series of nodes that are connected through associative links. Node is the term used to describe an information chunk that is stored in the hypermedia program. Information in a node may be represented through text, illustrations, or sounds. Associative links, which allow users to navigate among nodes, represent the main difference between traditional ways of presenting information on the computer and hypermedia (Jonassen, 1991).

Whereas traditional instruction often presents information sequentially to make the content easier to comprehend, hypermedia allows users to browse through an information base and to construct relationships between their personal experiences and the lesson. It is often claimed that in doing so learning becomes more meaningful as students generate webs of semantically and logically related information that accommodate the knowledge structure of the learner rather than that of the teacher or designer. Although hypermedia environments can be used to present information sequentially to students, when carefully designed users can create different diverse pathways through a lesson resulting in multiple cognitive representations of the content. By allowing exploration, students are encouraged to discover interrelationships that are often missed in traditional presentations of lesson content and to search for information that meets individual needs. Hypermedia is especially effective when users are encouraged to explore a database, to create links among information nodes, and even to modify a knowledge base based on new insight into content structure (Nelson & Palumbo, 1992).

Hypermedia and cooperative learning represent technologies that can make learning more meaningful. However, both must be managed carefully to achieve the intended outcomes. In cooperative learning, potentially damaging social effects often occur when individual accountability is not maintained. Similarly, hypermedia projects often focus on presenting information and rarely fulfill their promise as knowledge construction kits. Furthermore, although each can be used independently, the learning benefits may be magnified when they are combined. Although many computer lessons are designed for single users, the benefits appear to multiply when used collaboratively (Hooper, 1992).

Principle 3: Effective Instruction Should Build upon Students' Knowledge and Experiences and Be Grounded in Meaningful Contexts

Philosophical beliefs about how educational goals can best be achieved have shifted from emphasizing curriculum content to focusing on learners' knowledge and experiences (Pea & Gomez, 1992; Tobin & Dawson, 1992). During the 1960s and

1970s considerable emphasis was placed on curriculum projects that focused on the structural analysis of content. These projects produced curriculum materials that emphasized helping learners better understand lesson content. For many years, education followed a correspondingly curriculum-centered approach. Teaching focused on analyzing learning tasks and on identifying strategies to achieve specific learning outcomes.

Recently, research emphasis has shifted from examining the structure of curriculum materials to determining the cognitive state of the learner. Education is presently concerned less with transmitting the "optimal" structure of lesson content than on building onto the current knowledge level of the student. This perspective has implications for teaching with technology. First, instruction should attempt to build upon the experiential base of each student. What a student learns from education is, to a large extent, a function of prior knowledge. One role of technology, therefore, is to bridge personal experiences and formal instruction. Technology should also be sufficiently flexible to adapt to students' ongoing instructional needs. One of the hallmarks of a master teacher is the ability to recognize and repair student misunderstandings and misconceptions. When learning difficulties arise, therefore, technology-based instruction should be sufficiently flexible to adapt to student experiences.

Closely related to building upon the knowledge and experiences of students is the belief that instruction should be grounded in familiar contexts. Teachers often decontextualize instruction to stimulate transfer and to improve instructional efficiency (Merrill, 1991). Recently, however, researchers have argued that such practices actually hinder transfer. Instead, they claim, instruction should be rooted in real-life problem-solving contexts. One such approach, known as situated cognition (Brown, Collins, & Duguid, 1989), involves teaching across multiple contexts before generating rules. Grounding instruction in meaningful contexts appears to have both cognitive and affective benefits. One of the axioms of cognitive psychology is that learning occurs by building upon previously learned experiences. Teaching in familiar contexts appears to help learners to relate new information to those experiences. Contextualization also appears to have a strong motivational component. Learning in a familiar context may make learning more personally relevant than decontextualized learning (Keller & Suzuki, 1988).

Microworlds illustrate how technology can improve meaningfulness by building upon students' experiences and by providing a relevant learning environment. A microworld is a special learning environment that accurately models a phenomenon and adapts the complexity of instruction to match the learner's level of understanding. Rieber (1992) designed Space Shuttle Commander, a computer microworld to teach Newton's Laws of Motion. By exploring the microworld, students generate a visceral understanding of the interrelationships that exist among lesson concepts. Microworlds offer opportunities for students to transfer understanding to the real world and to examine and manipulate concepts in a manner that would otherwise be impossible. The microworld contains several levels of difficulty to accommodate varying levels of user expertise and introduces an element of fantasy to motivate learners by using the scenario of traveling through frictionless space in a space shuttle.

THEORY INTO PRACTICE

In this section we present three examples of educational products that incorporate many of the principles outlined earlier in the chapter. None of these products ensures that learning will take place. The key ingredient in each case is the idea technology employed by the teacher.

The Jasper Woodbury Problem Solving Series

The Adventures of Jasper Woodbury (Cognition and Technology Group at Vanderbilt, 1992) is a video package that reflects contemporary beliefs about learning and instruction. Important differences exist between the Jasper series and traditional educational television. Each episode of the Jasper videos presents instruction in a motivating and realistic environment that encourages students to explore and to identify and solve real problems. Furthermore, teachers are encouraged to blend idea technologies such as cooperative grouping and problem-based learning with the videos to make learning active, meaningful, and motivating. Perhaps the most striking difference between the Jasper materials and national educational television concerns the role played by the students. Educational television often transmits information to students who may, or may not, participate in the learning experience. In contrast, the Jasper series requires students to be actively engaged. While watching the video, students must collect information. Following each episode, a problem is presented. The problem challenges the students to use the information collected during the lesson to identify and solve sub-problems en route to solving the larger problem.

The Voyage of the Mimi

The Voyage of the Mimi is a multimedia curriculum package developed at the Bank Street College of Education that integrates print, video, and computer materials in learning about science and mathematics. Video is used to present the package's context for learning: a realistic, fictional account of the adventures of the crew of the Mimi, a boat hired by a team of scientists to study humpback whales (a second Mimi series has also been produced using the context of Mayan archaeology). The context was chosen based on research conducted at Bank Street that indicated that people, and especially children, share a general fascination with whales. Mathematics and science become the crew's most important tools as they conduct their whale research or engage in many other problem-solving activities. Video is also used to present a series of documentaries showing real scientists at work using many of the principles introduced in the dramatic episodes. The computer materials provide students with interactive activities, usually simulations and games, that closely mirror the adventures of the Mimi's crew in the video. The print-based materials include a text version of the video and consumable workbooks for the students to complete. The Mimi materials were developed to be sufficiently flexible to provide teachers with multiple entry levels to the materials (Martin, 1987). Teachers can choose to use the materials to augment or to replace all or part of their curriculum. The materials provide for the range of learning outcomes from initial concept formation to problem solving. The materials can also be used individually by students or cooperatively in groups.

The Geometric Supposer

The Geometric Supposer (Schwartz & Yerushalmy, 1985a) is a computer-based geometry tool that teaches deductive reasoning by providing students with opportunities to experiment with geometry. Traditionally, geometry teaching has employed passive instructional strategies by focusing on definitions, theorems, and proofs. In contrast, the Geometric Supposer stimulates active learning by encouraging learners to discover geometric properties (Schwartz, Yerushalmy, & Wilson, 1993).

The program allows students to perform two functions that are difficult to achieve in non-computer-based environments. First, it allows students to construct electronically any geometric shape that can be made with a straight edge and a compass. Moreover, the program "remembers" the construction and will repeat the procedure on similar shapes when instructed to do so. Second, the program can automatically measure and report any element of a construction, thus allowing users to instantaneously observe the outcomes of any manipulations of the geometric figures. Together, these features allow students to create constructions, hypothesize about geometric relationships, and test and observe the validity of their conjectures. For example, students studying relationships among the medians of a triangle may attempt to identify and test principles by examining results across several different cases (Schwartz & Yerushalmy, 1985b).

Putting It Together

It is important to recognize that the learning outcomes achieved using any of the materials outlined above will reflect the idea technology employed. The idea technology will also indicate the level of technology adoption to which the teacher has risen. Three idea technologies have been outlined by the Cognition and Technology Group at Vanderbilt (1992).

1. *Basics First* advocates mastering basic skills before attempting similar problems embedded in the video. Teachers who use this approach may have entered the utilization phase, but have not entered the integration phase. Few instructional differences would result if the videos were removed from the classroom. Similar problems could easily be generated from other sources.

2. *Structured Problem Solving* involves capitalizing on the design features inherent in the videos but restricts students' progress to prevent errors and disorientation. For example, teachers might use structured worksheets to guide students' progress. Teachers who focus on rigid lesson structuring may have reached the integration phase, but probably have not entered into reorientation.

3. *Guided Generation* involves using activities that reflect many of the principles outlined earlier in the chapter, that is, activities that help students to generate meaningful relationships. The teacher focuses on guiding students and exploring issues that may be novel or unfamiliar to both teacher and student. Teachers who use Guided Generation would probably have entered the reorientation or evolution adoption phases.

CONCLUSION

In this chapter we have examined why technology has failed to impact education in the past and have outlined the conditions necessary for technology to be used effectively in the future. To be used effectively, idea and product technologies must be united and teachers must venture beyond familiarization and utilization and into the integration, reorientation, and evolution phases of technology use. Teachers who learn to integrate technology may go on to reconceptualize their roles in the classroom. Guided by research findings from cognitive psychology and other related areas, teachers can create environments in which students actively engage in cognitive partnerships with technology.

REFERENCES

Brown, John, Allan Collins, and Paul Duguid. (1989). "Situated Cognition and the Culture of Learning." *Educational Researcher, 18*(1), 32–42.

Clark, Richard. (1983). "Reconsidering Research on Learning From Media." *Review of Educational Research, 53,* 445–459.

Cognition and Technology Group at Vanderbilt. (1992). "The Jasper Experiment: An Exploration of Issues in Learning and Instructional Design." *Educational Technology Research and Development, 40*(1), 65–80.

Dalton, David. (1989). "Computers in the Schools: A Diffusion/Adoption Perspective." *Educational Technology, 29*(11), 20–27.

Dede, Christopher. (1987). "Empowering Environments, Hypermedia and Microworlds." *The Computing Teacher, 15*(3), 20–24, 61.

Dwyer, David, Cathy Ringstaff, and Judy Sandholtz. (1991). "Changes in Teachers' Beliefs and Practices in Technology-Rich Classrooms." *Educational Leadership, 48*(8), 45–52.

Gagné, Ellen. (1985). *The Cognitive Psychology of School Learning.* Boston: Little, Brown and Company.

Hoffmeister, Joseph. (1990). "The Birth of Hyper-School." In S. Ambron and K. Hooper (Eds.). *Learning with Interactive Multimedia: Developing and Using Multimedia Tools in Education* (pp. 199–221). Redmond, WA: Microsoft Press.

Hooper, Simon. (1992). "Cooperative Learning and Computer-Based Instruction." *Educational Technology Research and Development, 40*(3), 21–38.

Jonassen, David. (1991). "Hypertext as Instruction Design." *Educational Technology Research and Development, 39*(1), 83–92.

Keller, John, and Katsuaki Suzuki. (1988). "Using the ARCS Motivation Model in Courseware Design." In D. Jonassen (Ed.), *Instructional Designs for Microcomputer Courseware* (pp. 401–434). Hillsdale, NJ: Lawrence Erlbaum Associates.

Kulik, James, Robert Bangert, and George Williams. (1983). "Effects of Computer-Based Teaching on Secondary School Students." *Journal of Educational Psychology, 75,* 19–26.

Marcinkiewicz, Heinrich. (1991). "The Relationships of Selected Personological Variables to the Use of Available Microcomputers by Elementary School Teachers." Doctoral dissertation, Pennsylvania State University.

Marcinkiewicz, Heinrich. (in press). "Computers and Teachers: Factors Influencing Computer Use in the Classroom." *Journal of Research on Computing in Education.*

Martin, C. Dianne, Rachelle Heller, and Emad Mahmoud. (1991). "American and Soviet Children's Attitudes Toward Computers." *Journal of Educational Computing Research, 8*(2), 155–185.

Martin, L. (1987). "Teachers' Adoption of Multimedia Technologies for Science and Mathematics Instruction." In R. D. Pea and K. Sheingold (Eds.). *Mirrors of Minds: Patterns of Experience in Educational Computing* (pp. 35–56). Norwood, NJ: Ablex Publishing Corporation.

Mayer, Richard. (1984). "Aids to Text Comprehension." *Educational Psychologist, 19,* 30–42.

Merrill, M. David. (1991). "Constructivism and Instructional Design." *Educational Technology, 31*(5), 45–53.

National Council of Teachers of Mathematics. (1989). *Curriculum and Evaluation Standards for School Mathematics.* Reston, VA: National Council of Teachers of Mathematics.

Nelson, Wayne, and David Palumbo. (1992). "Learning, Instruction, and Hypermedia." *Journal of Educational Multimedia and Hypermedia, 1,* 287–299.

Papert, Seymour. (1981). "Computer-Based Microworlds as Incubators for Powerful Ideas." In R. Taylor (Ed.). *The Computer in the School: Tutor, Tool, Tutee* (pp. 203–210). New York: Teachers College Press.

Pea, Roy, and Louis Gomez. (1992). "Distributed Multimedia Learning Environments: Why and How?" *Interactive Learning Environments, 2*(2), 73–109.

Perkins, David. (1992). "Technology Meets Constructivism: Do They Make a Marriage?" *Educational Technology, 31*(5), 18–23.

Reiser, Robert. (1987). "Instructional Technology: A History." In R. Gagné (Ed.). *Instructional Technology: Foundations* (pp. 11–48). Hillsdale, NJ: Lawrence Erlbaum Associates.

Rieber, Lloyd. (1992). "Computer-Based Microworlds: A Bridge Between Constructivism and Direct Instruction." *Educational Technology Research and Development, 40*(1), 93–106.

Rieber, Lloyd, and Paul Welliver. (1989). "Infusing Educational Technology into Mainstream Educational Computing." *International Journal of Instructional Media, 16*(1), 21–32.

Saettler, Paul. (1990). *The Evolution of American Educational Technology.* Denver, CO: Libraries Unlimited.

Salomon, Gavriel. (1984). "Television Is "Easy" and Print Is "Tough": The Differential Investment of Mental Effort in Learning as a Function of Perceptions and Attributions." *Journal of Educational Psychology, 76,* 647–658.

Savenye, Wilhelmina, Gayle Davidson, and Patricia Smith. (1991). "Teaching Instructional Design in a Computer Literacy Course." *Educational Technology Research and Development 39*(3), 49–58.

Schwartz, Judah, and Michel Yerushalmy. (1985a). "The Geometric Supposer." Pleasantville, N.Y.: Sunburst Communications.

Schwartz, Judah, and Michel Yerushalmy. (1985b). "The Geometric Supposer: An Intellectual Prosthesis for Making Conjectures." *The College Mathematics Journal, 18,* 58–65.

Schwartz, Judah, Michel Yerushalmy, and B. Wilson (Eds.). (1993). *The Geometric Supposer: What Is It a Case Of?* Hillsdale, NJ: Lawrence Erlbaum Associates.

Tobin, Kenneth, and George Dawson. (1992). "Constraints to Curriculum Reform." *Educational Technology Research and Development, 40*(1), 81–92.

DISCUSSION QUESTIONS

1. How do idea technologies and product technologies exemplify teachers' philosophical beliefs?

2. Can product technologies and idea technologies be integrated to provide effective use of educational technology? Why? Why not?

3. How can educational technology be effectively integrated with instructional approaches?

4. How does educational technology facilitate higher-order thinking skills?

5. How might educational technology result in a reconceptualization of teachers' roles?

24

Curriculum Trends Revisited

ALLAN C. ORNSTEIN

FOCUSING QUESTIONS

1. *What are some of the trends affecting curriculum?*
2. *How have these trends affected curricularists' thinking?*
3. *How might the integration of advanced technology into school-based curriculum impact student achievement?*
4. *What procedures will curricularists employ to design a relevant curriculum?*
5. *Which time-tested aspects of the curriculum are likely to continue in the future?*

Opinions differ on the directions education will take, and library shelves are filled with volumes describing current and anticipated changes in society and education. Despite disagreements, however, it is likely that certain trends in particular will increasingly affect curriculum planning in the near future. Some of the most important of these trends are noted in the discussion that follows.

The emerging curriculum responds to the urge to break away from traditional disciplines, to develop more interdisciplinary approaches. In the curriculum of the future, subject matter most likely will be less compartmentalized and more integrated and holistic. Although traditional subject boundaries will remain, there will be increased cross-subject material; knowledge will no longer be considered fragmented or linear but multidisciplinary and multidimensional; it will also be integrated with more visual and auditory resources and will rely less on verbal and reading materials.

ELECTRONIC EDUCATION

The advent of video technology has made available another valuable tool for instruction. Videotapes, cassettes, and disks can be used for instruction in classrooms, libraries, resource centers, and the student's home. Because the video can be played at any convenient time, the students never have to miss a lesson. Hundreds of catalogs offer videos on a wide range of subjects; in addition, many school systems and teachers have begun to produce their own videos for specific instructional purposes. With the help of a videoprinter, individual images from the screen—photographs, tables, graphs, or any other useful picture—can be printed on paper for further study.

Many videos interact with the viewer when used in conjunction with a computer. Realistic simulations and action-reaction situations can be presented as part of an instructional program. The program can tell the viewer whether a response is right or wrong—or the viewer can be offered a choice of options, and the program will then display the outcome of the option chosen. Interactive videos have an enormous teaching potential that educators are just beginning to explore. Such videos can be used either for individual lessons or for instruction in small groups.

Educators need to investigate ways to use the popularity of videogames for teaching purposes. Although videogames have been criticized for their escapism, they are by nature interactive: to each move by the player, the machine responds with a move of its own. Math, reading, and writing lessons can be written in a videogame format, and the student will find practice and drill more lively in a game atmosphere.

According to one estimate, by the year 2000 more than 20 percent of instructional tools will include computers and videos. Teachers must not only keep abreast of this changing video technology, but must also plan ways to integrate it into the curriculum. In an era when the number of videos rented from video stores surpasses the total number of books checked out of libraries, teachers should help students to become critical video consumers and to be aware of how visual images affect us as individuals and as a society (Ornstein, 1990, 1991).

Today, schools may select television programs specifically developed for educational purposes and have them beamed into the classroom by satellite. This is particularly useful for small, rural schools with limited local resources. Some home cable systems also carry educational programming, but its quantity and quality will increase only if educators demand this resource and use it.

Widely used in business and industry, teleconferences have begun to appear in school systems, usually as an experiment on the secondary level. In a typical conference, a resource person, teacher, or group of students is viewed through the television screen, talking to or instructing other students or participants. Viewers can watch as if they were across the table, although they may be thousands of miles away. The viewing audience can ask questions and make decisions about what further information should be presented.

The curriculum is going to come alive with interactive videos, satellite and cable networks, and teleconferences for most subject areas. The fact that there are already some two million computers in classrooms, and increasing at a rate of 100,000 per year, suggests the demise of what some call "pencil technology." The point will no longer be made by the pencil. And, similarly, the textbook as we know it is doomed to obsolescence. It will become incidental and probably take on different forms: talking to the student, monitoring his or her progress, and modifying content accordingly.

New forms of electronic knowledge will take shape—more personal, immediate, graphic, and rapid. Acquiring new knowledge will not be crucial, because no one will be able to keep pace with it; rather, being able to access it and being networked into a call system will be critical. People who lack information or who are unable to call for it and use it will become impotent on the job and in dealing on a daily basis with other people, service agencies, or institutions that have information.

TECHNICAL LITERACY

Because of the revolution in technology, the schools must now educate citizens to become familiar with computers, electronics, lasers, and robots. Computer literacy stands beside the three Rs as a fundamental skill. According to government projections to 1995, of the ten fastest-growing occupations, four require knowledge of computers (technician, systems analyst, programmer, and operator). Other trends suggest high-tech influence in such growth areas as biogenetics, computer/video software, robotics, telecommunications, microelectronics, toxic waste and pollution, space, and the oceans (Klode, 1991; *Occupational Projections and Training Data,* 1990). Soon there will exist technical occupations for which we do not yet even have names.

In a high-tech economy, workers will need to be better educated (compared to the industrial economy) and to have better cognitive, communication, and cooperative team skills. People at home and on the job will have calculators, computers, fax machines, and other technical tools to do their symbol crunching for them; however, they will have to decide what buttons to push and what the symbols mean. As the pace of technology accelerates, whole industries may be born, expand, and die in terms of peaks and valleys of the stock market; it will be impossible to predict the precise skills employees will need on the job, but they will need to be retrained periodically in order to compete on a global basis. In such an environment, it is likely that workers will be displaced from one job to another and will be required to retool and relearn new skills on the job; education will become a lifelong enterprise.

In cooperation with industry and government, schools must identify the emerging technologies and services and provide a curriculum that prepares students for viable careers. In part, this means educating future scientists who can design, develop, and apply the new technology. But not everyone needs to become a scientific expert. For many occupations, people simply need to understand the technological basics—what buttons to push under what conditions and how to make machines provide the service or information that they were designed to offer. Only a small percentage of the work force will require sophisticated technical or scientific knowledge, but many will need better cognitive and communication skills.

The National Science Teachers Association (NSTA) has endorsed a curricular approach called Science/Technology/Society, which emphasizes the social and technical aspects of science rather than pure science. One of the purposes of such programs is to help students prepare for the impact of technology on daily life. Some traditional vocational/industrial programs are also being enriched with a focus on technology, especially on computers and robotic design. In still other cases, the entire vocational and industrial arts program is being revamped to meet new technological requirements; this demands updated equipment, the integration of computers into courses, and continual interaction among schools, government, and the work force.

As the pace of technology accelerates, there is increasing need to develop a nationwide plan—involving education, industry, and government—that assesses the future occupational needs of society and establishes corresponding guidelines for schools. Cooperative planning is needed—now.

LIFELONG LEARNING

The trend toward lifelong learning is occurring in all modern societies as a result of the knowledge explosion and the rapid social, technological, and economic changes that force people to prepare for second or third careers and to keep themselves updated on new developments that affect their personal and social goals. Education will continue to become more a lifelong enterprise and increasingly will take place outside the confines of the traditional school. Taking note of these trends, the Carnegie Commission has developed the concept of a "step-in, step-out" educational system for lifelong learning. This means that people could move in and out of educational programs throughout their lives.

Some observers believe that much of the learning that has been provided by elementary, secondary, and postsecondary schools may be provided in the future by business and industry, especially to meet the needs of a skilled work force in high-tech and information-based industries (Hoyt, 1991; Magaziner and Clinton, 1992; Weisman, 1993). By 1989, in fact, employers were spending $250 billion annually in training; in comparison, colleges and universities spent only $120 billion (*Condition of Education,* 1991; *Digest of Education and Statistics,* 1990). Still other scenarios envision educating adolescents and adults through a network of community resources as well as small learning centers and libraries.

There is also growing concern about the rate of international illiteracy, about 1.1 billion (or 20%) worldwide (mostly involving Third World countries), including 23 to 25 million in the United States, which is the highest number in the industrialized world. Methods for eliminating illiteracy in the United States are mainly tied to adult education courses in basic education. Spending for adult education at the state and local levels increased 379 percent between 1980 and 1988, and the number of participants increased from 2 million to 3.1 million (*Adult Literacy,* 1990; *Digest of Education Statistics,* 1990). Adult education is expected to increase in the 1990s, especially in states in which there are large minority and immigrant populations.

INTERNATIONAL EDUCATION

Although historically the United States has taken a relatively isolationist position, the increasing interdependence among nations demands that Americans become knowledgeable about developments in distant lands. Oil prices in Saudi Arabia and Iran affect job opportunities in Houston, Denver, and Tulsa. Auto and steel production in Japan and Korea influences the local economy in Detroit and Pittsburgh. Deforestation in Brazil and Malaysia affects the atmosphere in New York and San Francisco. We truly inhabit a "global village" in which our standard of living and our national economy are virtually connected to events in other parts of the world.

Satellite and aerospace communications, instant television reporting, supercomputer networks, laser technology, and jet travel have made this planet seem smaller, and other people's problems (or strengths) are harder to ignore. About 20 million children in Third World countries die of starvation each year, and another 800 million (about 15% of humanity) go to bed hungry or malnourished. Considering the rapid worldwide growth in population and the increasing scarcity of world resources, these figures indicate a planet in transition that may soon be unable to sustain even the industrialized nations.

Another area of international education that U.S. schools may need to address in the future is foreign language instruction. The most common spoken language in the world is Mandarin, followed by English, Hindi, and Spanish. Japanese ranks tenth, and German and French rank much lower. Nearly all foreign language programs in American schools offer Spanish and French; in fact, 58 percent of secondary students enrolled in a foreign language study Spanish (Met, 1989). But

fewer than .01 percent of U.S. high school students study Japanese, and about .001 percent attempt Mandarin (Ornstein & Hunkins, 1993). Failure to train students in these languages may severely limit the future growth of U.S. trade and our understanding of other economic market places.

Education in America must become more widely international in scope. Educators might expand travel exchange programs and perhaps make study in another culture a requirement for graduation. There should be emphasis on international geography, history, political science, and economics. As the world becomes more interconnected and interdependent, such needs will become more evident and more funds may be devoted to the area of global curriculum.

ENVIRONMENTAL EDUCATION

Mounting concern over such problems as pollution, toxic waste, overpopulation, and depletion of food and natural resources has created demands for more knowledge and new programs in ecology and environmental education. Much of the relevant content has long been included in traditional earth sciences, biology, and geography courses and in conservation programs. The new demand calls for a more meaningful and better coordinated program that raises the theme of crisis.

The parade of grim environmental realities is a long one and is continually expanding. Scientists believe that the depletion of the earth's ozone layer (already depleted some 5%), caused chiefly by man-made chemicals used in the manufacture of some plastics and in aerosol sprays and cleaning solvents, will increase the incidence of skin cancer, cataracts, and immune system disorders; it may also damage crops, trees, and marine organisms worldwide. If the ozone layer fades over populated regions (there is evidence that such a hole may already exist over northeast portions of the United States), the results could be devastating. The greenhouse effect, which may warm the atmosphere and increase the sea level, may result in substantial harm to both farmlands and cities.

In addition, fish and wildlife, soil, water, and the air we breathe are often contaminated; the only debatable point is when the cumulative effects of all these poisons and toxic substances begin to affect our health. Many people believe that the entire ecological chain is in jeopardy; and some even predict that the great wars of the twenty-first century will be fought for clean water and soil.

Rather than terrifying students about ecological disaster, however, schools should prepare students for tomorrow's world by helping them understand how scientific, social, and political issues interact. Because mere possession of knowledge does not ensure proper action, the curriculum must also deal with the attitudes, values, and moral thinking that lead to responsible environmental behavior. Ecological literacy requires a comprehensive view of the modern world, of how fragile it is, and of how scientific, social, and political issues combine and lead to problems and/or solutions. It requires that schools take a more active role in requiring students to study the environment rather than expect government agencies and activist groups to manage or protect people from other people.

NUCLEAR EDUCATION

The nuclear standoff between the United States and the Soviet Union has ended, and we are now less vulnerable to world nuclear confrontation than we were during the last fifty years. Indeed, the threat of computer malfunction and subsequent nuclear disaster has declined dramatically. But the nuclear bomb club, which now includes more than twelve nations, is expanding. Some countries such as China, and private corporations in Germany and France, continue to sell their nuclear knowledge to Third World countries. Considering the possibility that terrorists may use nuclear devices for their own purposes, the world may not be that safe from nuclear threat after all.

Even peaceful uses of nuclear energy—power plants, medical facilities, radiation therapy, and nuclear medicines—have come to seem more problematical, especially since the disasters at Three Mile Island and Chernobyl. The entire world is affected by a serious meltdown—in terms of air, food, and water quality. Global weather patterns know no national boundaries; concentrated radiation can affect human populations thousands of miles away.

The waste products of nuclear facilities and toxic chemicals also present a continuing problem; where in this world can we bury them? Try to convince the residents of Maine or Michigan that it is to their advantage, or that it is their patriotic duty, to have a nuclear (or toxic) dump site in their backyards. For children to realize that nuclear destruction comes in various forms, and that they cannot always rely on adults to watch for their future, is very painful and fearsome.

Concern about nuclear energy has reached schools under such rubrics as "nuclear-sane programs," "peace education," and "peace-making strategies." In coming years these will continue to be important elements in a globally oriented curriculum. We must not reduce our concern about nuclear energy because of the demise of the Soviet Union; nuclear energy will play a great role in the future—and we will need a nuclear education program.

HEALTH EDUCATION
AND PHYSICAL FITNESS

Trends in the health of the U.S. population are producing new pressures to expand or reorient the curriculum. For example, the epidemic of AIDS (acquired immunodeficiency syndrome), with its dire risk to sexually active adolescents, has forced educators to confront the issue of student health in a new way. Predictions are that by the year 2000 some 40 to 50 million people around the world will be affected by the disease; the majority will be from Africa, but some four to five million will be Americans (Altman, 1991; Popham, 1993). Some educators see the AIDS epidemic as literally a life-or-death matter for their students. Schools have been slow, however, to include AIDS education in the curriculum.

One reason for the lack of AIDS education is the continued controversy over the disease and the recommended preventive measures. Many parents and educators have been particularly incensed by programs involving the distribution of condoms in big-city schools. A more basic reason for the lack of AIDS education, however, is that only twenty-seven states require any form of health or sex education, and American students average only 13.9 hours of such education annually. Moreover, nationwide there is only one certified health teacher for every 21,500 students (Manna & Symons, 1990; Miller & Becker-Dunn, 1993). Many educators believe that this shortage must and will be addressed in the future. Certainly AIDS education is going to be incorporated into the curriculum, as early as at the elementary grade level.

Dietary habits and exercise comprise another health concern. Citing medical evidence of high blood pressure and elevated blood fats and cholesterol counts among American youngsters, physicians have criticized the high-fat, burgers-and-fries diet common among school-age children. Many young students appear to be eating their way toward heart disease and other maladies. In addition, school children have been increasingly unable to pass basic physical fitness tests; they do poorly on measures of body development, strength, and flexibility. Television and video viewing habits (including salt and sugar-coated snacks) among American children and youth have contributed to this lack of fitness, and what we might call the "fat and flabby" generation.

Although the American adult population appears to have a love affair with physical fitness and sports, the schools ironically have cut back physical education and fitness programs because of budget considerations and the renewed stress on academic excellence. Educators frequently assert that we will need to rebuild these programs in the curriculum of the future. Some schools are already recognizing the need to provide better guidance for diet and exercise.

Sports, too, should be reoriented to increase the emphasis on aerobic and rhythmic activities (running, jumping, jogging, bicycling). By the end of the 1990s, progressive and far-sighted schools should be deemphasizing traditional competitive sports, which tend to cater to only a few students and involve activities that only the young pursue. Instead, schools increasingly should emphasize lifelong sports such as tennis, golf, biking, and swimming, as well as noncompetitive intramural activities in which the average athlete and even the nonathlete can participate.

The primary goal for physical and health programs is to have fun and socialize in sporting activities, not to compete and win, and to adopt lifelong exercise behavior. Some type A parents and coaches are going to have to be reprogrammed; winning and working out for three hours a day are appropriate for a very small percentage of students.

IMMIGRANT EDUCATION

Legal immigration now accounts for up to one-half of the annual growth in the U.S. population. It has already surpassed post–World War II rates and is approaching the peaks reached in the years prior to World War I. Despite its present economic ills, the United States still looks like the promised land to many people who are searching for a better life.

The new immigrant population differs in ethnic origins from that of the past. From 1930 to 1950, 80 percent of immigrants to the United States came from Western Europe and Canada. From 1970 through 1985, only 10 percent came from these countries; the leading source countries, with the highest first, were Mexico, the Philippines, South Korea, Taiwan, Vietnam, Jamaica, India, the Dominican Republic, and Guatemala. In tenth place, with two percent of the total, was Great Britain. Today as many as 90 to 95 percent of immigrants come from non-Western or Third World countries. Moreover, estimates of *illegal* immigration, mainly from Mexico, Central America, and the Caribbean, total about 1 million people per year, with approximately 500,000 establishing permanent residence (Fallows, 1991; Juffus, 1991). Partly as a result of these immigration trends, by the year 2000 nearly one-third of the U.S. population will be nonwhite and Hispanic, and in Arizona, California, Colorado, Texas, and New Mexico the proportion will approach 50 percent (Ornstein, 1984, 1989).

For some recent immigrants, life in America has been a remarkable success story. Many, however, face language barriers, ethnic prejudice, health problems, and a lack of good jobs. One difference is that the newcomers now enter a country that is vastly different from the open, economically booming America that absorbed the European masses with ease in prior decades. Moreover, hostility toward immigrants, especially illegal immigrants, is common, and born of economic and population pressures. Jobs are scarce in many parts of the country, and wages and unemployment trends in many sectors of the economy are affected by immigrants who are willing to work harder and for less money than Americans.

A significant number of immigrant families are "structurally poor," meaning that the family conditions are unstable or disorganized and the children have few chances to escape from poverty. Because of cultural differences in learning styles or thinking patterns, the children may be labeled "learning disabled" or "slow." Even when this is not the case, value hierarchies vary widely across cultures, so that immigrant children have diverse attitudes about school, teacher authority, gender differences, social class, and behavior in general.

To assist these new immigrants, many educators are suggesting an increase in compensatory and bilingual programs in the schools. A multicultural curriculum can also help immigrant children achieve acceptance and respect in their new country. But in the future, if present immigration trends continue, schools will have to go even further in adapting their curricula for students who have been transplanted from another land and another culture. We can expect our school budgets to be strained while we try to resolve the learning and linguistic problems that these children bring to school, and we will need to sensitize our teachers to immigrant customs and values, rather than mislabel many with such terms as "learning disabled," "behavioral disordered," "handicapped."

THE RETURN OF GEOGRAPHY

Most adults over forty remember geography as a required unit in their elementary school days and as a separate subject in high school that was taken for a half year along with civics or economics for the remaining half year. Those of us with good spatial relations and abstract abilities were able to appreciate the concept of longitude and latitude, topography and climate maps, and great circle routes. For others geography was a drudgery-filled requirement with names of far-off rivers and mountain ranges and hard-to-pronounce capitals that had little meaning to us.

During World War II and the Cold War period, geography was considered important for understanding international relations, economic power, military warfare, and U.S. and Allied activities in Europe and Asia. The subject was considered useful for explaining current events in the elementary grades and was considered one of the "essential" subjects needed for transmitting the nation's heritage and for guaranteeing international leadership.

However, geography gradually disappeared from the school curriculum; absorbed into social studies, it was often delegated to teachers who preferred to emphasize history. By 1960 only 14 percent of U.S. students in grades 7 to 12 were enrolled in geography courses, and in the mid-1970s the proportion dropped to 9 percent—a low point for the entire century (Gardner, 1986; Stoltman, 1990). Not only had geography been consolidated into social studies, it also was no longer a requirement for college admission.

As a result of this neglect, American high school and college students became geographically illiterate. A recent NAEP assessment of the nation's high school students revealed that only 42 percent could locate Nigeria on a map of Africa, and only 37 percent could find Southeast Asia on a world map (*The Geography Learning of High School Seniors,* 1990). In another survey, 39 percent of young adults living in Boston could not name the six New England states; in Dallas 25 percent could not identify the country that borders the United States to the south (Kearns, 1988).

The reform movement in education, starting with the publication of *A Nation at Risk* in 1983, has sounded the alarm. For the United States to remain a worldwide power, U.S. students must learn about the world around them, including its basic geography. Renewed emphasis on geography has become part of several different curriculum focuses, such as back-to-basics, cultural literacy, environmental education, and global education. As the drive toward restoring substantive content to the curriculum continues, geography will play an increasing role.

MIDDLE-GRADE EDUCATION

There is a growing recognition today that students between the ages of ten and fifteen are often distracted from their schoolwork because they are going through a time of rapid growth and development. Enormous variability exists among these students, even within the same age group and in the same classroom. The differences in physical, intellectual, and emotional development are so great that averages have little meaning. One eighth-grade student may be six feet and weigh two hundred pounds, and the student sitting next to him may be nearly two feet smaller and weigh half that amount.

The expanding use of middle schools is an attempt to make education more responsive to these students' social and psychological needs. Middle schools comprising grades 6 to 8 now enroll as many as 40 percent of U.S. students in this grade span. Schools concentrating on grades 7 and 8—also called middle schools—account for another 25 percent. Today only 17 percent of U.S. students in this grade range attend a school comprising grades 7 through 9, the traditional junior high school (Epstein & MacIver, 1988; Ornstein, 1992).

The difference between middle schools and junior highs is often confusing. Many middle schools were originally established for administrative reasons, such as the need to alleviate overcrowded elementary or high schools. Since the 1980s, however, middle schools have tended to rep-

resent a distinct way of thinking about the education of preadolescents and early adolescents. Compared to other secondary schools, middle schools put more emphasis on socialization, less on academics; more emphasis on intramural sports, less on interscholastic or competitive sports. There is more emphasis on the students' growth and development, not only on cognitive domains of learning. Their curricula are more interdisciplinary, and they offer more exploratory subjects, such as sex education, creative writing, and drama in blocks of ten to twelve weeks as opposed to traditional academic subjects for the entire term. Cooperative learning, heterogeneous grouping, flexible scheduling, and extended advisory periods are more common in middle schools than in junior high and high schools.

As middle schools become even more widespread, new curriculum approaches will continue to develop. Teacher education programs will also reflect the change. Until now, only a tiny percentage of teacher education programs have distinguished middle schools from elementary and secondary schools in their preservice programs. In the new future, however, teacher training institutions will focus increasingly on the skills and knowledge needed to teach in a middle school.

AGING EDUCATION

Unless the U.S. birth and death rates both dramatically increase, we are heading for a society in which the young will play a diminished role. Our society is rapidly aging, and all of us are on the same conveyor belt—the only difference being that we got on at different times. By the year 2020, increased longevity and the aging of the post–World War II baby-boom group will increase the number of elderly Americans (age 65 or older) to an estimated 51.4 million, or 17.3 percent of the projected U.S. population. By comparison, this age group included only 25.5 million people, or 11.3 percent of the population, in 1980 (*U.S. Population, Where We Are, Where We're Going,* 1992; Van Wishard, 1990).

The costs for medical and custodial care of elderly people will likely create an increasing burden on the younger working population. Moreover, the aging members of society constitute a growing political force, able to shift social spending dollars toward their own needs at the expense of school budgets. According to some projections, the increases in federal spending for Medicaid, Social Security, and old-age benefits will increase 73 percent between 1990 and 1995, after a 52 percent hike during the previous ten years, while spending on education dips 4 percent (Hadley & Zuckerman, 1990; Kaplan, 1991).

Given this "graying of America" and the issues it raises, some educators believe that schools must teach students to understand the problems and prospects of aging: how to cope with aging personally (even though it may seem distant when we are young) and how to help loved ones (parents and grandparents) successfully confront this stage of life. On another level, schools should attempt to counter many of the existing stereotypes about the elderly. Retirement ages are changing as people stay in the work force well past the age of sixty-five. We see more and more people in their seventies playing tennis and being actively involved in business and community affairs. Soon the curriculum may treat age stereotypes and age discrimination as another "ism," like racism and sexism, that students should learn to overcome.

Schools themselves should integrate semi-retired and retired people into the school work force, as volunteers, teacher aides, and resource people. The collective wisdom of these people is immense, and their political support for schools will become increasingly important. Most important, schools may be required to deal with shrinking budgets as our nation's priorities change from the youth to aging group.

FOR-PROFIT EDUCATION

A new form of separate and unequal schooling may increase in the years ahead. Privatization and profitization of education have appeared in the form of nationwide nursery schools, day-care and after-school centers, private coaching and sports centers, franchised tutoring centers, private college counseling services (aimed at selected colleges), private coaching for SAT and professional tests, corporate training schools, and contracted out-of-school services. All of these trends have one thing in common: they turn education into business by marketing educational services for a fee.

Although we have always had private alternatives to public education, a growing number of affluent families are willing to pay for various types of educational services to enhance their children's education and opportunities. Because of parental emphasis on the importance of education for their children's success, and fueled by the school choice and private school movements, entrepreneurs have rightly judged that there is a market for supplementary services—especially among well-to-do, high-driven parents.

The largest private learning centers, as of 1991, were the Britannica Learning Centers, with 86 centers in 8 states; Huntington Learning Centers, with 100 centers in 26 states; Kinder Learning Centers, with 1,250 centers in 41 states and 2 Canadian provinces; and Stanley Kaplan Educational Centers, with 125 permanent centers and nearly 500 temporary centers (Telephone conversations, 1991). About 3 to 5 percent of the U.S. school population participates in this type of proprietary school, twice the percentage that did so in 1987; the percentage is expected to increase further as the learning centers expand.

Some commentators have welcomed these private and profit-making schools as a means for radically changing American education. The present school structure, they contend, hinders school reform; educational services can be delivered more efficiently by the market system than by the government. Other observers argue that public education discriminates against taxpayers who do not have children in school. Some proponents of profit-making schools see a worldwide movement in industrialized countries to privatize education. In fact, it would not be surprising to see large computer or publishing companies such as Apple, IBM, Mac-millan, and World Encyclopedia enter the market or even begin to franchise education for-profit centers.

On the other hand, many educators believe the rise of for-profit education will widen the gap be-tween "have" and "have-not" children. Hourly fees for many learning centers and tutoring courses range from $15 to $50, a cost that prices out the great majority of parents. The price will probably increase as the demand for such services rises. To counter the trend, critics argue that public schools should offer more remedial education, supplemen-tary help, and enrichment programs—services that would benefit students and increase parents' confi-dence in local schools. In this way, the rise of pri-vate learning centers may soon stimulate changes in curriculum and instruction in the public schools.

FUTURISTIC EDUCATION

According to Toffler (1970), many people are sus-ceptible to "future shock," that is, they are unable to cope with the rapid change of today's society. As he puts it, "To survive, [and] to avert…future shock, the individual must become infinitely more adaptable and capable than ever before." The prin-cipal aim of education "must be to increase the in-dividual's 'cope-ability'—the speed and economy with which the person can adapt to continual change" (pp. 35, 402).

One way of preparing students for the future is through studying the future itself. New courses or programs, called futuristic studies, futuristics, or futurism, are now being offered at the college level, and they should soon filter down to second-ary schools. This field of study considers techno-logical developments and social events not as separate but rather as twin components that will determine our future. To generate accurate concep-tions of the future is no small task, but presenting the future as a formal object of study helps stu-dents learn the implications of rapid change and how society can adjust to these changes.

Educators have identified several areas of competence that are important in a future-oriented curriculum. An understanding of technology is critical, of course, particularly communications technology. Other subjects of study include plan-ning procedures, the organization of information, forecasting techniques, decision making, and working in groups and institutions. Students would be taught to think in multidimensional as well as linear ways. Finally, the curriculum would en-hance students' self-concepts so they do not feel powerless in a powerful society and would equip them to deal with the complexity of international power shifts and rapid change (Ornstein & Hunkins, 1989, 1993).

The future is always evolving; therefore, the curriculum must also be evolving. Whether in fu-turistic courses or in more standard ones, educators must begin to confront the twenty-first century. We must plan it now, but we must keep in mind that there are valuable historical lessons to remember and a rich culture that needs to be preserved.

CONCLUSION

Although the curriculum must evolve to serve a changing society, we caution the reader on several fronts. Change for the sake of change is not good; it must be tempered with wisdom, compassion, and justice. Schools throughout the ages have viewed their programs as being on the cutting edge of progress, and they have often been wrong. We may be misguided again as we view our schools and society; only the future will tell.

New knowledge, indeed, is not necessarily better than old knowledge. Are we to throw away most of Aristotle, Galileo, Kepler, Darwin, and Newton merely because they are no longer part of this century? If we stress only scientific and tech-nological knowledge, we could languish physi-cally, aesthetically, morally, and spiritually. As we try to maintain curriculum relevancy and plan for the future, there is no guarantee that we will not re-peat the mistakes of the past; as educators, we should never lose historical perspective.

What knowledge we select and how we orga-nize the curriculum require continual attention; we must learn to prune away old and irrelevant knowledge and to balance and integrate new knowledge into the curriculum. As we modify and update content, we must not throw away time-tested, enduring subjects such as literature, history, even music or art (or the three Rs at the elementary school level). Teachers, and especially curriculum specialists, must protect the schools and their students against fads and frills, and especially against extremism. They must keep in perspective the type of society we are, the values we cherish, and the educational aims we wish to achieve.

REFERENCES

Adult Literacy (1990). *Education Digest,* 56 (October), 42.

Altman, L. K. (1991). W. H. says 40 million will be infected with AIDS. *New York Times.* June 18, B8.

Condition of Education (1991). Washington, D.C.: U.S. Dept. of Education, Table 1:25-2, p. 225.

Digest of Education Statistics (1990). Washington, D.C.: U.S. Dept. of Education, Tables 229, 321, pp. 302, 322.

Epstein, J. L. and D. J. MacIver (1988). The middle school grades: Is grade span the most important issue? *Educational Horizons.* 67 (Winter), 88–94.

Fallows, J. (1983). The new immigrants. *Atlantic* (November), 45–68, 85–89.

Gardner, D. P. (1986). Geography in the school curriculum. *Annals of the Association of American Geographers.* Washington, D.C.: The Association.

The Geography Learning of High School Seniors (1990). Washington, D.C.: U.S. Dept. of Education.

Hadley, J. and S. Zuckerman (1990). Rising hospital costs. *Urban Institute Policy and Research Report,* 20 (Winter-Spring), 9–10.

Hoyt, K. (1991). Education reform and relationships between the private sector and education. *Phi Delta Kappan,* 72 (February), 450–452.

Juffus, J. (1991). *The Impact of the Immigration Reform and Control Act on Immigration.* Washington, D.C.: Urban Institute.

Kaplan, G. (1991). Suppose they gave an intergenerational conflict and nobody came. *Phi Delta Kappan,* 72 (May), K1–K12.

Kearns, D. T. (1988). An education recovery plan for America. *Phi Delta Kappan,* 69 (April), 565–570.

Klode, R. F. (1991). Integrated learning for a competitive workforce. *Phi Delta Kappan,* 72 (February), 453–455.

Magaziner, I. and H. R. Clinton (1992). Will America choose high skills or low wages? *Educational Leadership,* 49 (March), 10–14.

Manna, A. L. and C. W. Symons (1990). Promoting student health through children's literature. *Educational Horizons,* 69 (Fall), 37–43.

Met, M. (1989). Which foreign languages should students learn? *Educational Leadership,* 47 (September), 54–58.

Miller, L. and E. Becker-Dunn, (1993). HIV at school. *American School Board Journal,* 180 (February), 42–45.

Occupational Projections and Training Data (1990). Washington, D.C.: U.S. Dept. of Labor.

Ornstein, A. C. (1984). Urban demographics with educational implications. *Education and Urban Society,* 16 (August), 477–496.

Ornstein, A. C. (1989). Enrollment trends in big-city schools. *Peabody Journal of Education,* 66 (Summer), 64–71.

Ornstein, A. C. (1990). Bring telecommunications and videos into the classroom. *High School Journal,* 73 (April-May), 252–257.

Ornstein, A. C. (1991). Video technology and the urban curriculum. *Education and Urban Society,* 23 (May), 335–341.

Ornstein, A. C. (1992). Middle school notes: The troubled world of the adolescent. *Principal,* 72 (September), 49–52.

Ornstein, A. C. and F. P. Hunkins (1989). Curriculum futures: Review and outlook. *Kappa Delta Pi Record,* 25 (Summer), 107–111.

Ornstein, A. C. and F. P. Hunkins (1993). *Curriculum: Foundations, Principles, and Issues.* Boston: Allyn and Bacon.

Popham, W. J. (1993). Wanted: AIDS education that works. *Phi Delta Kappan,* 74 (March), 559–562.

Stoltman, J. P. (1990). Geography in the secondary schools: 1945–1990. *NASSP Bulletin,* 74 (December), 9–13.

Telephone conversations (1991). With David Hiatt, Vice President of Development, Kinder Learning Centers, July 11; Susan Meutchen, Manager of Franchise Services, Huntington Learning Centers, June 21; and Mary Verdon, Director of Public Relations, Britannica Learning Center, June 24.

Toffler, A. (1970). *Future Shock.* New York: Bantam Books.

U.S. Population: Where We Are, Where We're Going. (1992). Washington, D.C.: Population Reference Bureau.

Van Wishard, W. (1990). What in the world is going on? *Vital Speeches of the Day,* 74 (March), 314.

Weisman, J. (1993). Skills in the schools: Now it's business' turn. *Phi Delta Kappan,* 74 (January), 367–369.

DISCUSSION QUESTIONS

1. How can curricularists effectively integrate technology into curriculums for early childhood, elementary, middle school/junior high, secondary, and special education students?
2. What implications does the influx of electronic and technological capabilities have for lifelong learning?
3. What kinds of curricular changes will be needed to ensure that students can actively participate in a global economy?
4. How can schools and businesses work together to provide student learning?
5. What alternative conceptions of curriculum might be considered to effectively integrate the trends addressed in this article?

PRO-CON CHART 4

Should academic achievement be the main criteria for assessing student outcomes?

PRO	CON
1. Academic achievement standards provide an objective means for evaluating student outcomes.	1. Alternative forms of assessment provide a more comprehensive view of how well students are performing in school.
2. Achievement measures can be used to group students for instructional purposes or as objective criteria for college admission.	2. Teachers become locked into presenting content that they anticipate will be assessed by tests; subsequently, achievement tests drive the curriculum.
3. Measures of achievement provide feedback to teachers about effectiveness of their instruction.	3. Pressures of instructional assessment constrain the teachers' creativity and lead to trivialization of learning.
4. Academic achievement measures let students know how well they are doing in school and can serve as a motivator to do good work.	4. Students need different kinds of feedback and should receive praise for quality work in cognitive as well as in noncognitive domains.
5. The essence of schooling boils down to academic excellence.	5. Schools should address the cognitive, social, personal, and moral domains of learners.

CASE STUDY 4

An Advocate for Longer School Days

Jack Pierce, curriculum coordinator of Ipsid Elementary District, handed a written proposal to the superintendent, Dick Bosio, which suggested that the district lengthen the school day by forty minutes beginning in the fall. Pierce cited research to support his claim that academic learning time is the most important variable associated with student learning for most types of learners. He also reported research that showed significant relationships between increased academic time and gains in student achievement. While explaining his rationale for increasing the length of the school day, Pierce said he felt confident that overall the district would demonstrate an increase in students' Iowa Test of Basic Skills scores. He suggested that this change would probably satisfy the public that Ipsid was promoting excellence in education.

Pierce emphasized that since time spent on relevant academic tasks is measurable the district would be able to show that better test scores were the result of the increased academic instruction. Furthermore, he said that increased instructional time was advisable according to the research on teaching that emphasized student outcomes.

The Ipsid superintendent listened closely to Pierce's proposal. He had some concerns, but decided that Pierce had analyzed almost all the critical factors. Noting some of the considerations that might need to be addressed, Bosio thought to himself that because engaged time was equivalent to time devoted to actual work, asking teachers to stay a little longer each day would not be an issue. Bosio turned to Pierce and said, "I think this is a good idea. Go ahead and implement this change."

1. Assume you are Bosio and discuss how you would implement an extension of your school's instructional day by forty minutes.

2. Do you think that student achievement is directly correlated with academic engaged time? Why? Why not?

3. Based on your experience, what factors other than time on task influence student outcomes?

4. In what ways do the use of different instructional models influence student outcomes?

5. What alternatives might be considered to promote student outcomes instead of lengthening the school day?

6. What is the relationship between content, quality of teaching, academic engaged time, and student outcomes?

7. How do subject matter content and social atmosphere of the classroom affect academic engaged time?

PART FIVE

Curriculum and Supervision

INTRODUCTION

How do developments in supervision influence curriculum? What are the issues affecting views of supervision and leadership? How would new conceptions of supervision influence practice and professional programs of preparation?

In Chapter 25, Linda Behar-Horenstein and Allan Ornstein explore the relationship between curriculum, instruction, and supervision. They discuss how the principals' instructional leadership behavior is related to successful student outcomes. They describe how the principal can promote effective teaching by having a clear understanding of how curriculum, instruction, and supervision affect teaching, learning, and evaluation. In Chapter 26, Thomas Sergiovanni describes how conceptions of school leadership practice would be reconceived if the politics of division were replaced with the politics of virtue. He explores how the role of the principals as steward differs from perceptions of transformational leadership. He also claims that students as well as teachers will be able to embrace the concept of civic virtue.

In Chapter 27, Dennis Sparks and Susan Loucks-Horsley provide an overview of the models that characterize effective staff development. They discuss the theory and research that support each model. The authors also consider how organizational climate, administrative structures, policy, and participant involvement support or impede the implementation of each approach. Next, Beverly Showers and Bruce Joyce describe the purpose and practices essential to successful peer coaching. They suggest that schools consider redesigning their workplace cultures to facilitate the work of peer coaching teams and encourage teachers to collaborate on an improvement of their teaching practices.

In Chapter 29, Thomas Guskey discusses why professional program development is essential to educational reform. He identifies components that are characteristic of successful professional development programs. He offers suggestions for how successful development programs should be designed. In the final chapter of Part Five, Linda Behar-Horenstein and Ellen Amatea explain how the characteristics of a diverse school age population and contemporary society are influencing the role of school principals. They describe the changes that will be needed in the organizational context of schools to facilitate the development of collaborative relationships with students and families. They also suggest that a quality of school leadership, characterized by the development of an "outside-in" philosophy, is an effective response to the challenges presented by contemporary students and society.

25

Curriculum, Instruction, and Supervision: Essential Leadership Roles for Principals

LINDA S. BEHAR-HORENSTEIN
ALLAN C. ORNSTEIN

FOCUSING QUESTIONS

1. *In what ways has the principal's role changed?*
2. *What role should the principal play in relationship to students' learning activities? Why?*
3. *How can principals promote effective teaching?*
4. *What type of supervisory leadership behaviors are needed in today's schools?*
5. *In your opinion, why should principals have a clear understanding of the relationship between curriculum, instruction, and supervision?*

OVERVIEW OF THE RELATIONSHIP

To most educators, the relationship between curriculum, instruction, and supervision tends to be unclear. Ornstein (1986) suggests several reasons for the difficulty in identifying precise meanings for these terms. He claims that an absence of certification and numerous interpretations concerning what curriculum should encompass, what knowledge is of tangible substance, and what content and processes are essential have made it difficult to define curriculum. While there has been much discussion about the relationship between curriculum and instruction, reflected in the historical roots of curriculum as well as in current curriculum textbooks, discussions about curriculum and supervision have declined considerably in curriculum texts in the past few years (Ornstein, 1986). Over the years most supervisory texts have portrayed supervision as the major system and curriculum as a subsystem.

The number of supervisory personnel in curriculum fields has declined dramatically since the early 1980s. Principals and other administrators have had to assume greater responsibility for curriculum development at the local school and school district levels (Ornstein, 1986). The principal's role, as a result, has been expanded to include identifying staff development needs, leading curriculum change initiatives, selecting and organizing curriculum resources, improving curriculum communication, and working with teachers in and outside classrooms to organize and improve instruction and learning (Ornstein, 1986).

EMERGENT CONCEPTIONS OF CURRICULUM, INSTRUCTION, AND SUPERVISION

The importance of clarifying the principal's role has been highlighted by expectations that the principal take a more active role in assessing the efficacy of school curriculum. There has been movement away from the managerial, authoritarian, and top-down leadership styles that are typically associated with the science of administration (Lumdsen, 1993; Milstein, 1993; Thompson, 1991; Thomson, 1992, 1993) toward collegial and empowering forms of principal leadership. Concomitantly, changes in the mind-set about what principal leadership is have led to a reconceptualization of the principal's role. Postmodernists have also expanded the parameters of these discussions. They have criticized the technocratic and bureaucratic rules that they believe constrain principals from providing effective leadership. Furthermore, they have reprehended the field for not carefully considering the ways in which cultural, contextual, psychological, and sociological factors influence student learning and outcomes. While we believe that their concerns warrant thoughtful consideration, our emphasis will be on identifying ideas of curriculum, instruction, and supervision that synthesize traditional and humanistic conceptions. Although we will not discuss the postmodernist's view of curriculum, instruction, and supervision, we want the reader to understand that other conceptions of these components may have relevance.

Recent studies have demonstrated that principals have a strong impact on students' academic accomplishment (Heck, 1992; Krug, 1993; Rosenholtz, 1989). Similarly, changes in the governance of schools have led to the increased scrutiny of principals' supervision and the impact supervision has on student achievement (Association for Supervision and Curriculum Development, 1994). At national and local levels, substantial discussion has ensued about the need to ensure that future principals have the skills requisite to providing effective instructional leadership.

What are the important curriculum, instruction, and supervisory leadership behaviors that principals will be expected to perform? In this chapter, the authors identify a knowledge base of skills that they believe will promote effective

principal-based leadership in the curricular, instructional, and supervisory domains.

CURRICULUM

While a single definition of curriculum is not easily provided, in a broad context, curriculum refers to the "what" that is taught in schools. The curriculum may be the content, subject matter, skills, concepts, or principles to be learned by students. The official or taught content may not be synonymous with the intended, the tested, or the experienced curriculum. Johnston (1994) points out that many people outside the field of curriculum view the lack of a concise definition as a limitation. Moreover, many principals dismiss curriculum concerns as irrelevant to the tasks of administering schools (Milburn, 1994).

CURRICULAR LEADERSHIP BEHAVIORS

To respond effectively to the changes occurring in today's classrooms, principals need to have a working knowledge of curriculum processes. For a growing number of students, prepackaged textbooks and other supplementary materials do not adequately address their instructional needs. As a result, there is a pressing need to help teachers acquire the skills requisite to modifying the curriculum for individual students.

Three primary roles are served by principals who have an understanding of a curriculum knowledge base. First, having fundamental curriculum skills is integral to developing quality lessons and promoting successful student outcomes. Second, a knowledge base of curriculum practices helps principals to analyze the instructional difficulties that teachers may experience while attempting to match their teaching approaches with student's preferred learning styles (see Behar-Horenstein, 1994). Third, assuring that teachers acquire the principles of curriculum knowledge will encourage them to take on increasing responsibilities for curriculum decisions. Assuming increased responsibility is a way to help teachers become more responsive to students' needs (Johnston, 1994).

The principal plays a central role in creating an atmosphere in which learning activities can be made relevant to students' worlds. Having a knowledge base of curriculum-related processes and related principles permits principals to offer the resources that teachers and staff members need to effectively implement a curriculum that is consistent with the school's mission. For example, they can assist teachers in their efforts to develop curriculum guidelines, write learning objectives for groups of students in different grade levels and across content areas, develop individualized learning plans (IEPs), and identify instructional adaptations that integrate various learning styles, as well as address the cultural and linguistic diversity of student populations.

To help teachers to recognize the integral value of their work, principals should promote an understanding about the macrocurriculum. Viewing the curriculum from a macro perspective, rather than from within a micro or classroom context, emphasizes the interdisciplinary and complementary linkages among all subjects in the entire curriculum, rather than the boundaries associated with a separate subject focus. Understanding how contextually based grade-level instruction and learning activities fit into the total school curriculum helps teachers to appreciate how their work forms the basis for students' subsequent learning and synthesis of knowledge (Behar-Horenstein, 1994).

As local school reform initiatives continue to invite teachers into a dialogue about school reform, it is increasingly important that principals provide leadership that ensures that teachers acquire the procedural curriculum knowledge necessary to bring about changes in practice. Encouraging conscious decision making among teachers will lead to empowerment and participation. Assisting teachers with the acquisition of these skills will promote informed involvement in discussions about the most effective ways to promote student learning. Furthermore, exercising curriculum knowledge will empower teachers to examine crit-

ically the decisions that they make and encourage a thoughtful analysis of the issues, which will improve the educational experiences of their students (Behar, 1994; Johnston, 1994).

The following are essential curricular leadership behaviors for effective principals.

- Model an understanding of essential curriculum processes
- Assist teachers in modifying their curriculum
- Encourage teachers to acquire the knowledge base of essential curriculum practice and skills
- Encourage teachers to critically examine the congruence between their philosophy of teaching and learning and their own behaviors
- Promote an understanding about the macrocurriculum

INSTRUCTION

Instruction represents "how" the curriculum is taught. Instruction is often referred to as the instructional methods that teachers use in classrooms. This area has been strongly influenced by educational psychologists who have associated instruction with learning theory, theory-based matching of students and teachers, testing and evaluation, and scientific principles of teaching (Ornstein, 1986).

INSTRUCTIONAL LEADERSHIP BEHAVIORS

An essential function of the principal is to provide instructional leadership by overseeing teaching (Krug, 1993). To promote effective teaching, principals should encourage innovative teaching, model an array of instructional strategies, help teachers expand their ability to implement a variety of instructional methods, and provide opportunities for teachers to acquire the syntax and process components related to various teaching models identified by Joyce, Weil, and Showers (1992). Principals can be effective resources for their faculty by modeling the selection and implementation of appropriate instructional strategies. They should be able to recommend the appropriate teaching models for various teaching contexts. Moreover, they should help teachers develop the ability to use alternative instructional strategies.

Because the perspectives that students bring to the classroom are multiple, it is important that teachers present a variety of opportunities in which learning may take place. Carefully selecting among the appropriate teaching models and developing appropriate learning activities that incorporate a variety of learning and thinking styles are critical to successful student outcomes. Quality leadership must be provided to ensure that instruction is responsive to students' learning needs. Lesson planning should acknowledge the different ways that students perceive and gain knowledge, formulate ideas and think, and develop values and act (Behar-Horenstein, 1994). Principals can foster the successful student outcomes by guiding teachers to develop appropriate classroom instruction (Behar-Horenstein, 1995). They can help teachers to focus their instruction by posing the following questions for reflection:

- What type of orientation should the lesson provide? Will the lesson focus on acquiring new ideas and facts, learning problem solving, critical thinking skills, or a motor skill?
- What are the actual learning activities that should be provided?
- What role will the teacher play in instruction? Will classroom instruction be teacher led or teacher facilitated?
- What kind of learning environment and materials should the teacher select?
- What type of structure should the teacher provide in the classroom? (See Behar-Horenstein, 1994.)

The principal plays a key role in monitoring students' progress. Which aspects of schooling are evaluated, how the evaluation processes are carried out, and how the results are interpreted convey important information about the nature of schooling (Maehr, Midgley, & Urban, 1992). The principal is responsible for overseeing evaluation activities that focus on the determination of the effectiveness of classroom curriculum or student achievement, assessing teacher's instructional practices, or analyzing how textbook and supplementary materials affect student outcomes (Behar-Horenstein, 1995). Effective assessment of student performance depends on defining realistic goals, selecting appropriate assessment devices, and using assessment results to make decisions about the effectiveness of instruction (e.g., whether or not to modify the curriculum and instruction).

Principals should be able to determine the congruence between the taught curriculum, the tested curriculum, and the curriculum that is promoted in mission statements and curriculum policy manuals. Using the school or district's mission statement and departmental curriculum guidelines as the basis for comparison, they can determine the congruence between philosophical beliefs and actual practice (English, 1987).

Krug (1993) suggests that managing curriculum and instruction is one of the essential areas that compromises behaviors in which principals engage. Heck, Larsen, and Marcoulides (1990) also found that effective principals are directly involved in making decisions about curriculum and instructional strategies.

The following are essential instructional leadership behaviors for effective principals.

- Model the use of effective instructional strategies
- Promote professional development
- Evaluate student outcomes
- Promote the use of responsive and authentic forms of evaluation
- Demonstrate the use of varied evaluation strategies
- Examine the congruence between the taught and tested curriculum

SUPERVISION

Supervision represents the process in which the instructional and procedural functions of schools are assessed to determine their effectiveness in meeting the aims, goals, and objectives of the school curriculum.

SUPERVISORY LEADERSHIP BEHAVIORS

The paradigm in which most principals have been trained is a mechanistic one. School principals typically have been viewed as middle managers who oversee operations and seek to maintain order and conformity to the hierarchical structure of the institution (Behar-Horenstein & Amatea, 1995). Their primary role has been to reinforce procedures and ensure the integrity of existing power bases and roles. Their energies have been focused on dealing with the internal operation of the school and the persons in it.

Changes at sociopolitical levels suggest that principals for the 21st century will need to be able to cope with change processes and challenges associated with educating diverse student populations and to recognize the need for a broadened participation in the leadership process (Behar-Horenstein, 1995; Behar-Horenstein & Amatea, 1995). Rather than operating in isolation with little input from their faculty, principals must recognize the need for the help and cooperation of each other, as well as that of "outside" stakeholders, such as parents and the local community, to respond effectively to changing needs and trends. Principals need to encourage faculty to bring forth their ideas and influence the direction that their school actually takes. They also need to foster the faculty's ability to function as a team, see the interdependencies in their tasks, and take the initiative in cooperative planning, decision making, and problem solving. This approach to supervisory leadership recognizes that individual perspectives and skills can be integrated into a group synergy that represents something more than just the simple sum of each faculty member's skills (Behar-Horenstein & Amatea, 1995).

To realize shared ownership, principals will need to foster the development of group processing and communication skills. By creating an environment that fosters understanding and appreciation

for diverse viewpoints, they can provide opportunities that encourage all individuals to express their views during group decision-making activities (Behar-Horenstein, 1995). The commitment to consensus building can be demonstrated through their willingness to forge collaborative working relationships, engage in participatory decision making, and lead by consensus.

To assist teachers in improving instruction, principals will also need to become skilled in using a variety of supervisory techniques that acknowledge teachers' cognitive complexity and learning and teaching styles. Principals should be facile in directive, collaborative, and nondirective approaches to supervision. More importantly, they should know when it is appropriate to focus on maintaining quality control, encourage professional development, or foster teacher motivation (Sergiovanni, 1988).

The following are essential supervisory leadership behaviors for effective principals.

- Promote collaborative relationships
- Model participatory decision making
- Lead by consensus building
- Encourage teacher input
- Demonstrate reflective listening
- Encourage teachers to become reflective practitioners

CONCLUSION

To ensure that schools fulfill the purposes for which they were designed, we believe that clear conceptualizations of leadership behaviors are essential. We also believe that the principal's view of curricular, instructional, and supervisory relationships ought to acknowledge how cultural, contextual, psychological, and sociological factors influence students and teachers' behavior. In this chapter we have offered an overview of the emergent curricular, instructional, and supervisory skills that principals will need to be effective leaders.

In the area of curriculum we recommend that principals guide teachers in a critical analysis of the work that they do and the decisions that they make. We believe that the principal can be instrumental by encouraging teachers to analyze their thinking processes and actions.

In the area of instruction we suggest that principals can promote effective teaching. Principals can encourage teachers to use appropriate forms of student evaluation and acquire a repertoire of instructional strategies that invites all students into the learning process.

In the area of supervision, principals can help teachers to appreciate the need to create caring communities in which all students feel respected and can have a voice. Supervisory leadership that values diverse viewpoints, collaboration, and participation can become a potent force for school improvement.

REFERENCES

Association for Supervision and Curriculum Development. (1994). *Update, 36*(7). Alexandria, VA: Association for Supervision and Curriculum Development.

Behar, L. S. (1994). *The knowledge base of curriculum: An empirical analysis.* Lanham, MD: University Press of America.

Behar-Horenstein, L. S. (1994). What's worth knowing for teachers? *Educational Horizons, 73,* 37–46.

Behar-Horenstein, L. S. (1995). Promoting effective school leadership: A change-oriented model for the preparation of principals. *Peabody Journal of Education, 70*(3), 18–40.

Behar-Horenstein, L. S., & Amatea, E. S. (1995). Changing worlds, changing paradigms: Redesigning administrative practice for more turbulent times. *Educational Horizons, 75*(1), 27–35.

English, F. W. (1987). *Curriculum management for schools colleges businesses.* Springfield, IL: Charles C Thomas.

Heck, R. H. (1992). Principals' instructional leadership and school performance: Implications for policy development. *Educational Evaluation and Policy Analysis, 14*(1), 21–34.

Heck, R. H., Larsen, T. J., & Marcoulides, G. A. (1990). Instructional leadership and school achievement: Validation of a causal model. *Educational Administration Quarterly, 26,* 94–125.

Johnston, S. (1994). Resolving questions of "why" and "how" about the study of curriculum in teacher education programs. *Journal of Curriculum Studies, 26*(5), 525–540.

Joyce, B., Weil, M., & Showers, M. (1992). *Models of instruction* (4th ed.). Boston: Allyn & Bacon.

Krug, S. E. (1993). Leadership craft and the crafting of school leaders. *Phi Delta Kappan, 75,* 240–244.

Lumsden, L. (1993). *The new face of principal preparation.* Alexandria, VA: National Association of Elementary School Principals.

Maehr, M. L., Midgley, C., & Urban, T. (1992). School leader as motivator. *Educational Administration Quarterly, 28,* 410–429.

Milburn, G. (1994). The handbook of research on curriculum. *Journal of Curriculum Studies, 26*(1), 115–120.

Milstein, M. (1993). *Changing the way we prepare educational leaders: The Danforth experience.* Newbury Park, CA: Corwin Press.

Ornstein, A. C. (1982). Thinking small for the 1980s. *Clearing House, 55*(6), 279–280.

Ornstein, A. C. (1986). Curriculum, instruction, and supervision—Their relationship and the role of the principal. *NASSP Bulletin, 70*(489), 74–81.

Rosenholtz, S. J. (1989). *Teachers' workplace.* New York: Longman.

Sergiovanni, T. J. (1988). *Supervision: Human perspectives.* (4th ed.), New York: McGraw-Hill.

Thompson, S. D. (1991). Principals for America 2000. *Journal of School Leadership, 1*(4), 294–304.

Thomson, S. D. (1992). National standards for school administrators. *International Journal of Educational Reform, 1*(1), 54–58.

Thomson, S. D. (ed.) (1993). *Principals for our changing schools: The knowledge and skill base.* Fairfax, VA: National Policy Board for Educational Administration.

DISCUSSION QUESTIONS

1. Why does the relationship between curriculum, instruction, and supervision tend to be unclear among most educators?

2. What factors have affected changes in the principal's role?
3. What is the relationship between the principal's knowledge about curriculum principles and successful instruction?
4. How is a principal's instructional leadership behavior related to successful student outcomes?
5. Given the paradigms in which most principals were trained and the need for participatory supervisory leadership, what are the implications for program design at universities and colleges?
6. What changes would you like to see in professional programs that train aspiring principals? Why?

26

The Politics of Virtue: A New Framework for School Leadership

THOMAS J. SERGIOVANNI

FOCUSING QUESTIONS

1. *What is the politics of virtue?*
2. *In what ways are the politics of virtue and the democratic legacy related?*
3. *How would practice emanating from a pluralistic conception of politics influence school leadership?*
4. *What are the basic principles of formal organization theories?*
5. *If the politics of division were replaced with the politics of virtue, how would conceptions of leadership need to be redefined?*
6. *In what ways does the role of the principal as steward differ from current conceptions of school leadership?*
7. *What are the similarities and differences between conceptions of stewardship and transformational leadership?*

Margeret Mead once remarked, "Never doubt that a small group of thoughtful, committed citizens can change the world; indeed, it's the only thing that ever has." Her thought suggests that perhaps there is something to the 1,000 points of light theory of change. Is it possible to rally enough small groups of thoughtful and committed citizens to create the kind of schools we want? I think so, if we are willing to change the way politics is thought about in schools.

Rarely does a day go by without the media telling us still another story of divisions, hostilities, factions, and other symptoms of disconnectedness in schools. Teachers disagreeing over methods; parents bickering with teachers over discipline problems; board members squabbling over curriculum issues; administrators complaining about encroachments on their prerogatives; everyone disagreeing on sex education; and students, feeling pretty much left out of it all, making it difficult for everyone in the school by tediously trading their compliance and good will for things that they want. This mixture of issues and this mixture of stakeholders, all competing for advantage, resembles a game of bartering where self-interest is the motivator and individual actors engage in the hard play of the politics of division. The purpose of this game is to win more for yourself than you have to give back in return. Allison (1969) summarizes the game of *politics of division* as follows:

> Actions emerge neither as the calculated choice of a unified group nor as a formal summary of a leader's preferences. Rather the context of shared power but separate judgment concerning important choices determines that politics is the mechanism of choice. Note the environment in which the game is played: inordinate uncertainty about what must be done, the necessity that something be done

and crucial consequences of whatever is done. These features force responsible men to become active players. The *pace of the game*—hundreds of issues, numerous games, and multiple channels—compels players to fight to "get others' attention," to make them "see the facts," to assure that they "take the time to think seriously about the broader issue." The *structure of the game*—power shared by individuals with separate responsibilities—validates each player's feeling that "others don't see my problem," and "others must be persuaded to look at the issue from a less parochial perspective." The *rules of the game*—he who hesitates loses his chance to play at that point, and he who is uncertain about his recommendation is overpowered by others who are sure—pressures players to come down on the side of a 51–49 issue and play. The *rewards of the game*—effectiveness, i.e., impact on outcomes, as the immediate measure of performance—encourage hard play (p. 710).

The politics of division is a consequence of applying formal organization theories of governance, management, and leadership to schools. At root, these theories assume that human nature is motivated by self-interest and that leadership requires the bartering of need fulfillment for compliance. Would things be different if we applied community theories instead? Communities, too, "play the game" of politics. But it is a different game. It is a game of politics more like that envisioned by James Madison, Alexander Hamilton, John Jay, Thomas Jefferson, and other American Founders and enshrined in such sacred documents as the Declaration of Independence, the Constitution of the United States, and the amendments to that Constitution that represent a bill of rights and a bill of responsibilities for all Americans. It is a game called the politics of virtue—a politics motivated by shared commitment to the common good and guided by protections that ensure the rights and responsibilities of individuals.

CIVIC VIRTUE

Is it possible to replace the politics of division with a politics of virtue? I think so, if we are willing to replace the values that have been borrowed from the

world of formal organizations with traditional democratic values that encourage a commitment to civic virtue. This would entail development and use of different theories of human nature and leadership. For example, the rational choice theories of human nature we now use will need to be replaced with a normative and moral theory of human nature. And the executive images of leadership that we now rely on will need to be replaced with collegial images aimed at problem solving and ministering.

Creating a politics of virtue requires that we renew commitments to the democratic legacy that gave birth to our country. This is the legacy that can provide the foundation for leadership in schools. The American Founders had in mind the creation of a covenantal polity within which "The body is one but has many members. There can be unity with diversity.... The great challenge was to create a political body that brought people together and created a 'we' but still enabled people to separate themselves and recognize and respect one another's individualities. This remains the great challenge for all modern democracies" (Elshtain, 1994, p. 9). The cultivation of commitment to civic virtue is a key part of this challenge.

During the debate over passing the Constitution of 1787, America was faced with a choice between two conceptions of politics: *republican* and *pluralist*. In republican politics, civic virtue was considered to be the cornerstone principle—the prerequisite for the newly proposed government to work. Civic virtue was embodied in the willingness of citizens to subordinate their own private interests to the general good (e.g., see Sunstein, 1993) and was therefore the basis for creating a politics of virtue. This politics of virtue emphasized self-rule by the people, but not the imposition of their private preferences on the new government. Instead, preferences were to be developed and shaped by the people themselves for the benefit of the common good.

Haefele (1993) believes that it is easier to provide examples of how civic virtue is expressed than to try to define it with precision. In his words:

It is fashionable nowadays for both the left and the right to decry the loss of civic virtue; the left on such issues as industry rape of the environment and the right because of the loss of patriotism. Both sides are undoubtedly right, as civic virtue belongs to no single party or creed. It is simply a quality of caring about public purposes and public destinations. Sometimes the public purpose is chosen over private purposes. A young Israeli economist investigating a Kibbutz came across the following case. The Kibbutz had money to spend. The alternatives were a TV antenna and TV sets for everyone or a community meeting hall. The economist found that everyone preferred the TV option but that, when they voted, they unanimously chose the meeting hall. Call it enlightened self-interest, a community preference or something else, it is civic virtue in action (p. 211).

When the republican conception of politics is applied to schools, both the unique shared values that define individual schools as communities and our common democratic principles and conceptions of goodness that provide the basis for defining civic virtue are important.

The pluralist conception of politics differs from the republican. Without the unifying power of civic virtue, factions are strengthened and the politics of division reigns. In the ideal, the challenge of this politics is to play people and events in a way that the self-interests of individuals and factions are mediated in some orderly manner. "Under the pluralist conception, people come to the political process with pre-selected interests that they seek to promote through political conflict and compromise" (Sunstein, 1993, p. 176). Deliberate governmental processes of conflict resolution and compromise, of checks and balances, are needed in the pluralist view because preferences are not shaped by the people themselves as they strive to control self-interests that happen to dominate at the time.

Civic virtue was important to both Federalists, who supported the proposed Constitution, and Anti-Federalists, who opposed the Constitution, though it was the centerpiece of Anti-Federalist thinking. The Anti-Federalists favored decentralization in the form of democracy tempered by a commitment to the common good. The Federalists, by contrast, acknowledged the importance of civic virtue, but felt the pull of pluralistic politics

was too strong for the embodiment of virtue to be left to chance. They proposed a representative rather than a direct form of government that would be guided by the principles of a formal constitution that specified a series of governmental checks and balances to control factionalism and self-interest.

Both the positions of the Federalists and the Anti-Federalists have roles to play in the governance of schools. In small communities, for example, the politics of virtue expressed within a direct democracy that is guided by *citizen* devotion to the public good seems to make the most sense. Small schools and small schools within schools would be examples of such communities. They would be governed by autonomous school councils that are responsible for both educational policy and site-based management—both ends and means. This approach to governance represents a significant departure from present policies that allow principals, parents, and teachers in local schools to decide how they will do things, but not what they will do. The decisions that local school councils make would be guided by shared values and beliefs that parents, teachers, and students develop together. Schools, in this image, would not function as markets where self-interests reign or bureaucracies where entrenched rule systems reign, but as morally based direct democracies within which parents, teachers, and students, guided by civic virtue, make the best decisions possible for learning.

At the school district level, by contrast, the position of the Federalists might make the most sense. A representative form of government spearheaded by elected school boards, guided by an explicit constitution that contains the protections and freedoms needed to enable individual school communities to function both responsibly and autonomously, would be the model. School communities would have to abide by certain school district regulations regarding safety, due process, equity, fiscal procedures, and a few basic academic standards. But, beyond these, schools would be free to decide for themselves not only their management processes, but their policy structures as well. They would be responsible for deciding their own educational purposes, educational programs, scheduling and ways of operating, and means to demonstrate to the school district and to the public that they are functioning responsibly. Accountability in such a system would be both responsive to each school's purposes and, in light of those purposes, to tough standards of proof.

How can schools be held accountable for different standards? First, we will need to create standards for standards. Then we will be able to assess whether the standards that individual schools set for themselves are good ones. Once standards are accepted, each school is then assessed on its own terms. Here is how such a strategy would work: Schools make promises to the people; the promises must be good ones; school boards and states hold schools accountable for keeping their promises.

THE RATIONAL CHOICE QUESTION

Formal organization theories of human nature can be traced back to a few principles that are at the center of classical economic theory. Prime among them is the *utility function,* which is believed to explain all consumer behavior. The reasoning behind this belief is as follows. Humans are by their nature selfish. They are driven by a desire to maximize their self-interests and thus continually calculate the costs and benefits of their actions. They choose courses of action that either make them winners (they get a desired payoff) or keep them from losing (they avoid penalties). So dominant is this view and so pervasive is the concept of utility function that emotions such as love, loyalty, obligation, sense of duty, belief in goodness, commitment to a cause, and a desire to help make things better are thought to count very little in determining the courses of actions that humans choose. This view of human nature comprises a model of economics called *rational choice theory.*

Rational choice theory, expressed simply as "What gets rewarded gets done," undergirds much of the thinking in schools about how to motivate teachers to perform, how to introduce school improvement initiatives in schools, how to motivate people to accept change, and how to motivate students to learn and to behave. By emphasizing self-

interest, rational choice theory discourages the development of civic virtue.

Two additional motivational rules need to be recognized if we are to have a more complete picture of human nature: "What is *rewarding* gets done," and "What people value and believe in gets done." Both rules compel people to perform, improve, change, and meet their commitments from within, even if doing so requires that self-interest be sacrificed. Both rules address the intrinsic and moral nature of human nature. Both rules are essential to the cultivation of civic virtue.

IS CIVIC VIRTUE FOR STUDENTS, TOO?

Some readers might concede that perhaps we should move away from a rational choice view of motivation. Perhaps we should acknowledge the capacity of parents and teachers to respond less in terms of their self-interest and more in terms of what they believe is right and good. But what about students? Can they too respond to the call of virtue?

Children and young adults in schools have different needs and different dispositions. They function developmentally at different levels of moral reasoning than do adults. But the evidence is clear that students from kindergarten to grade 12 have the capacity to understand what civic virtue is and to respond to it in ways that are consistent with their own levels of maturation.

Reissman (1993) and several other teachers in New York City's District 25, for example, have been working with elementary school children (even first and second graders) on developing "bills of responsibilities." The bills are designed to teach the meaning of civic virtue and to introduce students to sources of authority that are more morally based than the usual behavioristic ways to get students to do things. Key is the emphasis on reciprocal responsibilities—a critical ingredient in community building. Communities of mind, for example, evolve from commitments to standards that apply to everyone in the school, not just to students. Thus, if students must be respectful, so must parents, teachers, principals, and everyone else who is a member of the school community or who visits the school.

Recent events at the Harmony School in Bloomington, Indiana, illustrate civic virtue in action (Panasonic Foundation, Inc., 1994). A well-known sculptor had removed his limestone rhinoceros from its place in front of an art gallery in Bloomington to keep it from being vandalized. The kindergarten through twelfth grade students at the Harmony School launched a campaign to return the rhino to Bloomington. They raised $6,000 and purchased the rhino, which now stands in front of the school for the entire community to enjoy.

Last year Harmony High School students decided that, instead of the traditional field trip to Chicago, they would go to Quincy, Illinois, where the Mississippi floods had devastated the city. One of the students explained, "They have plenty of food, and plenty of relief supplies, but they don't have anybody to help get life in order." Harmony students helped by clearing mud, garbage, and debris from the streets and by planting flowers and shrubs. Many similar stories, I know, are coming to your mind as you read about and think about the events at Harmony.

Harmony School is private, and Bloomington, Indiana, is hardly downtown Kansas City, Miami, or San Antonio. But students everywhere are pretty much the same. They have the capacity to care. They want to be called to be good, and they know the difference between right and wrong. The fact is that students, too, under the right conditions, not only will be responsive to the calls of civic virtue, but they need to be responsive if they are to develop into the kinds of adults that we want them to be.

NEW LEADERSHIP IMAGES

Replacing the politics of division with a politics of virtue requires a redefined leadership. Civic virtue is encouraged when leadership aims to develop a web of moral obligations that administrators, teachers, parents, and even students must accept. One part of this obligation is to share in the responsibility for exercising leadership. Another part of this obligation is to share in the responsibility for ensuring that leadership, whatever its source, is

successful. In this redefinition, teachers continue to be responsible for providing leadership in classrooms. But students, too, have a moral obligation to help make things work. They, too, provide leadership where they can and try as best they can to make the teacher's leadership effective. Similarly, administrators, parents, and teachers would accept responsibility together for the provision and the success of leadership.

Key to leadership in a democracy is the concept of social contract. Heifetz (1994) notes, "In part, democracy requires that average citizens become aware that they are indeed the principals, and that those upon whom they confer power are the agents. They have also to bear the risks, the costs, and the fruits of shared responsibility and civic participation" (p. 61).

It is through morally held role responsibilities that we can understand school administration as a profession in its more traditional sense. School administration is bound not just to standards of technical competence, but to standards of public obligation as well (Bellah et al., 1985, p. 290). The primacy of public obligation leads us to the roots of school leadership—stewardship defined as a commitment to administer to the needs of the school by serving its purposes, by serving those who struggle to embody these purposes, and by acting as a guardian to protect the institutional integrity of the school.

Principals function as stewards by providing for the overseeing and caring of their schools. As stewards, they are not so much managers or executives but administrators. According to Webster, to "manage" means to handle, to control, to make submissive, to direct an organization. "Superintend," in turn, means attending to, giving attention to, having oversight over what is intended. It means, in other words, supervision. As supervisor, the principal acts in loco parentis in relationship to students, ensuring that all is well for them. And as supervisor the principal acts as steward, guarding and protecting the school's purposes and structures.

Supervision in communities implies accountability, but not in the tough, inspectoral sense suggested by factory images of inspection and control. Instead, it implies an accountability embedded in tough and tender caring. Principals care enough about the school, the values and purposes that undergird it, the students who are being served, the parents whom they represent, and the teachers upon whom they depend that they will do whatever they can to protect school values and purposes, on the one hand, and to enable their accomplishment on the other.

In a recent interview, Deborah Meier, then co-director of the celebrated Central Park East Secondary School in New York City, was asked, "What is the role of the principal in an effective school?" (Scherer, 1995). Her response shows how the various ministerial roles of the principal are brought together by supervision understood as an expression of stewardship:

> Someone has to keep an eye on the whole and alert everyone when parts need close- or long-range attention. A principal's job is to put forth to the staff an agenda. The staff may or may not agree, but they have an opportunity to discuss it. I'll say, "Listen, I've been around class after class, and I notice this, don't notice this, we made a commitment to be accountable for one another, but I didn't see anybody visiting anybody else's class...." Paul [Schwartz, Meier's co-director] and I also read all the teachers' assessments of students. Once we noticed that the 9th and the 10th grade math teachers often said the kids didn't seem to have an aptitude for math. We asked the math staff, "How can these kids do nicely in 7th and 8th grade, and then seem inept in 9th and 10th? Are we fooling ourselves in 7th and 8th, or are we fooling ourselves in 9th and 10th? Because they are the same kids" (p. 7).

Meier and Schwartz both practiced leadership that is idea based. The source of authority that they appealed to are the values that are central to the school and the commitments that everyone has made to them. And because of this, their supervisory responsibilities do not compromise democratic principles, dampen teacher empowerment, or get in the way of community building. Both directors were committed to creating a staff-run school with high standards—one where staff must know each other, be familiar with each other's work, and know how the school operates. As Meier (1992) explained,

Decisions are made as close to each teacher's own classroom setting as possible, although all decisions are ultimately the responsibility of the whole staff. The decisions are not merely on minor matters—length of classes or the number of field trips. The teachers collectively decide on content, pedagogy, and assessment as well. They teach what they think matters...governance is simple. There are virtually no permanent standing committees. Finally, we work together to develop assessment systems for our students, their families, ourselves, and the broader public. Systems that represent our values and beliefs in as direct a manner as possible. (p. 607).

This process of shared decision making is not institutionalized into a formal system, but is embedded in the daily interactions of everyone working together.

In stewardship the legitimacy of leadership comes in part from the virtuous responsibilities associated with the principal's role and in part from the principal's obligation to function as the head follower of the school's moral compact. In exercising these responsibilities and obligations, it is not enough to make the right moves for just any purpose or just any vision. The noted historian and leadership theorist James MacGregor Burns (1978) pointed out that purposes and visions should be socially useful, should serve the common good, should meet the needs of followers, and should elevate followers to a higher moral level. He calls this kind of leadership *transformational.*

Many business writers and their imitators in educational administration have secularized this original definition of transformational leadership to make it more suitable to the values of formal organizations. They "conceive of transformation, not in Burns's sense of elevating the moral functioning of a polity, but in the sense of inspiration, intellectual stimulation, and personal considerations..., or altering the basic normative principles that guide an institution..." (Heifetz, 1994, pp. 228–289; see also Bass, 1985, and Hargrove, 1989). This revisionist concept of transformational leadership might be alright for managers and CEOs in business organizations. But when it comes to the kind of leadership that they want for their children's schools, few business persons are likely to prefer the corporate definition over Burns's original definition.

When principals practice leadership as stewardship, they commit themselves to building, serving, caring for, and protecting the school and its purposes. They commit themselves to helping others to face problems and to make progress in getting problems solved. Leadership as stewardship asks a great deal of leaders and followers alike. It calls both to higher levels of commitment. It calls both to higher levels of goodness. It calls both to higher levels of effort. And it calls both to higher levels of accountability. Leadership as stewardship is the *sine qua non* for cultivating civic virtue. Civic virtue can help to transform individual stakeholders into members of a community who share common commitments and who feel a moral obligation to help each other to embody those commitments.

Note: This chapter is drawn from *Leadership for the Schoolhouse: How Is It Different? Why Is It Important?* San Francisco: Jossey-Bass, 1996.

REFERENCES

Allison, G. T. 1969. Conceptual models and the Cuban missile crisis. *American Political Science Review,* 63 (3): 689–718.

Bass, B. M. 1985. *Leadership and performance beyond expectations.* New York: Free Press.

Bellah, R. N., and others. 1985. *Habits of the heart: Individualism and commitment in American life.* New York: HarperCollins.

Burns, J. M. 1978. *Leadership.* New York: HarperCollins.

Elshtain, J. B. 1994. Democracy and the politics of difference. *Responsive Community,* 4 (2): 9–20.

Haefele, E. T. 1993. What constitutes the American republic? In S. L. Elkin and K. E. Soltan, *A new constitutionalism.* Chicago: University of Chicago Press: 207–233.

Hargrove, E. C. 1989. Two conceptions of institutional leadership. In B. D. Jones (ed.), *Leadership and politics: New perspectives in political science.* Lawrence: University of Kansas Press.

Heifetz, R. 1994. *Leadership no easy answers.* Cambridge, MA: Harvard University Press.

Meier, D. 1992. Reinventing teaching. *Teacher's College Record,* 93(4): 594–609.

Panasonic Foundation. 1994. *Panasonic partnership program.* A newsletter of the Panasonic Foundation, 4 (1).

Reissman, R. 1993. A bill of responsibilities. *Educational Leadership,* 51(4): 86–87.

Samuelson, P. 1947. *Foundations of economic analysis.* Cambridge, MA.: Harvard University Press.

Scherer, M. 1995. On schools where students want to be: A conversation with Deborah Meier. *Educational Leadership,* 52(1): 4–8.

Sunstein, C. R. 1993. The enduring legacy of republicanism. In S. L. Elkin and K. E. Soltan, *A new constitutionalism.* Chicago: University of Chicago Press: 174–207.

van Mannen, M. 1991. *The tact of teaching: The meaning of pedagogical thoughtfulness.* Albany: State University of New York Press.

DISCUSSION QUESTIONS

1. What is the relationship between the politics of division and the application of formal organization theories of governance, management, and leadership in schools?

2. What are the implications of applying the politics of virtue to the practice of school leadership?

3. What are the disadvantages of applying rational choice theory to change initiatives and student motivation?

4. What evidence is there to support the belief that students of all ages have the capacity to understand and support civic virtue?

5. Why are the concepts of social contract and obligation key to the practice of leadership in a democracy?

6. In your opinion, is the notion of school leadership based on the politics of virtue a (a) practical, (b) feasible, or (c) desirable idea? Why? Why not?

27

Five Models of Staff Development for Teachers

DENNIS SPARKS
SUSAN LOUCKS-HORSLEY

FOCUSING QUESTIONS

1. *How are staff development and school restructuring initiatives related?*
2. *For what kind of person is the individually guided model of staff development most suitable?*
3. *How are cognitive levels and types of feedback related?*
4. *What activities are characteristic of the peer-coaching, clinical supervision, and evaluation supervisory approaches?*
5. *How can training facilitate school improvement efforts?*
6. *What are the common elements within organizations that have successful staff development programs?*
7. *How can staff development contribute to the professionalization of teaching?*

In the early 1970s, a growing concern about the effectiveness of inservice education resulted in a spate of studies to determine the attitudes of educators about these programs (Ainsworth, 1976; Brim & Tollett, 1974; Joyce & Peck, 1977; Zigarmi, Betz, & Jensen, 1977). The findings indicated nearly unanimous dissatisfaction with current efforts, but a strong consensus that inservice was critical if school programs and practices were to be improved (Wood & Kleine, 1987).

During the late 1970s and early 1980s, several major studies and reviews contributed to our understanding of the characteristics of effective staff development, focusing not on attitudes, but on actual practices (Berman & McLaughlin, 1978; Kells, 1980; Lawrence, 1974; Yarger, Howey, & Joyce, 1980). The resulting list of effective practices, well known by now, included:

- Programs conducted in school settings and linked to school-wide efforts
- Teachers participating as helpers to each other and as planners, with administrators, of inservice activities
- Emphasis on self instruction, with differentiated training opportunities
- Teachers in active roles, choosing goals and activities for themselves
- Emphasis on demonstration, supervised trials, and feedback; training that is concrete and ongoing over time
- Ongoing assistance and support available on request

Staff development came of age in the 1980s. It was the focus of countless conferences, workshops, articles, books, and research reports. State legislators and administrators of local school districts saw staff development as a key aspect of school improvement efforts. Many school districts initiated extensive staff development projects to improve student learning. Research on these projects and craft knowledge generated by staff developers have substantially advanced our understanding of effective staff development practices beyond the overview studies of the early 1980s referred to above.

INTRODUCTION

In spite of this recent intense, widespread interest in staff development, much remains to be learned about the process. This article organizes what is known about effective staff development into five models currently being espoused and used by staff developers. A review of the supporting theory and research on these models is followed by a description of what is currently known about the organizational context that is required to support successful staff development efforts. The conclusion discusses what can be said with confidence about effective staff development practice and what remains to be learned. First, however, are definitions of the key terms and a description of the literature that is used throughout the article.

Definitions

Staff development is defined as those processes that improve the job-related knowledge, skills, or attitudes of school employees. While participants in staff development activities may include school board members, central office administrators, principals, and non-certified staff, this article focuses on staff development for teachers. In particular, it examines what is known about staff development that is intended to improve student learning through enhanced teacher performance.

Two uses of the word "model" have been combined in an effort to both conceptualize staff development and make this conceptualization useful to staff developers. First, borrowing from Ingvarson's (1987) use of the term, a model can be seen as a design for learning which embodies a set of assumptions about (a) where knowledge about teaching practice comes from, and (b) how teachers acquire or extend their knowledge. Models chosen for discussion differ in their assumptions. Second, adapting Joyce and Weil's (1972) definition of a model of teaching, a staff development model is a pattern or plan which can be used to guide the design of a staff development program.

Each staff development model presented below is discussed in terms of its theoretical and research underpinnings, its critical attributes (including its underlying assumptions and phases of activities), and illustrations of its impact on teacher growth and development. The literature supporting these models is of several types. First, for each model, the theoretical and research bases that support its use in improving teachers' knowledge, skills, or attitudes are considered. The question asked was: Why should one believe that this model *should* affect teachers' classroom behavior? Second, program descriptions were reviewed in which these models were applied. The question asked was: What evidence exists that demonstrates that this model can be implemented by staff developers in schools and school districts? Third, data about outcomes were sought. The question asked was: What evidence indicates that this model actually makes a difference in teacher performance?

An Overview

This chapter presents five models of staff development: (a) individually-guided staff development, (b) observation/assessment, (c) involvement in a development/improvement process, (d) training, and (e) inquiry.

Individually-guided staff development refers to a process through which teachers plan for and pursue activities they believe will promote their own learning. The observation/assessment model provides teachers with objective data and feedback regarding their classroom performance. This process may in itself produce growth or it can provide information that may be used to select areas for growth.

Involvement in a development/improvement process engages teachers in developing curriculum, designing programs, or engaging in a school improvement process to solve general or particular problems. The inquiry model requires that teachers identify an area of instructional interest, collect data, and make changes in their instruction based on an interpretation of those data. The training model (which may be synonymous with staff development in the minds of many educators) involves teachers in acquiring knowledge or skills through appropriate individual or group instruction.

Next, this article examines the organizational context that is required to support these models. Our discussion includes organizational climate, leadership and support, district policies and systems, and participant involvement.

The final section looks for gaps in the knowledge base of staff development, identifying areas about which there is still more to learn and areas that as yet remain unexplored by researchers. The hope is that this chapter will serve as both a signpost for how far we have come in the past 20 years in our understanding of effective staff development practices and a spring-board for future research in this vital area.

Five Models of Staff Development

1. Individually-Guided Staff Development

Teachers learn many things on their own. They read professional publications, have discussions with colleagues, and experiment with new instructional strategies, among other activities. All of these may occur with or without the existence of a formal staff development program.

It is possible, however, for staff development programs to actively promote individually-guided activities. While the actual activities may vary widely, the key characteristic of the individually guided staff development model is that the learning is designed by the teacher. The teacher determines his or her own goals and selects the activities that will result in the achievement of those goals. Perhaps a sense of this model is best represented in an advertisement for the Great Books Foundation,

which reads: "At 30, 50, or 70, you are more self-educable than you were at 20. It's time to join a Great Books reading and discussion group."

Underlying Assumptions. This model assumes that individuals can best judge their own learning needs and that they are capable of self-direction and self-initiated learning. It also assumes that adults learn most efficiently when they initiate and plan their learning activities rather than spending their time in activities that are less relevant than those they would design. (It is, however, true that when individual teachers design their own learning there is much "reinventing of the wheel," which may seem inefficient to some observers.) The model also holds that individuals will be most motivated when they select their own learning goals based on their personal assessment of their needs.

Theoretical and Research Underpinnings. According to Lawrence's (1974) review of 97 studies of inservice programs, programs with individualized activities were more likely to achieve their objectives than were those that provided identical experiences for all participants. Theory supporting the individually-guided model can be found in the work of a number of individuals. Rogers' (1969) client-centered therapy and views on education are based on the premise that human beings will seek growth given the appropriate conditions. "I have come to feel," Rogers wrote, "that the only learning which significantly influences behavior is self-discovered, self-appropriated learning" (p. 153).

The differences in people and their needs are well represented in the literature on adult learning theory, adult development, learning styles, and the change process. Adult learning theorists (Kidd, 1973; Knowles, 1980) believe that adults become increasingly self-directed and that their readiness to learn is stimulated by real life tasks and problems. Stage theorists (Levine, 1989) hold that individuals in different stages of development have different personal and professional needs. Consequently, staff development that provides practical classroom management assistance to a 22-year-old beginning teacher may be inappropriate for a teaching veteran who is approaching retirement.

Learning styles researchers (Dunn & Dunn, 1978; Gregorc, 1979) argue that individuals are different in the ways they perceive and process information and in the manner in which they most effectively learn (e.g., alone or with others, by doing as opposed to hearing about). Research on the Concerns-Based Adoption Model (CBAM) (Hall & Loucks, 1978) indicates that as individuals learn new behaviors and change their practice, they experience different types of concerns that require different types of responses from staff developers. For instance, when first learning about a new instructional technique, some teachers with personal concerns require reassurance that they will not be immediately evaluated on the use of the strategy, while a teacher with management concerns wants to know how this technique can be used in the classroom.

Taken together, these theorists and researchers recognize that the circumstances most suitable for one person's professional development may be quite different from those that promote another individual's growth. Consequently, individually-guided staff development allows teachers to find answers to self-selected professional problems using their preferred modes of learning.

Phases of Activity. Individually-guided staff development consists of several phases: (a) the identification of a need or interest, (b) the development of a plan to meet the need or interest, (c) the learning activity(ies), and (d) assessment of whether the learning meets the identified need or interest. These phases might be undertaken informally and almost unconsciously, or they may be part of a formal, structured process. Each phase is explained in greater detail below.

With the identification of a need or interest, the teacher considers what he or she needs to learn. This assessment may be done formally (e.g., the completion of a needs assessment process or as a result of evaluation by a supervisor) or occur more spontaneously (e.g., a conversation with a colleague or reflection upon an instructional problem). The need or interest may be remedial (e.g.,

"I've really come to dislike my work because of the classroom management problems I'm having") or growth-oriented (e.g., "I'm intrigued by recent research on the brain and want to better understand its implications for student learning").

Having identified the need or interest, the teacher selects a learning objective and chooses activities that will lead to accomplishing this objective. Activities may include workshop attendance, reading, visits to another classroom or school, or initiation of a seminar or similar learning program.

The learning activity may be single session (e.g., attendance at a workshop on new approaches to reading in the content areas) or occur over time (e.g., examination of the research on retaining students in grade). Based on the individual's preferred mode of learning, it may be done alone (e.g., reading or writing), with others (e.g., a seminar that considers ways of boosting the self-esteem of high school students), or as a combination of these activities.

When assessing formal individually-guided processes the teacher may be asked to make a brief written report to the funding source or an oral report to colleagues. In other instances the teacher may simply be aware that he or she now better understands something. It is not uncommon that as a result of this assessment phase the teacher may realize how much more there is to be learned on the topic or be led to a newly emerging need or interest.

Illustrations and Outcomes. Individually guided staff development may take many forms. It may be as simple as a teacher reading a journal article on a topic of interest. Other forms of individually-guided staff development are more complex. For instance, teachers may design and carry out special professional projects supported by incentive grants such as a competitive "teacher excellence fund" promoted by Boyer (1983) or "mini-grants" described by Mosher (1981). Their projects may involve research, curriculum development, or other learning activities. While evidence of outcomes for such programs is not substantial, there are indications that they can empower teachers to address their own problems, create a sense of professionalism, and provide intellectual stimulation (Loucks-Horsley, Harding, Arbuckle, Dubea, Murray, & Williams, 1987). This strategy proved effective in New York City and Houston, where teachers were supported to develop and disseminate their own exemplary programs through Impact II grants. They reported changes in their classroom practices, as well as increases in student attendance, discipline, and motivation (Mann, 1984–85).

Teacher evaluation and supervision can be a source of data for individually guided staff development. McGreal (1983) advocates that goal setting be the principal activity of teacher evaluation. Supervisors would assist in the establishment of those goals based on the motivation and ability of the teacher. The type of goals, the activities teachers engage in to meet the goals, and the amount of assistance provided by supervisors would differ from teacher to teacher based upon developmental level, interests, concerns, and instructional problems.

Similarly, Glatthorn's (1984) "differentiated supervision" calls for "self-directed development" as one form of assistance to teachers. Self-directed development is a goal-based approach to professional improvement in which teachers have access to a variety of resources for meeting their collaboratively identified needs.

Research on teacher centers also demonstrates the value of individually guided staff development. Hering and Howey (1982) summarized research conducted on 15 teacher centers sponsored by the Far West Laboratory for Educational Research and Development from 1978 to 1982. They concluded that, "the most important contribution of teachers' centers is their emphasis on working with individual teachers over time" (p. 2). Such a focus on individual teachers is absent from many traditional staff development programs, which teacher centers appear to complement quite effectively.

Hering and Howey (1982) reported that minigrants of up to $750 provided by the St. Louis Metropolitan Teacher Center were used to fund a variety of classroom-oriented projects. Interviews with participants found that teachers made extensive use of the ideas and products they developed. Some of these projects eventually affected not only an individual classroom, but a school or the entire district. Regarding this project, Hering and Howey concluded:

> As would be expected, teachers who were given money and support reported high levels of satisfaction and a sense of accomplishment. Also not surprisingly, they developed projects anchored in the realities of the classroom and responsive to the needs and interests of their students. Perhaps most important, however, is the strong suggestion that they can, indeed, influence change and innovation in other classrooms, as well as their own, through projects they design at minimal costs. (p. 6)

Hering and Howey (1982) also report the findings for a study done on individualized services provided at the Northwest Staff Development Center in Livonia, Michigan. Even though these awards rarely exceeded $50, 78 percent of the recipients reported that they had considerable control over their own learning and professional development. Almost 85 percent of the recipients thought that these services made a substantive difference in their classrooms. In summarizing the value of individualized services, the researchers wrote, "Individual teacher needs and concerns have to be attended to, as well as school-wide collective ones, or enthusiasm for the collective approach will quickly wane" (p. 6).

While there are many illustrations of an individualized approach to staff development in the literature and many more in practice, research on its impact on teaching is largely perceptual and self-report. Perhaps as more resources are directed to supporting this strategy—particularly in the form of incentive grants to teachers—more will be learned about its contribution to teacher, as well as student, growth.

2. Observation/Assessment

"Feedback is the breakfast of champions" is the theme of Blanchard and Johnson's (1982) popular management book, *The One Minute Manager.* Yet many teachers receive little or no feedback on their classroom performance. In fact, in some school districts teachers may be observed by a supervisor as little as once every 3 years, and that observation/feedback cycle may be perfunctory in nature.

While observation/assessment can be a powerful staff development model, in the minds of many teachers it is associated with evaluation. Because this process often has not been perceived as helpful (Wise & Darling-Hammond, 1985), teachers frequently have difficulty understanding the value of this staff development model. However, once they have had an opportunity to learn about the many forms this model can take (for instance, peer coaching and clinical supervision, as well as teacher evaluation), it may become more widely practiced.

Underlying Assumptions. One assumption underlying this model, according to Loucks-Horsley and her associates (1987), is that "Reflection and analysis are central means of professional growth" (p. 61). Observation and assessment of instruction provide the teacher with data that can be reflected upon and analyzed for the purpose of improving student learning.

A second assumption is that reflection by an individual on his or her own practice can be enhanced by another's observations. Since teaching is an isolated profession, typically taking place in the presence of no other adults, teachers are not able to benefit from the observations of others. Having "another set of eyes" gives a teacher a different view of how he or she is performing with students.

Another assumption is that observation and assessment of classroom teaching can benefit both involved parties—the teacher being observed and the observer. The teacher benefits by another's view of his or her behavior and by receiving helpful feedback from a colleague. The observer benefits by watching a colleague, preparing the feedback, and discussing the common experience.

A final assumption is that when teachers see positive results from their efforts to change, they are more apt to continue to engage in improvement. Because this model may involve multiple observations and conferences spread over time, it can help teachers see that change is possible. As

they apply new strategies, they can see changes both in their own and their students' behavior. In some instances, measurable improvements in student learning will also be observed.

Theoretical and Research Underpinnings. Theoretical and research support for the observation/assessment model can be found in the literature on teacher evaluation, clinical supervision, and peer coaching. Each of these approaches is based on the premise that teaching can be objectively observed and analyzed and that improvement can result from feedback on that performance.

McGreal's (1982) work on teacher evaluation suggests a key role for classroom observation, but expresses a major concern about reliability of observations. The author points to two primary ways to increase the reliability of classroom observations. The first is to narrow the range of what is looked for by having a system that takes a narrowed focus on teaching (for instance, an observation system based on the Madeline Hunter approach to instruction), or by using an observation guide or focusing instrument. The second way is to use a pre-conference to increase the kind and amount of information the observer has prior to the observation. Glatthorn (1984) recommends that clinical supervisors (or coaches) alternate unfocused observations with focused observations. In unfocused observation the observer usually takes verbatim notes on all significant behavior. These data are used to identify some strengths and potential problems that are discussed in a problem-solving feedback conference. A focus is then determined for the next observation, during which the observer gathers data related to the identified problem.

Glickman (1986) suggests that the type of feedback provided teachers should be based on their cognitive levels. Teachers with a "low-abstract" cognitive style should receive directive conferences (problem identification and solution come primarily from the coach or supervisor); "moderate-abstract" teachers should receive collaborative conferences (an exchange of perceptions about problems and a negotiated solution); and "high-abstract" teachers should receive a non-directive approach (the coach or supervisor helps the teacher clarify problems and choose a course of action).

Peer coaching is a form of the observation/assessment model that promotes transfer of learning to the classroom (Joyce & Showers, 1982). In peer observation, teachers visit one another's classrooms, gather objective data about student performance or teacher behavior, and give feedback in a follow-up conference. According to Joyce and Showers (1983):

> Relatively few persons, having mastered a new teaching skill, will then transfer that skill into their active repertoire. In fact, few will use it at all. Continuous practice, feedback, and the companionship of coaches are essential to enable even highly motivated persons to bring additions to their repertoire under effective control. (p. 4)

Joyce (Brandt, 1987) says that up to 30 trials may be required to bring a new teaching strategy under "executive control." Similarly, Shalaway (1985) found that 10 to 15 coaching sessions may be necessary for teachers to use what they have learned in their classrooms.

Phases of Activity.   The observation/assessment model—whether implemented through evaluation, clinical supervision, or peer coaching—usually includes a pre-observation conference, observation, analysis of data, post-observation conference, and (in some instances) an analysis of the observation/assessment process (Loucks-Horsley et al., 1987). In the pre-observation conference, a focus for the observation is determined, observation methods selected, and any special problems noted.

During the observation, data are collected using the processes agreed upon in the pre-observation conference. The observation may be focused on the students or on the teacher, and can be global in nature or narrowly focused. Patterns found during instruction may become evident. Hunter (1982) recommends three points of analysis: (a) behaviors that contribute to learning, (b) behaviors that interfere with learning, and (c) behaviors that neither contribute nor interfere, but use time and energy that could be better spent.

In the post-observation conference both the teacher and observer reflect on the lesson and the observer shares the data collected. Strengths are typically acknowledged and areas for improvement suggested (by either the teacher or observer, depending upon the goals established in the pre-observation conference). An analysis of the supervisory (or coaching) process itself, while not necessarily a part of all forms of this model, provides participants with an opportunity to reflect on the value of the observation/assessment process and to discuss modifications that might be made in future cycles.

Illustrations and Outcomes.   Acheson and Gall (1980) report a number of studies in which the clinical supervision model has been accepted by teachers when they and their supervisors are taught systematic observation techniques. They further note that this process is viewed as productive by teachers when the supervisor uses "indirect" behaviors (e.g., accepting feelings and ideas, giving praise and encouragement, asking questions). While the authors report that trained supervisors helped teachers make improvements in a number of instructional behaviors, they were unable to find any studies that demonstrated student effects.

The most intensive and extensive studies of the impact of observation/assessment on learning come from the work of Showers and Joyce. Discussed in more detail in the training section, these authors and their associates have found that powerful improvements have been made to student learning when the training of teachers in effective instructional practices is followed by observations and coaching in their classrooms (Joyce & Showers, 1988). In a study that contrasted different sources of coaching, Sparks (1986) contrasted a workshop-only approach with peer coaching and with consultant coaching. Her findings indicated that peer coaching was most powerful in improving classroom performance.

The research, then, provides reason to believe that teacher behaviors can be positively influenced by the use of an observation/assessment model of staff development. It still remains to be learned, however, whether this model must be combined with particular kinds of training if student learning is to be enhanced.

3. Involvement in a Development/ Improvement Process

Teachers are sometimes asked to develop or adapt curriculum, design programs, or engage in systematic school improvement processes that have as their goal the improvement of classroom instruction and/or curriculum. Typically these projects are initiated to solve a problem. Their successful completion may require that teachers acquire specific knowledge or skills (e.g., curriculum planning, research on effective teaching, group problem-solving strategies). This learning could be acquired through reading, discussion, observation, training, and/or trial and error. In other instances, the process of developing a product itself may cause significant learnings (e.g., through experiential learning), some of which may have been difficult or impossible to predict in advance. This model focuses on the combination of learnings that result from the involvement of teachers in such development/improvement processes.

Underlying Assumptions. One assumption on which this model is based is that adults learn most effectively when they have a need to know or a problem to solve (Knowles, 1980). Serving on a school improvement committee may require that teachers read the research on effective teaching and that they learn new group and interpersonal skills. Curriculum development may demand new content knowledge of teachers. In each instance, teachers' learning is driven by the demands of problem solving.

Another assumption of this model is that people working closest to the job best understand what is required to improve their performance. Their teaching experiences guide teachers as they frame problems and develop solutions. Given appropriate opportunities, teachers can effectively bring their unique perspectives to the tasks of improving teaching and their schools.

A final assumption is that teachers acquire important knowledge or skills through their involvement in school improvement or curriculum development processes. Such involvement may cause alterations in attitudes or the acquisition of skills as individuals or groups work toward the solution of a common problem. For instance, teachers may become more aware of the perspectives of others, more appreciative of individual differences, more skilled in group leadership, and better able to solve problems. While the learnings may be unpredictable in advance, they are often regarded as important by teachers.

Theoretical and Research Underpinnings. We have chosen to represent curriculum development and school improvement as types of staff development; involvement in these processes nurtures teachers' growth. Others see staff development (perhaps viewed more narrowly as training) as a key component of effective curriculum development and implementation. As Joyce and Showers (1988) write, "It has been well established that curriculum implementation is demanding of staff development—essentially, without strong staff development programs that are appropriately designed a very low level of implementation occurs" (p. 44).

Whichever perspective one has, staff development and the improvement of schools and curriculum go hand in hand. Glickman (1986), who argues that the aim of staff development should be to improve teachers' ability to think, views curriculum development as a key aspect of this process. He believes that the intellectual engagement required in curriculum development demands that teachers not only know their content, but that they must also acquire curriculum planning skills. He recommends that curriculum development be conducted in heterogeneous groups composed of teachers of low, medium, and high abstract reasoning abilities. According to Glickman, the complexity of the curriculum development task should be matched to the abstract reasoning ability of the majority of teachers in the group.

Glatthorn (1987) describes three ways in which teachers can modify a district's curriculum guide. They may operationalize the district's curriculum guide by taking its lists of objectives and recommended teaching methods and turning them into a set of usable instructional guides. Or they may adapt the guide to students' special needs (e.g., remediation, learning style differences, etc.). Finally, teachers may enhance the guide by developing optional enrichment units. Glatthorn recommends that these activities be done in groups, believing that, in doing so, teachers will become more cohesive and will share ideas about teaching and learning in general, as well as on the development task at hand.

The involvement of teachers in school improvement processes, while similar in its assumptions and process to curriculum development, finds its research and theory base in other sources. General approaches to school improvement come from the literature on change and innovation. For example, Loucks-Horsley and Hergert (1985) describe seven action steps in a school improvement process that are based in research on implementation of new practices in schools (Crandall & Loucks, 1983; Hall & Loucks, 1978; Louis & Rosenblum, 1981). The research on effective schools underpins other approaches to school improvement (Cohen, 1981). Finally, an approach to school improvement through staff development developed by Wood and his associates was derived from an analysis of effective staff development practices as represented in the research and in reports from educational practitioners (Thompson, 1982; Wood, 1989). The result is a five-stage RPTIM model (Readiness, Planning, Training, Implementation, and Maintenance) used widely in designing and implementing staff development efforts (Wood, Thompson, & Russell, 1981). As a result of involvement in such improvement efforts, schools (and the teachers within them) may develop new curriculum, change reporting procedures to parents, enhance communication within the faculty, and improve instruction, among many other topics.

Phases of Activity.   This model begins with the identification of a problem or need by an individual, a group of teachers (e.g., a grade-level team or a secondary department), a school faculty, or a district administrator. The need may be identified in-

formally through discussion or a growing sense of dissatisfaction, through a more formal process such as brainstorming or the use of a standardized instrument (such as a school improvement survey or needs assessment), or through examination of student achievement or program evaluation data.

After a need has been identified, a response is formulated. This response may be determined informally or formally. In some cases, the necessary action may become immediately evident (e.g., the need for new lunchroom rules). At other times, teachers may need to brainstorm or search out alternatives, weigh them against a set of predetermined criteria, develop an action plan, and determine evaluation procedures. This process may take several sessions to complete and require consultation with a larger group (e.g., the schoolwide staff development committee may receive feedback on the tentative plan from the entire faculty).

Typically it becomes evident during this phase that specific knowledge or skills may be required to implement the plan. For instance, the faculty may decide that it wants to study several discipline systems before implementing the new lunchroom management system. The improvement of students' higher-order thinking may involve the selection of new textbooks, requiring that committee members better understand which features to look for in a textbook to support this goal. The development or selection of a new elementary science curriculum may require study of the latest research on science teaching and the examination of other curricula.

At this point the plan is implemented or the product developed. This process may take several days, several months, or several years. As a final step, the success of the program is assessed. If teachers are not satisfied with the results, they may return to an earlier phase (e.g., acquisition of knowledge or skills) and repeat the process.

Illustrations and Outcomes.   While teachers have long been involved in curriculum development, little research on the impact of these experiences on their professional development has been conducted. The research that has been done has assessed the impact of such involvement on areas other than professional development (for example, job satisfaction, costs, and commitment to the organization) (Kimpston & Rogers, 1987). Similarly, although the engagement of teachers in school improvement processes has increased in the last few years, little research has been conducted on the effects of that involvement on their professional development. There are, however, numerous examples that illustrate the various ways schools and districts have enhanced teacher growth by engaging them in the development/improvement process.

In the past few years, many state education agencies have supported implementation of state-initiated reforms through the encouragement (and sometimes mandating) of school improvement processes. For example, the Franklin County (Ohio) Department of Education used a staff development process to assist five school districts to meet mandated state goals (Scholl & McQueen, 1985). Teachers and administrators from the districts learned about the state requirements and developed goals and planning strategies for their districts. A major product of the program was a manual that included a synthesis of information and worksheets that could be used to guide small group activities in the five districts.

School districts have also initiated programs which involved teachers in improvement planning. In the Hammond (Indiana) Public Schools, decision making is school based (Casner-Lotto, 1988). School improvement committees (each composed of 15–20 members, including teachers, administrators, parents, students, and community members) received training in consensus building, brainstorming, creative problem solving, and group dynamics. After this training, each committee develops a "vision of excellence" for its school. As a result, schools have initiated projects in individualized learning, peer evaluation, cross-grade-level reading, and teacher coaching/mentoring.

Sparks, Nowakowski, Hall, Alec, and Imrick (1985) reported on two elementary school improvement projects that led to large gains on state reading tests. The first school's staff decided to review the reading curriculum and to investigate al-

ternative instructional approaches. Teachers task-analyzed the six lowest-scoring objectives on the state test, studied effective instructional techniques, and participated in self-selected professional growth activities. In 2 years the number of students who scored above the average rose from 72 percent to 100 percent. In the second school, teachers adopted a new reading series, revised the kindergarten program, and created a booklet that included practice test items and effective instructional practices for improving student achievement. The percentage of students achieving the reading objectives increased almost 20 percent in 3 years.

The Jefferson County (Colorado) School District has long involved teachers in curriculum development and adaptation (Jefferson County Public Schools, 1974). A cyclical process of needs assessment, curriculum objective statements, curriculum writing, pilot testing and evaluation, and district-wide implementation has been used on a regular basis in the major content areas. Teachers involved in writing and pilot test teams hone their skills as curriculum planners and developers and as masters of the new techniques that are incorporated into the curriculum (these have included such strategies as cooperative learning and individualized instruction). They also often take on the role of teacher trainers for the district-wide implementation that follows pilot and field tests (Loucks & Pratt, 1979).

E. J. Wilson High School in Spencerport (New York) is one of many across the country that has implemented elements of effective schools through a systematic school improvement process. Teachers in the school participate with building administrators on a Building Planning Committee which spearheads the achievement of "ideal practices" within the school through a seven-step process that engages the entire faculty in assessment, planning, implementation, and evaluation. As a result, the school climate and student achievement have improved, as have the knowledge, skills, and attitudes of the teachers involved. This school's outcome is representative of other schools that have implemented similar improvement processes (Kyle, 1985).

These state, school, and district-level efforts illustrate the wide variety of ways in which this model of staff development is being used. While the research and evaluation evidence regarding the impact of these processes on teacher knowledge and skills is not substantial, research does support many of the ingredients contained within these processes. These include commitment to the process by school and building administrators, which includes giving authority and resources to the team to pursue and then implement its agenda; development of knowledge and skills on the part of the teacher participants; adequate, quality time to meet, reflect, and develop; adequate resources to purchase materials, visit other sites, hire consultants to contribute to informed decision making; leadership that provides a vision, direction and guidance, but allows for significant decision making on the part of the teacher participants; and integration of the effort into other improvement efforts and into other structures that influence teaching and learning in the school (Loucks-Horsley et al., 1987). When these factors are present, a limited amount of research data and a great deal of self-report data indicate clearly that the desired outcomes of staff development are achieved.

4. Training

In the minds of many educators, training is synonymous with staff development. Most teachers are accustomed to attending workshop-type sessions in which the presenter is the expert who establishes the content and flow of activities. Typically the training session is conducted with a clear set of objectives or learner outcomes. These outcomes frequently include awareness or knowledge (e.g., participants will be able to explain the five principles of cooperative learning) and skill development (e.g., participants will demonstrate the appropriate use of open-ended questions in a class discussion). Joyce and Showers (1988) cite changes in attitudes, transfer of training, and "executive control" (the appropriate and consistent use of new strategies in the classroom) as additional outcomes. It is the trainer's role to select activities (e.g., lecture, demonstration, role-playing, simulation, micro-teaching) that will aid teachers in achieving the desired outcomes.

Whatever the anticipated outcomes, the improvement of teachers' thinking is an important goal. According to Showers, Joyce, and Bennett (1987):

> ...the purpose of providing training in any practice is not simply to generate the external visible teaching "moves" that bring that practice to bear in the instructional setting but to generate the conditions that enable the practice to be selected and used appropriately and integratively.... a major, perhaps the major, dimension of teaching skill is cognitive in nature. (pp. 85–86)

Underlying Assumptions. An assumption that undergirds the training model of staff development is that there are behaviors and techniques that are worthy of replication by teachers in the classroom. This assumption can certainly be supported by the large number of research-based effective teaching practices that have been identified and verified in the past 20 years (Sparks, 1983).

Another assumption underlying this model is that teachers can change their behaviors and learn to replicate behaviors in their classroom that were not previously in their repertoire. As Joyce and Showers (1983) point out, training is a powerful process for enhancing knowledge and skills. "It is plain from the research on training," they say, "that teachers can be wonderful learners. They can master just about any kind of teaching strategy or implement almost any technique as long as adequate training is provided" (p. 2).

Because of a high participant-to-trainer ratio, training is usually a cost-efficient means for teachers to acquire knowledge or skills. Many instructional skills require that teachers view a demonstration of their use to fully understand their implementation. Likewise, certain instructional techniques require for their classroom implementation that teachers have an opportunity to practice them with feedback from a skilled observer. Training may be the most efficient means for large numbers of teachers to view these demonstrations and to receive feedback as they practice.

Theoretical and Research Underpinnings. The theoretical and research underpinnings for the training model come from several sources, but the most recent and intensive research has been conducted by Joyce and Showers (1988). They have determined that, depending upon the desired outcomes, training might include exploration of theory, demonstration or modeling of a skill, practice of the skill under simulated conditions, feedback about performance, and coaching in the workplace. Their research indicates that this combination of components is necessary if the outcome is skill development.

In addition to those components identified by Joyce and Showers, Sparks (1983) cites the importance of discussion and peer observation as training activities. She notes that discussion is useful both when new concepts or techniques are presented and as a problem-solving tool after teachers have had an opportunity to try out new strategies in their classrooms. Training sessions that are spaced 1 or more weeks apart so that content can be "chunked" for improved comprehension and so that teachers have opportunities for classroom practice and peer coaching are shown to be more effective than "one-shot" training (Loucks-Horsley et al., 1987; Sparks, 1983).

Sparks (1983), Wu (1987), and Wood and Kleine (1987) point out the value of teachers as trainers of their peers. Sparks indicates that teachers may learn as much from their peers as from "expert" trainers. She also argues that school districts can afford the type of small-group training that she recommends when peers are used rather than more expensive external consultants. In reviewing the research, Wood and Kleine found that teachers preferred their peers as trainers. Wu's review of the research also confirmed this, finding that when their peers are trainers, teachers feel more comfortable exchanging ideas, play a more active role in workshops, and report that they receive more practical suggestions. There is, however, evidence that indicates that expert trainers who have the critical qualities teachers value in their peers (e.g., a clear understanding of how a new practice works with real students in real class-

room settings) can also be highly effective (Crandall, 1983).

Phases of Activities. According to Joyce and Showers (1988), "Someone has to decide what will be the substance of the training, who will provide training, when and where the training will be held and for what duration" (p. 69). While training content, objectives, and schedules are often determined by administrators or by the trainer, Wood, McQuarrie, and Thompson's (1982) research-based model advocates involving participants in planning training programs. Participants serve on planning teams which assess needs (using appropriate sources of data), explore various research-based approaches, select content, determine goals and objectives, schedule training sessions, and monitor implementation of the program.

Joyce and Showers (1988) point out that there are specific "learning-to-learn" attitudes and skills that teachers possess or can develop that aid the training process. They cite persistence, acknowledgment of the transfer problem (the need for considerable practice of new skills in the classroom), teaching new behaviors to students, meeting the cognitive demands of innovations (developing a "deep understanding" of new practices), the productive use of peers, and flexibility. The authors list several conditions of training sessions that foster these aptitudes and behaviors: adequate training, opportunities for collegial problem solving, norms that encourage experimentation, and organizational structures that support learning. Sparks' (1983) review of staff development research suggests that a diagnostic process (such as detailed profiles of teaching behaviors based upon classroom observations) may be an important first step in the training process.

After training, in-classroom assistance in the form of peer observation and coaching is critical to the transfer of more complex teaching skills (Joyce & Showers, 1988). The process of data gathering and analysis that accompanies most forms of peer observation is valuable to the observer as well as the observed teacher (Brandt, 1987; Sparks, 1986). A more thorough discussion of this topic can be found in the observation/assessment model described earlier in this article.

Illustrations and Outcomes.   The power of training to alter teachers' knowledge, attitudes, and instructional skills is well established. Its impact on teachers, however, depends upon its objectives and the quality of the training program. Joyce and Showers (1988) have determined that when all training components are present (theory, demonstration, practice, feedback, and coaching), an effect size of 2.71 exists for knowledge-level objectives, 1.25 for skill-level objectives, and 1.68 for transfer of training to the classroom. (The effect size describes the magnitude of gains from any given change in educational practice; the higher the effect size, the greater the magnitude of gain. For instance, an effect size of 1.0 indicates that the average teacher in the experimental group outperformed 84% of the teachers in the control group.) "We have concluded from these data," Joyce and Showers (1988) report, "that teachers can acquire new knowledge and skill and use it in their instructional practice when provided with adequate opportunities to learn" (p. 72). Coaching and peer observation research cited earlier in the observation/assessment model also supports the efficacy of training.

Wade (1985) found in her meta-analysis of inservice teacher education research that training affected participants' learning by an effect size of .90 and their behavior by .60. An effect size of .37 was found for the impact of teacher training on student behavior. Wade also concluded that training groups composed of both elementary and secondary teachers achieved higher effect sizes than did those enrolling only elementary or only secondary teachers.

Gage (1984) traces the evolution of research on teaching from observational and descriptive studies to correlational studies to nine experiments that were designed to alter instructional practices. "The main conclusion of this body of research," Gage wrote, "is that, in eight out of the nine cases, inservice education was fairly effective—not with all teachers and not with all teaching practices but

effective enough to change teachers and improve student achievement, or attitudes, or behavior" (p. 92).

Numerous specific illustrations of training programs are available that have demonstrated impact on teacher behavior and/or student learning. For instance, studies indicate that teachers who have been taught cooperative learning strategies for their classrooms have students who have higher achievement, display higher reasoning and greater critical thinking, have more positive attitudes toward the subject area, and like their fellow students better (Johnson, Johnson, Holubec, & Roy, 1984).

Good and Grouws (1987) describe a mathematics staff development program for elementary teachers. In this 10-session program teachers learned more about mathematics content and about instructional and management issues. As a result of the training, the researchers found changes in teachers' classroom practice and improved mathematics presentations. Student mathematics performance was also improved.

Kerman (1979) reports a 3-year study in which several hundred K–12 teachers were trained to improve their interactions with low-achieving students. The five-session training program included peer observation in the month interval between each session. The researchers found that low-achieving students in experimental classes made significant academic gains over their counterparts in control groups.

Rauth (1986) describes an American Federation of Teachers training program that brought research on teaching to its members. Teacher Research Linkers (TRLs) first determine which aspects of the research will be most valuable in their teaching. Between sessions they carry out implementation plans in their own classrooms. TRLs are then taught how to effectively share this research with their colleagues. A study of this program indicated that teachers made significant changes in their practice and that, in addition, their morale and collegiality increased dramatically.

Robbins and Wolfe (1987) discuss a 4-year staff development project designed to increase elementary students' engaged time and achievement.

Evaluation of the training program documented steady improvement for 3 years in teachers' instructional skills, student engaged time, and student achievement in reading and math. While scores in all these areas dropped in the project's fourth and final year, Robbins and Wolfe argue that this decline was due to insufficient coaching and peer observation during that year.

As the preceding discussion indicates, there is a much more substantial research literature on training than on the models presented earlier. Under the appropriate conditions, training has the potential for significantly changing teachers' beliefs, knowledge, behavior, and the performance of their students.

5. Inquiry

Teacher inquiry can take different forms. A high school teacher wonders if an alteration in her lesson plan from her first period class will produce improved student understanding in second period. A brief written quiz given at the end of the class indicates that it did. A group of teachers gathers weekly after school for an hour or two at the teacher center to examine the research on ability grouping. Their findings will be shared with the district's curriculum council. Several elementary teachers study basic classroom research techniques, formulate research questions, gather and analyze data, and use their findings to improve instruction in their classrooms.

Teacher inquiry may be a solitary activity, be done in small groups, or be conducted by a school faculty. Its process may be formal or informal. It may occur in a classroom, at a teacher center, or result from a university class. In this section teacher inquiry is explored as a staff development model.

Underlying Assumptions.   Inquiry reflects a basic belief in teachers' ability to formulate valid questions about their own practice and to pursue objective answers to those questions. Loucks-Horsley and her associates (1987) list three assumptions about a teacher inquiry approach to staff development:

- Teachers are intelligent, inquiring individuals with legitimate expertise and important experience.
- Teachers are inclined to search for data to answer pressing questions and to reflect on the data to formulate solutions.
- Teachers will develop new understandings as they formulate their own questions and collect their own data to answer them.

The overarching assumption of the model is that

> the most effective avenue for professional development is cooperative study by teachers themselves into problems and issues arising from their attempts to make their practice consistent with their educational values…. [The approach] aims to give greater control over what is to count as valid educational knowledge to teachers. (Ingvarson, 1987, pp. 15, 17)

Theoretical and Research Underpinnings.   The call for inquiry-oriented teachers is not new. Dewey (1933) wrote of the need for teachers to take "reflective action." Zeichner (1983) cites more than 30 years of advocacy for "teachers as action researchers," "teacher scholars," "teacher innovators," "self-monitoring teachers," and "teachers as participant observers."

More recently, various forms of inquiry have been advocated by a number of theorists and researchers. Tikunoff and Ward's (1983) model of interactive research and development promotes teacher inquiry into the questions they are asking through close work with researchers (who help with methodology) and staff developers (who help them create ways of sharing their results with others). Lieberman (1986) reports on a similar process in which teachers serving on collaborative teams pursued answers to school-wide rather than classroom problems. Watts (1985) discusses the role of collaborative research, classroom action research, and teacher support groups in encouraging teacher inquiry. Simmons and Sparks (1985) describe the use of action research to help teachers better relate research on teaching to their unique classrooms.

Glickman (1986) advocates action research in the form of quality circles, problem-solving groups, and school improvement projects as means to develop teacher thought. Cross (1987) proposes classroom research to help teachers evaluate the effectiveness of their own teaching. Glatthorn (1987) discusses action research by teams of teachers as a peer-centered option for promoting professional growth. Loucks-Horsley and her colleagues (1987) discuss teachers-as-researchers as a form of teacher development that helps narrow the gap between research and practice. Sparks and Simmons (1989) propose inquiry-oriented staff development as a means to enhance teachers' decision-making abilities.

One of the important tenets of the inquiry approach is that research is an important activity in which teachers should be engaged, although they rarely participate in it other than as "subjects." Gable and Rogers (1987) "take the terror out of research" by describing ways in which it can be used as a staff development tool. They discuss both qualitative and quantitative methodology, providing specific strategies that teachers can use in their classrooms. They conclude by saying "...the desire and ability to do research is an essential attribute of the professional teacher of the Eighties" (p. 695).

Phases of Activity.   While the inquiry model of staff development can take many forms, these forms have a number of elements in common. First, individuals or a group of teachers identify a problem of interest. Next, they explore ways of collecting data that may range from examining existing theoretical and research literature to gathering original classroom or school data. These data are then analyzed and interpreted by an individual or the group. Finally, changes are made, and new data are gathered and analyzed to determine the effects of the intervention.

This process can be adapted to the unique needs of a particular approach to inquiry. For instance, Hovda and Kyle (1984) provide a 10-step process for action research that progresses from identifying interested participants, through sharing

several study ideas, to discussing findings, to considering having the study published or presented. Glatthorn (1987) describes a four-step process for action research. Collaborative research teams (a) identify a problem, (b) decide upon specific research questions to be investigated and methodology to be used, (c) carry out the research design, and (d) use the research to design an intervention to be implemented in the school.

Watts (1985) describes "reflective conversations" in which teachers carefully observe and thoughtfully consider a particular child or practice. Using a standard procedure, the group shares observations, reviews previous records and information, summarizes their findings, and makes recommendations. As a final step, the group reviews the process to assess how well it went, looks for gaps, and identifies ideas to repeat in future conversations.

Organizational support and/or technical assistance may be required throughout the phases of an inquiry activity. Organizational support may take the form of structures such as teacher centers or study groups, or of resources such as released time or materials. Technical assistance may involve training in research methodologies, data-gathering techniques, and other processes that aid teachers in making sense of their experiences.

Illustrations and Outcomes.   The forms inquiry as a staff development model may take are limited only by the imagination. Simmons and Sparks (1985) describe a "Master of Arts in Classroom Teaching" degree designed to help teachers meet their individually identified improvement goals. Teachers in this program learn about educational research, identify and analyze classroom problems, pursue topics of professional interest, and improve their overall teaching ability. The authors report evidence of change in participant knowledge (e.g., concerning effective teaching-learning), thinking (e.g., enhanced problem-solving skills, increased cognitive complexity), and patterns of communication and collegiality.

Watts (1985) presents a number of ways in which teachers act as researchers. She discussed collaborative research in teacher centers funded by the Teachers' Center Exchange (then located at the Far West Laboratory for Educational Research and Development) that was conducted in the late 1970s and early 1980s. Fourteen projects were funded in which teachers collaborated with researchers on topics of interest to the individual teachers' center. Watts also described ethnographic studies of classrooms conducted collaboratively by teachers and researchers. In addition, she provided examples of classroom action research and teachers' study groups as forms of inquiry. Watts concluded that these three approaches share several outcomes. First, as a result of learning more about research, teachers make more informed decisions about when and how to apply the research findings of others. Second, teachers experience more supportive and collegial relationships. And third, teaching improves as teachers learn more about it by becoming better able to look beyond the immediate, the individual, and the concrete.

The effects of the teacher inquiry model of staff development may reach beyond the classroom to the school. An example of school-wide impact comes from the report of a high school team convened to reflect on a lack of communication and support between teachers and administrators (Lieberman & Miller, 1984). As a result of working together to define the problem, learn each other's perspectives, gather evidence, and formulate solutions, teachers and administrators address important school problems collaboratively. Note that there is a substantial overlap between this kind of "school-based" inquiry and some of the school improvement processes discussed earlier in the model described as involvement in a development/improvement process.

ORGANIZATIONAL CONTEXT

Teacher development in school districts does not take place in a vacuum. Its success is influenced in many ways by the district's organizational context (McLaughlin & Marsh, 1978; Sparks, 1983). Key organizational factors include school and district climate, leadership attitudes and behaviors, district policies and systems, and the involvement of participants.

While staff development fosters the professional growth of individuals, organizational development addresses the organization's responsibility to define and meet changing self-improvement goals (Dillon-Peterson, 1981). Consequently, effective organizations have the capacity to continually renew themselves and solve problems. Within this context, individuals can grow.

In earlier sections of this chapter, five models of staff development were discussed that have solid foundations in research and/or practice, and are being used in increasingly robust forms throughout the country today. While each model requires somewhat different organizational supports to make it successful, it is also true that research points to a common set of attributes of the organizational context without which staff development can have only limited success (Loucks-Horsley et al., 1987). In organizations where staff development is most successful:

- Staff members have a common, coherent set of goals and objectives that they have helped formulate, reflecting high expectations of themselves and their students.
- Administrators exercise strong leadership by promoting a "norm of collegiality," minimizing status differences between themselves and their staff members, promoting informal communication, and reducing their own need to use formal controls to achieve coordination.
- Administrators and teachers place a high priority on staff development and continuous improvement.
- Administrators and teachers make use of a variety of formal and informal processes for monitoring progress toward goals, using them to identify obstacles to such progress and ways of overcoming these obstacles, rather than using them to make summary judgments regarding the "competence" of particular staff members (Conley & Bacharach, 1987).
- Knowledge, expertise, and resources, including time, are drawn on appropriately, yet lib-

erally, to initiate and support the pursuit of staff development goals.

This section briefly highlights the research that supports these organizational attributes.

Organizational Climate

Little (1982) found that effective schools are characterized by norms of collegiality and experimentation. Simply put, teachers are more likely to persist in using new behaviors when they feel the support of colleagues and when they believe that professional risk taking (and its occasional failures) are encouraged. Fullan (1982) reports that the degree of change is strongly related to the extent to which teachers interact with each other and provide technical help to one another. "Teachers need to participate in skill-training workshops," Fullan writes, "but they also need to have one-to-one and group opportunities to receive and give help, and more simply to converse about the meaning of change" (p. 121).

Joyce and Showers (1983) point out that "in a loose and disorganized social climate without clear goals, reticent teachers may actually subvert elements of the training process not only for themselves but also for others" (p. 31). While teacher commitment is desirable, it need not necessarily be present initially for the program to be successful. Miles (1983) found that teacher/administrator harmony was critical to the success of improvement efforts, but that it could develop over the course of an improvement effort. Initially, working relationships between teachers and administrators had to be clear and supportive enough so that most participants could "suspend disbelief," believing that the demands of change would be dealt with together (Crandall, 1983). In their study of school improvement efforts that relied heavily on staff development for their success, both Miles and Crandall found that in projects where a mandated strategy caused some initial disharmony between teachers and administrators, the climate changed as the new program's positive impact on students became clear. When a new program was selected carefully and teachers received good training and support,

most who were initially skeptical soon agreed with and were committed to the effort. Showers, Joyce, and Bennett (1987) support the position that, at least initially, teachers' ability to use a new practice in a competent way may be more important than commitment.

Few would disagree with the importance of a school and district climate that encourages experimentation and supports teachers to take risks, i.e., establishes readiness for change (Wood, Thompson, & Russell, 1981). Yet a supportive context consists of more than "good feelings." The quality of the recommended practices is also critical. Research conducted by Guskey (1986) and Loucks and Zacchei (1983) indicates that the new practices developed or chosen by or for teachers need to be effective ones—effective by virtue of evaluation results offered by the developer or by careful testing by the teachers who have developed them. These researchers found that only when teachers see that a new program or practice enhances the learning of their students will their beliefs and attitudes change in a significant way.

Leadership and Support

According to the Rand Change Agent Study (McLaughlin & Marsh, 1978) active support by principals and district administrators is critical to the success of any change effort. According to McLaughlin and Marsh (1978):

> The Rand research sets the role of the principal as instructional leader in the context of strengthening the school improvement process through team building and problem solving in a "project-like" context. It suggests that principals need to give clear messages that teachers may take responsibility for their own professional growth. (p. 92)

Stallings and Mohlman (1981) determined that teachers improved most in staff development programs where the principal supported them and was clear and consistent in communicating school policies. Likewise, Fielding and Schalock (1985) report a study in which principals' involvement in teachers' staff development produced longer-term changes than when principals were not involved.

In their discussion of factors that affect the application of innovations, Loucks and Zacchei (1983) wrote "…administrators in successful improvement sites take their leadership roles seriously and provide the direction needed to engage teachers in the new practices" (p. 30).

According to Huberman (1983), teachers' successful use of new skills often occurs when administrators exert strong and continuous pressure for implementation. He argues that "…administrators, both at the central office and building levels, have to go to center stage and stay there if school improvement efforts are to succeed" (p. 27). While administrator presence is important, administrators must also act as gate-keepers of change so that "innovation overload" can be avoided (Anderson & Odden, 1986).

While much research points to administrators as being key leaders in staff development and change, it is also true that others can take on leadership and support roles—and may in fact be better placed to do so. Research on school improvement indicates that a team approach can help orchestrate leadership and support "functions" which can be shared by administrators (building and district level), district coordinators or staff developers, teachers, and external trainers and consultants (Loucks-Horsley & Hergert, 1985). For example, Cox (1983) reports that while principals seem to play an important role in clarifying expectations and goals and stabilizing the school organization, central office coordinators, who often know more about a specific practice, can effectively coach teachers in their attempts to change their classroom behavior. Coordinated leadership can also help avoid situations such as a school's textbooks and curriculum not matching the instructional models teachers are being taught to use (Fielding & Schalock, 1985).

District Policies and Systems

Staff development activities occur within the context of a school district's staff development program. According to Ellis (1989), a comprehensive staff development program includes a philosophy, goals, allocation of resources, and coordination. The philosophy spells out beliefs that guide the program. District, school, and individual goals (and their accompanying action plans) provide direction to staff development efforts. Resources need to be allocated at the district, school, and individual levels so that these goals have a reasonable chance of being achieved. Staff development programs need to be coordinated by individuals who have an assigned responsibility for this area. Ellis also supports the use of a district-level staff development committee to aid in coordination of programs.

The selection, incorporation, or combination of the models of staff development described in this chapter are the responsibility of the district's staff development structure. Decisions about their use need to match the intended outcomes if they are to be effective (Levine & Broude, 1989), but these decisions are also influenced by state and/or community initiatives aimed at the improvement of schools and/or teaching (Anderson & Odden, 1986).

Participant Involvement

Research clearly indicates that involving participants in key decisions about staff development is necessary for a program to have its greatest impact. According to Lieberman and Miller (1986), a supportive context for staff development requires both a "top-down" and "bottom-up" approach. The top-down component sets a general direction for the district or school and communicates expectations regarding performance. The bottom-up processes involve teachers in establishing goals and designing appropriate staff development activities.

The establishment of common goals is important to the success of staff development efforts (Ward & Tikunoff, 1981). Odden and Anderson's (1986) research indicates that a clearly defined process of data collection, shared diagnosis, and identification of solutions to problems must be employed during the planning phase. Collaboration, from initial planning through implementation and institutionalization, is a key process in determining these goals and in influencing lasting change (Lambert, 1984; McLaughlin & Marsh, 1978; Wood, Thompson, & Russell, 1981).

Lortie (1986) argues that when teachers perceive that they can participate in important school-level decisions, the relationship between the extra efforts required by school improvement and the benefits of these efforts becomes clearer. Following this argument, he recommends that schools be given relatively little detailed supervision, but be monitored instead for results based on explicit criteria.

Others report that, when teachers cannot be involved in initial decisions regarding staff development (e.g., when it is mandated by state legislation or when it supports the use of district-wide curriculum), their involvement in decisions about the "hows" and "whens" of implementation can be important to success. Furthermore, teachers' involvement in developing curriculum and as trainers for staff development programs can contribute in important ways to the success of an effort (Loucks & Pratt, 1979).

Odden and Anderson (1986) capture the reciprocal relationship between organization and individual development in this discussion of their research:

> When instructional strategies, which aim to improve the skills of individuals, were successful, they had significant effects on schools as organizations. When school strategies, which aim to improve schools as organizations, were successful, they had significant impacts on individuals. (p. 585)

The importance of paying attention to the context of staff development is underscored by Fullan (1982). He responds to educators who say that they cannot provide the elements required to support change (e.g., supportive principals, a 2- or 3-year time period for implementation):

> Well don't expect much implementation to occur...I say this not because I am a cynic but because it is wrong to let hopes blind us to the actual obstacles to change. If these obstacles are ignored, the experience with implementation can be harmful to the adults and children directly involved—more harmful than if nothing had been done. (p. 103)

CONCLUSION

Staff development is a relatively young "science" within education. In many ways the current knowledge base in staff development is similar to what was known about teaching in the early 1970s. During the 1970s and early 1980s research on teaching advanced from descriptive to correlational to experimental (Gage, 1984). With the exception of research on training, much of the staff development literature is theoretical and descriptive rather than experimental. The remaining two sections describe what can be said with some confidence about the research base for the staff development models and what remains to be learned.

What Can Be Said with Confidence

Staff development possesses a useful "craft knowledge" that guides the field. This craft knowledge includes ways to organize, structure, and deliver staff development programs (Caldwell, 1989). It has been disseminated in the past decade through publications such as *The Journal of Staff Development, Educational Leadership,* and *Phi Delta Kappan,* and through thousands of presentations at workshops and conventions. As a result, in the past 20 years hundreds of staff development programs have been established in urban, suburban, and rural school districts throughout the United States and Canada. This craft knowledge serves another useful purpose: It can guide researchers in asking far better questions than they could have asked a decade ago.

Of the five models discussed in this chapter, the research on training is the most robust. It is the most widely used form of staff development and the most thoroughly investigated. As a result, it is possible to say with some confidence which training elements are required to promote the attainment of specific outcomes. Likewise, research on coaching has demonstrated the importance of in-classroom assistance to teachers (by an "expert" or by a peer) for the transfer of training to the classroom.

The consensus of "expert opinion" is that school improvement is a systemic process (Fullan, 1982). This ecological approach recognizes that changes in one part of a system influence the other parts. Consequently, staff development both influences and is influenced by the organizational context in which it takes place. The impact of the staff development models that have been discussed depends not only upon their individual or blended use, but upon the features of the organization in which they are used.

While this appears to relate to the "art" of making staff development work (i.e., the judgment with which one combines and juggles the various organizational interactions), there is also much "science" that can be drawn from when it comes to the organizational supports necessary for effective staff development. Study after study confirms the necessity of:

- Schools possessing norms that support collegiality and experimentation
- District and building administrators who work with staff to clarify goals and expectations, and actively commit to and support teachers' efforts to change their practice
- Efforts that are strongly focused on changes in curricular, instructional, and classroom management practices with improved student learning as the goal
- Adequate, appropriate staff development experiences with follow-up assistance that continues long enough for new behaviors to be incorporated into ongoing practice

Interestingly enough, it appears that these factors apply to a wide variety of school improvement and staff development efforts. While there are little hard research data on some of the models discussed above (see next section), most if not all of these factors will certainly persist as being important, regardless of what is learned about other models.

What We Need to Learn More About

While the work of staff developers during the past decade has been grounded in theory and research from various disciplines (e.g., adult learning, organization development, training), the scientific base of their own practice (with the exception of training and coaching) is quite thin. Unfortunately, the systematic study of some of the models discussed earlier is difficult because their use is not widespread or because they have been implemented only recently as part of comprehensive staff development programs. Listed below are areas for further study.

1. We need research to determine the potency of the models described above (with the exception of training). We need to learn which models are most effective for which outcomes with which teachers. For instance, we might ask: How effective is individually-guided staff development for knowledge level outcomes for self-directed experienced teachers? Or: How effective is an inquiry approach in helping beginning teachers learn their craft?

2. We need a better understanding of the impact on student learning of the four non-training staff development models. Do non-training models alter teacher knowledge or skills in a way that improves student learning?

3. We need to know more about the impact on teachers of blending the models described above in a comprehensive staff development program. How are teachers' attitudes, knowledge, and skills altered when they choose among and blend various models as the means of reaching one or more "growth" goals? For instance, what would be the result if a teacher blended individually-guided staff development (e.g., reading research on tracking), observation/assessment (e.g., peer observation), and training (e.g., in cooperative learning) as means to alter classroom practices that are viewed as disadvantageous to a sub-group of students?

4. We need a systemic view of comprehensive staff development at the district level. Most districts provide a variety of staff development opportunities to teachers. Some purposely support individual, school-based, and district-based activities. We need descriptive studies of what these programs look like, both from the overall, coordination point of view, and from the individual teacher point of view. We need to know: How are goals set and coordinated? How are resources allocated? How equitable are opportunities for individual teachers?

How do different contextual factors (e.g., resources, state mandates) influence success?

5. *We need to understand more about the relative costs of different staff development models and combinations of the models.* Moore and Hyde (1978, 1979, 1981) have conducted some useful analyses of how many school district resources actually go for staff development purposes. But more micro-analyses would be useful to understand the cost-effectiveness of relatively labor-intensive models (e.g., coaching) versus those that rely only on the activity of a single teacher (e.g., individually-guided staff development).

6. *Finally, we need to look at staff development as it contributes to teacher professionalism and teacher leadership.* Many believe that teacher professionalism and leadership must characterize our education system in the future if that system is to survive. Yet there are as many different definitions of the terms as there are ideas of how to implement them. One role of staff development research is to help identify and clarify the various meanings given to these concepts. We then need descriptive studies of staff development's contributions to these efforts, with special attention to how these efforts influence the conduct of staff development.

It is possible that future research may contradict current craft knowledge (this, for example, has occurred with the learning that attitude change does not always have to precede behavior change), or, as is likely, future research will support current practice. Many questions about effective staff development remain unanswered. The need is great for well-designed, long-term studies of school improvement efforts that are based on staff development. The field of staff development seeks a solid base that moves beyond description and advocacy to a better understanding of those factors that support and improve classroom practice.

ENDNOTE

This chapter was adapted from "Models of Staff Development," in W. Robert Houston (Ed.), *Handbook of Research on Teacher Education*. New York: Macmillan, 1990.

REFERENCES

Ainsworth, A. (1976). Teachers talk about in-service education. *Journal of Teacher Education, 27,* 107–109.

Anderson, B., & Odden, A. (1986). State initiatives can foster school improvement. *Phi Delta Kappan, 67*(8), 578–581.

Berman, P., & McLaughlin, M. (1978). *Federal programs supporting educational change: Vol. 8. Implementing and sustaining innovation.* Santa Monica, CA: Rand Corporation.

Blanchard, K., & Johnson, S. (1982). *The one minute manager.* New York: William Morrow.

Boyer, E. (1983). *High school: A report on secondary education in America.* New York: Harper & Row.

Brandt, R. (1982). On improving teacher effectiveness: A conversation with David Berliner. *Educational Leadership, 40*(1), 12–15.

Brandt, R. (1987). On teachers coaching teachers: A conversation with Bruce Joyce. *Educational Leadership, 44*(5), 12–17.

Brim, J., & Tollett, D. (1974). How do teachers feel about inservice education? *Educational Leadership, 31,* 21–25.

Caldwell, S. (Ed.) (1989). *Staff development: A handbook of effective practices.* Oxford, OH: National Staff Development Council.

Casner-Lotto, J. (1988). Expanding the teacher's role: Hammond's school improvement process. *Phi Delta Kappan, 69*(5), 349–353.

Cohen, M. (1981). Effective schools: What the research says. *Today's Education, 70,* 466–469.

Conley, S., & Bacharach, S. (1987). The Holmes Group report: Standards, hierarchies, and management. *Teachers College Record, 88*(3), 340–347.

Crandall, D. (1983). The teacher's role in school improvement. *Educational Leadership, 41*(3), 6–9.

Crandall, D., & Loucks. S. (1983). *A roadmap for school improvement.* Executive summary of *People, policies, and practices: Examining the chain of school improvement.* Andover, MA: The NETWORK, Inc.

Cross, P. (1987). The adventures of education in wonderland: Implementing education reform. *Phi Delta Kappan, 68*(7), 496–502.

Dewey, J. (1933). *How we think.* Chicago, IL: Henry Regnery Co.

Dillon-Peterson, B. (1981). Staff development/organizational development—perspective 1981. In B. Dillon-Peterson (Ed.), *Staff development/organization development* (pp. 1–10). Alexandria, VA:

Association for Supervision and Curriculum Development.

Dunn, R., & Dunn, K. (1978). *Teaching students through their individual learning styles: A practical approach.* Reston, VA: Reston Publishing Co.

Ellis, S. (1989). Putting it all together: An integrated staff development program. In S. Caldwell (Ed.), *Staff development: A handbook of effective practices* (pp. 58–69). Oxford, OH: National Staff Development Council.

Fielding, G., & Schalock, H. (1985). *Promoting the professional development of teachers and administrators.* Eugene, OR: ERIC Clearinghouse on Educational Management. (ERIC Document Reproduction Service No. EA 017 747)

Fullan, M. (1982). *The meaning of educational change.* Toronto: OISE Press.

Gable, R., & Rogers, V. (1987). Taking the terror out of research. *Phi Delta Kappan, 68*(9), 690–695.

Gage, N. (1984). What do we know about teaching effectiveness? *Phi Delta Kappan, 66*(2), 87–93.

Glatthorn, A. (1984). *Differentiated supervision.* Alexandria, VA: Association for Supervision and Curriculum Development.

Glatthorn, A. (1987). Cooperative professional development: Peer-centered options for teacher growth. *Educational Leadership, 45*(3), 31–35.

Glickman, E. (1986). Developing teacher thought. *Journal of Staff Development, 7*(1), 6–21.

Good, T. (1981). Teacher expectations and student perceptions: A decade of research. *Educational Leadership, 38*(5), 415–422.

Good, T., & Grouws, D. (1987). Increasing teachers' understanding of mathematical ideas through inservice training. *Phi Delta Kappan, 68*(10), 778–783.

Gregorc, A. (1970). Learning/teaching styles: Their nature and effects. In *Student learning styles: Diagnosing and prescribing programs.* Reston, VA: National Association of Secondary School Principals.

Guskey, T. (1986). Staff development and the process of teacher change. *Educational Researcher, 15*(5), 5–12.

Hall, G., & Loucks, S. (1978). Teacher concerns as a basis for facilitating and personalizing staff development. *Teachers College Record, 80*(1), 36–53.

Hering, W., & Howey, K. (1982). *Research in, on, and by teachers' centers.* Occasional Paper No. 10. San Francisco, CA: Teachers' Center Exchange, Far West Laboratory for Educational Research and Development.

Hovda, R., & Kyle, D. (1984). A strategy for helping teachers integrate research into teaching. *Middle School Journal, 15*(3), 21–23.

Huberman, A. (1983). School improvement strategies that work: Some scenarios. *Educational Leadership, 41*(3), 23–27.

Hunter, M. (1982). *Mastery teaching.* El Segundo, CA: TIP Publications.

Ingvarson, L. (1987). *Models of inservice education and their implications for professional development policy.* Paper presented at a conference on "Inservice Education: Trends of the Past, Themes for the Future," Melbourne, Australia.

Jefferson County Public Schools (1974). *Report of the task force to define the process of developing curriculum.* Lakewood, CO: Author.

Johnson, D., Johnson, R., Holubec, E., & Roy, P. (1984). *Circles of learning.* Alexandria, VA: Association for Supervision and Curriculum Development.

Joyce, B., & Peck, L. (1977). *Inservice teacher education project report II: Interviews.* Syracuse, NY: Syracuse University.

Joyce, B., & Showers, B. (1982). The coaching of teaching. *Educational Leadership, 40*(1), 4–10.

Joyce, B., & Showers, B. (1983). *Power in staff development through research in training.* Alexandria, VA: Association for Supervision and Curriculum Development.

Joyce, B., & Showers, B. (1988). *Student achievement through staff development.* New York: Longman.

Joyce, B., & Weil, M. (1972). *Models of teaching.* Englewood Cliffs, NJ: Prentice-Hall.

Kells, P. (1981, January). Quality practices in inservice education. *The Developer.* Oxford, OH: National Staff Development Council.

Kerman, S. (1979). Teacher expectations and student achievement. *Phi Delta Kappan, 60*(10), 716–718.

Kidd, J. (1973). *How adults learn.* Chicago, IL: Follett Publishing Co.

Kimpston, R., & Rogers, K. (1987). The influence of prior perspectives, differences in participatory roles, and degree of participation on views about curriculum development: A case study. *Journal of Curriculum and Supervision, 2*(3), 203–220.

Knowles, M. (1980). *The modern practice of adult education.* Chicago, IL: Association/Follett Press.

Kyle, R. (Ed.) (1985). *Reaching for excellence: An effective school sourcebook.* Washington, DC: U.S. Government Printing Office.

Lambert, L. (1984). *How adults learn: An interview study of leading researchers, policy makers, and staff developers.* Paper presented at the annual meeting of the American Educational Research Association, New Orleans, LA.

Lawrence, G. (1974). *Patterns of effective inservice education: A state of the art summary of research on materials and procedures for changing teacher behaviors in inservice education.* Gainesville: University of Florida College of Education. (ERIC Document Reproduction Service No. ED 176 424)

Levine, S. (1989). *Promoting adult growth in schools: The promise of professional development.* Lexington, MA: Allyn & Bacon.

Levine, S., & Broude, N. (1989). Designs for learning. In S. Caldwell (Ed.), *Staff development: A handbook of effective practices.* Oxford, OH: National Staff Development Council.

Levine, S., & Jacobs, V. (1986). Writing as a staff development tool. *Journal of Staff Development, 7*(1), 44–51.

Lieberman, A. (1986). Collaborative research: Working with, not working on. *Educational Leadership, 43*(5), 28–32.

Lieberman, A., & Miller, L. (1984). *Teachers, their world and their work: Implications for school improvement.* Alexandria, VA: Association for Supervision and Curriculum Development.

Lieberman, A., & Miller, L. (1986). School improvement: Themes and variations. In A. Lieberman (Ed.), *Rethinking school improvement: Research, craft, and concept.* New York: Teachers College Press.

Little, J. (1982). Norms of collegiality and experimentation: Work-place conditions of school success. *American Educational Research Journal, 19*(3), 325–340.

Lortie, D. (1986). Teacher status in Dade County: A case of structural strain? *Phi Delta Kappan, 67*(8), 568–575.

Loucks, S., & Pratt, H. (1979). A concerns-based approach to curriculum change. *Educational Leadership, 37*(3), 212–215.

Loucks, S., & Zacchei, D. (1983). Applying our findings to today's innovations. *Educational Leadership, 41*(3), 28–31.

Loucks-Horsley, S., Harding, C., Arbuckle, M., Murray, L., Dubea, C., & Williams, M. (1987). *Continuing to learn: A guidebook for teacher development.* Andover, MA: Regional Laboratory for Educational Improvement of the Northeast and Islands, and the National Staff Development Council.

Loucks-Horsley, S., & Hergert, L. (1985). *An action guide to school improvement.* Alexandria, VA: Association for Supervision and Curriculum Development and Andover, MA: The NETWORK, Inc.

Louis, K., & Rosenblum, S. (1981). *Linking R & D with schools: A program and its implications for dissemination and school improvement policy.* Washington, DC: National Institute of Education.

Mann, D. (1984–85). Impact II and the problem of staff development. *Educational Leadership, 42*(4), 44–47.

Mathieson, D. (1987, December). Writing for professional growth. *The Developer.* Oxford, OH: National Staff Development Council.

McGreal, T. (1982). Effective teacher evaluation systems. *Educational Leadership, 39*(4), 303–305.

McGreal, T. (1983). *Successful teacher evaluation.* Alexandria, VA: Association for Supervision and Curriculum Development.

McLaughlin, M., & Marsh, D. (1978). Staff development and school change. *Teachers College Record, 80*(1), 69–94.

Miles, M. (1983). Unraveling the mystery of institutionalization. *Educational Leadership, 41*(3), 14–19.

Mosher, W. (1981). *Individual and systemic change mediated by a small educational grant program.* San Francisco, CA: Far West Laboratory for Educational Research and Development.

Odden, A., & Anderson, B. (1986). How successful state education improvement programs work. *Phi Delta Kappan, 67*(8), 582–585.

Rauth, M. (1986). Putting research to work. *American Educator, 10*(4), 26–31.

Robbins, P., & Wolfe, P. (1987). Reflections on a Hunter-based staff development project. *Educational Leadership, 44*(5), 56–61.

Rogers, C. (1969). *Freedom to learn.* Columbus, OH: Charles E. Merrill.

Scholl, S., & McQueen, P. (1985). The basic skills articulation plan: Curriculum development through staff development. *Journal of Staff Development, 6*(2), 138–142.

Shalaway, T. S. (1985). Peer coaching...does it work? *R & D Notes.* Washington, DC: National Institute of Education.

Showers, B. (1984). *Peer coaching: A strategy for facilitating transfer of training.* Eugene, OR: Center for Educational Policy and Management, University of Oregon.

Showers, B., Joyce, B., & Bennett, B. (1987). Synthesis of research on staff development: A framework for future study and a state-of-art analysis. *Educational Leadership, 45*(3), 77–87.

Simmons, J., & Sparks, G. (1985). Using research to develop professional thinking about teaching. *Journal of Staff Development, 6*(1), 106–116.

Sparks, G. (1983). Synthesis of research on staff development for effective teaching. *Educational Leadership, 41*(3), 65–72.

Sparks, G. (1986). The effectiveness of alternative training activities in changing teaching practices. *American Educational Research Journal, 23*(2), 217–225.

Sparks, G., Nowakowski, M., Hall, B., Alec, R., & Imrick, J. (1985). School improvement through staff development. *Educational Leadership, 42*(6), 59–61.

Sparks, G., & Simmons, J. (1989). Inquiry-oriented staff development: Using research as a source of tools, not rules. In S. Caldwell (Ed.), *Staff development: A handbook of effective practices* (pp. 126–139). Oxford, OH: National Staff Development Council.

Stallings, J., & Mohlman, G. (1981). *School policy, leadership style, teacher change, and student behavior in eight schools, final report.* Washington, DC: National Institute of Education.

Thompson, S. (1982). *A survey and analysis of Pennsylvania public school personnel perceptions of staff development practices and beliefs with a view to identifying some critical problems or needs.* Unpublished Dissertation, The Pennsylvania State University, University Park, PA.

Tikunoff, W., & Ward, B. (1983). Collaborative research on teaching. *The Elementary School Journal, 83*(4), 453–468.

Wade, R. (1985). What makes a difference in inservice teacher education? A meta-analysis of research. *Educational Leadership, 42*(4), 48–54.

Wanous, D., & Sparks, D. (1981). *Analysis of individualized teacher center services.* San Francisco, CA: Far West Laboratory for Educational Research and Development.

Ward, B., & Tikunoff, W. (1981, September). The relationship between inservice training, organizational structure and school climate. *Inservice, 7–8.*

Watts, H. (1985). When teachers are researchers, teaching improves. *Journal of Staff Development, 6*(2), 118–127.

Westbrook, C., Loomis, A., Coffina, J., Adelberg, J., Brooks, S., & Ellis, S. (1985). Classroom research: A promising model for staff development. *Journal of Staff Development, 6*(2), 128–132.

Wise, A., & Darling-Hammond, L. (1985). *Educational Leadership, 42*(4), 28–33.

Wood, F. (1989). Organizing and managing school-based staff development. In S. Caldwell (Ed.), *Staff development: A handbook of effective practices* (pp. 26–43). Oxford, OH: National Staff Development Council.

Wood, F., & Kleine, P. (1987). *Staff development research and rural schools: A critical appraisal.* Unpublished paper, University of Oklahoma, Norman.

Wood, F., McQuarrie, F., & Thompson, S. (1982). Practitioners and professors agree on effective staff development practices. *Educational Leadership, 43,* 63–66.

Wood, F., Thompson, S., & Russell, F. (1981). Designing effective staff development programs. In B. Dillon-Peterson (Ed.), *Staff development/organization development* (pp. 59–91). Alexandria, VA: Association for Supervision and Curriculum Development.

Wu, P. (1987). Teachers as staff developers: Research, opinions, and cautions. *Journal of Staff Development, 8*(1), 4–6.

Yarger, S., Howey, K., & Joyce, B. (1980). *Inservice teacher education.* Palo Alto, CA: Booksend Laboratory.

Zeichner, K. (1983). Alternative paradigms of teacher education. *Journal of Teacher Education, 34*(3), 3–9.

Zigarmi, P., Betz, L., & Jensen, D. (1977). Teacher preference in and perceptions of inservice. *Educational Leadership, 34,* 545–551.

DISCUSSION QUESTIONS

1. How is knowledge of adult learning theory integrated into the underlying assumptions of the five staff development models described?

2. In what ways can staff development programs aid teachers in school improvement or curriculum development?

3. What kind of staff development program would you design to assist your colleagues in mainstreaming students?
4. Discuss the similarities and differences between the inquiry model of staff development, reflective action, and an independent research initiative.
5. How do school district attitudes and climate variables influence staff development program efforts?

28

The Evolution of Peer Coaching

BEVERLY SHOWERS
BRUCE JOYCE

FOCUSING QUESTIONS

1. *What is the purpose of peer coaching?*
2. *What practices have been essential to the success of peer coaching?*
3. *What role should the school play in facilitating peer-coaching teams?*
4. *How does peer coaching differ from collegial coaching and cognitive coaching?*
5. *What are the principles of peer coaching?*

Fifteen years have passed since we first proposed peer coaching as an on-site dimension of staff development (Joyce and Showers, 1980). In the 1970s, evaluations of staff development that focused on teaching strategies and curriculum revealed that as few as 10 percent of the participants implemented what they had learned. Rates of transfer were low even for those who had volunteered for the training. Well-researched curriculum and teaching models did not find their way into general practice and thus could not influence students' learning environments.

In a series of studies beginning in 1980, we tested hypotheses related to the proposition that regular (weekly) seminars would enable teachers to practice and implement the content that they were learning. The seminars, or coaching sessions, focused on classroom implementation and the analysis of teaching, especially students' responses.

The results were consistent: Implementation rose dramatically, whether experts or participants conducted the sessions. Thus we recommended that teachers who were studying teaching and curriculum form small peer-coaching groups that would share the learning process. In this way, staff development might directly affect student learning.

Our central concern has been helping students to benefit when their teachers learn, grow, and change. In studying how teachers can create better learning environments for themselves (Joyce and Showers, 1995), we noted with interest a serendipitous by-product of the early peer-coaching studies: Successful peer coaching teams developed skills in collaboration and enjoyed the experience so much that they wanted to continue their collegial partnerships after they accomplished their initial goals. Why not create permanent structures, we wondered, that would enable teachers to study teaching on a continuous basis?

In working with this broadened view of peer coaching as a mechanism to increase classroom implementation of training, we evolved our present practice of organizing entire faculties into peer-coaching teams. We have been convinced throughout that peer coaching is neither an end in itself nor by itself a school improvement initiative. Rather, it must operate in a context of training, implementation, and general school improvement. There is no evidence that simply organizing peer coaching or peer study teams will affect students' learning environments. The study of teaching and curriculum must be the focus.

Here we examine the history of coaching, describe changes in the conduct of coaching, and make recommendations for its future, including its role as a component of staff development that drives organizational change.

HISTORY OF PEER COACHING

Pre-1980.   The processes of training and implementation have come under close scrutiny only in the last 25 years. Beginning in the mid-1950s, national movements to improve education focused on academic quality and social equality. By the early 1970s, educators recognized that many of those efforts, even when well funded and approved by the public, seldom led to changes. The lack of research on how people learn teaching strategies and how schools successfully disseminate innovations contributed to our failures. Educators assumed that teachers could learn new strategies, return to a school, and implement their new learning smoothly and appropriately. The organization of the schools did not support the intensive training efforts that occurred in summer institutes or workshops during the year, however. Initial diagnoses attributed the failure to flaws in the motivation, effort, and attitudes of the teachers, rather than to the state of the organization or the design of training.

1980–1987.   We began to believe that changes in the school organization and in training design could solve implementation problems or ease them greatly and that assigning the blame to teachers was erroneous. Our understanding of how people learn new behaviors and put them into practice has continuously evolved as a result of work by colleagues in schools and universities and our own efforts with teachers and schools.

When we first advanced the notion of coaching, we had just completed an exhaustive review of literature on training and presented our findings as a set of hypotheses about types of training likely to produce results. The training components discussed in that early work grew from what we found in the literature: theory presentation, practice, structured and open-ended feedback, and in-class assistance with transfer.

In 1980, we believed that "modeling, practice under simulated conditions, and practice in the classroom, combined with feedback" (Joyce and Showers, 1980, p. 384) were the most productive training design. We hypothesized that teachers attempting to master new curriculum and teaching approaches would need continued technical assistance at the classroom level. For purposes of research, we distinguished between the initial development of a skill that would permit a teacher to experiment with new teaching strategies and the classroom practice of that skill until it had become a part of the teacher's repertoire. At that time, training designs for skill development were much better developed than were designs for conditions that would lead to transfer.

In the early 1980s, we formally investigated the hypothesis that coaching, following initial training, would result in much greater transfer than would training alone (Showers 1982, 1984). We confirmed this hypothesis. We assumed that the coach needed to have more expertise in the content area and thus paired teachers with an outside consultant or an expert peer. The literature on supervisory practices and feedback influenced our thinking as we struggled to create the kind of structured feedback that appeared to facilitate skill development.

Results of our early studies showed that teachers who had a coaching relationship—that is, who shared aspects of teaching, planned together, and pooled their experiences—practiced new skills and strategies more frequently and applied them more appropriately than did their counterparts who worked alone to expand their repertoires. Members of peer-coaching groups exhibited greater long-term retention of new strategies and more appropriate use of new teaching models over time (Baker and Showers, 1984).

Coaching helped nearly all the teachers implement new teaching strategies. Equally important, teachers introduced to the new models could coach one another, provided that the teachers continued to receive periodic follow-up in training settings. Thus we recommended that schools organize teachers into peer-coaching teams and arrange school settings so that the teachers could work together to gain sufficient skill to affect student learning. We had moved from the 1950s and 1960s, where the probability of implementation was extremely low, to a very simple technology that virtually reversed the odds. The coaching process was added to the training paradigm, taking into account the two levels of skill development described above.

Current Practice. We conducted the early studies with individual teachers or small groups within a school. The next stage involved faculties that volunteered as a whole, which required collaborating with staffs to determine their students' most pressing needs, selecting appropriate content, helping them to design training, and assessing the impact on students. Increasingly, we have found that attention to the social organization is extremely important. We now ask entire faculties to decide whether they want the school site to work with us, and we discuss at length exactly how we might work together.

PRINCIPLES OF PEER COACHING

Numerous staff development practices are called "coaching." These include "technical coaching," "collegial coaching," "challenge coaching," "team coaching," "cognitive coaching," and uses of "peer coaching" (Garmston, 1987) to refer to the traditional supervisory mode of preconference, observation, and postconference. None of these should be confused with or used for evaluation of teachers.

Similar to our approach, technical coaching, team coaching, and peer coaching (as in peer clini-

cal supervision) focus on innovations in curriculum and instruction (Kent, 1985; Neubert and Bratton, 1987; Rogers, 1987), whereas collegial coaching and cognitive coaching aim more at improving existing practices (Garmston et al., 1993). All except team coaching differ from our practice in that their primary vehicle for improving or changing classroom instruction is verbal feedback.

Following are our principles of peer coaching.

1. When we work with entire faculties, *all teachers must agree to be members of peer-coaching study teams.* Teams must collectively agree to (a) practice or use whatever change the faculty has decided to implement; (b) support one another in the change process, including sharing planning of instructional objectives and developing materials and lessons; and (c) collect data about the implementation process and the effects on students relative to the school's goals.

2. We have found it necessary and important to *omit verbal feedback as a coaching component.* The primary activities of peer-coaching study teams are planning and developing curriculum and instruction in pursuit of shared goals. Especially when they are learning teaching strategies designed for higher-order outcomes, teachers need to think through their overarching goals, as well as the specific objectives leading to them. Collaborative planning is essential if teachers are to divide the labor of developing new lesson and unit sequences and use one another's products.

When teachers try to give one another feedback, collaborative activity tends to disintegrate. Peer coaches told us that they found themselves slipping into "supervisory, evaluative comments" despite their intentions to avoid them. Teachers shared with us that they expect "first the good news, then the bad" because of their past experiences with clinical supervision and admitted that they often pressured their coaches to go beyond technical feedback and give them "the real scoop." To the extent that feedback was evaluative or was perceived as evaluative, it was not meeting our original intention.

Remarkably, omitting feedback in the coaching process has not depressed implementation or student growth (Joyce and Showers, 1995), and the omission has greatly simplified the organization of peer coaching teams. In retrospect, it is not difficult to understand this finding. Learning to provide technical feedback required extensive training and time and was unnecessary after team members mastered new behaviors.

3. We have needed to redefine the meaning of "coach": *when pairs of teachers observe each other, the one teaching is the "coach," and the one observing is the "coached."* In this process, teachers who are observing do so in order to learn from their colleagues. There is no discussion of the observation in the "technical feedback" sense that we used in our early studies. Generally, these observations are followed by brief conversations on the order of "Thanks for letting me watch you work. I picked up some good ideas on how to work with my students."

4. *The collaborative work of peer-coaching teams is much broader than observations and conferences.* Many believe that the essence of the coaching transaction is to offer advice to teachers following observations. Not so. Rather, teachers learn from one another while planning instruction, developing support materials, watching one another work with students, and thinking together about the impact of their behavior on their students' learning.

RECOMMENDATIONS FOR TRAINING SESSIONS

Continuing concerns drive our work: how best to help teachers to teach students to build intellectual independence; reasoning and problem-solving capability; competence in handling the explosion of information and data; and, with the help of technology, the ability to navigate the information age. We believe that staff developers can assist educators by incorporating certain behaviors in their training sessions.

First, we can help schools and teams of teachers *redesign their workplaces.* Rather than simply advocating that schools provide time for collaborative planning and problem solving related to specific plans for change, we can provide time during training to address this problem. Reviewing Raywid's (1993) research on finding time for collaboration is one way to begin such a session.

Second, staff can *form peer-coaching teams on the first day of training.* When entire school faculties train together, they have many options for forming teams, and staff developers can facilitate discussion of those options. Faculties can also try out various formats, comparing the costs and benefits of alternative plans. A school attempting to develop an integrated curriculum as part of its improvement plan may want to experiment with cross-subject or cross-grade teams. Schools with a focus on multicultural curriculums may want to spread faculty expertise on various cultures among the teams. However a school forms its teams, it is useful for teachers to have immediate practice in working together toward shared goals.

Third, we can *provide examples of formats or structures for collaborative planning.* Many teachers have shared with us their difficulty in jointly performing an activity that they have traditionally done alone. A structured walk-through of a planning activity can allow teams to respond to questions within specific time frames, practice thinking aloud about what each person wants to accomplish, and identify overlap with their colleagues' agendas. A sample sequence might include the following:

- Think about your year's course. What are your big, overarching goals for your students?
- Now think about the first six weeks of school. What objectives will you need to accomplish if you are to meet your year's goals? How much time can you spend in review and still meet your objectives?
- What instructional strategies are most appropriate for the objectives you've set for the first six weeks? Are they consistent with your year-end goals?

• Given the overlap of objectives in your team, can you divide the labor and develop materials that others can use?

Fourth, peer-coaching study teams need to plan how they will *monitor implementation* of new initiatives and *determine the impact of each initiative on their students.* When whole schools agree on a specific change agenda, study teams may want to address in small groups how they will discover whether their efforts are having the desired effects and then combine their ideas in a whole-school session. Measuring the impact of planned change is critical to any school improvement effort. The training session is optimal for planning ministudies that teams can conduct throughout the year for this purpose.

COACHING AND SCHOOL IMPROVEMENT

Collaborative planning and data collection increase the time, and thus the cost, of staff development activities. To the extent that such activities result in greater clarity about means and ends, more thorough implementation of planned changes, and more immediate information about effects on students, the additional effort is well worth the investment.

Adding peer-coaching study teams to school improvement efforts is a substantial departure from the way that schools often embark on change efforts. On the surface, it appears simple to implement—what could be more natural than teams of professional teachers working on content and skills? It is a complex innovation only because it requires a radical change in relationships among teachers and between teachers and administrative personnel.

When staff development becomes the major vehicle for school improvement, schools should take into account both the structures and content of training, as well as the changes needed in the workplace to make possible the collaborative planning, decision making, and data collection that are essential to organizational change efforts. As we ponder ways to ensure that training and coaching fuel the school renewal process, we are also examining how the culture of the school can increasingly provide a benign environment for collective activity.

A cohesive school culture makes possible the collective decisions that generate schoolwide improvement efforts. The formation of peer coaching teams produces greater faculty cohesion and focus and, in turn, facilitates more skillful shared decision making. A skillful staff development program results in a self-perpetuating process for change, as well as new knowledge and skills for teachers and increased learning for students.

REFERENCES

Baker, R. G., and B. Showers (1984). *The Effects of a Coaching Strategy on Teachers' Transfer of Training to Classroom Practice: A Six-Month Follow-up Study.* Paper presented at the annual meeting of the American Educational Research Association, New Orleans, La.

Garmston, R. (1987). "How Administrators Support Peer Coaching," *Educational Leadership* 44, 5: 18–26.

Garmston, R., C. Linder, and J. Whitaker (1993). "Reflections on Cognitive Coaching," *Educational Leadership* 51, 2: 57–61.

Joyce, B., and B. Showers (1980). "Improving Inservice Training: The Messages of Research," *Educational Leadership* 37, 5: 379–385.

Joyce, B., and B. Showers (1995). *Student Achievement through Staff Development: Fundamentals of School Renewal,* 2nd ed. White Plains, N.Y.: Longman.

Kent, K. M. (1985). "A Successful Program of Teachers Assisting Teachers," *Educational Leadership* 43, 3: 30–33.

Neubert, G. A., and E. C. Bratton (1987). "Team Coaching: Staff Development Side by Side," *Educational Leadership* 44, 5: 29–33.

Raywid, M. A. (1993). " Finding Time for Collaboration," *Educational Leadership* 51, 1: 30–35.

Rogers, S. (1987). "If I Can See Myself, I Can Change," *Educational Leadership* 45, 2: 64–67.

Showers, B. (1982). *Transfer of Training: The Contribution of Coaching,* Eugene, Ore.: Center for Educational Policy and Management.

Showers, B. (1984). *Peer Coaching: A Strategy for Facilitating Transfer of Training.* Eugene, Ore.: Center for Educational Policy and Management.

DISCUSSION QUESTIONS

1. What factors were instrumental in the development of peer coaching?
2. Why did national efforts to improve academic quality and school inequality tend to fail?
3. Why was it necessary to omit verbal feedback as a coaching component?
4. Why should schools consider redesigning their workplaces?
5. How might an analysis of both school faculty's training needs and the characteristics of the workplace culture influence organizational change efforts?

29

Results-oriented Professional Development

THOMAS R. GUSKEY

FOCUSING QUESTIONS

1. *What is professional development?*
2. *What evidence is there to confirm that professional development programs are effective?*
3. *How can meta-analysis help to identify the elements of a successful professional development program?*
4. *In what ways does consideration of context influence the design of a professional development program?*
5. *Why should change efforts be introduced in a gradual and incremental fashion?*
6. *How are teamwork and collaboration related to successful professional development programs?*
7. *In what ways are support and pressure integral to successful professional development programs?*

Never before in the history of education has there been greater recognition of the importance of professional development. Every proposal to reform, restructure, or transform schools emphasizes professional development as a primary vehicle in efforts to bring about needed change. With this increased recognition, however, has come increased scrutiny.

Questions are being raised about the effectiveness of all forms of professional development. And with these questions have come increased demands for demonstrable results. Legislators, policy makers, funding agencies, and the general public all want to know if professional development programs really make a difference. If they do, what evidence is there to show that they are effective?

To address these questions, professional developers are considering more seriously the issues of program evaluation. They are beginning to gather information more regularly on the outcomes of professional development activities. And this information is no longer limited to surveys of teachers' attitudes and practices. Increasingly, information on crucial measures of student learning is also being considered (Guskey & Sparks, 1991).

But perhaps more importantly, professional developers are looking more seriously at the research on professional development in education. They are examining what is known about the various forms of professional development, not only for teachers but for all those involved in the educational process. They also are considering what is known about various organizational characteristics and structures, especially those that facilitate on-going professional growth.

This chapter will examine what that research says about the effectiveness of professional development. In particular, I will consider the mixed messages reformers are getting from this research and how we might make sense of those messages. I will then turn to a series of guidelines for professional development, drawn principally from the research on individual and organizational change. Finally, I will consider the potential impact of implementing these guidelines.

RESEARCH ON PROFESSIONAL DEVELOPMENT

The research base on professional development in education is extensive. For the most part, however, this research has documented the inadequacies of professional development and, occasionally, proposed solutions (Epstein, Lockard, & Dauber, 1988; Griffin, 1983; Guskey, 1986; Joyce & Showers, 1988; Lieberman & Miller, 1979; Orlich, 1989; Wood & Thompson, 1980, 1993).

Still, reformers attempting to make sense of these various solutions quickly find themselves faced with seemingly incompatible dichotomies. For instance:

• Some researchers suggest that professional development efforts designed to facilitate change must be teacher specific and focus on the day-to-day activities at the classroom level (McLaughlin, 1990; Weatherly & Lipsky, 1977; Wise, 1991). Others indicate that an emphasis on individuals is fundamental to progress, and more systemic or organizational approaches are necessary (Tye & Tye, 1984; Waugh & Punch, 1987).

• Some experts stress that reforms in professional development must be initiated and carried out by individual teachers and school-based personnel (Joyce, McNair, Diaz, & McKibbin, 1976; Lambert, 1988; Lawrence, 1974; Massarella, 1980). Others emphasize that the most successful programs are guided by a clear vision that tran-scends the walls of individual classrooms and schools, since individual teachers and school-based individuals generally lack the opportunity to conceive and implement worthwhile improvements (Barth, 1991; Clune, 1991; Mann, 1986; Wade, 1984).

• Some reviewers argue that the most effective professional development programs are those that approach change in a gradual and incremental fashion, not expecting too much at one time (Doyle & Ponder, 1977; Fullan, 1985; Mann, 1978; Sparks, 1983). Others insist that the broader the scope of a professional development program is, the more effort required of teachers, and the greater the overall change in teaching style attempted, the more likely the program is to elicit the enthusiasm of teachers and to be implemented well (Berman, 1978; McLaughlin & Marsh, 1978).

These and other similar dichotomies in the professional development literature leave reformers feeling confused. Many question how they can be expected to design and implement successful professional development programs when even researchers and experts in the field cannot agree on what should be done. While the critical issues seem clear, solutions remain illusive. As a result, reformers struggle desperately in their attempts to address educators' many and highly diverse professional development needs.

THE SEARCH FOR AN OPTIMAL MIX

A major problem in these efforts to identify elements of successful professional development programs is that they are generally looking for "one right answer." Most begin by gathering evidence from a variety of studies, investigations, and program evaluations. This evidence is then combined and synthesized to identify those characteristics that are consistently associated with some measure of effectiveness. The modern technique many researchers use to conduct such a synthesis is called *meta-analysis* (Hedges & Olkin, 1985).

In most cases, program effectiveness is judged by an index of participants' satisfaction with the program or some indication of change in participants' professional knowledge. Only rarely is change in professional practice considered, and rarer still is the assessment of any impact on student learning (Guskey & Sparks, 1991). The result of such an effort is usually a prescription composed of general practices described in broad and nebulous terms. Unfortunately, such prescriptions offer little guidance to practically minded reformers who want to know precisely what to do and how to do it.

What is neglected in nearly all of these efforts is the powerful impact of *context.* In fact, synthesizing the evidence across studies is done specifically to eliminate the effects of context, or to decontextualize the data. Yet, as Clark, Lotto, and Astuto (1984), Firestone and Corbett (1987), Fullan (1985), Huberman and Miles (1984), and others suggest, the uniqueness of the individual setting will always be a critical factor in education. While there may be some general principles that apply throughout, most will need to be adapted, at least in part, to the unique characteristics of that setting.

Businesses and industries operating in different parts of the country or in different regions around the world may successfully utilize identical processes to produce the same quality product. But reforms based on assumptions of uniformity in the educational system repeatedly fail (Elmore & McLaughlin, 1988). The teaching and learning process is a complex endeavor that is embedded in contexts that are highly diverse. This combination of complexity and diversity makes it difficult, if not impossible, for researchers to come up with universal truths (Guskey, 1993; Huberman, 1983, 1985).

We know with certainty that reforms in education today succeed to the degree that they adapt to and capitalize on this variability. In other words, they must be shaped and integrated in ways that best suit local values, norms, policies, structures, resources, and processes (Griffin & Barnes, 1984; McLauglin, 1990; Talbert, McLaughlin, & Rowan, 1993).

Recognizing the importance of contextual differences brings clarity to the dichotomies described earlier. That is, successful change efforts in some contexts require professional development that focuses on teacher-specific activities (Porter, 1986; Wise, 1991), while other contexts demand a more systemic or organizational approach (Sarason, 1990).

In some contexts, teacher-initiated efforts work best (Weatherley & Lipsky, 1977), while in others a more administratively directed approach may be needed (Mann, 1986). And while some contexts demand that professional development take a gradual approach to change (Sparks, 1983), others require immediate and drastic alterations at all levels of the organization (McLaughlin, 1990).

Acknowledging the powerful influence of context also shows the futility of any search for "one right answer." Rather than one right answer, there will be a collection of answers, each specific to a context. Our search must focus, therefore, on finding the *optimal mix*—that assortment of professional development processes and technologies that will work best in a particular setting.

We also must recognize, however, that the optimal mix in a particular setting changes over time. Contexts, like the people who shape them, are dynamic. They change and adapt in response to a variety of influences. Some of these influences may be self-initiated, while others are environmentally imposed. Because of this dynamic nature, the optimal mix for a particular context evolves over time, changing as various aspects of the context change. What works today may be quite different from what worked five years ago, but also is likely to be different from what will work five years hence.

GUIDELINES FOR SUCCESS

Because of the powerful and dynamic influence of context, it is impossible to make precise statements about the elements of an effective professional development program. Even programs that share a common vision and seek to attain comparable goals may need to follow very different pathways to succeed. The best that can be offered, therefore, are *procedural guidelines* that appear to be critical to the professional development process.

These guidelines are derived from research on professional development specifically and on the change process generally (Crandall et al., 1982; Fullan, 1991; Guskey, 1986; Huberman & Miles, 1984; Prochaska, DiClemente, & Norcross, 1992; McLaughlin, 1990). Rather than representing strict requirements, these guidelines reflect a framework for developing that optimal mix of professional development processes and technologies that will work best in a a specific context at a particular time.

In reviewing these guidelines, it is important to keep in mind that at present we know far more about professional development processes that fail than we do about those that succeed (Gall & Renchler, 1985; Showers, Joyce, & Bennett, 1987). There is no guarantee, therefore, that following these guidelines will result in successful professional development programs. Nevertheless, substantial evidence indicates that neglecting the issues described in these guidelines at best will limit success and, at worst, will result in programs that fail to bring about significant or enduring change.

1. *Recognize that change is both an individual and organizational process.* An important lesson learned from the past is that we cannot improve schools without improving the skills and abilities of the teachers and principals within them. In other words, we must see change as an *individual process* and be willing to invest in the intellectual capital of those individuals who staff our schools (Wise, 1991).

Success in any improvement effort always hinges on the smallest unit of the organization and, in education, that is the classroom (McLaughlin, 1991). Teachers are the ones chiefly responsible for implementing change. Therefore, professional development processes, regardless of their form (Sparks & Loucks-Horsley, 1989), must be not only relevant to teachers, but must directly address their needs and concerns (Hall & Loucks, 1978; Weatherly & Lipsky, 1977.)

Yet to see change as *only* an individual process can limit the effectiveness of professional develop-

ment. Even changes that are empowering bring a certain amount of anxiety. And teachers, like professionals in many fields, are reluctant to adopt new practices or procedures unless they feel sure that they can make them work (Lortie, 1975). To change or to try something new means to risk failure, and that is both highly embarrassing and threatening to one's sense of professional pride (Pejouhy, 1990).

Furthermore, it is important to keep in mind that organizations, like individuals, must change (Sarason, 1982; Shroyer, 1990; Waugh & Punch, 1987). To focus exclusively on individuals in professional development efforts and to neglect factors such as organizational features and system politics severely limit the likelihood of success (Berman, 1978; Clift, Holland, & Veal, 1990; Deal, 1987; Fullan & Pomfret, 1977; Parker, 1980). A debilitating environment can quash any change effort, no matter how much we exhort individuals to persist (Beane, 1991).

To focus on change as *only* an organizational matter, however, is equally ineffective. Fiddling with the organizational structure is a favorite device of educational policy makers and administrators, because it communicates to the public symbolically that they are concerned with the performance of the system. But, as Elmore (1992) argues, evidence is scant that such structural change leads in any reliable way to changes in how teachers teach, what they teach, or how students learn. McLaughlin (1990) describes this as the difference between macro-level concerns and micro-level realities. To facilitate change, we must look beyond policy and consider the embedded structure that most directly affects the actions and choices of the individuals involved.

The key is to find the optimal mix of individual *and* organizational processes that will contribute to success in a particular context. In some situations, individual initiative and motivation might be high, but organizational structures stand in the way of significant improvement. In others, progressive and supportive organizational structures may be in place, but the lack of personal incentives for collaboration and experimentation inhibit any meaningful change in classroom practice. Viewing change as both an individual *and* organizational process that must be adapted to contextual characteristics will help to clarify the steps necessary for success in professional development.

2. *Think big but start small.* There is no easier way to sabotage change efforts than to take on too much at one time. In fact, if there is one truism in the vast research literature on change it is that the magnitude of change that people are asked to make is inversely related to their likelihood of making it (Guskey, 1991). Professionals at all levels generally oppose radical alterations to their present procedures. Hence, the probability of their implementing a new program or innovation depends largely on their judgment of the magnitude of change required for implementation (Doyle & Ponder, 1977; Fullan, 1982; Mann, 1978).

Successful professional development programs are those that approach change in a gradual and incremental fashion. Efforts are made to illustrate how the new practices can be implemented in ways that are not too disruptive or require a great deal of extra work (Sparks, 1983). If a new program does require major changes, it is best to ease into its use rather than expect comprehensive implementation at once (Fullan, 1985).

But while the changes advocated in a professional development program must not be so ambitious that they require too much too soon, they need to be sufficient in scope to challenge professionals and kindle interest (McLaughlin, 1990). Crandall, Eisemann, and Louis (1986) argue that the greatest success is likely when the size of the change is not so massive that typical users find it necessary to adopt a coping strategy that seriously distorts the change, but large enough to require noticeable, sustained effort. Modest, narrowly conceived projects seldom bring about significant improvement. This is what is meant by "think big."

The key again is to find the optimal mix. Professional development efforts should be designed with long-term goals based on a grand vision of what is possible. A program might seek to have *all* students become successful learners, for example. At the same time, that vision should be accompanied by a strategic plan that includes specific incre-

mental goals for three to five years into the future, gradually expanding on what is successful in that context and offering support to those engaged in the change (Fullan, 1992; Louis & Miles, 1990).

3. *Work in teams to maintain support.* The discomfort that accompanies change is greatly compounded if the individuals involved perceive that they have no say in the process or if they feel isolated and detached in their implementation efforts. For this reason it is imperative that all aspects of a professional development program be fashioned to involve teams of individuals working together. This means that planning, implementation, and follow-up activities should be seen as joint efforts, providing opportunities for those with diverse interests and responsibilities to offer their input and advice (Massarella, 1980).

To ensure that the teams function well and garner broad-based support for professional development efforts, it is important that they involve individuals from all levels of the organization. In school improvement programs, for example, the best professional development teams include teachers, non-instructional staff members, and building and central office administrators (Caldwell & Wood, 1988).

In some contexts the involvement of parents and community members also can be helpful (Lezotte, 1989). Although the roles and responsibilities of these individuals in the professional development process will be different, all have valuable insights and expertise to offer.

Still, the notion of teamwork must be balanced. There is evidence to show, for instance, that large-scale participation during the early stages of a change effort is sometimes counterproductive (Huberman & Miles, 1984). Elaborate needs assessments, endless committee and task force meetings, and long and tedious planning sessions often create confusion and alienation in the absence of any action. Extensive planning can also exhaust the energy needed for implementation so that, by the time change is to be enacted, people are burned out (Fullan, 1991).

Furthermore, broad-based participation in many decisions is not always essential or possible on a large scale (Dawson, 1981; Hood & Blackwell, 1980). As Little (1989) argues, there is nothing particularly virtuous about teamwork or collaboration *per se.* It can serve to block change or inhibit progress just as easily as it can serve to enhance the process.

To facilitate change, teamwork must be linked to established norms of continuous improvement and experimentation. In other words, teamwork and collaboration must be balanced with the expectation that all involved in the process—teachers, administrators, and noninstructional staff members—are constantly seeking and assessing potentially better practices (Little, 1989). Such a balance promotes collegial interaction and acknowledges the naturally occurring relationships among professionals.

The most successful professional development programs, for example, are those that provide regular opportunities for participants to share perspectives and seek solutions to common problems in an atmosphere of collegiality and professional respect (Fullan, Bennett, & Rolheiser-Bennett, 1989; Little, 1982). Working in teams also allows tasks and responsibilities to be shared. This not only reduces the workload of individual team members, but it also enhances the quality of the work produced. Additionally, working in teams helps to focus attention on the shared purposes and improvement goals that are the basis of the professional development process in that context (Leithwood & Montgomery, 1982; Rosenholtz, 1987; Stevenson, 1987).

4. *Include procedures for feedback on results.* If the use of new practices is to be sustained and changes are to endure, the individuals involved need to receive regular feedback on the effects of their efforts. It is well known that successful actions are reinforcing and likely to be repeated, while those that are unsuccessful tend to be diminished.

Similarly, practices that are new and unfamiliar will be accepted and retained when they are perceived as increasing one's competence and effectiveness. This is especially true of teachers, whose primary psychic rewards come from feeling certain about their capacity to affect student

growth and development (Bredeson, Fruth, & Kasten, 1983; Guskey, 1989; Huberman, 1992).

New practices are likely to be abandoned, however, in the absence of any evidence of their positive effects. Hence, specific procedures to provide feedback on results are essential to the success of any professional development effort.

Personal feedback on results can be provided in a variety of ways, depending on the context. In professional development programs involving the implementation of mastery learning (Bloom, 1968, 1971), for example, teachers receive this feedback from their students through regular formative assessments (Bloom, Madaus, & Hastings, 1981).

In mastery learning classrooms, formative assessments are used to provide students with detailed feedback on their learning progress and to diagnose learning problems. As such, they can take many forms, including writing samples, skill demonstrations, projects, reports, performance tasks, or other, more objective assessment devices such as quizzes or tests. These assessments are then paired with corrective activities designed to help students to remedy any learning errors identified through the assessment.

But, in addition to the feedback that they offer students, formative assessments also offer teachers specific feedback on the effectiveness of their application of mastery learning. These regular checks on student learning provide teachers with direct evidence of the results of their teaching efforts. They illustrate what improvements have been made and where problems still exist. This information then can be used to guide revisions in the instructional process so that even greater gains are achieved (Guskey, 1985).

Of course, results from assessments of student learning are not the only type of personal feedback that teachers find meaningful. Brophy and Good (1974) discovered that providing feedback to teachers about their differential treatment of students resulted in significant change in their interactions with students.

Information on increased rates of student engagement during class sessions and evidence of improvements in students' sense of confidence or self-worth also have been shown to be powerful in reinforcing the use of new instructional practices (Dolan, 1980; Stallings, 1980). Information from informal assessments of student learning and moment-to-moment responses during instruction can also provide a basis for teachers to judge the effectiveness of alternative techniques (Fiedler, 1975; Green, 1983; Smylie, 1988).

Yet, despite its importance, procedure for gathering feedback on results must be balanced with other concerns. The methods used to obtain feedback, for example, must not be disruptive to instructional procedures. Furthermore, they should not require inordinate amounts of time or extra work from those engaged in the difficult process of implementation.

Timing issues are also critical, for it is unfair to expect too much too soon from those involved in implementation. As Loucks-Horsley et al. (1987) point out, this is analogous to pulling a plant out of the ground each day to check its roots for growth. In other words, the need for feedback must be adapted to the characteristics of the program and the setting. Feedback procedures must focus on outcomes that are meaningful to the professionals involved, but also timed to best suit program needs and the constraints of the context.

5. _Provide continued follow-up, support, and pressure._ Few persons can move from a professional development experience directly into successful implementation. In fact, few will even venture into the uncertainty of implementation unless there is an appreciation of the difficulties and potential problems involved (Fullan & Miles, 1992).

Fitting new practices and techniques to unique on-the-job conditions is an uneven process that requires time and extra effort, especially when beginning (Berman, 1978; Joyce and Showers, 1980). Guidance, direction, and support with pressure are crucial when these adaptations are being made (Baldridge & Deal, 1975; Fullan, 1991; Parker, 1980; Waugh & Punch, 1987).

What makes the early stages of implementation so complicated is that the problems encountered at this time are often multiple, pervasive, and unanticipated. Miles and Louis (1990) point out that developing the capacity to deal with these problems promptly, actively, and in some depth may be "the single biggest determinant of program success" (p. 60). And, regardless of how much advanced planning or preparation takes place, it is when professionals actually implement the new ideas or practices that they have the most specific problems and doubts (Berman, 1978; Fullan & Pomfret, 1977).

Support coupled with pressure at this time is vital for continuation. Support allows those engaged in the difficult process of implementation to tolerate the anxiety of occasional failures. Pressure is often necessary to initiate change among those with little self-impetus for change (Airasian, 1987; Huberman & Crandall, 1983). In addition, it provides the encouragement, motivation, and occasional nudging that many practitioners require to persist in the challenging tasks that are intrinsic to all change efforts.

Of all aspects of professional development, this aspect of support with pressure is perhaps the most neglected. It makes clear that, to be successful, professional development must be seen as a _process,_ not an event (Loucks-Horsley et al., 1987). Learning to be proficient at something new or finding meaning in a new way of doing things is difficult and sometimes painful. Furthermore, any change that holds great promise for increasing individuals' competence or enhancing an organization's effectiveness is likely to be slow and require extra work (Huberman & Miles, 1984). It is imperative, therefore, that improvement be seen as a continuous and ongoing endeavor (McLaughlin & Marsh, 1978).

If a new program or innovation is to be implemented well, it must become a natural part of practitioners' repertoire of professional skills and built into the normal structures and practices of the organization (Fullan & Miles, 1992; Miles & Louis, 1987). For advances to be made and professional improvements to continue, the new practices and techniques that were the focus of the professional development effort must be used automatically. And, for this to occur, continued support and encouragement, paired with subtle pressure to persist, are essential.

This crucial support with pressure can be offered in a variety of ways. McLaughlin and Marsh (1978) recommend that local resource personnel or consultants be available to provide on-line assistance when difficulties arise. They emphasize, however, that the quality of the assistance is critical and that it is better to offer no assistance than poor or inappropriate assistance.

Joyce and Showers (1988) suggest that support for change take the form of coaching—providing practitioners with technical feedback, guiding them in adapting the new practices to their unique contextual conditions, helping them to analyze the effects of their efforts, and urging them to continue despite minor setbacks. In other words, coaching is personal, practical, on-the-job assistance that can be provided by consultants, administrators, directors, or professional colleagues. Simply offering opportunities for practitioners to interact and share ideas with each other also can be valuable (Massarella, 1980; McLaughlin & Marsh, 1978).

Here, again, the notion of balance is critical. In some contexts a substantial amount of pressure from leaders may be necessary to overcome inertia, recalcitrance, or outright resistance (Mann, 1986). It is possible, for example, when making decisions about instructional practices to overemphasize teachers' personal preferences and underemphasize concern about student learning (Buchmann, 1986). Yet, in contexts where there is considerable individual initiative, such pressure may be seen as a strong-armed tactic and unprofessional (Leiter & Cooper, 1978). The key is to find the optimal mix for that context, understanding well the interpersonal dynamics of the individuals involved and the culture of the organization in which they work.

6. *Integrate programs.* More so than any other profession, education seems fraught with innovation. In fact, innovations seem to come and go in education about as regularly as the seasons change. Each year new programs are introduced in schools without any effort to show how they relate to the ones that came before or those that may come afterward. Furthermore, there is seldom any mention of how these various innovations contribute to a growing professional knowledge base. The result is an enormous overload of fragmented, uncoordinated, and ephemeral attempts at change (Fullan & Miles, 1992).

The steady stream of innovations in education causes many practitioners to view all new programs as isolated fads that will soon be gone, only to be replaced by yet another bandwagon (Latham, 1988). This pattern of constant, yet unrelated, short-term innovations not only obscures improvement and provokes cynicism, but it also imposes a sense of affliction. Having seen a multitude of innovations come into and go out of fashion, veteran teachers frequently calm the fears of their less experienced colleagues who express concern about implementing a new program with the advice, "Don't worry; this too shall pass."

If professional development efforts that focus on the implementation of innovations are to succeed, they must include precise descriptions of how these innovations can be integrated. That is, each new innovation must be presented as part of a coherent framework for improvement. It is difficult enough for practitioners to learn the particular features of one innovation, let alone to figure out how it can be combined with others. And, because no single innovation is totally comprehensive, implementing only one will leave many problems unresolved. It is only when several strategies are carefully and systematically integrated that substantial improvements become possible. Doyle (1992), Sarason (1990), and others also emphasize that coordinating programs and combining ideas release great energy in the improvement process.

In recent years, insightful researchers have described how different combinations of innovations can yield impressive results (e.g., Arredondo & Block, 1990; Davidson & O'Leary, 1990; Guskey, 1988, 1990a; Mevarech, 1985; Weber, 1990). In addition, several frameworks for integrating a collection of programs or innovations have been developed that practitioners are finding especially useful.

One example is a framework developed by Marzano, Pickering, and Brandt (1990) based on various dimensions of learning. Another developed by Guskey (1990b) is built around five major components in the teaching and learning process. These frameworks allow skilled practitioners to see more clearly the linkages between various innovations. They also offer guidance to the efforts of seriously minded reformers seeking to pull together programs that collectively address the problems that are most pressing in a particular context.

A crucial point here is that the particular collection of programs or innovations that is best undoubtedly will vary from setting to setting. As a result, the way linkages are established and applications integrated will need to vary as well.

Fullan (1992) stresses that "schools are not in the business of managing single innovations; they are in the business of contending with multiple innovations simultaneously" (p. 19). By recognizing the dimensions of learning that a particular innovation stresses or the components of the teaching and learning process that it emphasizes, savvy educators can pull together innovations that collectively address what is most needed in that context at a particular time.

CONCLUSION

The ideas presented in these procedural guidelines are not really new and certainly cannot be considered revolutionary. They may, in fact, appear obvious to those with extensive experience in the professional development process. Yet, as self-evident as they may seem, it is rare to find a professional development program today that is designed and implemented with thorough attention to these guidelines or the factors that underlie them. It is rarer still to find professional development programs that evaluate the implementation of these guidelines in terms of their effects on student learning.

What is evident from these guidelines is that the key to greater success in professional development, which translates to improvements in student learning, rests not so much in the discovery of new knowledge, but in our capacity to deliberately and wisely use the knowledge that we have. This is true

regardless of whether professional development is viewed as an integral part of one's career cycle, as a self-directed journey to find meaning and appreciation in one's work, or as a structured effort to keep professionals abreast of advances in their field. To develop this capacity requires a clear vision of the process by which those goals can be attained.

In the minds of many today, there is a clear vision of what would be ideal in professional development. That ideal sees educators at all levels constantly in search of new and better ways to address the diverse learning needs of their students. It sees schools as learning communities in which teachers and students are continually engaged in inquiry and stimulating discourse. It sees practitioners in education respected for their professional knowledge and pedagogic skill.

The exact process by which that vision can be accomplished, however, is blurred and confused. The reason, as we have argued here, is that the process is so highly contextualized. There is no "one right answer" or "one best way." Rather, there are a multitude of ways, all adapted to the complex and dynamic characteristics of specific contexts. Success, therefore, rests in finding the optimal mix of process elements and technologies that can then be carefully, sensibly, and thoughtfully applied in a particular setting.

While it is true that the ideas presented here offer an optimistic perspective on the potential of professional development in education, these ideas are not far-fetched. They illustrate that, although the process of change is difficult and complex, we are beginning to understand how to facilitate that process through pragmatic adaptations to specific contexts so that ongoing professional growth and improved professional practice are ensured. Doing so is essential to the improved learning of all students.

ENDNOTE

This chapter is adapted from a chapter in T. R. Guskey and M. Huberman (Eds.), *New Paradigms and Practices in Professional Development,* soon to be published by Teachers College Press. Copyright T. Guskey.

REFERENCES

Airasian, P. W. (1987). State mandated testing and educational reform: Context and consequences. *American Journal of Education, 95,* 393–412.

Arredondo, D. E., & Block, J. H. (1990). Recognizing the connections between thinking skills and mastery learning. *Educational Leadership, 47*(5), 4–10.

Baldridge, J. V., & Deal, T. (1975). *Managing change in educational organizations.* Berkeley, CA: McCutchan.

Barth, R. S. (1991). Restructuring schools: Some questions for teachers and principals. *Phi Delta Kappan, 73*(2), 123–128.

Beane, J. A. (1991). Sorting out the self-esteem controversy. *Educational Leadership, 49*(1), 25–30.

Berman, P. (1978). The study of macro- and micro-implementation. *Public Policy, 26*(2), 157–184. In P. Berman & M.W. McLaughlin (Eds.), *Federal programs supporting educational change. Vol. VIII: Implementing and sustaining innovations.* Santa Monica, CA: Rand Corporation.

Bloom, B. S. (1968). Learning for mastery. *Evaluation Comment, 1*(2), 1–12.

Bloom, B. S. (1971). Mastery learning. In J. H. Block (Ed.), *Mastery learning: Theory and practice.* New York: Holt, Rinehart & Winston.

Bloom, B. S., Madaus, G. F., & Hastings, J. T. (1981). *Evaluation to improve learning.* New York: McGraw-Hill.

Bredeson, P. V., Fruth, M. J., & Kasten, K. L. (1983). Organizational incentives and secondary school teaching. *Journal of Research and Development in Education, 16,* 24–42.

Brophy, J. E., & Good, T. L. (1974). *Teacher–student relationships: Causes and consequences.* New York: Holt, Rinehart & Winston.

Buchmann, M. (1986). Role over person: Morality and authenticity in teaching. *Teachers College Record, 87,* 529–543.

Caldwell, S., & Wood, F. (1988). School-based improvement—Are we ready? *Educational Leadership, 46*(2), 50–53.

Clark, D., Lotto, S., & Astuto, T. (1984). Effective schools and school improvement: A comparative analysis of two lines of inquiry. *Educational Administration Quarterly, 20*(3), 41–68.

Clift, R. T., Holland, P. E., & Veal, M. L. (1990). School context dimensions that affect staff development. *Journal of Staff Development, 11*(1), 34–38.

Clune, W. H. (1991). *Systemic educational policy.* Madison, WI: Wisconsin Center for Educational Policy, University of Wisconsin-Madison.

Crandall, D., Eiseman, J., & Louis, K. (1986). Strategic planning issues that bear on the success of school improvement efforts. *Educational Administration Quarterly, 22*(3), 21–53.

Crandall, D. P., Loucks-Horsley, S., Bauchner, J. E., Schmidt, W. B., Eiseman, J. W., Cox, P. L., Miles, M. B., Huberman, A. M., Taylor, B. L., Goldberg, J. A., Shive, G., Thompson, C. L., & Taylor, J. A. (1982). *People, policies, and practices: Examining the chain of school improvement.* Andover, MA: The NETWORK, Inc.

Davidson, N., & O'Leary, P. W. (1990). How cooperative learning can enhance mastery teaching. *Educational Leadership, 47*(5), 30–34.

Dawson, J. (1981). *Teacher participation in educational innovation: Some insights into its nature.* Philadelphia, PA: Research for Better Schools.

Deal, T. (1987). The culture of schools. In L. Sheive & M. Schoeheit (Eds.), *Leadership: Examining the elusive* (pp. 3–15). Alexandria, VA: Association for Supervision and Curriculum Development.

Dolan, L. J. (1980). *The affective correlates of home support, instructional quality, and achievement.* Unpublished doctoral dissertation, University of Chicago.

Doyle, D. P. (1992). The challenge, the opportunity. *Phi Delta Kappan, 73*(7), 512–520.

Doyle, W., & Ponder, G. (1977). The practical ethic and teacher decision-making. *Interchange, 8*(3), 1–12.

Elmore, R. F. (1992). Why restructuring alone won't improve teaching. *Educational Leadership, 49*(7), 44–48.

Elmore, R. F., & McLaughlin, M. W. (1988). *Steady work: Policy, practice, and reform in American education* (R-3574-NIE/RC). Santa Monica, CA: Rand Corporation.

Epstein, J. L., Lockard, B. L., & Dauber, S. L. (1988). *Staff development policies needed in the middle grades.* Paper presented at the annual meeting of the American Educational Research Association, New Orleans, LA.

Fiedler, M. (1975). Bidirectionality of influence in classroom interaction. *Journal of Educational Psychology, 67,* 735–744.

Firestone, W., & Corbett, H. D. (1987). Planned organizational change. In N. Boyand (Ed.), *Handbook of research on educational administration* (pp. 321–340). New York: Longman.

Fullan, M. G. (1982). *The meaning of educational change.* New York: Teachers College Press.

Fullan, M. G. (1985). Change processes and strategies at the local level. *Elementary School Journal, 85,* 391–421.

Fullan, M. G. (1991). *The new meaning of educational change.* New York: Teachers College Press.

Fullan, M. G. (1992). Visions that blind. *Educational Leadership, 49*(5), 19–20.

Fullan, M. G., & Miles, M. B. (1992). Getting reform right: What works and what doesn't. *Phi Delta Kappan, 73*(10), 745–752.

Fullan, M. G., Bennett, B., & Rolheiser-Bennett, C. (1989). *Linking classroom and school improvement.* Paper presented at the annual meeting of the American Educational Research Association, San Francisco, CA.

Fullan, M., & Pomfret, A. (1977). Research on curriculum and instruction implementation. *Review of Educational Research, 27*(2), 355–397.

Gall, M. D., & Renchler, R. S. (1985). *Effective staff development for teachers: A research-based model.* Eugene, OR: ERIC Clearinghouse on Educational Management, University of Oregon.

Green, J. (1983). Research on teaching as a linguistic process: A state of the art. In E. Gordon (Ed.), *Review of research in education* (Vol.10, pp. 151–252.). Washington, DC: American Educational Research Association.

Griffin, G. A. (Ed.) (1983). *Staff development. Eighty-second yearbook of the National Society for the Study of Education.* Chicago: University of Chicago Press.

Griffin, G. A., & Barnes, S. (1984). School change: A craft-derived and research-based strategy. *Teachers College Record, 86,* 103–123.

Guskey, T. R. (1985). *Implementing mastery learning.* Belmont, CA: Wadsworth.

Guskey, T. R. (1986). Staff development and the process of teacher change. *Educational Researcher, 15*(5), 5–12.

Guskey, T. R. (1988). Mastery learning and mastery teaching: How they complement each other. *Principal, 68*(1), 6–8.

Guskey, T. R. (1989). Attitude and perceptual change in teachers. *International Journal of Educational Research, 13*(4), 439–453.

Guskey, T. R. (1990a). Cooperative mastery learning strategies. *Elementary School Journal, 91*(1), 33–42.

Guskey, T. R. (1990b). Integrating innovations. *Educational Leadership, 47*(5), 11–15.

Guskey, T. R. (1991). Enhancing the effectiveness of professional development programs. *Journal of Educational and Psychological Consultation, 2*(3), 239–247.

Guskey, T. R. (1993, February). Why pay attention to research if researchers can't agree? *The Developer,* pp. 3–4.

Guskey, T. R., & Sparks, D. (1991). What to consider when evaluating staff development. *Educational Leadership, 49*(3), 73–76.

Hall, G. E., & Loucks, S. (1978). Teachers' concerns as a basis for facilitating and personalizing staff development. *Teachers College Record, 80,* 36–53.

Hedges, L. V., & Olkin, I. (1985). *Statistical methods for meta-analysis.* Orlando, FL: Academic Press.

Hood, P., & Blackwell, L. (1980). *The role of teachers and other school practitioners in decision-making and innovations.* San Francisco: Far West Laboratory.

Huberman, M. (1983). Recipes for busy teachers. *Knowledge: Creation, Diffusion, Utilization, 4,* 478–510.

Huberman, M. (1985). What knowledge is of most worth to teachers? A knowledge-use perspective. *Teaching and Teacher Education, 1,* 251–262.

Huberman, M. (1992). Teacher development and instructional mastery. In A. Hargreaves & M. G. Fullan (Eds.), *Understand teacher development* (pp. 122–142). New York: Teachers College Press.

Huberman, M., & Crandall, D. (1983). *People, policies and practice: Examining the chain of school improvement, Vol. 9. Implications for action: A Study of dissemination efforts supporting school improvement.* Andover, MA: The Network.

Huberman, M., & Miles, M. B. (1984). *Innovation up close: How school improvement works.* New York: Plenum.

Joyce, B., & Showers, B. (1980). Improving inservice training: The messages of research. *Educational Leadership, 37*(5), 379–385.

Joyce, B., & Showers, B. (1988). *Student achievement through staff development.* New York: Longman.

Joyce, B., McNair, K. M., Diaz, R., & McKibbin, M. D. (1976). *Interviews: Perceptions of professionals and policy makers.* Stanford, CA: Stanford Center for Research and Development in Teaching, Stanford University.

Lambert, L. (1988). Staff development redesigned. *Educational Leadership, 45*(8), 665–668.

Latham, G. (1988). The birth and death cycles of educational innovations. *Principal, 68*(1), 41–43.

Lawrence, G. (1974). *Patterns of effective inservice education: A state of the art summary of research on materials and procedures for changing teacher behavior in inservice education.* Tallahassee, FL: Florida State Department of Education.

Leiter, M., & Cooper, M. (1978). How teacher unionists view inservice education. *Teachers College Record, 80,* 107–125.

Leithwood, K., & Montgomery, D. (1982). The role of the elementary school principal in program improvement. *Review of Educational Research, 52,* 309–339.

Lezotte, L. W. (1989). The open book. *Focus in Change, 1*(2), 3.

Lieberman, A., & Miller, L. (1979). *Staff development: New demands, new realities, new perspectives.* New York: Teachers College Press.

Little, J. W. (1982). Norms of collegiality and experimentation: Workplace conditions of school success. *American Educational Research Journal, 19,* 325–340.

Little, J. W. (1989). *The persistence of privacy: Autonomy and initiative in teachers' professional relations.* Paper presented at the annual meeting of the American Educational Research Association, San Francisco.

Lortie, D. C. (1975). *Schoolteacher: A sociological study.* Chicago: University of Chicago Press.

Loucks-Horsely, S., Harding, C. K., Arbuckle, M. A., Murray, L. B., Dubea, C., & Williams, M. K. (1987). *Continuing to learn: A guidebook for teacher development.* Andover, MA: Regional Laboratory for Educational Improvement of the Northeast & Islands.

Louis, K. S., & Miles, M. B. (1990). *Improving the urban high school: What works and why.* New York: Teachers College Press.

Mann, D. (1978). The politics of training teachers in schools. In D. Mann (Ed.), *Making change happen* (pp. 3–18). New York: Teachers College Press.

Mann, D. (1986). Authority and school improvement: An essay on "Little King" leadership. *Teachers College Record, 88*(1), 41–52.

Marzano, R. J., Pickering, D. J., & Brandt, R. S. (1990). Integrating instructional programs through dimensions of learning. *Educational Leadership, 47*(5), 17–24.

Massarella, J. A. (1980). Synthesis of research on staff development. *Educational Leadership, 38*(2), 182–185.

McLaughlin, M. W. (1990). The Rand change agent study revisited: Macro perspectives and micro realities. *Educational Researcher, 19*(9), 11–16.

McLaughlin, M. W. (1991). Test-based accountability as a reform strategy. *Phi Delta Kappan, 73*(3), 248–251.

McLaughlin, M. W., & Marsh, D. D. (1978). Staff development and school change. *Teachers College Record, 80*(1), 70–94.

Mevarech, Z. R. (1985). The effects of cooperative mastery learning strategies on mathematics achievement. *Journal of Educational Research, 78,* 372–377.

Miles, M. B., & Louis, K. S. (1987). Research on institutionalization: A reflective review (pp. 24–44). In M. B. Miles, M. Ekholm, & R. Vandenberghe (Eds.), *Lasting school improvement: Exploring the process of institutionalization.* Leuven, Belgium: Acco.

Miles, M. B., & Louis, K. S. (1990). Mustering the will and skill for change. *Educational Leadership, 47*(8), 57–61.

Orlich, D. C. (1989). *Staff development: Enhancing human potential.* Boston: Allyn & Bacon.

Parker, C. A. (1980). The literature on planned organizational change: A review and analysis. *Higher Education, 9,* 429–442.

Pejouhy, N. H. (1990). Teaching math for the 21st century. *Phi Delta Kappan, 72*(1), 76–78.

Porter, A. C. (1986). From research on teaching to staff development: A difficult step. *Elementary School Journal, 87,* 159–164.

Prochaska, J. O., DiClemente, C. C., & Norcross, J. C. (1992). In search of how people change. *American Psychologist, 47,* 1102–1114.

Rosenholtz, S. (1987). Education reform strategies: Will they increase teacher commitment? *American Journal of Education, 95,* 534–562.

Sarason, S. (1982). *The culture of school and the problem of change.* Boston: Allyn & Bacon.

Sarason, S. (1990). *The predictable failure of educational reform.* San Francisco: Jossey-Bass.

Showers, B., Joyce, B., & Bennett, B. (1987). Synthesis of research on staff development: A framework for future study and a state-of-the-art analysis. *Education Leadership, 45*(3), 77–87.

Shroyer, M. G. (1990). Effective staff development for effective organizational development. *Journal of Staff Development, 11*(1), 2–6.

Smylie, M. A. (1988). The enhancement function of staff development: Organizational and psychological antecedents to individual teacher change. *American Educational Research Journal, 25*(1), 1–30.

Sparks, D., & Loucks-Horsley, S. (1989). Five models of staff development for teachers. *Journal of Staff Development, 10*(4), 40–57.

Sparks, G. M. (1983). Synthesis of research on staff development for effective teaching. *Educational Leadership, 41*(3), 65–72.

Stallings, J. (1980). Allocated academic learning time revisited, or beyond time on task. *Educational Researcher, 9*(11), 11–16.

Stevenson, R. B. (1987). Staff development for effective secondary schools: A synthesis of research. *Teaching and Teacher Education, 3*(2), 233–248.

Talbert, J. E., McLaughlin, M. W., & Rowan, B. (1993). Understanding context effects on secondary school teaching. *Teachers College Record, 95*(1), 45–68.

Tye, K. A., & Tye, B. B. (1984). Teacher isolation and school reform. *Phi Delta Kappan, 65*(5), 319–322.

Wade, R. K. (1984). What makes a difference in inservice teacher education? A meta-analysis of research. *Educational Leadership, 42*(4), 48–54.

Waugh, R. F., & Punch, K. F. (1987). Teacher receptivity to systemwide change in the implementation stage. *Review of Educational Research, 57*(3), 237–254.

Weatherley, R., & Lipsky, M. (1977). Street-level bureaucrats and institutional innovation: Implementing special education reform. *Harvard Educational Review, 47*(2), 171–197.

Weber, A. (1990). Linking ITIP and the writing process. *Educational Leadership, 47*(5), 35–39.

Wise, A. E. (1991). On teacher accountability. In *Voices from the field* (pp. 23–24). Washington, DC: William T. Grant Foundation Commission on Work, Family and Citizenship *and* Institute for Educational Leadership.

Wood, F. H., & Thompson, S. R. (1980). Guidelines for better staff development. *Educational Leadership, 37,* 374–378.

Wood, F. H., & Thompson, S. R. (1993). Assumptions about staff development based on research and best practice. *Journal of Staff Development, 14*(4), 52–57.

DISCUSSION QUESTIONS

1. Why is successful professional program development essential to educational reform?

2. What is the relationship between professional development and student outcomes?

3. Based on the research on professional development, how should such programs be redesigned?

4. In what ways is context critical to the impact of a professional development program?

5. Why is change considered both an individual and organizational process?

6. Why is feedback essential to professional development?

7. What can be done to ensure that the implementation of an innovation is successful?

30

Reconceiving the Principal's Role
for More Turbulent Times

LINDA S. BEHAR-HORENSTEIN
ELLEN S. AMATEA

FOCUSING QUESTIONS

1. *What factors in society are influencing the nature of work that principals do?*
2. *What are the implications of systemic transformation within the change process?*
3. *How have politics and special-interest groups influenced the behavior of school leaders?*
4. *What type of change will be needed in the organizational context of schools to facilitate the development of collaborative relationships with students and families?*
5. *How might principals' leadership behavior be influenced by developing an outside-in philosophy?*

As we move into the 21st century, there is an emergent need to view the student as client or customer, rather than product. Previously, school organizations and leadership emphasized a "one size fits all" approach to delivering instruction and managing student behavior. Recognizing the diversity of school age populations has resulted in a restructuring of the roles and work that school faculty and administrators are being asked to perform. What impact will adopting this perspective have on current forms of school leadership and staff organization? How will our beliefs about the ways in which staff communicate and make decisions need to change? How can the school organizational structures and current thought about models of leadership be adapted to foster greater staff flexibility and shared ownership in the decision-making processes that affect student outcomes?

Today's school administrators practice leadership in environments characterized by unparalleled complexity and change indigenous to a rapidly changing society.[1] The nature of these influences is notable in several arenas. In the supervisory domain, administrators have been expected to provide the appropriate support to staff who deal with an increasingly diverse student body. In the realm of educational goals and methods, they must select among an array of competing technologies and innovations and determine which are best suited to a pluralistic context. In the areas of social responsibility and politics, they must consider the voices of multiple stakeholders who hold variable standards on the correct or proper focus of and approach to education. Today's administrators must also contend with a rapidly changing sociopolitical context in which competitors jockey for limited financial resources. These conditions have prompted a reexamination of the current mind-sets governing how schools should operate and how administrators should function. This reexamination is, in turn, leading to the identification of new paradigms and competencies that might be used to foster successful adaptation to the demands of this turbulent environment.

In the past, school leaders were guided by the top-down managerial approaches undergirding the science of administration. They could comfortably provide a quality of leadership that tendered mechanistic solutions. However, social turbulence has disturbed the equilibrium that once coincided with the influence of a single paradigm. External pressures brought to bear by a more vocal public and a growing politicization inside the school have resulted in a reconsideration of past practices and a re-visioning of leadership behavior.[2] The notion of a quick fix of the school's social system will no longer suffice. Instead, the practice of administration must be directed toward change that provides for *systemic transformation*[3] guided by a self-organizing systems organizational model.[4]

We use the term *systemic transformation* to refer to the process of making critical changes to the cultural, structural, contextual, political, and organizational patterns within schools. The overarching framework implied by this process requires that school administrators develop the competencies needed to (1) formulate successful change, (2) identify directions and pathways to guide change, (3) catalyze staff's efforts into concerted actions, and (4) apply a flexible mind-set in which to consider issues and behaviors relevant to substantive change efforts. School administrators will need to communicate an actionable vision for restructuring the various elements of schools.

For example, if an administrator plans to detrack the school's curriculum, he or she must have a clear sense of how the curriculum will be reorganized to permit the formation of heterogeneous student groups. The school leader will need to identify alternative methods for reorganizing traditional curriculum and instructional practices as exemplified by a move from compartmentalized teaching to interdisciplinary instructional approaches. He or

she will need to guide the staff members' talents, collective synergy, and expression of ideas toward productive action. Finally, the administrator will need to be flexible about the emergence of contextually based processes. This type of leadership will encourage staff participation and a sense of volition, while creating interstices that permit professional growth.

In this chapter, the authors provide an overview of the complex and turbulent conditions that are challenging traditional assumptions of school administrative practice and examine why the original paradigm on which these practices were based is becoming obsolete. The authors then explore emerging ideas on how schools and administrators might operate and identify the alternative mind-set (i.e., paradigm) and competencies required. Finally, the authors discuss the implications of this alternative paradigm for the professional preparation of school administrators.

CONDITIONS FACING TODAY'S SCHOOL ADMINISTRATORS

There is a growing sense among school administrators that the business of operating and managing a school is growing more and more complex.[5] The facets of school life over which principals have operational authority have increased significantly during the past several decades. Not only are principals concerned with instructional effectiveness, student achievement, budgets, and schedules; they are often called on to coordinate an array of special social services for students and their families. In addition, there has been a significant increase in the number of outside stakeholders that administrators must consider. The context of operating schools and the design and delivery of educational services have become more complicated as a result of special-interest groups' influence (e.g., racial desegregation of the schools, increased access rights of women, rights of emotionally and physically handicapped students, and greater political involvement of religious fundamentalist groups). Moreover, there has been a growing demand for the diversification of instructional strategies and classroom management methods to meet the needs of the increased diversity of student "customer markets" that schools are expected to serve.[6] As more at-risk students requiring significantly different learning and management approaches enter school, the assumption that "one size fits all," under which many educators were originally trained, has been seriously challenged. Finally, numerous educational reforms legislated in the past decade have increased the level of regulatory pressures and the range of monitoring responsibilities that principals must shoulder.

This increase in the number of factors to consider in operating a school coincides with increased turbulence taking place in the broader external sociopolitical environment in which schools operate. Contributing to the change in these factors is the rapid turnover of ideas as to "best practices" for meeting instructional or behavioral goals. For example, as various therapeutic and educational specialties have expanded, a wider array of options has been advocated. Experts compete with each other in advocating "favorite solutions" to educational and social problems. This practice, also known as the "jumping on the bandwagon," is exemplified by the implementation of sweeping educational movements such as outcomes-based assessment before conclusive research findings have become available.

A second factor contributing to the increased rate of change is the growing politicization and organization of outside interest groups.[7] Today's special-interest groups are politically more active and appear to trust educators, policymakers, and government leaders less. Groups such as the religious right have demanded that their interests be represented in the school. Renewed attempts by legislators to mandate prayer in schools and limit the extent of sex education in the curriculum are priority goals for the religious right. By the same token, many of these parties no longer assume that professional educators know what is best for their children or can best represent their children's interests. Finally, another catalyst for change exists in the political, structural, and organizational framework of schools. Varied initiatives focused on restructuring the roles and relationships of school staff, both within the school and between the school and the

broader sociopolitical environment, are influencing the politics of school life.[8] Discussions regarding how technology should be used in the schools and the role of the arts in the curriculum are representative issues influencing the organization of schools. Debates about the most appropriate models of leadership for today's schools are influencing discussions about the structure of school leadership.

TRADITIONAL ASSUMPTIONS UNDERLYING THE ORGANIZATIONAL LIFE AND ADMINISTRATIVE PRACTICE WITHIN SCHOOLS

How are schools and school administrators responding to these changing conditions? The traditional paradigm in which most educational administrators and other school professionals have been trained is a mechanistic one modeled after the successfully managed high-volume, large-scale business enterprise that operated during the first half of this century. According to the social engineers and educators of this era, the problems involved in managing the delivery of educational services to students and across schools were just one level removed from those of mobilizing and coordinating productive units within a single firm. Viewing these as viable principles for effectively organizing school life, educators emulated them to coordinate the delivery of educational services on a massive scale. What were the principles of management that shaped educators' goals and public expectations about how schools were to be organized during the first half of the century? According to Reich,

> Scientific management rested upon three principles: specialization of work through simplification of individual tasks; predetermined rules to coordinate the tasks; and detailed monitoring of performance.... Job tasks were to be monitored through various data-gathering efforts—such as budget controls, task reports, and cost accounting....[9]

Social analysts maintained that one of the most immediate outcomes of this organizational model was that it separated the thinkers from the doers.[10] Those who planned the production also took responsibility for setting the rules and controls for production. However, these people were not the work force that produced or delivered those services.

Several consequences resulted from this organizational structure. First, it became next to impossible for individual workers at the "line" level to see the "bigger picture" of how their work interrelated with that of others in the organization. It was assumed that individuals needed to know only how to perform assigned tasks. Understanding the larger context of interrelated tasks was considered irrelevant. Second, the employees' responsibility and authority for production became indirect rather than direct. Authority rested in the codified rules and structure of the larger organization. Third, people began to assume that the individual worker did not have the ability to identify when or where the production process might be breaking down. Instead, the responsibility for anticipating errors or breakdowns rested exclusively at the top with the thinkers who established and designed the organization (and the methods for monitoring production), rather than at the bottom of the organization with the doers.

The power to make decisions in organizations operating from this traditional paradigm was based in a hierarchy of fixed roles, with decision making based on authority and tradition. Directions and commands were passed down the hierarchy from those at the top to those at the lower levels. As Reich asserts, "Specialization and simplification forced the development of management hierarchies, arranged like a pyramid. Each level up the hierarchy is responsible for a progressively larger part of the operations."[11] As might be inferred, in such organizations the values of stability, loyalty, and consistency of methods are highly prized, while independence, individuality, and diversity of response are discouraged.

The leadership styles of administrators guided by this traditional paradigm of organizational life emphasize mechanistic styles of thought and action. School administrators are viewed as mid-level managers who "oversee operations." Their responses range from maintaining order and conformity to the hierarchical structure of the institution to reinforcing procedures that ensure the integrity of existing power bases and roles.

Administrative functioning within this paradigm focuses on fixing problems and responding to the immediacy of an issue or crisis within the school. For example, in matters of student discipline, the principal's energies are usually dedicated to dealing with students as if they are objects. In dealing with issues related to teacher concerns, the focus centers on the immediate context of the situation, that of understanding the problem and delivering an effective and efficient response. Principals are not expected to analyze school-based situations beyond their surface manifestations. Rarely have alternative influences and reflection on the "bigger patterns" that might be driving a situation been given a primary emphasis.

By and large the mission of schools and the hierarchy of institutions maintains an affiliation with a mainstream curriculum philosophy that advocates the utilitarian and essentialist functions of schooling. The school administrator and staff usually direct their attention to dealing with the internal operation of the school and the people in it. Thus children are the exclusive focus ("in loco parentis") of one's attention to the exclusion of family members or other outside resources—despite ample evidence that school staff cannot do the job of educating a community's children alone.

One might think that this could not possibly be the organizational model on which our American educational system was based. After all, teachers have been considered professionals, thinkers no less. However, in many ways, teachers might be considered the mid-level staff in a school, and their students the "line." Metaphorically speaking, it is the students who have been considered the products of learning. However, to avert too individualized a view of the production process, consider how teachers are coordinated and controlled by a higher-level manager, the school principal, who in turn is monitored by an even higher authority level. Judging the value of the principal's leadership behavior is often reduced to measures of school achievement, such as test scores, graduation, or dropout rates.

EMERGING IDEAS ABOUT THE ORGANIZATIONAL LIFE AND ADMINISTRATIVE PRACTICE WITHIN SCHOOLS

Over the past seventy years, the traditional organizational paradigm undergirding the design of our nation's schools has resulted in some stunning accomplishments. Using a large-scale, high-volume production model of organizational life, we have been able to cover the high fixed costs of developing the specialized facilities and assembling the sizable professional staffs that our system of public schooling has required. These actions have resulted in the development of a stable and accessible educational system that has not a single peer in the Western world. Almost all our populace has had the opportunity to receive "free" educational services. The volume of individuals who successfully complete postsecondary education also speaks to the accessibility and stability of our educational system. Such advanced levels of education coupled with expanding job opportunities have resulted in developing a highly educated middle class who expect a certain standard of living and a substantial political voice.

However, the very stability of the current system of schooling that has resulted in these accomplishments now makes it difficult for American educators to respond to the complexity and change of the current era. Buffeted by diverse constituencies, each with its own agenda for education, the era in which one standardized, high-volume version of education would suit all students has become obsolete. It has given way to an era in which members of diverse communities are demanding that educational experiences be custom tailored to honor the distinctive values and beliefs of their constituencies. The call for responsive instruction is depicted by efforts to modernize teaching methods and technology and to individualize rather than standardize methods of instruction and evaluation.

Schools need an organizational structure that can adapt to changing mores and beliefs and diverse student needs. Changes in educational delivery and design require a much closer coordination of students and their families working in tandem with education professionals. Highly skilled and knowledgeable education professionals who are comfortable in their ability to interact with clientele, who can assess new situations, and who can tailor instruction to particular learning environments are needed. Such paradigmatic shifts necessitate that the organizational structure of schools be able to respond quickly to the changing markets and technologies. School leaders will need to anticipate and modify procedures quickly, rather than develop a reliable routine applicable to every student or situation.

Many educators believe that this new organizational paradigm will be more responsive to the complexity of demands of a more diverse student population, multiple stakeholders, and a rapidly changing technological and sociopolitical context. The politics and dynamics within school cultures are likely to undergo dramatic shifts. For example, school staff will need to respond to changes in their environment yet also maintain a stable and coherent identity, purpose, and vision for themselves. Within this framework, the staff will assume greater initiative and responsibility for the organization and its management by effectively "reading" the environment to anticipate trends in student and community needs. As a result, they will be expected to identify and implement pivotal changes in instructional methods, daily procedures, and services.

To encourage such flexibility and inventiveness requires a broadened ownership of the leadership process such that the local school staff is encouraged by the administrator to bring forth ideas and have a voice in influencing the direction that the school actually takes. This entails a different organizational structure, in which management and control are based on shared authority and "voluntary followership"[12] rather than administrative mandate. Because school professionals (e.g., administrators, teachers, counselors, reading specialists, curriculum specialists) have typically received standardized instructions about the maintenance of school routines and have traditionally performed domain-specific functions independently of one another, implementing this new paradigm would require that school professionals learn how to operate as members of integrated teams.

Rather than operating in isolation with little or no coordination of service delivery, the process of *systemic transformation* would require that school professionals recognize that they need to cooperate with each other and with outside stakeholders (such as students' families and community members) to respond effectively to changing needs. Staff would need to see the interdependencies in their tasks and to take the initiative in collective planning, decision making, and problem solving. The traditional top-down approach to decision making would need to be replaced by a new way of doing business. Individual perspectives and skills of staff would be integrated into group expression so that the collective capacity of the staff became something more than just the simple sum of its members' skills. As staff members became familiar that with each other's complementing talents, a synergy could develop that permitted the development of a stronger identification with and allegiance to the educational enterprise and the community of learners and families that the staff members serve.

This new paradigm for school organizations might be patterned after the innovative "self-organizing systems" organizational models now being developed in the business world. In response to increased turbulence, business leaders are moving beyond the bureaucratically structured large-scale organizations of the current century in search of more "self-organizing" models of production and management. As Morgan writes,

> Change demands innovation, and innovation demands that we unleash the creative potential in our people.... The need to remain open and flexible demands creative responses from every quarter, and many leading organizations recognize that human intelligence and the ability to unleash and direct that intelligence are critical resources.... Future managers will thus need to pay more attention to attracting the right people to their organization, de-

veloping human potential and fostering conditions that make this relevant and effective, and positioning and repositioning people so that they always contribute where they are most needed.[13]

What new types of competencies will school administrators need to implement this new "self-organizing system" model of school organization? A number of competencies identified for persons in leadership roles in the business world may have applicability for those in positions of leadership in schools. One competency mentioned by a number of different business leaders[14] is the leaders' ability to "look ahead" and see the "big picture," while noticing the relationships between certain events and their consequences in context-based situations. Although length of experience is regarded as pivotal to one's ability to see these interrelationships, "experience can only contribute to expertise if practitioners learn from it."[15] To develop the ability to see the underlying patterns linking certain events together, school administrators will need practice in seeing the connections between certain events and the beliefs and practices. Developing this type of perception will require the leader to rise above the immediate details, step back, and see the big picture in context.[16]

A second useful competency of successful leaders is the ability to "read" and anticipate environmental and social change. They will need to reframe problem areas "so that negatives become potential positives, opening up new areas for development in the organization."[17] Coupled with this proactive approach to problems as change opportunities, today's successful school leaders are shifting from managing from the *inside out* to leading from the *outside in*. This requires that the leader maintain close contact with the organization's changing environment to enhance its capacity to respond to challenges and opportunities. This outside-in philosophy contrasts with the inside-out philosophy implicit in the traditional organizational paradigm, in which managers relate to the environment in terms of what they and their colleagues want to do, rather than what is necessary to meet the challenge of social change and the demands of external stakeholders.

One current illustration of the shift in practice to an outside-in philosophy is depicted in the systematic attempts made by a number of school staffs to assess the needs of students' families more routinely. Practitioners are now giving greater attention to (1) responding to family and school needs, identifying what teachers, parents, and students perceive they need, and figuring out ways to address their concerns; (2) resolving conflicts between the needs of these different stakeholders; and (3) learning how to work collaboratively with families to foster students' academic growth.[18] Acknowledging the need to involve families in their children's schooling represents educators' ongoing effort to assess the school's strengths and weaknesses through the eyes of key stakeholders and to read the early warning signs of the transformations that may be required in one's organization.

Another key set of competencies centers on the leadership style and processes of the successful manager. According to Morgan,

> Managers of the future will have to view leadership as a "framing" or "bridging" process that can energize and focus the efforts of their employees in ways that resonate with the challenges and demands posed by the wider environment. This process requires many competencies, especially those that enable the leader to create or find the vision, shared understanding or sense of identity that can unite people in pursuit of relevant challenges; and to find means of communicating that vision in a way that makes it actionable.[19]

In the public schools, leadership has been based primarily on hierarchical management. Such approaches have led to the creation of rigid systems that depend on rules and procedures and encourage smoldering fires that require constant cure and aid.[20] However, hierarchical management does not encourage the analysis of or a focus on the underlying organizational problems. The shared leadership model, in contrast, requires orchestrating a process whereby the competing points of view of the staff coalesce into a cohesive vision.[21] The school leader would model this behavior by embracing a holistic view of the school environment and shaping the internal structures and processes while keeping the bigger picture in mind.

Finally, understanding how to manage the stress of change is an integral competency for today's school administrator. The future will continue to present many challenges to today's school leaders that will require an understanding of role transition and role strain. The kind of restructuring facing schools will necessitate substantial changes in the identity and understanding of tasks, behaviors, norms, and cultural values for educational administrators.[22] These changes will also require significant role adjustment. With each significant role change, the integrity of the self often experiences a sense of jeopardy.[23] For example, role strain may be experienced as feelings of a loss of control over particular position responsibilities, fear of failing in the implementation of the restructuring efforts, self-doubts about personal competence and the ability to be successful, or impatience, frustration, loss of identity, and increased uncertainty about significant changes in one's professional life and work. Maintaining an internal locus of control is a critical aspect for sustaining the adjustments endured during role transition. Bredeson[24] reports that personal factors such as leadership style, capacity for growth, tolerance, patience, and interpersonal communication are under the direct control of individuals. School environments characterized as nurturing and supportive will be important to educational leaders who are engaged in defining, renegotiating, and internalizing new mind-sets about their leadership role.

IMPLICATIONS FOR THE PROFESSIONAL PREPARATION OF SCHOOL ADMINISTRATORS

Clearly, the changing conditions and mind-sets reported here have already had a powerful impact on the agenda of school administrator training, both in terms of content and general thrust. Since 1987, reform of principal-preparation programs has been an issue of considerable scrutiny. Many programs have become more responsive to the challenges facing school principals.[25] The thinking underlying these preparation programs seems to mirror the paradigmatic changes taking place at a more global level in the world of business and commerce. Just as business management preparation is moving away from an exclusive emphasis on the acquisition of functional skills (such as marketing, planning, and finance) to more contextual mind-sets, postsecondary educational administration training programs, which previously accentuated planning, facilities, buses, and budgets, are now designing more holistic approaches to preparing principals. Graduate education models of administrative training reflect a movement away from the managerial top-down styles of leadership[26] to more collegial and empowering forms of leadership. Attempts to ensure an alignment between administrator preparation and practice have been authenticated by Thompson's[27] and Thomson's[28] identification of strategies and domain-specific skills. An emphasis on the development of group process skills, collaborative leadership styles, and communication skills,[29] participatory decision making and consensus building,[30] reflective thinking,[31] and mentoring[32] is now emerging.

Despite the structural changes taking place in some schools (such as the emergence of full-service schools), systemic change and fundamental shifts in philosophy have not taken place. Overseeing the totality of school functions requires leadership, not solely management. Understanding how management and leadership differ is an important concept in providing the kind of vision that is needed to restructure today's schools. Although management provides consistency, leadership, control, and efficiency, leadership is the catalyst for stimulating purpose, passion, and imagination.[33] Management is fundamental to an authoritarian-driven hierarchical structure that seeks to maintain fragmentation in organizational structures. In contrast, leadership offers an opportunity to reevaluate and restructure a system that is nonoperational, dysfunctional, or operating poorly by building bridges and alliances with colleagues and major stakeholders.

What are the implications for providing leadership in broader paradigmatic contexts? How will administrative practice for pluralistic contexts need to be redesigned? To be fully effective in applying these skills, school administrators will need competencies that are framed by an appreciation for the context in which they are attempting to implement these skills. For example, if the skills of participatory decision making and consensus building are applied without the type of leadership that expands the organizational paradigm, little in the way of a true change in the processes and practices of the organization will occur. Clearly, current school environments are influenced by a multiplicity of agendas, demands, and stakeholders. Given the complex and changing landscape of schools that principals of the twenty-first century are likely to inherit, they will need a revised set of competencies. These competencies will require their ability to try on a variety of different mindsets and to develop a guiding image of the organization. They will need to provide leadership that allows staff to mobilize their energies and adapt to change while maintaining stable operations within the school. Changing sociopolitical contexts and paradigms will require practitioners who can analyze the dynamics of pluralistic environments and respond to the needs of diverse constituencies. At the same time, school leaders will be expected to maintain high standards for instruction and demonstrate exemplary levels of student achievement. There is little doubt that school leaders will need a solid foundation in pedagogy augmented by skills encouraged in the professional development of artists and therapists—intuition, reflection, and interpersonal communication.

Currently, schools are not structured in ways that invite easy adaptation to student needs. As we begin to think about tailoring instructional strategies and interventions to fit diverse student needs, the paradigm that governs school organization will need to move toward heterarchically structured team roles and away from hierarchically structured compartmentalized roles. School administrators will need to encourage staff to embrace change rather than endure or resist it. The changing paradigm in school organization that we have discussed is one that views students, teachers, and principals in distinctly different roles than they have traditionally held. We propose that the vision of leadership and school organization shift to one in which the student is viewed as client and customer, rather than as a product, the teacher is seen as an innovator and initiator, rather than as the production unit, and the principal is viewed as an organizational leader, rather than as the production manager. Principals who can bring about effective instruction, foster a quality of leadership that encourages flexibility, open lines of communication, and invite negotiation among school staff hold the greatest potential for promoting successful student outcomes.

ENDNOTES

1. L. Darling-Hammond and A. C. Wise, "Beyond Standardization: State Standards and School Improvement," *Elementary School Journal* 85 (1985): 315–356; J. Hannaway, "Political Pressure and Centralization: The Case of School Districts," *Sociology of Education* 66, no. 3 (1993): 147–163; L. McNeil, *Contradictions of Control: School Structure and School Knowledge* (New York: Routledge & Kegan Paul, 1986); and J. Murphy, *Restructuring Schools: Capturing and Assessing the Phenomena* (New York: Teachers College Press, 1990).

2. Hannaway, "Political Pressure."

3. J. L. David and P. M. Shields, *From Effective Schools to Restructuring: A Literature Review* (Menlo Park, Calif.: SRI International, 1991); Murphy, *Restructuring Schools;* and M. S. Smith and J. O'Day, "Systematic School Reform," in *The Politics of Curriculum and Testing,* ed. S. Fuhrman and B. Malen (Philadelphia: Falmer, 1991), 233–267.

4. P. Senge, et al., *The Fifth Discipline Fieldbook* (New York: Doubleday, 1994).

5. Darling-Hammond and Wise, "Beyond Standardization"; Hannaway, "Political Pressure"; McNeil, *Contradictions of Control;* Murphy, *Restructuring Schools;* and J. F. Witte and D. J. Walsh, "A Systematic Test of the Effective Schools Model," *Educational Evaluation and Policy Analysis* 12 (1990): 188–212.

6. J. Chubb and T. Moe, *Politics, Markets, and American Schools* (Washington, D.C.: Brookings Institute, 1990); M. B. Miles, E. Farrar, and B. Neufield, *Review of Effective Schools Programs,* 3 vols. (Cambridge, Mass.: Huron Institute, 1983); and M. B. Miles and T. Kaufmann,

"Director of Effective Schools Programs," in *Reaching for Excellence: An Effective Schools Sourcebook,* Part 2, ed. R. Kyle (Washington, D.C.: U.S. Government Printing Office, 1985), 145–233.

7. Darling-Hammond and Wise, "Beyond Standardization"; Hannaway, "Political Pressure"; and McNeil, *Contradictions of Control.*

8. Hannaway, "Political Pressure"; D. E. Mitchell, "Alternative Approaches to Labor–Management Relations for Public Schools, Teachers and Administrators," in *The Politics of Reforming School Administration,* ed. J. Hannaway and R. Crowson (New York: Falmer, 1989), 161–182; and F. M. Newman, R. A. Rutter, and M. S. Smith, "Organizational Factors Affecting School Sense of Efficacy, Community, and Expectations," *Sociology of Education* 62 (1989): 221–238.

9. R. B. Reich, *The Next American Frontier* (New York: Penguin Books, 1983), 64–65.

10. J. D. Goldbar and M. Jelinek, "Plan for Economies of Scope," *Harvard Business Review,* 61 (1983): 141–148; Reich, *Next American Frontier;* and E. L. Trist, "The Evolution of Sociotechnical Systems as a Conceptual Framework and as an Action Research Program," in *Perspectives on Organization Design and Behavior,* ed. A. H. Van de Ven and W. F. Joyce (New York: Wiley, 1982).

11. Reich, *Next American Frontier,* 65.

12. Senge, et al., *Fifth Discipline Fieldbook.*

13. G. Morgan, *Images of Organizations* (Newbury Park, Calif.: Sage, 1986), 56–57.

14. G. Morgan, *Riding the Waves of Change: Developing Managerial Competencies for a Turbulent World* (San Francisco, Calif.: Jossey–Bass, 1988).

15. M. M. Kennedy "Inexact Science: Professional Education and the Development of Expertise," in *Review of Research in Education,* ed. E. Z. Rothkopf (Washington, D.C.: American Educational Research Association, 1987), 148.

16. Allison and Allison, "Both Ends of a Telescope: Experience and Expertise in Principal Problem Solving," *Educational Administration Quarterly* 29, no. 3 (1993): 302–322.

17. Morgan, *Riding the Waves,* 5.

18. J. L. Epstein, "Parent Involvement: State Education Agencies Should Lead the Way," *Community Education Journal* 14 (1987): 4–9; and H. M. Weiss and M. E. Edwards, "The Family-School Collaboration Project: Systemic Interventions for School Improvement" in *Home–School Collaboration,* ed. S. L. Christensen and J. C. Conoley (Silver Spring, Md.: National Association of School Psychologists, 1992), 215–243.

19. Morgan, *Riding the Waves,* 6.

20. L. G. Bolman and T. E. Deal, "Looking for Leadership: Another Search Party's Report," *Educational Administration Quarterly* 30, no. 1 (1994): 77–96.

21. Ibid.

22. P. V. Bredeson, "Letting Go of Outlived Professional Identities: A Study of Role Transition and Role Strain for Principals in Restructured Schools," *Educational Administration Quarterly* 29, no. 1 (1994): 34–68.

23. Z. S. Blau, *Old Age in a Changing Society* (New York: Franklin Watts, 1973).

24. Bredeson, "Letting Go."

25. L. S. Behar-Horenstein, "Promoting Effective School Leadership: A Change-oriented Model for the Preparation of Principals," *Peabody Journal of Education* 70, no. 3 (1995): 18–40.

26. L. Lumsden, *The New Face of Principal Preparation* (Alexandria, Va.: National Association of Elementary School Principals, 1993); M. Milstein, *Changing the Way We Prepare Educational Leaders: The Danforth Experience* (Newbury Park, Calif.: Corwin Press, 1993); S. D. Thompson, "Principals for America 2000," *Journal of School Leadership* 1, no. 4 (1991): 294–304; S. D. Thomson, "National Standards for School Administrators," *International Journal of Educational Reform* 1, no. 1 (1992): 54–58; and S. D. Thomson, ed., *Principals for Our Changing Schools: The Knowledge and Skill Base* (Fairfax, Va.:

National Policy Board for Educational Administration, 1993).

27. Thompson, "Principals."

28. Thomson, "National Standards"; and Thomson, ed., *Principals for Our Changing Schools.*

29. W. Worner, "The National Alliance at Virginia Tech: Making a Difference," *NASSP Bulletin* 78, no. 559 (1994): 57–61.

30. P. Thurston, R. Clift, and M. Schacht, "Preparing Leaders for Change-oriented Schools," *Phi Delta Kappan* 75 (1993): 259–265.

31. D. Gordon and M. Moles, "Mentoring Becomes Staff Development: A Case of Serendipity," *NASSP Bulletin* 78, no. 559 (1994): 66–71.

32. H. Luebkemann and J. Clemens, "Mentors for Women Entering Administration," *NASSP Bulletin* 78, no. 559 (1994): 42–45; N. A. Prestine and B. F. Le Grand, "Cognitive Learning Theory and the Preparation of Educational Administrators: Implications for Practice and Policy," *Educational Administrative Quarterly* 27, no. 1 (1991): 61–89; R. G. Stakenas, "Program Reform in Administrator Preparation," *NASSP Bulletin* 78, no. 559 (1994): 28–33; W. R. Synder, "A Very Special Specialist Degree for School Leaders," *NASSP Bulletin* 78, no. 559 (1994): 23–27; and Worner, "The National Alliance."

33. Bolman and Deal, "Looking for Leadership."

DISCUSSION QUESTIONS

1. How are the characteristics of a diverse school age population and contemporary society influencing the role of school principals?

2. How have the variables of school life over which principals have authority changed?

3. In what ways have traditional paradigms influenced the role of principals?

4. What successes within our nation's schools are attributable to the traditional organizational paradigm?

5. What are the implications for preparing school principals who can respond to the challenges presented by contemporary students and society?

PRO-CON CHART 5

Does site-based management improve staff morale?

PRO	CON
1. Site-based management encourages collaborative working relationships between teachers and administrators.	1. Teachers are not trained for shared leadership; instead of cooperating they often reopen old disagreements and old wounds.
2. Most teachers welcome the increased involvement and reach greater professional maturity; the result is improved school effectiveness.	2. Considerable time is devoted to discussing daily problems such as equipment needs, clerical routines, and working conditions; little time remains for the larger issue of school effectiveness.
3. Site-based management promotes participatory decision making between teachers and administrators as well as a commitment to long-range planning and budgeting.	3. School organizations ensure a clear division of administrative and teacher roles as well as an emphasis on short-term goals, often evidenced by achievement test scores and budget constraints.
4. Site-based management fosters improved school-community relations among teachers, administrators, parents, and community members.	4. Because of differences in expectations among participants, site based management often leads to conflict or to interference by individuals who lack expertise in school matters.
5. Site-based management empowers teachers and further enhances their professional status; it is important for teachers and administrators to work together for a common goal.	5. Teacher organizations empower teachers and enhance their professional status; it is important for teachers to retain their autonomy through professional associations.

CASE STUDY 5

Principals to Assume New Role as Curriculum Leaders

A memo from District Superintendent Harry Shaffer was sent to all of the district principals. The principals knew that Shaffer and the board expected them to begin directing all aspects of the curriculum including the planning, implementation, and evaluation components next year. The fifteen veteran principals, who had administrative experience in the range of five to twelve years, were not happy about receiving this mandate.

After describing his expectations, Shaffer asked if there were any questions. Sharon Flamb, who spoke on behalf of the principal group, voiced several problems with the new expectations. Flamb indicated that she had already assigned the curriculum planning and evaluation functions to her department chairpersons. She stated that curriculum implementation was the teacher's domain and any concerns about instructional practice could be addressed in teacher evaluation assessments. Flamb pointed out that the principals had not had any input on this decision and that Shaffer's action was felt both as a top-down mandate and as professionally insensitive to their roles. Finally, Flam suggested that asking principals to assume the role of instructional leader might be sound from a theoretical perspective, but it was not practical given all the responsibilities already assigned to the principals. Shaffer listened impatiently while Flamb spoke.

1. Using the information in this case study, indicate some of the actions that probably influenced Flamb's response.

2. Assume you are Shaffer. What actions will you take now?

3. What are some ways that the principals could have been involved in the decision-making process that was going to impact their responsibilities?

4. What are the advantages and disadvantages of having principals assume the responsibilities of an instructional leader?

5. What type of skills do principals need to supervise the curriculum?

6. What steps can be taken to train principals who lack adequate preparation in and knowledge of curriculum?

7. What should be the role of teachers in curriculum development and design?

8. Many perceive the role of the high school principal as akin to a manager. Do you agree with this perception? Why? Why not?

PART SIX

Curriculum and Policy

INTRODUCTION

In Part Six, the relationship between policy and curriculum is considered. How are issues of diversity, homosexuality, movement toward educational equity, and practice-based assessment influencing the curriculum? How are school reform and restructuring efforts affecting the curriculum? In what ways might greater involvement of families and communities affect student outcomes?

Geneva Gay describes the current state of multicultural educational practice. She examines the disparity between the theory and practice of multicultural education. She offers some strategies to ensure that practitioners can use the theoretical ideas proposed by multicultural educational theorists for the benefit of teaching and learning. Next, James Sears calls attention to the growing number of school-age children who come from nontraditional families. He suggests that educators need to be responsive to the issues that children with gay or lesbian parents might encounter in gender and social development, as well as in the classroom. He advocates integrating issues about homosexuality into the school curriculum. He also describes some ways that educators can assume proactive roles on behalf of lesbian, gay, or bisexual students and families.

In Chapter 33, Linda Darling-Hammond explains how assessment tools influence the conception and delivery of curriculum. She cites ways that assessment can be used for the improvement of teaching and learning, rather than as a means for sorting students and sanctioning educators. In Chapter 34, Elliot Eisner considers the factors that influence the success of school reform, including teacher, parent, and community views of education and the organizational dynamics within schools. He stresses how action research, qualitative forms of evaluation, and giving teachers a greater role in creating local policy might facilitate reform initiatives.

In Chapter 35, Michael Fullan discusses why efforts to bring about systemic reform tend to fail. He suggests that networking, reculturing, and restructuring are likely to facilitate successful systemic change. In the final chapter of this book, Joyce Epstein explores how partnerships between schools, families, and communities are likely to benefit school-age children. She cites the practices that are characteristic of successful school, family, and community partnerships programs at all grade levels. She describes the process that has been used by schools involved in school, family, and community partnership projects to develop more positive partnerships.

31

Bridging Multicultural Theory and Practice

GENEVA GAY

FOCUSING QUESTIONS

1. *What is the current state of multicultural educational practice?*
2. *How do current and past conceptualizations of multicultural education differ?*
3. *Why do most educators tend to find theoretical explanations intimidating?*
4. *In what ways do multicultural educational theorists and college and university professors envision a transformation of the K–12 educational process?*
5. *What fundamental components of multicultural educational theory tend to be misunderstood by educators?*
6. *What are the advantages of application models that are decontextualized?*

The current state of multicultural education is at once exciting and troubling. A significant part of this dilemma—and the one of interest here—results from disparities in the developmental growth of its theory and practice. Ideally, educational theory and practice develop in tandem, and the relationship between them is complementary, reciprocal, and dialectic. This is not yet happening, in any systematic way, in multicultural education. Its theoretical development is far outstripping its practical development, and its further refinement is stimulated more by proposals of what should be than by lessons learned from what is.

Multicultural theory is becoming more thorough, complex, and comprehensive, while its practice in K–12 and college classrooms continues to be rather questionable, simplistic, and fragmentary. This gap is growing exponentially; it fuels much of the current debate because critics fail to distinguish between the two in their critiques; and it limits the overall effectiveness of multicultural reform efforts.

These divergent growth patterns also make it difficult for multicultural advocates in different aspects of the educational enterprise to engage in constructive dialogue and to work as collaboratively as they might for the achievement of common goals. As a result, multicultural classroom instruction is often not synchronized with curriculum development. Policy statements governing school practices may specify that multiculturalism must be included in instructional materials and program designs, but routinely fail to make similar requirements for hiring personnel and for assessing the performance of students and teachers. Yet theorists consistently argue that, for multicultural education to be maximally successful, all parts of the educational system must be responsive to and inclusive of cultural diversity.

The gaps between multicultural theory and practice present some serious challenges and opportunities for future directions in the field. In this discussion, I will offer some thoughts about why these gaps exist and make some suggestions for how the challenges that they present might be addressed.

INVERSE GROWTH PATTERNS

According to George Beauchamp (1968), an essential function of educational theorizing is to constantly search for new conceptual ideas, understandings, and principles to describe, explain, and predict issues of interest or study. He adds that the theorist "seeks out new relationships by combining sets of events into a new universal set and then [proceeds] with the search for new relationships and new laws in a new theory" (p. 19). This search has both internal and external dimensions. It analyzes the components of an existing paradigm to achieve greater depths and clarity of meanings, while simultaneously bringing ideas and insights from other sources to bear on the phenomenon being studied.

For example, multicultural education was initially conceptualized as a discrete program of studies with heavy emphasis on teaching factual content about the histories, heritages, and contributions of groups of color. Over the last 25 years, this conceptualization has been reexamined, revised, and refined so that now multicultural education is conceived more as a particular ideological and methodological approach to the entire educational enterprise than a separate curriculum or program *per se.*

The relationships between culture, ethnicity, and learning, which are so central to multicultural education, are continually analyzed and reinterpreted. Different ways to systematize the implementation of commonly agreed upon elements of

multicultural education are constantly being proposed by various scholars. In the rhetoric of today's educational thinking, these processes might be coded as self-reflection, critical interrogation, knowledge reconstruction, meta-analyses or meta-cognition, and multiple perspectives. Thus, the evolvement of educational theory from inception to maturity is a self-renewing, regenerative process. One of its natural effects is the creation of subsidiary theories and conceptual models.

Even a cursory look at the scholarship of leading multiculturalists (see, for example, Banks & Banks, 1993, 1995; Hollins, King, & Hayman, 1994; Bennett, 1995; Sleeter, 1991; Sleeter & Grant, 1995; Foster, 1991) provides persuasive evidence of these processes taking place. Senior scholars are revisioning and elaborating on some of their earlier thinking, as well as using knowledge and interpretive filters from other disciplines to enrich, elaborate, and extend the conceptual contours, attributes, and principles of multicultural education.

Several specific examples illustrate this trend. In a recent publication, Gay (1994) explained the relationship between canonical principles of general education commonly endorsed by United States schools and those of multicultural education. She argued that these are fundamentally the same, with the only differences being in context and constituency. Multicultural education merely translates general educational principles to fit the specific contexts of ethnic and cultural diversity. Banks (1995) is now exploring intersections between feminist theory, knowledge reconstruction, and multicultural education, as well as ideological antecedents to it found in the thinking of early 20th century African-American educators. Bennett (1995) and Nieto (1992), along with Banks and many others, evoke democratic principles and ethics to support their claims about the multicultural imperative in education. Sleeter and Grant (1995), King (1994, 1997), Ladson-Billings (1994), and Darder (1992) incorporate ideas from critical theory, postmodernism, social reconstructionism, and political empowerment into their explanations of the essential goals, purposes, and anticipated outcomes of multicultural education. Other theorists are beginning to establish direct linkages between economic development, international diplomacy, and being responsive to cultural diversity in the educational process.

This "conceptual webbing" is producing both encouraging and disturbing results for multicultural education. It is stimulating and enriching discussions among theorists about the necessities, contours, and potentialities of multicultural education. The thoughts and ideas that result from these discussions are at increasingly higher levels of sophistication, abstraction, and complexity. In this sense, the field is developing the way it should from the perspective of theory development. As any kind of educational theory matures, its ideological contours become more complex and abstract, and thus it moves further and further away from direct and immediate translation to classroom application.

Ironically, these theoretical strengths are also the nemesis of multicultural education practice. Rather than enlightening practitioners and stimulating them to higher levels of instructional action, complex theoretical explanations often have the reverse effects. They can intimidate, confuse, overwhelm, and incapacitate classroom teachers. The language used to express key ideas and concepts becomes more esoteric, thereby making them less clear to everyone except other theorists with similar developmental status and understanding. More attention is devoted to conceptualizing than to actualizing multicultural components and characteristics. That is, as theorists prescribe and visualize what should be done, they speak increasingly in terms of ideals, without clearly articulating directions for how these are to be operationalized in practice.

This situation is complicated even further by differences in the ideological ideas, disciplinary emphases, and maturational levels of theorists themselves. Some multiculturalists are influenced heavily by history and sociology, while others speak through the conceptual and linguistic filters of politics, psychology, anthropology, and pedagogy. Consequently, classroom teachers and school administrators are left to their own devices to translate theory to practice. Frequently, what they do in practice is inconsistent with or even violates what is meant by the theory.

Thus, while multicultural theorists argue that cultural diversity should be infused into the learning experiences of all students regardless of the ethnic demographics of specific school and classroom sites, practitioners still tend to make its implementation contingent on the presence of specific ethnic groups of color. If there are no African-American, Latino, Native-American, or certain Asian-American students enrolled in their schools, they find it difficult to see the relevance of doing multicultural education. When theorists propose that the K–12 educational process be transformed by cultural diversity, they mean that the most fundamental and deeply ingrained values, beliefs, and assumptions, which determine all educational policies, content, procedures, and structures, will be revolutionized by being culturally pluralized.

However, their college and university counterparts do not necessarily conceive of transformation in the same way. They, as well as many K–12 practitioners, use a more restricted notion of transformation as simply "change." They assume that multicultural transformation is accomplished by merely including information about ethnically diverse individuals and achievements into the content of instruction, or disciplinary canons. In this sense, the curriculum of a United States literature course is thought to have been transformed when writings by authors of color and females are routinely included for study. These conceptions and practices fail to realize that curriculum involves more than content, that the educational enterprise is not analogous to curriculum, and that the mere presence of ethnic information is not enough to constitute transformation.

These kinds of discrepancies in meaning between theorists and practitioners are understandable, given their differential levels of mastery of and maturity in the field. But they also are confusing and can have negative effects on the overall advancement of multiculturalism in all levels of the educational enterprise. They place both the practitioners and the theorists in reactive rather than proactive positions. The practitioners are faced with having to explain away their unintended misinterpretations and possible accusations that theorists are too esoteric in their explanations of key multicultural ideas. The theorists feel the need to reexamine and reexplain their intended original meanings to avoid future misinterpretations. This "back-stepping" slows down the forward thrust and continuous development of multicultural education in both theory and practice.

A strongly endorsed theoretical idea that is often misunderstood and is another powerful illustration of the lack of operational bridging between multicultural educational theory and practice is infusion. Virtually every multicultural theorist supports the idea that cultural diversity should be an integral part of the total educational experiences of all students in all school settings. This means it should influence the contexts and structures of teaching and learning, as well as their content and text. Stated somewhat differently, all policies, programs, and procedures in school curriculum, instruction, administration, guidance, assessment, and governance should be responsive to cultural diversity. This responsiveness is multidimensional, too, including recognition, knowledge, acceptance, respect, praise, and promotion. But very few theorists explain how to actually do these all-encompassing mandates in the various dimensions of the educational enterprise.

What do school principals do to multiculturalize the different tasks that comprise their administrative and leadership functions? What are the operational steps and decision-making points involved in multiculturalizing the curriculum creation process? How can these general principles be specified in different domains of learning such as math, science, reading, and social studies? How does one make the content as well as the administrative styles of student assessment culturally pluralistic? These are the kinds of questions that remain after most theoretical pronouncements are made regarding multicultural education infusion. They must be answered more precisely in order to establish better connections between theory and practice.

The few attempts that are made to create these bridges often are unsuccessful because they tend to be "finished or product examples" of what infusion looks like, instead of clearly articulated and functional explanations of the processes of infusion itself. For example, theorists may present illustrations of multiculturally infused reading units, but fail to explain how decisions about their specific components were made or why they embody and personify different principles of multicultural education.

Consequently, these samples are of limited value in empowering other educators to create similar ones and thereby continue to advance the development of multicultural education practice. This places practitioners in a situation of trying to imitate or replicate the sample lessons without being sufficiently informed about how the original decisions were made. The results are not very successful, which can cause instructional program designers to become frustrated and discouraged. This frustration then becomes a convenient excuse for them to abandon future efforts to implement multicultural education in their classrooms.

Another tension between multicultural theory and practice is the fact that many application models suggested for classroom use are decontextualized. They are not connected in any systematic way to what teachers routinely do in the day-to-day operations of their curricula and classrooms. Excellent books that present authentic and accurate portrayals of different ethnic groups' cultures, contributions, and experiences are now available. A wide variety of richly textured and significant learning activities has been developed for teaching various aspects of multicultural education, such as prejudice reduction, ethnic identity development, intergroup relations, and self-esteem.

Despite their inherent worth, decontextualized multicultural activities are of limited use in classrooms because the authors do not explain where and how they fit into typical instructional tasks and responsibilities. If, for example, designers were to demonstrate how learning nonpejorative terms for ethnic groups can be incorporated into standard vocabulary lessons in reading instruction, how ethnic population statistics can be used in teaching math skills such as proportions, ratios, and graphing, and how participating in interethnic group social exchanges approximates some of the skills social studies teach about international diplomacy, classroom teachers may be more willing and capable of using them.

Without this functional contextualization, teachers are likely to continue to perceive multicultural education as an intrusive addition to an already overburdened workload, or something that requires extra efforts and special skills. It then becomes very easy for them to dismiss the idea of cultural diversity without due consideration because they "don't have time to teach anything else," or because "it jeopardizes other important things that must be taught, such as basic literacy skills."

Another occurrence common to the profession that causes a split between theory and practice is variability in the positional responsibilities of the membership. Educational theorists tend to be more highly specialized in selected aspects of a discipline than school practitioners. They have the luxury of concentrating their professional activities on fewer things and becoming more thoroughly involved in exploring even deeper conceptual parameters and possibilities of their areas of expertise.

By comparison, school practitioners tend to be more generalists than specialists and are more engaged in applying than creating new knowledge. The more deeply involved they are in a pedagogical field, the more devoted they become to improving its practical applications. It seems only natural that these positional emphases would produce more divergent than convergent developments. As the field of study advances, both groups grow in clarity and coherency, but in opposite directions—practice seeks increasing conciseness, while theory searches for greater complexity. These kinds of developments support the need for specialists who can translate theory to practice.

These patterns of professional participation are evident in the field of multicultural education. Most nationally-known multiculturalists are scholars and specialists whose units of study and analysis are precollegiate educational programs,

processes, and practices. Their suggestions and proposals are ideal prescriptions about what cultural education should be.

By comparison, most school practitioners are specialists in something other than multicultural education, such as reading, history, math, or science instruction. They are concerned more with realistic and functional descriptions of what to do and how—about cultural diversity in relation to their other pedagogical responsibilities.

When these different professionals appeal to each other to satisfy their respective needs, they are often disappointed and may even doubt the value of each other's contributions because their quality may not be readily apparent in other domains of operations. Thus, when multicultural practitioners appeal to theorists for suggestions on how cultural diversity should be taught, they expect procedural specificities, but get conceptual guidelines instead. They are advised to be integrative, authentic, and transformative. These are great principles, but they do not have any action directives.

Conversely, when theorists look to practitioners for evidence of the application of conceptual ideas in classroom actions, they expect composites and systems of varieties of methods, materials, and tools, since concepts embed a multitude of action possibilities. Instead, they frequently see isolated activities and fragmented events.

These situations are understandable from the perspective of both the theorist and the practitioner. Multicultural theorists should be pursuing deeper conceptual understandings and explanations of the field, and practitioners should be looking for more pragmatic ways to implement cultural diversity in the classroom. It does little toward advancing both theory and practice for either to indict the other for not being maximally accountable for quality performance. Theorists should not be expected to perform as practitioners do; nor should practitioners be held accountable for being theorists. Both should be valued for their respective skills and functions. Yet, the need to establish better linkages between multicultural education theory and practice is imperative. Therefore, individuals who can translate theoretical ideas to the functional operations of actual classroom instruction can contribute significantly to the overall development of the field.

BUILDING BETTER BRIDGES BETWEEN THEORY AND PRACTICE

Two ideas are discussed here to illustrate how multicultural education theory and practice can be linked closer together. One involves approaches to multicultural education implementation, and the other has to do with the personal and professional empowerment of teachers in cultural diversity. Hopefully, they are instructive of the kinds of opportunities this challenge offers for enriching current developments in the field, as well as adding new dimensions of growth in the future.

All major multicultural scholars have developed models of different approaches to implementing cultural diversity in classroom curriculum and instruction. In some form or another, they include variations of inclusion, infusion, deconstruction, and transformation. The progression of these is from teaching information about ethnic groups in rather fragmentary, haphazard, and additive ways; to incorporating cultural pluralism throughout the educational process systemically and systematically; to using culturally pluralistic knowledge, perspectives, and experiences as criteria for reexamining the basic premises and assumptions on which the U.S. educational system is grounded; to creating new educational and social systems that are based on the ethics, morality, and legalities of cultural diversity.

Embedded in all these models are ideas of historical context, developmental growth, and increasing referential and conceptual complexity. Each model also conveys the message that some approaches to dealing with cultural diversity are inherently better than others, and everyone should aim to adopt these. It will help to establish closer and more functional linkages between multicultural theory and practice if those conceptualizations were reconsidered to be more developmental than hierarchical.

Rather than continuing to argue that there is a single best way to do multicultural education to which everyone should adhere, it is more feasible, pragmatic, inclusive, and empowering to legitimize multiple levels of appropriateness in participation. Currently, the theoretical message is that efforts to do multicultural education are inadequate if they are not at least at the infusion and preferably the transformation level. To impose these expectations on everyone is unrealistic. Educators just entering the field of multiculturalism simply do not have the background information, the pedagogical skills, or the personal confidence needed to fully understand what infusion and transformation are, least of all how to translate these ideals to practice. When they try to do so, the results are disastrous for everyone concerned—the professionals, the students, and the field.

The theoretical ideas of developmental progression and appropriateness have far greater potential for improving the quality of participation of educators at various stages of personal growth and professional positions in the promotion of multicultural education, as well as closer synchronizing its theory and practice. Developmental progression means that people's understanding of and capabilities in multicultural education move through different stages of conceptualization and practice, that each stage has inherent worth and legitimacy, and that the emergence of more advanced stages is contingent on the development of earlier, more basic stages. It also means that there is growth potential within each stage.

While the inclusion of ethnic content into selective curriculum lessons or units of instruction is a more rudimentary and basic approach to multicultural education than transforming the entire schooling enterprise, it has conceptual value and practical utility. Educators have to master this approach before they move on to more advanced levels of implementation. They have to learn how to do good multicultural lessons before they can design effective units on cultural diversity or redesign topics in other subjects so that they include multicultural perspectives. Teachers most certainly cannot deconstruct the cultural hegemony ingrained in their instructional styles or make them multiculturally responsive until they have learned a great deal about how cultural elements of different ethnic groups are embedded in the rituals and routines of teaching and learning.

Viewing multicultural education theory and practice as developmental and progressional enfranchises more people to be active advocates. Relatively few educators are ready now to actually transform the educational system so that it reflects cultural diversity in all of its content, values, and structures, even though they may believe this is necessary. Therefore, if its practice were solely dependent on them, very little would be accomplished. As others engage in practical actions at other levels of conceptualization, the number of advocates who promote diversity increases significantly. The field needs these numbers to create a critical mass of change agents who can affect the educational system at multiple levels and in diverse ways. Diversified personnel with differentiated abilities and skills are imperative to operationalize the multicultural mandate of systemic reform.

These ideas of involving individuals at various levels of complexity and using a variety of techniques to incorporate cultural diversity in the educational enterprise are highly consistent with the nature of the field. The heart of multicultural education is diversity and plurality. Just as advocates demand that these principles be applied in teaching students about cultural differences, the field should apply similar criteria to itself. If it does, then both multicultural theory and practice must provide opportunities for educators in various stages of professional development to be involved in a variety of ways in promoting cultural diversity that are legitimized and compatible with their capabilities. They also should have the chance to improve the quality of their present state of being before they are expected to move to new planes of performance. These ideas evoke the learning principles of readiness and prerequisites. Just as classroom teachers use them to help to guide their students' learning, similar applications should be made to the professional growth of teachers in cultural diversity.

More systematic ways to empower practice are needed within each of the developmental stages of multicultural education theory. These can be ac-complished by carefully analyzing essential components of teaching functions endemic to each stage and then demonstrating how these can be modified to illustrate stage-related principles of multicultural education. Four brief examples will suffice to illustrate this point. A powerful feature of the *inclusion* stage of multicultural education theory and practice is the concept of heroism. Students are introduced to a host of ethnic individuals who have made major contributions to their own cultural groups, as well as to U.S. society and humankind. The theoretical idea of selecting authentic ethnic individuals and artifacts to be taught can be applied in practice by teachers understanding what is a cultural hero or heroine according to the standards of different ethnic groups. Using these as criteria to select candidates for this distinction will help educators to avoid using their own cultural standards to select heroes and then imposing them on students from other ethnic groups. Understanding cultural standards of heroism and how different candidates manifest them thus empowers teachers and curriculum designers to select better examples of ethnic heroes and contributions to teach to students.

At the *infusion* level of multicultural education, implementation educators can be empowered in practice by demonstrating how the typical components of curriculum development can be culturally diversified. For example, how can sensitivity to cultural diversity be embedded in a curriculum rationale, statement of goals and objectives, content and learning objectives, and students' performance assessment? Other natural infusion opportunities can be identified by analyzing the teaching act to determine things that teachers routinely do and then changing them to be responsive to cultural diversity. The notions of influencing that which is habitual, routine, and fundamental in the educational process are central to the multicultural education infusion. Because teacher talk is a major component of instruction and affects culturally diverse students differently, it should be a primary target for multicultural infusion. But, in order to do this well, how teachers talk needs to be carefully analyzed and then changed accordingly. This analysis might include the kinds of questions asked of which students, turn-taking rules, wait time for re- sponses, and mechanisms used to convey praise and criticism to students.

At the essence of *deconstruction* approaches to multicultural education is what is often referred to as critique, interrogation, and knowledge recon- struction. In practice, this means that students are groomed to be healthy skeptics who are constantly questioning existing claims to social and academic truths and accuracy in search of new explanations and to determine if the perspectives of different eth- nic and cultural groups are represented. Nothing is considered sacrosanct, infallible, perfect, totally finished, or purely objective. Students are taught how to discern authors' biases, determine whose story is being told and validated from which van- tage point, and how to engage in perspective taking, as well as how to be self-monitoring, self-reflective, and self-renewing, especially in relation to issues of cultural diversity. These are the behavioral or prac- tical manifestations of such deconstructive princi- ples as multiple perspectives, giving voice, and the positionality of knowledge.

In practice, *transformative* approaches to mul- ticultural education focus on constructing new real- ities, new systems, and new possibilities. They are the action response to deconstructive processes. Whereas deconstruction focuses on thinking and imagining new explanations of culturally pluralis- tic social situations, transformation takes the revi- sioning processes to their ultimate conclusion by acting on the mental constructions. This building of new systems that are fully culturally pluralistic may include models, facsimiles, simulations, and actual creations. In creating them, students are engaged in various forms of social and political actions, both within and outside of schools, that symbolize their moral and ethical commitments to freedom, equal- ity, and justice for culturally diverse peoples.

CONCLUSION

The challenges posed by the need to bridge multi- cultural education theory and practice require that one be able to think analytically about current de- velopments to explicate their most salient inter-

secting possibilities. With some careful thinking from individuals with the necessary expertise, it is possible to generate a whole new body of research and scholarship in multicultural education that demonstrates, with operational clarity, how theo- retical principles can be translated into actual prac- tices in schools and classrooms.

However, the act of creating these strategies will prompt yet another generation of multicultural theorizing. But this evolving vitality and potential should not be seen as a problem to the field. As long as multicultural education has the regenera- tive power to create new thoughts, critiques, possi- bilities, and proposals for its own refinement, it is alive and well both as a theoretical endeavor and a practical necessity.

REFERENCES

Banks, J. A. (1995). The historical reconstruction of knowledge about race: Implications for transfor- mative teaching. *Educational Researcher,* 24 (20), 18–25.

Banks, J. A., & Banks, C. A. M. (Eds.) (1993). *Multicul- tural education: Issues and perspectives.* Boston: Allyn & Bacon.

Banks, J. A., & Banks, C. A. M. (Eds.) (1995). *Hand- book of research on multicultural education.* New York: Macmillan.

Beauchamp, G. A. (1968). *Curriculum theory* (2d. ed.). Wilmette, IL: Kagg Press.

Bennett, C. I. (1995). *Comprehensive multicultural edu- cation: Theory and practice* (3rd ed.). Boston: Al- lyn & Bacon.

Darder, A. (1991). *Culture and power in the classroom: A critical foundation for bicultural education.* New York: Bergin & Garvey.

Foster, M. (Ed.) (1991). *Readings on equal education. Volume II: Qualitative investigations into schools and schooling.* New York: AMS Press.

Gay, G. (1994). *At the essence of learning: Multicultural education.* West Lafayette, IN: Kappa Delta Pi.

Hollins, E. R., King, J. E., and Hayman, W. C. (Eds.) (1994). *Teaching diverse populations: Formulating a knowledge base.* Albany, NY: State University of New York Press.

King, J. E. (1994). *Teaching diverse populations: Formu- lating a knowledge base.* Albany, NY: State Univer- sity of New York Press.

King, J. E. (1997). *Preparing teachers for cultural diversity.* New York: Teachers College Press.

Ladson-Billings, G. (1994). *The dreamkeepers: Successful teachers of African-American children.* San Francisco: Jossey-Bass Publishers.

Nieto, S. (1992). *Affirming diversity: The sociopolitical content of multicultural education.* New York: Longman.

Sleeter, C. E. (Ed.) (1991). *Empowerment through multicultural education.* Albany, NY: State University of New York Press.

Sleeter, C. E., & Grant, C. A. (1995). *Making choices for multicultural education: Five approaches to race, class, and gender* (2d ed.). Columbus, OH: Merrill.

DISCUSSION QUESTIONS

1. Why is there a disparity between the theory and practice of multicultural education?
2. In your opinion, how can educators bridge the gap between the theory and practice of multicultural education?
3. How can multicultural educational theorists help practitioners to use the theoretical ideas that they propose for the benefit of teaching and learning?
4. In what way does the notion of developmental progression and appropriateness have greater potential for improving the practice of multicultural education?
5. What ideas does the author suggest to empower practice?
6. What type of preservice training should be offered to ensure that novice teachers can effectively implement the ideals proposed by multicultural educational theorists?

32

Challenges for Educators:
Lesbian, Gay, and Bisexual Families

JAMES T. SEARS

FOCUSING QUESTIONS

1. *What are the major types of families in the United States today?*
2. *What seems to be the most influential factor in deciding whether to award custody or visitation rights when a gay, lesbian, or bisexual parent or couple is involved?*
3. *What are some of the difficulties that children with gay or lesbian parents might experience in gender development? Social development? The school classroom?*
4. *In what ways can accepting the values associated with lesbian or gay parenting benefit society?*
5. *How can educators help to dispel the myths and ignorance regarding children of lesbian and gay parents?*
6. *How can issues of homosexuality be integrated into the school curriculum?*
7. *Should issues of homosexuality be integrated into the school curriculum? Why? Why not?*
8. *In what ways can conversations between educators and lesbian, gay, and bisexual adults be helpful?*

Kim and Carolyn, a Boston area lesbian couple, took in Earl, a Black deaf boy, who at the time was five years old. Kim is also deaf, although she can speak and lip-read…. Eventually Kim and Carolyn were formally approved as Earl's foster parents by Massachusetts social workers. Several years later the two women adopted Earl…. [At age 11] Earl is a child who is different. He is deaf in a hearing world; Black in a predominantly white community; and the son of [white and Asian] lesbians in a largely heterosexual culture. (Sands, 1988, pp. 46–47, 50)

Since I made the decision seven years ago to become a parent through anonymous donor insemination, the question that others have asked most frequently is, "But how are you going to explain this to your child?"…During breakfast today, in the middle of a discussion about Velcro closings on shoes, Jonathon [her five year old son], asked why he has only a mom and some people have a mom and a dad. I explained that there are all kinds of families in the world and gave lots of examples of those he knows: some with, some without kids; some big, some small. We talked about the fact that from the time I was 15, I just had a dad and no mom. I explained that there are no set rules for who family members can be; rather, families are people who love and are there for one another. (Blumenthal, 1990/91, p. 45)

The seven-year-old daughter [Alicia] asked her father some questions about "Gene" (the lover), *and the father answered them honestly, explaining that he loved Gene and he loved Mommy. The daughter did not seem concerned, but shortly afterward she asked her mother, "Do you still love Daddy?" Mother assured her that she did. "Do you love Gene?" the daughter asked. "He's my friend," her mother answered, "but I love your father." (Matteson, 1987, p. 151)*

Jennifer sits down at the kitchen table to eat her cereal and juice. "What will you be doing at school, today?" asks Patsy, her mother. "Mrs. Thomkins says we will make Christmas trees today." Patsy's husband, Bill, pours another cup of coffee and says: "Well, I guess that means that we won't have to go and chop down a tree this year!" "Oh, no!" Jennifer exclaims, "We're going to make them out of paper. When are we going to get our tree?" "Well," Patsy's mother says, "When Pam's ship returns for Christmas next week. Until then, you and Bill can talk about where we should go this year for our tree." Jennifer finishes her meal, kisses her mother and Patsy's husband goodbye. "Oh, I almost forgot. Where's Bob?" Bob, Bill's lover of five years, sits in the living room reading the morning paper. "I'm out here, Jennifer. Give me a kiss before you go to school."—An Alabama family (circa 1991)

The traditional American family—to the degree that it ever existed—represents a minority of all households in the United States today (Kamerman & Hayes, 1982). There are three major types of American families: families of first marriage, single-parent families, and families of remarriage. Less than one in four students comes to school from a home occupied by both biological parents. Single-parent households account for about one-quarter of all American families; about one of every two African-American children (one of every four white children) lives with a lone parent (Glick, 1988). If current trends continue, six out of ten children will be part of a single family sometime before they become 18 years of age (Bozett & Hanson, 1991). These single households are generally the product of divorce or separation. Remarried families account for one in six households with nearly 6 million stepchildren (Glick, 1987).

In recent years, alternative family arrangements have emerged in which either one or both partners are a self-identified lesbian, gay man, or bisexual person (Alpert, 1988; Pollack & Vaughn, 1989; Schulenberg, 1985).[1] Children, like Jennifer, from these alternative marriages may be the product of a prior marriage in which the partner has custody or visiting privileges or the gay or lesbian couple's decision, like Kim and Carolyn, to adopt (Jullion, 1985; Ricketts & Achtenberg, 1987).[2] Other children, like Alicia, may live in a biologically traditional family but have one or both parents who are openly bisexual (Matteson, 1985; 1987). Children, like Jonathon, may also come to school from households of a lesbian or bisexual woman who has elected to bear and raise the child following artificial insemination or the departure of the father (Pies, 1985; 1987). And, of course, the parents of many other children never choose to disclose their bisexuality or homosexuality to their family (Green & Clunis, 1989).

The publications on alternative families such as *Jenny Lives with Eric and Martin* (Bosche, 1983), *How Would You Feel If Your Dad Was Gay?* (Heron & Maran, 1990), and *Daddy's Roommate* (Wilhoite, 1990), as well as the controversy surrounding the New York City Public Schools' adoption of the Rainbow Curriculum and the subsequent dismissal of its superintendent, Frank Fernandez, may mean that few of our students will understand the true diversity among the families whose children attend their schools. Deleting lesbian, gay, and bisexual families from the school curriculum, however, does not remove them from the day-to-day realities of school life. If we are to truly serve all of our students, then educators must become more aware of the challenges facing lesbian, gay, and bisexual parents and their children.

CHALLENGES FACING LESBIAN, GAY, AND BISEXUAL PARENTS

How, the average person wants to know, can a lesbian possibly be a mother? If heterosexual intercourse is the usual prerequisite for maternity, how is it possible for women who by definition do not engage in heterosexual behavior to be mothers? If motherhood is a state which requires the expression of nurturance, altruism, and the sacrifice of sexual fulfillment, how can a lesbian, a being thought to be oversexed, narcissistic, and pleasure oriented, perform the maternal role? How can women who are "masculine," aggressive, and assumed to be confused about their gender be able to behave appropriately within its boundaries or to assume the quintessentially womanly task of motherhood? If lesbians are women whose lives are organized in terms of the relentless pursuit of clandestine pleasures, if lesbians are women who behave as quasi-men and who have been poorly socialized into their gender roles, then how can they expect to provide adequate models of feminine behavior to their children, to prepare them for their own sexual and parental careers? (Lewin & Lyons, 1982, p. 250)

Such questions pose challenges to women (and men) who are homosexual but choose parenting. While the assumptions underlying many of these questions are flawed (Sears, 1991a), the coupling of parenthood with homosexuality to form categories of lesbian mothers and gay fathers may appear contradictory. This contradiction, however, is of social not biological origin.

The difficulties confronted by acknowledged lesbian mothers or gay fathers are, in many ways, similar to those faced by single parents and divorced households, with the significant exception of the additional burden of wrestling with the social stigma associated with homosexuality. Two of the greatest challenges are securing or maintaining custody of their children and disclosing their homosexuality to their children.

Legal Barriers

In child custody decisions the judge has a wide leeway within common law to provide for the "best interest of the child" and not to interfere with existing custody arrangements unless there have been "material changes in circumstances" (Achtenburg, 1985; Basile, 1974; Payne, 1977/78). While heterosexual mothers have generally not lost custody of their children for unfitness, the sexual orientation of a parent has played a promi-

nent role in both circumstances (Pagelow, 1980; Rivera, 1987).

In general, gay fathers seeking custody face the double burden of being male where the female is presumed more nurturant and of being homosexual where heterosexual is considered normal. Moreover, in those cases involving a son the court appears more concerned with issues of sexual development than those involving daughters (Miller, 1979b), and in custody disputes involving lesbian mothers, the woman loses 85 percent of those cases that go to trial (Chesler, 1986). A disproportionate number of cases are between the mother and another relative (Hitchens, 1979/80), and in cases where lesbian mothers are provided custody, the courts have often demanded the absence of same-sex lovers in the household. One lesbian who won provisional custody of her five-year-old son lamented:

> That is unjust! They don't put those kinds of restrictions on a heterosexual mother...for 13 years I'm forbidden to set up a living relationship with a sexual partner of my choice. Sure, I don't have to be celibate—I can sneak out somewhere or I can send my son away—but I want to be free to set up my home with someone I love. It's much better for a child to have more than one parent figure—I can't possibly be available to answer all of my child's needs alone. (Pagelow, 1980, p. 194)

In deciding whether to award custody or even visiting privileges to a homosexual parent or to allow a lesbian or gay couple to adopt a child, judges often base their decisions on other unsubstantiated judicial fears such as "turning" the child into a homosexual, molesting the child, stigmatization of the child, and AIDS (Hitchens, 1979/80; Payne, 1977/78; Polikoff, 1987; Rivera, 1987). The willingness of the courts to entertain homosexuality as a factor for denying custody or restricting visiting rights has not escaped the attention of many lesbian mothers who, though themselves not a party to legal action, fear such a possibility (Kirkpatrick, Smith, & Roy, 1981).

Nonbiological parents and lesbians or gay men wishing to adopt also face significant legal hurdles. Six jurisdictions in the United States have ruled in favor of adoptions by same-sex parents (Alaska, Washington, Oregon, California, Minnesota, and the District of Columbia), and while only two states (Massachusetts and Florida) specifically prohibit gay men or lesbians from being foster or adoptive parents, most courts and agencies have allowed sodomy statutes (applicable in twenty-five states), prejudicial attitudes, or myths and stereotypes to affect their decision. In Minnesota, for example, one lesbian was denied visitation rights to a child she had raised with her former partner, and in Wisconsin the court refused to enforce a co-parenting contract signed by two former lovers. Even in states that have ruled in favor of adoptions, there remains bureaucratic and political resistance and, if approved, joint adoptions by gay men or lesbians are unusual (Achtenburg, 1985; Ricketts & Achtenberg, 1987).

Only recently have educational associations, state departments of education, and school districts developed policies and programs regarding the discrimination and harassment of homosexual students or the inclusion of sexual orientation issues in the school curriculum; little attention has been given to children with a lesbian or gay parent. As I will discuss in the final section of this chapter, these policies and programs, however, cannot only have a positive effect on the lesbian, gay, or bisexual student but also on the heterosexual student who comes from such an alternative family structure.

Disclosure to Children

Some, if not most, of our children from such families have not been told of their parent's sexual identity (Bozett, 1980: Miller, 1979a). In heterosexually coupled families with a gay, lesbian, or bisexual spouse, underlying tensions may create home problems (e.g., marital discord, emotional detachment from the child), which manifest themselves in a child's school behavior or academic achievement (Harris & Turner, 1985/86; Lewis, 1980, Matteson, 1987). In those families, for example, where gay fathers have not disclosed their sexual identity to their children, Miller (1979b) found "their fathering is of lower quality than the fathering of more overt respondents.... The guilt many of these men experienced over being homosexual manifested itself in over-indulgent behavior.... Data also indicate that respondents living with their wives tended to spend less time with their children" (p. 550). Educators who are aware of this social phenomenon can integrate this knowledge with their classroom assessment while respecting the confidentiality of the family.

Parents often fear the impact of such disclosure on their children. In deciding whether to disclose the parent's sexual identity, the most common parental fears are rejection from the child, inability of the child to understand, and child rejection from peers (Shernoff, 1984; Wyers, 1984, 1987). The difficulties faced by the gay or bisexual partner in "coming out" to a child are well articulated by Matteson (1987) following his analysis of a nonclinical sample of forty-four spouses in a mixed-orientation marriage:

> Since the beginning, I've been saying, "next year I'm leaving as soon as the children are bigger." Now that they are in college, I can't leave because they are my judges. They'd never forgive me for doing this all these years to their mother." (p. 145; quoted from Miller, 1978, p. 217)

The most common time for such disclosure is during a separation or a divorce or when the gay parent elects to enter into a domestic partnership (Bozett, 1981b; Miller, 1978). In the case of still-married bisexual spouses, somewhere between one-third to one-half of their school-age children have been informed (Coleman, 1985; Wolf, 1985). The mean age of gay parental self-disclosure or child discovery ranges from 8 to 11 years of age (Turner, Scadden, & Harris, 1985; Wyers, 1984). According to Bozett (1987b),

> The means by which the father discloses takes several forms. For example, with small children the father may disclose indirectly by taking children to a gay social event or by hugging another man in their presence. Both indirect and direct means may be used with older children in which the father also discusses his homosexuality with them. (p. 13)

Studies of gay parents and their children report different findings regarding the child's reaction (Bozett, 1980; Harris & Turner, 1985/86; Lewis, 1980; Miller, 1979b; Paul, 1986; Pennington, 1987; Turner, Scadden, & Harris, 1985; Wyers, 1987). In her clinical study of thirty-two children from twenty-eight lesbian-mother families, Pennington (1987) found the differing "children's reactions to mother 'coming out' generally range from 'Please, can't you change, you're ruining my life!' to 'I'm proud of my mom, and if other kids don't like it, then I don't want that kind of person to be my friend'" (p. 66). In his study of forty gay fathers, Miller (1979b), on the other hand, found all of their children to have reacted more positively than their fathers had anticipated. Furthermore, "children who showed the greatest acceptance were those who, prior to full disclosure, were gradually introduced by their parents to homosexuality through meeting gay family friends, reading about it, and discussing the topic informally with parents" (p. 549). In general, these and other studies (e.g., Gantz, 1983; Lamothe, 1989; Schulenburg, 1985) found the parent–child relationship was ultimately enhanced by such disclosure.

CHALLENGES FACED BY CHILDREN WITH LESBIAN, GAY, OR BISEXUAL PARENTS

> Susan expected her family to be thrilled that she was finally "settling down" after a decade of working as a lawyer. Her mother's first reaction [to Susan's interest in having a baby], however, was "But you're not married!" After Susan explained that she was still lesbian and planned to raise the child with her lover, Susan's mother wondered, "But is it fair to the child? Everyone else will have a father; she'll feel different, she'll be treated badly." (Rohrbaugh, 1989, pp. 51–52)

In the past, concerns about children growing up in a homosexual household focused on the household as the potential problem. Children were believed to be at a higher risk of developing a gender-inappropriate identity or sex-typed behaviors, acquiring a homosexual orientation, or exhibiting behavioral or psychological problems. While these fears are unjustified, the difficulties of growing up in a lesbian, gay, or bisexual household are linked to the homophobia and heterosexism pervasive in our society and tolerated, if not magnified, in our public schools.

Impact of Parental Sexual Orientation on Children

As the discussion of gay parenting becomes more public, fears about a child living with a lesbian or gay parent have been expressed. One concern is that the child may become homosexual or experience sexual harassment from either the parent or parental friends. Though persons generally do not identify themselves as gay or lesbian until their late teens or early twenties (Sears, 1991a; Rust, 1993), there is no greater likelihood that a son or daughter of a homosexual parent may declare a homosexual identity than those children from heterosexual households (Bozett, 1981a, 1981b; Gottman, 1990; Green, 1978, Miller, 1979b; Paul, 1986). Furthermore, there is no empirical evidence that such children living with lesbian or gay parents face any greater danger of sexual harassment or molestation than those living with heterosexual parents (Hotvedt & Mandel, 1982; Miller, 1979b).

Another concern is that children living in homosexual families may suffer in gender development or model "inappropriate" sex role behaviors. Here research studies present a mixed picture. While some studies have found that homosexual parents, like their heterosexual counterparts, encourage their child's use of sex-typed toys (Golombok, Spencer, & Rutter, 1983; Gottman, 1990; Harris & Turner, 1985/86; McGuire & Alexander, 1985; Kirkpatrick, Smith, & Roy, 1981; Turner, Scadden, & Harris, 1985), others have reported the opposite finding, including a greater emphasis on paternal nurturance or less preference for traditional sex-typed play (Hotvedt & Mandel, 1982; Scallen, 1981).

In general, studies comparing lesbian or gay men as parents with heterosexual single parents (Bigner & Jacobsen, 1989; Kirkpatrick, Smith, & Roy, 1981; Lewin & Lyons, 1982; Scallen, 1981) portray families that are either similar to the heterosexual norm or that excel in socially desirable ways (e.g., androgynous parenting behaviors, more child-centered fathers). Though the studies cited in this chapter varied in their methodology and samples, none found homosexuality to be incompatible with fatherhood or motherhood. Furthermore, these studies do not reveal parenting patterns that would be any less positive than those provided by a heterosexual parent (e.g., Bozett, 1985; Golombok, Spencer, & Rutter, 1983; Hoeffer, 1981; Robinson & Skeen, 1982).

In fact, those men who are most open about their homosexuality, compared with other homosexual fathers, display fatherhood traits that many professionals consider to be desirable. These fathers, for example, used corporal punishment less often, expressed a strong commitment to provide a nonsexist and egalitarian home environment, and were less authoritarian (Miller, 1979b). Similar findings were available for lesbian mothers. For example, in comparing black lesbian with black heterosexual mothers (Hill, 1981), the lesbians were found to be more tolerant and treated their male and female children in a more sex-equitable manner.

Those fathers and mothers who were the most publicly "out" were most likely to provide a supportive home environment. Ironically, given custody or visiting concerns as well as the general level of homophobia in society, those parents who are the most candid may be most vulnerable to denial of their parenting rights and visible targets for antigay harassment of themselves and their children.

Impact of Homophobia and Heterosexism on Children

The most commonly experienced problem or fear confronting children, most notably adolescents, from lesbian or gay households is rejection or harassment from peers or the fear that others would assume that they, too, were homosexual (Bigner & Bozett, 1990; Bozett, 1987a; Lewis, 1980; Paul, 1986; Wyers, 1987). An anecdote told to Pennington (1987) by a daughter of a lesbian mother illustrates the genuine acceptance of children *prior* to encountering stereotypes and harassment in school:

When I was around five, my mom and Lois told me they were lesbians. I said good, and thought I want to be just like my mom. Well, when I reached about the fifth grade…I heard kids calling someone a faggot as a swear word, and I thought, "My God, they're talking about my mom." (p. 61)

Based on his study of sixteen children with a gay or bisexual father, Paul (1986), as well as others (e.g., Riddle & Arguelles, 1981), found that it was during adolescence that these children had the most difficult time coping with their father's sexuality. An excerpt from a case study, written by a family psychotherapist (Corley, 1990) who worked with the two lesbians, Jane and Marge, and their eight children—a family for more than 10 years—is illustrative. During the next three years of therapy, the family began their first open discussions about the special relationship between the two women and the feelings of their children. The therapist continues:

Marge's two boys had difficult adjusting to do…. By now everyone at their school knew Joe and Tom had two mothers. Both of them had come to their school as the primary parent. The children started to tease them about having "lesbos" for parents. Both of the boys [in their early teens] were rather stout in nature so many fights erupted over the teasing they received. Since Joe and Tom were embarrassed over what the children at school were saying, they usually told the teachers and principal that there was no reason for the fights. When Jane and Marge would question them about the fights, they would equally clam up…. Because of the lack of intervention, the boys continued to get in trouble at school and started to act out in other ways. Although the boys were only average students, they always passed. Now they were bringing home failing marks. Since these were the first failing grades for either of them, Jane and Marge felt the situation would improve. Unfortunately, the grade situation only deteriorated. Several parent conferences were called at school. Although both women showed up at the conferences together, nothing was ever mentioned about the family unit or their relationship. It was not until the family came into therapy that the boys revealed they were having problems. (p. 80)

A prominent researcher in the study of children of gay fathers, Frederick Bozett (1980), relays a similar anecdote from a 14-year-old boy whose gay father had made several school visits:

"All his jewelry was on. The teachers knew he was gay, and all the kids saw him and figured it out. It was obvious. They started calling me names like 'homoson.' It was awful. I couldn't stand it. I hate him for it. I really do" (p. 178).

According to Bozett (1987a), children generally use one of three "social control strategies" to deal with their parent's homosexuality. The first, *boundary control,* is evidenced in the child's control of the parent's behavior, the child's control of his or her own behavior vis-à-vis his or her gay parent, and the child's control of others' contact with the parent. Some of these controls are evidenced in an interview with two adolescent girls, both of whom have lesbian parents:

> Margo: I try and hide stuff when people walk in, but probably most of my friends know.
>
> Interviewer: Do they ever ask you directly?
>
> Tania: My friends don't. My mother's girlfriend doesn't live with us. My mom keeps stuff out but I make a point of putting it away when someone is going to come over....
>
> Margo: I used to always walk between my mother and Cheryl. I used to make Cheryl walk at the curb and my mother inside and I'd walk right in the middle.... So it wouldn't be really obvious. But it probably was.... People say, "Why do they live together?" And you make up all these stories and they don't even fit together.... My mother tries to make up stories sometimes, but it doesn't work because they make no sense. "Oh my girlfriend, my brother's ex-wife's sister...." I used to be real embarrassed. One of my girlfriends asked me once and I was really embarrassed. I was like "No! What are you talking about? Where did you get that idea from?" But it turned out that her mother was gay too. (Alpert, 1988, pp. 100–102)

The second controlling strategy, *nondisclosure,* is evidenced in the child's refusal to share (and in some cases deny) their parent's homosexuality. One lesbian woman, discussing the difficulties she faced in her daughter's denials, commented,

> When I asked Noelle [now age 13] what she would say if anybody asked her about me she said she would deny it. I was very very hurt. I talked it over with Cathy (a lesbian and a close friend). She said

her son ... had got into a fight at school about her and had come home really upset.... She told him that she didn't expect him to fight her battles for her.... That was fine by her and that really helped me because I realized I should not expect Noelle to fight my battles either.... I actually did tell my children that if they want to deny it that's fine and I think that helped them because they were caught a bit between loyalties. (Lesbian Mothers Group, 1989, p. 126).

Some children, however, also employ nondisclosure to protect the parent who might be vulnerable to a child custody challenge or to job discrimination (Paul, 1986).

The third controlling strategy, *disclosure,* is evidenced by a child's selective sharing of this personal information. In Miller's (1979b) study of gay fathers, one 17-year-old son stated, "I don't tell people if they're uptight types or unless I know them well. I've told my close friends and it's cool with them" (p. 548). In Gantz's (1983) study, a 13-year-old child of a household with two lesbians noted, "I've told one person.... We'd go do stuff like shoot pool and all that down in his basement. I just told him, you know, that they were gay.... I didn't know how he'd react. He said he'd keep it a secret, so that made me feel a little better" (p. 68). Another male respondent commented, "You have to be sure they won't tell somebody else. I was worried [about] people knowing [because] I was afraid of what they'd think of me; maybe it would be embarrassing" (Bozett, 1987a, p. 43).

Furthermore, according to Bozett (1987a), several factors influence the degree to which children employ one or more of these strategies. Those children who identify with the father because of their behavior, life-style, values, or beliefs are less likely to use any social control strategy, whereas children who view their father's homosexuality as "obtrusive," who are older, or who live with their father are more likely to employ these strategies.

Studies on children from gay families or homosexual mothers and fathers have been conducted within a Euro-American context. Only one study has examined minority homosexual parents (Hill, 1981), and there has been no research directed at minority children of a gay parent. Anecdotal writings by persons of color who are homosexual parents, however, convey some dissimilarities with their Anglo counterparts. For example, Lorde (1987) writes,

> Black children of lesbian couples have an advantage because they learn, very early, that oppression comes in many different forms, none of which have anything to do with their own worth ... I remember that for years, in the name-calling at school, boys shouted at Jonathan not—"Your mother's a lesbian"—but rather "Your mother's a nigger." (p. 222)

Research into the unique difficulties confronting lesbian or gay young adults who must cope with their emerging homosexual identity within the context of a nondominant culture underscores the difficulties of being a minority within a minority and suggests differences that minority children with gay or lesbian parents might confront (Sears, 1991a; Johnson, 1981). Morales (1990) explains:

> What does it mean to be an ethnic minority gay man or lesbian? For ethnic minority gays and lesbians, life is often living in three different communities: the gay/lesbian community, the ethnic minority community, and the predominantly heterosexual white mainstream society. Since these three social groups have norms, expectations, and styles, the minority lesbian or gay man must balance a set of often conflicting challenges and pressures. The multiminority status makes it difficult for a person to become integrated and assimilated. (p. 220)

This was evident in my study of young lesbian and gay African-American southerners (Sears, 1991a). Irwin, a working class black man, for example, states, "When you're black in a black society and you're gay it's even harder. Blacks don't want it to be known because they don't want to mimic or imitate white people. They see it as a crutch and they don't want to have to deal with it" (p. 135). Malcolm comments, "If they are going to see you with a man at all, they would rather see you with another black man.... If they think you're gay and you're with a white man, they think that he's your sugar daddy or you're a snow queen" (p. 138). This is also evident in the anecdotal and autobiographical writings by people of color (e.g., Beam, 1986; Moraga

& Anzaldua, 1981; Smith, 1983). A Chinese American (Lim-Hing, 1990/91), for example, writes about her family's reactions to her lesbianism:

> The implicit message my family gave me was not so much a condemnation as an embarrassed tolerance inextricably tied to a plea for secrecy.... At the end of my stay [with my father], he asked me if "they" would pick me up at Logan, although he knows Jacquelyn's name. My father's inability to accept my being a lesbian is related to his more traditional values: family first, make money and buy land, don't stand out. (p. 20)

A Puerto Rican (Vazquez, 1992) expresses his anger at racism encountered within the Anglo gay community: "I won't lay in my own bed with some Euro-American and do Racism 101. Nor do I want to sit down with the cute white boy I'm dating and deconstruct the statement 'I love sleeping with Puerto Ricans'" (p. 90).

Children from some minority families may have a particularly difficult time coping with the homosexuality of a parent or may choose to cope with the information in a culturally different manner than researchers such as Bozett have found. Whether it is a child "coming out" to his family, a parent disclosing her homosexual orientation to the children, or both revealing this information to their extended family, they do so within different cultural contexts, perhaps facing greater risks than their Euro-American counterparts. Morales (1990) writes that

> "Coming out" to the family tends to involve both the nuclear and extended family systems. Such a family collective is the major support system for the ethnic persons and is the source of great strength and pride .... For minority lesbians and gays coming out to the family not only jeopardizes the intrafamily relationship, but also threatens their strong association with their ethnic community. As a result minority gays and lesbians may run the risk of feeling uprooted as an ethnic person. (p. 233)

Other difficulties faced by both Anglo and minority children of lesbian, gay, and bisexual parents may be the same as children from other families experiencing marital discord or integrating a new adult into the household (Hotvedt &

Mandel, 1982; Miller, 1979b; Weeks, Derdeyn, & Langman, 1975). Like children of heterosexual divorces, adolescents generally experience the most difficult period of adjustment during the first year of separation. In one of the first studies of gay fathers and their children, Miller (1979b) found "problems of sexual acting out" in the biographies of forty-eight daughters and forty-two sons. Only

> two daughters reported premarital pregnancies and abortions; one admitted to engaging in some prostitution. Two interviewed offspring had problems in school, and one had had professional counseling for emotional difficulties. As studies of children of divorced heterosexual parents have revealed similar problems...these concerns may not result so much from the father's homosexuality as from family tensions surrounding marital instability, divorce, and residential relocation. Anger and bitterness toward parents are common to children with disrupted families, and respondents in this study were not immune to such feelings. (p. 547)

In another study matching separated or divorced lesbian mothers with heterosexual mothers and using a variety of questionnaires, attitudes scales as well as interviews for both parents and preadolescent children (ages 3 to 11), Hotvedt & Mandel (1982) concluded that there was "no evidence of gender identity conflict, poor peer relationships, or neglect" (p. 285). These findings were extended by Huggins (1989), who examined children's self-esteem through interviews and surveys of thirty-six adolescents whose head of household was lesbian. Compared with a matched-set of heterosexual single female parents, Huggins concluded that "the mother's sexual object choice does not appear to influence negatively the self-esteem of her adolescent children.... the assumption that children of lesbian mothers are socially stigmatized by their mothers' sexual choice is not borne out by this study" (p. 132).

While this study does not imply that these children experienced no difficulties because of the stigma of homosexuality, it does mean that "the development of self-esteem is primarily influenced by the interaction between children and their parents or primary caregivers" (Huggins,

1989; p. 132). For example, one study found that one out of two children of lesbian mothers experienced relationship problems with other people due to the stigma of their mother's sexual identity (Wyers, 1987), and another (Lewis, 1980) concluded that

> Although the findings are similar to those...of children of divorce, the particular issue of acceptance of the "crisis" is dissimilar.... Children's initial reaction to divorce was denial of pain: follow-up one year later revealed more open acceptance of the hurt. One reason for this difference may be that children of divorce have community support for their pain; children of lesbians do not. (p. 199)

Of course, parenting by lesbians, gay men, and bisexuals presents society with alternative approaches to family life that can challenge oppressive sexist and heterosexist myths and stereotypes. Pollack (1989), though acknowledging the legal necessity for demonstrating the sameness between homosexual and heterosexual families, challenges the "underlying assumption that the lesbian mother should be judged on how well she compares to the heterosexual norm." For example, do we really believe that, as a society, we want to foster the continued sex-role education of children?

Pollack argues that, rather than accepting the values associated with the heterosexual family, lesbian and gay parenting affords opportunities to challenge these norms in society and in the upbringing of their children. The "possible benefits of being a child of a lesbian mother" include "the children of lesbians may become aware (perhaps more so than other children) of their responsibility for themselves and their choices" (p. 322). For example, one study (Harris & Turner, 1985/86) reported that lesbian mothers tended to use their homosexuality in a positive manner through assisting their children to accept their own sexuality, adopt empathetic and tolerant attitudes, and consider other points of view.

Central to the problems faced by children of lesbian and gay parents are the heterosexism and homophobia rampant in today's society. Homophobia—an irrational fear and hatred of homosexuals (Weinberg, 1972)—manifests itself in students' negative attitudes and feelings about homosexuality, and the institutionalization of sodomy statutes that deny rights of sexual expression among persons of the same gender, thus restricting the legal definition of marriage and family. Heterosexism—the presumption of superiority and exclusiveness of heterosexual relationships—is evidenced in the assumption that parents of all children are heterosexual or that a heterosexual adult will *prima facie* be a better parent than one who is homosexual.

As two leading researchers on gay parenting stated, "Much ignorance regarding homosexuality is due to the propagation of myths. It is important for educators in many disciplines and at all educational levels to dispel myths, impart facts, and promote values clarification" (Bigner & Bozett, 1990, p. 168). It is at this juncture that educators' concern for the student with a newly identified lesbian or gay parent is married to their concern for the gay or lesbian student and for the heterosexual student harboring intensely homophobic feelings and attitudes. Each of these students can benefit from honest discussion about homosexuality in the school (Sears, 1987, 1991b), the adoption and implementation of antiharassment guidelines (Sears, 1992d), the portrayal of the contributions and rich history of lesbians, gay men, and bisexuals (Sears, 1983), and the provision of gay-affirmative counseling services (Sears, 1989c).

Based on her interviews with children with lesbian mothers, Lewis (1980) concurred:

> The children of lesbians seem not to have peer support available to them, since most of these children have either pulled away from their friends altogether or maintained friends but with a sense of their own differentness. Children of lesbians have been taught the same stereotypical myths and prejudices against homosexuals as the rest of society. Better understanding is needed about available family support systems and other systems that should be provided. These might include peer supports as well as educational supports, for example, dissemination of information about homosexuality. (p. 202)

HOMOSEXUALITY AND THE SCHOOLS

Though some teachers, administrators, and guidance counselors are reluctant to discuss homosexuality in schools (Sears, 1992a, 1992b), every major professional educational association has adopted resolutions calling on schools to address this topic. Some school districts have adopted specific programs and policies, and a variety of recommendations have been made to integrate issues relating to homosexuality in the school curriculum. Educators who assume proactive roles not only benefit lesbian, gay, and bisexual students but are making inroads into the institutionalized homophobia and heterosexism that make school life more difficult for children from homosexual families.

Gay and Lesbian Students and Professional Standards

Professional educational associations have adopted policies affirming the worth and dignity of lesbians, gay men, and bisexuals and/or calling for an end to statutes, policies, and practices that effectively condone discrimination and harassment on the basis of sexual identity. Educators, school board members, and parents who have spearheaded these efforts acknowledge the simple social fact that being sexually different in a society of sexual sameness exacts a heavy psychological toll. Struggling to cope with their sexual identity, these students are more likely than other youth to attempt suicide, to abuse drugs or alcohol, and to experience academic problems (Gibson, 1989; Hetrick & Martin, 1987; Martin & Hetrick, 1988; Sears, 1989b; Teague, 1992; Zera, 1992). Other youth coping with their same-sex feelings may not display these symptoms but may excel in schoolwork, extracurricular activities, or sports as a means of hiding their sexual feelings from themselves or others (Sears, 1991a). By hiding, however, their emotional and sexual development languishes (Martin, 1982).

Five states (Massachusetts, New Jersey, Wisconsin, Hawaii, and Minnesota) have adopted some type of antidiscrimination statutes. For example, Wisconsin's statute Section 118.13 reads, in part,

No person may be denied admission to any public school or be denied participation in, be denied the benefits of or be discriminated against in any curricular, extracurricular, pupil services, recreational, or other program or activity because of the person's sex, race...marital or parental status, sexual orientation.

As part of the process of implementing its statute, the Wisconsin Department of Public Instruction issued a fifty-nine page booklet that noted that "the board shall adopt instructional and library media materials selection policies stating that instructional materials, texts, and library services reflect the cultural diversity and pluralist nature of American study" and cited lesbian and gay students as one underrepresented group.

Finally, many major educational organizations, such as the National Educational Association, American Federation of Teachers, and the Association for Supervision and Curriculum Development, have adopted statements affirming the rights of homosexual and bisexual students in K–12 schools and calling on their members to undertake proactive measures to combat the heterosexism and homophobia that are rampant in our nation's schools. For example, the American School Health Association issued a policy statement on gay and lesbian youth in schools, which stated, in part, that

> School personnel should discourage any sexually oriented, deprecating, harassing, and prejudicial statements injurious to students' self-esteem. Every school district should provide access to professional counseling, by specially trained personnel for students who may be concerned about sexual orientation.

School Policies and Programs

Since the late 1980s, the invisibility of homosexuality in education has lessened. Evidence of its being less invisible includes extensive sex education courses in this nation's schools (Haffner, 1990; Sears, 1992c), with some systems including units on homosexuality (Sears, 1991b); the first public funding of a school serving homosexual students, The Harvey Milk School, by the New York City public school system (Friends of Project 10, 1991;

Rofes, 1989); the institution of the first gay-affirmative counseling service in a public high school, Project 10 within the Los Angeles Unified School District (Rofes, 1989); the election of the nation's first openly gay school board member in San Francisco; and the formation of the Lesbian and Gay Studies special interest group of the American Educational Research Association (Grayson, 1987).

Several school districts have adopted antiharassment guidelines. In 1987, the Cambridge (MA) public schools included in their policies the following statement:

> *Harassment on the basis of an individual's sexual preference or orientation is prohibited. Words, action or other verbal, written, or physical conduct which ridicules, scorns, mocks, intimidates, or otherwise threatens an individual because of his/her sexual orientation/preference constitutes homophobic harassment when it has the purpose or effect of unreasonably interfering with the work performance or creating an intimidating, hostile, or offensive environment. (Peterkin, 1987)*

More recently, in 1991, the St. Paul school board passed a human rights policy forbidding discrimination on the basis of "sexual or affectional orientation." Several large urban school districts (e.g., New York, Washington, DC, Cincinnati, Los Angeles, Des Moines, San Francisco) have implemented antigay and lesbian discrimination policies. Perhaps the most publicized effort to meet the needs of homosexual students has been the funding of a public alternative school for gay and lesbian youth in New York City and the development of counseling services expressly for this target population in Los Angeles. The Harvey Milk School, established in 1985 under the sponsorship of the Hetrick–Martin Institute, serves about forty students who are unable to function in the conventional school setting (Rofes, 1989). In Los Angeles, Project 10 at Fairfax High School has received international attention for the gay-affirmative services provided by its counseling staff. And, in 1993, the school district, under the auspices of Project 10, hosted the first conference for their high school gay youth at nearby Occidental College.

These policies and programs not only have a positive impact on the gay, lesbian, and bisexual student, but on heterosexual students, faculty, and staff, who often harbor homophobic feelings or heterosexist attitudes. Thus, these policies and programs can help to create a supportive school climate for heterosexual students who come from lesbian, gay, or bisexual households.

Curriculum and Staffing Recommendations

Elsewhere (Sears, 1987; Sears, 1992b; Sears, 1991b) I have discussed the importance of integrating issues of homosexuality into the school curriculum. Briefly, when the issue of homosexuality appears in the school curriculum, the most likely subjects to be targeted are science in the form of human physiology or health in the form of HIV/AIDS prevention (Sears, 1992c). In contrast, I believe, sexuality can serve as a transformative tool for thinking about the construction of one's sexual identities vis-à-vis the interrelationships among language, history, and society (Carlson, 1992; Macanghaill, 1991). As such, sexuality no longer becomes the province of sex educators teaching separate units within physical education or biology, but becomes a major strand woven throughout the curriculum (Sears, 1991b).

Educators have long argued that schools ought to be an embryonic environment for engaging young people in the art of democratic living and, in the process, moving society further along its democratic path (Dewey, 1916; Giroux, 1988; Rugg, 1939). In fact, however, the hidden curriculum of school fosters conformity and passivity, while seldom encouraging critical thinking, ethical behavior, and civic courage (Giroux, 1988; McLaren, 1991, 1993). Within this environment, controversial ideas and individual differences are seldom welcomed. The discussion of homosexuality, the treatment of lesbian, gay, and bisexual students, and the restrictive definition of family are some of the most glaring examples.

Specific strategies and materials that foster an awareness of homosexuality and homosexual persons already have been proposed or developed (e.g., Friends of Project 10, 1991; Goodman, 1983;

Hubbard, 1989; Krysiak, 1987; Lipkin, 1992; Sears, 1983; Wilson, 1984). Educators have been admonished by scholars and activists alike to sit down and talk with bisexual, lesbian, and gay adults to learn first hand about the special problems they faced in school; the importance of lesbian and gay educators as role models for homosexual students has been stressed, as has the need for public school systems to follow the lead of communities such as Berkeley and Cambridge in adopting antislur policies and nonharassment guidelines (Griffin, 1992; Hetrick & Martin, 1987; Kissen, 1991; Martin & Hetrick, 1988; Peterkin, 1987; Rofes, 1989; Sears, 1987; Sears, 1993; Slater, 1988; Stover, 1992). In some schools, anti-homophobia workshops with heterosexual students and educators have been conducted (Schneider & Tremble, 1986; Stewart, 1984). Professional educators as well as lesbian and gay activists ask, at the very least, for the construction of a nonjudgemental atmosphere in which homosexual-identified students can come to terms with their sexuality, the acquisition by school libraries of biographical books where students can discover the homosexuality of some famous people, and the integration of references to homosexual men and women as well as the topic of homosexuality into the high school curriculum (Jenkins, 1990; Sears, 1983, 1988b).

It should be noted that there is no legal justification for systematically barring discussion of homosexuality and the inclusion of the contributions of lesbian, gay, and bisexual artists, politicians, scientists, and athletes from the school curriculum. A United States Court of Appeals ruling that a state statute prohibiting educators and school staff from "advocating, soliciting, or promoting homosexual activity" was unconstitutional was let stand due to a deadlock Supreme Court vote (*National Gay Task Force* v. *Board of Education of the City of Oklahoma,* 1984). Nevertheless, the integration of lesbian, gay, and bisexual topics or persons into the school curriculum appears too radical for many educators. Too few administrators refuse to acquiesce to a scissors and paste mentality of curriculum development in which only the most mundane, least controversial material survives the scrutiny of self-appointed moral vigilantes or the self-censorship of timid school officials (Sears, 1992d; Summerford, 1987; Tabbert, 1988).

In such an Orwellian school world, the curriculum is carefully crafted to omit (without the appearance of omission) the homoerotic imagery in the poetry of Walt Whitman, Sappho, and Langston Hughes or the visual arts of Donatello, Marsden Hartley, and Robert Mapplethorpe; the conflict between racial and sexual identities present in the literature of James Baldwin, Yukio Mishima, and Toni Morrison; or the conflict between the professional and personal lives of computer inventor Alan Turing, sports heroes David Kopay and Martina Navratilova, and political activists Eleanor Roosevelt and Susan B. Anthony. Just as sexuality is extracted from life and compartmentalized into units of sexuality, education, so, too, is bisexuality and homosexuality exorcised from the body politic and tucked away in the curriculum closet.

In each of these areas, educators can play an important role in reducing homophobia and heterosexism. In the process, they can directly counter those litigants who petition courts to deny custody or visitation rights to lesbian or gay parents due to the fear of a "definite possibility of peer ridicule in the future" (Hitchens, 1979/80, p. 90).

SUMMARY OF RESEARCH

Studies on bisexual and homosexual parenting as well as on children of lesbians and gay men are far from complete. There are, however, some suggestive findings:

- Children are less accepting when a same-sex parent "comes out" than when a parent of the other gender discloses sexual identity.
- Children of a lesbian or gay parent are no more likely to define themselves as homosexual than children of heterosexual parents, nor are they any more likely to display atypical sex role preferences.
- Lesbian, gay, and bisexual parents often seek to provide children with a variety of gender role models.

- The earlier the disclosure to the child is, the fewer problems in the parent–child relationship.
- Children of a lesbian or gay parent follow typical developmental patterns of acquiring sex role concepts and sex-typed behaviors.
- Children of homosexual parents who have experienced marital turmoil face similar difficulties common to children of divorce.
- Gay fathers may have a more difficult time disclosing their sexuality to their children than lesbian mothers, children of gay fathers are less likely to know of their parents' sexual identity, and the coming out process is more difficult for gay fathers with children at home.
- Sons are less accepting when learning their parent is gay than are daughters.
- As children enter adolescence, there is a greater likelihood that they will experience peer harassment about their parents' sexual identity and engage in a variety of self-protective mechanisms.
- Gay fathers are more likely to report their children experiencing difficulty with peer harassment because of the parent's homosexuality.

Recommendations for Educators

In several studies, researchers have noted the important role that educators can play in reducing the homophobia and heterosexism that create difficult environments for children of lesbian or gay families to learn in and for their parents to visit. Based on these and other writings (e.g., Clay, 1990; Casper & Wickens, 1992), educators should

- Redesign school paperwork in order to be inclusive. Replace words such as "mother" and "father" with "parent" or "parent 1, parent 2."
- When establishing associations such as parent–teacher organizations, develop assistance for single-parent families (e.g., child-care) and create or identify a safe space for homosexual parents (e.g., support groups). Encouraging gay parents to share their family status with school officials is important. Based on his extensive research with children of gay fathers, Bozett (1987a) states that

It is best for school officials to know about the father's homosexuality, especially if the father has child custody. Knowing about the family can alert school personnel to problems which may have the home situation as their genesis. Likewise, if the father is known about by school officials, both the father and his lover may participate in school affairs, attend school functions, or the lover may pick the child up at school all without the parents or the child having to make elaborate explanations. (p. 53)

- Represent family and cultural diversity in classroom materials and books, on bulletin boards, and in everyday teaching practices.
- Ensure that books depicting alternative family patterns are included in school libraries (see the following resource section for a few recommendations).
- Sensitize teachers and prepare guidance counselors to work with children as well as their gay parent as they confront issues ranging from the child's need for self-protection to the parent's need for respect for their sexual choices.
- Provide role models of gay or lesbian parents for students. Examples should reflect a multicultural emphasis, rather than reinforcing the stereotype of homosexuality existing only within the white community. Since some children in every school will identify themselves as lesbian or gay, it is important for them to have positive parenting role models should they elect to bear or foster children as adults.
- Inform parents of any sexual harassment or intimidation directed at their child.
- Modify the school's antislur and antiharassment policy to include sexual orientation and equally enforce violations against this policy.
- Interview potential teachers and counselors to determine their professional experiences and personal attitudes in working with several minorities.
- Revise hiring policies and procedures to enhance the likelihood of recruiting sexual minority faculty.
- Develop and publicize a counseling service for students who wish to discuss issues related to sexual identity.

- Hold a series of informal faculty meetings with gay and lesbian parents and faculty to identify needs and possible solutions.
- Meet with support services personnel (e.g., media specialists, counselors) to determine the adequacy of resource materials available for students and faculty about homosexuality and bisexuality.
- Review and revise accordingly student and faculty school-sanctioned activities that discriminate on the basis of sexual orientation (e.g., Junior ROTC, school dances, job-recruitment fairs).
- Review school textbooks for biased or misleading information about lesbians, gays, and bisexuals.
- Review the school curriculum to identify areas within *every* subject matter where relevant information (people, places, events) about lesbians, gay men, and bisexuals can be included.
- Engage teachers and administrators in formal activities that address the cognitive, affective, and behavioral dimension of homophobia.
- Develop prejudice awareness among student leaders through after-school workshops.
- Invite former students and members of the community to address the student body on issues relating to homosexuality.

Resources for Educators

There is a wide selection of books, organizations, and journals appropriate for adults interested in lesbian and gay parents or their children. These include the following:

Alpert, H. (1988). *We are everywhere: Writings by and about lesbian parents.* Freedom, CA: Crossing Press.

Boys of Lesbian Mothers. 935 W. Broadway, Eugene, OR 97402.

Chain of Life. A newsletter for lesbian and gay adoptees. Box 8081, Berkeley, CA 94707.

Children of Gay/Lesbians. 8306 Wilshire Blvd., Suite 222, Beverly Hills, CA 90211.

Empathy: An interdisciplinary journal for persons working to end oppression based on sexual identities. Published twice a year (individuals $15, institutions $20), this 100+ page journal regularly includes essays on alternative family structures and issues relating to lesbian, gay, and bisexual youth. PO Box 5085, Columbia, SC 29250.

Gay and Lesbian Parents Coalition International. An advocacy and support group for lesbian and gay parents with a quarterly newsletter. PO Box 50360, Washington, DC 20091.

Gay Fathers (1981). *Some of their stories, experience, and advice.* Toronto: Author.

Gay Fathers Coalition, Box 50360, Washington, DC 20004.

Gay Parents Support Packet. National Gay Task Force, 80 Fifth Ave., Room 506, New York, NY 10011.

Jenkins, C. (1990, September 1). "Being gay: Gay/lesbian characters and concerns in young adult books." *Booklist,* 39–41.

Jullion, J. (1985). *Long way home: The odyssey of a lesbian mother and her children.* Pittsburgh, PA: Cleis.

MacPike, L. (1989). *There's something I've been meaning to tell you.* Tallahassee, FL: Naiad Press.

Parents and Friends of Lesbians and Gays. PO Box 27605, Washington, DC 20038-7605.

Pollack, S., & Vaughn, S. (1987). *Politics of the heart: A lesbian parenting anthology.* Ithaca, NY: Firebrand.

Rafkin, L. (1990). *Different mothers: Sons and daughters of lesbians talk about their lives.* Pittsburgh, PA: Cleis.

Schulenburg, J. (1985). *Gay parenting: A complete guide for gay men and lesbians with children.* Garden City, NY: Doubleday.

Wolf, V. (1989). "The gay family in literature for young people." *Children's Literature in Education, 20*(1), 51–58.

ENDNOTES

1. These real-world vignettes reflect the variety of lesbian, gay, and bisexual families. While the number of children of lesbian, gay, and bisexual parents is speculative, researchers cite a range of 6 to 14 million children (Bozett, 1987a; Rivera, 1987; Schulenberg, 1985). Empirical data, which are subject to sampling problems, suggest that approximately one in five lesbians and one in ten gay men have children (Bell & Weinberg, 1978; Jay & Young, 1979), with estimates of upward of 1.5 million lesbians living with their children (Hoeffer, 1981). Until recently, these children were the result of defunct heterosexual relationships or marriages in which a spouse's homosexuality remains undisclosed (Brown, 1976; Green, 1987; Miller, 1979a).

Studies on lesbian and gay parents and their families have been limited in terms of sample size and methodology. For example, some studies (e.g., Weeks, Derdeyn, & Langman, 1975) have been clinical case studies and others have relied on anecdotal evidence (e.g., Alpert, 1988; Brown, 1976; Mager, 1975); others have studied small (10 to 40) groups of homosexual parents identified through gay-related organizations (e.g., Scallen, 1981). Only a few studies have used larger samples with more sophisticated research designs (e.g., Bigner & Jacobsen, 1989; Hotvedt & Mandel, 1982). There have been no ethnographic, longitudinal, or nation-wide studies conducted. Furthermore, researchers generally have compared homosexual single parents with single heterosexual parents and, occasionally, homosexual parents living with a domestic partner with remarried heterosexual couples. Due to their incompatibility, no comparisons between homosexual parented households with the "traditional" two-parent heterosexual families have been made. Furthermore, few of these studies present statistical analyses, control for the presence of a male role model in the home, take into account the desire to appear socially acceptable, include a majority of adolescent subjects, or focus on bisexual parents (Gottman, 1990). Finally, only a handful of studies have directly interviewed, surveyed, or observed children raised by a father or mother who is homosexual (Bozett, 1980; 1987b; Green, 1978; Huggins, 1989; Paul, 1986). For a review of much of this literature, see Bozett (1989).

2. One tragedy of failures to challenge successfully state sodomy statutes in the courts and the legislature is the difficulty that lesbians, gay men, or bisexuals have in obtaining child custody or visiting privileges in divorce hearings or approval from adoption agencies even for children whose prospects for adoption are slim, such as an older child or an HIV-infected baby (Hitchens, 1979/80; Payne, 1977/1978; Ricketts & Achtenberg, 1987; Rivera, 1987).

REFERENCES

Achtenburg, R. (1985) *Sexual orientation and the law.* New York: Clark–Boardman.

Alpert, H. (1988). *We are everywhere: Writings by and about lesbian parents.* Freedom, CA: Crossing Press.

Basile, R. (1974). "Lesbian mothers and custody and homosexual parents." *Women's Rights Law Reporter, 2,* 3–25.

Beam, J. (Ed.) (1986). *In the life: A black gay anthology.* Boston: Alyson.

Bell, A., & Weinberg, M. (1978). *Homosexualities.* New York: Simon & Schuster.

Bigner, J., & Bozett, F. (1990). "Parenting by gay fathers." In F. Bozett & M. Sussman (Eds.), *Homosexuality and family relations* (pp. 155–175). New York: Haworth Press.

Bigner, J., & Jacobsen, R. (1989). "Parenting behaviors of homosexual and heterosexual fathers." In F. Bozett (Ed.), *Homosexuality and the family* (pp. 173–186). New York: Haworth Press.

Blumenthal, A. (1990/1991). "Scrambled eggs and seed daddies: Conversations with my son." *Empathy,* 2(2), 45–48.

Bosche, S. (1983). *Jenny lives with Eric and Martin.* London: Gay Men's Press.

Bozett, F. (1980). "Gay fathers: How and why gay fathers disclose their homosexuality to their children." *Family Relations,* 29, 173–179.

Bozett, F. (1981a). "Gay fathers: Evolution of the gay-father identity." *American Journal of Orthopsychiatry,* 51, 552–559.

Bozett, F. (1981b). "Gay fathers: Identity conflict resolution through integrative sanctions." *Alternative Lifestyles,* 4, 90–107.

Bozett, F. (1985). "Gay men as fathers." In S. Hanson & F. Bozett (Eds.). *Dimensions of fatherhood* (pp. 327–352). Beverly Hills, CA: Sage.

Bozett, F. (1987a). "Children of gay fathers." In F. Bozett (Ed.), *Gay and lesbian parents* (pp. 39–57). Westport, CT: Praeger.

Bozett, F. (1987b). "Gay fathers." In F. Bozett (Ed.), *Gay and lesbian parents* (pp. 3–22). Westport, CT: Praeger.

Bozett, F. (1989). "Gay fathers: A review of the literature." In F. Bozett (Ed.), *Homosexuality and the family* (pp. 137–162). New York: Haworth Press.

Bozett, F., & Hanson, S. (1991). "Cultural change and the future of fatherhood and families." In F. Bozett & S. Hanson (Eds.), *Fatherhood and families in cultural context* (pp. 263–274). New York: Springer.

Brown, H. (1976). "Married homosexuals." In H. Brown (Ed.), *Familiar faces, hidden lives* (pp. 108–130). New York: Harcourt Brace Jovanovich.

Carlson, D. (1992). "Ideological conflict and change in the sexuality curriculum." In J. Sears (Ed.), *Sexuality and the curriculum* (pp. 34–57). New York: Teachers College Press.

Casper, V., & Wickens, E. (1992). "Gay and lesbian parents: Their children in school." *Teachers College Record,* 94 (1).

Chesler, P. (1986). *Mothers on trial: The battle for children and custody.* New York: McGraw-Hill.

Clay, J. (1990). "Working with lesbian and gay parents and their children." *Young Children,* 45(3), 31–35.

Coleman, E. (1985). "Bisexual women in marriages." *Journal of Homosexuality,* 11, 87–100.

Corley, R. (1990). *The final closet.* N. Miami, FL: Editech Press.

Dewey, J. (1916). *Democracy and education: An introduction to the philosophy of education.* New York: Macmillan.

Friends of Project 10 (1991). *Project 10 handbook: Addressing lesbian and gay issues in our schools* (third edition). Los Angeles, CA: Author (ERIC Reproduction No. ED 337567).

Gantz, J. (1983). "The Weston/Roberts family." In J. Gantz (Ed.), *Whose child cries: Children of gay parents talk about their lives* (pp. 49–96). Rolling Hills Estate, CA: Jalmar Press.

Gibson, P. (1989). "Gay male and lesbian youth suicide." *Report of the Secretary's Task Force on Youth Suicide. Volume 3: Prevention and interventions in youth suicide.* Washington, DC: U.S. Department of Health and Human Services.

Giroux, H. (1988). *Teachers as intellectuals: Toward a critical pedagogy of learning.* Boston: Bergin & Garvey.

Glick, P. (1987). *Remarried families, stepfamilies and stepchildren.* Paper presented at the Wingspread Conference on the Remarried Family, Racine, Wisconsin.

Glick, P. (1988). "Fifty years of family demography: A record of social change." *Journal of Marriage and the Family,* 50(4), 861–873.

Golombok, S., Spencer, A., & Rutter, M. (1983). "Children in lesbian and single-parent households: Psychosexual and psychiatric appraisal." *Journal of Child Psychology and Psychiatry,* 24, 551–572.

Goodman, J. (1983). "Out of the closet by paying the price." *Interracial Books for Children,* 9(3/4), 13–15.

Gottman, J. (1990). "Children of gay and lesbian parents." In F. Bozett & M. Sussman (Eds.), *Homosexuality and family relations* (pp. 177–196). New York: Haworth Press.

Grayson, D. (1987). "Emerging equity issues related to homosexuality in education." *Peabody Journal of Education,* 64(4), 132–145.

Green, G. (1987, August 28). *Lesbian mothers.* Paper presented at the Annual Convention of the American Psychological Association: ERIC Reproduction No. ED 297205.

Green, G., & Clunis, D. (1989). "Married lesbians." In E. Rothblum & E. Cole (Eds.), *Lesbianism: Affirming nontraditional roles* (pp. 41–50). New York: Haworth Press.

Green, R. (1978). "Sexual identity of 37 children raised by homosexual or transsexual parents." *American Journal of Psychiatry,* 135(6), 692–697.

Griffin, P. (1992). "From hiding out to coming out: Empowering lesbian and gay educators." In K. Harbeck (Ed.), *Homosexuality and Education.* New York: Haworth Press.

Haffner, D. (1990). *Sex education 2000: A call to action.* New York: SIECUS.

Harris, M., & Turner, P. (1985/1986). "Gay and lesbian parents." *Journal of Homosexuality,* 12(2), 101–113.

Heron, A., & Maran, M. (1990). *How would you feel if your dad was gay?* Boston: Alyson.

Hetrick, E., & Martin, A. D. (1987). "Developmental issues and their resolution for gay and lesbian adolescents." *Journal of Homosexuality,* 14(1/2), 25–43.

Hill, M. (1981). "Effects of conscious and unconscious factors on child reacting attitudes of lesbian mothers." (Doctoral dissertation. Adelphia University). *Dissertation Abstracts International,* 42, 1608B.

Hitchens, D. (1979/1980). "Social attitudes, legal standards, and personal trauma in child custody cases." *Journal of Homosexuality,* 5(1/2), 89–95.

Hoeffer, B. (1981). "Children's acquisition of sex role behavior in lesbian-mother families." *American Journal of Orthopsychiatry,* 51(31), 536–544.

Hotvedt, M., & Mandel, J. (1982). "Children of lesbian mothers." In W. Paul, J. Weinrich, J. Gonsiorek, & M. Hotvedt (Eds.). *Homosexuality: Social, psychological, and biological issues* (pp. 273–285). Beverly Hills, CA: Sage.

Hubbard, B. (1989). *Entering adulthood: Living in relationships. A curriculum for grades 9–12.* Santa Cruz, CA: Network Publications.

Huggins, S. (1989). "A comparative study of self-esteem of adolescent children of divorced lesbian mothers and divorced heterosexual mothers." In F. Bozett (Ed.), *Homosexuality and the family* (pp. 123–135). New York: Haworth Press.

Jay, K., & Young, A. (1979). *The gay report.* New York: Summit.

Jenkins, C. (1990, September 1). "Being gay: Gay/lesbian characters and concerns in young adult books." *Booklist,* 39–41.

Johnson, J. (1981). *Influence of assimilation on the psychosocial adjustment of black homosexual men.* (Unpublished doctoral dissertation, California School of Professional Psychology, Berkeley, CA) *Dissertation Abstracts International* 42, 11, 4620B.

Jullion, J. (1985). *Long way home: The odyssey of a lesbian mother and her children.* Pittsburgh, PA: Cleis.

Kamerman, S., & Hayes, C. (1982). "Families that work." In S. Kamerman & C. Hayes (Eds.), *Children in a changing world.* Washington, DC: National Academy Press.

Kirkpatrick, M., Smith, C., & Roy, R. (1981). "Lesbian mothers and their children: A comparative study." *American Journal of Orthopsychiatry,* 51(3), 545–551.

Kissen, R. (1991). *Listening to gay and lesbian teenagers.* Paper presented at the Annual Meeting of the National Council of Teachers of English, Seattle, WA. (ERIC Reproduction No. ED 344220.)

Krysiak, G. (1987). "Very silent and gay minority." *School Counselor,* 34(4), 304–307.

Lamothe, D. (1989). *Previously heterosexual lesbian mothers who have come out to an adolescent daughter: An exploratory study of the coming out process.* (Unpublished doctoral dissertation, Antioch University, Yellow Spring, OH.) *Dissertation Abstracts International* 50, 5, 2157B.

Lesbian Mothers Group. (1989). "A word might slip and that would be it." Lesbian mothers and their children. In L. Holly (Ed.), *Girls and sexuality: Teaching and learning* (pp. 122–129). Milton Keynes: Open University.

Lewin, E., & Lyons, T. (1982). "Everything in its place: The coexistence of lesbianism and motherhood." In W. Paul, J. Weinrich, J. Gonsiorek, & M. Hotvedt (Eds.), *Homosexuality: Social, psychological, and biological issues* (pp. 249–273). Beverly Hills, CA: Sage.

Lewis, K. (1980). "Children of lesbians: Their points of view." *Social Work,* 25(3), 198–203.

Lim-Hing, S. (1990/1991). "Dragon ladies, snow queens, and Asian-American dykes: Reflections on race and sexuality." *Empathy,* 2(2), 20–22.

Lipkin, A. (1992). "Project 10: Gay and lesbian students find acceptance in their school community." *Teaching Tolerance, 1* (2), 24–27.

Lorde, A. (1987). "Man child: A black lesbian feminist's response." In S. Pollack & J. Vaughn (Eds.), *Politics of the heart: A lesbian parenting anthology* (pp. 220–226). Ithaca, NY: Firebrand.

Macanghaill, M. (1991). "Schooling, sexuality and male power: Towards an emancipatory curriculum." *Gender and Education,* 3(3), 291–309.

Mager, D. (1975). "Faggot father." In K. Jay & A. Young (Eds.), *After you're out* (pp. 128–134). New York: Gage.

Martin, A. D. (1982). "Learning to hide: The socialization of the gay adolescent." In S. Feinstein & J. Looney (Eds.), *Adolescent psychiatry: Developmental and clinical studies* (pp. 52–65). Chicago: University of Chicago Press.

Martin, A. D., & Hetrick, E. (1988). "The stigmatization of gay and lesbian adolescents." *Journal of Homosexuality,* 15(1–2), 163–185.

Matteson, D. (1985). "Bisexual men in marriages: Is a positive homosexual identity and stable marriage possible?" *Journal of Homosexuality,* 11, 149–173.

Matteson, D. (1987). "The heterosexually married gay and lesbian parent." In F. Bozett (Ed.), *Gay and lesbian parents* (pp. 138–161). Westport, CT: Praeger.

McGuire, M., & Alexander, N. (1985). "Artificial insemination of single women." *Fertility and Sterility,* 43, 182–184.

McLaren, P. (1991). "Critical pedagogy: Constructing an arch of social dreaming and a doorway to hope." *Journal of Education,* 173 (1), 9–34.

McLaren, P. (1993). *Schooling as a ritual performance* (second edition). London: Routledge.

Miller, B. (1978). "Adult sexual resocialization: Adjustments toward a stigmatized identity." *Alternative Lifestyles,* 1, 207–234.

Miller, B. (1979a). "Unpromised paternity: The lifestyles of gay fathers." In M. Levin (Ed.), *Gay men: The sociology of male homosexuality* (pp. 239–252). New York: Harper & Row.

Miller, B. (1979b). "Gay fathers and their children." *Family Coordinator,* 28(4), 544–552.

Moraga, C., & Anzaldua, G. (Eds.). (1981). *This bridge called my back: Writings by radical women of color.* Watertown, MA: Persephone Press.

Morales, E. (1990). "Ethnic minority families and minority gays and lesbians." In F. Bozett & M. Sussman (Eds.), *Homosexuality and family relations* (pp. 217–239). New York: Haworth Press.

National Gay Task Force v. *Board of Education of the City of Oklahoma.* State of Oklahoma, 729 Fed.2d 1270 (1984). 33 FEP 1009 (1982).

Pagelow, M. (1980). "Heterosexual and lesbian single mothers: A comparison of problems, coping, and solutions." *Journal of Homosexuality,* 5(3), 189–204.

Paul, J. (1986). "Growing up with a gay, lesbian or bisexual parent: An exploratory study of experiences and perceptions." (Unpublished doctoral dissertation, University of California, Berkeley.) *Dissertation Abstracts International* 47, 7, 2756A.

Payne, A. (1977/1978). "Law and the problem patient: Custody and parental rights of homosexual, mentally retarded, mentally ill, and incarcerated patients." *Journal of Family Law,* 16(4), 797–818.

Pennington, S. (1987). "Children of lesbian mothers." F. Bozett (Ed.), *Gay and lesbian parents* (pp. 58–74). New York: Praeger.

Peterkin, R. (1987, June 11). Letter to Administrative Staff: Anti-harassment guidelines. Cambridge, MA.

Pies, C. (1985). *Considering parenthood.* San Francisco: Spinster's Ink.

Pies, C. (1987). "Considering parenthood: Psychosocial issues for gay men and lesbians choosing alternative fertilization." In F. Bozett (Ed.), *Gay and lesbian parents* (pp. 165–174). Westport, CT: Praeger.

Polikoff, N. (1987). "Lesbian mothers, lesbian families: Legal obstacles, legal challenges." In S. Pollack & J. Vaughn (Eds.), *Politics of the heart: A lesbian parenting anthology* (pp. 325–332). Ithaca, NY: Firebrand.

Pollack, S. (1989). "Lesbian mothers: A lesbian-feminist perspective on research." In S. Pollack & J. Vaughn (Eds.), *Politics of the heart: A lesbian parenting anthology* (pp. 316–324). Ithaca, NY: Firebrand.

Pollack, S., & Vaughn, J. (Eds.) (1989). *Politics of the heart: A lesbian parenting anthology.* Ithaca, NY: Firebrand.

Ricketts, W., & Achtenberg, R. (1987). "The adoptive and foster gay and lesbian parent." In F. Bozett (Ed.), *Gay and lesbian parents* (pp. 89–111). Westport, CT: Praeger.

Riddle, D., & Arguelles, M. (1981). "Children of gay parents: Homophobia's victims." In I. Stuart & L. Abt (Eds.), *Children of separation and divorce.* New York: Von Nostrand Reinhold.

Rivera, R. (1987). "Legal issues in gay and lesbian parenting." In F. Bozett (Ed.), *Gay and lesbian parents* (pp. 199–227). Westport, CT: Praeger.

Robinson, B., & Skeen, P. (1982). "Sex-role orientation of gay fathers versus gay nonfathers." *Perceptual and Motor Skills,* 55, 1055–1059.

Rofes, E. (1989). "Opening up the classroom closet: Responding to the educational needs of gay and lesbian youth." *Harvard Educational Review,* 59(4), 444–453.

Rohrbaugh, J. (1989). "Choosing children: Psychological issues in lesbian parenting." In E. Rothblum & E.

Cole (Eds.), *Lesbianism: Affirming nontraditional roles* (pp. 51–64). New York: Haworth Press.

Rugg, H. (1939). *Democracy and the curriculum: The life and progress of the American school.* New York: Appleton–Century.

Rust, P. (1993). " 'Coming Out' in the age of social constructionism: Sexual identity formation among lesbian and bisexual women." *Gender and Society,* 7 (1), 50–77.

Sands, A. (1988). "We are family." In H. Alpert (Ed.), *We are everywhere* (pp. 45–51). Freedom. CA: Crossing Press.

Scallen, R. (1981). *An investigation of paternal attitudes and behaviors in homosexual and heterosexual fathers.* (Unpublished doctoral dissertation. California School of Professional Psychology, Los Angeles, CA.) *Dissertation Abstracts International 42,* 9, 3809B.

Schneider, M., & Tremble, B. (1986). "Training service providers to work with gay or lesbian adolescents: A workshop." *Journal of Counseling and Development,* 65(2), 98–99.

Schulenberg, J. (1985). *Gay parenting.* Garden City, NY: Doubleday.

Sears, J. (1983). "Sexuality: Taking off the masks." *Changing Schools,* 11, 12–13.

Sears, J. (1987). "Peering into the well of loneliness: The responsibility of educators to gay and lesbian youth." In Alex Molnar (Ed.), *Social issues and education: Challenge and responsibility* (pp. 79–100). Alexandria, VA: Association for Supervision & Curriculum Development.

Sears, J. (1988b). "Growing up gay: Is anyone there to listen?" *American School Counselors Association Newsletter,* 26, 8–9.

Sears, J. (1989b). "The impact of gender and race on growing up lesbian and gay in the South." *NWSA Journal,* 1(3), 422–457.

Sears, J. (1989c). "Counseling sexual minorities: An interview with Virginia Uribe." *Empathy,* 1(2), 1, 8.

Sears, J. (1991a). *Growing up gay in the South: Race, gender, and journeys of the spirit.* New York: Haworth Press.

Sears, J. (1991b). "Teaching for diversity: Student sexual identities." *Educational Leadership,* 49, 54–57.

Sears, J. (1992a). "Educators, homosexuality, and homosexual students: Are personal feelings related to professional beliefs?" *Journal of Homosexuality,* 29–79.

Sears, J. (1992b). "The impact of culture and ideology on the construction of gender and sexual identities: De-veloping a critically-based sexuality curriculum." In J. Sears (Ed.), *Sexuality and the curriculum: The politics and practices of sexuality education* (pp. 169–189). New York: Teachers College Press.

Sears, J. (1992c). "Dilemmas and possibilities of sexuality education: Reproducing the body politic." In J. Sears (Ed.), *Sexuality and the curriculum: The politics and practices of sexuality education* (pp. 19–50). New York: Teachers College Press.

Sears, J. (1992d). "Responding to the sexual diversity of faculty and students: An agenda for critically reflective administrators." In C. Capper (Ed.), *The social context of education: Administration in a pluralist society* (pp. 110–172). New York: State University of New York Press.

Sears, J. (1993). "Alston and Everetta: Too risky for school?" In R. Donmoyer & R. Kos (Eds.). *At-risk students* (pp. 153–172). New York: State University of New York Press.

Shernoff, M. (1984). "Family therapy for lesbian and gay clients." *Social Work,* 29(4), 393–396.

Slater, B. (1988). "Essential issues in working with lesbian and gay male youths." *Professional Psychology: Research and Practice,* 19(2), 226–235.

Smith, B. (Ed.) (1983). *Home girls: A black feminist anthology.* New York: Kitchen Table: Women of Color Press.

Stewart, J. (1984). "What non-gay therapists need to know to work with gay and lesbian clients." *Practice Digest,* 7(1), 28–32.

Stover, D. (1992). "The at-risk kids schools ignore." *Executive Educator,* 14 (3), 28–31.

Summerford, S. (1987). "The public library: Offensive by design." *Public Libraries,* 26(2), 60–62.

Tabbert, B. (1988). "Battling over books: Freedom and responsibility are tested." *Emergency Librarian,* 16(1), 9–13.

Teague, J. (1992). "Issues relating to the treatment of adolescent lesbians and homosexuals." *Journal of Mental Health Counseling,* 14 (4), 422–439.

Turner, P., Scadden, L., & Harris, M. (1985, March). *Parenting in gay and lesbian families.* Paper presented at the First Annual Future of Parenting Symposium, Chicago.

Vazquez, R. (1992). "(No longer) sleeping with the enemy." *Empathy,* 3(1), 90–91.

Weeks, R., Derdeyn, A., & Langman, M. (1975). "Two cases of children of homosexuals." *Child Psychiatry and Human Development,* 6(1), 26–32.

Weinberg, G. (1972). *Society and the healthy homosexual.* New York: St. Martin's Press.

Wilhoite, M. (1990). *Daddy's roommate.* Boston: Alyson.

Wilson, D. (1984). "The open library." *English Journal,* 43(7), 60–63.

Wolf, T. (1985). "Marriages of bisexual men." *Journal of Homosexuality,* 4, 135–148.

Wyers, N. (1984). *Lesbian and gay spouses and parents: Homosexuality in the family.* Portland, OR: School of Social Work, Portland State University.

Wyers, N. (1987). "Homosexuality in the family: Lesbian and gay spouses." *Social Work,* 32(2), 143–148.

Zera, D. (1992). "Coming of age in a heterosexist world: The development of gay and lesbian adolescents." *Adolescence,* 27 (108), 849–854.

DISCUSSION QUESTIONS

1. Why does the sexual orientation of a parent play a prominent role in child custody cases?
2. According to research studies, what is the child's typical reaction to learning that a parent is gay or lesbian?
3. How do homophobia and heterosexism affect children of gay or lesbian parents?
4. What are some of the social control strategies that children use to deal with their parent's homosexuality?
5. Why should educators assume proactive roles on behalf of lesbian, gay, or bisexual students and families?
6. According to the author, how can discussions about sexuality be transformative?
7. How should preservice teacher education programs prepare future teachers to respond to issues faced by students of gay and lesbian parents?

33

Performance-based Assessment and Educational Equity

LINDA DARLING-HAMMOND

FOCUSING QUESTIONS

1. *What is authentic assessment?*
2. *In what ways do proposals for authentic assessment differ?*
3. *What issues are associated with the nature of assessment tools?*
4. *How do assessment tools influence curriculum and instruction?*
5. *What is the difference between testing and assessment?*
6. *How does the quality of teacher instruction influence educational equity?*
7. *What role should teachers play in developing and using authentic assessment? Why? Why not?*
8. *In what ways can assessment be used to measure student success in a continuous and authentic fashion rather than as a means to sort students and sanction educators?*

The use of educational testing in the United States has been criticized for its inequitable effects on different populations of students. Many assume that new forms of assessment will lead to more equitable outcomes. The author argues in this chapter, however, that alternative assessment methods, such as performance-based assessment, are not inherently equitable and that educators must pay careful attention to the ways that the assessments are used. Some school reform strategies, for example, use assessment reform as a lever for external control of schools. These strategies are unlikely to be successful, and the assessments are unlikely to be equitable because they stem from a distrust of teachers and fail to involve teachers in the reform processes.

The author argues instead for policies that ensure "top-down support for bottom-up reform," where assessment is used to give teachers practical information on student learning and to provide opportunities for school communities to engage in "a recursive process of self-reflection, self-critique, self-correction, and self-renewal." Ultimately, then, the equitable use of performance assessments depends not only on the design of the assessments themselves, but also on how well the assessment practices are interwoven with the goals of authentic school reform and effective teaching.

In recent years, the school reform movement has engendered widespread efforts to transform the ways in which students' work and learning are assessed in schools. These alternatives are frequently called performance-based or "authentic" assessments because they engage students in "real-world" tasks, rather than multiple-choice tests, and evaluate them according to criteria that are important for actual performance in a field of work (Wiggins, 1989). Such assessments include oral presentations, debates, and exhibitions, along with collections of students' written products, videotapes of performances and other learning occasions, constructions and models, and their solutions to problems, experiments, or results of scientific and other inquiries (Archbald & Newman, 1988). They also include teacher observations and inventories of individual students' work and behavior, as well as of cooperative group work (National Association for the Education of Young Children [NAEYC], 1988).

Much of the rationale for these initiatives is based on growing evidence that traditional norm-referenced, multiple-choice tests fail to measure complex cognitive and performance abilities. Furthermore, when used for decision making, they encourage instruction that tends to emphasize decontextualized, rote-oriented tasks imposing low cognitive demands, rather than meaningful learning. Thus, efforts to raise standards of learning and performance must rest in part on strategies to transform assessment practices.

In addition, efforts to ensure that *all* students learn in meaningful ways resulting in high levels of performance require that teachers know as much about students and their learning as they do about subject matter. However, teachers' understandings of students' strengths, needs, and approaches to learning are not well supported by external testing programs that send secret, secured tests into the school and whisk them out again for machine scoring that produces numerical quotients many months later. Authentic assessment strategies can provide teachers with much more useful classroom information because they engage teachers in evaluating how and what students know and can do in real-life performance situations. These kinds of assessment strategies create the possibility that teachers will not only develop curricula aimed at challenging performance skills, but that they will also be able to use the resulting rich information about student learning and performance to shape their teaching in ways that can prove more effective for individual students.

Recently, interest in alternative forms of student assessment has expanded from the classroom-based efforts of individual teachers to district and statewide initiatives to overhaul entire testing programs so that they become more performance based. Major national testing programs, such as the National Assessment of Educational Progress and the College Board's Scholastic Assessment Tests (formerly the Scholastic Aptitude Tests), are also undergoing important changes. These programs are being redesigned so that they will increasingly engage students in performance tasks requiring written and oral responses in lieu of multiple-choice questions focused on discrete facts or decontextualized bits of knowledge.

However, proposals for assessment reform differ in several important ways: (1) in the extent to which they aim to broaden the roles of educators, students, parents, and other community members in assessment; (2) in the extent to which they aim to make assessment part of the teaching and learning process and use it to serve developmental and educational purposes, rather than sorting and screening purposes; (3) in the extent to which they anticipate a problem-based interdisciplinary curriculum or a coverage-oriented curriculum that maintains traditional subject area compartments for learning; and (4) in the extent to which they see assessment reform as part of a broader national agenda to improve and equalize educational opportunities in schools. Some see assessment reform as part of a broader agenda to strengthen the national educational infrastructure (the availability of high-quality teachers, curriculum, and resources) and to equalize access so that all students start from an equal platform for learning. Others, however, view performance-based assessment as a single sledgehammer for change, without acknowledging other structural realities of schooling, such as vast inequalities in educational opportunities.

These differences in approaches to assessment reform predict very different consequences for the educational system and dramatically different consequences for those who have been traditionally underserved in U.S. schools—students in poor communities, "minorities," immigrants, and students with distinctive learning needs. In this chapter, I argue in particular that *changes in the forms of assessment are unlikely to enhance equity unless we change the ways in which assessments are used as well:* from sorting mechanisms to diagnostic supports, from external monitors of performance to locally generated tools for inquiring deeply into teaching and learning, and from purveyors of sanctions for those already underserved to levers for equalizing resources and enhancing learning opportunities.

The extent to which educational testing serves to enhance teaching and learning and to support greater equality or to undermine educational opportunity depends on how a variety of issues is resolved. Among these are issues associated with the nature of assessment tools themselves:

• Whether and how they avoid bias
• How they resolve concerns about subjectivity versus objectivity in evaluating student work
• How they influence curriculum and teaching

A second set of issues has to do with whether and how assessment results are used to determine student placements and promotions, to reinforce differential curriculum tracking, or to allocate rewards and sanctions to teachers, programs, or schools.

A final set of issues concerns the policies and practices that surround the assessment system and determine the educational opportunities available to students to support their learning. A fundamental question is whether assessment systems will support better teaching and transform schooling for traditionally underserved students or whether they will merely reify existing inequities. This depends on the extent to which they promote equity in the allocation of resources for providing education, supports for effective teaching practices, and supports for more widespread school restructuring.

MOTIVATIONS FOR ASSESSMENT REFORM

The current movement to change U.S. traditions of student assessment in large-scale and systemic ways has several motivations. One is based on the recognition that assessment, especially when it is used for decision-making purposes, exerts powerful influences on curriculum and instruction. It can drive instruction in ways that mimic not only the content, but also the format and cognitive demands of tests (Darling-Hammond & Wise, 1985; Madaus, West, Harmon, Lomax, & Viator, 1992). If assessment exerts these influences, many argue, it should be carefully shaped to send signals that are consistent with the kinds of learning desired and the approaches to curriculum and instruction that will support such learning (Cohen & Spillane, 1992; O'Day & Smith, 1993).

A second and somewhat related motive for systemic approaches to assessment reform stems from the belief that if assessment can exert powerful influences on behavior it can be used to change school organizational behavior as well as classroom work. The idea of using assessment as a lever for school change is not a new one: many accountability tools in the 1970s and 1980s tried to link policy decisions to test scores (Linn, 1987; Madaus, 1985; Wise, 1979). Unfortunately, these efforts frequently had unhappy results for teaching and learning generally and for schools' treatment of low-scoring students in particular. Research on these initiatives has found that test-based decision making has driven instruction toward lower-order cognitive skills. This shift has created incentives for pushing low scorers into special education, consigning them to educationally unproductive remedial classes, holding them back in the grades, and encouraging them to drop out (Allington & McGill-Franzen, 1992; Darling-Hammond, 1991, 1993; Koretz, 1988; Shepard & Smith, 1988; Smith, 1986). In addition, school incentives tied to test scores have undermined efforts to create and sustain more inclusive and integrated student populations, as schools are punished for accepting and keeping students with special needs and are rewarded for keeping such students out of their programs through selective admissions and transfer policies. Those with clout and means "improve" education by manipulating the population of students that they serve (Smith, 1986). Schools serving disadvantaged students find it increasingly hard to recruit and retain experienced and highly qualified staff when the threat of punishments for low scores hangs over them. Thus, such policies exacerbate rather than ameliorate the unequal distribution of educational opportunity.

Nonetheless, a variety of proposals has recently been put forth that involves the use of mandated performance-based assessments as external levers for school change (Commission on Chapter I, 1992; Hornbeck, 1992; O'Day & Smith, 1993). Even those who do not endorse such proposals share the view that assessment can promote change. Other proposals, raised from a different philosophical vantage point and envisioning different uses of assessment, suggest the use of alternative classroom-embedded assessments as internal supports for school-based inquiry (Darling-Hammond & Ascher, 1990; Wolf & Baron, in press).

A third reason for assessment reform addresses concerns about equity and access to educational opportunity. Over many decades, assessment results have frequently been used to define not only teaching, but also students' opportunities to learn. As a tool for tracking students into different courses, levels, and kinds of instructional programs, testing has been a primary means for limiting or expanding students' life choices and their avenues for demonstrating competence. Increasingly, these uses of tests are recognized as having the unintended consequence of limiting students' access to further learning opportunities (Darling-Hammond, 1991; Glaser, 1990; Oakes, 1985).

Some current proposals for performance-based assessment view these new kinds of tests as serving the same screening and tracking purposes as more traditional tests (Commission on the Skills of the American Workforce, 1990; Educate America, 1991; National Center on Education and the Economy, 1989). The presumption is that more "authentic" assessments will both motivate and sort students more effectively. Others see a primary goal of assessment reform as transforming the purposes and uses of testing as well as its form and content. They argue for shifting from the use of assessment as a sorting device to its use as a tool for identifying student strengths and needs so that teachers can adapt instruction more successfully (Darling-Hammond, Ancess, & Falk, 1995; Gla-

ser, 1981, 1990; Kornhaber & Gardner, 1993). Given the knowledge now available for addressing diverse learning needs and the needs of today's society for a broadly educated populace, the goals of education—and assessment—are being transformed from deciding who will be permitted to become well-educated to helping to ensure that everyone will learn successfully.

Clearly, the current press to reform assessment entails many motivations and many possible consequences, depending on decisions that are made about (1) the nature of the "new" assessments, (2) the ways in which they are used, and (3) the companion efforts (if any) that accompany them to actually improve education in the schools.

In this chapter I outline the range of equity issues that arise with respect to testing generally and with respect to proposals for the development of new "authentic" assessments specifically. I argue that the outcomes of the current wave of assessment reforms will depend in large measure on the extent to which assessment developers and users

- Focus on both the quality and fairness of assessment strategies
- Use assessments in ways that serve teaching and learning, rather than sorting and selecting
- Develop policies that are congruent with (and respectful of) these assessment goals, as well as with assessment strategies and limitations
- Embed assessment reform in broader reforms to improve and equalize access to educational resources and opportunities
- Support the professional development of teachers along with the organizational development of schools so that assessment is embedded in teaching and learning and is used to inform more skillful and adaptive teaching that enables more successful learning for all students

USES AND CONSEQUENCES OF TESTING

Historical Perspectives

For over 100 years, standardized testing has been a tool used to exert control over the schooling process and to make decisions about educational entitlements for students. Testing proved a convenient instrument of social control for those superintendents in the late nineteenth century who sought to use tests as a means for creating the "one best system" of education (Tyack, 1974). It also proved enormously useful as a means of determining how to slot students for more and less rigorous (and costly) curricula when public funding of education and compulsory attendance vastly increased access to schools in the early twentieth century.

Given the massive increase in students, the limits of public budgets, and the relatively meager training of teachers, strategies were sought to codify curriculum and to group students for differential instruction. IQ tests were widely used as a measure of educational input (with intelligence viewed as the "raw material" for schooling) to sort pupils so that they could be efficiently educated according to their future roles in society (Cremin, 1961; Cubberly, 1919; Watson, in press). Frequently, they were used to exclude students from schooling opportunities altogether (Glaser, 1981).

Though many proponents argued that the use of these tests as a tool for tracking students would enhance social justice, the rationales for tracking—like those for using scores to set immigration quotas into the United States—were often frankly motivated by racial and ethnic politics. Just as Goddard's 1912 data—"proving" that 83 percent of Jews, 80 percent of Hungarians, 79 percent of Italians, and 87 percent of Russians were "feebleminded"—were used to justify low immigration quotas for those groups (Kamin, 1974), so did Terman's test data "prove" that "[Indians, Mexicans, and Negroes] should be segregated in special classes.... They cannot master abstractions, but they can often be made efficient workers" (Terman, cited in Oakes, 1985, p. 36). Presumptions like these reinforced racial segregation and differential learning opportunities.

Terman found many inequalities in performance among groups on his IQ test, which was adapted from Binet's work in France. Most, but not all of them, seemed to confirm what he and presumably every "intelligent" person already knew: that various groups were inherently unequal in their mental capacities. However, when girls scored higher than boys on his 1916 version of the Stanford–Binet, he revised the test to correct for this apparent flaw by selecting items to create parity among genders in the scores (Mercer, 1989). Other inequalities—between urban and rural students, students of higher and lower socioeconomic status, native English speakers and immigrants, whites and blacks—did not occasion such revisions, since their validity seemed patently obvious to the test makers.

The role of testing in reinforcing and extending social inequalities in educational opportunities has by now been extensively researched (Gould, 1981; Kamin, 1974; Mercer, 1989; Oakes, 1985; Watson, in press) and widely acknowledged. It began with the two fallacies that Gould describes: the fallacy of reification, which allowed testers to develop and sell the abstract concept of intelligence as an innate, unitary, measurable commodity; and the fallacy of ranking, which supported the development of strategies for quantifying intelligence in ways that would allow people to be arrayed in a single series against each other (Gould, 1981). These two fallacies—recently debunked (though not yet dismantled) by understandings that intelligence has many dimensions (Gardner, 1983; Sternberg, 1985)—were made more dangerous by the social uses of testing as a tool for allocating educational and employment benefits rather than as a means for informing teaching and developing talents.

Negative Consequences of Standardized Testing

Current standardized tests are widely criticized for placing test takers in a passive, reactive role (Wigdor & Garner, 1982), rather than one that engages their capacities to structure tasks, produce ideas, and solve problems. Based on outmoded views of learning, intelligence, and performance, they fail to measure students' higher-order cognitive abilities or to support their capacities to perform real-world tasks (Resnick, 1987a; Sternberg, 1985).

In a seminal paper on the past, present, and future of testing, Glaser (1990) makes an important distinction between testing and assessment. These two kinds of measurement have different purposes and different social and technical histories. Glaser describes testing as aimed at selection and placement: it attempts to predict success at learning by "measur[ing] human ability prior to a course of instruction so that individuals can be appropriately placed, diagnosed, included or excluded" (p. 2). Assessment, on the other hand, is aimed at gauging educational outcomes: it measures the results of a course of learning. What is important for testing is the instrument's predictive power, rather than its content. What is important for assessment is the content validity of an approach—its ability to describe the nature of performance that results from learning.

Recently, another validity construct has emerged: *consequential validity,* which describes the extent to which an assessment tool *and the ways in which it is used* produce positive consequences both for the teaching and learning process and for students who may experience different educational opportunities as a result of test-based placements (Glaser, 1990; Shepard, 1993). This emerging validity standard places a much heavier burden on assessment developers and users to demonstrate that what they are doing works to the benefit of those who are assessed and to the society at large. The emergence of this standard has led many educators and researchers to question test-based program placements for students and to press for forms of assessment that can support more challenging and authentic forms of teaching and learning. Some test developers are just beginning to understand that the criteria against which their products are being evaluated are changing.

For most of this century, much of the energy of U.S. measurement experts has been invested in developing tests aimed at ranking students for sorting and selecting them into and out of particular placements. Standardized test developers have devoted much less energy to worrying about the properties of these instruments as reflections of— or influences on—instruction (Wigdor & Garner, 1982). As a consequence, the tests generally do not reflect the actual tasks that educators and citi-

zens expect students to be able to perform, nor do they stimulate forms of instruction that are closely connected to the development of performance abilities. Similarly, to date, though awareness levels are heightened, virtually no attention has been paid to the consequences of test-based decisions in policy discussions about developing new assessment systems.

These shortcomings of U.S. tests were less problematic when they were used as only one source of information among many other kinds of information about student learning and when they were not directly tied to decisions about students and programs. However, as test scores have been used to make important educational decisions, their flaws have become more damaging. As schools have begun to "teach to the tests," the scores have become ever poorer assessments of students' overall abilities, because class work oriented toward recognizing the answers to multiple-choice questions does not heighten students' proficiency in aspects of the subjects that are not tested, such as analysis, complex problem solving, and written and oral expression (Darling-Hammond & Wise, 1985; Haney & Madaus, 1986; Koretz, 1988).

As the National Assessment of Educational Progress (NAEP) found, "Only 5 to 10 percent of students can move beyond initial readings of a text; most seem genuinely puzzled at requests to explain or defend their points of view." The NAEP assessors explained that current methods of testing reading require short responses and lower-level cognitive thinking, resulting in "an emphasis on shallow and superficial opinions at the expense of reasoned and disciplined thought, … [thus] it is not surprising that students fail to develop more comprehensive thinking and analytic skills" (NAEP, 1981, p. 5).

During the 1970s, when test-oriented accountability measures were instituted in U.S. schools, there was a decline in public schools' use of teaching methods appropriate to the teaching of higher-order skills, such as research projects and laboratory work, student-centered discussions, and the writing of essays or themes (National Center for Education Statistics [NCES], 1982, p. 83). Major studies by Boyer (1983), Goodlad (1984), and Sizer (1985) documented the negative effects of standardized testing on teaching and learning in high schools, while the disadvantage created for U.S. students by the rote learning stressed in U.S. standardized tests has been documented in international studies of achievement (McKnight et al., 1987).

The effects of basic skills test misuse have been most unfortunate for the students that they were most intended to help. Many studies have found that students placed in the lowest tracks or in remedial programs—disproportionately low-income and minority students—are most apt to experience instruction geared only to multiple-choice tests, working at a low cognitive level on test-oriented tasks that are profoundly disconnected from the skills that they need to learn. Rarely are they given the opportunity to talk about what they know, to read real books, to write, or to construct and solve problems in mathematics, science, or other subjects (Cooper & Sherk, 1989; Davis, 1986; Oakes, 1985; Trimble & Sinclair, 1986). In short, they have been denied the opportunity to develop the capacities that they will need for the future, in large part because commonly used tests are so firmly pointed at educational goals of the past.

Thus, the quality of education made available to many students has been undermined by the nature of the testing programs used to monitor and shape their learning. If new performance-based assessments point at more challenging learning goals for all students, they may ameliorate some of this source of inequality. However, this will be true only to the extent that teachers who serve these students are able to teach in the ways demanded by the assessments—that is, in ways that support the development of higher-order thinking and performance skills and in ways that diagnose and build on individual learners' strengths and needs.

The Uses of Assessment Tools in Decision Making

As noted earlier, testing policies affect students' opportunities to learn in other important ways. In addition to determining whether students graduate,

tests are increasingly used to track students and to determine whether they can be promoted from one grade to the next. Research suggests that both practices have had harmful consequences for individual students and for U.S. achievement generally. If performance-based assessments are used for the same purposes as traditional tests have been, the outcomes for underserved students are likely to be unchanged.

Tracking. In the United States, the process of tracking begins in elementary schools with the designation of instructional groups and programs based on test scores and becomes highly formalized by junior high school. The result of this practice is that challenging curricula are rationed to a very small proportion of students. Consequently, few U.S. students ever encounter the kinds of curricula that most students in other countries typically experience (McKnight et al., 1987). As Oakes (1986) notes, these assignments are predictable:

> One finding about placements is undisputed.... Disproportionate percentages of poor and minority youngsters (principally black and Hispanic) are placed in tracks for low-ability or non-college-bound students (NCES, 1985; Rosenbaum, 1980); further, minority students are consistently underrepresented in programs for the gifted and talented. (College Board, 1985, p. 129)

Students placed in lower tracks are exposed to a limited, rote-oriented curriculum and ultimately achieve less than students of similar aptitude who are placed in academic programs or untracked classes. Furthermore, these curricular differences explain much of the disparity between the achievement of white and minority students and between those of higher and lower income levels (Lee & Bryk, 1988; Oakes, 1985). In this way, the uses of tests have impeded rather than supported the pursuit of high and rigorous educational goals for all students.

Grade Retention. In addition, some U.S. states and local districts have enacted policies requiring that test scores be used as the sole criterion for decisions about student promotion from one grade to the next. Since the student promotion policies were enacted, a substantial body of research has demonstrated that the effects of this kind of test-based decision making are much more negative than positive. When students who were retained in grade are compared to students of equal achievement levels who were promoted, the retained students are consistently behind on both achievement and social–emotional measures (Holmes & Matthews, 1984; Shephard & Smith, 1986). As Shephard and Smith put it, "Contrary to popular beliefs, repeating a grade does *not* help students gain ground academically and has a negative impact on social adjustment and self-esteem" (1986, p. 86).

Furthermore, the practice of retaining students is a major contributor to increased dropout rates. Research suggests that being retained increases the odds of dropping out by 40 to 50 percent. A second retention nearly doubles the risk (Mann, 1987; see also Carnegie Council on Adolescent Development, 1989; Massachusetts Advocacy Center, 1988; Wehlage, Rutter, Smith, Lesko, & Fernández, 1990). Thus, the policy of automatically retaining students based on their test-score performance has actually produced lower achievement for these students, lower self-esteem, and higher dropout rates for them and for the nation.

Graduation. Perhaps the ultimate test-related sanction for students is denying a diploma based on a test score. The rationale for this practice is that students should show that they have mastered the "minimum skills" needed for employment or future education in order to graduate. The assumption is that tests can adequately capture whatever those skills are. While this appears plausible in theory, it is unlikely in reality, given the disjunction between multiple-choice tests of decontextualized bits of information and the demands of real jobs and adult tasks (Bailey, 1989; Carnevale, Gainer, & Meltzer, 1989; Resnick, 1987b). In fact, research indicates that neither employability nor earnings are significantly affected by students' scores on basic skills tests, while chances of employment and welfare dependency are tightly linked to graduation from high school (Eckland, 1980; Gordon & Sum, 1988; Jaeger, 1991). Thus, the use of tests as a sole determinant of graduation imposes heavy personal and societal costs, without obvious social benefits.

Rewards and Sanctions. Finally, a few states and districts have also tried to use student test scores to allocate rewards or sanctions to schools or teachers. President Bush's proposal for a National Test included a suggestion to allocate some federal funds based on schools' scores on the "American Achievement Tests" (U.S. Department of Education, 1991). An independent commission on Chapter I has recently proposed, over the formal dissent of a number of its members, a rewards and sanctions system for Chapter I programs based on aggregate "performance-based" test scores (Commission on Chapter I, 1992). An analogous policy proposal has been enacted, though not yet implemented, for use with performance-based tests in the state of Kentucky. There, all schools that do not show specified percentage increases in student achievement scores each year will automatically suffer sanctions, which may include actions against staff. Those that meet the standards will be financially rewarded (Legislative Research Commission, 1990, p. 21).

Oblivious to the fact that schools' scores on any measure are sensitive to changes in the population of students taking the test and that such changes can be induced by manipulating admission, dropouts, and pupil classifications, the policy will create and sustain a wide variety of perverse incentives, regardless of whether the tests are multiple choice or performance oriented. Because schools' aggregate scores on any measure are sensitive to the population of students taking the test, the policy creates incentives for schools to keep out students whom they fear may lower their scores—children who are handicapped, limited English speaking, or from educationally disadvantaged environments. Schools where average test scores are used for making decisions about rewards and sanctions have found a number of ways to manipulate their test-taking population in order to inflate artificially the school's average test scores. These strategies include labeling large numbers of low-scoring students for special education placements so that their scores won't "count" in school reports, retaining students in grade so that their relative standing will look better on "grade-equivalent" scores, excluding low-scoring students from admission to "open enrollment" schools, and encouraging such students to leave schools or drop out (Allington & McGill-Franzen, 1992; Darling-Hammond, 1991, 1993; Koretz, 1988; Shepard & Smith, 1988; Smith, 1986).

Smith explains the widespread engineering of student populations that he found in his study of a large urban school district that used performance standards as a basis for school-level sanctions:

> Student selection provides the greatest leverage in the short-term accountability game…. The easiest way to improve one's chances of winning is (1) to add some highly likely students and (2) to drop some unlikely students, while simply hanging on to those in the middle. School admissions is a central thread in the accountability fabric. (1986, pp. 30–31)

This kind of policy, which rewards or punishes schools for aggregate test scores, creates a distorted view of accountability, in which beating the numbers by playing shell games with student placements overwhelms efforts to serve students' educational needs well. Equally important, these policies further exacerbate existing incentives for talented staff to opt for school placements where students are easy to teach and school stability is high. Capable staff are less likely to risk losing rewards or incurring sanctions by volunteering to teach where many students have special needs and performance standards will be more difficult to attain. This compromises even further the educational chances of disadvantaged students, who are already served by a disproportionate share of those teachers who are inexperienced, unprepared, and underqualified.

Applying sanctions to schools with lower test score performance penalizes already disadvantaged students twice over: having given them inadequate schools to begin with, society will now punish them again for failing to perform as well as other students attending schools with greater resources and more capable teachers. This kind of reward system confuses the quality of education offered by schools with the needs of the students that they enroll; it works against equity and integration and against any possibilities for fair and open school choice by discouraging good schools from opening their doors to educationally needy students. Such a reward structure places more emphasis on score manipulations and student assignments or exclusions than on school improvement and the development of more effective teaching practices.

POLICIES FOR BUILDING AN EQUITABLE SYSTEM

Improving Teacher Capacity

Because this nation has not invested heavily in teacher education and professional development, the capacity for a more complex, student-centered approach to teaching is not prevalent throughout the current teaching force. Furthermore, because teacher salaries and working conditions are inadequate to ensure a steady supply of qualified teachers in poor districts, low-income and minority students are routinely taught by the least experienced and least prepared teachers (Darling-Hammond, 1991; Oakes, 1990). Differences in achievement between white and minority students can be substantially explained by unequal access to high-quality curriculum and instruction (Barr & Dreeben, 1983; College Board, 1985; Darling-Hammond & Snyder, 1992a; Dreeben, 1987; Dreeben & Barr, 1987; Dreeben & Gamoran, 1986; Oakes, 1990).

From a policy perspective, perhaps the single greatest source of educational inequity is this disparity in the availability and distribution of highly qualified teachers (Darling-Hammond, 1990). Providing equity in the distribution of teacher quality will be required before changes in assessment strategies result in more challenging and effective instruction for currently underserved students. This, in turn, requires changing policies and long-standing incentive structures in education so that shortages of well-prepared teachers are overcome, and schools serving poor and minority students are not disadvantaged by lower salaries and poorer working conditions in the bidding war for good teachers. Fundamental changes in school funding are essential to this task. Since revenues in poor districts are often half as great as those in wealthy districts, state aid changes that equalize district resources are the first step toward ensuring access to qualified teachers (Darling-Hammond, in press).

This crucial equity concern is finally gaining some attention in the rush to improve schools by testing. The recent report of the National Council on Education Standards and Testing (NCEST), while arguing for national performance standards for students, acknowledged the importance of "school delivery standards" for educational improvements to occur. The Council's Standards Task Force noted:

> If not accompanied by measures to ensure equal opportunity to learn, national content and performance standards could help widen the achievement gap between the advantaged and the disadvantaged in our society. If national content and performance standards and assessment are not accompanied by clear school delivery standards and policy measures designed to afford all students an equal opportunity to learn, the concerns about diminished equity could easily be realized. Standards and assessments must be accompanied by policies that provide access for all students to high quality resources, including appropriate instructional materials and well-prepared teachers. High content and performance standards can be used to challenge all students with the same expectations, but high expectations will only result in common high performance if all schools provide high quality instruction designed to meet the expectations. (NCEST, 1992, pp. E12–El3)

Delivery standards make clear that the governmental agencies that are imposing standards on students are simultaneously accepting responsibility for ensuring that students will encounter the opportunities necessary for their success (Darling-Hammond, 1993). Though this may seem a straightforward prerequisite for making judgments about students or schools, it marks an entirely different approach to accountability in U.S. education than the one that has predominated for most of the last two decades and is widespread today. Earlier approaches to outcomes-based accountability legislated minimum competency tests and sometimes punished schools or students with low scores without attempting to correct the resource disparities that contributed to poor performance in the first place.

Ensuring that all students have adequate opportunities to learn requires enhancing the capacity of all teachers—their knowledge of students and subjects and their ability to use that knowledge—by professionalizing teaching. This means that teacher education policies must ensure that *all* teachers have a stronger understanding of how children learn and develop, how assessment can be used to evaluate what they know and how they learn, how a variety of curricular and instructional strategies can address their needs, and how changes in school and classroom organization can support their growth and achievement.

Such teacher capacities are also important for supporting the promise of authentic assessment to enable richer, more instructionally useful forms of evaluation that are also fair and informative. A major reason for the advent of externally controlled, highly standardized testing systems has been the belief that teachers could not be trusted to make sound decisions about what students know and are able to do. The presumed "objectivity" of current tests derives both from the lack of reliance on individual teacher judgment in scoring and from the fact that test takers are anonymous to test scorers (hence, extraneous views about the student do not bias scoring).

Of course, many forms of bias remain, as the choice of items, responses deemed appropriate, and content deemed important are the product of culturally and contextually determined judgments, as well as the privileging of certain ways of knowing and modes of performance over others (García & Pearson, 1994; Gardner, 1983; Sternberg, 1985;

Wigdor & Garner, 1982). And these forms of bias are equally likely to plague performance-based assessments, because the selection of tasks will rest on cultural and other referents, such as experiences, terms, and exposures to types of music, art, literature, and social experiences that are differentially accessible to test takers of different backgrounds.

If assessment is to be used to open up as many opportunities as possible to as many students as possible, it must address a wide range of talents, a variety of life experiences, and multiple ways of knowing. Diverse and wide-ranging tasks that use many different performance modes and that involve students in choosing ways to demonstrate their competence become important for this goal (Gordon, no date; Kornhaber & Gardner, 1993). Substantial teacher and student involvement in and control over assessment strategies and uses are critical if assessment is to support the most challenging education possible for every student, taking full account of his or her special talents and ways of knowing. As Gordon puts it,

> The task is to find assessment probes which measure the same criterion from contexts and perspectives which reflect the life space and values of the learner…. Thus options and choices become a critical feature in any assessment system created to be responsive to equity, just as processual description and diagnosis become central purposes. (no date, pp. 8–9)

The objective of maintaining high standards with less standardization will demand teachers who are able to evaluate and eliminate sources of unfair bias in their development and scoring of instructionally embedded assessments and who can balance subjectivity and objectivity, using their subjective knowledge of students appropriately in selecting tasks and assessment options while adhering to common, collective standards of evaluation. These same abilities will be crucial for other assessment developers. In many respects, even greater sensitivity to the sources of bias that can pervade assessment will be needed with forms that frequently eliminate the anonymity of test takers,

drawing more heavily on interpersonal interaction in tasks and on observations on the part of teachers.

"Top-down Support for Bottom-up Reform"

The need for greater teacher knowledge and sensitivity in developing and using authentic assessments in schools will cause some to argue that they should not be attempted, that externally developed and scored "objective" tests are safer for making decisions because local judgment is avoided. However, the argument for authentic assessments rests as much on a changed conception of the *uses* of assessment as on the *form* in which assessment occurs. Rather than being used largely to determine how students rank against one another on a single, limited dimension of performance so as to determine curriculum or school placements of various kinds, many reformers hope that assessment can be used to *inform and improve* teaching and learning.

In this view, assessment should be integrally connected to the teaching and learning process so that students' strengths and needs are identified, built on, and addressed. School-wide assessments should continually inform teachers' collective review of their practice so that improvements in curriculum, instruction, and school organization are ongoing. Thus, students should actually *learn* more as a result of assessment, rather than being more precisely classified, and schools should be able to inquire into and improve their practices more intelligently, rather than being more rigidly ranked. Assessment should increase the overall amount of learning and good practice across all schools, rather than merely measuring how much of a nonexpanding pool of knowledge is claimed by different students and schools.

If authentic assessment is to realize its potential as a tool for school change, however, policies must enable assessments to be used as a vehicle for student, teacher, and school development. Like students, teachers also learn by constructing knowledge based on their experiences, conceptions, and opportunities for firsthand inquiry. They must be deeply engaged in hands-on developmental work if they are to construct new understandings of the teaching–learning process and new possibilities for their own practices in the classroom and in the school. They must come to understand the kinds of higher-order learning and integrated performance goals of current school reforms from the inside out if they are to successfully develop practices that will support these goals. They must create partnerships with parents and students toward the achievement of jointly held goals if the will to change is to overcome the inertia of familiar patterns.

This suggests a policy paradigm that provides "top-down support for bottom-up reform," rather than top-down directives for school-level implementation. Different policy proposals envision different uses for performance-based assessments. State and local district initiatives vary in their views of the uses of assessment results and of the role of school and teacher participation in assessment development and use. At one end of the continuum is a state like Kentucky, where performance-based assessments are to be developed externally and used at every grade level above grade three, not only to rate children but also to allocate rewards and sanctions to schools. Because the planned system intends to continue the tradition of development and management of most testing by agencies external to the school—and the uses of such tests for individual and organizational decision making—the costs of developing Kentucky's state assessment system are now estimated at over $100 million, excluding implementation costs (Wheelock, 1992).

Some state programs plan to change the nature of existing standardized tests, but not the locus of control of test items, scoring, and uses of results. Tests will still be used primarily for ranking students and schools and controlling instruction from outside the school. Similarly, some proposals for national testing envision NAEP-like instruments used to rank schools, districts, and states on measures that use more performance-oriented tasks, but these would enter and leave schools on "testing days" just as current assessments do.

Due to their intended uses, such tests will need to be carefully controlled and managed to ensure scoring reliability and security. This means that lo-

cal teachers, parents, and students can have little voice in choices of tasks and assessment opportunities or the means of configuring them; that those assessments that count will still be occasional and threatening, rather than continuous and developmental; that the strategies for assessment will be limited to what can be managed with external development and reliable scoring at "reasonable" costs; and that the learning available to school people will be limited to that which can occur at several removes from hands-on participation.

If performance-based assessments are used in the same fashion as current externally developed and mandated tests are used, they are likely to highlight differences in students' learning even more keenly, but they will be unlikely to help teachers to revamp their teaching or schools to rethink their ways of operating. If they arrive in secured packets and leave in parcels for external scoring, teachers will have only a superficial understanding of what the assessments are trying to measure or achieve. If assessments are occasional externally controlled events used primarily for aggregated measures of student achievement levels, they are unlikely to be constructed in ways that provide rich information about the processes of student learning and their individual, idiosyncratic approaches to different kinds of tasks and opportunities. Consequently, teachers will have little opportunity to use the results to understand the complex nuances of student learning in ways that support more successful instruction and little information on which to act in trying to rethink their daily practices. They will have no new grist for ongoing conversations with parents and with their peers about the insights and dilemmas raised through an ongoing, integrated, collaborative process of teaching, learning, and assessment.

Furthermore, if the results are used to allocate rewards and sanctions for students, teachers, and/or schools, the assessments will inspire fear and continual game playing to manipulate student populations, but they will be unlikely to open up the kinds of honest inquiry and serious innovation needed to stimulate new learning and transform practices in fundamental ways.

Another approach is exemplified in states such as New York, Vermont, Connecticut, and California. These states envision carefully targeted state assessments at a few key developmental points that will provide data for informing policy-makers about program successes and needs, areas where assistance and investments are needed, and assessment models for local schools. Meanwhile, locally implemented assessment systems—including portfolios, projects, performance tasks, and structured teaching observations of learning—will provide the multiple forms of evidence about student learning needed to make sound judgments about instruction. In these models, assessment is used as a learning tool for schools and teachers, rather than as a sledgehammer for sorting and sanctioning.

In the New York Plan, state assessments will provide comparable data on student performances on a periodic sampling basis, including data from longer-term projects and portfolios as well as controlled performance tasks. In addition, investments in the development of local assessment systems will support schools in developing continuous, multifaceted records of achievement and information about students in authentic performance situations. Supports for school learning and equalization of resources are also included through a newly proposed equalizing formula for school funding (including an add-on factor for rates of poverty) and a school quality review process to support teacher and school learning (New York Council, 1992). Both California and New York are currently piloting such practitioner-led school review processes modeled, in part, after long-standing practices of Her Majesty's Inspectorate in Great Britain.

Reformers hope that these initiatives will use assessment as a vehicle for student development and adaptive teaching, rather than as a tool for sorting, screening, and selecting students out of educational opportunities. They also intend for assessment to inform teacher and school learning so that the possibilities of multiple pathways to student success are enhanced. These kinds of initiatives acknowledge the need to experiment with diverse methods for assessment that can support Gardner's (1991) conception of "individually configured excellence"—efforts that will tap the multiple intelligences and potentials of students obscured by traditional testing practices.

Many schools, reform networks, and professional organizations have already made inroads in the development of such assessments and their use for supporting teaching and learning. Strategies for assessing learning through exhibitions, portfolios, projects, and careful observations of children have been invented and shared among grassroots school reform initiatives stimulated by such organizations as the Coalition of Essential Schools, Project Zero, the Foxfire Teacher Outreach Network, the North Dakota Study Group, the Prospect Center, and other networks of progressive schools, along with organizations such as the National Association for Education of Young Children, the National Council of Teachers of Mathematics, and other professional associations.

These approaches to assessment development aim at strengthening teaching and learning at the school level by engaging students in more meaningful, integrative, and challenging work and by helping teachers to look carefully at performance, to understand how students are learning and thinking, to reflect on student strengths and needs, and to support them with adaptive teaching strategies.

Where these efforts are underway, changes in teaching and schooling practices occur—especially for students who are not as often successful at schoolwork. Kornhaber and Gardner (1993) illustrate how students whose strengths, interests, and talents are not visible on standardized tests can be understood and better taught. They describe how varied classroom opportunities for performance and assessments can illuminate productive "entry points" that build on children's developed intelligences and extend them into new areas of learning. Case studies of the use of such instruments as the Primary Language Record (Barrs, Ellis, Hester, & Thomas, 1988; Centre for Language in Primary Education (CLPE], 1990), an observational tool for teachers to document student language and literacy development in diverse performance contexts, also demonstrate how developing teachers' capacities to look closely at students' work and learning strategies helps them to provide more supportive experiences, especially for students who have previously had difficulties in learning or whose first language is not English (Falk & Darling-Hammond, 1993).

Teacher learning about how to support student learning has also occurred as teams of teachers have developed authentic assessment strategies at New York's International High School, whose population is 100 percent limited-English-proficient immigrants. Portfolios, projects, and oral debriefings on the work of cooperative learning groups have become the primary instruments for judging the effectiveness of both students' progress and teachers' own instruction. Students' portfolios and products are evaluated by the students themselves, their peers, and their teachers. These multiple perspectives on student work along with student evaluations of courses provide teachers with a steady stream of feedback about their curriculum and insights about individual students. This system of assessment makes the act of teaching itself an act of professional development, because teachers analyze student responses and use them in the development of their pedagogy. The press to cover content has been supplanted by the press to support students in successful learning, with extraordinary results for student success (Ancess & Darling-Hammond, in press).

At International, Central Park East Secondary School, the Urban Academy, and other urban high schools engaged in portfolio assessment for graduation, students who would normally fail in central city schools succeed—graduating and going on to college at rates comparable to affluent suburban schools (Darling-Hammond, Ancess, & Falk, 1995; Darling-Hammond et al., 1993). As teachers learn about how students approach tasks, what helps them learn most effectively, and what assessment tasks challenge and support the kinds of learning desired, they find themselves transforming both their teaching and their assessment strategies. The more information that teachers obtain about what students know and think, as well as

how they learn, the more capacity they have to reform their pedagogy and the more opportunities they create for student success.

These and other assessment initiatives that embed authentic assessment in the ongoing processes of teaching and curriculum development share Glaser's (1990) view that schools must move from a selective mode "characterized by minimal variation in the conditions for learning" in which "a narrow range of instructional options and a limited number of paths to success are available" (p. 16) to an adaptive mode in which "conceptions of learning and modes of teaching are adjusted to individuals—their backgrounds, talents, interests, and the nature of their past performances and experiences" (p. 17). Fundamental agreement with this view leads to a rejection of the traditional uses of testing, even performance-based testing, as an externally controlled tool for the allocation of educational opportunities, rewards, or sanctions. As students are offered wider opportunities for learning and the assessment of their achievement becomes an integral part of learning and teaching, tests are required that provide multidimensional views of performance.

As an alternative to past uses of standardized testing, Glaser (1990) proposes the following criteria for evaluating how new assessments should be designed and used:

1. *Access to educational opportunity:* Assessments should be designed to survey possibilities for student growth, rather than to designate students as ready or not ready to profit from standard instruction.

2. *Consequential validity:* Assessments should be interpreted and evaluated on the basis of their instructional effects, that is, their effectiveness in leading teachers to spend time on classroom activities conducive to valuable learning goals and responsive to individual student learning styles and needs.

3. *Transparency and openness:* Knowledge and skills should be measured so that the processes and products of learning are openly displayed. The criteria of performance must be transparent, rather than secret, so that they can motivate and direct learning.

4. *Self-assessment:* Because assessment and instruction will be integrally related, instructional situations should provide coaching and practice in ways that help students to set incremental standards by which they can judge their own achievement and develop self-direction for attaining higher performance levels.

5. *Socially situated assessment:* Assessment situations in which the student participates in group activity should increase. In this context, not only performance, but also the facility with which a student adapts to help and guidance can be assessed.

6. *Extended tasks and contextualized skills:* Assessment should be more representative of meaningful tasks and subject matter goals. Assessment opportunities will themselves provide worthwhile learning experiences that illustrate the relevance and utility of the knowledge and skills that are being acquired.

7. *Scope and comprehensiveness:* Assessment will attend to a greater range of learning and performance processes, stimulating analysis of what students can do in terms of the cognitive demands and performance skills that tasks entail, as well as their content.

These guidelines suggest strategies for creating assessment systems that serve the daily, intimate processes of teaching and learning. Though a continuing role for external assessments that provide information for policymakers and guideposts for district and school analysis is legitimate, the broader vision of school restructuring demands a much more prominent and highly developed role for school-based assessment initiatives as well.

The Relationship of Assessment Reform to School Restructuring

At the policy level, the different approaches to developing and using performance-based assessments reflect different theories of organizational change and different views of educational purposes. One view seeks to induce change through extrinsic rewards and sanctions for both schools and students, on the assumption that the fundamental problem is a lack of will to change on the part of educators. The other view seeks to induce change by building knowledge among school practitioners and parents about alternative methods and by stimulating organizational rethinking through opportunities to work together on the design of teaching and schooling and to experiment with new approaches. This view assumes that the fundamental problem is a lack of knowledge about the possibilities for teaching and learning, combined with lack of organizational capacity for change.

The developmental view of assessment seeks to create the conditions that enable responsible and responsive practice, including teacher knowledge, school capacity for improvement and problem solving, flexibility in meeting the actual needs of real people, shared ethical commitments among staff, and appropriate policy structures that encourage, rather than punish, inclusive education (Darling-Hammond & Snyder, 1992b). An emphasis on controlling school and classroom work through externally applied assessment schemes makes it difficult to produce this kind of practice.

Senge (1992) explains why organizational controls operating through extrinsic rewards and sanctions undermine the development of learning organizations:

> Making continual learning a way of organizational life…can only be achieved by breaking with the traditional authoritarian, command and control hierarchy where the top thinks and the local acts, to merge thinking and acting at all levels. This represents a profound re-orientation in the concerns of management—a shift from a predominant concern with controlling to a predominant concern with learning. (p. 2)

His assertion is borne out by research on necessary factors for restructuring schools. David (1990) describes the restructuring districts she studied:

> Teachers and principals are asked to experiment and to continuously assess the effects of their experiments…. District leaders encourage school

staff to learn from their successes and their mistakes. School staffs are urged to experiment without fear of punishment for failures. These districts are moving from the known to the unknown, so risks are an essential part of progress. All the districts face the challenge of getting teachers and principals to imagine new ways of organizing their roles and their work. They recognize that risk taking requires knowledge of what to do and how to judge it as well as support and flexibility. (pp. 226–227)

Thus, support for learning and risk taking are strengthened by opportunities for evaluating the results of that learning when a safe environment for innovation has been created. Engaging teachers in assessment is a critical aspect of that process. That engagement becomes a powerful vehicle for professional development, supporting teachers in looking at and understanding student learning, in investigating the effects of teaching on learning, and in transforming their practices so that they become more effective. It is this insight into what students are really doing, thinking, and learning that is one of the greatest contributions of authentic assessment to teacher development.

This insight is greatly encouraged by opportunities for teachers to evaluate and document students' work in ways that help the teachers attend to what students can do, how they approach their work, and what types of teaching approaches seem to support what kinds of learning. In the parlance of many currently proposed performance assessment schemes, this kind of insight might be supported by participation in "scoring" activities; however, the kind of teacher participation needed for full attention to student learning must extend beyond evaluations of discrete pieces of work against a common grid or rubric. A focus on distinct tasks scored against necessarily narrowed and standardized criteria can be periodically helpful, but a more comprehensive view of teaching, learning, and the diverse capacities of students is needed to ensure that teachers have the understandings that they need to help students to learn. This learner-centered information can only be derived from extensive involvement in looking at children and their work from many different vantage points.

Kanevsky (1992), a teacher, explains the Descriptive Review process, a collaborative means for evaluating student learning and growth:

> The assessment we use determines the way we see children and make educational decisions…. Because the Descriptive Review is a collaborative process, it can contribute to the current efforts to restructure schools. The Descriptive Review process allows teachers to hear individual voices and to pursue collaborative inquiry. As teachers draw upon their experiences and knowledge, they begin to envision new roles for themselves and new structures for schools. They are also creating a body of knowledge about teaching and learning that starts with looking at a particular child in depth and ends with new insights and understandings about children and classrooms in general.
>
> Teachers must have opportunities to participate in an educational community; to examine what they care about and what is important for children; to have ongoing, thoughtful conversations about teaching and learning in order to plan meaningful restructuring. (p. 57)

CONCLUSION

I have argued here that, for all the promise of more authentic and performance-based forms of assessment, their value depends as much on how they are used and what supports for learning accompany them as on the new technologies that they employ. Changing assessment forms and formats without changing the ways in which assessments are used will not change the outcomes of education. In order for assessment to support student learning, it must include teachers in all stages of the process and be embedded in curriculum and teaching activities. It must be aimed primarily at supporting more informed and student-centered teaching, rather than at sorting students and sanctioning schools. It must be intimately understood by teachers, students, and parents so that it can help them to strive for and achieve the learning goals that it embodies. It must allow for different starting points for learning and diverse ways of demonstrating competence. In order for schooling to improve, assessment must also be an integral part of ongoing teacher dialogue and school development.

In short, we must rethink the uses of assessment, since we have entered an era when the goal of schooling is to educate all children well, rather than selecting a "talented tenth" to be prepared for knowledge work. In addition, we must publicly acknowledge that inequalities in access to education must be tackled directly if all students are to be well educated. Testing students will not provide accountability in education while some students receive only a fraction of the school resources that support the education of their more privileged counterparts. For all students to receive high-quality instruction from highly qualified teachers, financial investments in schooling must be equalized across rich and poor communities.

With these supports, authentic assessment strategies can help schools to become educational communities committed to self-determined common values. When this happens, all members of the community become learners struggling to construct knowledge that they can individually and collectively use to achieve their goals. The development and practice of authentic assessment cast teachers in the role of problem framers and problem solvers who use their classroom and school experiences to build an empirical knowledge base to inform their practice and strengthen their effectiveness. When supported by adequate resources and learning opportunities for teachers, authentic assessment increases the capacity of schools to engage in a recursive process of self-reflection, self-critique, self-correction, and self-renewal. As schools thus become learning organizations, they can increase their capacity to ensure that all their students learn. Under these conditions, assessment may work on behalf of equity in education, rather than perpetuating the "savage inequalities" (Kozol, 1991) that now exist.

ENDNOTE

This article was originally prepared for the Symposium on Equity and Educational Testing and Assessment, sponsored by the Ford Foundation, Washington, DC, March 11–12, 1993.

REFERENCES

Allington, R. L., & McGill-Franzen, A. (1992). Unintended effects of educational reform in New York. *Educational Policy, 6,* 397–414.

Ancess, J., & Darling-Hammond, L. (in press). *Authentic assessment as an instrument of learning and evaluation at International High School.* New York: Columbia University, Teachers College, National Center for Restructuring Education, Schools, and Teaching.

Archbald, D. A., & Newman, F. M. (1988). *Beyond standardized testing: Assessing authentic academic achievement in the secondary school.* Reston, VA: National Association of Secondary School Principals.

Bailey, T. (1989). *Changes in the nature and structure of work: Implications for skill requirements and skill formation* (Technical Paper No. 9). New York: Columbia University, Teachers College, National Center on Education and Employment.

Barr, R., & Dreeben, R. (1983). *How schools work.* Chicago: University of Chicago Press.

Barrs, M., Ellis, S., Hester, H., & Thomas, A. (1988). *The primary language record.* London: Inner London Education Authority Centre for Language in Primary Education.

Boyer, E. L. (1983). *High school.* New York: Harper & Row.

Carnegie Council on Adolescent Development (1989). *Turning points: Preparing youth for the 21st century.* New York: Carnegie Corporation of New York.

Carnevale, A. P., Gainer, L. J., & Meltzer, A. S. (1989). *Workplace basics: The skills employers want.* Alexandria, VA: American Society for Training and Development.

Centre for Language in Primary Education (1990). *The reading book.* London: Inner London Education Authority.

Cohen, D. K., & Spillane, J. P. (1992). Policy and practice: The relations between governance and instruction. In G. Grant (Ed.), *Review of research in education, Vol. 18* (pp. 3–50). Washington, DC: American Educational Research Association.

College Entrance Examination Board (1985). *Equality and excellence: The educational status of black Americans.* New York: Author.

Commission on Chapter I (1992). *High performance schools: No exceptions, no excuses.* Washington, DC: Author.

Commission on the Skills of the American Workforce (1990). *America's choice: High skills or low wages.* Rochester, NY: National Center on Education and the Economy

Cooper, E., & Sherk, J. (1989). Addressing urban school reform: Issues and alliances. *Journal of Negro Education, 58,* 315–331.

Cremin, L (1961). *The transformation of the school: Progressivism in American education, 1876–1957.* New York: Vintage Books.

Cubberly, E. P. (1919). *Public education in the United States: A study and interpretation of American educational history.* Boston: Houghton Mifflin.

Darling-Hammond, L. (1990). Teacher quality and equality. In J. Goodlad & P. Keating (Eds.), *Access to knowledge: An agenda for our nation's schools* (pp. 237–258). New York: College Entrance Examination Board.

Darling-Hammond, L. (1991). The implications of testing policy for quality and equality. *Phi Delta Kappan, 73,* 220–225.

Darling-Hammond, L. (1993). Creating standards of practice and delivery for learner-centered schools. *Stanford Law and Policy Review, 4,* 37–52.

Darling-Hammond, L. (in press). Inequality and access to knowledge. In J. Banks (Ed.), *Handbook of multicultural education.* New York: Macmillan.

Darling-Hammond, L., & Ascher, C. (1990). *Accountability in big city schools.* New York: Columbia University, Teachers College, National Center for Restructuring Education, Schools, and Teaching, and Institute for Urban and Minority Education.

Darling-Hammond, L., & Snyder, J. (1992a). Traditions of curriculum inquiry. The scientific tradition. In P. Jackson (Ed.), *Handbook of research on curriculum* (pp. 41–78). New York: Macmillan.

Darling-Hammond, L., & Snyder, J. (1992b). Reframing accountability for learner-centered practice. In A. Lieberman (Ed.), *The changing contexts of teaching: 91st Yearbook of the National Society for the Study of Education* (pp. 11–36). Chicago: University of Chicago Press.

Darling-Hammond, L., & Wise, A. (1985). Beyond standardization: State standards and school improvement. *Elementary School Journal, 85,* 315–336.

Darling-Hammond, L., Snyder, J., Ancess, J., Einbender, L., Goodwin, A. L., & Macdonald, M. (1993). Creating learner-centered accountability. New York: Columbia University, Teachers College, National Center for Restructuring Education, Schools, and Teaching.

Darling-Hammond, L., Ancess, J., & Falk, B. (1995). *Authentic assessment in action: Case studies of students and schools at work.* New York: Teachers College Press.

David, J. (1990). Restructuring in progress: Lessons from pioneering districts. In R. Elmore (Ed.), *Restructuring schools: The next generation of educational reform* (pp. 209–250). San Francisco: Jossey-Bass.

Davis, D. G. (1986, April). *A pilot study to assess equity in selected curricular offerings across three diverse schools in a large urban school district: A search for methodology.* Paper presented at the annual meeting of the American Educational Research Association, San Francisco.

Dreeben, R. (1987). Closing the divide: What teachers and administrators can do to help black students reach their reading potential. *American Educator, 11*(4), 28–35.

Dreeben, R., & Barr, R. (1987, April). *Class composition and the design of instruction.* Paper presented at the annual meeting of the American Education Research Association, Washington, DC.

Dreeben, R., & Gamoran, A. (1986). Race, instruction, and learning. *American Sociological Review, 51,* 660–669.

Eckland, B. K. (1980). Sociodemographic implications of minimum competency testing. In R. M. Jaeger & C. K. Tittle (Eds.), *Minimum competency achievement testing: Motives, models, measures, and consequences* (pp. 124–135). Berkeley, CA: McCutchan.

Educate America (1991). *An idea whose time has come: A national achievement test for high school seniors.* Morristown, NJ: Author.

Falk, B., & Darling-Hammond, L. (1993). *The primary language record at P.S. 261.* New York: Columbia University, Teachers College, National Center for Restructuring Education, Schools, and Teaching.

García, G., & Pearson, D. (1994). Assessment and diversity. In L. Darling-Hammond (Ed.), *Review of research in education, 20.* Washington, DC: American Educational Research Association.

Gardner, H. (1983). *Frames of mind.* New York: Basic Books.

Gardner, H. (1991). *The unschooled mind.* New York: Basic Books.

Glaser, R. (1981). The future of testing: A research agenda for cognitive psychology and psychometrics. *American Psychologist, 36,* 923–936.

Glaser, R. (1990). *Testing and assessment: O tempora! O mores!* Pittsburgh, PA: University of Pittsburgh, Learning Research and Development Center.

Goodlad, J. I. (1984). *A place called school: Prospects for the future.* New York: McGraw-Hill.

Gordon, E. (no date). *Implications of diversity in human characteristics for authentic assessment.* Unpublished manuscript, Yale University, New Haven, CT.

Gordon, B., & Sum, A. (1988). *Toward a more perfect union: Basic skills, poor families, and our economic future.* New York: Ford Foundation.

Gould, S. J. (1981). *The mismeasure of man.* New York: W.W. Norton.

Haney, W., & Madaus, G. (1986). *Effects of standardized testing and the future of the national assessment of educational progress.* Chestnut Hill, MA: Center for the Study of Testing, Evaluation, and Educational Policy.

Holmes, C. T., & Matthews, K. M. (1984). The effects of nonpromotion on elementary and junior high school pupils: A meta-analysis. *Review of Educational Research, 54,* 225–236.

Hornbeck, D. (1992, May 6). The true road to equity. *Education Week,* pp. 33, 25.

Jaeger, R. M. (1991, June 5). *Legislative perspectives on statewide testing: Goals, hopes, and desires.* Paper presented at the American Educational Research Association Forum, Washington, DC.

Kamin, L. (1974). *The science and politics of IQ.* New York: Wiley.

Kanevsky, R. D. (1992). The descriptive review of a child: Teachers learn about values. In *Exploring values and standards: Implications for assessment* (pp. 41–58). New York: Columbia University, Teachers College, National Center for Restructuring Education, Schools, and Teaching.

Koretz, D. (1988). Arriving in Lake Wobegon: Are standardized tests exaggerating achievement and distorting instruction? *American Educator, 12*(2), 8–15, 46–52.

Kornhaber, M., & Gardner, H. (1993). *Varieties of excellence: Identifying and assessing children's talents.* New York: Columbia University, Teachers College, National Center for Restructuring Education, Schools, and Teaching.

Kozol, J. (1991). *Savage inequalities: Children in America's schools.* New York: Crown.

Lee, V., & Bryk, A. (1988). Curriculum tracking as mediating the social distribution of high school achievement. *Sociology of Education, 61,* 78–94.

Legislative Research Commission (1990). *A guide to the Kentucky Education Reform Act of 1990.* Frankfurt, KY: Author.

Linn, R. L. (1987). Accountability: The comparison of educational systems and the quality of test results. *Educational Policy, 1*(2), 181–198.

Madaus, G., West, M. M., Harmon, M. C., Lomax, R. G., & Viator, K. A. (1992). *The influence of testing on teaching math and science in grades 4–12.* Chestnut Hill, MA: Boston College Center for the Study of Testing, Evaluation, and Educational Policy.

Madaus, G. F. (1985). Public policy and the testing profession—You've never had it so good? *Educational Measurement: Issues and Practice, 4,* 5–11.

Mann, D. (1987). Can we help dropouts? Thinking about the undoable. In G. Natriello (Ed.), *School dropouts: Patterns and policies* (pp. 3–19). New York: Teachers College Press.

Massachusetts Advocacy Center and the Center for Early Adolescence (1988). *Before it's too late: Dropout prevention in the middle grades.* Boston: Author.

McKnight, C. C., Crosswhite, F. J., Dossey, J. A., Kifer, E., Swafford, S. O., Travers, K. J., & Cooney, T. J. (1987). *The underachieving curriculum: Assessing U.S. school mathematics from an international perspective.* Champaign, IL: Stipes.

Mercer, J. R. (1989). Alternative paradigms for assessment in a pluralistic society. In J. A. Banks & C. M. Banks (Eds.), *Multicultural education* (pp. 289–303). Boston: Allyn & Bacon.

National Assessment of Educational Progress (1981). *Reading, thinking, and writing: Results from the 1979–80 National Assessment of Reading and Literature.* Denver, CO: Education Commission of the States.

National Association for the Education of Young Children (January, 1988). NAEYC position statement on developmentally appropriate practice in the primary grades, serving 5 through 8 year-olds. *Young Children, 47*(1), 64–84.

National Center for Education Statistics (1982). *The condition of education, 1982.* Washington, DC: U.S. Department of Education.

National Center for Education Statistics (1985). *High school and beyond: An analysis of course-taking patterns in secondary schools as related to student characteristics.* Washington, DC: U.S. Government Printing Office.

National Center on Education and the Economy (1989). *To secure our future: The federal role in education.* Rochester, NY: Author.

National Council on Educational Standards and Testing (1992). *Raising standards for American education.* Washington, DC: Author.

New York Council on Curriculum and Assessment (1992). *Building a learning-centered curriculum for learner-centered schools: Report of the Council on Curriculum and Assessment.* Albany, NY: New York State Education Department.

Oakes, J. (1985). *Keeping track: How schools structure inequality.* New Haven, CT: Yale University Press.

Oakes, J. (1986). Tracking in secondary schools: A contextual perspective. *Educational Psychologist, 22,* 129–154.

Oakes, J. (1990). *Multiplying inequalities: The effects of race, social class, and tracking on opportunities to learn mathematics and science.* Santa Monica, CA: RAND.

O'Day, J. A., & Smith, M. S. (1993). Systemic school reform and educational opportunity. In S. Fuhrman (Ed.), *Designing coherent education polity: Improving the system* (pp. 250–311). San Francisco: Jossey–Bass.

Resnick, L. B. (1987a). *Education and learning to think.* Washington, DC: National Academy Press.

Resnick, L. (1987b). Learning in school and out. *Educational Researcher, 16,* 13–20.

Rosenbaum, J. E. (1980). Social implications of educational grouping. In D. C. Berliner (Ed.), *Review of Research in Education, 8* (pp. 361–401). Washington, DC: American Educational Research Association.

Senge, P. M. (1992). *Building learning organizations.* Framingham, MA: Innovation Associates.

Shepard, L. (1993). Evaluating test validity. In L. Darling-Hammond (Ed.), *Review of Research in Education, Vol. 19* (pp. 405–450). Washington, DC: American Educational Research Association.

Shepard, L., & Smith, M. L. (1986). Synthesis of research on school readiness and kindergarten retention. *Educational Leadership, 44*(3), 78–86.

Shepard, L. A., & Smith, M. L. (1988). Escalating academic demand in kindergarten: Counterproductive policies. *Elementary School Journal, 89,* 135–145.

Sizer, T. (1985). *Horace's compromise.* Boston: Houghton Mifflin.

Smith, F. (1986). *High school admission and the improvement of schooling.* New York: New York City Board of Education.

Sternberg, R. J. (1985). *Beyond IQ.* New York: Cambridge University Press.

Trimble, K., & Sinclair, R. L. (1986, April). *Ability grouping and differing conditions for learning: An analysis of content and instruction in ability-grouped classes.* Paper presented at the annual meeting of the American Educational Research Association, San Francisco.

Tyack, D. (1974). *The one best system.* Cambridge, MA: Harvard University Press.

U.S. Department of Education (1991). *America 2000: An education strategy.* Washington, DC: Author.

Watson, B. (in press). *Essays from the underside.* Philadelphia: Temple University Press.

Wehlage, G. G., Rutter, R. A., Smith, G. A., Lesko, N., & Fernández, R. R. (1990). *Reducing the risk: Schools as communities of support.* New York: Falmer Press.

Wheelock, A. (1992). *School accountability policies: Implications for policy making in Massachusetts.* Paper prepared for the Massachusetts Department of Education.

Wigdor, A. K., & Garner, W. R. (Eds.) (1982). *Ability testing: Uses, consequences, and controversies.* Washington, DC: National Academy Press.

Wiggins, G. (1989). Teaching to the (authentic) test. *Educational Leadership, 46*(7), 41–47.

Wise, A. E. (1979). *Legislated learning.* Berkeley, CA: University of California Press.

Wolf, D. P., & Baron, J. B. (in press). A realization of a national performance-based assessment system. In D. Stevenson (Ed.), *Promises and perils of new assessments.* Englewood Cliffs, NJ: Lawrence Erlbaum.

DISCUSSION QUESTIONS

1. What is the rationale for using authentic assessment in measuring student outcomes?

2. According to the author, how must educators use assessment results if we wish to enhance equity?

3. Historically, how has testing been used in schools?

4. How do testing policies affect students' opportunities to learn?

5. What is the relationship between teacher training, incentive structures, school funding, and building an equitable system of assessment?

6. In your opinion, can authentic assessment be used to inform and improve teaching and learning? Why? Why not?

34

Educational Reform and the Ecology of Schooling

ELLIOT W. EISNER

FOCUSING QUESTIONS

1. *Why do teachers tend to resist reform efforts?*
2. *What procedures will be necessary to assist teachers with reform initiatives?*
3. *How can contextualized in-service programs benefit a teacher's professional development?*
4. *In what ways do parent and community views of education influence reform?*
5. *How does the ecology of the school affect reform?*
6. *In what ways will action research impact the relationship between universities and schools?*
7. *Should teachers be given the responsibility to establish local educational policy?*
8. *What alternative conceptions of curriculum programming might facilitate school reform?*

The aspiration to reform schools has been a recurrent theme in American education. This aspiration frequently is stimulated by changes outside the United States. For example, the successful launching of *Sputnik I* on October 4, 1957, was sufficiently traumatic to our sense of national security to motivate the Congress of the United States to provide funds for the development of curricula in science and mathematics in order to "catch up with the Russians." During the 1960s over $100,000,000 was spent in building new programs in these fields and in retraining teachers. Despite all the effort and all the money, there is little that now remains in American schools that reflects the aspirations of the curriculum reform movement of the 1960s: Few of

the curricula are to be found. *Sputnik I* motivated many, but its educational residue is difficult to find.

Since *Sputnik I,* American schools have been subjected to numerous reform efforts. The latest was initiated at a presidentially sponsored education summit on April 18, 1991, a summit attended by the nation's governors, by the U.S. Secretary of Education, and by educators holding positions of high office, to announce Bush's new plans for educational reform. Yet only a few years earlier another president supported another effort at educational reform. *A Nation at Risk,* a document that enjoyed the highest level of visibility of any American educational policy paper published during this century, caught not only the attention but the enthusiasm of almost everyone.[1] Despite these reform efforts, the major features of schools remain largely as they were. What went wrong? Is there anything to learn from past efforts that might make current efforts more successful? This chapter first describes some of the conditions that make change in school difficult and then presents a potentially useful framework for developing a more effective agenda for school reform.

SCHOOLS AS ROBUST INSTITUTIONS

One thing is clear: It is much easier to change educational policy than to change the ways in which schools function. Schools are robust institutions whose very robustness provides a source of social stability.[2] But what is it about schools that makes them so stable? Consider the following nine factors.

INTERNALIZED IMAGES
OF TEACHERS' ROLES

The images of what teachers do in classrooms, how they teach and organize children and tasks, are acquired very early in a child's life. In one sense, teaching is the only profession in which professional socialization begins at age five or six—when children begin school. In no other field do children have as much systematic opportunity to learn what a professional does in his or her work. Indeed, many children spend more time with their teachers than with their parents. This fact of early professional socialization should not be underestimated. Many young adults choose teaching because of their image of teachers and this image is not unrelated to what they believe being a teacher entails. Images of teaching and ways of being a teacher are internalized early in a child's life and bringing about significant changes in the ways in which teachers function requires replacing old images with new, more adequate ones. When a university teacher education program tries to promulgate a new image of teaching, but sends its young, would-be teachers back to schools that are essentially like the ones in which they were socialized, the prospects for replacing the old ideas in the

all too familiar contexts in which new teachers work are dimmed: The new wine is changed when it is poured into the old bottle.

ATTACHMENT TO FAMILIAR
PEDAGOGICAL ROUTINE

Being a teacher, if it requires any set of skills and understandings, requires the ability to manage a group of children so that the class remains coherent and intact; nothing can be done if the class as such is in a state of disarray. But matters of management are only one part of the equation. The other is having something to teach. Teachers acquire a useful pedagogical repertoire by virtue of their experience in classrooms and that repertoire includes some degree of mastery of both the content they wish to teach and the methods and tactics through which to teach it.[3] This repertoire is extremely important to teachers, for it provides them with a source of security and enables them to cope with pedagogical demands efficiently. If a teacher does not know what to teach or is insecure about a subject, attention must be paid to matters of content. This can exacerbate both problems of management and problems of pedagogy. It is difficult to be pedagogically graceful when you are lost in unfamiliar territory. Teachers are often reluctant to relinquish teaching repertoires that provide an important source of security for them. New content areas might require new pedagogical routines. Given the overload that teachers typically experience in school—large numbers of students and many courses or subjects to teach—economy of effort is an important value.[4] Familiar teaching repertoires provide economy of effort; hence changes in schools that require new content and new repertoires are likely to be met with passive resistance by experienced teachers who have defined for themselves an array of routines they can efficiently employ. To make matters even less promising for school reform, few efforts at reform in the United States have provided time for teachers to develop mastery of new content or the skills required for new forms of teaching. Typically, new expectations for teachers are "add-ons" to already overloaded curricula and very demanding teaching schedules.

RIGID AND ENDURING STANDARDS FOR APPROPRIATE BEHAVIOR

A third source of school stability resides in the persistence of school norms. Every social occasion from the birthday party to the funeral service is pervaded by social norms that prescribe implicitly, if not always explicitly, ways to be in the world. Schools are no different. What teachers are supposed to be, how children are supposed to behave, what constitutes an appropriate and fair set of expectations for a subject, are defined by the norms of schooling. These norms have been described by Dreeben, Jackson, Lortie, Lightfoot, Powell, and Eisner, and decades earlier by Waller.[5] In the past two decades educational scholars on the political Left such as Apple and Giroux have also examined the ways in which the pervasive and sometimes covert norms of schooling shape attitudes, create inequities, and often reproduce the inequities of the society at large.[6] Undoubtedly, some of their observations are correct, but my point here is not so much to make a statement about what Bourdieu has called "cultural reproduction"[7] as to make it plain that if schools are to seriously address matters of intellectual development, the cultivation of sensibility, and the refinement of the imagination, changes must be made in educational priorities. Such changes will require institutional norms different from those now salient in schools.

Norms, after all, reflect values. They adumbrate what we care about. Trying to convert schools from academic institutions—institutions that attempt to transmit what is already known—into intellectual ones—institutions that prize inquiry for its own sake—will require a change in what schools prize. Most efforts at school reform fail to address this challenge. The tack taken in most educational policy papers is typically superficial and the language is technical. The problem is often thought to be solvable by curriculum "installation"; we are to "install" a new curriculum and then "align it" with other curricula. We typically employ a language of change that reveals a shallow and mechanistic conception of what real change requires. Policymakers cannot install new norms in schools any more than they can install new teaching methods. Both need careful cultivation and nurture. By persisting in using inappropriate mechanical metaphors for thinking about the process of school reform, we persist in misconceptualizing the problem and undermining genuine change.

TEACHER ISOLATION

A fourth factor that thwarts school reform is the fact that in the United States, we have structured schools and defined teaching roles in ways that make improved teaching performance difficult to achieve. Consider the ways in which teachers are insulated and isolated from their colleagues. Teaching, by and large, in both elementary and secondary schools is a lonely activity. It is not that teachers have no contact with people; after all, they are with students all day. The point is that they have very little contact with other adults in the context of their classrooms. Some school districts in the United States and some enlightened policies provide teachers with aides and with special assistance by certified professionals, but these human resources are relatively rare. Most teachers spend most of their time in their own classrooms, closed environments, with twenty-five to thirty-five children or adolescents. Of course, there are occasions—lunchtime and the occasional staff meeting, for example—where teachers see each other, but seldom in the context of teaching. Even teachers who have worked in the same school for twenty years are likely to have never seen their colleagues teach.

The result of professional isolation is the difficulty that teachers encounter in learning what they themselves do in their own classrooms when they teach. Classrooms, unlike the rooms in which ballerinas practice their craft, have no mirrors. The only mirrors available to teachers are those they find in their students' eyes, and these mirrors are too small. Hence the teacher, whether elementary or secondary, must learn on his or her own, usually by reflecting on how things went. Such personal reflection is subject to two forms of ignorance, one type remediable, the other not.

The two types of ignorance I speak of are primary and secondary ignorance. Primary ignorance about teaching, or about anything else for that matter, is when you do not know something but you *know* that you do not know it. In such a situation, you can do something about it. Secondary ignorance is when you do not know something but do *not know* you do not know it. In this case, you can do nothing about the problem. The professional isolation of teachers fosters secondary ignorance. How can a teacher learn that he or she is talking too much, not providing sufficient time for student reflection, raising low-order questions, or is simply boring students? Teachers unaware of such features of their own performance are in no position to change them. Educational reform efforts that depend on new and better approaches to teaching yet make it difficult for teachers to learn about their own teaching are destined to have a poor prognosis for success. Despite what seems obvious, we have designed schools both physically and organizationally to restrict the teacher's access to other professionals. Discretionary time for teachers is limited and although the school principal could make the time to provide teachers with useful feedback, he or she often does not have the inclination or the skills or is so preoccupied with other matters of lesser importance that attention to the improvement of teaching becomes marginalized. As a result, it is not unusual for teachers to feel that no one really cares about the quality of their work.[8]

INADEQUACIES OF IN-SERVICE EDUCATION

In-service education is the major means used in the United States to further the quality of teaching. But in-service education typically means that teachers will attend meetings or conferences to hear experts (often university professors who have had little contact with schools) provide advice on the newest developments in teaching mathematics, social studies, or the language arts. The assumption is that once teachers are exposed to such wisdom,

they will implement the practices suggested in their own classrooms. The in-service seminar is one in which the advice-giver typically has never seen the teachers who comprise the audience. The advice-giver does not know the teachers' strengths or their weaknesses. The situation is much like a voice coach giving advice to a singer whom he or she has never heard sing. General recommendations go only so far.

Thus, we try to improve teaching by asking teachers to leave their classrooms so that they can travel to distant locations in order to get general advice from people who have never seen them teach. One does not need to be a specialist in learning theory to know that for complex forms of human action, general advice is of limited utility. Feedback needs to be specific and focused on the actor in context. What we do, however, is decontextualize in-service education and, as a result, weaken its potential usefulness.

My remarks should not be interpreted to mean that in-service programs for teachers cannot be useful, but that in-service education without some direct observation of teachers in the context of their own classrooms is not likely to be adequate. In this case, as in so many others, we have greatly underestimated what it will take to improve what teachers actually do in their own classrooms.

CONSERVATIVE EXPECTATIONS FOR THE FUNCTION OF SCHOOLS

Another factor that contributes to the robust quality of schools and their resistance to change is that the expectations of both students and parents regarding the function of schools and the forms of practice that are appropriate are usually conservative. What does a good teacher do? What kinds of questions are appropriate for students to ask? How much freedom should teachers provide? What kinds of problems and projects should students be asked to engage in? How should students be evaluated? Should they have any role in their own assessment? Answers to each of the foregoing questions are related to expectations of what schools, classrooms, and teachers should be. The expectations of parents and students are often quite traditional on such matters.

The call for "back to basics"—a return to the educational practices of the past—is regarded by many as the way to save American schools from mediocrity or worse. Familiar practices are not threatening; the past almost always has a rosy glow. Practices that violate tradition are often regarded as subversive of high-quality education. School reform efforts that challenge tradition can be expected to encounter difficulties, especially from the segment of the population that has done well in socioeconomic terms and has the tendency to believe that the kind of schooling that facilitated their success is precisely the kind their own children should receive.

Expectations by students for practices with which they are familiar go beyond general forms of teaching practice; they include expectations for the way in which specific subjects should be taught. For example, students whose experience in art classes has not included learning about the history of art or writing about the qualities of particular works of art may regard such practices as distasteful; for many students reading and writing have no place in an art class. A program in social studies that requires group cooperation on project-centered work can be regarded as inappropriate by students whose concept of social studies is one that is devoted exclusively to individual tasks. Parents whose experience in learning mathematics emphasized drill and practice may regard an arithmetic program oriented toward the practical applications of arithmetic as less intellectual and less rigorous. The point here is that educational consumers can exercise a conservative function in the effort at educational reform. It is difficult for schools to exceed in aim, form, and content what the public is willing to accept.

DISTANCE BETWEEN EDUCATIONAL REFORMERS AND TEACHERS IMPLEMENTING CHANGE

Reform efforts in American education are almost always from the top down. For whatever reason, ed-

ucational policymakers mandate change, often through national or state reports or through new educational legislation that sends the message of changed policies to those "on the front line." The tacit assumption is that once new policies are formulated, a stream of change will begin to flow with little further assistance. When assistance is provided it sometimes comes in the form of new policy papers, curriculum guides, and district conferences. Typically, the structural conditions of schools stay the same. Teachers remain on the receiving end of policy and have little hand in its formation.

The attraction of providing teachers with a hand in shaping educational policy is quite limited if one believes educational practice, at its best, will be uniform across school districts and geographic regions. If one's model of ideal educational practice is one of standardized practice, the way in which an efficient manufacturing plan might function, giving 2½ million American teachers the opportunity to determine what is best for their own school or school district can appear chaotic or even nihilistic. Thus, there is a real tension in the process of school reform. At one end there is the desire to create a uniform and "equitable" program for children and adolescents, regardless of who they are or where they live. This requires centralized decision making. At the other end is the realization that unless teachers feel some commitment to change, they are unlikely to change. To feel such commitment it is important for teachers to have the opportunity to participate in shaping the change process.

Many veteran teachers, those who have seen educational reforms come and go, are skeptical about new reforms and respond with passive resistance: They simply ride out the new policies. This can be done without much difficulty for two reasons. First, educational reform policies come and go about every five or six years and are more visible in the media than in the classroom. Second, once the classroom door is closed, the ways in which teachers teach are essentially a private affair. Elementary school principals rarely monitor teaching practice closely, and, at the secondary level, they do not have the subject-matter expertise in a wide variety of fields to do so.

The growing desire to engage teachers in the change process has led to the notion of "teacher empowerment." In general, the idea is that, as important stakeholders in what schools do, teachers need to have authority to plan and monitor the quality of the educational process in their schools. The effort, in a sense, is to democratize educational reform by giving teachers a say-so in what happens. This say-so includes defining curricular goals and content, improving teaching practice, and developing ways to assess what children experience during the school day. In some cases, it includes decision making about budget allocations through a process called site-based management.

A practice related to this general thrust of teacher improvement is called *action research.* Action research is intended to encourage teachers to collaborate with other teachers and, at times, with university professors in order to undertake research in their own school or classroom.[9] The aim of the enterprise is to stimulate professional reflection by encouraging teachers to take a more reflective intellectual role in understanding and improving their own teaching practice.

It is not yet clear just how many teachers are interested in being "empowered." It is not yet clear how many teachers want to do educational research. It is not yet clear how many teachers are interested in assuming larger responsibilities such as the formulation of educational policy. Many teachers gain their deepest satisfaction in their own classroom. The classroom is their professional home and they are not particularly interested in collaboration or in doing educational research. As I indicated earlier, conceptions of the teacher's role are acquired early in development and teachers are often comfortable with these conceptions. If a bird has been in a cage for a decade and suddenly finds the door open, it should not be too surprising if the bird does not wish to leave. The familiar is often more comfortable than the uncertainty of the unknown.

Empowering teachers is more complex than I have suggested. When innovative reform policies are formulated or new aims or programs presented, they are often prescribed *in addition* to what teachers are already doing; they are add-ons. Given that the teacher's day is already quite demanding, it should come as no surprise that taking on added responsibilities for the formulation of policy or for monitoring the school should be regarded by some as an extra burden. Put more bluntly, it is unrealistic to expect overworked teachers who have very little discretionary time in the school day to be more active in their school without some relief from some of their current responsibilities. To provide relief will require restructuring. Restructuring is likely to require money, something that is in scarce supply in many school districts. As a result, much of the activity in the context of school reform is more at the level of rhetoric than at the level of practice.

As educational reformers have become increasingly aware of the difficulty of bringing about significant change in the ways in which schools function, they have talked about the restructuring of schools.[10] For this term, which to me generates an image of fundamental rather than superficial change, there are almost as many meanings as there are writers. In my discussions with school principals and school superintendents, "restructuring" meant to them changing the ways in which funds were allocated rather than reconceptualizing the organization, content, and aims of schools. Conceptualized in terms of financial resource allocation, the power of the concept was neutralized.

Another complexity regarding teacher empowerment involves the question of authority and responsibility. If teachers are given the authority to change local educational policy in their schools, will they assume responsibility for the consequences of those policies? If so, how will those consequences be determined? What will be the responsibilities of the school district's superintendent and the district central office staff? Just what is the appropriate balance between authority and responsibility and who is responsible for what when responsibility and authority are localized?

These questions are not yet resolved. The recent interest in giving teachers a genuine role in the reform of schools is seen by many (including me) as salutary, but how lines of authority and responsibility are to be drawn is far from clear. Can genuine school improvement occur without commitment from teachers? It seems unlikely. Just how can such commitment be developed? These questions are on the current agenda of school reform in the United States.

ARTIFICIAL BARRIER BETWEEN DISCIPLINES AND BETWEEN TEACHERS

An eighth factor that impedes school reform pertains to the ways in which the school itself is organized. One of the most problematic features in the organization of schools is the fact that they are *structurally fragmented,* especially at the secondary level. By structurally fragmented I refer to the fact that curricula are divided and organized into distinct subject matters that make it difficult for students to make connections between the subjects they study.[11] In the United States, secondary school students will typically enroll in four to six subjects each semester. As a result, teachers must teach within narrow time blocks. They teach four to seven classes each day, see 130 to 180 students each day; students must move every fifty minutes to another teacher who teaches them another subject. There is no occupation in American society in which workers must change jobs every fifty minutes, move to another location, and work under the direction of another supervisor. Yet this is precisely what we ask of adolescents, hoping, at the same time, to provide them with a coherent educational program.

Structural fragmentation also pertains to the fact that the form of school organization that we have created isolates teachers. And as I have already indicated, isolation makes it difficult for teachers to receive critical and supportive feedback about their work. Teachers experience little colleagueship in the context of the classroom, and of course it is in the context of a classroom that the real business of education is played out. Unless there is significant change in the way in which teachers and students live and work together, any significant change in schools is illusory.

Because the forms of school organization are cultural rather than natural entities, they need not be regarded as being of necessity; that is, they can be other than the way they are. Moses did not receive instructions about school organization on Mount Sinai, at least as far as I know. Yet we persist in maintaining school structures that might not be in the best interests of either teachers or students. I can tell you that the organizational structure and the curricular requirements of the secondary school I attended forty years ago are quite like the organizational structure and curricular requirements secondary school students encounter today. How much structural and curricular overlap is there between the secondary school you attended and today's secondary schools?

FECKLESS PIECEMEAL EFFORTS AT REFORM

The last factor that impedes significant educational reform is the piecemeal and superficial way in which reformers think about educational reform. Minor efforts at change are eventually swamped by the factors in the school that do not change. Robust systems can withstand minor incursions. Thus the need, I believe, is to think about school reform ecologically, or at least systemically. Aspects of schooling that remain constant militate against those features of schooling that are being changed. For example, efforts to help teachers learn how to teach inductively are not likely to succeed if the evaluation system the school employs rewards other types of teaching. Efforts to encourage teachers to engage in reflective teaching are likely to be feckless if teachers have no time during the school day for reflection. Efforts to create intellectual coherence in the student's understanding are likely to fail if the form that the curriculum takes makes coherence impossible. Improvement in teaching is unlikely as long as teachers get no useful feedback on the work they actually do in their own classrooms.

It is important in educational reform to think big even if one must start small. There needs, I believe, to be an overall conception of what schools are as forms of shared communal life as well as persuasive and attractive visions of what such shared living might become. The next section describes a means for securing a better understanding of what schools are as living organisms. The last section provides a model or framework that identifies important candidates for educational change.

Schools as Living Systems

The place to begin school reform is in the effort to understand the ways that schools actually function, what it is they teach both implicitly and explicitly, and how they reward the people who spend so much of their lives there. Unfortunately, the effects of efforts at school reform are based on the results of standardized achievement testing and the results of such testing say little about the processes that lead to them. We cannot know much about the educational quality of schools simply by examining test scores. We need a finer, more refined screen, one that focuses on the processes as well as the outcomes of schooling.

Much recent research in the United States has focused on the quality and process of schooling.[12] Some of these students have used ethnographic research methods or modifications of such methods.[13] Some studies have been rooted in critical approaches[14] and others in methods derived from the arts and humanities.[15] As a result of this work a number of salient features of schools, many of which are quite common across a variety of schools, have been identified: structural fragmentation, teacher isolation, didactic teaching, treaties between teachers and students, the particular ways in which effective teachers and school administrators relate to students, the emphasis on extrinsic rewards, and the like. How salient are these features? Are there important differences? How can we know?

The only way I know to discover the salient and significant features of schools is to look. The implications of what is found will depend on what is found and on the educational values that give direction to the schools themselves.

To look at schools as I have suggested is not enough. Anyone can look. The trick is to see. Seeing requires an enlightened eye. It requires schemata through which different genres of teaching can be appreciated.[16] It is a mistake to assume that all good teaching has identical characteristics, that one size fits all. Thus, to see what happens in classrooms requires a willingness and a set of sensibilities and schemata that can pick up the distinctive features of particular types of teaching. These types of teaching are not simply generic. They emerge within the constraints and possibilities of particular subject matters—*what* one teaches counts. As Stodolsky says, "the subject matters."[17] Even more than this, any given subject matter—history, for example, or mathematics—can have a wide variety of aims and methods. Perceiving school processes requires an understanding of the types of teaching possible within the subject-matter field and an awareness of the varieties of quality that can be manifested within each.

This chapter is not the place to describe in detail the forms of perception and description of life in schools I have in mind. Readers interested in what I have called "educational connoisseurship" and "educational criticism" can find the approach described in a variety of articles and particularly in my latest book.[18] The point is that school reform should begin with a decent understanding of the schools themselves, not with old memories of schooling held by middle-aged men and women working in institutions far removed from schools. A major part of the current investment in school reform should be aimed, in my opinion, at trying to understand such processes as how teaching takes place in particular fields, what constitutes the implicit as well as the explicit norms of the school, the sense that students make of what they study, the aims that teachers say are important and the relationship of those aims to what they do in their classrooms. It should also deal with the intellectual quality of what is taught and the procedures that are used in the classroom to motivate and reward students and teachers. The aim of such inquiry is to secure an organic, cultural picture of schools as places to be. The basic questions direct attention to the value of what goes on in them. Such questions are easy to raise but difficult to answer, yet unless they are raised educational reform is likely to be predicated on very partial forms of understanding of what schools are like for teachers and students.

As I have indicated, the kind of study I am suggesting is one that is organic or cultural. To study schools in this way is likely to require an approach to educational research that is *qualitative* in character. It is an approach that pays attention to the processes of schooling and to the context in which those processes occur. I know of no way to find out what schools are like except by going to schools themselves to see, to describe, to interpret, and to evaluate what is occurring. Such an understanding can provide a foundation for reform that addresses what is genuinely important in education.

Five Major Dimensions of School Reform

In the final section of this chapter, I identify five dimensions of schooling that I believe must be considered in order to think comprehensively about the reform of schools. I call these dimensions the *intentional,* the *structural,* the *curricular,* the *pedagogical,* and the *evaluative.*

My thesis is that meaningful and educationally significant school reform will require attention to each of these dimensions. Attention to one direction without attention to the others is not likely to lead to change. Where change does occur, it is likely to be temporary and superficial.

The intentional refers to what it is that schools are intended to accomplish. What really counts in schools? Defining intentions pertains to both the general aims of schooling and the aims of the particular subject matters being taught. Consider, for example, intentions that are typically *not* given high priority in schools or in reform efforts: fostering a desire to continue learning what schools teach, the development of curiosity, stimulating the ability to think metaphorically, creating a caring attitude toward others, the development of productive idiosyncrasy, the ability to define one's own goals and the ability to pursue them, the ability to raise perceptive questions about what one has studied. An argument for each of these intentions could be made that is cogent and relevant to the world in which children live. If such intentions were taken seriously, their ramifications for educational practice would be considerable. My point here is not to advocate such intentions (although I

do not reject them) but rather to illustrate the idea that the conventional intentions schools serve are not necessarily the most important ones. What is important will depend on an argued set of educational values and an understanding of the students and society schools serve.

Most efforts at school reform operate on the assumption that the important outcomes of schooling, indeed the primary indices of educational success, are high levels of academic achievement as measured by standardized achievement tests. Just what do scores on academic achievement tests predict? They predict scores on other academic achievement tests. But schools, I would argue, do not exist for the sake of high levels of performance in the context of schools, but in the context of life outside of the school. The significant dependent variables in education are located in the kinds of interests, voluntary activities, levels of thinking and problem solving that students engage in when they are not in school. In other words, the real test of successful schooling is not what students do in school, but what they do outside of it.

If such intentions were genuinely central in our educational planning, we would probably make other arrangements for teaching, curriculum, and evaluation than those we now employ. Significant new intentions are likely to require new ways of leading educational lives.

The structural aspects of schooling pertain to the ways in which we have organized subjects, time, and roles. I have already alluded to the fact that we structure subjects by type. We use what Bernstein has called a collection-type curriculum.[19] Each subject is bounded and kept distinct from others. This boundedness is reinforced by how time is allocated, what is taught, and in some secondary schools, where on the school campus a subject matter department is located. In some schools there is a section of the school devoted exclusively to the sciences, another to the fine arts, another to business and computer studies. We emphasize separateness and reinforce that separateness through a departmentalized structure.

Departmentalization might be, in the long run, the most rational way to structure schools, but it is not the only way. My aim here is not to advocate a particular change, but to problematize the structures we have lived with for so long that we come to think about them as natural entities rather than as the results of decisions that could have been otherwise. Is a departmentalized structure the best way to organize schools? It depends on a set of educational values and an exploration of alternative modes of organization. In the United States very few efforts at school reform—open schooling being a vivid exception—have tried to restructure schools. The curriculum reform movement of the 1960s attempted to create curricula designed to fit into existing school structures. Can new messages change the school or will the school change the messages?

The structure of the school also influences the way in which roles are defined. In American schools there are basically two roles for adults: teacher and principal. The teacher spends his or her day with children or adolescents. The principal seldom is responsible for teaching functions and has far more discretionary time than do teachers. If a teacher wants to secure more professional life-space, he or she must leave teaching and become a school administrator. Once such a decision is made, for all practical purposes, there is no return to the classroom—as the caterpillar, once it becomes a butterfly, remains a butterfly until it dies.

Working as an educator in a school need not be limited to two roles, nor must these roles be conceived of as "permanent." Schools can be structured so that teachers who are interested can devote some years or parts of some years to curriculum development, to the design of better evaluation methods for their school, to serving as mentors to beginning teachers. Teachers could create liaisons with community agencies such as museums, hospitals, cultural centers, retirement homes, in order to secure services that could enhance and enrich school programs. Teachers could devote time to research in their own school and assist parents with children who are having difficulty in school. There is a host of possible roles that could make important generic contributions to a school's way of life, but for these contributions to be made, educators need to create school structures that permit them to be developed. American schools, with few exceptions,

are structured to inhibit these roles rather than to encourage their formation. The paradigms we have internalized about the nature of schooling—the way time is allocated, the way subjects are defined, the way in which roles are specified—are so strong that efforts at reform are typically conceptualized to fit into the constraints of those structures, thus defining the parameters within which reform efforts are to occur.

The curricular is the third dimension that needs attention in any effort to create genuinely significant educational reform. Decisions about curriculum can be made about several of its features. Among the most important are those about the content that is to be provided, about the kind of activities that are to be used to help students experience that content, and the way in which the curriculum itself is to be organized. As I have indicated, most efforts at curriculum reform in the United States have left the organization of curriculum intact: Separate subjects separately taught has been the dominant mode of organization, although at the elementary level such organization is less prevalent than at the middle or secondary school levels. Yet in spite of frequent admonitions by educational scholars to reduce curriculum fragmentation,[20] the separation of subject matters persists and is supported by the infrastructure of professional education: testing programs, university admissions criteria, teacher training programs, specialization among subject-matter teachers. This collection-type form of curriculum organization[21] is not the only way in which curriculum can be organized. Whether it is the most appropriate form, given the potential costs of other forms of organization, depends upon our educational intentions. If integration of learning is desired, separation may indeed be problematic. Again, my point here is not to argue for a specific form of curriculum reorganization as much as to urge the careful rethinking of the organization that now prevails.

What is taught in the first place is of primary importance. One way to increase the probability that something *will not be learned* is to ensure that it *will not be taught,* that is, to make a subject matter a part of a *null curriculum.*[22] The fine arts are often relegated to this position. For many citizens the arts are someone else's pleasures. Large and important legacies of culture go unseen, unheard, unread, and as a result, unloved. Schools perpetuate this state of ignorance by withholding from the young important parts of their cultural legacy. The list could be expanded.

Regarding the activities that allow students to grasp or experience what is taught in schools, according to Goodlad, the lecture still dominates at the secondary school level.[23] Students typically have few opportunities to formulate their own questions and to pursue them. They are expected to do what the teacher requests; their role is in the application of means rather than the formulation of ends. They become, says Apple, deskilled, unable to formulate the aims and goals they seek to attain.[24]

The provision of opportunities for students to define at least some of their purposes is arguably an important educational aim and the ability to do so an important educational achievement. To what extent does it occur? Genuine reform of schools will require attention not only to intentions and school structure, but to the content, tasks, and forms of organization of the school curriculum. Which aspects of curricula should receive attention will depend on what is now occurring in schools; the only way to know that is to go to the schools to see.

The fourth dimension needing attention in genuine school reform is *the pedagogical* aspects of educational practice. If the curriculum is the systole of education, teaching is the diastole. No curriculum teaches itself and how it is mediated is crucial. In fact, I find it useful to distinguish between the *intended* curriculum and the *operational* curriculum.[25] What we plan to teach—materials, outlines, projected activities and goals—constitutes the intended curriculum. The operational curriculum is the curriculum that is played out in the context of classroom life. In this process pedagogy plays a crucial role. When programs call for new teaching skills that teachers do not possess— inductive teaching, for example—teachers understandably use the skills they possess and these may not be adequate to the task.

No intended curriculum can be followed by teachers as a script; the classroom is too uncertain a place for recipes. The professional teacher needs to use the curriculum as a resource, as an amplifier of his or her own ability. Different teachers need different amounts of guidance and specificity. Thus, the pedagogical is a central aspect of school reform. Unless classroom practices change, changes on paper, whether in policy or in curriculum, are not likely to be of much consequence for students.

How can students of education know about the ways in which teaching occurs? What are the strengths teachers possess and what are their weaknesses? Are there important educational consequences on both sides of the ledger? These questions are, of course, easy to pose but difficult to answer. At minimum, qualitative studies of classroom life must be undertaken. Such studies could provide the basis on which effective change strategies could be initiated and could provide a focus for efforts aimed at pedagogical issues. *Both* curriculum and pedagogy need to be seen in context and both need attention for strengthening school reform.

Finally, the fifth dimension needing attention in school reform is *the evaluative*. It makes no sense whatsoever to write policy papers about educational reform and to prepare syllabi and curriculum guides for teachers that advocate a new direction for educational practice and continue to assess the outcomes of schooling on instruments that reflect older, more traditional views. Yet, this is what we often do. Consider the proposition that good schools increase individuality and cultivate productive idiosyncrasy. Consider the idea that good schools increase differences among students, not diminish them. If we truly embraced these views, how could we go about evaluating the educational effectiveness of schools? Would commensurability remain an important criterion? What kinds of opportunities could be provided to students to develop what they have learned? To what extent would we use closed-ended examinations?

High-stake assessment procedures symbolically and practically represent what "higher-ups" care about and performance on such procedures significantly affects both the options students have and the professional reputation of teachers. How outcomes are evaluated is a major agent influencing what teachers and school administrators pay attention to. Thus, the redesign of assessment instruments so that they provide information about what teachers and others care about most from an educational perspective is a fundamental aspect of school reform. Schools cannot move in one direction and assess teachers and students using procedures that represent values in quite another direction.

Evaluation, however, should not be conceived of exclusively in terms of outcome assessment. Evaluation, it seems to me, should be regarded as an educational medium. The processes of teaching and the quality of what is taught, as well their outcomes, are the proper subject matter of an adequate approach to educational evaluation. If the quality of the content being taught is poor, it does not matter much if the quality of teaching is good. Indeed, if the content being taught is pernicious, excellence in teaching is a vice.

Evaluation is an aspect of professional educational practice that should be regarded as one of the major means through which educators can secure information they can use to enhance the quality of their work. Evaluation ought to be an ongoing part of the process of education, one that contributes to its enhancement, not simply a means for scoring students and teachers.

CONCLUSION

These factors, the *intentional,* the *structural,* the *curricular,* the *pedagogical,* and the *evaluative,* are all important and interacting dimensions of schooling. Collectively they constitute a kind of ecology of schooling. To bring about reform in schools that is more than superficial and short-term requires attention to all of them.

To consider these dimensions not simply as an academic enterprise but as an activity leading to an agenda that can be acted on is the tough test of educational reform efforts. In some way that agenda has to be set. In setting this agenda teachers will need to be involved, as well as school administrators who themselves are not afraid of new forms of practice. The details of this agenda—the role, for example, that universities might play in school reform—cannot be addressed in this chapter. Yet unless the plan for school reform is comprehensive, it is likely to leave little residue in the long run. We sometimes say in the United States that educational reform is like a pendulum swing—we go back and forth. Pendulums are objects that move without going any place. Recognizing the ecological character of schools and facing up to the magnitude of the task of educational reform are important beginning efforts in dismounting from the pendulum.

ENDNOTES

1. USA Research. *A Nation at Risk: The Full Account* (Cambridge: USA Research, 1984).

2. Larry Cuban, "Reforming Again, Again, and Again," *Educational Researcher* 19, no. 1 (January–February 1990): 3–13.

3. David Berliner, "In Pursuit of the Expert Pedagogue," *Educational Researcher* 15, no. 7 (1986): 5–10.

4. D. Flinders, "What Teachers Learn from Teaching: Educational Outcomes of Instructional Adaptation" (Ph.D. diss., Stanford University, 1987).

5. Robert Dreeben, *On What Is Learned in School* (New York: Addison-Wesley, 1968); Philip W. Jackson, *Life in Classrooms* (New York: Holt, Rinehart & Winston, 1968); Dan C. Lortie, *School Teacher: A Psychological Study* (Chicago: University of Chicago Press, 1975); Sara Lawrence Lightfoot, *The Good High School: Portraits of Character and Culture* (New York: Basic Books, 1983); Arthur G. Powell, Eleanor Farrar, and David K. Cohen, *The Shopping Mall High School: Winners and Losers in the Educational Marketplace* (Boston: Houghton Mifflin, 1985); Elliot W. Eisner, *What High Schools Are Like: Views from the Inside* (Stanford: Stanford School of Education, 1985); and Willard W. Waller, *The Sociology of Teaching* (New York: John Wiley, 1932).

6. Michael Apple, *Education and Power* (Boston: Routledge & Kegan Paul, 1982); and Henry Giroux, *Critical Pedagogy, the State, and Cultural Struggle* (Albany: University of New York Press, 1989).

7. Pierre Bourdieu, *Reproduction in Education's Society and Culture* (London: Sage Publications, 1977).

8. Eisner, *What High Schools Are Like.*

9. J. M. Atkin, "Can Educational Research Keep Pace with Educational Reform?" *Kappan* 71, no. 3 (November 1989): 200–05.

10. *Restructuring California Education: A Design for Public Education in the Twenty-first Century, Recommendations to the California Business Round Table* (Berkeley: B. W. Associates, 1988).

11. Eisner, *What High Schools Are Like.*

12. John I. Goodlad, *A Place Called School: Prospects for the Future* (New York: McGraw-Hill, 1984); Theodore R. Sizer, *Horace's Compromise: The Dilemma of the American High School* (Boston: Houghton Mifflin, 1984); Powell, Farrar, and Cohen, *The Shopping Mall High School*; and Eisner, *What High Schools Are Like.*

13. H. Wolcott, *The Man in the Principal's Office* (Prospect Heights, Ill.: Waveland Press, 1984).

14. P. Willis, *Learning to Labor* (Lexington: D.C. Heath, 1977).

15. Lightfood, *The Good High School.*

16. Elliot W. Eisner, *The Enlightened Eye: Qualitative Inquiry and the Enhancement of Educational Practice* (New York: Macmillan, 1991).

17. S. S. Stodolsky, *The Subject Matters* (Chicago: University of Chicago Press, 1988).

18. Eisner, *The Enlightened Eye.*

19. Basil Bernstein, "On the Classification and Framing of Educational Knowledge," in *Knowledge and Control,* ed. M. Young (London: Collier-Macmillan, 1971), pp. 47–69.

20. Eisner, *What High Schools Are Like*; and Sizer, *Horace's Compromise.*

21. Bernstein, "On the Classification and Framing of Educational Knowledge."

22. Eisner, *What High Schools Are Like.*

23. Goodlad, *A Place Called School.*

24. Apple, *Education and Power.*

25. Eisner, *What High Schools Are Like.*

DISCUSSION QUESTIONS

1. If teachers were to assume the responsibility of creating local educational policy, should they be held accountable for the consequences of those policies? Why? Why not?

2. How does the organization of schools impede or support reform efforts?

3. How can qualitative forms of evaluation facilitate reform?

4. What role should universities play in local school reform?

5. What voice should students have in reform initiatives?

35

Turning Systemic Thinking on Its Head

MICHAEL G. FULLAN

FOCUSING QUESTIONS

1. *Why are efforts to bring about educational reform continually fraught with barriers?*
2. *What is meant by the term systemic reform?*
3. *What are the essential questions to ask when attempting to implement a systems change?*
4. *What are the limitations of networking?*
5. *How are the activities envisioned by systemic reformers likely to influence (a) conceptions of a teacher, (b) the design and culture of schools, (c) teacher preparation, and (d) the day-to-day role of the teacher?*

Overload and fragmentation are two major barriers to education reform, and they are related. Overload is the continuous stream of planned and unplanned changes that affect the schools. Educators must contend constantly with multiple innovations and myriad policies, and they must deal with them all at once. Overload is compounded by a host of unplanned changes and problems, including technological developments, shifting demographics, family and community complexities, economic and political pressures, and more. Fragmentation occurs when the pressures—and even the opportunities—for reform work at cross purposes or seem disjointed and incoherent.

Overload and fragmentation combine to reduce educators' motivation for working on reform. Together they make the situation that the schools face seem hopeless, and they take their toll on the most committed, who find that will alone is not sufficient to achieve or sustain reform.

This situation would seem to be an ideal candidate for *systemic reform,* which promises to align the different parts of the system, focus on the right things, and marshal and coordinate resources in agreed on directions. The idea of systemic reform is to define clear and inspiring learning goals for all students, to gear instruction to focus on these new directions, and to back up these changes with appropriate governance and accountability procedures.

In this chapter, I first want to present evidence that there is a fundamental flaw in the reasoning that leads us to conclude that we can resolve the problem by attending to systemic alignment. Then I will make the case that we must turn the question on its head and ask not how we can make the system cohere, but rather how we can help educators to achieve greater coherence in their own minds and efforts. Finally, I will describe the main implications for evaluating systemic reforms at the level of practice.

THE FALSE ASSUMPTION
OF SYSTEMIC REFORM

There is an overwhelming amount of evidence that educational change is inherently, endemically, and ineluctably *nonlinear.* This means that the most systemically sophisticated plan imaginable will unfold in a nonlinear, broken-front, back-and-forth manner. It will be fragmented.

This conclusion is both theoretically and empirically compelling. Dynamically complex societies, to use Peter Senge's phrase, could not operate in any other way.[1] In *Change Forces* I describe in some detail why this must be the case—why nonlinearity is built into the very dynamics of chance. For a taste of this line of argument, consider the following:

> Take any educational policy or problem and start listing all the forces that could figure in the solution and that would need to be influenced to make for productive chance. Then, take the idea that unplanned factors are inevitable—government, policy changes or gets constantly redefined, key leaders leave, important contact people are shifted to another role, new technology is invented, immigration increases, recession reduces available resources, a bitter conflict erupts, and so on. Finally, realize that every new variable that enters the equation—those unpredictable but inevitable noise factors—produces ten other ramifications, which in turn produce tens of other reactions, and on and on.[2]

No amount of sheer brilliance, authority, or power could possibly resolve the problem of nonlinearity, because it is organically part and parcel of the way complex societies *must* evolve. The rational trap, then, is to take as one's central purpose the strategy of making the system cohere objectively.

As will become clear, I am not arguing for neglecting systemic reform. It will "help" to work on alignment, clarity, and consistency of policy. Rather, I would suggest that we avoid becoming preoccupied with *orchestrating* the coherence of the system, that we realize the fundamental limitations of this line of thinking, and that we take different strategic actions.

Moreover, I am not claiming that systemic reformers think purely rationally or that they fail to build in flexibility and the ability to meet contingencies. I make a more fundamental point: that we must develop a neglected aspect of our thinking that is well grounded in the lessons of reality—in the way successful change does occur, not on how it should occur.

Ironically, current systemic reform initiatives may actually exacerbate the problems of overload and fragmentation. What looks like clarity at the top may increase clutter at the bottom. There is no reason to assume that the debate about systemic reform has so far added one iota of clarity to the confusing picture faced by the majority of teachers.

ACHIEVING GREATER COHERENCE
ON THE GROUND

As we work on clarifying what students should know and be able to do (and I agree that this represents one essential lever for reform), we must focus on what is the critical implementation issue: *only when greater clarity and coherence are achieved in the minds of the majority of teachers will we have any chance of success.* Therefore, the central question is what combination of strategies will have the best chance of achieving greater shared, subjective clarity on a wide scale. Put another way, clarity must be achieved on the receiving end more than on the delivery end.

As it turns out, we know a fair amount about what kinds of strategies are more effective. We still do not know how to achieve comprehensive reform on a wide scale, but we know much more about some of the components necessary. Incidentally, there is considerable evidence that neither top-down nor bottom-up strategies work by themselves.[3] But what are some of the strategies that are most promising?

It is easier to identify systemiclike changes in the top half of the system than in the bottom half. At or near the top, the kinds of changes needed are, first, the development of inspiring goals and visions for teaching and learning, which can be expressed through curriculum and instructional frameworks, and, second, the development of the technology of corresponding assessment. California represents one of the clearest examples of this sort of effort.

Such endeavors have the potential for helping, but they are plagued by three problems, all of which undercut their effectiveness at the bottom. First, the politics of dynamically complex societies ensure that these new directions will be nonlinear. To cite the California example again, that state is experiencing setbacks as a result of political wrangling. This nonlinearity, according to theory (and so far to practice), is normal.

Second, if those at the top make the seemingly rational mistake of thinking and acting as if the new framework were "something to be implemented"—through credentialing, accountability schemes, or even orchestrated training—they misunderstand how change works, and they ultimately defeat their own purpose.[4] Kentucky represents an example of this tendency, although, depending on preexisting conditions, it may be necessary to start with system-level restructuring.[5]

Third—and we are still at the early stages of working this out—a new realization about systemic reform has entered the equation. Not only does the education system need to become more coherent internally, but it must also become more coherently related, as a system, to other social and economic services and agencies. Even the most obviously necessary coordination across government departments and bureaucracies can hardly be described as systemically driven.

All of this is to say that those at the top, as well as those at the bottom, have to turn systemic thinking on its head. They have to ask how we can focus our efforts at the bottom so that there is some chance to achieve widespread improvement under the conditions of nonlinearity in the "big" system.

The question here is not how do we cope despite the system, a question I addressed in *Change Forces*. Instead, the question is what the top and the bottom can do *in combination* that will maximize the impact on learning outcomes. Let's be clear about the scope of the problem. Assuming that the top has already worked on matters of vi-

sion and direction, it would probably have done so in collaboration with various parts of the system. This process would have mobilized only a small percentage of those who need to become involved—probably 5 percent at most. What strategies, then, are going to be most effective in working with the remaining 95 percent?

Two powerful sets of strategies are now underway, and, taken together, they seem likely to bring about the changes at the bottom that will be necessary for systemic change to occur on a large scale. One is the set of strategies that can be described under the broad label of *networking*. The other involves the longer-term strategies of changing the conditions and the nature of learning and teaching through *reculturing* and *restructuring*.

The most action-oriented, immediate set of strategies involves purposeful, structured networking, which Bill Honig has described as

> a large-scale attempt to link significant numbers of schools through support networks organized around powerful visions or themes for improvement. This approach was designed to extend reform to those schools that were willing to change but were stymied without some organized assistance.[6]

In addition to being purposeful, the strategic and tactical features of networks include:

- Ongoing, systematic multilevel staff development (usually involving identified teacher leaders within each school and external staff developers)
- Multiple ways to share ideas, including telecommunication, cross-visitation, and workshops
- Integration with schoolwide and districtwide priorities and mechanisms, including leadership of school principals, collective actions by the majority of teachers, community development, school improvement plans under district auspices, growth-oriented performance appraisal schemes, and teacher union interest in professional development
- A commitment to and a preoccupation with inquiry, assessment of progress, and continuous improvement

This network strategy assumes that people need integrating (coherence-making) mechanisms, that continuous skills development is essential, that people need to experience new kinds of environments with regard to pressure and support, and that change requires external facilitation to support internal capacity building.

For the sake of argument, I might suggest that networking, when practiced on a significant scale, might increase the involvement of teachers in systemic reform from our hypothetical 5 percent to some 30 percent to 40 percent. Networks have two limitations, however. The first stems from the fact that there are frequently multiple networks on the scene. To participate in any one network does not necessarily resolve the fragmentation problem, because it represents just one among many projects. The second problem is that networks do not really *replace* existing working conditions, but rather are grafted on. This is why the second set of strategies—reculturing and restructuring—is so essential.

Reculturing refers to the process of developing new values, beliefs, and norms. For systemic reform it involves building new conceptions about instruction (e.g., teaching for understanding and using new forms of assessment) and new forms of professionalism for teachers (e.g., building commitment to continuous learning and to problem solving through collaboration). Restructuring concerns changes in the roles, structures, and other mechanisms that enable new cultures to thrive.

To put it bluntly, existing school cultures and structures are antithetical to the kinds of activities envisioned by systemic reform. Thus, until these more basic conditions begin to change, the best networking efforts will fall short. Incidentally, such restructuring attempts as site-based management typically change structures—leaving the culture intact.[7] We have begun to make progress in developing these collaborative work cultures.[8] Donahoe advocates redesigning not only structure and culture but time as well:

> No matter how unthinkable radical change in the school day may be, the school simply cannot continue to function traditionally, with a compressed academic day during which each teacher sticks to his or her own room and duties.[9]

What is at stake here is a fundamental redefinition of teachers and professionals that includes radical changes in teacher preparation, in the design and culture of schools, and in teachers' day-to-day role. The role of the teacher of the future will be both wider and deeper, involving at least six domains of commitment, knowledge, and skills: teaching and learning, collegiality, context, continuous learning, moral purpose, and change process.[10]

As I indicated above, in some large jurisdictions networking has probably mobilized as many as one-third of teachers to move in the direction implied by reculturing. They have not yet accomplished radical redesign of their own schools, let alone of the host of other schools. What is needed now is "to move to scale" by enabling the majority of teachers and schools to operate in these ways and thereby create the critical mass of new norms necessary to sustain a culture of systemic reform. The need to move to scale and some ideas for doing so have been identified by Honig and by Simmons and Mazany.[11]

In summary, systemic reform is partly a matter of redesigning the objective systems of interrelationships so that obvious structural faults are corrected. However, it mainly involves strategies (such as networking and reculturing) that help to develop and mobilize the conceptions, skills, and motivation in the minds and hearts of scores of educators. The ultimate test for reducing overload and fragmentation is whether teachers feel that greater coherence has been achieved.

EVALUATING SYSTEMIC REFORM

Several implications for evaluating systemic reform can be derived from the foregoing discussion. First, protocols can be developed for assessing how much objective alignment exists in the policies and procedures of specific jurisdictions (e.g., districts, states, nations), including linkages that exist between education and other providers of social services.

Second, developing and regularly administering assessments of what students are learning is essential. The data must be properly disaggregated, and progress (i.e., movement from a given starting point to the time of assessment) must be the focus.

Third, and here is where it gets appropriately messy, one can gather data on a number of proxy measures of systemic reform, as indicated by the state of the networking activities associated with particular initiatives. How much ongoing staff development is there within the network and of what quality? How active and effective are multilevel relationships with, for example, external facilitators? What is the quality of product and problem sharing? How integrated is network activity with district and schoolwide priorities and planning and implementation procedures? What links exist between school and community development? How much built-in monitoring is there (inquiry, assessment, examination of data, action)?

Fourth, are the cultures and structures of schools and classrooms changing to favor greater collaboration, radical new uses of time, and continuous teacher development, including stronger links with preservice programs? Is the role of the teacher becoming more sophisticated, and is the quality of the teaching profession improving? Do teachers have greater self-respect and societal respect?

Fifth, in a kind of backward mapping exercise, we should be gathering data on how well teachers understand the new things that they are expected and wanting to do. Do they perceive a degree of overall coherence about their work and about major policies? Do they find the work overwhelming or not? Are they critical consumers of new ideas?

I have to say that these measures are just as important as student performance measures, because you cannot improve student learning for all or most students without improving teacher learning for all or most teachers.

I believe that one of the main reasons that teachers seem to be constantly defending themselves from external critics is that they cannot explain themselves adequately. Critics are increasingly using clear language and specific examples in their charges, while educators are responding with philosophical rationales (e.g., we

are engaged in active learning). Abstract responses to specific complaints are not credible.

What does it mean to say that educators cannot explain themselves adequately? Perhaps teachers do not fully understand what they are doing, or perhaps they are simply unable to articulate it. Systemic reform, if it works, will mean that educators will achieve greater coherence and improved ability to explain what they do—all the more so because they will be working continuously with parents and communities.

Finally, the kinds of systemic reforms we are talking about increase the capacity of systems to manage change on a continuous basis. "Systems" have a better track record of maintaining the status quo than they have of changing themselves. This is why attempting to change the system directly, through regulation and structural reform, does not work. It is people who change systems, through the development of new critical masses. Once a critical mass becomes a majority, we begin to see the system change. The lesson of systemic reform is to look for those strategies that are most likely to mobilize large numbers of people in new directions. Evaluation should focus on this development, not because it will always result in clear measures, but because such a focus will propel the very changes essential for systemic breakthroughs.

ENDNOTES

1. Peter Senge, *The Fifth Discipline* (Garden City, N.Y.: Doubleday, 1990).
2. Michael Fullan, *Change Forces: Probing the Depths of Educational Reform* (Bristol, Pa.: Falmer Press, 1993), p. 19.
3. Michael Fullan, "Coordinating Top-down and Bottom-up Strategies for Educational Reform." In Susan Fuhrman and Richard Elmore, eds., *The Governance of Curriculum* (Alexandria, Va.: Association for Supervision and Curriculum Development, 1994), pp. 186–202.
4. David L. Clark and Terry A. Astuto, "Redirecting Reform: Challenges to Popular Assumptions about Teachers and Students." *Phi Delta Kappan,* March 1994, pp. 512–20; and Fullan, *Change Forces.*
5. Betty E. Steffy, *The Kentucky Education Reform* (Lancaster, Pa.: Technomic, 1995).
6. Bill Honig, "How Can Horace Best Be Helped?" *Phi Delta Kappan,* June 1994, p. 794.

7. Fullan, *Change Forces.*

8. Michael G. Fullan and Andy Hargreaves, *What's Worth Fighting for in Your School?,* 2nd ed. (New York: Teachers College Press, 1996).

9. Tom Donahoe, "Finding the Way: Structure, Time, and Culture in School Improvement," *Phi Delta Kappan,* December 1993, p. 301. See also Mary Anne Raywid, "Finding Time for Collaboration," *Educational Leadership,* September 1993, pp. 30–34.

10. Michael Fullan, "Teacher Leadership: A Failure to Conceptualize." In Donovan R. Walling, ed., *Teachers as Leaders: Perspectives on the Professional Development of Teachers* (Bloomington, Ind.: Phi Delta Kappa Educational Foundation, 1995), pp. 241–53.

11. Honig, op. cit.; John Simmons and Terry Mazany, "Going to Scale: Extending the Best Practices of Reform to All Chicago Public Schools," unpublished paper, Participation Associates, Chicago; and Michael Fullan, "Broadening Teacher Leadership," in Sarah Caldwell, ed., *New Directions in Staff Development* (Oxford, Ohio: National Staff Development Council (forthcoming).

DISCUSSION QUESTIONS

1. In what way is the process of systemic reform fundamentally flawed?
2. How does the dynamic of nonlinearity affect systemic reform initiatives?
3. According to the author, how are networking, reculturing, and restructuring likely to facilitate successful systemic change?
4. In what ways do existing school cultures and structures mitigate against systemic reform initiatives?
5. What type of evaluation can be used to assess the effectiveness of systemic reform?

36

Creating School, Family, and Community Partnerships

JOYCE L. EPSTEIN

FOCUSING QUESTIONS

1. *How have federal, state, and local policies influenced the development of school, family, and community partnerships?*
2. *How does an interest in the welfare of students influence the development of partnerships between schools, families, and communities?*
3. *How do family-like schools and traditional schools differ?*
4. *What is the role of the teacher and school principal in developing positive relationships with families?*
5. *What practices are common across all successful school, family, and community partnership programs at all grade levels?*
6. *Who should be responsible for creating family, school, and community partnerships: (a) teachers, (b) administrators, (c) parents, (d) students, or (e) local taxpayers? Why?*

The way schools care about children is reflected in the way schools care about the children's families. If educators view children simply as *students,* they are likely to see the family as separate from the school. That is, the family is expected to do its job and leave the education of children to the schools. If educators view students as *children,* they are likely to see both the family and the community as partners with the school in children's education and development. Partners recognize their shared interests in and responsibilities for children, and they work together to create better programs and opportunities for students.

There are many reasons for developing school, family, and community partnerships. They can improve school programs and school climate, provide family services and support, increase par-

ents' skills and leadership, connect families with others in the school and in the community, and help teachers with their work. However, the main reason to create such partnerships is to help all youngsters to succeed in school and in later life. When parents, teachers, students, and others view one another as partners in education, a caring community forms around students and begins its work.

What do successful partnership programs look like? How can practices be effectively designed and implemented? What are the results of better communications, interactions, and exchanges across these important contexts? These questions have challenged research and practice, creating an interdisciplinary field of inquiry into school, family, and community partnerships with "caring" as a core concept.

The field has been strengthened by supporting federal, state, and local policies. For example, the Goals 2000 legislation sets partnerships as a voluntary national goal for all schools: Title I specifies and mandates programs and practices of partnership in order for schools to qualify for or maintain funding. Many states and districts have developed or are preparing policies to guide schools in creating more systematic connections with families and communities. These policies reflect research results and the prior successes of leading educators who have shown that these goals are attainable.

Underlying these policies and programs are a theory of how social organizations connect: a framework of the basic components of school, family, and community partnerships for children's learning; a growing literature on the positive and negative results of these connections for students, families, and schools; and an understanding of how to organize good programs. In this chapter I summarize the theory, framework, and guidelines that have assisted the schools in our research projects in building partnerships and that should help any elementary, middle, or high school to take similar steps.

OVERLAPPING SPHERES OF INFLUENCE: UNDERSTANDING THE THEORY

Schools make choices. They might conduct only a few communications and interactions with families and communities, keeping the three spheres of influence that directly affect student learning and development relatively separate. Or they might conduct many high-quality communications and interactions designed to bring all three spheres of influence closer together. With frequent interactions between schools, families, and communities, more students are more likely to receive common messages from various people about the importance of school, of working hard, of thinking creatively, of helping one another, and of staying in school.

The *external model* of overlapping spheres of influence recognizes that the three major contexts in which students learn and grow—the family, the school, and the community—may be drawn together or pushed apart. In this model, there are some practices that schools, families, and communities conduct separately and some that they conduct jointly in order to influence children's learning and development. The *internal* model of the interaction of the three spheres of influence shows where and how complex and essential interpersonal relations and patterns of influence occur between individuals at home, at school, and in the community. These social relationships may be enacted and studied at an *institutional* level (e.g., when a school invites all families to an event or sends the same communications to all families) and at an *individual* level (e.g., when a parent and a teacher meet in conference or talk by phone). Connections between schools or parents and community groups, agencies, and services can also be represented and studied within the model.[1]

The model of school, family, and community partnerships locates the student at the center. The inarguable fact is that students are the main actors in their education, development, and success in school. School, family, and community partnerships cannot simply produce successful students. Rather, partnership activities may be designed to engage, guide, energize, and motivate students to produce their own successes. The assumption is that, if children feel cared for and encouraged to work hard in the role of student, they are more likely to do their best to learn to read, write, and calculate, to learn other skills and talents, and to remain in school.

Interestingly, and somewhat ironically, studies indicate that students are also crucial for the success of school, family, and community partnerships. Students are often their parents' main source of information about school. In strong partnership programs, teachers help students to understand and conduct traditional communications with families (e.g., delivering memos or report cards) and new communications (e.g., interacting with family members about homework or participating in parent, teacher, student conferences). As we gain more information about the role of students in partnerships, we are developing a more complete understanding of how schools, families, and communities must work with students to increase their chances for success.

How Theory Sounds in Practice

In some schools there are still educators who say, "If the family would just do its job, we could do our job." And there are still families who say, "I raised this child; now it is your job to educate her." These words embody the theory of *separate spheres of influence.* Other educators say, "I cannot do my job without the help of my students' families and the support of this community." And some parents say, "I really need to know what is happening in school in order to help my child." These phrases embody the theory of *overlapping spheres of influence.*

In a partnership, teachers and administrators create more *familylike* schools. A familylike school recognizes each child's individuality and makes each child feel special and included. Familylike schools welcome all families, not just those that are easy to reach. In a partnership, parents create more *schoollike* families. A schoollike family recognizes that each child is also a student. Families reinforce the importance of school, homework, and activities that build student skills and feelings of success. Communities, including groups of parents working together, create schoollike opportunities, events, and programs that reinforce, recognize, and reward students for good progress, creativity, contributions, and excellence. Communities also create *familylike* settings, services, and events to enable families to better support their children. *Community-minded* families and students help their neighborhoods and other families. The concept of a community school is reemerging. It refers to a place where programs and services for students, parents, and others are offered before, during, and after the regular school day.

Schools and communities talk about programs and services that are "family friendly," meaning that they take into account the needs and realities of family life in the 1990s, are feasible to conduct, and are equitable toward all families. When all these concepts combine, children experience *learning communities* or *caring communities.*[2]

All these terms are consistent with the theory of overlapping spheres of influence, but they are not abstract concepts. You will find them daily in conversations, news stories, and celebrations of many kinds. In a familylike school, a teacher might say, "I know when a student is having a bad day and how to help him along." A student might slip and call a teacher "mom" or "dad" and then laugh with a mixture of embarrassment and glee. In a schoollike family, a parent might say, "I make sure my daughter knows that homework comes first." A child might raise his hand to speak at the dinner table and then joke about acting as if he were still in school. When communities reach out to students and their families, youngsters might say, "This program really made my schoolwork make sense!" Parents or educators might comment, "This community really supports its schools."

Once people hear about such concepts as familylike schools or schoollike families, they remember positive examples of schools, teachers, and places in the community that were "like a family" to them. They may remember how a teacher paid individual attention to them, recognized their uniqueness, or praised them for real progress, just as a parent might. Or they might recall things at home that were "just like school" and supported their work as a student, or they might remember community activities that made them feel smart or good about themselves and their families. They will recall that parents, siblings, and other family members engaged in and enjoyed educational activities and took pride in the good schoolwork or homework that they did, just as a teacher might.

How Partnerships Work in Practice

These terms and examples are evidence of the *potential* for schools, families, and communities to create caring educational environments. It is possible to have a school that is excellent academically but ignores families. However, that school will build barriers between teachers, parents, and children—barriers that affect school life and learning. It is possible to have a school that is ineffective academically but involves families in many good ways. With its weak academic program, that school will shortchange students' learning. Neither of these schools exemplifies a caring educational environment that requires academic excellence, good communications, and productive interactions involving school, family, and community.

Some children succeed in school without much family involvement or despite family neglect or distress, particularly if the school has excellent academic and support programs. Teachers, relatives outside the immediate family, other families, and members of the community can provide important guidance and encouragement to these students. As support from school, family, and community accumulates, significantly more students feel secure and cared for, understand the goals of education, work to achieve to their full potential, build positive attitudes and school behaviors, and stay in school. The shared interests and investments of schools, families, and communities create the conditions of caring that work to "overdetermine" the likelihood of student success.[3]

Any practice can be designed and implemented well or poorly. And even well-implemented partnership practices may not be useful to all families. In a caring school community, participants work continually to improve the nature and effects of partnerships. Although the interactions of educators, parents, students, and community members will not always be smooth or successful, partnership programs establish a base of respect and trust on which to build. Good partnerships withstand questions, conflicts, debates, and disagreements; provide structures and processes to solve problems; and are maintained—even strengthened—after differences have been resolved. Without this firm base, disagreements and problems that are sure to arise about schools and students will be harder to solve.

What Research Says

In surveys and field studies involving teachers, parents, and students at the elementary, middle,

and high school levels, some important patterns relating to partnerships have emerged.[4]

- Partnerships tend to decline across the grades, *unless* schools and teachers work to develop and implement appropriate practices of partnership at each grade level.
- Affluent communities currently have more positive family involvement, on average, *unless* schools and teachers in economically distressed communities work to build positive partnerships with their students' families.
- Schools in more economically depressed communities make more contacts with families about the problems and difficulties their children are having, *unless* they work at developing balanced partnership programs that include contacts about positive accomplishments of students.
- Single parents, parents who are employed outside the home, parents who live far from the school, and fathers are less involved, on average, at the school building, *unless* the school organizes opportunities for families to volunteer at various times and in various places to support the school and their children.

Researchers have also drawn the following conclusions.

- Just about all families care about their children, want them to succeed, and are eager to obtain better information from schools and communities so as to remain good partners in their children's education.
- Just about all teachers and administrators would like to involve families, but many do not know how to go about building positive and productive programs and are consequently fearful about trying. This creates a "rhetoric rut," in which educators are stuck, expressing support for partnerships without taking any action.
- Just about all students at all levels—elementary, middle, and high school—want their families to be more knowledgeable partners about schooling and are willing to take active roles in assisting communications between home and school. However, students need much better information and guidance

than most now receive about how their schools view partnerships and about how they can conduct important exchanges with their families about school activities, homework, and school decisions.

The research results are important because they indicate that caring communities can be built, on purpose; that they include families that might not become involved on their own; and that, by their own reports, just about all families, students, and teachers believe that partnerships are important for helping students to succeed across the grades.

Good programs will look different in each site as individual schools tailor their practices to meet the needs and interests, time and talents, ages and grade levels of students, and their families. However, there are some commonalities across successful programs at all grade levels. These include a recognition of the overlapping spheres of influence on student development; attention to various types of involvement that promote a variety of opportunities for schools, families, and communities to work together; and an Action Team for School, Family, and Community Partnerships to coordinate each school's work and progress.

SIX TYPES OF INVOLVEMENT; SIX TYPES OF CARING

A framework of six major types of involvement has evolved from many studies and from many years of work by educators and families in elementary, middle, and high schools. The framework (summarized in the accompanying tables) helps educators to develop more comprehensive programs of school and family partnerships and also helps researchers to locate their questions and results in ways that inform and improve practice.[5]

Each type of involvement includes many different *practices* of partnership (see Table 36.1). Each type presents particular *challenges* that must be met in order to involve all families and needed *redefinitions* of some basic principles of involvement (see Table 36.2). Finally, each type is likely to lead to different *results* for students, for parents, for teaching practice, and for school climate (see Table 36.3). Thus, schools have choices about

which practices will help achieve important goals. The tables provide examples of practices, challenges for successful implementation, redefinitions for up-to-date understanding, and results that have been documented and observed.

Charting the Course

The entries in the tables are illustrative. The sample practices displayed in Table 36.1 are only a few of hundreds that may be selected or designed for each type of involvement. Although all schools may use the framework of six types as a guide, each school must chart its own course in choosing practices to meet the needs of its families and students.

The challenges shown (Table 36.2) are just a few of many that relate to the examples. There are challenges, that is, problems, for every practice of partnership, and they must be resolved in order to reach and engage all families in the best ways. Often, when one challenge is met, a new one will emerge.

The redefinitions (also in Table 36.2) redirect old notions so that involvement is not viewed solely as or measured only by "bodies in the building." As examples, the table calls for redefinitions of workshops, communication, volunteers, homework, decision making, and community. By redefining these familiar terms, it is possible for partnership programs to reach out in new ways to many more families.

The selected results (Table 36.3) should help to correct the widespread misperception that any practice that involves families will raise children's achievement test scores. Instead, in the short term, certain practices are more likely than others to influence students' skills and scores, while other practices are more likely to affect attitudes and behaviors. Although students are the main focus of partnerships, the various types of involvement also promote various kinds of results for parents and teachers. For example, the expected results for parents include not only leadership in decision making, but also confidence about parenting, productive curriculum-related interactions with children, and many interactions with other parents

TABLE 36.1 Epstein's Framework of Six Types of Involvement and Sample Practices

Type 1 Parenting	Type 2 Communicating	Type 3 Volunteering	Type 4 Learning at Home	Type 5 Decision Making	Type 6 Collaborating with Community
Help all families to establish home environments to support children as students.	Design effective forms of school-to-home and home-to-school communications about school programs and children's progress.	Recruit and organize parent help and support.	Provide information and ideas to families about how to help students at home with homework and other curriculum-related activities, decisions, and planning.	Include parents in school decisions, developing parent leaders and representatives.	Identify and integrate resources and services from the community to strengthen school programs, family practices, and student learning and development.
Sample Practices	**Sample Practices**	**Sample Practices**	**Sample Practices**	**Sample Practices**	**Sample Practices**
Suggestions for home conditions that support learning at each grade level.	Conferences with every parent at least once a year, with follow-ups as needed.	School and classroom volunteer program to help teachers, administrators, students, and other parents.	Information for families on skills required for students in all subjects at each grade.	Active PTA/PTO or other parent organizations, advisory councils, or committees (e.g., curriculum, safety, personnel) for parent leadership and participation.	Information for students and families on community health, cultural, recreational, social support, and other programs or services.
Workshops, videotapes, computerized phone messages on parenting and child rearing at each age and grade level.	Language translators to assist families as needed.	Parent room or family center for volunteer work, meetings, resources for families.	Information on homework policies and how to monitor and discuss schoolwork at home.	Independent advocacy groups to lobby and work for school reform and improvements.	Information on community activities that link to learning skills and talents, including summer programs for students.
Parent education and other courses or training for parents (e.g., GED, college credit, family literacy).	Weekly or monthly folders of student work sent home for review and comments.	Annual postcard survey to identify all available talents, times, and locations of volunteers.	Information on how to assist students to improve skills on various class and school assessments.	District-level councils and committees for family and community involvement.	Service integration through partnerships involving school; civic, counseling, cultural, health, recreation, and other agencies and organizations; and businesses.
Family support programs to assist families with health, nutrition, and other services.	Parent–student pickup of report card, with conferences on improving grades.	Class parent, telephone tree, or other structures to provide all families with needed information.	Regular schedule of homework that requires students to discuss and interact with families on what they are learning in class.	Information on school or local elections for school representatives.	Service to the community by students, families, and schools (e.g., recycling, art, music, drama, and other activities for seniors or others).
Home visits at transition points to preschool, elementary, middle, and high school. Neighborhood meetings to help families to understand schools and to help schools understand families.	Regular schedule of useful notices, memos, phone calls, newsletters, and other communications.	Parent patrols of other activities to aid safety and operation of school programs.	Calendars with activities for parents and students at home.	Networks to link all families with parent representatives.	Participation of alumni in school programs for students.
	Clear information on choosing schools or courses, programs, and activities within schools.		Family math, science, and reading activities at school.		
	Clear information on all school policies, programs, reforms, and transitions.		Summer learning packets or activities.		
			Family participation in setting student goals each year and in planning for college or work.		

TABLE 36.2 Challenges and Redefinitions for the Six Types of Involvement

Type 1 Parenting	Type 2 Communicating	Type 3 Volunteering	Type 4 Learning at Home	Type 5 Decision Making	Type 6 Collaborating with Community
Challenges	**Challenges**	**Challenges**	**Challenges**	**Challenges**	**Challenges**
Provide information to *all* families who want it or who need it, not just to the few who can attend workshops or meetings at the school building.	Review the readability, clarity, form, and frequency of all memos, notices, and other print and nonprint communications.	Recruit volunteers widely so that *all* families know that their time and talents are welcome.	Design and organize a regular schedule of interactive homework (e.g., weekly or bimonthly) that gives *students* responsibility for discussing important things they are learning and helps families to stay aware of the content of their children's classwork.	Include parent leaders from all racial, ethnic, socioeconomic, and other groups in the school.	Solve turf problems of responsibilities, funds, staff, and locations for collaborative activities.
Enable families to share information with schools about culture, background, children's talents and needs.	Consider parents who do not speak English well, do not read well, or need large type.	Make flexible schedules for volunteers, assemblies, and events to enable parents who work to participate.		Offer training to enable leaders to serve as representatives of other families, with input from and return of information to all parents.	Inform families of community programs for students, such as mentoring, tutoring, business partnerships.
Make sure that all information for and from families is clear, usable, and linked to children's success in school.	Review the quality of major communications (newsletters, report cards, conference schedules, and so on).	Organize volunteer work; provide training; match time and talent with school, teacher, and student needs; and recognize efforts so that participants are productive.	Coordinate family-linked homework activities, if students have several teachers.	Include students (along with parents) in decision-making groups.	Assure equity of opportunities for students and families to participate in community programs or to obtain services.
	Establish clear two-way channels for communications from home to school and from school to home.		Involve families and their children in all important curriculum-related decisions.		Match community contributions with school goals; integrate child and family services with education.

Redefinitions

"Workshop" to mean more than a *meeting* about a topic held at the school building at a particular time. "Workshop" may also mean making information about a topic available in a variety of forms that can be viewed, heard, or read anywhere, anytime, in varied forms.

Redefinitions

"Communications about school programs and student progress" to mean two-way, three-way, and many-way channels of communication that connect schools, families, students, and the community.

Redefinitions

"Volunteer" to mean anyone who supports school goals and children's learning or development in any way, at any place, and at any time—not just during the school day and at the school building.

Redefinitions

"Homework" to mean not only work done alone, but also interactive activities shared with others at home or in the community, linking schoolwork to real life.

"Help" at home to mean encouraging, listening, reacting, praising, guiding, monitoring, and discussing— not "teaching" school subjects.

Redefinitions

"Decision making" to mean a process of partnership, of shared views and actions toward shared goals, not just a power struggle between conflicting ideas.

Parent "leader" to mean a real representative, with opportunities and support to hear from and communicate with other families.

Redefinitions

"Community" to mean not only the neighborhoods where students' homes and schools are located but also any neighborhoods that influence their learning and development.

"Community" rated not only by low or high social or economic qualities, but by strengths and talents to support students, families, and schools.

"Community" means all who are interested in and affected by the quality of education, not just those with children in the schools.

429

TABLE 36.3 Expected Results of the Six Types of Involvement for Students, Parents, and Teachers

	Type 1 Parenting	Type 2 Communicating	Type 3 Volunteering	Type 4 Learning at Home	Type 5 Decision Making	Type 6 Collaborating with Community
Results for Students	Awareness of family supervision; respect for parents.	Awareness of own progress and of actions needed to maintain or improve grades.	Skill in communicating with adults.	Gains in skills, abilities, and test scores linked to homework and classwork.	Awareness of representation of families in school decisions.	Increased skills and talents through enriched curricular and extracurricular experiences.
	Positive personal qualities, habits, beliefs, and values, as taught by family.	Understanding of school policies on behavior, attendance, and other areas of student conduct.	Increased learning of skills that receive tutoring or targeted attention from volunteers.	Homework completion.	Understanding that student rights are protected.	Awareness of careers and of options for future education and work.
	Balance between time spent on chores, on other activities, and on homework.	Informed decisions about courses and programs.	Awareness of many skills, talents, occupations, and contribution of parents and other volunteers.	Positive attitude toward schoolwork.	Specific benefits linked to policies enacted by parent organizations and experienced by students.	Specific benefits linked to programs, services, resources, and opportunities that connect students with community.
	Good or improve attendance.	Awareness of own role in partnerships, serving as a courier and communicator.		View of parent as more similar to teacher and of home as more similar to school.		
	Awareness of importance of school.			Self-concept of ability of learner.		
For Parents	Understanding of and confidence about parenting, child and adolescent development, and changes in home conditions for learning as children proceed through school.	Understanding school programs and policies.	Understanding teacher's job, increased comfort in school, and carry-over of school activities at home.	Know how to support, encourage, and help student at home each year.	Input into policies that affect child's education.	Knowledge and use of local resources by family and child to increase skills and talents or to obtain needed services.
	Awareness of own and others' challenges in parenting.	Monitoring and awareness of child's progress.	Self-confidence about ability to work in school and with children or to take steps to improve own education.	Discussions of school, classwork, and homework.	Feelings of ownership of school.	Interactions with other families in community activities.
	Feeling of support from school and other parents.	Responding effectively to students' problems.	Awareness that families are welcome and valued at school.	Understanding of instructional program each year and of what child is learning in each subject.	Awareness of parents' voices in school decisions.	Awareness of school's role in the community and of community's contributions to the school.
		Interactions with teachers and ease of communication with school and teachers.	Gains in specific skills of volunteer work.	Appreciation of teaching skills.	Shared experiences and connections with other families.	
				Awareness of child as a learner.	Awareness of school, district, and state policies.	

For Teachers	For Teachers	For Teachers	For Teachers	For Teachers	For Teachers
Understanding families' backgrounds, cultures, concerns, goals, needs, and views of their children. Respect for families' strengths and efforts. Understanding of student diversity. Awareness of own skills to share information on child development.	Increased diversity and use of communications with families and awareness of own ability to communicate clearly. Appreciation for and use of parent network for communications. Increased ability to elicit and understand family views on children's programs and progress.	Readiness to involve families in new ways, including those who do not volunteer at school. Awareness of parents' talents and interests in school and children. Greater individual attention to students, with help from volunteers.	Better designing of home-work assignments. Respect of family time. Recognition of equal helpfulness of single-parent, dual-income, and less formally educated families in motivating and reinforcing student learning. Satisfaction with family involvement and support.	Awareness of parent perspectives as a factor in policy development and decisions. View of equal status of family representatives on committees and in leadership roles.	Awareness of community resources to enrich curriculum and instruction. Openness to and skill in using mentors, business partners, community volunteers, and others to assist students and augment teaching practice. Knowledgeable, helpful referrals of children and families to needed services.

and the school. The expected results for teachers include not only improved parent–teacher conferences or school–home communications, but also better understanding of families, new approaches to homework, and other connections with families and the community.

Most of the results noted in Table 36.3 have been measured in at least one research study and observed as schools conduct their work. The entries are listed in positive terms to indicate the results of well-designed and well-implemented practices. It should be fully understood, however, that results may be negative if poorly designed practices exclude families or create greater barriers to communication and exchange. Research is still needed on the results of specific practices of partnership in various schools, at various grade levels, and for diverse populations of students, families, and teachers. It will be important to confirm, extend, or correct the information on results listed in Table 36.3 if schools are to make purposeful choices among practices that foster various types of involvement.

The tables cannot show the connections that occur when one practice activates several types of involvement simultaneously. For example, volunteers may organize and conduct a food bank (Type 3) that allows parents to pay $15 for $30 worth of food for their families (Type 1). The food may be subsidized by community agencies (Type 6). The recipients might then serve as volunteers for the program or in the community (perpetuating Type 3 and Type 6 activities). Or consider another example. An after-school homework club run by volunteers and the community recreation department combines Type 3 and Type 6 practices. Yet it also serves as a Type 1 activity, because the after-school program assists families with the supervision of their children. This practice may also alter the way homework interactions are conducted between students and parents at home (Type 4). These and other connections are interesting, and research is needed to understand the combined efforts of such activities.

The tables also simplify the complex longitudinal influences that produce various results over time. For example, a series of events might play out as follows: The involvement of families in reading at home leads students to give more attention to reading and to be more strongly motivated to read. This, in turn, may help students to maintain or improve their daily reading skills and then their reading grades. With the accumulation over time of good classroom reading programs, continued home support, and increased skills and confidence in reading, students may significantly improve their reading achievement test scores. The time between reading aloud at home and increased reading test scores may vary greatly, depending on the quality and quantity of other reading activities in school and out.

Or consider another example. A study by Seyong Lee, using longitudinal data and rigorous statistical controls on background and prior influences, found important benefits for high school students' attitudes and grades as a result of continuing several types of family involvement from the middle school into the high school. However, achievement test scores were not greatly affected by partnerships at the high school level. Longitudinal studies and practical experiences that are monitored over time are needed to increase our understanding of the complex patterns of results that can develop from various partnership activities.[6]

The six types of involvement can guide the development of a balanced, comprehensive program of partnerships, including opportunities for family involvement at school and at home, with potentially important results for students, parents, and teachers. The results for students, parents, and teachers will depend on the particular types of involvement that are implemented, as well as on the quality of the implementation.

ACTION TEAMS FOR SCHOOL, FAMILY, AND COMMUNITY PARTNERSHIPS

Who will work to create caring school communities that are based on the concepts of partnership? How will the necessary work on all six types of involvement get done? Although a principal or a teacher may be a leader in working with some families or with groups in the community, one person cannot create a lasting, comprehensive program that involves all families as their children progress through the grades.

From the hard work of many educators and families in many schools, we have learned that, along with clear policies and strong support from state and district leaders and from school principals, an Action Team for School, Family, and Community Partnerships in each school is a useful structure. The action team guides the development of a comprehensive program of partnership, including all six types of involvement, and the integration of all family and community connections within a single, unified plan and program. The trials and errors, efforts and insights of many schools in our projects have helped to identify the five important steps that any school can take to develop more positive school, family, community connections.[7]

Step 1: Create an Action Team

A team approach is an appropriate way to build partnerships. The Action Team for School, Family, and Community Partnerships can be the "action arm" of a school council, if one exists. The action team takes responsibility for assessing present practices, organizing options for new partnerships, implementing selected activities, evaluating next steps, and continuing to improve and coordinate practices for all six types of involvement. Although the members of the action team lead these activities, they are assisted by other teachers, parents, students, administrators, and community members.

The action team should include at least three teachers from different grade levels, three parents with children in different grade levels, and at least one administrator. Teams may also include at least one member from the community at large and, at the middle and high school levels, at least two students from different grade levels. Others who are central to the school's work with families may also be included as members, such as a cafeteria worker, a school social worker, a counselor, or a school psychologist. Such diverse membership ensures that partnership activities will take into ac-

count the various needs, interests, and talents of teachers, parents, the school, and students.

The leader of the action team may be any member who has the respect of the other members, as well as good communication skills and an understanding of the partnership approach. The leader or at least one member of the action team should also serve on the school council, school improvement team, or other such body, if one exists.

In addition to group planning, members of the action team elect (or are assigned to act as) the chair or cochair of one of six subcommittees for each type of involvement. A team with at least six members (and perhaps as many as twelve) ensures that responsibilities for leadership can be delegated so that one person is not overburdened and that the work of the action team will continue even if members move or change schools or positions. Members may serve renewable terms of two to three years, with replacement of any who leave in the interim. Other thoughtful variations in assignments and activities may be created by small or large schools using this process.

In the first phase of our work in 1987, projects were led by project directors (usually teachers) and were focused on one type of involvement at a time. Some schools succeeded in developing good partnerships over several years, but others were thwarted if the project director moved, if the principal changed, or if the project grew larger than one person could handle. Other schools took a team approach in order to work on many types of involvement simultaneously. Their efforts demonstrated how to structure the program for the next set of schools in our work. Starting in 1990, this second set of schools tested and improved on the structure and work of action teams. Now, all elementary, middle, and high schools in our research and development projects and in other states and districts that are applying this work are given assistance in taking the action team approach.

Step 2: Obtain Funds and Other Support

A modest budget is needed to guide and support the work and expenses of each school's action team. Funds for state coordinators to assist districts and schools and funds for district coordinators or facilitators to help each school may come from a number of sources. These include federal, state, and local programs that mandate, request, or support family involvement, such as Title I, Title II, Title VII, Goals 2000, and other federal and similar state funding programs. In addition to paying the state and district coordinators, funds from these sources may be applied in creative ways to support staff development in the area of school, family, and community partnerships; to pay for lead teachers at each school; to set up demonstration programs; and for other partnership expenses. In addition, local school–business partnerships, school discretionary funds, and separate fund-raising efforts targeted to the schools' partnership programs have been used to support the work of their action teams. At the very least, a school's action team requires a small stipend (at least $1,000 per year for three to five years, with summer supplements) for time and materials needed by each subcommittee to plan, implement, and revise practices of partnership that include all six types of involvement.

The action team must also be given sufficient time and social support to do its work. This requires explicit support from the principal and district leaders to allow time for team members to meet, plan, and conduct the activities that are selected for each type of involvement. Time during the summer is also valuable—and may be essential—for planning new approaches that will start in the new school year.

Step 3: Identify Starting Points

Most schools have some teachers who conduct some practices of partnership with some families some of the time. How can good practices be organized and extended so that they may be used by all teachers, at all grade levels, with all families? The action team works to improve and systematize the typically haphazard patterns of involvement. It starts by collecting information about the school's present practices of partnership, along with the views, experiences, and wishes of teachers, parents, administrators, and students.

Assessments of starting points may be made in a variety of ways, depending on available resources, time, and talents. For example, the action team might use formal questionnaires[8] or telephone interviews to survey teachers, administrators, parents, and students (if resources exist to process, analyze, and report survey data). Or the action team might organize a panel of teachers, parents, and students to speak at a meeting of the parent–teacher organization or at some other school meeting as a way of initiating discussion about the goals and desired activities for partnership. Structured discussions may be conducted through a series of principal's breakfasts for representative groups of teachers, parents, students, and others; random sample phone calls may also be used to collect reactions and ideas; or formal focus groups may be convened to gather ideas about school, family, and community partnerships at the school.

What questions should be addressed? Regardless of how the information is gathered, some areas must be covered in any information gathering.

- *Present strengths.* Which practices of school, family, and community partnerships are now working well for the school as a whole? For individual grade levels? For which types of involvement?
- *Needed changes.* Ideally, how do we want school, family, and community partnerships to work at this school three years from now? Which present practices should continue and which should change? To reach school goals, what new practices are needed for each of the major types of involvement?
- *Expectations.* What do teachers expect of families? What do families expect of teachers and other school personnel? What do students expect their families to do to help them to negotiate school life? What do students expect their teachers to do to keep their families informed and involved?
- *Sense of community.* Which families are we now reaching, and which are we not yet reaching? Who are the hard-to-reach families? What might

be done to communicate with and engage these families in their children's education? Are current partnership practices coordinated to include all families as a school community? Or are families whose children receive special services (e.g., Title I, special education, bilingual education) separated from other families?

• *Links to goals.* How are students fairing on such measures of academic achievement as report card grades, on measures of attitudes and attendance, and on other indicators of success? How might family and community connections assist the school in helping more students to reach higher goals and achieve greater success? Which practices of school, family, and community partnerships would directly connect to particular goals?

Step 4: Develop a Three-year Plan

From the ideas and goals for partnerships collected from teachers, parents, and students, the action team can develop a three-year outline of the specific steps that will help the school to progress from its starting point on each type of involvement to where it wants to be in three years. This plan outlines how each subcommittee will work over three years to make important incremental advances to reach more families each year on each type of involvement. The three-year outline also shows how all school, family, and community connections will be integrated into one coherent program of partnership that includes activities for the whole school community, activities to meet the special needs of children and families, activities to link to the district committees and councils, and activities conducted in each grade level.

In addition to the three-year outline of goals for each type of involvement, a detailed one-year plan should be developed for the first year's work. It should include the specific activities that will be implemented, improved, or maintained for each type of involvement; a time line of monthly actions needed for each activity; identification of the subcommittee chair who will be responsible for each type of involvement; identification of the teachers, parents, students, or others (not necessarily action

team members) who will assist with the implementation of each activity; indicators of how the implementation and results of each major activity will be assessed; and other details of importance to the action team.

The three-year outline and one-year detailed plan are shared with the school council and/or parent organization, with all teachers, and with the parents and students. Even if the action team makes only one good step forward each year on each of the six types of involvement, it will take eighteen steps forward over three years to develop a more comprehensive and coordinated program of school, family, and community partnerships.

In short, based on the input from the parents, teachers, students, and others on the school's starting points and desired partnerships, the action team will address these issues.

• *Details.* What will be done each year, for three years, to implement a program on all six types of involvement? What, specifically, will be accomplished in the first year on each type of involvement?

• *Responsibilities.* Who will be responsible for developing and implementing practices of partnership for each type of involvement? Will staff development be needed? How will teachers, administrators, parents, and students be supported and recognized for their work?

• *Costs.* What costs are associated with the improvement and maintenance of the planned activities? What sources will provide the needed funds? Will small grants or other special budgets be needed?

• *Evaluation.* How will we know how well the practices have been implemented and what their effects are on students, teachers, and families? What indicators will we use that are closely linked to the practices implemented to determine their effects?

Step 5: Continue Planning and Working

The action team should schedule an annual presentation and celebration of progress at the school so that all teachers, families, and students will know about the work that has been done each year to build partnerships. Or the district coordinator for school, family, and community partnerships might arrange an annual conference for all schools in the district. At the annual school or district meeting, the action team presents and displays the highlights of accomplishments on each type of involvement. Problems are discussed and ideas are shared about improvements, additions, and continuations for the next year.

Each year the action team updates the school's three-year outline and develops a detailed one-year plan for the coming year's work. It is important for educators, families, students, and the community at large to be aware of annual progress, of new plans, and of how they can help.

In short, the action team addresses the following questions: How can it ensure that the program of school, family, and community partnership will continue to improve its structure, processes, and practices in order to increase the number of families who are partners with the school in their children's education? What opportunities will teachers, parents, and students have to share information on successful practices and to strengthen and maintain their efforts?

CHARACTERISTICS OF
SUCCESSFUL PROGRAMS

As schools have implemented partnership programs, their experience has helped to identify some important properties of successful partnerships.

• *Incremental progress.* Progress in partnerships is incremental, including more families each year in ways that benefit more students. Like reading or math programs, assessment programs, sports programs, or other school investments, partnership programs take time to develop, must be periodically reviewed, and should be continuously improved. The schools in our projects have shown that three years is the minimum time needed for an action team to complete a number of activities on each type of involvement and to establish its work

as a productive and permanent structure in a school.

The development of a partnership is a process, not a single event. All teachers, families, students, and community groups do not engage in all activities on all types of involvement all at once. Not all activities implemented will succeed with all families. But with good planning, thoughtful implementation, well-designed activities, and pointed improvements, more and more families and teachers can learn to work with one another on behalf of the children whose interests they share. Similarly, not all students instant!y improve their attitudes or achievements when their families become involved in their education. After all, student learning depends mainly on good curricula and instruction and on the work completed by students. However, with a well-implemented program of partnership, more students will receive support from their families, and more will be motivated to work harder.

• *Connection to curricular and instructional reform.* A program of school, family, and community partnerships that focuses on children's learning and development is an important component of curricular and instructional reform. Aspects of partnerships that aim to help more students succeed in school can be supported by federal, state, and local funds that are targeted for curricular and instructional reform. Helping families to understand, monitor, and interact with students on homework, for example, can be a clear and important extension of classroom instruction, as can volunteer programs that bolster and broaden student skills, talents, and interests. Improving the content and conduct of parent, teacher, and student conferences and goal-setting activities can be an important step in curricular reform; family support and family understanding of child and adolescent development and school curricula are necessary elements to assist students as learners.

The connection of partnerships to curriculum and instruction in schools and the location of leadership for these partnership programs in district departments of curriculum and instruction are important changes that move partnerships from being peripheral public relations activities about parents to being central programs about student learning and development.

• *Redefining staff development.* The action team approach to partnerships guides the work of educators by restructuring staff development to mean colleagues working together and with parents to develop, implement, evaluate, and continue to improve practices of partnership. This is less a "dose of inservice education" than it is an active form of developing staff talents and capacities. The teachers, administrators, and others on the action team become the "experts" on this topic for their school. Their work in this area can be supported by various federal, state, and local funding programs as a clear investment in staff development for overall school reform. Indeed, the action team approach as outlined can be applied to any or all important topics on a school improvement agenda. It need not be restricted to the pursuit of successful partnerships.

It is important to note that the development of partnership programs would be easier if educators came to their schools prepared to work productively with families and communities. Courses or classes are needed in preservice teacher education and in advanced degree programs for teachers and administrators to help them to define their professional work in terms of partnerships. Today, most educators enter schools without an understanding of family backgrounds, concepts of caring, the framework of partnerships, or the other "basics" I have discussed here. Thus most principals and district leaders are not prepared to guide and lead their staffs in developing strong school and classroom practices that inform and involve families. And most teachers and administrators are not prepared to understand, design, implement, or evaluate good practices of partnership with the families of their students. Colleges and universities that prepare educators and others who work with children and families should identify where in their curricula the theory, research, policy, and practical ideas about partnerships are presented or where in their programs these can be added.[9]

Even with improved preservice and advanced coursework, however, each school's action team will have to tailor its menu of practices to the needs and wishes of the teachers, families, and students in the school. The framework and guidelines offered in this chapter can be used by thoughtful educators to organize this work, school by school.

THE CORE OF CARING

One school in our Baltimore project named its partnerships the "I Care Program." It developed an I Care Parent Club that fostered fellowship and leadership of families, an *I Care Newsletter,* and many other events and activities. Other schools also gave catchy, positive names to their programs to indicate to families, students, teachers, and everyone else in the school community that there are important relationships and exchanges that must be developed in order to assist students.

Interestingly, synonyms for "caring" match the six types of involvement: Type 1, parenting: supporting, nurturing, and rearing; Type 2, communicating: relating, reviewing, and overseeing; Type 3, volunteering: supervising and fostering; Type 4, learning at home: managing, recognizing, and rewarding; Type 5, decision making: contributing, considering, and judging; and Type 6, collaborating with the community: sharing and giving.

Underlying all six types of involvement are two defining synonyms of caring: trusting and respecting. Of course, the varied meanings are interconnected, but it is striking that language permits us to call forth various elements of caring associated with activities for the six types of involvement. If all six types of involvement are operating well in a school's program of partnership, then all these caring behaviors could be activated to assist children's learning and development.

Despite real progress in many states, districts, and schools over the past few years, there are still too many schools in which educators do not understand the families of their students; in which families do not understand their children's schools; and in which communities do not understand or assist the schools, families, or students. There are still too many states and districts without the policies, departments, leadership, staff, and fiscal support needed to enable all their schools to develop good programs of partnership. Yet relatively small financial investments that support and assist the work of action teams could yield significant returns for all schools, teachers, families, and students. Educators who have led the way with trials, errors, and successes provide evidence that any state, district, or school can create similar programs.[10]

Schools have choices. There are two common approaches to involving families in schools and in their children's education. One approach emphasizes conflict and views the school as a battleground. The conditions and relationships in this kind of environment guarantee power struggles and disharmony. The other approach emphasizes partnership and views the school as a homeland. The conditions and relationships in this kind of environment invite power sharing and mutual respect and allow energies to be directed toward activities that foster student learning and development. Even when conflicts rage, however, peace must be restored sooner or later, and the partners in children's education must work together.

NEXT STEPS:
STRENGTHENING PARTNERSHIPS

Collaborative work and thoughtful give and take among researchers, policy leaders, educators, and parents are responsible for the progress that has been made over the past decade in understanding and developing school, family, and community partnerships. Similar collaborations will be important for future progress in this and other areas of school reform. To promote these approaches, I have established a national network of Partnership-2000 Schools to link state, district, and other leaders who are responsible for helping their elementary, middle, and high schools implement programs of school, family, and community partnerships by the year 2000. The state and district coordinators are supported for at least three years by sufficient staff and budgets that enable them to help increasing numbers of elementary, middle, and high schools in their districts to plan, imple-

ment, and maintain comprehensive programs of partnership.

Partnership-2000 Schools was aided in putting the recommendations of this chapter into practice in ways that are appropriate to their locations. Implementation includes applying the theory of overlapping spheres of influence, the framework of six types of involvement, and the action team approach. Researchers and staff members at Johns Hopkins disseminate information and guidelines, send out newsletters, and hold optional annual workshops to help state and district coordinators to learn new strategies and share successful ideas. Activities for leaders at the state and district levels, school-level programs, and successful partnership practices are shared.

The national network of Partnership-2000 Schools began its activities in the fall of 1995 and will continue until at least the year 2000. The goal is to enable leaders in all states and districts to assist all their schools in establishing and strengthening programs of school, family, and community partnership.[11]

ENDNOTES

1. Joyce L. Epstein, "Toward a Theory of Family–School Connections: Teacher Practices and Parent Involvement," in Klaus Hurrelmann, Frederick Kaufmann, and Frederick Losel, eds., *Social Intervention: Potential and Constraints* (New York: DeGruyter, 1987), pp. 121–36; idem, "School and Family Partnerships," in Marvin Alkin, ed., *Encyclopedia of Educational Research,* 6th ed. (New York: Macmillan, 1992), pp. 1139–51; idem, "Theory to Practice: School and Family Partnerships Lead to School Improvement and Student Success," in Cheryl L. Fagnano and Beverly Z. Werber, eds., *School, Family and Community Interaction: A View from the Firing Lines* (Boulder, Colo.: Westview Press, 1994), pp. 39–52; and idem, *School and Family Partnerships: Preparing Educators and Improving Schools* (Boulder, Colo.: Westview Press, forthcoming).

2. Ron Brandt, "On Parents and Schools: A Conversation with Joyce Epstein," *Educational Leadership,* October 1989, pp. 24–27; Epstein, "Toward a Theory"; Catherine C. Lewis, Eric Schaps, and Marilyn Watson, "Beyond the Pendulum: Creating Challenging and Caring Schools," *Phi Delta Kappan,* March 1995, pp. 547–54; and Debra

Viadero, "Learning to Care," *Education Week,* October 26, 1994, pp. 31–33.

3. A. Wade Boykin. "Harvesting Culture and Talent: African American Children and Educational Reform," in Robert Rossi, ed., *Schools and Students at Risk* (New York: Teachers College Press, 1994), pp. 116–39.

4. For references to studies by many researchers, see the following literature reviews: Epstein, "School and Family Partnerships"; idem, *School and Family Partnerships,* and idem. "Perspectives and Previews on Research and Policy for School, Family, and Community Partnerships," in Alan Booth and Judith Dunn, eds., *Family–School Links: How Do They Affect Educational Outcomes?* (Hillsdale, N.J.: Erlbaum, 1996). Research that reports patterns of involvement across the grades for families with low and high socioeconomic status, for one- and two-parent homes, and on schools' programs of partnership includes Carol Ames, with Madhab Khoju and Thomas Watkins, "Parents and Schools: The Impact of School-to-Home Communications on Parents' Beliefs and Perceptions." Center on Families, Communities, Schools, and Children's Learning, Center Report 15, Johns Hopkins University, Baltimore, 1993; David P. Baker and David L. Stevenson, "Mothers' Strategies for Children's School Achievement: Managing the Transition to High School," *Sociology of Education,* vol. 59, 1986, pp. 156–66; Patricia A. Bauch, "Is Parent Involvement Different in Private Schools?," *Educational Horizons,* vol. 66, 1988, pp. 78–82; Henry J. Becker and Joyce L. Epstein, "Parent Involvement: A Study of Teacher Practices," *Elementary School Journal,* vol. 83, 1982, pp. 85–102; Reginald M. Clark, *Family Life and School Achievement: Why Poor Black Children Succeed or Fail* (Chicago: University of Chicago Press, 1983); Susan L. Dauber and Joyce L. Epstein, "Parents' Attitudes and Practices of Involvement in Inner-city Elementary and Middle Schools," in Nancy Chavkin, ed., *Families and Schools in a Pluralistic Society* (Albany: State University of New York Press, 1993), pp. 53–71; Sanford M. Dornbusch and Philip L. Ritter, "Parents of High School Students: A Neglected Resource," *Educational Horizons,* vol. 66, 1988, pp. 75–77; Jacquelynne S. Eccles, "Family Involvement in Children's and Adolescents' Schooling," in Booth and Dunn, op, cit.; Joyce L. Epstein, "Parents' Reactions to Teacher Practices of Parent Involvement," *Elementary School Journal,* vol. 86, 1986, pp. 277–94; idem, "Single Parents and the Schools: Effects of Marital Status on Parent and Teacher Interactions," in Maureen Hallinan, ed., *Change in Societal Institutions* (New York: Plenum, 1990), pp. 91–121; Joyce L. Epstein and Seyong Lee, "National Patterns of School and Family Connections in the Middle Grades," in

Bruce A. Ryan and Gerald R. Adams, eds., *The Family–School Connection: Theory, Research, and Practice* (Newbury Park, Calif.: Sage, forthcoming); Annette Lareau, *Home Advantage: Social Class and Parental Intervention in Elementary Education* (Philadelphia: Falmer Press, 1989); and Diane Scott-Jones, "Activities in the Home That Support School Learning in the Middle Grades," in Barry Rutherford, ed., *Creating Family/School Partnerships* (Columbus, Ohio: National Middle School Association, 1995), pp. 161–81.

5. The three tables update earlier versions that were based on only five types of involvement. For other discussions of the types, practices, challenges, redefinitions, and results, see Epstein, "School and Family Partnerships"; Lori Connors Tadros and Joyce L. Epstein, "Parents and Schools," in Marc H. Bornstein, ed., *Handbook of Parenting* (Hillsdale, N.J.: Erlbaum, 1995); Joyce L. Epstein and Lori Connors Tadros, "School and Family Partnerships in the Middle Grades," in Rutherford, op. cit.; and idem, "Trust Fund: School, Family, and Community Partnerships in High Schools," Center on Families, Communities, Schools, and Children's Learning, Center Report 24, Johns Hopkins University, Baltimore, 1994. Schools' activities with various types of involvement are outlined in Don Davies, Patricia Burch, and Vivian Johnson, "A Portrait of Schools Reaching Out: Report of a Survey on Practices and Policies of Family–Community–School Collaboration," Center on Families, Communities, Schools, and Children's Learning, Center Report 1, Johns Hopkins University, Baltimore, 1992.

6. Seyong Lee, "Family–School Connections and Students' Education: Continuity and Change of Family Involvement from the Middle Grades to High School" (doctoral dissertation, Johns Hopkins University, 1994). For a discussion of issues concerning the results of partnerships, see Epstein, "Perspectives and Previews." For various research reports on results of partnerships for students and for parents, see Joyce L. Epstein, "Effects on Student Achievement of Teacher Practices of Parent Involvement," in Steven Silvern, ed., *Literacy Through Family, Community, and School Interaction* (Greenwich, Conn.: JAI Press, 1991), pp. 261–76; Joyce L. Epstein and Susan L. Dauber, "Effects on Students of an Interdisciplinary Program Linking Social Studies, Art, and Family Volunteers in the Middle Grades," *Journal of Early Adolescence,* vol. 15, 1995, pp. 237–66; Joyce L. Epstein and Jill Jacobsen, "Effects of School Practices to Involve Families in the Middle Grades: Parents' Perspectives," paper presented at the annual meeting of the American Sociological Association, Los Angeles, 1994; Joyce L.

Epstein and Seyong Lee, "Effects of School Practices to Involve Families on Parents and Students in the Middle Grades: A View from the Schools," paper presented at the annual meeting of the American Sociological Association, Miami, 1993; and Anne T. Henderson and Nancy Berla, *A New Generation of Evidence: The Family Is Critical to Student Achievement* (Washington, D.C.: National Committee for Citizens in Education, 1994).

7. Lori Connors Tadros and Joyce L. Epstein, "Taking Stock: The Views of Teachers, Parents, and Students on School, Family, and Commmunity Partnerships in High Schools," Center on Families, Communities, Schools, and Children's Learning, Center Report 25, Johns Hopkins University, Baltimore, 1994; Epstein and Tadros, "Trust Fund"; Joyce L. Epstein and Susan L. Dauber, "School Programs and Teacher Practices of Parent Involvement in Inner-City Elementary and Middle Schools," *Elementary School Journal,* vol. 91, 1991, pp. 289–303; and Joyce L. Epstein, Susan C. Herrick, and Lucretia Coates, "Effects of Summer Home Learning Packets on Student Achievement in Language Arts in the Middle Grades," *School Effectiveness and School Improvement,* in press. For other approaches to the use of action teams for partnerships, see Patricia Burch and Ameetha Palanki, "Action Research on Family–School–Community Partnerships," *Journal of Emotional and Behavioral Problems,* vol. 1, 1994, pp. 16–19; Patricia Burch, Ameetha Palanki, and Don Davies, "In Our Hands: A Multi-Site Parent–Teacher Action Research Project," Center on Families, Communities, Schools, and Children's Learning, Center Report 29, Johns Hopkins University, Baltimore, 1995; Don Davies, "Schools Reaching Out: Family, School, and Community Partnerships for Student Success," *Phi Delta Kappan,* January 1991, pp. 376–82; idem, "A More Distant Mirror: Progress Report on a Cross-national Project to Study Family–School–Community Partnerships," *Equity and Choice,* vol. 19, 1993, pp. 41–46; and Don Davies, Ameetha Palanki, and Patricia D. Palanki, "Getting Started: Action Research in Family–School–Community Partnerships," Center on Families, Communities, Schools, and Children's Learning, Center Report 17, Johns Hopkins University, Baltimore, 1993. For an example of an organizing mechanism for action teams, see Vivian R. Johnson, "Parent Centers in Urban Schools: Four Case Studies," Center on Families, Communities, Schools, and Children's Learning, Center Report 23, Johns Hopkins University, Baltimore, 1994.

8. Surveys for teachers and parents in the elementary and middle grades and for teachers, parents, and students in high school, developed and revised in 1993 by Joyce L. Epstein, Karen Clark Salinas, and Lori Connors Tadros, are available from the Center on Families, Communities, Schools, and Children's Learning at Johns Hopkins University.

9. Mary Sue Ammon, "University of California Project on Teacher Preparation for Parent Involvement. Report I: April 1989 Conference and Initial Follow-up," mimeo. University of California, Berkeley, 1990; Nancy F. Chavkin and David L. Williams, "Critical Issues in Teacher Training for Parent Involvement," *Educational Horizons,* vol. 66, 1988, pp. 87–89; and Lisa Hinz, Jessica Clarke, and Joe Nathan, "A Survey of Parent Involvement Course Offerings in Minnesota's Undergraduate Preparation Programs," Center for School Change, Humphrey Institute of Public Affairs, University of Minnesota, Minneapolis, 1992. To correct deficiencies in the education of educators, I have written a course text or supplementary reader based on the theory, framework, and approaches described in this chapter. See Epstein, *School and Family Partnerships.* Other useful readings for a university course include Sandra L. Christenson and Jane Close Conoley, eds., *Home–School Collaboration: Enhancing Children's Academic Competence* (Silver Spring, Md.: National Association of School Psychologists, 1992); Fagnano and Werber, op. cit.; Norman Fruchter, Anne Galetta, and J. Lynne White, *New Directions in Parent Involvement* (Washington, D.C.: Academy for Educational Development, 1992); William Rioux and Nancy Berla, eds., *Innovations in Parent and Family Involvement* (Princeton Junction, N.J.: Eye on Education, 1993); and Susan McAllister Swap, *Developing Home–School Partnerships: From Concepts to Practice* (New York: Teachers College Press, 1993).

10. See, for example, Gary Lloyd, "Research and Practical Application for School, Family, and Community Partnerships," in Booth and Dunn, op cit.; Wisconsin Department of Public Instruction. *Sharesheet: The DPI Family–Community–School Partnership Newsletter,* August/September 1994; and the special section on parent involvement in the January 1991 *Phi Delta Kappan.*

11. For more information about the national network of Partnership-2000 Schools, send the name, position, address, phone, and fax numbers of the key contact for your school, state, or district to Dr. Joyce L. Epstein, Director, Center on School, Family, and Community Partnerships, 3505 N. Charles St., Baltimore, MD 21218, or visit the Network's Website (http://scov.csos.jhu.edu/p2000/p2000.html).

DISCUSSION QUESTIONS

1. In what ways is partnership between families and schools likely to benefit children?
2. What conclusions have been drawn by researchers about the relationship between families and schools?
3. What suggestions for practice logically follow from the redefinitions of basic principles of involvement identified by Epstein?
4. How will increased family involvement influence student (a) outcomes, (b) attitudes, and (c) behaviors?
5. How might the types of involvement identified by Epstein be used in developing partnership programs?
6. What steps have been suggested by schools involved in school, family, and community partnership projects to develop more positive partnerships?

PRO-CON CHART 6

Should parent voice be a major consideration in determining where students attend school?

PRO	CON
1. The public school system is a monolithic structure that fosters middle class conformity.	1. School choice will promote a dual class educational system, schools for the rich and schools for the poor.
2. Public schooling perpetuates the existing power structure, including the subordination effects of class, caste, and gender.	2. Parental choice will breed intolerance for diversity and will further religious, racial, and socioeconomic isolation.
3. The reduced quality of public education necessitates that parents be given options in order to locate better learning environments.	3. Transporting students out of neighborhoods is costly for school districts and is time consuming for students.
4. Increasing choices means expanding educational opportunities for low income and minority students.	4. Choice may not increase equity. In fact, it may lead to further segregation of low-income and minority students.
5. Competitive schools should stimulate statewide efforts to implement school reform.	5. Choice is not a solution for securing adequate funding, upgrading teachers' pedagogical skills, or reforming education.

CASE STUDY 6

School Board Debates Bilingual Education Program

"There can be no debate," demanded school board member Ricardo Del Rotberg. "Public education monies should be used for educating students in English only. Bilingual education is poor use of the community's tax dollars." Following this fiery opening statement, people in the gallery sat momentarily stunned. The entire community knew that this school year was sure to be contentious. No one doubted that the school board members were deeply divided over the issue of providing bilingual education to immigrant children.

After a long silence, board member Evita Ellmano moved toward the microphone. She reminded the board that the number of immigrant children attending district schools was increasing dramatically each year. She cited research showing that children who were given several years of instruction in their native langauge learned English faster and were successful academically. Ellmano also read results from the district's test scores, which demonstrated that students for whom English was not their dominant language lagged significantly behind other students academically. Del Rotberg retorted that it was his belief that multilingual education is an ill-founded practice that seeks to instill pride in students with low self-esteem. He also suggested that the school board lobby for legislation declaring English to be the nation's official language.

School board president, Sarah Turner could no longer remain silent. She reminded board members that schools are obligated to help all students to live up to their fullest potential and to provide an education in their native language. Turner remarked that schools must embrace and value the traditions and cultures of all students. Moreover, she commented that bilingual education had become a target for people who opposed immigration. Finally, she stated that all teachers should be competent enough to teach their subject matter in at least one foreign language. Immediately, the teachers in the audience roared with protest. Turner pounded her gavel for nearly eight minutes to restore order. Meanwhile, several security personnel came to the meeting room to encourage calmness.

Consider the following questions:

1. What information should be obtained to clarify the facts reflective of both factions?

2. What members of the community should become involved in discussions related to bilingual education programs?

3. Should teachers be expected to retool their pedagogical skills and learn to teach their subject matter in a foreign language? Why? Why not?

4. Are there programmatic alternatives to providing bilingual education to immigrant children?

5. Do schools have a responsibility in maintaining the ethnic culture of immigrant children?